Lifting the Lid

Lifting the Lid

Inside Cheltenham & Tewkesbury Councils

LES GODWIN

THE CHOIR PRESS

First published in the United Kingdom in 2015 by
The Choir Press

ISBN 978–1–909300–81–1

CONTENTS

Introduction

This is not an autobiography, it was never meant to be, but it is a story about a small group of people who were so dismayed at the bureaucracy that pervaded the corridors of power in local government that they wanted to change it.

This is my personal account of how these people came together in February 1976 and formed a successful independent group determined to challenge the unfair changes that were being imposed on them as a result of boundary changes.

I have put the events in chronological order from the date in February 1976 when more than eighty people sat in a far from warm school hall and expressed their concerns at the way local government was going. It was very much a people's group and they wanted the group to gain access to the corridors of local government power and above all else, they wanted the group to speak up on behalf of the local residents.

The sceptics in the communities and the local press wrote us off in no time at all, many thought we would not last a month let alone a year but thirty eight years later we are still a force in local government. We haven't changed but the problems we have had to deal with now are much greater and more complex than they ever were in 1976.

The book is not just a retrospective account of the People Against Bureaucracy Group. It deals with past events and reveals the substance and background of some of the most tumultuous times and costly decisions ever made by a local authority. The reckless investment of £22.5 million of Council taxpayers' money on the Money Markets; the investment of money in the Icelandic banks and the costly pursuit of its former managing director to the Royal Courts of Justice are just some of the issues the book will try to explain.

The effects of the extravagant behaviour of the local authority are still present and the cost is being borne with grim determination to ensure that the events will never be repeated again.

Human behaviour is difficult to explain: how one human being treats another in the quest for revenge and the lengths to which they will go, will never be understood, but I do try to find answers to the questions.

Whilst this is a personal account of my period of service to the community as well as the history of the People Against Bureaucracy Group, it records the major events of my time. Not all bad by any means, and the good times are recorded too.

The book is not written as a retrospective diary of events, nor a precise chronology of events through my period of office. Each year brought different themes that were important and interesting, and I try to illuminate them for what they were, not as I would have liked them to be.

*

The book is also a guide or an aide-memoire to those individuals and groups who find themselves in similar circumstances with their local authority and want to do something about it.

The reason the People Against Bureaucracy Group has been successful is because the group of people who came together in February 1976 have remained loyal throughout the years.

They believe in keeping party politics out of local government; they believe in open government and the democratic system.

The PAB Group of councillors also believe in the freedom of each individual to question and to speak with an open mind, and always to put people before party politics.

If this means that a community and its local authority area becomes a better place to live with these principles as its bedrock, then this is where I belong and where I always want to be.

Finally, I would like to thank all those people who made the creation of the People Against Bureaucracy Group possible in 1976 and the members and supporters who have sustained it over the following years.

I am sure they will continue to do so in the years ahead.

CHAPTER 1

Boundary Changes For Good Or Bad?

"When it is not necessary to change, it is necessary not to change."
Lord Falkland (1614–43)

It was a time of change, uncertainty and confusion. It was as if the smog of the towns banished by the Clean Air Act, 1956, had sought sanctuary in the council offices of the land.

It was the early 1970's. The Second World War had left its legacy of considerable debt still gripping the population. From Derby to Durham, from Dover to Dunstable and beyond, the nation wanted to enjoy a better standard of living. Yet there would soon be the highest interest rates within living memory, either to gladden the hearts of savers, or to plunge those about to take out a mortgage into despair.

Out of this melting pot came the reorganisation of local government in 1974. Would this serve the needs of the local population better than in the past? Could there have been a more efficient system? What could locals do to improve matters where appropriate?

This story offers hope and it gives heart to those who feel that the weight of officialdom is too heavy, or even misguided at times.

To set the scene, the few pages in the rest of this chapter will give a brief outline of the shape of local government through time. They will also describe the essential details of the geography of the area concerned in this book, so that you may have an appreciation of the effect of different proposals on those living in this area – basically North Gloucestershire.

We are concerned chiefly with three towns, Gloucester, Cheltenham and Tewkesbury. Gloucester, as capital of the County, has a long history dating back to AD 46. The city was founded by the Romans and granted its first charter in 1155 by King Henry II. Gloucester is a Cathedral city as well as being a port and dockland area.

The wharfs, warehouses and the docks themselves fell into disrepair until they were renovated in the 1980's. The docklands area is now an attractive shopping area with large open spaces and interesting museums.

The population of Gloucester is around 124,000.

Tewkesbury is an ancient settlement, nestling at the confluence of the Rivers Severn and Avon. It is a town of medieval splendour, whose expansion was curtailed by the rivers and their associated flood plains. It is now (2011) a thriving town, very little altered through time. It is one of the must-see places to visit by tourists to the North Cotswold region of the county.

It has a population of about 10,000.

Cheltenham, by contrast, was more of a market town and staging post, until its spa fame overtook it in the 18th Century. In the 19th Century education became its dominating feature together with horse-racing, and, in the 20th Century, its music and other festivals found their place.

Its medieval Parish Church is still in regular use.

The population of Cheltenham is about 110,000.

Turning now to the administration of local government, County Councils came into being in 1888 and soon after in 1889 County Boroughs were created, which meant that a large borough or a city was independent of county council control.

Originally ten county boroughs were proposed; Bristol, Hull, Newcastle-upon-Tyne, Nottingham, Birmingham, Bradford, Leeds, Liverpool, Manchester and Sheffield, but an additional 61 county boroughs were created as areas grew in size. The Local Government Act, 1972 abolished them.

County boroughs were recognised as being politically independent from the county councils and they were the major centres of activities for people and employment within their county council areas.

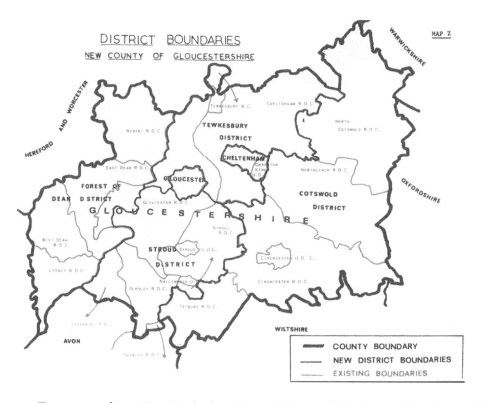

To accommodate a New Tewkesbury Borough Council, the changed boundaries of Gloucestershire in 1974

The Local Government Act, 1894 created a second tier of local government; all administrative counties and county boroughs were divided into either rural or urban districts, which allowed more local administration. The Act also reformed municipal boroughs and provided for the establishment of civil parishes.

In Gloucestershire, the Cheltenham Rural District Council was created and so too the Gloucester Rural District Council; and in Cheltenham there was the Charlton Kings Urban District Council, which had unprecedented powers for the local Charlton Kings area.

The name Charlton Kings comes from Anglo-Saxon times and its urban district status was ended with the local government reorganisation in 1974. It became a civic parish and now has its own parish council.

Until 1974, Tewkesbury Town had Borough status by virtue of various charters going back to 1109, but, the Local Government Act, 1972, created a new enlarged Tewkesbury Borough Council, which included the rural districts of Cheltenham and Gloucester.

Apart from boundary changes that were made by the Boundary Commission in 1990, which marginally reduced the size of the area, there have been no other significant changes since 1974.

Following the end of the second world war there was an uneasy period in local government when it was generally accepted that changes to the structure were urgently required if obvious cases of duplication of services were to end.

In 1958, a Local Government Commission was set up to review local government across the country resulting in the creation of several county boroughs and a reduction in the number of small rural district councils.

The Commission originally discussed the abolition of parish councils, but, the Secretary of Association of Parish Councils (NACP) argued the case for their retention and the Commission subsequently agreed that parish councils should be preserved.

Because of its historical past and the many charters made going back as far as 1109 when Tewkesbury was first made a free borough by Robert, Earl of Gloucester, a recognised statement was issued as follows:

> "In 1974 by virtue of the Local Government Act, 1972, Tewkesbury became part of a new enlarged Tewkesbury Borough Council with the addition of the Rural District of Cheltenham and a part of the Rural District of Gloucester. By virtue of the Royal Charter of Queen Elizabeth II, the District of Tewkesbury was given the Status of a Borough and any powers to appoint local officers of dignity. Any privileges or rights belonging immediately before 1st April, 1974 to the Mayor, Aldermen and Burgesses of the earlier Borough of Tewkesbury could be exercisable by the Council of the Borough of Tewkesbury in respect of the whole of the new Borough."

It was not long before the population of the new Tewkesbury Borough Council area began to show their resentment when the first act of the new administration was to announce that they intended to build new council offices on land at Tewkesbury Park at a cost of £1,250,000.

This large expenditure was based on the assumption of the new administration that the three existing, although scattered, council offices in Cheltenham, Gloucester and Tewkesbury would bring in nearly £450,000.

The intention was to finance the construction by selling the two Rural District Council offices in Imperial Square, Cheltenham and Brunswick Road, Gloucester, plus the Tewkesbury Council offices in Oldbury Road, Tewkesbury. But, as there were no ready buyers in the market at the time, this proved to be a serious obstacle in the plans of the new administration.

Many people thought that the new administration had over-valued the three properties and it came as a shock to learn that the former Cheltenham Rural District Offices in Imperial Square had been sold for £114,000, which was little more than half of the valued price of £200,000 that the new authority had expected to achieve.

Although this sum was a long way short of the financial advice they had been given, it was a vast improvement on the offer by one company of £70,000, which, thankfully, was rejected by the new administration.

All credit was due to Tewkesbury Borough Council for not accepting the offer and waited for a better deal to be forthcoming. However, the general feeling at the time, was that if the new administration had been less optimistic about the value of the former three premises, would they have gone ahead with building a centralised headquarters on Tewkesbury Park?

This question was put repeatedly by both councillors and local ratepayers, but the answers given were often negative.

Up Hatherley, a rural village and one of the parishes around the periphery of Cheltenham was proud of its historical past although the inevitable residential extensions into the rural countryside were dreaded by many local residents.

Rural Districts were created in 1894 by the Local Government Act, 1894 at the same time as Urban District Councils.

These Rural Districts were established for the sole purpose of administration of predominantly rural areas at a level lower than the existing county councils.

They had elected Rural District Councils (RDC's) which inherited the functions of the earlier sanitary districts, which were based on Poor Law Unions, but they also had wider authority over matters such as planning, council housing, recreation grounds and cemeteries.

Major services such as education, highways, waste and refuse collection were the responsibility of the county councils.

In 1930 there were 787 rural districts in England and Wales and each parish was represented by one or more councillors.

The gradual urbanisation of some of the rural parishes led to them being redefined as either semi-rural parishes, or, being totally subsumed into the existing urban districts and newly formed boroughs.

Other rural districts were either too small or not viable and by 1965 the number of rural districts had been reduced to 473.

All rural districts in England and Wales were abolished in 1974, by virtue of the Local Government Act, 1972 and they were merged with the urban districts or boroughs, which provided a uniform pattern of districts based on both urban and rural areas.

I moved to the Up Hatherley area in 1962 and, like other local residents, was satisfied with the autonomous position of Cheltenham Rural District Council whose main concern it seemed, was getting the best value for money it could for the ratepayers who resided in the peripheral parishes around Cheltenham.

The separation of the rural district council from the political machinations of Cheltenham Borough Council was welcomed as future chapters will show, but, we were not aware that sweeping changes would come along which would change life as we knew it for ever.

I was elected to the Up Hatherley Parish Council in 1968 and became chairman in 1972 replacing the Reverend Cecil Smith who had been chairman of the council for many years.

If someone had told me at the time that in a few years I would be experiencing the most dramatic changes in local government and witnessing the reckless spending of council money by a newly formed borough council, I would not have believed them. Neither would I have believed that it was possible for a council to continually make decisions without consultation with the people who paid the bills and, on occasions, did not even bother to consult with the elected members of the new council before making a decision.

There was so much wrong with the way the new administration were conducting their business. The council had a 'deaf ear' to any criticism that ratepayers across the whole of the administration area were making. Hardly a day went by without someone contacting me with their complaints and my only response at the time was to urge them to repeat their concerns through the medium of the local press.

By the early part of 1976 I felt that it was time for local ratepayers to stand up and be counted and with this in mind I decided to call a meeting in Lakeside School, Up Hatherley, to air my views and to see and hear whether other ratepayers felt the same way. The result was quite remarkable and it lead to the creation of a 'voice of the people' group, which had immediate and astounding results. It was called The People Against Bureaucracy Action Group.

CHAPTER 2

Why People Against Bureaucracy?

It is an inevitable defect, that bureaucrats will care more for routine than for results.
The English Constitution (1867) 'On Changes of Ministry'

With the encouragement of other disillusioned residents I decided in February 1976 to book Lakeside School for a public meeting. The criterion for booking a school hall had to be for a community purpose, so it was true to state on the form that it was to talk about local government.

Permission was granted and I then wrote a public notice that even now I believe was bland in the extreme. It was as follows:

> "If you are as fed up with Tewkesbury Borough Council as I am then come to a public meeting at Lakeside School, Up Hatherley, on Friday, February 20th at 7.30 p.m."

Grasping my advert I went to the offices of the *Gloucestershire Echo* to enquire how much it would cost for such an advert to be published. The lady behind the desk told me it would cost £5 and whether or not it was the look on my face that prompted a further comment, she quickly added that it would be for one night only, unless I was prepared to pay for more nights at a reduced rate.

I told the now disappointed lady that it would not be necessary and we agreed a night for publication and I handed over the five pounds.

It was not easy scanning the pages of the evening paper expecting to see my advert prominently displayed when in reality it consisted of just a few lines.

Eventually, I found the advert tucked between two large commercial adverts and my face dropped because it seemed to me that its position in the evening paper would not guarantee a wide readership.

My wife Pamela who was always a reliable sounding board was sceptical, as were friends of mine whom I had informed of the meeting, about the smallness of the advert in the local evening paper.

Friday, 20th February 1976 was a typical February day, cold with an occasional break in the clouds that allowed the sun to come through. By evening it had become colder although I was grateful that it wasn't raining.

My wife broke my train of thought by asking me to forecast how many I thought would turn up for the meeting. Not a pessimist by nature I ventured with a figure of around twelve or fourteen. She laughed and suggested it would be more like half a dozen. In any event she added, "What are you going to say?"

That was a point I had not considered too seriously. I certainly didn't have a script although I did have a list of subjects in my mind that I wanted to talk about.

I knew there were matters that had been a source of concern to local residents, and I knew there was still the fear of the unexpected by those who had been resident in the peripheral parishes around Cheltenham.

Since the new administration had been in place the number of meetings held behind closed doors had prompted several adverse reports in the local newspaper and critical letters appeared in the press condemning the practice.

The *Gloucestershire Echo* went as far as to publish a lengthy report by its 'Political Correspondent' on the proposed reorganisation and boundary changes and suggested that the local ratepayer would be required to pay more money for reduced services and at the same time have more local government bureaucracy to contend with.

The report was well received by *Echo* readers and many supported the article through the letter pages.

The reported purchase of land at Tewkesbury Park to accommodate the construction of new expensive council offices had gathered interest once the new administration started to find its feet.

Many residents living in parishes around Cheltenham were concerned that green belt land around their villages would be the subject of urban extensions by the new administration and many expressed a wish for more protective policies to protect the green belt land.

And of course, many shared the views of the local newspaper that the residents of Gloucestershire needed another bout of local government reorganisation like 'a hole in the head'.

All this and many more ideas were buzzing around in my head as I left home shortly before 7.20 p.m. to go to Lakeside School and address the small or large crowd that perhaps had gathered at the school to hear what I had to say.

As I approached the school, I could see in the half light from the street lamp, what appeared to be a large group of people in the school grounds. Surely, this couldn't possibly be people waiting to go into the school to hear what I had to say about local government reorganisation.

Had these people actually seen the small advert in the local paper and been curious enough to hear what I had to say about the dreadful Tewkesbury Borough Council? Perhaps there was another social activity going on at the school that I had not been told about. My mind started to play tricks, was I going to be told that my meeting, for which I had paid the princely sum of five pounds, could only take place in one of the classrooms because the main hall had been booked. The thought of adults sitting in the children's small desks and trying to be comfortable was worrying.

All this went through my mind as I approached the school gates, but it was a great moment of relief as a muffled cheer went up as they saw me, which became louder when someone in the large group shouted with a loud voice, "Come on Godwin – we are waiting for you, have you got the key?"

I couldn't believe it, but I was greatly relieved.

My shocked response to the crowd was that 'the caretaker had the key and I would go and get it.' It was a lame response, but it gave me the chance to turn and run at full speed to the caretaker's house, which fortunately for me was only a few hundred yards from Lakeside School.

My loud banging on the caretaker's door brought a quick response from him. He recognised me immediately, looked at his watch showing it was a few minutes to 7.30 p.m., and commented with what sounded like a half-apology for not being there, but with a sarcastic expostulation that he would be amazed if there were more than half a dozen people waiting to be let into the school.

He wasn't impressed at all when I suggested to him that he might find more than a hundred people there, and I begged him to 'please hurry before some of the crowd start to get impatient and go back home.'

To his credit, he grabbed his coat from behind the door and the two of us hurried back along Hatherley Road. As we approached the school the sound of loud cheering came from members of the public who had gathered outside the main door followed by appreciative clapping.

Once inside the building the caretaker opened the main hall, and without being asked a number of residents started to put out rows of chairs to accommodate the increasing numbers of interested people. The best sight of all, on what turned out to

Lakeside School, Up Hatherley, where the inaugural meeting of the People Against Bureaucracy Group (PAB) took place in February 1976

be quite a memorable occasion, was the look on the caretaker's face as people filed in to the school hall. It was a sight to behold.

I believe he was genuinely surprised at the number of people who had turned up and he wished the meeting well as he told me he would be back at 9.00 p.m. to lock the doors of the school.

As I pondered about the message I was about to deliver, I noticed that the chairs had been set out in meticulous rows and the people sitting on them had a look of expectation on their faces: I started to get nervous. Dismissing this from my mind I climbed the stairs to the stage and peered into the well-lit room hoping to see faces that I might know, which I knew would be a source of encouragement to me.

I was not too worried about what I had to say to the large gathering, but my train of thought was interrupted when I spotted in the audience a former Leader of the Conservative group on Cheltenham Borough Council. He was a well known local businessman who had been an outspoken person on all kinds of issues affecting the town. I could not believe my eyes.

Knowing that he had been Mayor of Cheltenham on two occasions and known for his political views, I wondered whether he had come to the meeting to listen and then argue against the measures I would be urging the meeting to take.

His name was Terry Joyner.

Terry Joyner former Conservative mayor of Cheltenham and the first vice-chairman of PAB in 1976

Douglas Grazier, first chairman of PAB, with his wife Margaret

Notwithstanding the small shock to my system seeing him sitting in the audience, but next to him sat another prominent member of the Borough Council, albeit from the other side of the political spectrum, who like his political adversary was a well-known local member of the community.

His name was Douglas Grazier.

Doug was a senior member of the Cheltenham Labour Party and he was also chairman of the Education Committee. The education department was transferred to the County Council in later years, but whilst it was part of Cheltenham Borough Council, it was a very powerful body as local residents at the time would testify.

Doug Grazier will be remembered as the person who played a prominent part in the creation of Bournside Comprehensive School.

I welcomed everyone to the meeting and explained the background of the Redcliffe-Maud Report on the boundary changes and, more importantly, the effect that the changes had already made on the lives of residents living outside the town of Tewkesbury.

I explained to the audience that an important matter still to be determined was the question of whether the county of Gloucestershire should consist of five districts or six, which was of paramount importance prior to the final decision on the changes proposed in the Maud Report. The problem, as I saw it, was that the small town of Tewkesbury and the vast areas of land with its numerous hamlets and villages could not be divided between the other five districts in the county.

The only other option on offer was to create a new borough district centred on Tewkesbury, which would include all 57 villages and hamlets from Twyning in the north of the county to Cowley in the south. Unfortunately, for the peripheral parishes around Cheltenham and Gloucester, it was decided later to include these semi-rural district areas into the newly created council area.

Tewkesbury Borough Council was formed on April 1st 1974.

I told the audience that this had probably been done to give some weight to the officers in the Tewkesbury Town Hall, who would be expected to take on the new and extra responsibilities for a much larger area.

It was my view that the Maud Report had caused the 'biggest geographical blunder in the history of local government.'

From the applause I received it was evident that most people in the school hall agreed with me.

'Did the audience think', I asked, 'that the old Tewkesbury Town Hall staff had the wherewithal to take on the demanding tasks of a new borough district.'

Again, a resounding, no!

I was warming to the occasion and to the audience too. I explained the detail of the controversial land deals, as I understood them, the purchase of Tewkesbury Park from money not yet acquired from the sale of the existing rural district offices. And, in my view, that the allegations made that many important decisions were continually taken behind closed doors were well-founded.

I told the meeting the first two years had passed since the reorganisation of local government and looking back of those years I had come to the conclusion they had been a disaster. The newly created Tewkesbury Borough Council consisted mainly of Conservative party members and people who called themselves 'independents'. "It did not take long", I told the meeting, "for time to prove that these so-called 'independent' people were not independent at all, but were members of the Conservative party who believed they would appeal to a wider section of the community if they were not labelled 'Conservative'".

I had held the view for some time that if there were to be 'independent' members of Tewkesbury Borough Council they needed to be the genuine article, honest with the electorate and free from any political pressures.

When questioned by the local press about their independence, some openly admitted that it was better for them, in electoral terms, to stand as 'independent' candidates rather than 'Conservative' in order to get themselves elected. Is there dishonesty in politics? It seems as though it starts from the moment some people put their names on the nomination papers.

"Bureaucracy", I claimed, "was a form of government that was based on the power of the officials who controlled the detail of both public and private life to the detriment of individual free thinking and enterprising people".

In other words, a culture of 'we know what is best for the people who pay their taxes'.

It was my view, I told the meeting, that if we were going to achieve anything at all by the end of the evening, it should be to set up a new group of people totally divorced from party politics whose main aim should be to persuade the new administration that nothing less than 'putting people first and before party politics' would be acceptable to this new group.

There was another roar of approval from the meeting and several people asked whether this would apply to the imposition of the new refuse collection system that was being imposed on the rural population?

I pointed out to the meeting that Up Hatherley Parish Council was totally opposed to the introduction to the new scheme because no-one had been consulted and it appeared that Tewkesbury Borough Council were adopting a 'take it or leave it' approach to the problem.

I explained to the meeting that the Public Health Act, 1936, spelt out the duties of a local council regarding the refuse collection system, and importantly, in one particular section of the Act, the procedures that a local authority should undertake should they wish to change the system of refuse collection.

It was my view that this procedure had not been followed by the council.

In the rural district council areas, the collection of refuse had been undertaken by what was called a 'back gate to back gate' system, which meant that the refuse collectors collected bins from the back of the property and returned the dustbins to the place where they had found them. The reason for this kind of system had been based on the fact that the rural areas had more than the normal number of long drives to properties; the previous Rural District Councils had accepted this position and supported the view that it was too much for householders to be expected to take the dustbins to the collector rather than the other way around.

The view of the local parish council was that the introduction of the new system, without consultation with residents, should be challenged.

Many residents in the audience agreed with this statement and some stood up and claimed, without reservation, that they would not comply with Tewkesbury Borough Council's instructions and would refuse to carry their dustbins to the kerbside.

It was clear that tempers were being raised by some groups of people in the audience and I was somewhat relieved when the figure of Terry Joyner rose from the centre of the hall shouting 'Mr Chairman' above the din that was being created. Eventually, his plea was listened to and an air of silence prevailed in the hall whilst Terry Joyner addressed the members of the public.

Mr Chairman' he repeated, 'it is clear that the majority of people in the hall are opposed to a number of things that you have outlined in your speech to us.' Much to my great relief, Terry Joyner broke the increasing tension in the hall by introducing Douglas Grazier to the meeting, who was sitting next to him.

He explained that both he and Doug Grazier had spent what seemed like a lifetime in local politics, each on opposing political sides in the Council chamber and they were now sick and tired of the political banter that had done little to improve the quality of life for local people, nor had it done anything to promote the well-being of Cheltenham.

He told the audience that he had spoken to Doug Grazier on the telephone when the advertisement appeared in the local press.

They had agreed that they should attend the meeting to express support for an independent cause, which on the face of it, could be a much better deal for local people than the political infighting and arguments that had prevailed in the council chamber for many years.

He also believed that should a report of the meeting appear in the local press, it would cause consternation among his 'political' friends and it might even mean that after a lifetime in the Conservative Party 'he would no longer be welcome'.

My joy at hearing this message was understandable and I immediately applauded Terry Joyner for his outspoken words, and the audience followed my example by clapping and shouting to the top of their voices, which took some time for me to bring a bit of decorum back to the meeting.

It was by natural instinct that I invited Terry and Doug Grazier to join me on the platform, which they did, and the meeting then took on a new dimension.

Doug explained to the audience that he, like Terry, had spent a lifetime as a member of a main stream political party. He was disappointed that 'party political' wrangling had dampened the enthusiasm of many good, hard-working councillors, not least because political infighting prevented progress being made to deal with the increasing number of problems facing the town.

To the amusement of the audience he described how Cheltenham Borough councillors would debate until midnight who should become the next mayor of Cheltenham, but spend little time on matters of importance.

Doug was clearly proud of the fact that in spite of their political views, he and Terry Joyner had come together to fight for the first mixed comprehensive school and sixth form centre in the southern part of Cheltenham.

Doug explained how difficult this phase had been, even though many of Terry's Conservative colleagues were against the idea in the early stages of debate.

Reverting back to the main purpose of the meeting, Doug Grazier admitted that when the news broke in 1973 that Cheltenham Rural District Council (RDC) would be swallowed up in a new Tewkesbury District the chairman of the RDC, Councillor R.C. Meadows, welcomed it with open arms.

He had made a public statement at the Watson Hall, Tewkesbury, claiming "If we can't make a go of it then something will have gone terribly wrong".

Doug Grazier said "Three years later the RDC's chairman 's words had come home to haunt him as things had gone terribly wrong and the local taxpayer had had to pay the bill"..

The audience cheered and someone shouted "but what are we going to do about it" which brought more applause. This was my cue to announce to the meeting that I was prepared to form an Action Group and invited Doug Grazier and Terry Joyner to be the first chairman and deputy chairman of the group.

Thankfully, both Terry and Doug accepted my proposal. At this point, someone suggested we needed a suitable name for the action group, which hopefully would change things for the better and bring a bit of pride back into local government affairs.

It dawned on me, looking into the faces of so many concerned local ratepayers, many had probably travelled quite long distances in order to attend the meeting and give support to a cause, which they believed might just be the right antidote to shake up the new local authority.

This is what I said to the audience,

> "You people have come here tonight because you are already fed up with the bureau-cratic nonsense that has been pouring out of the new Tewkesbury District; why don't we call ourselves The People Against Bureaucracy Action Group"?

The applause was deafening. My suggestion wasn't that awe-inspiring, but it seemed to click with those in the hall. I went on to say that 'as Doug and Terry were prepared to be our first chairman and deputy chairman, I was prepared to act as the Honorary Secretary, if the meeting agreed'.

This brought more cheering and by the time this had ended another person stood up in the middle of the school hall and announced in a loud voice "The People Against Bureaucracy Action Group now has its first Tewkesbury councillor, because I am currently an independent councillor who serves on the Cheltenham Rural District Council. My name is Bill Norton and I am now the People Against Bureau-cracy Action Group councillor for Up Hatherley".

The cheering that greeted that announcement must have been unprecedented for a public meeting of this kind. With the cheering and back slapping, Bill Norton was clearly delighted with his announcement.

For me, the night was getting better with every passing minute and there was still more to come as a lady stood up and told the meeting that she was Mrs Bunty Griffiths from Shurdington.

She told the meeting that she had been involved with accountancy during her working life and she would willingly act as the Honoury Treasurer of the Action Group if it was going to raise funds for its activities.

Praise and thanks from Doug and Terry certainly pleased Mrs Griffiths who then joined the rest of us on the platform.

I quickly recapped that we now had a chairman, a deputy chairman, a secretary and a treasurer and a first People Against Bureaucracy Action Group councillor. It seemed to me that the 'Action Group' was on its way.

"Mr Godwin", I heard a voice behind me saying, "I think you should ask the audience if they would agree to a fifty pence subscription so that we can start the organisation off on the right foot".

Most of the audience had heard what Bunty Griffiths had said and they were in full agreement, but I added that they would need to give the Hon Treasurer their names and addresses with their fifty pence pieces so that we could start off with a proper paid-up membership list of interested people.

Co-operation was the order of the night and I honestly believe that if I had asked the audience to go with me and jump in the nearest lake they would have done so.

It was some time before the last person 'signed in' and paid the fifty pence and I could see that the caretaker, who had been standing just inside the hall for the past twenty minutes, was getting weary of waiting. I offered him my apologies for being later than I had originally envisaged.

He understood and he wished us well, because like the audience, he had seen something rather unique in the last twenty minutes, the formation of the first independent, non-political 'action group' in Cheltenham. He also had the good grace to say that he hoped we would succeed – we promised him we would.

As the caretaker started to turn off some of the lights, Bunty Griffiths told us that there were 87 paid-up members and she confirmed that each one had given their home address. The list revealed a membership of people from eleven different wards, from Cowley in the south to Tewkesbury in the north. Most of the names were from the peripheral parishes on the edge of Cheltenham such as Bishops Cleeve, Leckhampton, Prestbury and The Reddings.

The four people who were last to leave Lakeside School hall that night were Doug Grazier, Terry Joyner, Bunty Griffiths and me. We felt a little exhausted but well pleased with the night's work. We promised to telephone each other in the next few days to start an organisation chart.

We all shook hands and agreed that we had been very successful in launching a 'people's group' called the People Against Bureaucracy Action Group.

We were on our way.

CHAPTER 3

Moving Forward

"Forward, forward let us range, let the great world spin forever down the ringing grooves of change."
Locksley Hall by Alfred, Lord Tennyson (1842)

Terry Joyner telephoned me on the following Monday morning 23rd February as I was descending the stairs to enjoy my first cup of tea of the day. He wanted me to know a few important facts concerning himself and his vision for the future.

He told me that he was no longer a member of the Conservative Party and, in his words, 'far better for me to opt out rather than the party to kick me out'.

Secondly, he thought I should know that he had his own business in Cheltenham, which was a firm supplying office equipment, both retail and wholesale, and he wanted to offer any help he could to the Group by providing paper, printing and anything else that a newly formed group would require.

I regarded that as excellent news and I told him so particularly as we needed to produce some kind of basic membership card for those who had joined the group on the previous Friday.

Terry suggested that he should contact Doug Grazier, the new group chairman, with a view to holding a meeting in Terry's office on Wednesday, 25th February.

At Terry's suggestion, I should invite our PAB councillor who would be useful in telling the meeting exactly what was going on in the offices of Tewkesbury District Council and to include the new Hon. Treasurer Mrs Bunty Griffiths.

Terry suggested that the meeting should take place in his office after the staff had departed and he further suggested that we go to the meeting prepared with ideas of how we could take the PAB Action Group forward.

After my conversation with Terry Joyner I was suddenly overwhelmed with calls from people wanting to know what had happened at the public meeting in Lakeside School the previous Friday evening.

Several local newspaper reporters telephoned asking for interviews about the meeting; what the outcome had been and what our intentions were regarding the local authority's current activities.

The local radio stations too followed in similar fashion with requests for me to explain in detail the events of the previous Friday night. Their insistence was worrying, not least because they talked as if some gigantic earth-shattering moment had taken place in the history of local government at the meeting, which of course, was not the case.

Perhaps it had been an important moment for those attending the meeting, but nothing like the 'spin' the press and media were trying to put on it.

It was never my intention to go down the road the media were trying to lead me and I must have sounded most negative with my replies to their numerous questions. It never crossed my mind during the course of the previous Friday evening that there were members of the press present. None had been invited, which probably explained the reason for their telephone calls.

I learned quickly to treat the press with caution – in time it paid off.

Whatever thoughts I may have held during the course of the day came to an abrupt end when I saw the evening edition of the *Gloucestershire Echo*, which proclaimed in banner headlines,

FACELESS OFFICERS RUNNING COUNCIL

The article went on to claim that "faceless officers were running Tewkesbury Borough Council and not the elected councillors". These were the words, according to the press, from Councillor W. W. Norton, who went on to claim that 'councillors were not considering matters on behalf of their electorate'.

It was a relief to continue reading that Cllr Norton was one of several speakers at the inaugural meeting of the PAB Action Group held in Lakeside School, a group, according to the article, which was 'dedicated to challenging certain decisions and allegedly wasteful spending by Tewkesbury Borough Council'.

There was more; Cllr Norton had stated that 'he had been criticised by the chief executive (Mr K. E. S. Smale) for daring to criticise officers, but in his opinion, the officers were servants of the people and if he, as an elected councillor, found fault with them then in his opinion, they should be named.'

As I continued to read the several column inches of reporting it became apparent that there had been a reporter present in the inaugural meeting and by the look of the detailed reporting contained in the article he, or she, had done a thorough job.

It was of special interest to read Bill Norton's comments at the inaugural meeting because they not only refreshed my memory of the various speeches made at the meeting, but they also contained valuable points.

The comments would become the bedrock of the PAB group when dealing with the events that would surely follow.

The *Echo* reported a valuable part of Bill Norton's speech when he claimed that "When local government was reorganised, the point was made early on by the Borough Council officers that the parish councils with their grass roots opinions, would be fully consulted on issues affecting their parishes, but what has happened – just secret meetings".

Bill Norton's advice, according to the *Gloucestershire Echo* was

"If the meeting wanted to do anything to change the present situation, it needed to find candidates for the May elections who were prepared to question things, especially officers' reports. Council officers put forward facts and figures but they are not always right and needed to be challenged".

I took up the call from Bill Norton and urged everyone present to work towards finding candidates for the council places in each ward at the May elections.

I told the meeting that I had already received calls from interested people in Prestbury and the Bishops Cleeve area, which suggested that the new PAB Action Group would field several candidates at the elections on May 6th 1976.

I had gone to the inaugural public meeting on February 20th with no prepared speech or notes, so, I was more than pleased to have read the *Gloucestershire Echo's* account of my speech.

The report devoted a lot of space to the purpose of the meeting and it made the point that the meeting had "effectively got the People Against Bureaucracy Action Group off the ground".

The *Echo* reported "It was the brainchild of Les Godwin, who was chairman of the Up Hatherley Parish Council and a severe critic of Tewkesbury Borough Council". That was certainly true, and I was eager to read on.

According to the article, I had also told the audience that 'I had been worried about the extravagant spending by the Borough Council and it needed to be checked'. I had also protested vigorously, the report said, 'against the decision of the council to go ahead with a downgraded system of refuse collection without prior consultation with the parish councils or with the local people'.

I remembered telling the meeting that the downgraded system would only affect the rural parishes that previously formed part of the former Cheltenham Rural District Council. In spite of the fact that the Leader of the Council claimed that the new scheme would save the council £12,000, the decision to provide radio telephones at a cost of £6,100 in the cars of senior officers still went ahead.

The important part of my speech that I recall telling the meeting was that many elderly residents from a wide area had contacted me expressing their concerns about having to carry their household refuse bins from the back of their houses to the front kerbside of their properties. They had expressed the view that the present system was working well and should be left alone. It was because of this that I suggested to the meeting that unless proper talks and consultation with both the residents and the parish councils took place then we should resist it. The ball, I remember saying was clearly in the council's court.

The *Echo* also stressed the point that I had told the meeting that other matters of wasteful expenditure by Tewkesbury Borough Council included £1,267,450 on a new administrative building in Tewkesbury, in spite of the fact that the council could only expect to receive £447,000 from the sale of the district offices in Cheltenham and Gloucester.

Other expenditure of £321,607 on the Roses Theatre and £50,000 on the refurbishment of a Baptist Chapel in Tewkesbury were costs that would also have to be borne by the council's taxpayers.

I told the meeting that I had been dismayed when I heard the news that the council administration planned to buy the Cotswold Hills golf course for £28,000 and I cheekily added 'that it was probably to enable their hard-working officers to relax at the end of a busy day of spending'. Whilst it brought a round of applause from the audience, it did seem to me that the new administration had embarked on a spending spree with ratepayers' money as if the pound note had suddenly gone out of fashion.

The *Echo* further reported that I had told the meeting that the district auditor was having difficulty in 'clearing the books' for the period 1974/75 and it begged the question whether the books had been cleared for the period 1973/74. Several rumours and reports in the local press had made local residents very suspicious about the running of the new administration, and therefore they had every right to be concerned.

The reporter ended his article by telling the readers that I would be 'launching a petition inviting people who opposed the new front-gate refuse collection system to sign if they did not intend to conform to the instructions issued by Tewkesbury Borough Council'. This was great stuff and I was very pleased.

So, all in all, the meeting had gone very well and the report in the *Gloucestershire Echo* had managed to get everything, or at least most of the salient points made at the meeting, in print for their readers to read.

It had crossed my mind as I read the press article that the staff at the new Tewkesbury Borough Council offices would not be pleased to read about the criticisms levelled at them by people attending an inaugural meeting of an ad hoc group of people. As it turned out, I was right in my assumptions and the rebuttals came fast and sometimes furious from leading members of the council.

Meanwhile, Up Hatherley Parish Council called a special meeting to discuss the question of costs associated with a possible High Court injunction to stop Tewkesbury Borough Council from imposing the revised refuse collection service.

The Parish Council had invited a local firm of solicitors to address them on the cost of a high court action and particularly the fees that would be asked for by a barrister whose job it would be to take the case to the court.

In my position as chairman of the council I explained to the members that there would be a cost for seeking Counsel's opinion on whether the council had sufficient grounds to seek an injunction against Tewkesbury Borough Council. We would also need to know whether we had any chance of preventing the council from introducing a revised and downgraded system of refuse collection based on the provisions of the Public Health Act, 1936.

We knew that ninety per cent of the parish had voiced their opposition to the new system only a few weeks earlier; and we knew that Tewkesbury Borough Council had given its approval for the new refuse scheme to start on April 1st 1976.

Other parishes had met and given their support to Up Hatherley Parish Council, and according to the various reports received showed that they too would not be complying with the new downgraded system.

The solicitor, Ray Tarling from Robinsons Solicitors, answered several questions from members of the parish council about possible costs, the process of going to the high court and the chances of an injunction being obtained.

In his view, based on the facts as he knew them, the parish council's chances of obtaining an injunction were very high.

On that advice, the Parish Council agreed to go ahead and seek Counsel's opinion. Parish councillors also agreed to set aside sufficient money to cover the costs, including the cost of seeking the injunction in the high court. The total cost would be met from the general purposes fund of the parish council.

The special parish council meeting was an open meeting and a number of local residents were present. The report of the meeting in the *Gloucestershire Echo* the following night brought an official response from Tewkesbury Borough Council.

Ronald Wheeler was regarded as a quiet man, a good listener, always smartly dressed and he had a liking for cheroots. Ron had been the assistant clerk to the Cheltenham Rural District Council, and after the boundary changes in 1974 became the Borough Secretary of the new Tewkesbury Borough Council.

Setting up of the new local authority had not been easy for Ron, not least, because he was obliged to take on staff from the former RDC offices as well as the staff from Tewkesbury Town Council. The mix of people from two different environments was tricky to handle and Ron was anxious to make the new local authority work smoothly.

He always listened intently to what was said and often gave the impression he was on the side of councillors as well as giving assurances to his staff that they were right and everything was working well.

The refuse dispute with Up Hatherley Parish Council was a test of his skills, but in my view, he could have handled the affair in a more constructive way.

For example, he could have arranged a meeting with my parish council, or he could have contacted me as chairman of the council to discuss the problem, but he did neither, which only created a difficult stalemate.

Instead of talking to me, the parish council or the solicitor we had engaged, he proudly claimed through the local press that the new system of refuse collection across the whole of the borough was "an effort to curb unnecessary expenditure".

He readily agreed that the new system would require "neighbourliness and goodwill to make the system work" but he failed to talk to those who were adamantly opposed to the new system.

I responded immediately to the Borough Secretary's claim by accusing him of 'fudging the issue' by claiming that the saving of a paltry £17,500 was important to the ratepayers, when at the same time his new administration had indicated that it was about to embark on a new council office project at a cost of £1.25 million. For good measure, I told the *Echo* readers that on top of that the council intended to spend £300,000 on a film theatre plus other expensive innovations.

I could not see how a saving of £17,500 out of a total cost for refuse collection of

£247,000 was of such importance that it needed to be imposed on local people irre-spective of the consequences it would create and contrary to the requirements of the Public Health Act, 1936.

After all, if the new administration was really serious in their attempt to save ratepayers' money, they should have been sending teams of efficiency experts into the three inherited council offices to see how inefficient they were and, where necessary, carry out improvements.

I suggested to the Borough Secretary that the new administration should look at council staff levels as a starting point and then look at the salaries of his staff, which in my opinion, were inflated when judged against comparable rates of workers in the private sector.

This was rejected.

A cut of just one per cent of staff salaries would have gone a long way towards saving money and the Borough Council would have had good reason not to impose an unwelcome new refuse system on local residents.

Meanwhile, not least because it had become clear that Tewkesbury Borough Council had no intention of reaching a compromise, Up Hatherley Parish Council agreed to continue the fight against the council. It was not long before other parishes in the former rural district area soon followed our lead.

It has always been my view that all council meetings should be open to the general public especially when matters to be discussed are of public interest.

Tewkesbury Borough Council held different views about this and there was growing evidence that in spite of complaints, several meetings were being held behind closed doors on subjects of interest to the general public.

The dispute between Up Hatherley Parish Council and the council over the refuse collection system was a classic example. A meeting of the Environmental Services Committee (ESC) had met to decide what to do to counteract the chal-lenges being made by the parish council; this meeting was held behind closed doors which meant that the press and public were excluded.

We will never know the details of that meeting although it did not take much effort to work out what the principal subject was on the committee agenda.

The *Gloucestershire Echo* reporter, along with members of the public, was told by the chairman that he could not remain in the committee room to report the proceedings. In spite of his protestations he was told to leave the room.

It was a bad move by the chairman because it was inevitable that the *Echo* reporter would report to his editor and relate to him the events surrounding the 'secret meeting' of the ESC, which had been held in the council offices.

Just as I had predicted, the subsequent story in the *Gloucestershire Echo* condemned the practice of 'secret meetings' calling for more openness. Further-more, the editor joined in the fray by using his editorial column to ask the question *'When is a public matter confidential?'*

'Presumably' said the editor, answering his own question, *'when the outcome will*

affect every ratepayer under Tewkesbury Borough Council's dustbin lids'.

I think the *Echo* readership understood the subtlety of the editor's comments.

The editor went further and questioned, on behalf of his readers, *'why the district's elected representatives are so reluctant to talk about such things in public. The issue has been smouldering like a rubbish tip for months'* he said *'and then out of the blue we came upon a copy of the minutes of a meeting held behind closed doors.'*

The next piece of the editorial made me smile as I read *'We did not steal the papers; we did not "bug" the meeting; we did not do a Watergate, we were handed the document on a platter.'*

My smile was like the look on the cat's face when presented with an enticing saucer of cream. The *Echo* editor was experiencing what we had suspected for a long time and no-one it seemed had given us the credit that we deserved.

At least the local press had experienced the strong arm of the Borough Council when they decided which meetings should be held in private and who should be allowed to attend.

In conclusion, the Editor wrote that he had been notified by the council that 'some of his reporters' articles were not accurate'. That was like a red rag to a bull and the editor responded crisply to the accusation, *"Prove it"* he wrote and continued *"If there were less cloak and gag 'em stuff in the Tewkesbury district, there would be less dissatisfaction among ratepayers".*

Well, I couldn't agree more, could I?

It was becoming clearer to me that in order for any group to succeed against the weight of bureaucracy in local government it was necessary to have the local press on our side. As a newly formed PAB Action Group, we quickly won the hearts and minds of the reporters and the sub-editors of the *Gloucestershire Echo*. We would not have succeeded without their support and in later chapters it will be seen what an important part the press, and particularly the *Gloucestershire Echo*, played in putting PAB on the map and keeping us there. The local media supported our cause and their contributions and support had kept us in the forefront of local politics in 1976and continued to do so for many years to come.

Throughout April 1976 the local newspaper concentrated on any matter that was connected to the refuse dispute between Up Hatherley Parish Council and Tewkes-bury Borough Council. Black plastic bags of refuse were piling up in the gardens and driveways of residents in parishes across the district as they determinedly defied the council and its new refuse collecting system.

This scenario quickly gave the local press photographers the golden opportunity to fill their local newspapers with eye-catching photographs.

Meanwhile, Tewkesbury Borough Council's Policy and Resources Committee (P&R) met in April to consider a request from the solicitors representing Up Hatherley Parish Council asking for an "unequivocal assurance within seven days that the Borough Council would abandon its plans to alter its refuse collection service on 1st April. The solicitors informed the Borough Council that "The request was also made on behalf of other parish councils who were supportive of the Up Hatherley Parish Council's cause".

The P & R rejected the request.

The solicitors informed Up Hatherley Parish Council that a writ had been prepared which made the point clear that 'unless Tewkesbury Borough Council gave an unequivocal assurance within seven days that the scheme would be abandoned the writ would be issued and served without further notice'.

They reminded the council that "if there was not a favourable response an immediate application would be made to the High Court for an injunction to restrain the council from implementing their objectionable scheme."

This brought a swift response from the mayor, Cllr the Hon. Alasdair Andrew Orr Morrison, who quickly assembled his senior officers together to discuss the possible writ and to decide what their response should be.

The council's solicitor Michael Mortimer, advised the officers that "if an injunction was sought then it would be open to the council to claim that it was endeavouring to comply with guidance from the Department of the Environment in order to save money". (Thirty five years later that still seems to be the council's answer to solve every problem)

Adding to his advice, Mr Mortimer suggested that the council "Would need to point out in court that a large proportion of ratepayers in the Borough were already dealing with their dustbins in the manner requested by the council".

What the council and Mr Mortimer continually failed to explain to the wider community was that areas other than the peripheral parishes had always experienced a front gate to front gate collection service and they knew and expected nothing else from the council.

The peripheral parishes, forced into a new Tewkesbury district area against their wishes, were entitled under the Public Health Act, 1936, to 'be informed by proper consultation before changes to a refuse system took place'.

Mr Mortimer and the council knew this and they also knew that any proposal to change the system had to be supported by a local bylaw.

This is what the Act called for and that was all the local residents who were affected by the new service wanted the council to respond to.

Either it was too much bother for them to undertake this task, or the council wanted to stamp its authority on these belligerent people in the former rural district council areas before too much time had elapsed.

When I challenged Cllr Morrison on this point he denied that such a thought had entered their heads, but he did concede that if Up Hatherley Parish Council did go to the High Court and win, then it would mean that the council would be required to change the system for every other parish and town in the new Tewkesbury Borough Council area.

This, of course, was scare mongering, just as his claim that the change would cost the Tewkesbury ratepayers £50,000 and that an extra supplementary rate would have to be levied.

I had a lot of time for the Hon. Alasdair Morrison. In spite of his background, he was the son of Viscount Dunrossil, he was a very 'down-to-earth' person who I believe genuinely wanted to do what he thought was best for the new council area. He was always easy to talk to, but usually conceded very little.

Apart from becoming mayor of Tewkesbury in 1976, he also became High Sheriff of Gloucestershire in 1983.

He lived in Maisemore and he died 5th December 2009.

I explained to the mayor the position his council was in; the council could leave the back gate to front gate collection system in the peripheral parishes as it currently stood, or he could make provision for a bye-law, which would give him the power to do what he and the council wanted to do.

I believed it was touch-and-go at this point and the situation wasn't helped by staff from the Borough Engineer's Department who were putting notices through every door in the peripheral parishes telling householders that unless they carried their refuse bins to the end of their drives week commencing 8th April their refuse would not be collected.

It seemed to me that we had no choice but to take on the council and pursue our challenge in the High Court.

CHAPTER 4

The Challenge

"One never notices what one has done, one can only see what remains to be done."
Marie Curie

The People Against Bureaucracy Action Group (PAB) was finding its feet and progressing slowly during the months following its inauguration. It had been preparing the ground for getting PAB councillors elected to the new Tewkesbury Borough Council.

Several members of Up Hatherley Parish Council had joined the PAB Group, which meant that we had close connections with what was going on in Up Hatherley as well as in other parishes.

Whilst the Action Group had not come out in early support of Up Hatherley Parish Council this was simply because we had been 'learning the ropes' as they say, about how to get councillors elected; and we were desperate to get candidates for the four vacant seats in Bishop's Cleeve.

We knew that fighting these four seats would be a major test for PAB, not least because the result would either indicate that we had the support of local people, or we were perhaps, just wasting our time.

At the PAB management meetings we comforted ourselves by agreeing that win or lose it would be a good opportunity to learn how to conduct elections and hopefully, how to win them.

It was a massive learning curve for all of us and we didn't lack enthusiasm.

The committee felt that a low profile was needed if we were to be successful in the forthcoming May 1976 elections, rather than pursue a 'drum banging' campaign about the changes we would make if we were elected.

Some members thought the refuse dispute should be at the forefront of our campaign, whilst others thought the 'card' should be played only if the situation demanded it.

In the end, we left it up to the judgement of the candidates who in any event, would be required to answer the questions that might be put to them by local residents.

There was no doubt that the refuse dispute was a topic of conversation wherever we went and we couldn't ignore it. The local press made sure that it was going to be at the forefront of everyone's mind and helped with its continuous coverage of the subject.

Even though we didn't want to use it as a political football during the election period, we did agree that the refuse dispute should be placed on the next management meeting for discussion. Notwithstanding our position on support for the dispute, the three candidates in Bishop's Cleeve did use it as a platform whenever they spoke at public meetings.

The candidates received excellent support from the local residents leading up to the elections and it became increasingly clear that their success was becoming assured as each day passed.

Bishop's Cleeve is a large village near Cheltenham. It lies at the foot of Cleeve Hill, the highest point of the Cotswolds.

It was part of the Cheltenham Rural District Council and later would become a much larger parish administered by the new Tewkesbury Borough Council.

The village dates back to the 8th century and records of its existence can be found in the Domesday Book of 1086.

Whilst its history is assured, it was about to embark on another historical moment by being the centre stone of an emerging non-political independent group that would prove its worth for many years to come.

Several Bishop's Cleeve residents who attended the inaugural meeting had joined PAB, so a strong base had been created.

We knew that Bill Norton had already pronounced that he was the first PAB councillor on Tewkesbury Borough Council, and in spite of our early apprehension about getting people to stand for election, we quickly found three members who lived in Bishop's Cleeve willing to become candidates in the forthcoming elections.

They were Sylvia Hughes, Mike Beresford and Alan New.

I was delighted to have three willing candidates, but I was surprised to learn that a fourth candidate had not been included in the PAB list of candidates. There were four seats to be contested in the elections, and if we were so confident of winning three seats in Bishop's Cleeve then it seemed to me that we should put up four candidates.

My concerns got through to the candidates who came to see me one evening to explain the reason why a fourth candidate was not being sought.

They were confident of winning three of the four seats, but at the same time they also had a great deal of respect and sympathy for one of the Bishop's Cleeve councillors currently on Tewkesbury Borough Council. Apparently, the councillor had devoted much of his life working for Bishop's Cleeve and its residents and the PAB candidates did not want to unseat him.

The councillor was Eric Foster, a retired Squadron Leader who had spent his new-found spare time working for the Bishop's Cleeve community. He had been a parish councillor in the village for as long as most people could remember; he had been chairman of the parish council and was always willing and ready to give support for anything that needed to be done to improve the village.

Eric wasn't getting any younger and many local people openly expressed the view that he should stand down. It was also true that the young people in Bishop's Cleeve believed he did not represent their views on the needs of young people in the village. Nevertheless, the three PAB candidates still regarded him as a dedicated community person and they really didn't want to see him defeated at the forthcoming elections.

It was a very commendable position to take and it soon became clear to me that nothing I said would alter their opinions.

The elections duly took place and just as Sylvia, Mike and Alan had predicted, we won three of the four seats in the Bishop's Cleeve ward with Squadron Leader Foster retaining his seat as an Independent, but with the lowest number of votes of the four candidates.

Eric knew that his re-election as a councillor was due entirely to the generosity of the PAB candidates. He wouldn't join the PAB group, but he worked with them on matters that affected the Bishop's Cleeve area.

I am sure Eric Foster knew that had we fielded four candidates he would not have been re-elected.

It was an interesting result because Sylvia Hughes received 946 votes, Alan New 910 and Mike Beresford 835.

Squadron Leader Foster won the fourth seat with just 662 votes.

The sitting Conservative members were all defeated and they included Mrs Gabrielle Ward the vice-chairman of the council's Recreational and Cultural Services Committee and one of the longest serving councillors.

By the time nominations closed for the May 1976 elections the PAB group had nominated ten candidates. By the time the votes had been counted we found we had won six of the ten seats. It was quite an achievement.

As I said earlier, it was a learning curve for PAB and we had come through with flying colours; it seemed that the local electors wanted us to succeed.

There was no doubt that the success at the polls would give us a sound base from which the Group could go forward.

None of the successful candidates had any experience of council work, or how council committees worked. Their lack of experience, however, didn't lessen their enthusiasm to attend their first meetings and to put forward their strongly held views. They believed they were on a mission, and they desperately wanted to represent the views of the people who had elected them to office.

In the Prestbury ward we had three candidates, and whilst the Group failed to win any of the seats, we had come extremely close to doing so.

Prestbury had been a solid Conservative area for decades. So solid, in fact, that no-one bothered to stand against the sitting councillors.

We decided it was a situation that needed to be changed. As a result of our efforts, we polled nearly 32 per cent of the votes in a ward that had not seen a council election for more years than anyone could remember.

Prestbury village lies on the lower slopes of the Cotswold escarpment, about two miles from the town of Cheltenham. Although it is an outlying village to the north east of the town, it has now become part of Cheltenham Borough Council area following boundary changes adopted in 1991.

Whether administered by Tewkesbury Borough Council or Cheltenham Borough Council, it has always managed to preserve its semi-rural identity and retain its unique village character.

With its historic buildings and their attractive settings, Prestbury has always been a much sought-after place to live. The old part of the village centred on St. Mary's Church, The Burgage, Lake Street and the High Street, is in stark contrast to the large areas of modern development that has taken place in recent years.

The Cotswold Area of Outstanding Natural Beauty covers a large area of land to the east and south east of Prestbury, and land to the north of the village is designated Green Belt.

Both protected areas are important to the setting of the Prestbury. Following representations to the council, the Prestbury Conservation Area was established and adopted in 2009.

As a result of the boundary changes in 1991 Prestbury was seconded from the jurisdiction of Tewkesbury Borough Council to Cheltenham Borough Council.

Although I lived in Up Hatherley I decided I would accept the challenge along with Mike Hunt and Peter Richmond to fight the local election in Prestbury on behalf of PAB in 1976. Because of its past electoral history it seemed a good opportunity to use the election as an exercise in electioneering in a safe Conservative seat. It could turn out to be an asset when the next elections took place in 1980.

It soon became apparent that the 1976 election was going to be a straight fight in Prestbury between the PAB candidates and the Conservatives.

Our failure to find a fourth candidate was disappointing.

Eventually, an independent candidate emerged (not associated with PAB) and this gave the election more balance, and with it more choice for the electors. His name was John Cornwell.

Canvassing, knocking on doors, talking to people as they went about their daily business, talking to them at the local shop and occasionally over a pint of beer was a new experience for me.

I talked to parents as they collected their children from St. Mary's Infant School. I made the mistake of asking them if they had any problems getting their children to and from school, and believe me, they had plenty; and they didn't waste any time telling me what they were.

A footpath from one of the big estates to the school, known as The Pieces, was in a poor state and they wanted it cleaned up and made more 'user friendly'. They were also concerned about road safety immediately outside St. Mary's School, and both issues were important to them.

Surprisingly, some parents expressed the view that they were pleased they were going to have the chance to participate in a local election, which they believed had been denied them in previous years.

In spite of what the cynics say, some people do want to participate in the democratic system, which is why they vote.

Looking back, I realise the importance of the 1976 election. I learned from the people I talked to about their concerns, and I listened to their aspirations, which were no different from mine. I had no doubt in my mind that this was something I wanted to do; if I could improve the quality of life for people in any small way, then that would be an enormous bonus for me as well.

I still had to wait for two more years to pass before I could start on the long journey of being a councillor, but I have never regretted the choice I made at the time, and there is still a bit more time left for me to achieve further successes before I call it a day.

In the early days of electioneering people wrote to the local press asking questions about PAB credibility; they wanted to know who we were, where did we come from and what were our motives.

Others wanted to know why these independent people, who claimed they were against bureaucracy, wanted to stand against the long-standing Conservative members of the council – it was simply unheard of.

It was brought to my notice that a prominent member of the Prestbury community had been heard suggesting that we were really 'closet communists' trying to take over the establishment. Further information revealed that it was part of the tactics of those whom we were trying to remove from the council chamber, and it was likely to last for a long time.

For many years, Prestbury residents had not concerned themselves about local elections at any level, mainly because the local population had been content to leave the political situation 'to those best used to managing it', a saying often used when we were talking to local residents.

Because of this attitude there had been a continuous process of Conservative party members being elected unopposed on both the parish council and the Cheltenham Rural District Council. Hardly anyone I spoke to could remember the last time an election took place for any of the local government seats.

In the Prestbury ward, Conservative councillors Mrs Rosemary Gregory, Lt. Col Aubrey Nichols and Mr Timothy Spencer-Cox were recognised as the respected stalwarts of the village and were often re-elected unopposed.

Mrs Gregory, a character of the age, chairman of the parish council and "the woman who wore large hats" as she was often described to me, lived in Lake House in Lake Street at the time.

Lake House which dates back to 1647 is a fine building, but the lake itself, which used to exist in front of Lake Farm, disappeared during the last century.

Lake Street is historical and dates back to medieval times and many of its buildings are listed and afforded protection from demolition and change. It is classified as an important street in the Prestbury Conservation Area.It was also a street where you needed a 'bob-or-two' if you were going to remain there for a long time.

Lt Col Aubrey Nichols, a lovely man who never missed an opportunity to tell me he was a staunch Conservative but often admitted to me, confidentially of course, that he had a lot of time for the principles of PAB.He was very much a military man, a stiff upper-lip man who was always smartly dressed and had an air of authority about him. He had presence.

Later years, when I was canvassing in the Prestbury High Street, where he lived with his wife, he confessed to me that he had been voting for PAB candidates for some time because he thought "they have been doing a damned fine job for the village". Well done Aubrey, I always swore I would never tell anyone and I didn't until I started writing this book.

This was a defining moment for me because it taught me never to accept the age old saying that opinions never change; they can and they often do, and like immovable objects can sometimes be moved quite easily too.

Looking at the recorded Conservative vote in the 1976 elections and comparing it to their vote in every election leading up to the election in 2010, it can be seen that opinions can change and they can remain constant for a number of years.

One of the interesting things about canvassing is the experience one gains from meeting people. Some people appear to take things too seriously and others go to the other extreme and try to belittle, or poke fun at whatever one is trying to do. Nevertheless, it is all good fun and good for keeping one's feet firmly on the ground.

Whilst canvassing in 1976 I came across a fellow who was overjoyed to see me, not just to tell me that he was going to vote for me, but to tell me that he had received a visit the previous night from Aubrey Nichols.

Not surprisingly, Aubrey had wanted the householder and his family to vote for him. According to the householder, he introduced himself as Lt. Colonel Nichols and he was seeking the householder's support at the forthcoming election.

What was your reply, I asked.

> "I told him that I was Private Tomkins, formally of the Gloucestershire Regiment and no way would I be voting for him."

I couldn't help it, but I burst out laughing, possibly because of the spontaneity of the occasion. The way it was said was so funny and we both laughed, but what the householder didn't know was that I could imagine the look on the face of Aubrey Nichols as he received the comment.

As I walked back down the drive I wondered whether I had just experienced a sign of the times – I bet Aubrey did because canvassing was a new experience for him. In the past there had been no elections – all he had to do was to sign the 'acceptance of office' papers which entitled him to represent Prestbury for another four years.

Timothy Spencer-Cox was well known as an accomplished horse rider in the Cheltenham Racecourse circle. He spent a lot of his time horse riding around the parish and he had links with local equestrian centres.

He was a long-serving member of the National Pony Club, which was founded in 1929 and he became its chairman in 1997.

*

The result of the election was a severe shock to the Conservative Party and its supporters as they realised that the PAB candidates had secured 32 per cent share of the votes against the Conservatives' 37 per cent. They probably regarded it as an electoral disaster.

They had come close to losing their seats to a group of unknowns, so they were instinctively concerned about their futures on the local councils.

For PAB it was a moral victory if nothing else.

I polled 965 votes, Mike Hunt 927 and Peter Richmond 912.

CHAPTER 5

Magistrates' Court

"Justice is the constant and perpetual wish to render to everyone his due".
Justinian (AD 483– 565)

David John Hall was a civil servant who lived in Up Hatherley. He was vice chairman of the parish council and one of a number of residents who refused to place his refuse bin at the front of the house. He decided to summon Tewkesbury Borough Council in the magistrates' court for 25 pence a day for every day they failed to collect his refuse from or near the back door of his property.

At a court hearing in July 1976, he told the local magistrates that before initiating its controversial front gate-to-front gate refuse collection service, the council should have made a bye-law before changing the system. This was a provision in the Public Health Act, 1936.

Mr Hall explained to the court that the parish of Up Hatherley consisted of many new open plan estates without front gates and with long driveways. He was concerned, and so were other local residents, that rubbish in paper sacks or plastic bags, if put out overnight, would be exposed to bad weather: high winds could damage the bags and expose the content, which in turn would attract vermin.

There was a possibility that the roads could become strewn with unsightly rubbish, blown about by the wind, and this would also be unhygienic and would lower the quality of life for residents.

His comments were heard in silence apart from the occasional 'hear hear' from members of the public, which brought a disapproving look from the chairman of the court, Mr Bernard Ward.

David Hall was warming to the occasion when he explained to the court that they should not be looking at a parish situation where the majority of residents live in large houses with drive-in and drive-out driveways. Neither did his parish have rows of terraced houses where collections are made on the day that the rubbish bins are put out by the householders.

"In any event" said Mr Hall, and this one of his strong points, "If Tewkesbury Borough Council was intent on changing its refuse collection service then they had a duty to provide a refuse container that was up to doing the job".

He had given the council seven days notice to collect four weeks of refuse from his property, and as they had failed to do this without a reasonable excuse under Section 72 of the Public Health Act 1936, he was entitled to 25 pence per day from the expiry of the notice.

David Hall, although vice chairman of the parish council, brought the case to court as a private individual, and he faced a strong team from Tewkesbury Borough Council, which included a barrister and the council's solicitor Mr Michael Mortimer.

There was no doubt that the council took the matter very seriously and had no intention of losing the case against Mr Hall. They knew that if they could not successfully defend their position in the magistrates' court, they would have to consider the possibility of taking the matter to a higher authority, or admit that their attempt to change the system without a bye-law was wrong.

The Borough Council officers knew that if they lost the case in the Magistrates' Court then their chances of winning a possible high court challenge would be weakened.

David Hall continued his evidence by telling the court that he had received a reply from Tewkesbury Borough Council on 4th June 1976, confirming that no bye-law had been made by the council concerning the change in the refuse collection system.

He told the court in a loud voice *"This was the whole point of me bringing the action before the court. By not making a byelaw, the council was in breach of the Public Health Act 1936"*.

He was sympathetic towards the council's case of wanting to change the refuse collection system, but *"they should do it within the framework of the law"* he said.

He told the court that prior to the reorganisation in 1974 the residents of Up Hatherley had a refuse collection system which was advertised in leaflets that were regularly distributed to householders telling them "their dustbins would be collected and returned to the place where they normally stood".

"'That was the system" he said *"and everyone had been satisfied with the service"*.

In answer to a question put to Mr Hall from the court it appeared that 'Tewkesbury Borough Council had assured local residents that the re-organisation of local government would mean 'better government and better services', but what it meant in reality, was the council posting a notice on notice boards around the parish in March, telling residents that their refuse collection service would change to a front-gate to front-gate system from 1st April 1976'.

There had been no consultation with the parish council and as far as I know the local councillor, Bill Norton, had not been made aware of the changes either.

David Hall's case was that the Borough Council had not given the local residents a chance to discuss the matter, nor the opportunity to raise objections that could have been considered by a higher authority. He made it clear to the court that this was the basis of his case together with the council's non-compliance with the requirements laid down in the Public Health Act; he appealed to the court to find his case proved against the local authority.

The barrister, Mr Desmond Keane, acting for the local authority, asked Mr Hall whether he agreed 'that the level of refuse service to be provided by a local authority was a matter to be decided by that authority and that the Borough Council had the discretion to improve or change the system?'

Mr Hall replied that he had agreed with the point from the beginning, but it was not the point he had been making in his submission. He emphasised again in the strongest possible terms that the changes could only be made providing the council acquired a bylaw in accordance with the requirements of the Public Health Act.

Mr Keane then asked Mr Hall

"If the council did not provide a bylaw, would he expect the council to collect his rubbish from any part of his premises wherever he decided to leave it, either indoors or outdoors?"

Mr Hall sensibly replied, *"I would expect the local authority to collect it from where it stands near my back gate, as they have done for the past twelve years"*.

Undaunted, Mr Keane then asked Mr Hall whether he had considered that the council was perhaps asking him and other residents to assist the council in the execution of their duties.

There was a gasp from the members of the public as they sat in the public gallery, straining their ears to catch every word that was being said. When the barrister explained to Mr Hall *"It was only a request from the Borough Council asking for a degree of reasonable co-operation, not a requirement"*.

This brought another gasp from the gallery and there were clear signs from Mr Bernard Ward's body language that he would not be in the mood for any disruption from those present in the public gallery.

There was no doubt that David Hall was up to the task of putting his case to the court, and he gave the impression he was winning the argument. He had a smile on his face when he replied to the barrister, and at the same time looking hard towards the chairman of the bench, *"If it was a request Mr Keane, then that would imply that there would be no sanctions against me. This has not happened. I have not had my refuse collected for the past ten weeks."*

The Leader of the Council, Councillor the Hon. Alasdair Andrew Orr Morrison, who was called as a witness for the council, told the court "Prior to the decision by the council on 20th January, there had been considerable discussion to rationalise the refuse system throughout the area".

This statement by Cllr Morrison was met with stony silence from the public gallery, many attending because there had been a distinct lack of discussion with members of the public prior to implementation of the new refuse scheme.

David Hall in cross-examination refuted the claim about prior discussion, pointing out that it had been the lack of consultation at the heart of the public's concerns. He asked Cllr Morrison whether his council had considered making a bylaw before changing the system.

In reply, Cllr Morrison admitted that they had considered it but had decided that it was not necessary in law, and it was undesirable for a number of reasons.

The Borough Surveyor, Paul Fearnside, another witness for the council, told the court that there were over 700 residents in the Tewkesbury Borough area who had

Front-gate dustbin row: councillor to seek court order

COUN. L. G. GODWIN, chairman of Up Hatherley Parish Council, wants to take out an injunction stopping Tewkesbury Borough Council from implementing a new refuse collection scheme in the area, he said at last night's parish council meeting.
—Go?

FRONT-GATE DUSTBIN PLAN APPROVED

TEWKESBURY BOROUGH COUNCIL'S environmental services committee yesterday agreed to recommend, as their first option, that a rationalised front-gate to front-gate refuse collection service be introduced in the whole borough area.

Mrs Godwin adds another bag to her increasing pile of rubbish this morning.

Mrs Godwin putting out her black bags of rubbish.

not complied with the new system since it was introduced, but the number was diminishing week by week.

He also claimed that he had not heard of any other local authority applying a by-law in order to change a system of refuse collection, but when challenged on this point, he admitted that 'a recent survey revealed that 16 local authorities had by-laws governing their refuse collection systems'.

The barrister in summing up on behalf of the council told the court that the council were acting in a reasonable manner. He suggested to the court that the decision taken by the council was based on reason and not on prejudice or any 'extraneous situation'.

He concluded, *"The council provided a service and they could expect reasonable co-operation if you wanted to avail yourself of that service."*

Mr Hall, in his summary, fell back on his earlier claim that the Public Health Act 1936, made it clear that if a local authority wanted to change the system of refuse collection then they should apply a bylaw. The section in the Act was very clear and he thought that a clause in such an important piece of legislation was a protection against local authorities wanting to impose an inferior system of refuse collection on their ratepayers.

In his final plea to the court, *"If the Council was intent on changing the style of refuse collection, then surely they had a duty to provide refuse containers that were up to the job. Plastic bags are inadequate"*, he said.

He also made the point *"If proper consultation had taken place with the parish council about the changes, we would have been able to discuss the matter of suitable containers along with the provision of a bylaw"*.

After an all day hearing the presiding chairman of the court, Mr Bernard Ward, declared that there were many facets to the case and a lot of paperwork to study. He announced that the case would be adjourned for two weeks and then a court decision would be made.

Upon resumption two weeks later, Mr Ward told the court "The bench had considered all the submissions made and they considered that the local authority had the power to make a bylaw but they had decided not to".

"We also think" he continued "that it was reasonable for the local authority not to exercise that power."

The chairman concluded *"We feel the local authority had reasonable excuse, having regard to the needs of the community as a whole, and the need to provide a uniform service to the whole of the area"*.

David Hall, clearly disappointed at the decision of the court, as were the large number of residents in the public gallery, stated that in spite of the court decision, it was still a matter of principle and he would consider appealing against the decision.

"What is the point of having such a clause in an Act of Parliament if courts can ignore it?" he said.

The PAB Group having kept a careful eye on the proceedings in the courtroom, soon came to the opinion that any changes they were hoping to make in the way the local authority conducted its business were going to be difficult to achieve.

It seemed to me and other members of the PAB Group that even when it appeared the law was on the side of the individual, it was bureaucracy that won in the end.

Whilst the court case was not the end of the refuse dispute, and there will be more on the subject later, it was the forerunner to the eventual implementation of the green wheeled bin service by Tewkesbury Borough Council, and later adopted by other local authorities across the country.

If only we had known at the time that this was going to happen – but hindsight is a wonderful thing, and of course, a crystal ball would have been useful too.

CHAPTER 6

Protecting The Green Belt

Protection is not a principle, but an expedient.
Benjamin Disraeli, House of Commons, 17th March 1845

Terry Joyner was true to his word and provided everything the PAB group needed to get its message across to the residents of Cheltenham and to those who lived in the outlying villages. Terry owned the Leicester Office Equipment business in Cheltenham and he not only provided printing facilities, but allowed the PAB management committee to meet in his office after the staff had left the premises.

The group had made an early impression in the Tewkesbury Borough Council areas, not least because of its three councillors from Bishop's Cleeve and the incisive inputs that came from Bill Norton. They were determined to prove that the PAB group had a serious message to get across to the electorate. The PAB group as a whole supported the attempt by Up Hatherley Parish Council to keep their long-standing refuse collection system, and they also intended to pursue with the utmost vigour the defence of the green belt in the Tewkesbury council area.

During those early years, we arranged meetings in eleven different venues in eleven different villages where we thought the protection of the green belt would be of paramount importance to the local people. It sounds a simple enough task, but to most members of the group it meant that a lot of research into possible venues was needed in the first instance; what facilities did some of the more remote villages have for holding a meeting; who did one book a room with; and how much would it cost?

With some villages we had to admit defeat because the booking clerk was unsure whether a meeting about the green belt might be considered to be a 'political meeting', which seemed a vacuous comment to me because the meeting was going to explain to the local residents the possible dangers of development in the green belt, and how we would argue against it whenever it came up for discussion in the council chamber.

There was also the matter of advertising each of the eleven events, the distribution of leaflets and payment for the cost of the rooms. Probably because of the adrenaline or the exuberance of everyone in those early days of the PAB group, members seemed willing to put their hands in their pockets to pay the costs.

The eleven meetings attracted over 1300 people, which speaks for itself, and taking into account that the one venue in Winchcombe was poorly attended, [about thirty turned up], the average attendance was well over a hundred residents.

Because of its importance the green belt was always going to be a topic of interest for councillors and local residents whenever there was a threat of development. It will be referred to frequently throughout the remaining chapters.

The PAB councillors meanwhile were asking as many questions as they could and seldom accepted the reports by officers at face value.

Bill Ferguson, a veteran reporter for the *Gloucestershire Echo* wrote an article on 7th December 1976 headed "The trouble with Tewkesbury council" and it caused a great deal of discussion and it prompted several local residents and council officers to respond to it.

Bill wrote that the "much maligned Tewkesbury Borough Council's illness is self-induced and its wounds self-inflicted". He continued by writing that the council had been content to 'amble along' since its formation in 1974, but the local elections in 1976 had changed all that and it had "jolted this happy band of legislators in their comfortable chairs". He referred to the fact that the elections had "brought a new body of opinion, representatives of a movement born out of disquiet and concern at the council's performance, who had taken their seats in the council chamber – representatives of the People Against Bureaucracy movement".

This was the part in the article that I liked the most: "Immediately an air of disquiet, if not disapproval, became apparent in the chamber. The new councillors, sitting as PAB members and keeping their political views to themselves, had obviously upset this well-ordered assembly".

On the same page as the article was a large photograph of the council chamber showing the horseshoe shape of the seating arrangement. On one side sat the Conservative councillors plus the so-called independents, and on the other side sat councillors from the Labour Party and the Liberal Alliance.

Observing the entrance of the PAB councillors from the public gallery, it was clear that no-one in the chamber was going to move closer to allow the three Bishop's Cleeve and one Up Hatherley councillors from taking their seats. The Borough Secretary, Ron Wheeler, appeared to guide the councillors to a table in front of the dais where the mayor and the Borough Secretary sat.

This seemed to me at the time to be an unfortunate way to treat my colleagues, not least because they would have to sit with their backs to the rest of the council-lors in the chamber, but also because it looked like an act of meanness.

I made representations to Ron Wheeler and he assured me the seating for PAB councillors was a temporary arrangement and it did change, but it took much longer than it should have done.

Bill Ferguson's excellent article went into further detail about the arrival of the PAB councillors in the council chamber who apparently 'asked questions on virtually every subject within the council's sphere – housing, recreation, health and welfare, finance. Especially finance'.

As the *Echo* report stated "They were only indulging in the task for which they were elected". It was also true as the article explained that some local authorities allowed the Press and public into subcommittee meetings, others, including

Tewkesbury Borough Council – did not. This was a matter of concern to the PAB councillors who believed that any meeting behind closed doors was not good for local democracy, and it prevented ratepayers from knowing how their money was being spent.

Not only did the council prevent the Press and public from attending certain meetings, but occasionally an elected councillor was asked to leave the room if he or she was not a member of the committee. As the new PAB councillors were on a learning curve in their first six months on the council, it wasn't a surprise to know that they were anxious to attend all the meetings, including those where they were not members, but willing to observe what was going on.

This too upset the old guard who immediately suspected the PAB councillors of wanting to 'spy on their colleagues' and who might reveal to the excluded press and public what was going on behind closed doors.

The editor of the *Gloucestershire Echo* put it in simple words: "When is a public matter confidential? Presumably when the outcome will affect every ratepayer under Tewkesbury Borough Council's dustbin lids. The council's environmental services committee went into secret session to discuss their continuing saga which might well be called The Great Dustbin Dilemma".

The editor couldn't understand why the district's elected representatives were so reluctant to talk about such things in public 'as the issue had been smouldering like a rubbish tip for months'.

Cllr Sylvia Hughes tried to remain in a finance subcommittee meeting as an observer, for no other reason but to listen to the debate on the district auditor's second interim report. Once again, this was another occasion when 'the old guard', by their actions, appeared to be nervous about PAB councillors listening to debates that concerned public finance.

I was not aware of the problem until I read the report in the local newspaper. Seemingly, the Press were allowed to stay to hear what the interim report contained, but not an elected councillor. This seemed rather odd.

In the newspaper article it reported that two councillors had objected to Cllr Hughes remaining in the room; one was Eric Foster, who readers will recall in an earlier chapter, was allowed to keep his seat on the council largely because the PAB group agreed to nominate three candidates in Bishop's Cleeve rather than four.

His proposal was disgraceful and his actions would not be forgotten at the next local government elections.

Even today, councils in most areas are reluctant to allow the press and public into meetings in case it might be too much for the general public to hear. The Local Government Act 1972 – Exempt Information, made it easier for 'secret' meetings to take place, but with the content of the meeting disguised as 'confidential'.

1976 and 1977 were hectic periods for me. There were so many things going on at the same time I found it difficult to cope with them all. As chairman of Up Hatherley Parish Council, I was constantly involved with the refuse dispute: I was secretary to a newly formed independent group: arranging the public meetings and speaking at them on the matter of defending the green belt: being a member of the magistracy: earning a living and being the guardian angel of a growing family.

And not forgetting I was a dedicated sportsman that meant absence from home through the winter and summer months particularly at weekends.

It took up a lot of valuable time, but the successes achieved over thirty eight years, have been enormous. Not least, we have given local residents across a wide area a choice about who should represent them in the council chamber – a political party, or a dedicated independent group of people who believed that 'party politics' had no place in the affairs of local government.

As this was the bedrock of what PAB members believed, we spent a good deal of time in Terry Joyner's office in the early days agreeing a 'statement of aims' which we felt should be widely publicised. The message was simple; we would fight against bureaucracy, defend the green belt, put the needs of people before politics and oppose secret meetings.

The 'aims' of the group have been updated from time to time to meet the changes that have occurred in local government which will be referred to in later chapters.

Terry Joyner quickly endeared the membership to the art of communication, which included the publication of a PAB *Newsletter*. He was adamant that if we were to succeed with what he called 'our dedicated mission' it was essential to keep the voting population with us.

He was right of course, and the group have published a twice yearly *Newsletter* since 1976, informing local residents of what we had been doing, including the failures as well as the achievements.

In the May 1977 edition of the *Newsletter*, Terry Joyner wrote the following forward:

"The Action Group can be proud of its achievements to date, but none is more important than the abolition of secret meetings held by Tewkesbury Borough Council. Ever since the formation of the Action Group, through its publications and public meetings, we have attacked the system of 'secret meetings'. We believed, in fact, one of our original claims set out quite clearly to abolish secret meetings and decisions, that the Press and general public had a democratic right to attend any meeting which the council might hold. Now, through the pressures of the Action Group and particularly by the efforts of the four PAB councillors, all subcommittee meetings held by Tewkesbury Borough Council are open to the Press and public.

The golden prize for their efforts was the eventual acceptance by the council that the Finance subcommittee should also operate under the eye of public scrutiny.

So my message is quite clear – keep up the good work and enjoy yourselves in the process. We have done a lot for which we can be proud, and with everyone's support we can achieve a great deal more".

Terry Joyner (Vice-chairman)

The message was warmly received by most readers of the PAB *Newsletter*. There were those, of course, no matter what successes we achieved, who would write to the local newspaper complaining about anything that did not conform to their beliefs.

Several letter-writers to the local newspaper were critical of my stand against the new council refuse bin collection system, stating that they believed that the alleged saving of money would ultimately mean they would have less council tax to pay.

This was a misunderstanding of the workings of council; they also believed that it was not important for the Public Health Act 1936 to be upheld.

One of several letters to the newspaper supported me and one letter "urged me to continue the fight against the Borough council and suggested that if I decided to contest the next council election in Prestbury, he would do everything he could to get me elected".

I smiled as I read his closing paragraph: "It is a pity some of our Borough representatives don't follow Mr Godwin's example and do some bleating. They could find plenty to bleat about".

I hadn't seen the alleged critical letter to the Press about my 'bleating' but if my challenge to the bureaucrats is called 'bleating' then I would have been all for it.

I hadn't known then (1977) that I would be contesting a by-election in Prestbury a year later, and I have no idea whether he helped me to become a borough councillor or not.

One of the four successful Conservative candidates in 1976 was a local resident called Robert Jackson. He lived in the Wyman's Brook estate and he was a member of Prestbury Parish Council. He worked for G.C.H.Q., and in his spare time he assisted with the distribution of bus tokens to the elderly for the council.

I don't know how much of his spare time the issuing of bus tokens would entail, but out of the blue in July 1978 came a report that Robert Jackson would be resigning from Tewkesbury Borough Council because he had been posted overseas.

In those days, Prestbury consisted of two wards – St. Nicholas and St. Mary's.

As there were four seats on the council, three were allocated to the larger ward of St. Mary's and one seat to represent the St Nicholas ward.

Robert Jackson represented the St. Nicholas ward.

The PAB Group immediately called a special meeting of its management committee to discuss the situation and to decide whether to nominate a candidate for the impending by-election. There was a unanimous decision that we should contest the by-election and the thought of having another chance to put someone up against an establishment character was exciting. I recall the air of excitement in Terry Joyner's office, but it didn't last because as in every case since, the difficulty was finding a candidate who was suitable and willing to be nominated.

Finding a candidate who is local is always the best option. When it becomes impossible to find such a person then several names are suggested and each name is carefully considered.

Several members of the committee urged me to stand, and I remember being equally adamant by telling the meeting that the electors of Prestbury would not vote for a person who lived in Up Hatherley if they had the chance to vote for a person who lived in the local area.

The discussion on trying to find a candidate went on for some time, covering the same ground over and over again. It was getting late and it seemed as though the meeting would continue until a name was forthcoming.

The fatal mistake I made at the time was to suggest to the committee that all we needed to do on this occasion, as it was only a by-election, was to put forward a name as 'a paper candidate' to ensure that the seat would be contested. This would prevent the inevitable Conservative candidate from being elected unopposed.

I was immediately nominated to be the 'paper candidate' in the forthcoming by-election. The chairman called for a show of hands, which was agreed nem con (I abstained) and the meeting closed immediately.

It was so swift I hardly had chance to blink let alone anything else.

Terry Joyner, twice mayor and a former leader of the Conservative group on the council knew a golden opportunity and when to take it. And before I realised what I had done, it seemed as though I was in my car and driving home in what I can only call a state of bewilderment.

I broke the news to my wife as gently as I could, and surprisingly she accepted what had happened, but she was also concerned that I had too much to do already and offered words of comfort. She may also have thought that the seat was a fairly safe seat for the Conservatives, which it was, but I felt relieved if nothing else.

Like the inaugural meeting in Lakeside School in 1976, this particular meeting of the PAB Group was another turning point that changed the course of my life, and one that I have never regretted.

The by-election was called for 14th September 1978 and the Conservatives made an early announcement that their candidate would be a local man whose name was John Cann. He lived on the western edge of Prestbury.

When I talked to knowledgeable people in the parish, I discovered that he was unknown in the centre of the village. His election address was bland and it talked about the reasons why he thought the 'modern Conservative Party had more appeal to him than did socialism', which I'm sure had little appeal to many of the voters in the St. Nicholas ward.

I read his election address, which was lacking in substance and based on politics rather than the needs of the community; I was spurred on in a way I would not have thought possible a few weeks before.

Graham Vero was another candidate who intended standing as an independent (which didn't help my cause). He claimed in his election address that he was a dog lover and he enjoyed walking his dog across the local green spaces. He claimed he was totally independent.

My election address, on the other hand, had been well crafted by Terry Joyner and Doug Grazier and was excellent. I used the same photograph on the front of the leaflet that I had supplied to the local newspaper, which they had regularly used to associate me with the ongoing refuse dispute. Reports of the debates at the parish council meetings were always reported.

Inside my election address I asked the electorate the following question:

"What Have Tewkesbury Borough Council Done For You"?

I answered the question for them by listing the items the council had provided such as new council offices at a cost of £1.5 million: a film theatre at a cost of £320,000 and they had at the same time subsidised the swimming pool to the tune of £40,000. I then asked the electors whether any of the expenditure had occurred in Prestbury and provided the answer by telling them that the expenditure was all in the town of Tewkesbury.

On the other side of the page I set down what I would try to achieve to improve the quality of life for the residents of Prestbury. I told the electors: "It was time for a change, and the change could be achieved with an independent voice unfettered by 'party politics' representing the true interests of the electorate". I told the electors I would fight bureaucracy that was all too evident in the council chamber, and I offered them a better deal if they voted for me. I must admit that for a 'paper candidate' I was making a strong case for the electors to vote for me.

Knocking on doors and talking to people has always been a pleasure for me. Seldom do I meet a rude and disgruntled resident during an election campaign, and that has been the case throughout my long association with the parish of Prestbury. Only my opponents used my Up Hatherley address as a means of trying to defeat me, and I hardly ever met someone who objected to me trying to represent their area when I lived so far away. In fact, it became a useful tool in my favour, because I could easily explain that the needs and aspirations of Prestbury people were no different from the needs and aspirations of people who happen to be my neighbours living in similar houses on the other side of town.

The plus side has always been the pleasure of hearing what people have to say about the needs of a particular area. Whilst they are interested in the way a local council operates, they are never slow to tell you about the difficulties they have had trying to get the council to meet what they believe are their rights. Inevitably they add the usual caveat that they pay their rates, are law-abiding citizens and they deserve a better service from those responsible.

I agreed with this line in 1978, not because I was seeking their vote, but having seen and experienced what had taken place in the new Tewkesbury Borough Council since 1974 – I was on their side.

When I knocked on doors and introduced myself, the residents often remarked "you are the refuse dispute man" which sometimes followed with a handshake, which was always a good sign. To listen to those people then, the phrase 'we are all in this together' now, would never have been more applicable.

Three days before the election, I held a public meeting in St. Nicolas Church Hall in Swindon Lane. In the invitation to local residents I asked them to consider "why their rates were so high; whether they thought they were getting value for money; did they consider their views were being adequately represented; and did they think that Tewkesbury Borough Council was an efficient council".

Around thirty people attended the meeting to hear my answers to the questions I had posed in the invitation. It was clear from the residents' comments and questions that they were not pleased with the council on many issues.

I was satisfied that the meeting had achieved what I hoped it would do.

A question from a woman who alleged she was speaking on behalf of several parents from the area concerned the safety of local children going to school. She told me that the local children attending the Swindon Village School had to cross the railway level crossing at the western end of Swindon Lane.

The problem was a daily congestion of mothers with buggies, unaccompanied children and cars at the gates, which in those days were manually operated.

I gave the typical reply from a person trying to get elected; I understood the problem and promised that if I was successful on polling day, I would give it my full attention.

In my attempt to become a councillor I was on tenterhooks all day Thursday 14th September. During the counting of the votes, which didn't take long due to a low turnout of 25 per cent, I watched nervously as the other 'independent' seemed to be getting more votes than me. Then another ballot box was opened and as the votes lay on the table, it looked as though there were more votes for me than for the other two candidates.

What a relief when the last votes were counted – it was a close thing. I polled 598 votes, John Cann 555 and Graham Vero 230. There was even more relief when I realised that I had won an election, which I was not supposed to, because I was only a 'paper candidate'. Not only had I stopped an easy win for the Conservative group, but I had become a borough councillor to add to the cares of being chairman of Up Hatherley Parish Council.

The look on the faces of the local Conservative hierarchy at the end of the count was a sight I shall never forget. I am sure they had thought that the seat was safe and it did not augur well for the council elections in May 1979.

I slept well that night; there were no wild celebrations following the win, although the other PAB councillors were ecstatic about the increase in PAB numbers on Tewkesbury Borough Council.

The following morning I set down a list of things that I would be taking up with the borough council. The list was long and I remembered drawing a red flag in the corner of the paper, which was to constantly remind me that I would have to go through all this again when the next cycle of local elections came up next year.

My first task was to look into the matter of road safety for the children going to and from school along Swindon Lane and across the railway level crossing.

I decided the best way to deal with this would be to see what was actually happening along Swindon Lane, which would mean getting across to Swindon Lane before the children and their parents started out on their journeys.

The Wyman's Brook estate where the majority of children live is on the south side of Swindon Lane. The north side is mainly open fields with sporadic development.

There is a footpath on the south side of the lane that goes all the way down to the level crossing, and this was where the problem lay.

As I walked down towards the level crossing I could see the manually controlled barrier being closed by the railway gatekeeper. Once closed, the build up of traffic was swift and the matter of child safety immediately became apparent as the children crossed over to the other side of the road. The children as well as adults were putting their hands on the bonnets of the cars in a gesture of 'please stop' as the cars were slowly coming to a halt. It was a bizarre situation.

Once I reached the gates I could see the problem more clearly – the pedestrian gate was on the other (north) side to the footpath, which meant that all pedestrian users had to cross in front of the cars in order to get to the gate. It was a crazy situation and it seemed worse when the barriers were opened and children and parents streamed across the level crossing. There was no control.

When school was over the parents and children went through the same procedure whenever the pedestrian gate was opened. And of course, this procedure happened throughout the day and throughout the year for the children and other pedestrian users. The remedy was simple – the pedestrian gate needed to be relocated on the south side of Swindon Lane, but why had the situation existed for so long?

I contacted British Rail (the name at the time) and the county highway authority and we all agreed to meet on site. To my great relief, both representatives agreed that it was a dangerous situation that could be remedied by transferring the gate from the north to the south side of the lane.

We then walked over the crossing and considered what would happen once the gate was relocated on the south side of Swindon Lane. There is a T junction at the end of the lane and the children would need to cross another road called Wyman's Lane in order to continue their journey to school. The Swindon Village School lies in a northerly direction along Wyman's Lane.

The county highway engineer came up with the answer – a pedestrian controlled crossing in Wyman's Lane. The children and parents, once they had crossed the road in safety, could then take a footpath across a public park, which was a direct route to the school and a safer one.

Job done, and for once a job carried out expeditiously without bureaucratic hold-ups, which had been the usual hallmark of council behaviour when problems needed to be resolved.

The early years of PAB had been momentous: a growing membership, public meetings around the county, press conferences, the refuse dispute and social events that included dinner dances and other forms of entertainment.

The management committee met regularly, sometimes at a different venue in order to encourage more people in the area to join the group.

Several key members who worked for GCHQ were posted to overseas posts, and we had what seemed to be a regular change in members of the management committee. Harry Tebbs, a member who lived in Swindon Village, agreed to take on the role of treasurer after Bunty Griffiths stood down, and at his first meeting announced that "the group needed to increase its funding if we were going to fight future elections". He was right of course, the fifty pence membership fee was not going to take us very far unless additional income was found elsewhere.

The committee came up with the usual things such as holding regular jumble sales, which in those days were very popular; social events that were profit-making rather than a non-profit social occasion were regularly suggested.

Terry Joyner in his usual way came up with a suggestion. He lived at Kings Farm, Woodmancote, with his wife Barbara and their family. The house was fairly large and the garden was expansive. He suggested that a wine and cheese party could be held at Kings Farm from 8:00 p.m., to 10:00 p.m. with the proceeds from the ticket sales being donated to PAB. Needless to say, the wine and cheese parties of which there were several were always over-subscribed, but the people who were lucky to obtain tickets also became committed members of the PAB Group. These parties made the group financially sound and the publicity we got from them was enormous.

Whilst fund-raising is important to any group like PAB, it was also important to deal with the issues that affected the lives of individuals and local communities. The issues were many and they all received equal treatment.

All councils have strong Local Plan policies which include the protection of the green belt and green open spaces in local communities. The boundaries and sometimes the wordings of the policies can be open to different interpretations by planning officers in order to support their recommendations for development. And often the planning committee members are not sufficiently bothered to take the time or the effort to read what the policies say or what they were designed to do.

The matter of planning control and their consequences, which in some cases ended with disastrous results for a community, will be examined in more detail in later chapters.

A resident who lived in the centre of Prestbury village was concerned that the rear area of a garage, which in his opinion had always been an open space, was gradually being turned into a storage and vehicle parking area. When I visited the area to see what the problem was all about, I saw not just an open space, but a garden with flowers and grass. The cars on site were beginning to encroach on the grassed area and if the business expanded then it would not be long before the open space would be lost. Careful investigation revealed that the owner of the garage had been given planning permission to store vehicles at the rear of the premises, but the permission had run out of time, which is usually five years.

At the subsequent planning meeting I proposed that enforcement action should be taken by the council against the garage owner for contravention of planning control. I reminded the committee that when planning permission was given in 1971 for the erection of a workshop at the rear of the garage, it was on the condition that the rear of the site should be kept as a garden and not used for storage or parking of vehicles. This condition was agreed by the committee to ensure that the amenities of the adjoining residents were not harmed.

The borough solicitor, John Daniels, came to the rescue of the garage owner by telling the committee that in his opinion, the work had begun before the expiration of the five year planning period. I had already contacted someone from the advisory service of the *Journal of Planning and Environmental Law* who cast doubts on the opinion of Mr Daniels.

But when it came to the vote, the planning committee members did what they will usually do, put their hands up for the applicant even when substantive professional advice and evidence to the contrary is provided by other competent people.

In time, the garage business ended, the owner sold out to a developer and the area is now developed.

I didn't know at the time, but this open space was the first of many I would be defending throughout the thirty six years of my time as a borough councillor.

I have to admit that my success rate has not been good for the simple reason that those who have been elected to protect these important areas for the benefit of the local communities, have not been sufficiently diligent and have often succumbed to the rhetoric of the planning officers.

Up Hatherley Parish Council, with the support from other parish councils continued their dispute with Tewkesbury Borough Council (TBC) over the changed method of the refuse collection system. I was now in a different position with the dispute – an elected borough councillor as well as chairman of the parish council.

The change of position meant that one of its own councillors would be going to the High Court to sue the council of which he was a member. At the time it sounded bizarre, but it was a situation that was going to be repeated again when litigation was chosen as the only way forward for resolving disputes.

I went to the Royal Courts of Justice in June 1976 with Graham Daniel, a solicitor from Robinsons & Co, to listen to Mr Justice Kusak in chambers consider two applications concerning the refuse dispute. The first application was a request by TBC asking the High Court judge to strike out the action by Up Hatherley Parish Council, but this was refused. As regards the second, Mr Michael Mortimer the borough solicitor represented TBC, and he gave documentary evidence to support TBC's case. I did not see the documents so I have no idea what they contained.

The Up Hatherley application was for an interlocutory injunction, following the issue of a writ to stop TBC from introducing the new system of kerbside collection, and for a reversion to the old back door to back door collection system.

The judge was reminded of the purpose of the Public Health Act 1936 by the parish council's barrister and he made several legal points concerning the Act.

Following the submissions by both sides the judge refused the interlocutory injunction pending a full hearing of the parish council's case.

Whilst this was disappointing it did indicate that the Up Hatherley Parish Council's case had substance and it would be up to the parish council and the local community to decide whether they wanted to spend a large sum of money to stop the unwanted new system of refuse collection being implemented.

On the way back to Cheltenham I pondered on a number of possibilities concerning my next actions and the actions of all the parishes that had supported us in our stance. I knew that I would be expected to hold a special meeting for Up Hatherley residents to explain what had happened in the High Court. I would also need to tell them of the possible large financial burden that they might have to bear if we lost the case. The parishioners had borne the cost so far, but would they be willing to go the extra mile and challenge TBC at a full hearing in the High Court? If there was a plus side, I suppose it was the fact that TBC would have to continue with the existing method of collection until a high court decision was made, which could take some time. It was enough to put a wry smile on my face as Graham Daniel drove along the A40 to Cheltenham.

The following months were taken up with endless meetings about the refuse dispute with TBC, and on every occasion the *Gloucestershire Echo* were eager to know when and where the meetings would be taking place, so that they could report them. To their credit, and with appreciation from me and others engaged in the dustbin saga, their reports were excellent.

The news of the dispute went out on the news lines and it prompted an article in the *Daily Telegraph* on 16th April 1979 giving details of the dispute between Up Hatherley Parish Council and the local authority. It brought a letter in my mail the following day from the Society of Local Council Clerks, asking me if the *Daily Telegraph* report was correct.

Another letter came from a councillor in Port Talbot who wrote that "he had read an article in the *Sunday Express* concerning the difficulty we were experiencing with the refuse collection system". He claimed that the local authority in Port Talbot had done a similar exercise there in breach of the Public Health Act 1936. Apparently, the objectors solved their problems after receiving advice that under chapter 49, paragraph 72 of the Act, they could serve a notice on the council informing them that domestic refuse was ready for collection, in accordance with the Public Health Act 1936. The notice requested the council to collect the refuse accordingly. The Port Talbot councillor informed me in his letter that the dispute was resolved after five weeks. Whether this meant that the council continued with the old system, the letter does not say, but it was interesting, none the less.

Another letter from a lady in Chalfont St. Peter gave information of a successful claim in the High Court by her father in 1928 on the same subject. Other letters came from Plympton, London and West Lothian, all offering advice and wishing Up Hatherley Parish Council well in their endeavours to achieve a satisfactory result in the High Court. Another letter from a gentleman who lived in Telford suggested not to bother with the High Court, but to ask the Health and Safety at Work executive to act on our behalf. We did not however follow his suggestion.

Paul Fearnside, the Borough Engineer and Surveyor, wrote to me on the 18th April 1979 stating that a part of the report in the *Daily Telegraph* was incorrect. I had made reference to the plight of elderly and disabled people who could claim exemption from the new system, but only if it was working correctly. Mr Fearnside suggested that I was implying that these people may suffer at some time, which he disputed because his refuse men had 'exemption lists' and he doubted whether the old and disabled would be overlooked by the refuse collectors. Although there had been a number of complaints, Mr Fearnside doubted the accuracy of the claims.

Around the same time, numerous articles and cartoons appeared in national papers, and one particularly caught my eye, which I believe was in the *Daily Mail*. The article was accompanied by a cartoon showing a woman struggling to carry her dustbin out to the lorry, whilst the refuse collector, with cigarette in hand, is leaning against the wall with a smug look on his face. If there was sufficient space it would be interesting for readers to read the article in full, but here are the opening paragraphs, which I believe give the reader a taste of what the journalist Sally Brompton had in mind when she wrote the article:

> "An extraordinary revolution has taken place on Britain's doorsteps. As a nation we have become psychologically dominated by our dustmen. We humour them, kowtow to them and frequently bribe them – and half the time we end up emptying our dustbins ourselves.
>
> As one householder put it: 'I always feel my dustman is doing me a favour when he empties my bins'.
>
> It is indeed, something of a national phenomenon how our dustmen have succeeded in browbeating us all into a state of cringing obedience.
>
> A young woman in Westminster volunteers to drag her black plastic bags to the pavement's edge – 'just to help them out'. Yet around 5 per cent of her rates is going towards having her rubbish removed from her doorstep.
>
> Ironically, it is now that their pay, perks and conditions are better than ever, that the dustmen have managed to get the upper-hand over us".

I know the article is dated, but at the time it was a hard-hitting article that did no harm to our fight against the new refuse collection system.

The refuse dispute was not the only thing that occupied my mind during 1977 and 1978. The matter concerning meetings behind closed doors was becoming more serious. The PAB group were determined to stop this practice by TBC, and we knew that the only way to bring 'secret meetings' to the attention of the public was to give it as much publicity as possible.

In March 1977 I was made aware that a meeting of councillors had been called by the council to discuss informally matters affecting the Tewkesbury Borough Council area – so I went along to hear what they had to talk about. Even though the meeting was supposed to be 'informal' (whatever that means) neither I nor the local journalists were allowed to remain in the room. A quick chat with my PAB councillors resulted in a letter to the local newspaper in which I warned TBC that "if they continued to operate in this way, then the PAB Group would continue to keep a watching brief on behalf of the ratepayers".

The letter seemed a good opportunity to ask TBC some important questions about the finances of the council, which I believe had been discussed at the 'secret' informal meeting. I asked the council the following questions: Was it true that by April 1977 the ratepayers would have to find £700,000? Was it correct that land purchased in 1974 had now been sold for £300,000, and was this at a loss? Was it true that the taxpayer would be asked to spend £93,000 to refurbish the Old Baptist Chapel in Tewkesbury? And did the council recently agree to purchase land at Ashchurch for a sum in excess of £335,000? Why the council thought fit to exclude the Press and public from this meeting was beyond me at the time, because it was inevitable that such information would become known to the general public sooner rather than later.

Needless to say, I didn't get a response from anyone in the council, either by telephone or by way of a reply in the local newspaper.

Once I had won the by-election in September 1978 and joined the other PAB councillors on TBC, we held meetings to discuss our plans.

We decided we would do our best to stop meetings taking place behind closed doors and we would challenge everything that was being proposed by the council if there was the slightest hint that the proposals would harm individuals or the local communities. We would continue to protect the green belt wherever and whenever it was under threat; if necessary by way of holding further meetings in villages across the Tewkesbury Borough area.

At the end of 1978 we met as a group of PAB councillors to assess our value as representatives of the people. We believed we had done a good job and this was borne out by the increase in our membership and the encouraging letters written to the local newspaper. We had supplied a great deal of useful information for the PAB *Newsletter* and we were confident we could increase our representation on the council in May 1979.

CHAPTER 7

Roses All The Way – Far From It

Mankind always sets itself only such problems as it can solve; since, looking at the matter more closely, it will always be found that the task itself arises only when the material conditions for its solution already exist or are at least in the process of formation.

Karl Marx 1818 – 1883

The PAB management committee knew that 1979 was going to be a tough year for the group. We didn't have a lot of money in our account and we desperately wanted to increase our quota of councillors on TBC.

Harry Tebbs the treasurer, reported a continuing increase in membership and warned that the forthcoming elections might mean the candidates being asked to contribute to their election address. This did not seem too big a burden to bear, and I reminded the meeting that I had paid for my own literature in the recent by-election.

Doug Grazier, the chairman, commented that the style of the by-election address was good and should be used as a template for the forthcoming May elections, providing the candidates were in agreement.

We decided to contest eight wards where we thought we might do well, not least because we had held public meetings in each of the areas since our inaugural meeting, and as the chairman put it "It was a good opportunity to see whether our message and activities had done any good in any of the eight wards". Amongst the eight seats to defend were Bishop's Cleeve, Up Hatherley and Prestbury St. Nicholas. Harry Tebbs told the meeting that he would like to contest the Swindon Village ward as a Residents candidate rather than as a PAB candidate.

It was a strange request, but understandable. Swindon Village in those days was a small village with a very close-knit community where Harry was involved in several village activities. As he put it to the meeting "My chances of winning the seat would be assured if I stand as a Residents candidate, whereas I may not be successful if I stand for PAB". It was logical, knowing the area as he did, and at the time it made sense.

The management committee agreed that the annual meeting of the group should be in Lakeside School, Up Hatherley on 16th February and the PAB candidates, once they had been endorsed by the committee, would hold public meetings in the Prestbury and Bishop's Cleeve wards.

The closing date for nominations was 5th April and we nominated fifteen names to contest elections in eight wards. Prestbury and Bishop's Cleeve had four seats, Leckhampton three and the other wards had either one or two.

The public meetings were very successful with Doug Grazier and Terry Joyner performing well. We were very confident and everyone seemed to be responding well to the occasion.

Having won the by-election, I was automatically nominated for one of the four seats in Prestbury, and my PAB colleagues were Andrew Cornish, Alan Marshall and David Herson. Andrew, like the other two, was a local man and he had worked with local charities including the Multiple Sclerosis Society and the Association of Transport for the Disabled. Alan Marshall was a Civil Engineer and a master house builder. David Herson was a Senior Scientific Officer at GCHQ. It was a formidable team.

Squadron Leader Foster had decided not to stand in the Bishop's Cleeve election, which was just as well, because we were determined this time to contest all four seats. Sylvia Hughes and Mike Beresford decided to stand again and we had two further nominees in Barbara Aston and Paul Hughes (not related to Sylvia).

Bill Norton sought re-election in Up Hatherley: he was returned unopposed.

In the Leckhampton ward we nominated Jeremy Evans and Harry Welsby as 'paper candidates' and they did well to record nearly one thousand votes.

We also nominated candidates in Shurdington, Staverton, Alderton and Winchcombe and while we failed to win any of those seats, each PAB candidate polled in excess of 40 per cent of the votes, which by any standards were incredible results.

I felt that if we could keep the interest alive in those areas we could make further gains in future elections. And of course, as Harry Tebbs had predicted, he won Swindon Village with a vote in excess of fifty per cent.

Bishop's Cleeve candidates returned the best results, winning all four seats with nearly forty per cent of the votes. Sylvia Hughes and Mike Beresford each polled nearly 2,000 votes in an 81 per cent turnout.

Barbara Aston and Paul Hughes each polled in excess of 1,500 votes – it was an incredible achievement for the candidates and for PAB.

We had similar success in Prestbury winning three of the four seats – David Herson just missed out: Rosemary Gregory scraped in, but only just. The voters rejected two of the 'old guard', Timothy Spencer-Cox and Col Aubrey Nicholls, who both lost their seats.

I polled nearly 2,300 votes and topped the poll, Andrew Cornish was second with 2,072 votes and Alan Marshall polled 1,792 votes, which taken along with the Bishop's Cleeve result, was quite a night for the PAB group. We now had eight PAB councillors on TBC with Cllr Harry Tebbs as an addition whenever the need arose. Now it seemed, we could start to make our presence felt in the council meetings as well as the council chamber.

We caused another disappointment for the local hierarchy in Prestbury by winning three seats on the parish council. Andrew Cornish topped the poll, which meant that Rosemary Gregory, who came third, ceased to be chairman of the council. She had been chairman of the parish council for many years, but after May 3rd she became just an ordinary member of the parish council.

Although we had not been slow in raising issues with TBC since our inauguration in 1976, the pressure was stepped up after the May 1979 elections. Local residents had become increasingly worried about the amount of expenditure being proposed by the council, much of it seemingly out of proportion to the requirements of the area. As reported on previous pages, the expenditure was always spent on the town of Tewkesbury, which aggravated local residents who lived in the outlying villages and in the peripheral parishes around Cheltenham.

Ever since the 1974 boundary changes, people who lived on the outskirts of Cheltenham found it odd having to pay their rates to TBC whilst using the public services provided by Cheltenham Borough Council (CBC). This was a subject that came up repeatedly on the doorstep and at our public meetings, and we knew that as we gained more information, we would be expected to give an opinion on why this continued to be the case.

By the end of 1979 we were engaged in discussions on all sorts of problems that concerned local residents. In Swindon Lane, for example, having been successful in getting the improvements at the railway level crossing, we were asked by local residents to obtain a Weight Restriction Order on Swindon Lane to reduce the number of heavy goods vehicles using it as a short-cut to the M5 motorway.

We carried out a weekly survey of traffic movements and found that there were a large number of articulated vehicles using Swindon Lane. We noted too that a number of HGV's that travelled along the lane turned left into Windyridge Road, using it as a shortcut to Tewkesbury Road. Other heavy vehicles travelled the length of Swindon Lane and across the level crossing in order to gain access to the Kingsditch Lane Trading Estate. Both routes chosen by the drivers were unacceptable for the local residents and PAB councillors contacted the county surveyor at Gloucestershire County Council to arrange a meeting with him to discuss the 'heavy lorry' situation in Swindon Lane.

It was our intention to persuade him that a 7.5 tonnes weight restriction order was necessary as quickly as possible. We thought it would be easy, but it was far from being easy – every obstacle it seemed was put in our path to stop the order from being made.

Whilst the county surveyor listened carefully to what we had to say, he seemed more anxious to tell us about the difficulties that would be encountered in getting an order rather than giving our request a sympathetic hearing. We held several meetings with officers from TBC, the county council, the police and representatives from the haulage association between 1980 and 1990. And in 1991 we had to go through the whole matter again with officers responsible for highway matters in CBC before we finally succeeded in getting a weight restriction order. This should indicate how difficult it was to break down the bureaucracy that prevails in local government, and to show how long it can take before community improvements can be achieved. Whilst local residents still complain about large vehicles using Swindon Lane, the fact is that before the weight restriction was in place, anything from 20 to 25 'heavy lorries' per day used Swindon Lane, but now the figure is no more than six. Vehicles over 7.5 tonnes are exempt from the prohibition order if they are delivering to commercial properties in Windyridge Road, but not the trading estate.

Meanwhile, the Roses Film Theatre, which had been built on the site of the former Sabrina Cinema in 1973 at a cost of £300,000 and opened by her HRH Princess Anne in October 1975, was in danger of closing down. Members of the recreational and cultural services committee were told that the Gloucester-based Courtyard Arts Trust (CAT), who had been running the theatre as an arts centre in association with TBC from 1975 to 1980, had decided to withdraw from their agreement with the council.

This was a bitter blow to everyone and there was intense speculation about the reasons why the agreement had been cancelled. We knew there was concern about the financial situation, which had not been helped by low attendances at the theatre since its opening night. Another factor that came to light was that CAT had operated the theatre with just two people, which was totally inadequate, but it was understandable if they had insufficient resources.

PAB asked questions about the financial arrangements and we were told that TBC had guaranteed a payment of £5,000 to CAT, which in those days may have seemed a large sum of money. Even with the money, we came to the conclusion it was an insufficient amount unless the theatre was full every night, which, at the time, was proving to be impossible. PAB councillors also asked questions about the maximum number of seats that the theatre held; and the pricing arrangements.

From the answers given, it was apparent that even if the theatre was full each night, the profit from the ticket sales would be small. We suggested that because the theatre was small and had relatively fewer seats than the average size local theatre, the price of the tickets needed to be increased. This suggestion was not well-received on the grounds that the theatre users would stay away, or attend other theatres.

Whilst this was a good point, PAB councillors responded by suggesting that if there was an improvement in the quality of the shows, then perhaps people may become willing to pay more for their tickets.

Ron Wheeler, the Borough Secretary, was reported in the *Gloucestershire Echo* saying: *"The council would take over the responsibility for paying the accounts, but within the budget figure already mentioned. He agreed that the withdrawal of CAT from the Roses Theatre would be in the interests of both organisations because of financial pressures."*

At the next TBC meeting, when councillors were told that £276,000 in cuts had to be made in keeping with Government guidelines, the mayor, Cllr Mrs Anderson, stated that she did not want details of the cuts to be discussed at the council meeting as the press were in attendance, and suggested that the details of the cuts should only be discussed in committee. The proposal was totally unacceptable to PAB councillors – committee meetings were notorious for being held behind closed doors, and the proposal by the mayor was obvious in its intention.

According to the *Echo,* I told the council:

> "It was unfair on the ratepayers to have to pay for the upkeep of the Roses Theatre. I was not in favour of closing the theatre, but it should not be a burden on the ratepayers. But even if the loan charges on the original building were ignored, the council would still be losing around £40,000 a year on the theatre, and on that basis, it should be offered to private enterprise."

To support my proposal, I suggested that if a buyer came forward, it would be worth it to offer a grant of £15,000 per year, especially if the private company made a success of the theatre.

I am sure long-serving councillors will agree with me when I write that there is a 'not-made-here' syndrome, which operates in council offices. It is a system where a councillor will suggest an improvement to an existing policy, or a change to the method of doing things, and the officers or the ruling administration, or both, will give the proposer a 'hundred or more reasons why it couldn't possibly be done'. Tewkesbury Borough Council was no different to other organisations.

In 1980, my suggestion that the Roses Theatre should be offered to private enterprise was rejected, but later that year it was leased to the well-known comedian/actor Stan Stennett, who apart from being a successful actor with the television soap opera *Crossroads*, set up his own company (The Stennett Company) which ran the Roses Theatre between 1980 and 1993.

I have no doubt that the council probably claimed (behind closed doors) that leasing the theatre to a private enterprise company had always been their long-term solution to the problem.

The theatre flourished for a number of years under the leadership of Stan Stennett and his son, but for reasons unknown to me, the Stennett Company lost their fight to renew their lease of the theatre in 1993.

The Roses Theatre is probably best remembered for the last performance of Eric Morecambe (Morecambe and Wise) on 27th May 1984 when Eric, unfortunately, suffered a heart attack and collapsed in his dressing room at the end of his one-man performance. He was taken to Cheltenham General Hospital and died later that night.

TBC appointed a London based theatre company, The *Crummels Theatre Company*, who after nearly a year of closure due to essential maintenance and refurbishing work, reopened the theatre in November 1994. This new arrangement did not last long because The *Crummels Theatre Company* ran into financial difficulties, went into liquidation and the Roses Theatre closed again in 1995. Later that year, the Roses Theatre Trust was formed and they won a 21 year licence to run the theatre. It reopened in 1996 with Robert Hamlin as its Theatre Director.

Robert had been Director of the Belgrade Theatre in Coventry from 1980 and he was succeeded as Director of the Roses Theatre in 2006 by Deborah Rees.

The Roses Theatre certainly had its ups and downs as well as excellent occasions when memorable actors came to Tewkesbury to perform there. It is a delightful theatre, more seating has been added, and I am pleased to say, at the time of writing this chapter, the theatre is doing very well and it is worth a visit at any time.

In 1980, Up Hatherley Parish Council carried out a referendum on whether the residents wanted to go the 'extra mile' with the refuse dispute and allow the High Court to decide whether TBC had breached the Public Health Act 1936.

The parish council explained the facts again to the local residents at a public meeting, and emphasised to them that in order to try to overturn the borough council's intention to impose the new scheme, a barrister would be required to present the parish council's case in the high court. "This would be expensive", they were told.

A referendum was held in the parish hall in order to gauge public opinion, and the count of votes was overseen by Ron Wheeler and members of his staff. It was a close run election with 93 residents supporting the parish council and 85 against – a majority of eight.

I was disappointed with the result because only 21.6 per cent of the residents showed sufficient interest in the referendum, and presumably the dispute, so the parish council would have a difficult decision to make. The low poll and the closeness of the vote was enough for me to be as neutral as possible when the parish council debated at the next council meeting what the next steps should be. Up to the day of the parish council meeting, I tried to arrange meaningful discussions with officers at TBC to see if a compromise could be reached. My attempts at trying to reach a compromise were not reciprocated.

I was sure that TBC were gambling on the local residents backing down when they were asked to vote in the referendum. I was also sure that they were convinced that Up Hatherley residents would vote a resounding 'no' once they were inside the polling station. It didn't work out quite as they had hoped, and the look on the face of Ron Wheeler during the count indicated that the vote might not go the way he and his council colleagues had secretly wanted.

As it turned out, the parish council decided by a small majority not to go ahead with the High Court case. Although the democratic vote supported going ahead by a small majority, the fact that such a small turnout of electors had made the decision was a source of concern. It may have been the right decision by the parish council-lors not to go ahead, even though there was a small majority in favour of doing so. But the burden of the cost to be borne by nearly 80 per cent of the parishioners was disconcerting.

Of course, the opportunity for me to go back to the Royal Courts of Justice to give evidence on behalf of the parishioners was not going to happen after all. But no-one could doubt the honesty and determination that had been displayed by a small rural village against the might of the 'Big Brother' tactics used by Tewkesbury Borough Council.

Once the dispute had ended the borough council provided black plastic bags to households in the peripheral parishes, allegedly to replace the heavy metal bins that were heavy to lift when they were full, especially by the elderly.

But by the time residents had got used to the black plastic bags splitting and the contents blown up the road on a regular basis; or the urban foxes had clawed their way in the plastic bag for a meal, a new document came out from TBC. It was called 'Proposals for a wheeled bin refuse collection system': it was dated 1986. The document was the work of Peter Eccleshare, the Borough Technical Officer; it was a revelation.

But, it is worth remembering that during the court case David Hall brought against the council in 1976, he made the point that if the council were committed to introducing a refuse collection system that was efficient, easy to use and hygienic (such as the system in use in Scandinavia), then he would withdraw his objection to the imposition of a "front gate collection service."

Peter Eccleshare was a North Country man who never failed to tell everyone he spoke to that it was better 'up-north' than it was 'down-south'. He was a great character and a dedicated officer of the borough, and I admired him for his openness and his apparent desire to help the borough whenever he could. From his report it was clear that since the end of the refuse dispute, he had been visiting other local authority areas to see the different systems of refuse collection being used. I can only presume that he found a local authority that operated the 'wheeled bin system' and found out the name of the company that supplied them.

The company was called Perstop Form Waste Management, which was located in Buckinghamshire. The principal advantage of the 'wheeled bin' was the mobility of it, plus the fact that the refuse collector where the bins were in operation, no longer had to handle other people's refuse. This appealed to Peter Eccleshare and the historical facts prove that we should be grateful that it did. In his report he set out the background, the operational and financial implications of the scheme and his recommendations. He recommended that the council should give the wheeled bin system a six month's trial on two domestic refuse rounds. Studies should be carried out on the full implications of the system and that financial provisions should be made to enable a full system to become operational by 1987/88.

The rest, as they say, is history, and the green wheeled bin system was introduced as Peter Eccleshare had proposed; it has been in operation ever since. Not only that, but local authorities across the country have followed the example of TBC and introduced the same system – so in a way, everyone should be grateful to the little group of Up Hatherley residents who dug their heels in against bureaucracy, and protested against the actions of others.

By the end of 1980 I was exhausted. The refuse dispute and the creation of PAB had been time-consuming. I informed Up Hatherley Parish Council that I would be standing down as chairman of the council at the end of April 1981. I would remain a member of the council, but I would be taking a back seat and concentrating on local matters that did not require me to spearhead them.

I had been chairman for nine years, probably during the council's most difficult period, but by the end of my chairmanship, no-one could say that they had never heard of Up Hatherley – we were not just a peripheral village on the edge of Cheltenham, but a strong community voice.

My parish council colleagues were gracious with their comments at the May 1981 annual parish council meeting. The vice-chairman David Hall presented me with a gift and a signed card, which indicated that I had been chairman of the parish council for the period 1972 to 1981. I was even more delighted when David Hall agreed to take on the task of parish council chairman.

I told the parish council members I was sure the new chairman would carry on the traditions of this parish, which had made its mark during my time on the council.

However, it was not long before the residents of Up Hatherley received another blow when news in July 1981 suggested that a developer wanted to build on green belt land between Up Hatherley and Leckhampton. It was a bitter blow because the land belonged to a well-known local farmer, whose family had owned the farmland on the south side of the parish for many years.

The parish council immediately took steps to find out the detail of the proposal before any discussions between the developer and the borough council took place. It was not good news; we learned to our dismay that the scheme proposed the construction of 2,250 dwellings with no community facilities and a very small area of green public space.

The parish council met and decided that the parish council should resist the proposal on three fronts,

1) to oppose development because part of it was on green belt land,
2) to reduce the number of dwellings in the planning proposal and
3) to ensure that community facilities such as a school, shops, a library and a doctor's surgery and more public spaces were included in the proposal.

These were ambitious demands, but we were determined to get the best possible result for the parish.

Although the site was outside the Cheltenham Borough boundary, CBC immediately took an interest in what might or might not be developed. They tried hard to persuade TBC that all the houses should be built in Up Hatherley and The Reddings rather than in Leckhampton.

Whilst the PAB Group were not directly involved with the development proposals, we supported the parish council's aim to try and protect the green belt. The application was refused by the planning committee, but the appeal inspector overturned the decision. He agreed with many of the proposals in the parish council submission, such as reducing the number of dwellings to allow room for substantial community facilities, and increasing the amount of public green open spaces.

As it turned out, the developer built a large new housing estate (Greatfield Park), and the community gained large green open spaces, a school, a library and a shopping area, which were not in the original proposals.

The hours of discussions and arguments had paid off in the end.

In 1981 the PAB Group were warned about a possible move by CBC to extend its boundaries. They had written to the Boundary Commission asking them to look at its boundaries with a view of allowing the Cheltenham Borough Council area to expand. The council were concerned about its 'tight' boundaries, and with an expanding population and industrial companies anxious to set up new businesses, it needed more space for development.

The original request was for an extension of its boundaries, which would have included large villages such as Bishop's Cleeve and Shurdington. It was too ambitious and doomed to fail from the outset.

CBC's fall-back position was to ask the Commission to look at an alternative and modest proposal, which was to include the peripheral parishes; Up Hatherley, Badgeworth, Uckington, Leckhampton, Prestbury and Swindon within an extended Borough boundary.

Not surprisingly, the news about possible district boundary changes brought a swift response from TBC and from people living in the affected areas. The general view regarding the first option was that neither TBC nor the residents were interested in Cheltenham's 'village grabbing' proposal and reports in the press seemed to bear this out. But residents living in the peripheral parishes did not express the same view. They were prepared to listen to the pros and cons of such a transfer before making up their minds.

The proposals also prompted the PAB Group to start a campaign giving local residents a chance to air their views on whether they wanted their local ward or parish to remain in TBC or whether they supported the transfer to CBC.

As was often the case, Up Hatherley Parish Council was in the forefront of asking the local community to make a decision about boundary changes. In June 1981, they held a referendum asking parishioners to say 'yes' or 'no' to the transfer of the parish into CBC. The response was incredible.

Eighty per cent of the electorate voted – 554 votes to 115 instructed the parish council to inform the Boundary Commission that they wanted to be part of Cheltenham borough. It proved that local democracy worked well at the grass roots level, if the opportunity is given to the community.

Meanwhile, householders in Leckhampton claimed they had been left in the dark about boundary changes and I was asked to arrange a public meeting to explain the purpose of boundary changes should the Commission agree. The public meeting was arranged for September 3rd in the United Reformed Church Hall in Salisbury Avenue, Leckhampton, "to give the local people an opportunity to air their views on boundary changes." The meeting room was packed and the opinions expressed were the same as those made in other places; "… they were part of Cheltenham and not

Tewkesbury; they used the Cheltenham services and not Tewkesbury's; and CBC was a better run council than TBC."

I explained to the meeting that we had held local referendums in two areas so that we could gauge the support or opposition to boundary changes. I also told the audience that it was always better for a parish council to hold a referendum rather than a group such as PAB. "In Prestbury" I said, "in spite of our efforts to give the local community an opportunity to express their views, the chairman of the parish council, Rosemary Gregory, could only express anger at the efforts of the PAB group to hold a parish referendum."

Cllr James Graham, chairman of Leckhampton Parish Council, who attended the PAB meeting, told the audience "He knew of only one person who had wanted a public meeting", and in any event he claimed, "local residents knew that they could put questions about any subject, including boundary changes, at the annual meeting of the council, which was open to the public." Not surprisingly, his comments were met with derision from the audience – one person thought the chairman of the council was out of touch with the needs of the community. It was an interesting meeting and did no harm to the PAB Group at all.

In the December issue of the PAB *Newsletter,* we invited all residents in Prestbury of voting age to complete a ballot form asking them to indicate a preference for remaining with TBC or becoming part of the Cheltenham district. By the middle of January 1982, sixty per cent returned their ballot forms – 55 per cent were in favour of transferring to Cheltenham and 45 per cent were in favour of staying within the Tewkesbury area. Not a big majority, but the result was clear. And it prompted the chairman of Prestbury parish council to report to the *Gloucestershire Echo* that the ballot "was ill-timed and biased", but her words surprised no-one; if the result had been the other way round; would she have made the same observations?

The years 1981 and 1982 were noted for the proposed district boundary changes by the Boundary Commission, but there were other important matters taking place that concerned local residents across the whole of the Tewkesbury Borough Council area.

PAB councillors had been aware for some time that the green belt land surrounding Cheltenham was under attack from developers, just as we forecast it would be at the various public meetings we had held in wards and villages since 1976. I have already referred to the large estate on part of the green belt land at Up Hatherley, but now land at Prestbury, Leckhampton and The Reddings, was also in danger of being developed.

We opposed the applications in every case and we tried hard to urge the planning authorities that 'brownfield sites' should be developed first before green belt land was considered. We also believed that the loss of any green areas within a community would be harmful to the local environment; a view we have continued to hold for more than thirty years.

One area of land that has been under threat from developers since 1970, and still continues to be, is the land on the north side of Swindon Lane. The land has always been important because of its openness and because it acts as a buffer between Prestbury and Bishop's Cleeve, preventing the coalescence of those two settlements.

In 1981, the PAB Group learned that J. A. Pye (Oxford) Estates Limited had been given first option by the owners to develop the land providing they could obtain planning permission from the council. The construction company had previously been successful with an appeal to build 70 houses on land adjacent to the Prestbury Racecourse (see chapter 8), so when the planning application to develop the Hunting Butts field was submitted and rejected by the planning committee, it was a great relief to the local residents.

The application subsequently went to appeal; PAB councillors knew that the land on the north side of Swindon Lane had been classified only as 'Interim Green Belt' land, which meant it was vulnerable until a re-classification made it 'non-developable' land. Thankfully, the planning inspector rejected the appeal on the grounds that it would give rise to further development on other parts of the land on the north side of Swindon Lane, which would lead inevitably lead to the coalescence of the two settlements.

The local residents were delighted, but the PAB councillors quickly realised what a close thing it had been, and began a campaign to make the 'interim' land 'Statutory Green Belt Land' which would give it a longer period of protection. This was harder than we thought it would be – to keep land in an interim state was easier for development to take place. Developers raised objections to an alteration to the status of the land, as we knew they would. It was therefore an enormous relief when the Planning Policy Guidance (PPG2) document was published in 1995 advising local planning authorities that they should include green belt policies for consideration when producing their Local Plans.

Even though an updated version of PPG2 in 2001 confirmed that Green Belts must be protected and should include a 'presumption against inappropriate development within a green belt' statement, it still did not stop numerous attempts by developers to submit planning applications to develop land in Swindon Lane and other areas; it continues to be an ongoing battle even in 2014.

Some of these applications will be discussed in detail in later pages of the book.

In political terms, life is never easy as a councillor, which I am sure many dedicated councillors will agree. From the moment the PAB Group was formed in 1976, we found ourselves at odds with the principal leaders on Tewkesbury Borough Council. The refuse dispute had been a parish council matter, but there were many other faults with the way the council was being administered. Some of the faults were so bad we felt we would not be doing our job unless we questioned the decisions on expenditure and procedures that were often impracticable. In spite of constant criticisms levelled at us, we constantly questioned what was going on in the meetings and in the council offices.

We knew we were not popular and our efforts were often snubbed by those at the top of the administration (officers as well as councillors), and at times they made the lives of PAB councillors very difficult. Among those who seemed to enjoy the cut-and-thrust of local politics was the Leader of the Council, the Honourable Alasdair Morrison.

He was an intelligent man and often had a word with me after a meeting to explain the point he had failed to get across during a heated exchange in committee. Alasdair had been doing the job for a long time, whereas I was new and on a long learning curve; he knew everything about local government whereas I knew very little. Nevertheless, we respected each other's point of view and we never fell out completely over any issue. At least that was the case until he spoke to a journalist from the *Daily Telegraph* in the weeks leading up to the May 1979 borough council elections.

Apparently, the *Sunday Express* on 15th April 1979 contained an article about the refuse dispute between Up Hatherley Parish Council and Tewkesbury Borough Council, which was leading to a possible High Court case.

The *Daily Telegraph* believed it was an interesting story and one of their reporters had the task of contacting me, Ron Wheeler, the Borough Secretary and Alasdair Morrison, to check the story for accuracy and in common with the usual practice, to ask each of us for a comment. In my telephone conversation with the journalist I explained to him that it was a parish council matter and not a PAB one. This prompted more questions and I told the journalist that in my view the parish council had a good case should they decide to go to court.

Alasdair Morrison, on the other hand, took the opportunity to accuse me of "electioneering". This is what Mr Morrison allegedly said to the *Telegraph* reporter:

> "Mr Godwin is one of five members of People Against Bureaucracy Action Group on the council. They attack virtually everything the council does. It is significant that the matter has been raised again by them within three weeks of our elections."

I thought it was a spiteful comment and each time I read the article I became more convinced that the statement was inaccurate and libellous.

On 23rd April 1979 I sought the advice of solicitors Robinson, Tarling and Company, who confirmed my belief that the article libelled me. I made it clear to them that I was seeking an unqualified apology from Mr Morrison, with an undertaking from him not to repeat the libel. My solicitors wrote to Mr Morrison making the request and "... reminded him that the refuse dispute was nothing to do with the PAB Group." They suggested to him that his comments inferred that "I was using the dustbin dispute for publicity which was unfair, improper and was an underhanded electioneering ploy by him."

The letter was long and finished with the following words:

> "Our client is a man of excellent reputation in the community having served his local community for many years, and in addition is one of Her Majesty's Justices of the Peace. To imply, as you have done, that he would be prepared to stoop to a shabby and unfair electioneering advantage is a serious attack upon his integrity. We are instructed to say that our client will issue proceedings against you for damages

unless an unqualified apology and an undertaking not to repeat the libel, together with agreement to indemnify him in respect of his legal costs is received by us within fourteen days."

The words used were strong and I pondered on them for some time before I came to the conclusion that the solicitors know what they are doing and I should simply sit back and see what happens.

The "strong words" didn't impress Alasdair Morrison who replied on May 7th with a curt three-line response to my solicitors that said: *"I have your letter dated April 24th. I cannot see how in the circumstances you can think that any apology is called for."*
I was not surprised by Alasdair's response – I had got to know him well in a short space of time, and my guess was that he regarded it as an affront to his position as Leader of the Council by this 'upstart from Up Hatherley'.

I had no intention of taking the matter to the High Court, but I began to wonder what a barrister with knowledge of these things would make of the issue. I knew it would cost me a sum that I could ill afford, but I was intrigued about the principles of libel law; it might be an exercise that would satisfy my curiosity and might come in useful later. I instructed my solicitors to seek legal advice from their barrister.

On 1st June 1979 I received a copy of Advice from Conrad Seagroatt of 1, Kings Bench Walk, London, who stated in his opening comments that "There is a good basis for an action for libel."

The Advice quoted several instances of case law and concluded by stating that "Mr Morrison knew that his words were going to be published by a national newspaper, and in his statement he claimed that Mr Godwin contacted the *Daily Telegraph*, when in fact it was the other way round."

The Advice was long and good, and it certainly opened my eyes to issues which I had not even given a second thought. For example, Conrad Seagroatt when dealing with the issue in relation to an election to a local authority claimed that "Malice appears to be attached to the statement, which would rule out any defence of fair comment." He also referred to what he called "the significant fact that the member of the PAB Group who was offering himself to the electors of Up Hatherley (Bill Norton) was unopposed, and if Morrison knew this, the comment suggesting political advantage must be known by him to be false. The absence of any genuine belief in the truth of the comment is conclusive proof of malice."

Following conversations with my solicitors, I made the decision to issue a writ against Alasdair Morrison in the hope that it might convince him that a simple apology was all that was needed to stop the matter from going any further. It didn't happen the way I thought it would and my solicitors were soon informed by Oswald Dickson, Collier and Co, Essex Street, London, that they would be acting for Mr Morrison.

On 10th December 1979 I received a copy of Mr Morrison's Defence, which claimed that the words reported in the *Daily Telegraph* were not defamatory. It then set out in great detail every comment reported in the local press, allegedly made by me, which had criticised Tewkesbury Borough Council and the way they were conducting their business since 1976.

It included reports in the *Gloucestershire Echo* over a long period of time, and it recorded the historical facts about the formation of the 'People Against Bureaucracy Action Group' and its aims of "giving a voice to the little people against the might of the bureaucratic machine." This section of the Defence was true. It quoted chapter and verse the refuse collection dispute, which obviously the Defence intended linking the two together. The quotes contained in the PAB election leaflets were repeated in full, but seemed to bear no relationship to the words that were reported in the *Daily Telegraph* article. What it did reveal was that Mr Morrison and the Tewkesbury Borough Council hierarchy had been irritated and upset by my words over the first three years of the PAB Group's existence. This was good news; reading about their displeasure not only pleased me, and did not fill me with any regrets. As far as I was concerned there was still a long way to go if the council had no intention of changing its ways.

In my letter to Robinson & Tarling and Company on 3rd January 1980, in response to the Morrison Defence, I admitted that "I had criticised the council in the past for its mishandling of ratepayers' money," and I suggested that "there was every reason that I would continue to do so and perhaps with more ferocity than I have done so in the past." Mr Morrison's Defence that I had unfairly criticised the council's financial competence was not borne out by the facts. The Roses Theatre, the Swimming Baths, the parks and open spaces, were all being run at a loss.

Each of the issues that Mr Morrison raised in his Defence document I answered by quoting the facts as they were recorded in council or committee minutes at the time.

In the meantime, my solicitors received further Advice from the barrister, which they passed on to me. Mr Seagroatt wrote: "I have a feeling that we have stirred up a hornet's nest here. There is a history of intense conflict between Mr Godwin and Tewkesbury Borough Council." He went on to claim that "... the sting has largely gone with the withdrawal of the Up Hatherley action; there were two matters wholly distinct as there were two different parties involved, though Mr Godwin was the guiding light of the Parish Council. If the libel was proved, it will not attract substantial damages – only nominal at best and the costs will certainly outweigh them."

It had not been my intention to go to court, only to obtain an apology from Alasdair Morrison, but I could see from the legal advice I was receiving that with no apology forthcoming the whole issue could develop into a slanging match between me and Mr Morrison. That would be doing no good to either side and I was not in the mood for it to be so.

In March 1980, I instructed my solicitors to talk to Mr Morrison's solicitors who would suggest to them "As there had been a great deal of co-operation between Mr Morrison, the council and me over recent weeks, and in order for this new spirit to continue and develop, I will discontinue my claim, providing both sides pay their own costs." It sounded like a simple solution, but it was far from that and the exchange of letters between the two legal sides went on for several more months. Neither side would give an inch; readers may be surprised to know that the matter was not settled until May 1981, when the solicitors acting for Mr Morrison reported that their client had agreed to pay his own costs so that normal service could be resumed at the council offices.

It would be easy to assume from what had been said and printed that relations between me and Mr Morrison were fragile and bitter, but that was not the case – we still expressed differences of opinion on certain things, but we chatted to each other after a meeting and on one occasion went to a nearby public house for a social drink and a chat.

Councillor Jack Denley was a farmer, born and bred in Woodmancote, near Cheltenham, and represented the ward for many years. He was a large rotund figure and looked every bit a farmer by his demeanour, and his chosen words. He was an Independent councillor although he made it known that he supported the Conservative cause. There wasn't much that Jack didn't know about any subject, so he told his colleagues, and he was never at a loss for words when expressing his views even if he offended others in the process. He often spoke to me with his concerns about the disagreements between Alasdair Morrison and me, always urging me to shake Cllr Morrison's hand and to be friends.

At around this time, Jack was 'in-line' to take on the responsible job of Mayor of Tewkesbury. In his role as deputy mayor he requested that I should have a word with him in the parlour after a particular council meeting.

A strange request to make and I wondered if I had done something wrong that had upset the council hierarchy. I need not have worried because all Jack wanted to do was to have a quiet word with me about his forthcoming mayoral ceremony. There was more to it though than seeking my advice about the ceremony, as he wanted me to second the proposal at the inaugural ceremony that he should become Mayor of Tewkesbury in 1981. In the view of Jack Denley, my presence on the stage would show everyone present that there was no animosity between members of the council, in spite of the bad press the council had received in the previous years.

It seemed a good idea and I agreed to his request.

He gave me a few details about himself, which I felt I could use in my speech, and I assured him that I would be on my best behaviour and would not say anything other than to 'sing his praises' and assure those present that he would do a good job as mayor of the town.

About a week later I received a hand written note from Jack, informing me that the Leader of the Council, Alasdair Morrison, had agreed to propose him as mayor for the period 1981/82. Furthermore, Alasdair was apparently delighted that I had agreed to second his proposal. There is no doubt that Jack thought it would be a good thing for the council if we were seen together on the stage, "doing what was necessary", using his words.

Good old Jack – he never failed to come up with some novel way of dealing with a difficult situation. Even to this day, I am not sure who Jack approached first; not that it would have made any difference to my decision to second the proposal.

Earlier in the year, PAB councillor, Mike Beresford, who had represented Bishop's Cleeve since 1976, resigned from the PAB Group. As vice chairman of the TBC finance subcommittee, he took exception to my expressing the view that some of the decisions taken by the committee appeared to be made for 'political purposes'.

Not only was this my view, but the view of a number of people who had written to the *Gloucestershire Echo* supporting my comments. Others went further, including some residents in Bishop's Cleeve, who suggested that Cllr Beresford should resign his seat and allow a by-election to take place. This would have been a rather drastic step to take and from his answers to his critics, Mike Beresford had no intention of taking such a course of action.

It is worth recording that the PAB management committee members had discussed the topic of the annual nominations for borough council committee chairmen and vice-chairmen each year on several occasions.

The general view expressed was that PAB councillors would be wise not to accept these positions for a while until more experience of borough council procedures was obtained. It was not a hard-and-fast rule, just an observation, which seemed to be accepted.

Although unease had been expressed by both Mike Beresford and Harry Tebbs whenever the topic was discussed and following their interventions, it was agreed that should any PAB councillor be offered the position of vice-chairman it should be accepted.

It did seem sensible for the councillors to wait a few more years before we took on the responsibilities of either a committee chairman, or a nomination to become the mayor of the town, should they be offered.

Both Mike and Harry objected to this rule, and from their submissions to the management committee, it seemed that both councillors had been approached by senior councillors about the possible responses from the PAB Group should they be nominated. In later years, both councillors accepted positions of chairmen of committees and both became mayors of Tewkesbury Borough Council. Harry Tebbs in 1983 and Mike Beresford in 1995.

CHAPTER 8

Trusting The People

"Democracy is the worst form of government except all those other forms that have been tried from time to time."

Winston Churchill
(speech in the House of Commons, 11th November 1947)

The four years since the 1979 local elections passed quickly and the PAB Group were soon back on the local election trail. In 1983, we had to defend the Borough Council seats we had previously won; increase our efforts to win more seats; and increase our voting numbers.

Parish council seats also came up for election that year, and in order to sustain levels of continuity at all levels of local government, we agreed that we needed to find parish council candidates in 1983 as well. The management committee instructed me to do whatever I could to persuade members to stand at all the local elections, which was a tall order.

Meanwhile, Christine Adamson, a PAB member who lived in Stoke Orchard, was campaigning to get the National Coal Board Research Establishment at Stoke Orchard to restrict and control the amount of pollution, which she claimed "was putting local residents' health at risk."

Christine was also the leader of the Stoke Orchard Residents' Association and was often reported in the local press urging the Research Establishment and Tewkesbury Borough Council to eliminate, as she put it, "the smoke and the obnoxious smells from the site." Stoke Orchard is a small village to the north-west of Cheltenham; it is twinned with neighbouring Tredington, and is close to other villages such as Elmstone-Hardwicke and Bishop's Cleeve.

The National Coal Board (NCB) was established in 1947 to run the nationalised coal industry. Its Coal Research Establishment (CRE) was set up in 1950 by its director of research Jacob Bronowski, and was located on the former Gloster Aircraft Company factory site, adjacent to the RAF Stoke Orchard air base.

PAB councillors held meetings in the village, organised by Chris Adamson, and they were always well-attended.

I found it easy to talk to the senior figures at the CRE who gave me the impression that they understood entirely the reasons why the local people were complaining. They assured me they were doing all they could to improve the situation. We held discussions with environmental health officers at the council offices who assured us that they were having a degree of co-operation from the CRE, but could not guarantee any permanent solution to the complaints of the local residents. The only solution to the problem was the closure of the research centre, and Christine Adamson never missed an opportunity at our management meetings to emphasise this point.

It was a long and painful period for Stoke Orchard residents until the news came through that the government intended to close the CRE by the end of 1997 or early 1998.

The CRE site has now been demolished and cleared. It is currently being developed by Bloor Homes who will construct 120 houses, a village hall and a village shop as well as other community amenities, which will more than double the size of the village.

The PAB Group had only been in existence for a short period of time, but it attracted every problem being encountered by communities within the Tewkesbury Borough Council area. Stoke Orchard was only one of many.

At a public meeting in the old village library in Prestbury, villagers heard from Mr Bill Strachan, a Tewkesbury Borough Council planning officer, that the planning committee had discussed the possibility of a 'retirement home for the clergy' on a popular section of green space land in The Burgage. He told the meeting "no planning application had been submitted, but the planning committee were in favour in principle."

The information was not well received by the audience and several people expressed their disappointment in the planning officer's comments.

Dermot Cusack, who lived opposite the land, told the meeting that the land had been used for cattle grazing for years. He wanted the land to be preserved and described the proposed building as an "H Block covering 29,000 square feet." John Hellier, another local resident, revealed that the land "Had been bequeathed to the church by Major Capel, and he had made it clear in his will that the land should not be built on."

The Capel family, like the Baghot family, had lived in Prestbury for centuries. The records show that William Capel had a house in Prestbury on the west side of The Burgage in 1679 and the purchase of land and houses by the Capel family continued throughout the 18th century. The estates and properties continued to grow and the family was one of the principal land owners in the village right up to the Second World War. Major Christopher Capel, who died in 1964, gradually sold off most of the estate, and at the time of his death only one house and the surrounding grounds still belonged to him. The grounds occupied most of the east side of The Burgage and almost reached the churchyard. The house, known as Prestbury House, was built c. 1700; it became a hotel for a time, but has now been returned to a family home. The Capel family had a close relationship with the church, and records show that Major Capel bequeathed a lot of land to his descendants, and it would not have surprised me if the words of John Hellier proved to be correct.

However, we listened intently to the debate, and particularly the words of Mr Strachan, which indicated that the planning committee members had committed themselves at pre-planning discussions with representatives from the Church of England Pension Board.

This had been a mistake, in my view.

Pre-planning discussions before any application is submitted should be nothing more than 'listening and explaining planning policy' to the applicant. If advice is asked for, then it should be given, but nothing more.

The *Gloucestershire Echo* published a good report of the meeting in the 15th March 1983 edition of their newspaper. The caption read: "Vicars' home plan gets massive thumbs-down". It gave a fair report of what individual residents had said about the proposal, and their reaction to the words of Mr Strachan that ". . . the building would commence next year and be completed in the following year" adding "although there is no application yet."

The announcement by Bill Strachan about a possible development that might take place was bizarre – I had never heard of such an arrangement by the planning committee, let alone a declaration by a planning officer indicating that the matter was 'all cut and dried'. It was an affront to normal planning practices.

As one of the local councillors for Prestbury I expressed my views at the meeting. According to the *Gloucestershire Echo* report, the following is a part of what I said to the meeting:

> "It was wrong for the proposal to have been given a pre-hearing by the committee, which seems to have come about by the Pension Board taking the initiative. If the parish had been given the same chance of putting its views to the planning committee as the Board, there might not have been a need to have had a public meeting.
>
> It would become difficult for planning committee members to change their minds having agreed in principle to the building."

The *Echo* report concluded by saying that the chairman Mrs Rosemary Gregory rebuked Cllr Godwin for his comments and added "You are not a parishioner." The words from my old adversary were greeted with boos from some people in the audience, and the insult, for that is what it was, made not one iota of difference to my opinion about the possible loss of the land, or the unusual way the planning department had responded to the proposal by the Church of England Pension Board. The harsh words by Mrs Gregory did not do her prospects much good; she lost her seat in the local elections that took place on 5th May 1983, whereas I was re-elected with a substantial majority.

We continued our campaign to stop Tewkesbury Borough Council from holding meetings in private, particularly if they concerned matters about which the public had the right to know.

In August 1983 I received a number of telephone calls from people living in Staverton, which is a small village between Cheltenham and Gloucester. It is a rural settlement, and is the home of the Dowty Rotol and Messier-Dowty aircraft components factories. It is also the location of the Gloucestershire Airport, previously Staverton Airport along with RAF Staverton, a dog-training centre, which relocated in 1951 to RAF Netheravon in Wiltshire.

The commercial activity in Staverton was in stark contrast to the quiet rural retreat of the village. It had a parish council of seven members in 1983 and a long-serving chairman called William Newton, a farmer whose family had farmed in the village for several generations. William (known as Bill) was also the borough councillor, and many councillors found that Bill could be a 'crusty' individual at times, conservative in everything he said and did, and would not accept change unless he was forced to comply with it. Bill was the patriarch figure in Staverton and what Bill said, was listened to with awe by the villagers.

Those who had contacted me had, apparently, tried to attend the monthly meetings of Staverton Parish Council. But when they arrived they found the door locked, although they could hear voices coming from inside.

The villagers told me that they had tried to gain entry to the parish council meetings on three consecutive months, and their knocking on the door finally brought a response from a member of the council, who told the villagers that the parish council meeting was 'in private'.

I didn't want to get involved in what was a village matter – I was already in Bill Newton's book as a trouble-maker – so my advice to the villagers was to contact the *Gloucestershire Echo* who would be interested. The villagers took my advice and on Monday 15th August 1983, the editor wrote the following comment in his editorial:

> "How fortunate it is for ratepayers that not all local authorities run their affairs like Staverton Parish Council. If they were to do so then the public would never get to know what was being done, or not being done, on their behalf.
>
> Three successive monthly meetings at Staverton Parish Council have been held behind closed doors – and tonight's session is also scheduled to be a secret affair, too.
>
> The law is quite plain – monthly meetings must be open unless the council decides to go "into committee" to discuss matters that must be debated in private.
>
> But the council must pass a formal resolution before excluding the public and must state good reasons for doing so.
>
> Staverton's chairman admits they have never bothered to take resolutions or to state reasons for exclusion. It is time they embraced democracy. It is an insult for authorities elected by the public to treat the people they represent with such disdain."

It was a very good editorial and it helped to stop parish councils like Staverton from holding meetings behind closed doors, and Bill Newton never knew that it was one of his Borough Council colleagues who had set it up.

One of my community duties in Up Hatherley in the early 1980's was to arrange summer fun-days on Fernleigh Green in the centre of the village. The fun-days were mainly for the children during the day and a relaxing evening of light music and refreshments for the parents, organised by me as a mark of appreciation for their contribution to the day's events. It was nothing special – a simple formula that cost little and was easy to arrange. It was my way of saying 'thank you' and it became very popular.

I arranged for the green to be marked out with running lines, and with the help of the mums and dads we organised sack races; egg-and-spoon races; three-legged races and sprints for the children of various ages. It brought enormous pleasure to the young and old alike, especially the mums' egg-and-spoon race. It was good fun; it ended with tea, sandwiches and cakes for the children, which had been provided by the parents. After the final races, small prizes were presented to the children. There was a break for two hours and then the evening was arranged for the older members of the community to enjoy. By arrangement, they brought their own chairs; chatted with their neighbours; enjoyed a drink and listened to recorded music provided by the residents.

One or two of the romantics would dance to the music, although it must have been difficult to do on the grass. The whole day was excellent and relaxing; it was a community activity which we had often talked about, but had never put into practice. I organised the event for three years and just as I imagined, it became more popular each year, and the children's races became more competitive.

My house overlooked the green and in the weeks prior to the fun-day, Pam and I would spend many happy moments watching the children practising their three-legged runs, or the juggling of spoons with the eggs, which they carefully held to make sure the egg didn't fall to the ground. Watching their efforts to get it right before the fun-day was quite amusing.

Following each fun-day, I received many comments from residents thanking me for arranging the day, which I believed would go on forever. But, as so often happens, one or two residents who over-looked Fernleigh Green began a campaign to stop it. They alleged that "Men were urinating at the rear of my property" and some claimed that the music had kept their children awake. (An analysis showed that the people who had complained did not have children).

Why the objectors should claim that male residents would want to urinate at the rear of their properties when home toilet facilities were available was ridiculous. The music, which was played on the other side of the green, away from the properties of the complainants, could hardly be heard. I checked this out on more than one occasion.

The objectors took the matter up with the parish council, who much to my surprise, took sides with the few against the views of the majority.

For me, this had become the last straw. I had believed that the efforts I had put in over the previous twenty years to bring the community together, which included the carol singing on the green on Christmas Eve, should have warranted support from the parish council. The objectors, who were fortunate to be facing the green, had adopted a manner that suggested to me that they thought the green open space belonged to them.

> "We were not against the children using the green in the afternoon" they said, but "we were against the parents having a social evening on the green that included wine and music."

It seemed that wine and mince pies with singing on the green was acceptable on Christmas Eve, but wine and refreshments with music on a summer evening was not. The parish council, unfortunately, agreed with this view, which left me with no other choice but to resign from Up Hatherley Parish Council.

I wrote to the chairman, David Hall, on 8th May tendering my resignation. In my letter I included the following words:

> "In my view the parish council lost its credibility on the night of Wednesday 2nd May, when it preferred to accede to the demands of a vociferous minority whose spurious claims gained more favour than the wishes of the majority, who desired the 'fun-day' to continue on the green in its entirety.
>
> Democracy, for what it is worth, received a jolt on May 2nd, when a majority view of at least 16 to 1 was swept aside by the parish council to the cheers of the selfish minority."

David Hall wrote to me on 10th May expressing his reluctance to accept my resignation. He referred to the past work I had done for the parish and the council for the previous twenty years. It was a memorable letter, which had shown appreciation for the contribution I had made to the parish; it even mentioned the frailty of the democratic process, which was my reason for resigning.

Democracy is a form of government that allows eligible citizens to have an equal say in the decisions that are made – it is the rule of the people. It instils in me a passion to defend its meaning even though it has been misused throughout the centuries.

By 1984 my workload on Tewkesbury Borough Council (TBC) had increased, and the growing number of PAB Group events, plus a number of public meetings, meant that I had very little time for anything else. With an influx of new members, the shape of the Group changed. Doug Grazier had resigned and became honorary President of PAB. Terry Joyner had retired early, sold his office equipment business in Cheltenham and moved to the Isle of Wight. Andrew Cornish took on the role of chairman and David Hyett became vice-chairman – Vivien Park (a teacher in Charlton Kings) became the treasurer. The Group's management committee met bi-monthly and we held an AGM before the start of each financial year.

The AGM provided information to members and it gave them the opportunity to know more about the work of its councillors at all levels of local government. It still does this, and we have included invitations to well-known public figures who give informative and entertaining talks on their work and aspirations.

It continues to be a well-attended event each year.

At the 1984 AGM the management committee presented a document to the meeting entitled "Aims and Objectives", for their approval.

The opening paragraph explained that PAB was a non-political group of concerned ratepayers in the TBC area whose aims and objectives were as follows:

1. To improve the relationship between the ratepayer and the council.
2. To achieve the abolition of secret meetings and decisions.
3. To widen the distribution of community funds to parish councils.
4. To constructively criticise the policies and expenditure of the council.
5. To seek the abandonment of the new Front Gate to Back Gate refuse collection service.

The reverse side of the document showed "The achievements so far" which, readers might guess, filled the page, but it only listed the most important achievements.

The news from the council between 1980 and 1984 had always seemed to be bleak – each announcement from TBC was not good for the local taxpayers.

One of the announcements confirmed that the losses on the Tewkesbury Swimming Pool "now stood at just under £600,000". But as Mr Mike Hudson, the Borough Treasurer, explained, "The sum had amassed over the previous eleven years."

Concern about the loss of green belt land across the area had become a worrying factor. Whilst TBC, to their credit, had done everything possible to prevent the green belt land in their area from being developed, they had experienced difficulty in defending it. The green belt policies were sound enough, and they knew that they had support from PAB councillors and others whenever land was under threat from developers.

In the early 1980's there was adequate land for residential development; local planning authorities were obliged to demonstrate that they held a 5 year supply of land suitable for residential development. In spite of this, and the fact that central government had endorsed the national green belt policies, we found that central government could not be relied upon to support its own policies.

In 1980, J. A. Pye (Oxford) Estates Limited had been refused planning permission by TBC planning committee to construct 70 dwellings and estate roads on land to the south of Cheltenham Racecourse. Because of the decision, the Secretary of State, the Right Honourable Michael Heseltine, M.P., called for an inquiry, which was held in the Tewkesbury Borough Council offices on 14th October 1980. It lasted three days.

The Council for the Protection of Rural England complained that the proposal to create a 'buffer zone' or public open space was inadequate. They also thought "It would damage the rural aspect of Prestbury to an unacceptable extent by bringing suburban development into the adjacent countryside."

The Steeplechase Company (Cheltenham) reminded the Planning Inspector that the racecourse held the internationally famous Cheltenham Gold Cup, along with other important races during the National Hunt Festival.

The Inspector was told that the races "...were watched by many thousands of race-goers as well as viewed by millions on television throughout Britain and other parts of Europe. The popularity and prestige of the racecourse creates a particular responsibility for ensuring that its setting at the foot of the Cotswold Escarpment and close by Cleeve Hill is not harmed."

The residents of Lake Street expressed their concerns about the increase in surface water and the possible inadequacy of the sewage system. They feared that permission for 70 dwellings would lead to further proposals to develop other land north of the Lake Street line.

Prestbury Parish Council were opposed to the proposals on the grounds that the parish had not been identified as an area for housing growth in the Gloucestershire Structure Plan. It had concerns about the traffic implications in the Lindens Estate, which had been endorsed by a large number of local residents who had signed a petition.

PAB councillor Andrew Cornish, who lived in Linden Close, gave a detailed account of what he considered would be serious traffic problems if the proposal went ahead.

CBC in their submission to the Examination in Public of the Structure Plan on September 10th 1980 had made it clear where they stood regarding the application by stating "The council had to rely mainly on adjacent local authorities for the provision of housing land to cater for the needs of Cheltenham." CBC expressed the view that "Modifications to the Green Belt proposals would provide a desirable degree of flexibility." This view was not shared by the PAB Group.

As the public inquiry continued the matter of the 'Interim Green Belt Policy' was debated at length, and as I mentioned in the previous chapter, unless steps were taken as a matter of urgency, to make the 'interim' policy permanent, then more valuable green belt land would be lost.

We were not going to get support from the developers, nor did it appear from Cheltenham Borough Council. The reasons were obvious.

However, the basic point that continued to be discussed was the original Inspector's letter which included the following:

> "Although opinion is not unanimous as to the best possible method of providing Cheltenham Racecourse with a pleasant setting, there exists a broad consensus supporting the idea of the need to ensure in future that this internationally renowned sporting centre is protected from insensitive development of its surroundings."

The Inquiry Inspector agreed with this, but suggested that the land in the proposal "... includes a substantial area of inconspicuous low ground." In recommending to the Secretary of State that the appeal should be allowed, the Inspector commented:

"In the light of the functions of the proposed Green Belt defined in the interim policy and the proposed County Structure Plan documents, there would seem to be little reason for regarding this proposal as conflicting with them, especially as it affords the possibility of enhancing the setting of Cheltenham Racecourse, a major landscape element in any Green Belt deliberations that should not be disregarded."

It was an argument that could not be refuted, but it did endorse the PAB belief that the 'Interim Green Belt' policy was worthless, and we supported the Gloucestershire Structure Plan and its green belt policies.

The Linden Close cul-de-sac was extended and the construction of a new road included a closed end to prevent through traffic. This was welcomed.

There was every indication that permanent green belt proposals would soon be approved, which was essential if we were to succeed in keeping Prestbury and Bishop's Cleeve from merging. In 1984, a TBC document outlining future housing developments for the Cheltenham Policy Area showed that Bishop's Cleeve was regarded as a residential growth area and was identified for up to 1,000 houses during the then current Local Plan period.

Even with an established statutory green belt area, PAB councillors knew that attempts would continue to be made to breach the green belt to the north of Cheltenham. One attempt was made in March 1984 when an outline planning application for the erection of one dwelling and two dwellings on 0.75 hectares of land off New Barn Lane, Prestbury was submitted. The land belonged to the owner of The Chase, New Barn Lane, Prestbury, but the application was submitted by Bovis Homes, who probably had the 'first option' on the land if a planning application was successful. Apart from the application for one and two dwellings, Bovis Homes applied for permission to erect 46 dwellings on 2.54 hectares on other land adjacent to The Chase with in and out access through Apple Close. [The Linden Estate] All three applications were refused by TBC. Bovis Homes Ltd., immediately went to appeal; a local inquiry was opened on Wednesday 11th April 1984.

The planning applications had not come as a surprise to residents living in the immediate area once the J. A. Pye development had been completed. The problem for Bovis Homes, of course, was that the land had been proposed as permanent green belt, and with the emerging Structure Plan about to be approved by the Secretary of State the chances of success with the planning appeal had been reduced.

I attended the local inquiry and spoke on behalf of the local residents. I informed the Planning Inspector that local residents had been disappointed with the recent Pye appeal decision. I explained to him that "Residents and the local councillors were of the opinion that the protection of the Green Belt had been established, yet it had been fractured by insensitive development across the town in recent years." I also stated it was important that the green belt line around the north side of Cheltenham should be drawn to ensure no extension of urban development into the surrounding countryside took place. I suggested it would give better protection to the setting of the Racecourse.

The outcome of the inquiry was that the proposal to erect two dwellings was dismissed, but the erection of one dwelling was allowed. The outline proposal to erect 46 dwellings on 2.54 hectares of land was also dismissed. Thankfully, the land has remained untouched since the erection of the single dwelling, which is good news for the community and the Racecourse.

Even as we approached the end of the year there were two important planning applications submitted for the development of green belt land. One was on the north side of Swindon Lane, Prestbury, and the other was a proposal to develop farm land in Leckhampton Lane, Shurdington.

Mr Bromley Finney, who lived in The Paddocks, Swindon Lane, with his wife, contacted me in August 1984 to ask whether I would support a planning application for the erection of four bungalows on the land adjacent to his house. I told him that the land was in the green belt and the 1981 decision by the Planning Inspector on the Hunting Butts would almost certainly attract a recommendation to refuse by the TBC planning department.

I made it clear to Mr Finney that I would oppose any attempt to breach the Green Belt policy that was currently in existence. He was not pleased with my response, but I had given him my honest opinion.

As expected, the planning committee refused the application and Mr Finney went to appeal to see whether the Planning Inspector agreed with the decision. The appeal was by written representations, which meant that Mr Finney and any local objectors could write letters to the Planning Inspectorate. The Inspector visited the site on the 4th January 1985.

In his decision letter the Inspector had come to the view that any further development on the north side of Swindon Lane would harm the rural appearance and character of the area. He also stated that he attached great importance to the land being in the Green Belt, and he could find no grounds to justify an exception to the green belt policies. The appeal was dismissed.

In the other case, Robert Antony Homes Limited, applied to Tewkesbury Borough Council in 1984 for outline planning permission for the residential development of land off Leckhampton Lane, Shurdington. It was refused. The company went to appeal and a public inquiry took place on the 28th November and the 11th December 1984.

The matter of the green belt designation of the area was challenged by the developer and the Planning Inspector made the following observation:

> "I consider the boundary of the green belt in this area to have been defined in accordance with well established policies and plans which have the effect of generally restricting development to the area north of the Shurdington Road, which forms the greater part of the village, while prohibiting non-essential development within the green belt."

The developer then questioned whether the location of the site was considered to be in open countryside, or related to the village of Shurdington. The Inspector considered that the site was open countryside on the edge of the village and he came to the conclusion that should he allow the appeal then it would extend the built-up area of the village north-eastward between the trunk road A46 and Leckhampton Lane making it difficult to resist further planning applications for the development of other nearby sites.

The Inspector dismissed the appeal.

Both decisions were important, but the Leckhampton Lane was especially important at the time, and it has been quoted as a bench-mark decision in later appeals. Although, it must be said, with the introduction of the National Planning Policy Framework (NPPF) in March 2012, a planning application is more likely to succeed now than fail.

It was with great sorrow that we learned of the sudden death of Terry Joyner on January 1st 1987 at his home on the Isle of Wight.

The news came as a shock to his friends and former colleagues at Cheltenham Borough Council, and the news was particularly devastating to members of the PAB Group; Terry had helped to make PAB possible in both words and deeds from the beginning; he was an inspiration to all who met him.

The sad thing about Terry's death was that he was only 53 years of age, which meant it was a very sad loss for his family who had been looking forward to a long retirement in a very pleasant part of the country. The funeral was held on 8th January 1987 on the Isle of Wight and many local councillors attended. A memorial service was held in Cheltenham on 16th March 1987. The service was conducted by the Rector of Cheltenham, Canon Geoffrey Hart.

The bad news continued in 1987 with the loss of PAB councillors in the local elections. We failed to hold on to several seats in Bishop's Cleeve, and we actually lost one of our seats in Prestbury to a well-known local Conservative, John Hamey.

It was the first time we had experienced a rejection by the electors, but 1987 saw a surge nationally in the fortunes of the Conservative Party, and the new name for the Liberals (The Alliance Party) seemed to attract votes where people had previously voted for other candidates.

1987 was also the year when Chris Burke, won a seat for Labour on Tewkesbury Borough Council. Paul Fearnside, the Borough Surveyor and Engineer, resigned following a special private meeting of the council in November 1987. The *Gloucestershire Echo* called the resignation "a mystery" and tried to get an explanation from the TBC executive regarding the reasons behind the resignation.

The council were tight-lipped about it and Mr Fearnside would only concede that it was a personal matter between himself and the council. Mr Fearnside's responsibilities covered several departments; too many we believed. Some had performed well, but other departments had been a source of concern to many councillors. Twelve months earlier there had been a motion of no confidence in Mr Fearnside, but this had been defeated.

The high cost of renewing the council's depot in Prestbury had resulted in an overspend of the budget and was a subject often talked about in the tearoom, but seldom in committee. It was my opinion that the sudden departure of a chief officer warranted a public explanation by Ron Wheeler the Borough Secretary. Even though I had threatened to reveal the reasons behind the resignation unless an official explanation was given within 14 days, nothing was forthcoming. It was a threat that I had no intention of keeping and it didn't work. The departure is still a secret matter as far as I know.

The Technical Services Department was completely re-organised, which meant that had Mr Fearnside remained in his post he would have become redundant; he should have stayed and waited until the council asked him to go.

CHAPTER 9

Farewell Tewkesbury Borough – Hello Cheltenham Borough

For ever, and forever, farewell, Brutus! If we do meet again, we'll smile indeed! If not, 'tis true this parting was well made.

William Shakespeare (Julius Caesar act 5)

The Local Government Boundary Commission for England (LGBCE) was the statutory body established under the Local Government Act 1972 to look at local authority boundaries in periods of not less than ten years or more than fifteen years from 1974 onwards.

Readers will know from a previous chapter that Cheltenham Borough Council (CBC) had wanted the Boundary Commission to agree changes to their boundaries that would have doubled its size. CBC submitted two plans to the Commission. One plan included parishes and villages within a ten mile radius from the centre of the town, which, if it had been allowed, would have had serious consequences for Tewkesbury Borough Council (TBC).

The other plan was based on a five mile radius (see below).

Gloucester City Council (GCC) had also submitted proposals and had they been allowed by the Commission, they too would have added to TBC's problems.

The LGBCE took their time in coming to their final decision in 1991, probably because they had been inundated with representations from residents and local organisations throughout the 1980's accusing Cheltenham and Gloucester councils of 'land-grabbing'.

Not all residents in the peripheral parishes were anxious to leave Tewkesbury; some residents in Prestbury, for example, were so incensed by the possibility of a transfer that they started a petition against the proposals.

The petition, which attracted over 1,000 names, along with letters of objection, were placed in a council bin and delivered to Nicholas Ridley, MP, Secretary of State, and Member of Parliament for the Tewkesbury consistency.

He met the delegation from Prestbury on 17th May 1988 outside the House of Commons and thanked them for their efforts. But, as is often the case, the petition fell on deaf ears and no account was taken of those directly affected by the change.

An exception to the rule was Up Hatherley parish council, who held a 'parish poll', and 80 per cent of its residents voted. When the votes were counted it revealed that 80 per cent of the total poll voted in favour of 'going into Cheltenham'.

The *Gloucestershire Echo* covered this story and several other ones.

In one 1984 edition they claimed "If the councils (Cheltenham and Gloucester) are successful, Tewkesbury Borough's population will be halved and, more serious still, so would its rateable value."

It should not be assumed that TBC ignored the threat to their existence; they had taken the threat so seriously that they employed two officers full time to find out the intentions of their neighbouring councils, and to inform them with strong words that they would not concede any part of their area to them.

CBC's alternative proposal was to seek permission to extend its boundaries which would have included parishes and villages within a five mile radius. This was a modest proposal in comparison to the other one, and, if approved by the LGBCE, it would only have included the peripheral parishes around Cheltenham.

That is not to say that it would not have had any effect on TBC, because it did. Contrary to the view at the time, TBC officers were generous enough to announce that it was not true they would be glad to see the back of PAB from the council chamber. They were also complimentary by saying that the PAB councillors had established a presence in the council that had been recognised by several senior council officers. One chief officer was kind enough to tell me that we were always strong in debate and reliable members of the council. That was good news, especially as we had been very critical of the way the council had been run from 1976, [their handling of the changes to the refuse collection system] and throughout the 1980's [profligate with their spending of ratepayers' money].

It seemed that our earlier criticisms of the council had been sufficiently constructive to bring forward more robust policies on matters such as the green belt, and an end to 'secret' committee meetings.

From conversations with TBC officers, it seemed that our efforts to protect the green belt across the whole of the Tewkesbury area had been welcomed.

There was no doubt that the council's green belt policies had been made stronger, and subsequent development only happened in places that were more acceptable to local residents – and open green spaces too were given a measure of protection.

But it should not be presumed that these successes and our strong commitment to the protection of the green belt were always supported by the opposition groups, far from it. Neither did they change their opinions when the peripheral parishes were transferred to CBC.

However, the same opposition councillors who had previously supported development in the green belt soon changed their minds when they realised that the green belt land in the Tewkesbury area was to be treated in a similar way to the green belt land that surrounded Cheltenham.

The realisation did not come about over-night, and we shall learn later how difficult it became to get the CBC Liberal Democrat administration to support the green belt and its associated policies throughout the 1990's.

Following the announcement by the LGBCE in May 1991, the peripheral parishes of Prestbury, Swindon, Up Hatherley and Leckhampton, were transferred from TBC to CBC.

Whilst the loss of the parishes had been difficult for TBC, it was not easy for the PAB group either. Our representation was now split between the two councils, and it weakened our position.

In spite of what has been written in the previous chapters, there was a great deal of sadness in leaving TBC. The break with our councillor colleagues in Bishop's Cleeve and the inevitable loss of membership in the rural areas would soon become a serious matter for the PAB group. Whilst every effort was made to support the PAB councillors with their work on TBC, the task became too great and we eventually lost our representation on the council.

Undaunted by this fact, the PAB councillors who transferred to CBC, soon realised that it would mean having to start all over again even though a great deal of expertise had been acquired during our time spent as TBC councillors. We were ready to play our part on Cheltenham Borough Council.

The Mayor of Cheltenham, Cllr Bill Bullingham, invited the new councillors from Tewkesbury to the parlour for tea and biscuits. The mayor welcomed everyone to CBC and hoped that we would all make a contribution to the town and the running of the council. We chatted about different matters concerning both local authorities and after twenty minutes or so the meeting was brought to an end with the mayor wishing everyone well.

I was impressed with the mayor's parlour; it contained memorabilia of past occasions for the town and previous mayors. I wondered whether I would get another chance to take a closer look at what was a very impressive display, especially the display of gifts from other towns and cities on the continent.

On the way out I went into the council chamber, which seemed old and uninviting compared to the modern chamber in the TBC building. Apart from that, my first impressions had been good.

My early years as a member of CBC were uneventful. PAB councillors became members of the various committees, choosing the subject that appealed to them – mine was planning, mainly because my period on the TBC planning committee had been interesting.

My time there had taught me the importance of consistency in the planning process if we truly wanted to protect the historical and environmental importance of the town. Policies that have been agreed to protect local environments are essential, providing officers and councillors adhere to them. The planning committee also taught me that only by having robust planning policies and strategies that looked forward, could a council plan for the future economic needs of its area.

The news that the Department of the Environment (DoE) had released a consultative draft Planning Policy Guidance Note (PPG2) on Green Belts in 1994 was welcomed in most quarters. The purpose of PPG's was a means by which Central Government set out its policy advice to local authorities. A green belt policy is for controlling urban growth; originally it was an idea for establishing a ring of protected countryside around a settlement where development would be resisted.

The most important attribute of green belts is their openness, which has remained the main thrust of green belt policies.

The Town and Country Planning Act 1947 allowed local authorities to include green belt proposals in their development plans. In 1955, the Minister of Housing, Duncan Sandys, encouraged local authorities around the country to consider protecting land around their towns and cities by the formal designation of clearly defined green belt boundaries.

This message was taken up by most local authorities, but the amount of protected land turned out to be very limited. Bearing in mind that green belt land has been lost to development in the intervening years, it is worth noting that an estimate of green belt land remaining in England at 31st March 2010 was only 1,639,560 hectares, which is about 13 per cent of the land area of the country.

The Gloucestershire green belt between Cheltenham and Gloucester was incorporated into the Gloucestershire Development Plan First Quinquennial Review published in 1960. It was considered "essential to preserve the open character of the land between the towns of Cheltenham and Gloucester and to prevent these communities merging into one another."

In 1981, the Gloucestershire Structure Plan extended the green belt to the north of Cheltenham (Swindon Lane) to prevent the coalescence of Cheltenham with Bishop's Cleeve.

The Gloucestershire green belt is relatively small when compared with other green belts. It does not surround the county's two main urban areas where alternative constraints on development exist. The main purpose of the green belt in the Cheltenham and Gloucester area has been to uphold the green belt policy and prevent the coalescence of the city and the town.

The Gloucestershire County Council Environment Committee met on 15th June 1994 to consider the report of Mr T. Smith, the county planning officer, on the various implications of the draft PPG2.

The report explained that Central Government saw the major aims of green belts as being the prevention of urban sprawl and the merging of settlements. That long held position had stood the test of time, and the publication of PPG2 served to strengthen existing green belt policies and the creation of new policies where they did not exist.

Mr Smith reported that central government had also set out other aims in its draft PPG2: to protect areas of open countryside around urban areas; to encourage the use and re-use of land in urban areas; and to preserve the setting and character of historic towns.

Whilst accepting these important points, the county planning officer suggested that some of the green belt designations and the relationships between town and country had become less distinct since the green belt policies were first introduced in the mid 1950's. He also conceded that green belts determine the shape and pattern of settlements, and should, therefore, be an integral part of the development plan process.

PPG2 was released on 24th January 1995 and it formed the basis on which green belt policies in local government development plans should be established. The guidance outlined the history and extent of green belts and their purpose. Each local authority set down its own green belt policies, and providing they showed "urban containment", they would be approved by the Secretary of State.

However, the county planning officer, in his report, recognised that not all green belts were of the highest environmental quality, particularly areas on the edge of the larger urban areas. He suggested that whenever this was found to be the case, then each local authority should take the necessary action to improve the environmental quality of the green belt land.

Whilst the suggestion was sound, I have no news that the local authorities actually carried out work to strengthen sections of green belt land in the Cheltenham and Tewkesbury areas. Whilst PPG2 effectively proscribed new development and prevented urban sprawl, it also allowed certain types of development to take place in the green belt, which included infilling and a limited amount of extensions to villages. [This was an important issue for a local authority such as Tewkesbury, which has more than fifty villages and hamlets within its boundaries].

The matter of infilling and limited expansion would always be contentious, not least when areas of green belt included employment sites, or sites that had amenity uses, and they became the subject for expansion and development.

Whilst I welcomed the purpose of PPG2, I was concerned about some aspects of its proposals, which I described at the time as woolly. It was non-specific, for example, on what could or could not be built on green belt land. It suggested that park and ride sites could be acceptable, but gave no indication of what should be the scale of development and the appropriateness of the use.

The county planning officer suggested to the Environmental Committee in his report that they should exercise caution in designating park and ride development within green belt areas. He thought *"This part of the guidance could prove to be the thin end of the wedge by attracting other development pressures around such transport interchanges."*

The county planning officer was right. Whilst park and ride facilities are good for reducing the number of cars entering and leaving a town centre, they are also a 'blot-on-the-landscape'. PAB councillors have repeatedly urged the council to develop underground parking facilities in Cheltenham but to no avail. Underground parking at Hyde Park in London and the one in our twin town of Annecy are good examples of what can be achieved.

Most of the issues that arose during the consultation period of the PPG2 were resolved, and there is no doubt that if the guidance document had not been approved in 1995, then our landscapes would look entirely different today. However, I am aware that throughout the period 1995 until the present day, there have been numerous attempts to breach green belt policies and to ignore the principles contained in PPG2. Unfortunately, some of the attempts have been successful and the details will be included in later chapters.

The next chapters will also show that both planning officers and planning committees have been responsible for 'unwanted' development in the green belt in spite of the advice in PPG2.

In March 2012, Central Government introduced a National Planning Policy Framework (NPPF); it swept away all the planning policy guidance documents (including PPG2).

Thankfully, the NPPF document includes a chapter entitled 'Protecting Green Belt land', which repeats the recognised main purposes of green belt protection. It also suggests that existing green belts should be re-defined, but in order to do this the local plan would need to be updated, which CBC was not prepared to do. A review and update would not have allowed new areas of green belt to be established, but it would have been an opportunity to redefine existing green belt if they no longer served the purposes defined in the PPG2 document, or the new NPPF.

Whilst I have no problem with the proposals for the green belt, I do believe the NPPF document is like 'the curate's egg' – good in parts; it leaves a number of loopholes for developers to exploit.

Within weeks of its publication, there have been attempts to breach what protection there is of important tracts of land. And with the increasing pressure on councils to provide more dwellings in the next twenty years, there will be most likely few occasions when anyone can report that green belt land or open green fields have been saved for the benefit of a community.

There had been ominous warning signs of what was likely to happen to areas of green belt and open green spaces as early as January 1995.

Towards the end of 1994, TBC published its proposals for a new statutory district-wide Local Plan. It was a draft document that went out for public consultation between 30th November 1994 and 13th January 1995.

Policies in a local plan should relate

a) to the development or use of land,
b) improvements and protection of the physical environment in the area it covers, and
c) the management of local traffic.

It should express precisely the council's intent on the above matters, and in order to receive the Secretary of State's approval, it should also conform to the Gloucestershire County Structure Plan.

The TBC area covered a large amount of open countryside embracing areas of outstanding natural beauty and acres of green belt land. They were concerned that a great deal of their green belt land abuts the boundaries of Cheltenham and Gloucester, and, not surprisingly, wanted to strengthen their policies in order to prevent the land being used for development.

CBC had done exactly the same thing in 1993 when their plan went out for public consultation.

In the introduction to their new plan, TBC stated that its intention was to strengthen their green belt policy by making it clear that they start from the presumption against new development unless there are exceptional circumstances to do otherwise. They also recognised that the planning policy guidance document PPG2 referred to "inappropriate development" whereas TBC preferred the more robust wording of "no new development".

TBC proposed adding the white land at Homecroft Drive/Tewkesbury Road, (including the Civil Service sports ground), to the status of green belt.

The white land at Farm Lane/Kidnappers Lane, Leckhampton, was also included in their green belt policy, claiming that it would ensure that the land was kept open and free from development in the future.The existing green belt area that included Staverton Airport was also important to Tewkesbury council; its status ensured that Cheltenham and Gloucester did not become one large conurbation. But, for the airport to remain viable, a certain amount of commercial development would be needed in the areas that had already been delineated for employment purposes.

With this in mind, TBC proposed a new policy:

> "Within that part of the Airport that lies within the Green Belt, as defined on the proposals map, there will be a strong presumption against new structure or buildings unless they are essential to the operation of the Airport; and cannot be accommodated within the identified employment areas that are excluded from the Green Belt."

Should park and ride proposals come forward, TBC introduced a new clause in its policy that stated "Park and Ride facilities will not normally be acceptable in the Green Belt".

To any rational thinking person the proposals were moderate and should have been regarded as a step in the right direction for both TBC and her adjoining neighbours. But this did not prove to be the case. CBC went completely over the top and questioned whether TBC were justified in making their proposals in order to retain the openness of the green belt.

PAB councillors took the opposite view and argued that TBC were entitled to strengthen their proposals; it was a sign of determination to protect what they had and to add protection where it did not exist.

Even though we had only recently become Cheltenham councillors, we spoke out in defence of what the Tewkesbury councillors wanted to do, which didn't improve our popularity in CBC at the time. The response by CBC to their neighbour's proposals was quite amazing. The chief planning officer was instructed to study the TBC Local Plan proposals and report to the planning committee on 19th January 1995.

Subsequently, the chief planning officer, in his report, restricted his comments to the matters which were important to Cheltenham as an adjoining local authority.

He objected to the five new policies that TBC had proposed. He reminded the planning committee that the Tewkesbury Road sports ground belonged to CBC and the development along the south side of the road was restricted to a small area. He recognised that TBC wanted to prevent any extension of the built-up area, but doubted whether adding the sports ground to their green belt portfolio was warranted and necessary. The sports ground was on a short lease to the Cheltenham Civil Service Association, and CBC could either cancel it, or not renew it. The land would then become available for development.

Following the planning meeting, PAB councillors held talks with CBC officers in an effort to extend the lease of the sports ground to the Civil Service. We argued that it would encourage them to make improvements to the clubhouse and ground with no cost to the ratepayer.

CBC took some time to come back to us with an answer but without any explanation, we learned that the lease had been extended to a longer period.

On the main point of the TBC proposals, CBC objected to the inclusion of the words "the council would be against new development" which they claimed, overruled the PPG2 wording "against inappropriate development".

When it suited them, the planning department had often used the phrase 'inappropriate development' in order to prevent planning applications from being approved, although an explanation of what 'inappropriate' meant has never been given.

As far as a park and ride facility was concerned, the council believed it was an important component in their policy for reducing car use, pollution, congestion and accidents in Cheltenham. Therefore, for their neighbours to exclude park and ride sites in their green belt policy was not, according to CBC, in the spirit and intention of PPG2.

Regarding Staverton Airport – the Chief Planning Officer said the Tewkesbury proposals would prevent other development taking place within the identified employment areas.

The Chief Planning Officer's recommendations, after a lengthy debate, were accepted by the planning committee members. I voted against the report.

Following the committee decision, the report went to full council for approval on Monday 23rd January 1995.

According to the minutes of that meeting, Cllr Hazel Langford (Liberal Democrat), representing Leckhampton and Up Hatherley, moved a motion approving the lodging of the objections to the TBC Local Plan proposals as recommended by the Chief Planning Officer.

The motion was seconded by Cllr David Lawrence (Liberal Democrat). The motion was carried – 33 votes in favour and 3 votes against with one member abstaining. A few years later, Cllr Lawrence was appointed to the Board of the Airport and did a good job in helping to steer the Board to a profitable position.

It was another case of a Liberal Democrat saying one thing and doing another, or a good example of how dangerous it is at a local level to have such things as a 'three line whip' placed on councillors at a political meeting, prior to a council or a planning meeting.

Following the decision by the council, I wrote to Ron Wheeler, Borough Secretary and Chief Executive of TBC, dissociating the PAB group from the decision that had been taken.

It is worth recording that *Echo* staff attended the council meeting on 23rd January 1995 when the TBC proposals were debated, but not a word was printed in the newspaper the following day.

Why the *Echo* preferred to remain silent on this important issue is a mystery – it will be up to its readers to draw their own conclusions.

If the *Echo* editorial had asked me, I could have told them that the two main political parties had held group meetings before the start of the council meeting – no doubt to ensure that all the councillors in the respective political groups would oppose the TBC green belt proposals.

However, opposition to the proposals by CBC made little difference to the determination of TBC to strengthen its green belt policies. This was good. I was convinced that the decisions by the main opposition parties on the council would come back to haunt them, and it did when the question of how much green belt land should be sacrificed for development was put to them in 2012.

The political parties have never seemed to grasp the fact that protecting the green belt is not a one-off exercise; it is a continuing process until such times as a review, followed by public consent, changes the green belt boundaries.

The behaviour of CBC councillors at that time prompted PAB councillors to hold further meetings in the areas where green belt land existed and particularly where they were under threat. All we could do was to report to the local residents the outcome of the debate in the council chamber, and to warn them of the possibility that green belt land and open spaces in their communities may be threatened by developers in the future. We urged them to write to Tewkesbury Borough Council supporting their efforts to strengthen their green belt proposals.

I contacted Jo Pyatt, a local reporter, to inform her of the series of meetings the PAB group intended to hold to alert local residents to the possible dangers to the green belt. She wrote an article in her newspaper outlining the programme and the purpose behind the PAB meetings.

She reported that the first meeting of the campaign would be held in the Hillview Community Centre, Up Hatherley, followed by meetings in Warden Hill, The Reddings and Swindon Village.

Jo Pyatt reported:

> "Councillor Godwin welcomed moves by Tewkesbury Borough Council to strengthen its green belt policy in its local plan, although Cheltenham Borough Council has objected to them. The reason for the objections is because the land Tewkesbury wants to bring into line with its policies; Uckington, Southam, Staverton, Shurdington and The Reddings, belongs to Cheltenham Borough Council."

By objecting to the plans, and providing it remained 'white land', it would be easier for CBC to allow development of the land in the future, but if it was designated green belt then it would become more difficult.

Not surprisingly, the article prompted a number of letters from residents, most of which supported my views rather than the views that had been expressed by the Liberal Democrats.

One thing was clear from the council decision – we all knew where the Liberal Democrats stood as far as protection of the green belt was concerned: support for non-airport related commercial and industrial development at Staverton Airport, which could lead to less green belt land separating Cheltenham and Gloucester: no support for 'white land' to become green belt at either Tewkesbury Road, or Farm Lane, Leckhampton: and support for a park and ride facility on the green belt within the Cheltenham boundary.

Graham Buckley, a reporter for the local newspaper *Independent*, wrote a story for his newspaper headed "Green belt row – fear of end to buffer between town and city". The article, published on 2nd February 1995, reported on my opposition to the objections by CBC to the amendments to the Tewkesbury Borough local plan.

He was interested to know more about my efforts to persuade the members of the Cheltenham council to support the Tewkesbury local plan proposals, which would create more green belt land, and protect the airport from creeping development.

I told him that the motion by the Liberal Democrats, which had support from a number of Conservative councillors, clearly demonstrated that 'the green belt was not safe in the hands of Cheltenham Borough Council'.

Cllr Hazel Langford immediately took umbrage over the article and wrote a letter to the *Independent* refuting my claim that CBC, and presumably her motion to council, did not in any way dilute the efforts of TBC to strengthen their green belt. If that was the case then why did she propose the motion? Furthermore, why did CBC ask its Chief Planning Officer to write a report, which resulted in him recommending to council that it should object to five of the TBC green belt proposals?

It did not come as a surprise to learn that other senior Liberal Democrat councillors were making supporting comments about the use of green belt land for development purposes in the local newspapers.

Prior to the council meeting on 23rd January 1995, I wrote to County Councillor Kit Braunholtz (Liberal Democrat), about the proposed changes that TBC intended to make to strengthen their green belt policies – I also alerted him to the fact that his political colleagues were going to move a motion opposing the changes by TBC.

He replied on 31st January saying:

"He was glad Tewkesbury is proposing to strengthen their Green belt policy", but he then went on to say, *"I also believe that the concept of 'keeping Gloucester and Cheltenham apart at all costs is really not what the green belt policy should be doing – I would actually prefer to see development, for instance, at Staverton Airport, than see it all around the fringes of Cheltenham, which is what I fear may happen if we do not allow it there. On grounds of sustainability, therefore enabling people to live near their work, and on good public transport, I will probably support what you clearly oppose, the development of Staverton Airport."*

The content of the letter was a shock; it was also contradictory.

My reply was immediate and I went straight to the point by accusing Cllr Braunholtz of hypocrisy. How could he support the strengthening of the TBC green belt policies and at the same time advocate the development of housing on Staverton Airport? I suggested that he clearly did not understand the functions of the green belt if he believed that it was not the intention of green belt policy to prevent the coalescence of Cheltenham and Gloucester.

In my opinion it was monstrous to suggest that development at Staverton Airport was permissible in order to avoid any development on the fringes of Cheltenham.

I received a six page letter from Cllr Braunholtz on 7th February 1995, and not surprisingly, the first paragraph stressed that he resented my accusation of hypocrisy. He then went on to repeat some of the points he had made in his earlier letter to me. The main issue continued to be that the land between Cheltenham and Gloucester should be developed in a controlled manner, which would help to protect the countryside. [The land between Gloucester and Cheltenham is countryside].

The next part of his letter was unbelievable – after all my years of campaigning to keep the green belt free of development, here was a county councillor who would be making decisions on behalf of the wider community, saying:

"It seems to me sensible to use the existing transport corridor between Cheltenham and Gloucester (Golden Valley bypass), to enable sustainable development to happen. This does not mean that Cheltenham and Gloucester would lose their identities – rather a greater Churchdown would develop between them. I certainly would not be in favour of this essentially 'linear city' developing sideways to form a metropolis – ideally everyone would live within half a mile of open countryside to one side or the other. The south side the railway might well be the limit of the development. It was not the most favourable alternative to which we might be forced to choose, but it was better than development round the outskirts of Cheltenham."

He could not, it seemed, understand that the green belt and the countryside is of the same value, and they both require our protection.

Following the exchange of letters an article appeared in the local newspaper headed 'A corridor of homes could meet needs'. It reported that Cllr Braunholtz believed that "The land between Cheltenham and Gloucester could be developed to solve a housing shortage. He believed creating a corridor of housing between the two areas should be looked at as a serious option. He claimed that the land between the Golden Valley bypass and Cheltenham Road East, including Staverton Airport, could be built on, but he admitted, the development would go against green belt policy".

He told the reporter that *"It is going to involve obliterating some pleasant country-side, annoying people who live there."*

That was an understatement to say the least.

The article brought about a spate of letters to the newspaper, not one, I recall, in support of what Cllr Braunholtz had suggested.

Unfazed by the number of critical letters to the press, he wrote an article in the *Gloucestershire Echo* in February 1995 saying that he thought it would be totally wrong to allow a farmer to erect a goat shed for his animals on the slopes of Leck-hampton Hill, because the land in question was one of the most important green belt sites in Cheltenham. This was true, but the existing green belt policies would have allowed a shed to be constructed if it was for farming or agricultural purposes. He should have known this.

A rather odd comment to make in a local newspaper following his recent comments that acres of green belt land could be sacrificed for development between Cheltenham and Gloucester. This land, like the land at Staverton Airport, was under the protection of TBC.

I made this clear in my letters to the *Gloucestershire Echo* in January 1995 and it prompted Cllr Braunholtz to write to me again on 31st January justifying his opinions. I replied immediately saying that it was clear that he did not understand the functions of green belt policy, if he could suggest, as he did, that it was not the intention of a green belt policy to prevent the coalescence of Cheltenham and Gloucester.

The following is an abstract of the most critical paragraph in my letter:

> "It is monstrous to suggest that development at Staverton should take place whilst at the same time your organisation, which goes under the name 'Leckhampton Green Land Action Group' (Leglag) constantly seeks my support to protect the green belt land and associated local plan policies. This is double- talk. Apparently, it is alright to protect the green belt at Leckhampton, but too bad for the residents at Staverton and elsewhere, where apparently, development can take place. I shall do my best to expose this hypocrisy whenever I can."

I thought it appropriate for me to write to Ron Wheeler, chief executive of TBC on 25th January 1995 to inform him that the CBC planning committee meeting on 19th January had approved the proposal to oppose the TBC intentions to strengthen their green belt policies. I also wanted Ron Wheeler to know that Colin Nye, who was chief executive of CBC at the time, had rebutted my claim that development at Staverton would bring about the coalescence of Cheltenham and Gloucester. He had also made a statement that the chief executive of TBC was supportive of his views on Staverton Airport stating that the airport should be commercially developed with the subsequent loss of green belt land.

A paragraph of my letter stated:

"Mr Nye seemed to forget that I had spent many years on Tewkesbury Borough Council, and that I was knowledgeable of your views and the views of the council. Unfortunately, many of my member colleagues fell for the persuasive tongue of Mr Nye, and believed his claim that you supported his view. Unless things have changed over recent years, I am still of the opinion that you and your council are determined to protect the green belt at Staverton. I hope you can confirm this view."

I did not receive a reply from Mr Wheeler, so I wrote to him again on 3rd March 1995 reminding him of his failure to answer my letter. It took another two weeks before I received a reply on 15th March, although we had spoken on the telephone about the matter. Whilst a telephone call is helpful, it is a poor substitute for a letter; a record that cannot be changed.

This is an extract from Ron Wheeler's letter:

"Your objection to any attempt to weaken the green belt is wholly consistent with the contributions you made when you were a Tewkesbury Borough councillor. The situation in connection with Staverton Airport is very clear. Officers at TBC in the process leading up to formal consideration of the district-wide local plan, certainly looked specifically at the pressure between Gloucester and Cheltenham, which included the land held for airport purposes.

Before approving a consultation report, my officers dealt with individual working groups for every parish area, and listened to the parish councils. The decision to maintain a policy that would allow airport related uses only is a clear and definitive one and so far as I can recall produced no dissent whatsoever amongst the elected members.

In a meeting some time ago, which included the airport manager, Colin Nye, chief executive of CBC, plus Mr Reg Ward, I warned that any ambition in relation to the airport area that was merely intended to enhance the equity would come up against the Tewkesbury Council's firm policy."

The message in the letter was positive and perhaps in hindsight it should have been distributed to other interested parties.

In April 1995, a letter signed by County Cllr Braunholtz and Borough Cllr Langford, was distributed to residents in the Warden Hill and Up Hatherley areas accusing me of being against the new South West Distributor Road that skirted around Warden Hill, Up Hatherley and The Reddings.

It was another piece of Liberal Democrat propaganda, making sure it gave the readers only half the story. What it didn't say was that in order to construct the road, a huge swathe of green belt land would be sacrificed and the cost of the road would not be economically viable when set against the county council's anticipated usage of the road by local residents.

Whilst it was true that it would be a short-cut for drivers travelling from the A46 to the Golden Valley bypass and along the A40 to Gloucester, there was no advantage for local residents wanting to travel to Cheltenham. The direct route to town has been and has continued to be along the Hatherley Road.

This has proved to be the case since the GCC-built section of the road from Cold Pool Lane to Arle Court was opened in September 1994.

In 2013 (19 years later), its usage is still 20 per cent below capacity. It also concerned me that once the road had been constructed there would be proposals for the land on the urban side of the road to be developed.

Development has happened, just as I forecast it would. But the selling point by the County highways department was the assurance that the road would create a permanent buffer between the urbanised side of the road and the green belt land on the other side. I asked them for a guarantee that the green belt would be secure in perpetuity, but my request was refused.

I was also concerned that following the construction of the road, a move would be made to construct a park and ride facility on green belt land adjacent to the new distributor road.

The letter by Cllrs Braunholtz and Langford ended with them accusing Up Hatherley parish council of writing "untrue statements in its April community magazine." The magazine allegedly accused Cllr Langford "of being in favour of developing green field sites for things like park and ride."

She claimed this was untrue, but admitted that "... the council is planning park and ride, which we both support."

Was there a difference between the two comments – I don't think so.

The letter was a deception. They claimed that all that was at stake for the local residents was a distributor road, which would become a major asset for the local residents, plus a park and ride facility, albeit in the green belt, which they (the residents) should all welcome.

The councillors had conveniently forgotten the 'warnings' in the County Planning Officer's report regarding park and ride sites "attracting other development pressures."

Looking now at the creeping development that has occurred in the vicinity of the park and ride site at Grovefield Way and in Hatherley Lane since 1995, one can only concede that the County Planning Officer's warnings were absolutely right. Unfortunately, those in charge of the well-being of the local community chose to ignore them.

The area of green belt now consists of two large stores (one includes a petrol filling station); 3,384 square metres of office accommodation; a pet shop and a large business park, which has recently been given planning approval following an appeal.

The park and ride facility was opened on 31st August 1997 (with around 150 spaces) and was extended to 360 spaces on 2nd May 1998.

Originally, the land belonged to Dowty Equipment Limited, and under a Section 106 agreement the land was transferred from Dowty to Gloucestershire County Council (GCC). When the South West Distributor Road was under construction in the early 1980's, some of the earth from the road building was spread over the land that was to become the park and ride site.

CBC helped GCC subsidise the running costs of the park and ride until 2005.

Planning consent was obtained to increase the number of spaces to 550, which was partly funded by GCHQ. This extension was opened in 2006. I am told that GCC still funds the site costs, which are approximately £50,000 per year.

The park and ride facility at the Cheltenham Racecourse followed a similar pattern. It started off in the 1990's as an unofficial park and ride site used by a bus operator called Circle Line until it was bought out by Stagecoach. In the year 2000, GCC invested through its local transport plan, sufficient funds to construct a large tarmac car park complete with bus shelters, and a 15 minute frequency service to town by Stagecoach. Initially, it operated without public subsidy, but later with funding offered by central government, Stagecoach invested in new buses and the council invested in new bus shelters for the new route 'D', which ran from Up Hatherley to the town centre, and later to Bishop's Cleeve.

Prior to 2005, CBC funded the site lease costs, which amounted to £60,000 annually, payable to the Racecourse Company. GCC took over this cost after 2005. In 2011, the public sector subsidy ended. The service continues to be run with no costs to the taxpayer.

Meanwhile, County Councillor Braunholtz, undaunted by my rebuttal of his suggestions, attended the May public meeting of Up Hatherley parish council.

During the adjournment, which allowed members of the public to speak or ask questions, Cllr Braunholtz spoke about two matters. Firstly, he accused parish councillor David Hall of allowing development in the green belt: he was referring to the remaining undeveloped land on the urban side of the South West Distributor Road. This had been earmarked for development once the road had been constructed in any event.

Secondly, he claimed that he had been misquoted in an article published in the local parish magazine concerning his support for development in the green belt.

Whilst Cllr Hall declined the opportunity to rebut the claims of Cllr Braunholtz at the parish council meeting, he did write a letter to the county councillor on 19th May 1995, regarding the inaccuracies in his statement at the meeting.

Cllr Hall, in his letter to Cllr Braunholtz, explained that the County Structure Plan had been available for public consultation in the mid 1970's. He wrote:

"At the time, the parish council had lobbied strongly for no growth in the Up Hatherley area, arguing for the existing green belt line to be held, which was the opposite of what you had alleged."

Cllr Hall was annoyed by the charge that he had been happy to allow houses to be built up to the new road when he was a member of Tewkesbury Borough Council. He reminded Cllr Braunholtz that the article in the Hatherley and Reddings magazine was a report of his statement to the parish council meeting when the matter of green belt protection had been debated. His comments had been recorded by the parish council clerk and they were reproduced in the magazine so that local residents in the two areas could read what had been said. He quoted the article:

"Kit Braunholtz gave an overview of the whole business, and thought that the green belt shouldn't be too restrictive and spoke of the possibility of a corridor of development between the two towns making it into a linear city".

David Hall made a generous offer in his letter –

"If this report is false in any material sense, please let me know, and your complaint will be tested at the next parish council meeting by those who were present at the meeting. If you did not attempt to give an overview of the whole business of the green belt; did not say that the green belt should not be too restrictive; didn't speak about the possibility of a corridor of development along the line of the Golden Valley bypass, linking the towns in the form of a linear city, then I will be only too pleased to make an apology on behalf of the parish council. I would also register it as such in the next issue of the said magazine."

As far as I am aware, Cllr Braunholtz did not respond to David Hall's offer, so I can only assume that the record in the minutes of the parish council meeting and the article in the local magazine were correct.

Handing a petition to Cllr Derek Davies in 1995 supporting the protection of Green Belt policies in the TBC Local Plan

Local residents were rightfully concerned about the loss of valuable Green Belt land around Cheltenham, particularly at Arle Court and Staverton Airport. PAB councillors came up with the idea that signatures on a petition should be collected at the various meetings we intended to hold about the pressures on the green belt. When the meetings were concluded we had collected 337 names on the petition and on behalf of the PAB Group, I presented it to Tewkesbury Borough Council on 3rd August 1995. The petition simply called on the council to stand firm on its green belt policies.

The petition was presented to Cllr Derek Davies, the chairman of the TBC planning committee, Chris Shaw the borough planning officer and Ron Wheeler, the chief executive. I was accompanied by David Hall, chairman of Up Hatherley parish council and Danny Judge, chairman of Staverton parish council.

The event was covered by the local *Independent* newspaper, but I have no record that the *Gloucestershire Echo* took any part in the photograph sessions, or printed an article about the event.

"David Hall", wrote the *Independent,* "claimed that CBC was not capable of handling its green belt responsibility. He was fearful that the green belt land between Cheltenham and Gloucester will disappear forever unless somebody makes a stand." David was right, once the green belt is developed, the land is gone forever.

The recorded event in the *Independent* brought a flurry of letters to its editor, some of which criticised the Liberal Democrats for trying to 'sabotage TBC's plans'. Others warned the readers that the criticism by the Liberal Democrats was contrary to what they had published in their political leaflets, and not for the first time came the charge that 'they say one thing and do another'.

Whilst this was good copy for the *Independent*, it was also good for the PAB image. We had been supporting the green belt intentions of TBC for some time, which had not been welcomed by the CBC administration. It must have been irksome, to say the least, for them to read about members of its own council supporting the proposals of another local authority.

Whether the administration liked it or not, PAB councillors intended to go on speaking in support of policies that would protect the peripheral parishes around Cheltenham, whether it was the green belt or any other issues.

Our motto has always been to be honest with our comments, and to be consistent with our support for sound planning policies.

Chris Shaw wrote to me on 26th July 1995 thanking me for the petition and told me that it had been registered as a representation supporting the green belt policies of TBC's local plan.

The document went out for public consultation in November 1995. Earlier I wrote about the attempt by a developer in 1995 to develop unallocated land to the east of Kidnappers Lane and Farm Lane. Following refusal of the application by the planning committee the applicant went to appeal.

The hearing was well attended by members of the public who tried hard to persuade the planning inspector (should he dismiss the appeal) to make the land green belt. Of course, the inspector did not have the power to order this change of status, but he did make the point that because the land played an important role in keeping Leckhampton and Shurdington apart, the land was worthy enough to be treated as though it was green belt.

Whilst this was a crumb of comfort for the local residents, it was never going to be strong enough to stop any unwanted development.

The inspector dismissed the appeal and his comments were a powerful signal to future would-be developers, but it did not please everyone who lived in the Leckhampton area – many wanted the land to be made green belt.

I took the view that it was a 'half-way house' decision, but because a planning inspector had made the comment, it seemed to me that a strong point had been established that would enable the PAB group to try to get the local council to include the 'white land' in its green belt portfolio. After all, TBC had been successful in amending some of their planning policies, so it was worth trying to persuade the Cheltenham councillors, if nothing else.

I called a meeting of PAB councillors in October 1995, to discuss the Farm Lane decision, mainly to see if there was a course of action we could take that would protect the land from development. We came to the conclusion that we needed to go further than the planning inspector and try to get the white land in the Leckhampton area designated green belt.

Cllr Andrew Cornish told the meeting that the Liberal Democrats had called an Extraordinary Meeting of the Council for 9th November 1995, to amend three minor policies in the Local Plan following the recent review. He reminded us that all amendments to the local plan had to be approved by the council before it could be adopted.

There was no doubt that it would be a good opportunity for PAB to propose a fourth amendment asking for the land at Kidnappers Lane and Farm Lane to be designated green belt thereby giving it better protection.

It also fitted in well with our earlier position of supporting the changes to the TBC green belt policies. We decided that we would propose an additional amendment to the Local Plan at the Extraordinary Council Meeting on 9th November.

It was suggested that I should talk to the Conservative group leader about our amendment, and to find out whether they would support it. We knew that seeking an amendment to the Local Plan would upset the Liberal Democrats, because they had already exposed their position on the green belt. Their colours had been well and truly tied to the mast when they refused to accept the amendments to the TBC green belt policies.

It was agreed that as group leader I should propose the amendment, with Cllr John Newman seconding it.

The amendment read as follows:

"This Council, mindful of the strong wishes of the people living in the south west of Cheltenham to maintain a green environment in their part of the town, seeks to designate the area of unallocated land lying to the east of Kidnappers Lane and Farm Lane as green belt, making it abundantly clear to all that there exists a clear presumption against this land being used for residential development".

There was only one item on the agenda for the Extraordinary Meeting, which read – The Local Plan: Proposed changes to modify document.

At the meeting of 9th November, Cllr Barry Anderson, chairman of the planning committee, referred to the seminars which had been held on major topics relating to the review of the local plan. He reported that the proposed changes had been circulated and they would be debated after the amendment proposed by Cllr Godwin.

He then invited me to move the PAB motion.

I thanked the chairman for his introduction and proceeded to outline the principal details of the recent planning inquiry where the inspector had told local residents that the land was worthy of being designated green belt.

I reminded the council that The Lanes development at the northern end of Farm Lane had been completed in 1990, which meant that there would be pressure to extend the development at some time in the future and we should take steps now to protect the land.

The inspector had helped the local authority by saying that although he could not designate the land as green belt, it should be treated as such should planning applications come forward. He had emphasised the importance of the land, which was a benefit to the community and it was an important tract of land for keeping the local settlements apart.

Cllr Newman formally seconded the proposal.

In anticipation that the Liberal Democrats might vote against the PAB motion, I requested the mayor to hold a recorded vote. This can only be agreed if nine or more members of the council rise from their seats. A sufficient number of PAB and Conservative councillors did this, which triggered the recorded vote.

The request for the recorded vote was not supported by the Liberal Democrats.

The result of the vote was as follows: For the PAB amendment: Cllr Les Freeman (mayor), Cllrs Buckland, Cornish, Mrs Fletcher, Godwin, Newman, Mrs Pennell, Pennington and Todman. Total 9 votes. Against the motion: Cllr Mrs Thornton (deputy mayor), Cllrs Anderson, Barnes, Cameron, Mrs Cassin, Mrs Clarke, Mrs Gray, Miss Griggs, Mrs Grundy, Miss Hall, Harvey, Mrs Hawkins, Jordan, Mrs Langford, Lawrence, Lee, Lloyd, McKinlay, Oates, Prince, Mrs Townsend and Worth. Total 22 votes. Cllr M. Hale (Labour) abstained. The mayor then formally declared the amendment lost.

I was naturally disappointed, but we were heartened by the fact that once again when the Liberal Democrats had the opportunity to do something worthwhile for a community, they had failed. The thought had crossed my mind as the votes were being recorded, that it might be a decision that the Liberal Democrats might regret in the future should further attempts be made to develop the same tract of land.

Remember the names of those who voted, because as we come closer to the present day, you will read that some of the same people are still on the council, but they have either changed their opinion, or latterly realised that there are votes to be had if they support a community group that wants to protect the green belt.

The minutes of the meeting do not record that any debate on the PAB motion took place. Perhaps at their pre-council meeting the Liberal Democrats had decided to say nothing and their members were instructed to vote against it.

Whatever their reasons, they had forgotten the sterling work of Don Horwood, the father of the Cheltenham member of parliament, Martin Horwood, who had been instrumental in forming the Leglag group in order to protect the Leckhampton land.

The Leglag group had good intentions and often came up with sensible suggestions, and probably, to give it more clout, Lib/Dem councillors became members of the action group in its early days; the same situation still exists in 2014.

Don Horwoood was noted for his fight to protect the green belt and to save the countryside whenever he could, but it seems to me that newer generations do not have the same aspirations.

Don wrote to me on 25th July 1994 enclosing a copy of a letter that Leglag had sent to the chief planning officer at TBC criticising his department for the way they had dealt with a proposal to erect a double garage and other changes on the Leckhampton farm site.

Don explained in his letter to me that the Leckhampton farm development (as he called it)

> "... sits right in the middle of the green open area known as Leckhampton Glebe, or in planning terms, Leckhampton white land, which our group was formed to protect from development. It is in a highly sensitive location in an area which is the subject of considerable local interest and concern. Furthermore, it is contrary to the terms of the current Local Plan which requires that this land be treated as Green Belt. It was only given planning approval in January this year because of the outline planning permission previously given to a significantly different scheme on the same site by Tewkesbury Borough Council back in 1988. In these circumstances it is clearly important that any new proposal affecting the site should be subject to the normal applications procedure, and that there should be no suggestion of additions being 'slipped in through the back door'".

It was an interesting letter and I am pleased that I kept it. The letter and subsequent ones at the time, plus the letters from Leglag must have been known to the Liberal Democrat councillors, so why did they vote against the PAB amendment?

Was it because the elapse of time from July 1994 to November 1995 had confused them, or was it a simple case that PAB had recognised the importance of such a move, whereas the administrative group on the council had failed to see its importance at the time? But there was still a long way to go before this could be clarified, and the matter of the park and ride facility was still unresolved.

Park and ride had become an issue that stirred the local population into a kind of frenzy, similar to the occasion we had experienced with the imposition of the refuse collection system in 1976. The decision of the CBC planning committee on Thursday 27th July 1995 to allow the park and ride facility at Arle Court brought scores of letters to the editor of the *Gloucestershire Echo* and the *Cheltenham News.* They all criticised the planning committee and called on them to resign. Thankfully, they excluded me in their demands.

"Go-ahead given to park on green belt" claimed the *Echo.* "The councillors have ignored the protests from residents in The Reddings who fear the scheme will ruin the countryside." Its editorial, in support of the article by Mark Bradley, stated "Park and ride idea a disaster."

The article alleged that the planning chairman, Cllr Barrie Anderson (Lib/Dem), and his deputy chairman, Cllr Hazel Langford (Lib/Dem), were in favour of the park and ride facility being located on green belt land. "The chairman" he said, "thought that with a bit of landscaping the site will look better than it does now." Not an inspiring piece of leadership from the chairman, who clearly did not understand the purpose of the green belt or the worth of green belt policies in the CBC's Local Plan.

His deputy suggested that "We should try it – and we must get on with it".

According to the article by Mark Bradley, a senior Lib/Dem councillor John Oates, told the meeting that he had not detected overwhelming opposition to the application when he attended a public meeting in The Reddings community centre the previous Monday, because only 50 people had turned up to the meeting to protest.

But, the record shows that if he had not stormed out of the public meeting claiming the meeting was biased against park and ride schemes, he would have seen that 99 per cent of the 70 members of the public (not 50 as he claimed) when a vote was taken, did not support the scheme.

The public meeting attracted Lib/Dem councillors from several wards across the town (Cllr Oates lived in the Clarence Square area of Cheltenham), and it even attracted the chairman of the planning committee, Cllr Anderson, who lived in Winchcombe.

The truth of the matter was that the community centre was full, and as I looked around the room before I gave my speech, I spotted the Liberal Democrats sitting in a group in the centre of the hall. They were laughing and joking amongst themselves; it looked false and they appeared to be adopting a carefree manner to try and indicate that it was not an important occasion.

They gave me the impression that a public meeting on the park and ride facility in the nearby Arle Court area would be either 'good fun', or an opportunity to exert their perceived authority at the public meeting. When the meeting started I was determined that they would follow the normal rules of debate – and apart from the demonstration of intolerance from Cllr Oates, who stormed out of the meeting, it all went well.

What puzzled me on the night, and I still do not know the answer to the question, was the reasoning behind the Lib/Dem councillors' decision to be at the meeting. They had already made it clear where they stood on green belt issues – what else could they say on the subject? Of course, if they had been there to gauge the views of the local residents before the vote at the planning meeting the following Thursday, then that could only be regarded as a worthwhile reason to be there. As it turned out – it was the furthest thing from their minds.

The report of the meeting by Mark Bradley, prompted the residents of Northbank Close, The Reddings, to send a letter to the *Gloucestershire Echo* expressing their concerns regarding the public meeting and the park and ride proposals. The letter was headed "Who cares for our green belt?"

They wrote:

"Local people care very strongly about the conservation of the green belt and do not want any intrusion into this. They also feel The Reddings and Up Hatherley have had more than their fair share of development. One councillor stormed out of the meeting stating that it was biased, but no mention was made in the report of Coun Les Godwin's words about the recent developments and the possible developments in the area and the fact that the green belt should be preserved".

They concluded their letter by saying

"The planning committee decided to grant this application despite residents' opposition. The rape of the Reddings continues".

They were harsh words, simply because they felt they had been let down by the planning system. If the aim of the park and ride facility was to reduce the number of cars in the centre of town, then it has to be said that twenty years later that goal has still not been achieved.

As far as I was concerned, the planning meeting on Thursday 27th July was a farce. The comments from the chairman and others in support of the application for the park and ride facility in the green belt were spiced with sarcasm against those who thought the application should be refused. The standard of debate was poor and it was clear from the start that the minds had already been made up by the committee members.

Mark Bradley, in his *Echo* article, wrote that Cllr Jackie Fletcher (Conservative) who represented The Reddings ward, "*Wondered whether proper consultation with drivers had taken place to ascertain whether they would use the park and ride facility. She had grave concerns about the threat to the green belt and added that it should be conserved at all costs."*

[Unfortunately, Cllr Fletcher's concerns were not long-lasting – at a meeting of the council on 5th September 2013, she, along with others, voted to allow large scale developments to take place on green belt land in South Cheltenham].

Tewkesbury Borough Council, whose area the park and ride scheme borders, opposed the application because it was an unacceptable intrusion into the green belt. Their letter of objection made no difference – their opposition to the scheme was rejected by the planning committee.

As a last resort, I proposed that as the possible usage of the facility was unknown, the application should be approved on a six-month trial basis using the disused Dowty car park before a final decision on the proposed park and ride site was taken. It would also have been a good use of a brownfield site rather than going into green belt territory. I argued that after the six month trial period, the planning committee would have a better idea about the usage, and could then make a more sustainable judgement on the proposal.

My proposal was rejected, but the editorial of the *Echo* on 28th July 1995 wrote that my proposal *"was along the right lines, having a six-month trial before agreeing to build on the green belt"*.

In its final paragraph, the editorial suggested *"The whole strategy is a disaster. Here we are building white elephants on the edge of town – and we'll still have traffic jams in the town centre"*.

Another idea close to my heart was whether the proposed site was the best one for the purpose of getting drivers out of their cars and on the buses. I asked the planning committee to consider whether the proposed park and ride facility was at the wrong end of the Golden Valley bypass? I suggested that if the intention of the facility was to reduce the number of vehicles entering Cheltenham, then it would make more sense to have a park and ride facility at Elmbridge Court, which is at the Gloucester end of the Golden Valley bypass.

My theory was that if drivers intended to use the park and ride service at Arle Court, should we not provide the facility at the start of their journey in Gloucester rather than provide it halfway along the A40 route into Cheltenham.

This suggestion, along with the question of seeking facts from the drivers through a questionnaire before we made a final decision, received negative answers from the planning officers and supercilious comments from the Liberal Democrats. To emphasise this, Cllr Oates claimed in one of his pointless comments that "there was no difference in this application to an application for a chip shop in Bath Road."

The chairman added another comment that suggested that the local residents should be grateful for the park and ride facility rather than the site being used for houses. However, housing is dealt with under housing and green belt policies, which are totally different to the policies covering park and ride proposals.

It did not fill me with much confidence regarding future planning applications, and my confidence today is very much at the same level as it was in 1995.

When the vote was taken there were 10 votes in favour with 2 against.

Nearly twenty-years later the Joint Core Strategy (JCS) contained a proposal for a park and ride facility at Elmbridge Court – better late than never. I wonder if it will take another twenty years before CBC and the County Council realise that underground parking is urgently needed in Cheltenham.

The discussions leading up to the publication of the JCS in 2013 brought a further change of attitude by the political parties: later chapters will explain how the decision-makers tried to circumvent some parts of the JCS and whether they were successful or not.

The decision by the planning committee was a disappointment; it caused me to write to the Secretary of State, the Rt Hon John Gummer, MP.

The letter asked him to 'call-in' the planning application for the park and ride scheme at Arle Court, Cheltenham. The letter, dated 4th August 1995 reminded him that the park and ride proposal would be on land that had only recently been designated as green belt and therefore the decision by the planning committee was a departure from the Cheltenham Borough Council's Local Plan and disregarded the advice contained in PPG2.

It seemed appropriate for me to mention to him that the cost of the scheme was estimated at £550,000; GCC providing £400,000 of that sum.

I reminded him that GCC had recently written to him asking him to prevent further capping of the council on the grounds that the council did not have sufficient money to provide adequate schooling for the county's children. The fact that the request by GCC was refused may have been because the Department of the Environment thought that the county's spending priorities needed to be more carefully assessed.

I received a copy of a letter dated 9th August 1995, which had been sent by Nick Hayward, CBC Head of Strategic Planning to the County Planning Officer at Shire Hall, Gloucester. The letter stated that CBC expected GCC to be more supportive of the Arle Court Park and Ride proposal. It reminded the county planning officer that the county surveyor had taken a more positive view of the application.

Obviously, there was disagreement in the GCC camp, but the part of the letter that surprised me referred to a joint study that had been undertaken by county and borough officers confirming "... there is no suitable non-green belt land in the vicinity."

Clearly, this was untrue.

The concluding paragraph in Nick Hayward's letter confirmed that "The CBC planning committee had granted planning permission at its meeting on 27th July, but because it was a departure from the development plan it had been referred to the Government Office for the South West." That part was true, at least.

Whilst I waited for a decision by John Gummer MP, I received a letter from Michael Smith, the CBC Head of Engineering, informing me that GCC had published its draft Transport Plan for Gloucestershire. The plan set out GCC's policies and proposals for transport in the county, up to the year 2011.

I was convinced that as soon as the matter of the park and ride had been resolved, the PAB group would be dealing with transport issues raised by our supporters and the local residents, who would be affected by the proposals.

Meanwhile, I received a letter from Sir Paul Beresford on 11th September 1995 in reply to my letter to John Gummer asking him to call-in the application by CBC for a park and ride facility at Arle Court.

Sir Paul Beresford was a Minister in the Department of the Environment.

The letter revealed that CBC was directed on August 23rd not to grant planning permission without special authorisation from the Secretary of State. According to the Minister, "It would allow the Secretary of State more time to consider the issue arising, including the joint local authority study into the existence and suitability of alternative sites." The letter concluded,

> "A decision on whether to call-in the application will be reached as quickly as possible after a copy of the joint study has been received, taking into account the views that you have expressed."

I was pleased with the letter, but horrified to think that the 'joint study' that I referred to above, contained a deliberate lie. If the Secretary of State was going to make his decision on a false premise that could result in a false decision, then it would be a decision based on a lie rather than based on facts.

The *Gloucestershire Echo* pre-empted the Secretary of State's decision on 12th December 1995 with the headline "Parking plan on the way."

The article by Tim Oliver suggested that the first phase of the £8 million park and ride scheme could be built within a year. He was careful to add that the Secretary of State has yet to decide whether to hold a public inquiry, so that objections that had been raised could be considered.

Apparently, other sites such as the A4019 Tewkesbury Road and Henley Bank, Brockworth had been considered, but were lower down the priority list. But if CBC or the county council is really concerned about the flow of traffic into Cheltenham, surely it would make sense to install park and ride as a priority on all the gateways into the town – not just one.

Before the end of the year, there was another shock for the local communities; a proposal to build a new town between Staverton and Boddington (a small rural village), was announced by Gloucestershire County Council (GCC).

In December 1995, *Gloucestershire Echo* told its readers "New homes bombshell" with a sub-heading explaining "Houses planned for green belt".

After all the work we had done throughout 1995, the news came as a shock to PAB members and to the residents living in the affected areas. The article suggested that a new town bigger than Bishop's Cleeve could be built in the middle of green belt land near Cheltenham. It claimed that the new town would be bigger than the combined size of Bishop's Cleeve, Gotherington and Woodmancote, concluding that it was part of the blueprint for development up to 2011 to meet the needs of the proposed County Structure Plan.

The news outraged TBC and from the reports expressed by many parish councils the proposal was going to be debated long and hard before any final decision was taken.

Mr Paul Fountain, assistant county planning officer, told the GCC panel that Gloucestershire will need 53,000 new homes in the next 15 years. He told the *Echo* that 23,000 new houses are already earmarked and an extra 10,000 will come from in-fill developments. That leaves the county council 20,000 homes short. The article is interesting because it goes on to report that the houses are needed for two main reasons: people are living longer; and Gloucestershire has become a magnet for jobseekers from other regions.

According to Mr Fountain, "The only solution is to build two new towns: one near Staverton and another west of Stonehouse near junction 13 of the M5 motorway."

The news was shattering, and I had to admit that it had been a well-kept secret – I was comforted by the fact that so far it was only a county council proposal.

The *Gloucestershire Echo* did its usual thorough job of interviewing local people and local councillors. It was interesting to read their comments about the new town proposal. Mr Mike Prosser, a Brockworth parish councillor is alleged to have said: *"We don't want any more houses built in Brockworth. I don't think it could take it. The increase in traffic alone would be horrendous and the green belt is being encroached on already."*

Mr Bob East, a member of Bishop's Cleeve parish council and a Tewkesbury Borough councillor, was also reported as saying: *"We are thrilled that Bishop's Cleeve has been spared. We have always objected to more construction in Bishop's Cleeve without more basic infrastructure like schools and libraries."*

I have quoted the comments because Bishop's Cleeve has suffered from large-scale development in the area since 1995 and can no longer be recognised as a rural village. In 2013 a planning appeal for another 1,100 homes was allowed by the Planning Inspectorate.

The Brockworth area too has experienced some development since 1995, but it will have been very little when compared to the development proposals in the Joint Core Strategy. Large scale developments are currently scheduled to take place in several areas to meet the anticipated housing demand.

Perhaps in hindsight, it would have been better for the Bishop's Cleeve and Brockworth councillors to have supported a new town development and their villages would have retained their status.

CHAPTER 10

Becoming Deputy Mayor

"A party of order or stability, and a party of progress or reform, are both necessary elements of a healthy state of political life".

John Stuart Mill 1806–73
English philosopher and economist

The debate and arguments about the protection and loss of green belt land continued well into 1996. In fact, as the next chapters will show, it has always been an important issue for the residents of Cheltenham and the surrounding areas.

And if anyone thought that 1995 was a difficult year, then the following year turned out be even more dramatic. The protection of the green belt had always been a PAB priority, so we were concerned about the accelerating loss of green belt land throughout 1996. The future of the green belt did not look good with the news that the construction of a park and ride facility in rural Up Hatherley was likely to take place; also on the cards was the possibility of a North West bypass around Swindon Village and the urban extension of parishes on the north west and the south west areas of the town. Already, many hectares of good quality agricultural land had been lost, due in no small part to the inability of councillors to understand the purpose of the green belt. Politics had entered into the debate on whether the land should be protected or not and that was not helpful.

While we waited patiently for the Secretary of State to announce whether the park and ride planning permission should be subject to a public inquiry, County Cllr Andy Cornish, who was a member of the county environment committee, suggested that part of the land at the Government Communications Headquarters (GCHQ) would be more suitable for a park and ride facility than the land in Hatherley Lane. He proposed that the alternative site should be investigated.

Mr N C Nelder, the county council's general manager, wrote to Cllr Cornish on 6th February 1996, to explain that as the GCHQ site is not in the green belt, and on the right side of the road for entering Cheltenham, an investigation would take place and a detailed assessment would be made.

It was a sensible and a worthwhile suggestion, but we feared that it would not be regarded as such by Cheltenham Borough Council (CBC) or Gloucestershire County Council (GCC) because they had made an early decision on the site and were also financially committed to it.

The chances of a sensible decision being made would be slight.

Why the GCHQ site was not included as an alternative site in the joint study submitted to the Secretary of State was beyond me. We rely on council officers to do the right thing when a matter has been proposed and debated in a meeting, and that should have meant including the alternative site in the submission to the Secretary of State.

I know the suggestion was not in line with what the officers wanted, which is perhaps why it was conveniently forgotten.

On 7th June 1996, Michael Smith sent out a letter to all councillors informing them that the Secretary of State "did not propose to intervene in the planning application for the construction of the park and ride facility at Arle Court". I had expected a direct reply from the Secretary of State considering I had taken the trouble to write to him outlining the background to the application. It struck me as the height of bad manners, so I wrote to him again on 11thJune 1996, reminding him that it had taken twelve months for the 'not to intervene' decision to be made. My letter again suggested that alternative brownfield sites should be used rather than the green belt land being proposed. My letter also gave me the opportunity to include the GCHQ site that was under investigation by the county council environment division; if the officers were not going to mention it, then I would.

My concluding paragraph read as follows:

> "I must make it clear that I am not against the principle of park and ride, but I do believe that vacant, unused and derelict sites should be used first rather than the easy option of development on a green belt site.
>
> I hope you will take another look at the detail of the application along with the information I have outlined above".

I received another letter from Sir Paul Beresford on 11th July 1996 thanking me for my letter to the Secretary of State.

He went on to refer to the Government 'attaching great importance to the protection of the green belt'. He wanted to assure me that 'development in such areas is always scrutinised very carefully when they are referred to the Secretary of State'. His final paragraph read:

> "In this particular case, the decision to allow Cheltenham Borough Council to determine the planning application as they see fit was only taken after a full and careful examination of all the issues involved.
>
> I have reviewed the matter in the light of your comments, but I remain of the view that the application is one that can properly be left to the local planning authority. Although I understand your concern that development at Arle Court might be seen as a precedent, each application must be considered on its merits, and I am confident that local planning authorities are conscious of that long established convention".

I did not have the same amount of confidence in the planning system that Sir Paul Beresford obviously had, but it was comforting to know that my letter had prompted an investigation about the issues I had raised, and had been discussed at such a high level of government.

But, what was the sense in allowing green belt land to be breached when two brownfield sites were available?

In my view, the Secretary of State and his Ministers had made the wrong choice, and their decision (allowing the local authority to determine the planning application) did enormous damage to a large swathe of valuable countryside in south west Cheltenham from which it has never recovered.

The decision meant that it was the end of the line as far as resistance to the planning application was concerned, but the Minister's decision did seem to be a contradiction of the Government's own guidance about protection of the green belt as set out in policy guidance document PPG2.

All boroughs, cities and some district councils are led by a Mayor. This has been a long-standing tradition which means that the local authority has approved rules and procedures to ensure that the election of the mayor is carried out annually.

The word "Mayor" derives from the Latin word "magnus", meaning great. The Office of Mayor, together with the Doomsday Book and the feudal system, were concepts brought to this country by the Normans. According to some accounts, the first English Mayor was Henry Fitz-Allen who was appointed Mayor of London 1189 by Richard I.

The role of the mayor and his or her presence adds enormous value to a local authority's standing, as well as to the usual fund-raising events that follow on behalf of the council.

The title of Magistrate was often attached to the mayor's role, and he was able to administer punishment for transgressions, including having people placed in the stocks. Thankfully, those days are long gone.

The procedure for appointing a mayor in Cheltenham is now done on a rotational basis according to the number of years a councillor has served on the council. It is not a system I support, because it can create a continuous line of mayors from one political party over a long period of time, particularly if one political party has a large majority on the council.

Prior to the current procedure, mayors were nominated by each political party on a proportional basis each year. Whilst the party with most councillors could expect more appointments from their ranks, at least the smaller groups could expect to be invited to provide a name for the position of mayor from time to time.

The elected mayor has the assistance of a deputy mayor, who is also nominated by a political group. In previous years it did help to produce a balance to the mayoralty if the mayor and the deputy came from different political groups. These days, one can expect the mayor and the deputy mayor to come from the same group in an almost endless procession for the reasons I have mentioned above.

Each mayor serves a term of office lasting one year.

The Cheltenham Town Hall, which is a public venue and not the seat of the borough council, was built in 1902/03. It has been the traditional venue for the mayor-making ceremony and it is held in the main hall.

The magnificent floral display at the Cheltenham Town Hall 1997. Never to be repeated at future mayor-making ceremonies

The main hall holds around 900 people and for the mayor-making ceremony it was always beautifully decorated with a large array of flowers supplied by the council's own garden nursery. I have used the past tense because the floral decoration that was part of the mayor-making celebration for as long as anyone can remember was reduced and finally ended in the years following the mayor-making ceremony in 1997.

Simon Lee was the Head of Parks and Landscapes, and responsible for making sure that the floral displays in the parks and gardens in the town were of the highest quality. His dedication to his job brought many successes in the Heart of England in Bloom competitions, and the parks and gardens were regular winners of the national Britain in Bloom competition, in the city category.

As a result of the town's continuing successes, it was chosen to represent the United Kingdom in the European Entente Florale competition, and received the Prix European d'Excellence award.

Simon was a man with a likeable personality and a good disposition, and a dedicated officer of the council. He was good at his job and also a dependable friend, whose company I often enjoyed.

In 1999, Simon was the lead officer in the Montpellier Gardens historic restoration plan project, which formed the basis of a successful bid to the Heritage Lottery Fund and the renovation of the gardens. He was mainly responsible for the Winston Churchill Gardens gaining the first Green Flag award for a Cheltenham park; the Parks Ranger Scheme covering Leckhampton Hill and the Griffiths Avenue Nature Reserve are testaments to Simon's achievements.

Before he left the council in 2001 to become the Superintendant of Hampstead Heath at the City of London Corporation, Simon Lee lent his talents in other directions, including acting. He was a keen member of The Keep Cheltenham Tidy Group, and the group put on a show for around 2000 children at the Everyman Theatre, where Simon played the part of Dame Tidy in an anti-litter pantomime to encourage children to dispose of their litter in the proper bins.

As always, Simon was a roaring success and the children loved him.

His abilities did not rest there; he took on the role of a male model to showcase clothing made from discarded litter, which was performed at the Queen Mother's Birthday Awards ceremony in Park Lane, London. Something very similar to this was performed by Simon and other council officers as part of the mayor's 'Fashion Show' in the Town Hall, in aid of my charities in September 1997. (More about this later)

The mayor-making ceremony is attended by local dignitaries and prominent business people – and of course, the families and relations of the mayor and the deputy mayor. The deputy mayor is always on hand to fill in when required, and he or she will acquire knowledge from watching the mayor at functions; listening to the speeches; and watching closely at the council meetings to see how the mayor deals with the council agenda. The deputy mayor is expected to become the town mayor the following year so it is important for the deputy mayor to be aware of what is going on, and a good mayor will either invite the deputy mayor to accompany him or her occasionally to a civic function, or ask the deputy mayor to carry out the function on their behalf, in order to get 'a feel for the job'.

In January 1996, the PAB group was invited to nominate a person to become deputy mayor for the period 1996 to 1997. This came as a bit of a shock to the group, especially as PAB councillors had only transferred from TBC in 1991.

The deputy mayor in 1995 was Cllr Mrs Pat Thornton, who had been nominated to be Mayor of Cheltenham in May 1996. Cllr Thornton was a Liberal Democrat, and as readers will know, PAB councillors could hardly be regarded as their bosom pals, so this was something that the PAB group needed to take into account.

We were also mindful of the fact that should the group decline the offer to fill the role in 1996; it could be some time before a PAB councillor was next invited.

The PAB group debated the invitation from the council, and remembering the occasion in 1978 when I suggested we should provide 'a paper candidate' for a council by-election, I decided to remain silent during the discussions.

It was interesting listening to the plaudits and the platitudes levelled at the secretary of the group: the person with the most experience; the leader of the group; the longest serving PAB councillor. Nevertheless, I still remained silent. Eventually, something had to give, and I was politely asked to take on the role, which would mean becoming mayor in May 1997.

The role, if I agreed to do it, would be seen, according to my colleagues, as 'a rather large feather in the rather small PAB hat'. As secretary of the group, I had been the first to be aware of the invitation from the council, so naturally, I had been mulling over the pros and cons of what would be involved if I was invited by the group to take on the role, and what my reaction would be. I came to the conclusion that apart from the possible political conflict, it would be nothing more than an extra job to do on top of what I was already doing as a councillor, group leader and secretary to the PAB group. There had been a certain amount of reluctance on my part to take on the role of deputy mayor, but with the prospect of the PAB group being side-lined for the job of mayor in the future, I agreed to accept the nomination.

The hardest part of my decision was the thought that I would have to break the news to my wife when I returned home from the meeting, and I knew it was not going to be easy.

On the way home I went through the various options of how I would tell Pam – in the end I settled for "You will not believe this, but I have been nominated to become the deputy mayor in May." Almost before I had completed the sentence, Pam said "You haven't". This was followed by "Don't expect me to come traipsing round with you at the functions, because you know I don't like being in the forefront at public events – you love it, I don't."

This was true – Pam had always worked hard for me and the PAB cause behind the scenes, but she was a naturally shy person when it came to the matter of meeting people she did not know. I knew from past experiences that it was going to be a testing time for Pam, but I was also sure she would rise to the occasion.

Apart from the obvious questions that needed sensible answers, I didn't prolong the discussion any longer than needed. There were still a lot of council business and PAB matters to deal with before the mayor-making ceremony took place in May. The period leading up to it would be carefully nurtured by me so that when the day arrived, Pam would be fine.

Thankfully, Pam soon got into the swing of things, much to my relief, and with the family around her to give support, there was very little to worry about. Once the mayor-making ceremony was over, the mayor invited everyone to stay for tea and cakes, which most people did, and it was an occasion when everyone spoke to people they didn't know, The Town Hall was full of friends and families of the mayor and deputy mayor, and Pam became even more at ease. Finally, Pam admitted that she had enjoyed the occasion, even when she was sitting on the platform receiving a bouquet of flowers. I was sure it was a good sign for the future.

The new municipal year in 1996 began quietly, but it was a strange feeling to be sitting alongside the mayor as she chaired her first council meeting. I looked at the place where I normally sat and wondered whether any of my colleagues would move up and fill the space. It gave me an eerie feeling.

I listened intently as the council meeting progressed, making a note from time to time, and holding my tongue when normally I would be speaking out.

As each month went by I became more confident about the job of deputy mayor, but I was anxious to get involved with matters outside the council chamber – I began to wonder when that would start.

I received a telephone call from a journalist by the name of Stuart Millson. He introduced himself as a freelance journalist who had been following with interest in the national press my attempts to 'save the green belt' as he put it, and he wanted to interview me as a first step towards a published article on the subject in the autumn edition of *The Country Lover's Magazine* in 1996.

We had several telephone conversations about most of the green belt issues that I have recorded in this book, and I was impressed with Stuart Millson's knowledge of each of the subjects with which I had been involved. This enabled us to get on well.

On 12th June 1996, I received a letter from Stuart Millson enclosing a copy of the commissioned article, which was to appear in the magazine. I was invited to phone through any corrections if I thought they were needed. I was informed that his agent had read the article and had passed it on for publication. I read the 1,400 word article with foreboding in case I had made a mistake in any of the information I had given to Stuart Millson, but no, it was an excellent article and it certainly didn't require any corrections from me.

I was sent a complimentary copy of the magazine, which is one of my treasured possessions; it promoted PAB and the work we had done over many years trying to convince councillors, officers and central government that the green belt was special and should be protected.

The autumn edition of the magazine article covered three pages, and its caption was eye-catching – "A DEVELOPMENT TOO FAR". There were excellent photographs of views, one taken from Frocester Hill to the Cotswold Scarp and the Severn; another of Goodrich Castle, and a lovely photograph of Lower Slaughter, Gloucestershire. This was the opening paragraph of the article by Stuart Millson:

"Yard after yard of newspaper column has been swallowed up as campaigning journalists, lamenting the loss of our Green Belt and countryside, have roared into battle on behalf of rural England. Barely a week goes by without a story breaking on the vexed issue of development, new housing and road building; of a landscape that once contained farms, foxes and pheasants being transformed by the treacle-like spread of the urban world".

It was a great opening to the article that went on to explain what had been happening in the Cheltenham and Gloucester areas during the 90's: loss of green belt and the creeping urbanisation of the countryside. This was true and twenty years later, history is repeating itself.

The article is obviously too long to quote in full, but some paragraphs summed up the situation in 1996, neither has it changed one bit in the years that followed. The article is a stark warning that people and groups like PAB should be forever vigilant and never give up the battle that Stuart Millson referred to.

> "To the money-is-everything developer, the architect of mass-housing, the self-appointed bureaucrat obsessed with statistics, the Green Belt is a waste of useful space. The swathe of semi-countryside, home to many wild animals, plants and remnants of still-viable woodland, is prime building land. Ideal for identikit houses in soulless estates, ideal for park-and-ride sites, and just the thing for the odd industrial estate, the Green Belt is at the heart of the battle for the future of the countryside. And that battle is being fought harder than ever before, with some sad losses".

The long process of the interviews with Stuart Millson had been worthwhile when I read the words "Occasionally we come across stories that fill us with hope – stories of how impending and irreversible changes in the name of progress have been challenged. One such story comes from Gloucestershire".

The article then carefully went through the numerous instances I have already mentioned in the previous chapters, but his attention had been drawn to the green belt land between Cheltenham and Gloucester. He wrote:

> "Approximately half way between Cheltenham and Gloucester, in the heart of the local green belt, lay the village of Staverton, which was home to the county's small, light-traffic airport. Already bitter arguments have been raging over the future of this valuable soil, with Cheltenham Borough Council attempting to undermine its Green Belt status. The danger here is that Cheltenham and Gloucester could be turned into a single conurbation".

Stuart Millson then assured readers that "... fortunately Staverton is safe, at least for the moment, but only because of the endless questioning, delving and lobbying conducted by the pro-green belt side".

The article was long and each of the problems I have referred to in the previous pages were explained in detail; it left the reader in no doubt what had been at risk for a long time in Gloucestershire and it was a timely reminder to those who lived in rural areas that the countryside was at risk.The article is still worth reading today.

The events that occurred in the 90's are sadly being repeated again in 2013/14 with green fields at risk and developers waiting patiently, with their cheque books at the ready.

This is Stuart Millson's final paragraph:

"Today, however, idealised images and memories frozen from the 1950's may be the only means we have of seeing the Gloucestershire, and indeed the England we once knew. It is a sobering thought that the only guarantee for countryside preservation comes from the vigilance of individuals, such as Councillor Les Godwin, and the painstaking work of bodies as influential as CPRE whose campaigns have done so much to protect a wide variety of endangered rural areas. But let us hope that the people of the country will stand firm against the mindless over-development now being foisted upon them, and that the thin green line will hold for a few more years to come."

By and large, Stuart's hopes were somewhat realised for the next 15 year period, although the 'battle' had been hard and some important tracts of land lost to development. There is still more to do and the final chapters will describe how difficult the challenges have been to defend the green belt, open green spaces and even green spaces to the rear of private properties.

The preparation of the 'Second Review' of the Gloucestershire Structure Plan followed by public consultation was ongoing throughout the 1990's. Critical comments from the public and commercial organisations where addressed. It was finally approved on 17th November 1999.

The purpose of the Structure Plan is to set out the strategic framework for the use and development of land across the county during a set period of time. In this particular case, the Plan Period was 1991 to 2011. It is from the Structure Plan that each district council prepares their Local Plans, so there are a number of issues to be taken into consideration.

The list of headings is extensive, but the heading that always attracts the most attention is the county council's proposal for the number of houses that should be constructed during the Structure Plan period. The figure can never be precise, but around 53,000 across the six districts was proposed, of which 7,350 was apportioned to the Cheltenham district.

Once housing figures are published they attract a lot of media attention and become a topic of conversation in public places. Scores of letters are written to the local paper, and it also becomes an excuse for opposition groups to become more active than usual, trying to convince the voting public that they are opposed to house building plans in their areas. An editorial in the *Gloucestershire Echo* (6th June 1996) suggested that the proposals contained in the draft Structure Plan "were poppycock". I didn't see the editor's Opinion so I cannot comment on it, but whatever it contained, it was enough to cause County Councillor Kit Braunholtz to reach for his pen again and write a letter to the editor of the *Gloucestershire Echo*. The letter, which had a headline "Yes we do need all these houses", challenged the content of the *Echo* Opinion, which had criticised the county council, and presumably its councillors, by implying that 'the local authorities had more regard for making money than to the good of Gloucestershire.'

Cllr Braunholtz did not agree and then went on to explain: *"As someone who has been involved in the process from the start, I can assure you that you are entirely wrong. Making money has not been a consideration at all, either for the officers who drew up the plan or for the councillors over-seeing the process".*

His letter went on to explain that the proposed 53,000 houses over the twenty year period worked out at 2,650 per year and added: *"It is a lot of houses, but why do we need them, mainly because we are better off than we used to be and can afford to live apart from our parents, our children, our spouses – and increasingly we do. Inevitably, building so many houses and flats will damage some attractive parts of the county".*

Cllr Braunholtz concluded his letter by suggesting that 'if the process of house building was slowed down, the county council would fall foul of central government policy. It would also lead to a housing shortage in five or ten years' time'.

As the historical facts show, the 53,000 dwellings were built in Gloucestershire during the twenty year period, and the 7,350 allocation for Cheltenham was reached long before the end of the plan period.

Now, in 2014, with the introduction of the Joint Core Strategy (JCS) we have been going through the same arguments about the number of houses that are required in the county in the next twenty year period as we did in the period prior to 1991. Opposition groups have been formed and Kit Braunholtz, a member of the Leckhampton Green Land Action Group (Leglag), who is no longer a county councillor, is opposed to the house building figures published by the JCS team. He is strongly opposed to any loss of land for houses in the Leckhampton area where he lives. There will be a lot more on this subject in later chapters.

Occasionally, I deputised for the mayor when she had other engagements, and one such occasion was an invitation to attend the annual July open day at Glenfall House, Charlton Kings, Cheltenham. Glenfall House is set in four acres of landscaped gardens, which feature an orchard and several scenic walks. Beyond the grounds there are public footpaths and bridleways into the Cotswold countryside. The house is currently owned by the Gloucester Diocese and it has been used as a Christian retreat since 1993; it was always regarded as "one of the premier Diocesan retreat houses in the country." Pam and I looked forward to our first official visit on behalf of the council. It turned out to be one of those memorable occasions that we often refer to during a light-hearted discussion about our visit. Firstly, we had to travel to Glenfall House in our old Ford Consul estate; secondly, we were greeted by a gentleman from the Glenfall House committee, who thought at first we were an invited couple for the 'open day' event. He was about to direct us to the public car park when he noticed my deputy mayor's chain of office around my neck.

"I am so sorry" said the man, who was clearly embarrassed by the situation, who then pointed me to a 'reserved' place for the mayor's car outside the main door of the house. It was difficult to know who was most embarrassed. Pam and I could understand the committee man's predicament; he was expecting a Daimler to arrive, instead he got a Ford Consul estate. The look on the gentleman's face was a sight to behold, and we often have a laugh about it.

As for the day itself, it was a delight to be there. We quickly realised that the charm of Glenfall House is due to its setting – the views all round are lovely and the quietness of the place is something special. There are several paths within the grounds and one becomes acutely aware that there is no traffic noise, only the continuous singing of the birds which filled the country air. It seemed a magical place to be, and we quickly became in love with the place, just as others have been.

Pam and I became members of the "Friends of Glenfall House" following our visit, and we have spent many hours of relaxation walking around the lovely gardens and taking in the sheer joy of the place. Most of the garden work at Glenfall is done by volunteers, chief among them has been Bob and Barbara Lyle from Prestbury, who redesigned the gardens and looked after them for many years. The gardens are a great credit to them.

Unfortunately, Bob died a few years ago, but Barbara continued with her voluntary work to recreate the gardens as they were in Victorian times. In appreciation of Barbara's work there is a plaque erected in the garden dedicated to Barbara for all the work she has done in restoring the gardens to their former glory.

Sadly, for financial reasons, the Diocese decided in 2013 that it could no longer afford to keep Glenfall House open. This is a great pity because apart from the quiet retreat that it has been, it was a great place for meeting people and to make lasting friendships.

Pam and I, like many others will miss it – that's for sure.

Barabara Lyle died in 2014.

I was invited to go to the Cheltenham Cricket Festival, which is held on the Cheltenham College sport's ground each year around July/August time, but the invitation didn't arrive in the usual way, in fact it arrived in a bizarre way, as it turned out. Cllr John Todman, who was leader of the Conservative group at the time, innocently asked me whether I was looking forward to going to the cricket festival. I replied negatively to the question, adding that I would only be going if I managed to get a ticket.

John looked puzzled at my answer and pressed me further; it appeared that John was a committee member of the Cheltenham business community, who had hired a marquee for one of the days during the festival period and they wanted someone from the mayoralty to attend. Apparently, the mayor could not go and John Todman assumed that the deputy mayor would automatically fill the role. This explained the original puzzled look on his face. "No, I had not received an invitation, but I was available to attend if it was not too late" I said.

Cricket, along with football, had been an important part of my life for many years, and when my playing days were over, the next best thing to do was to watch those who play the game for a living. John knew about my cricket past and said he would find out what had happened to the invitation and he promised he would get back to me. It was several days before John Todman contacted me again, to tell me that the invitation had gone to the mayor in the usual way, but as the mayor could not, or did not want to attend the cricket festival, she had passed the invitation on to her daughter, who, allegedly, was pleased to attend on her behalf. My immediate reaction to the news was to let it stay as it was – it was not sufficiently important to go to the extreme of rescinding the original invitation, and issuing another one to me. It was no big deal. John Todman would not hear of it. He told me that the error would be rectified as quickly as possible. I heard later that he had been furious with those associated with the 'business fraternity's day at the festival'. It may have been good for John's ego, but it didn't help me, in fact, once the mayor had been told of the changes to the arrangements for the cricket festival, she immediately laid the blame at my door and as a result I suffered a long period of 'silent contempt' from Cllr Thornton. It was unfair, because I had nothing to do with it – I just did what I was asked to do.

Apart from the unpleasant side of the invitation, I did enjoy the cricket and I met a few old cricket friends that helped to make the day go well. I also had the chance to meet Vicky Tuck who was the Principal designate for the Cheltenham Ladies' College. She was due to take up her appointment on the 1stSeptember 1996 and she was, as she put it, 'getting the feel of Cheltenham and its special occasions', and of course, enjoying the cricket. She was very pleasant company, and very knowledge-able about the town and its traditions. She agreed that we were going to see a lot of each other when I became mayor, because she had what she called 'progressive ideas involving young people from outside the college'. It sounded a good idea to me, not least because the Ladies' College had a reputation of being a bit 'stuffy' at the time.

There were changes in the mayor's office in 1996. The ever-present incumbent who had been the mayor's secretary for years, decided to retire. A young woman called Sue Hemp was interviewed for the job. She was offered the post and started work in the early part of 1996. I liked Sue; she was an interesting person to talk to; she was always positive and she had a good sense of humour. I was also keen to cement our relationship knowing that I would have to rely on Sue's efforts and expertise during my mayoral year 1997/98.

Imagine my shock when Sue told me after six months into the job that she had decided to leave CBC. She was keen to tell me that she enjoyed being the mayor's personal assistant (PA), but unfortunately, she alleged, "There was a clash of personalities between the mayor and herself, and she felt she could no longer continue doing the job." From my long experience in personnel management, I knew that this was one of the insurmountable problems of the working environ-ment; no matter how hard one might try to get people to like each other, it is an impossible task.

I tried hard to dissuade Sue from leaving, by suggesting to her that if she could 'grit her teeth' for a few more months, then things would get better. I failed to get Sue to change her mind, neither would she tell me what was at the bottom of the problems she had been facing, but I did have sympathy for her.

When she left CBC at the beginning of 1997 and the job was advertised inter-nally, Maggie Handson, who was currently the PA to the chief executive Lawrence

Davison, successfully applied for the vacant post and became the personal assistant to the mayor in February 1997

Maggie had always been a popular figure in the chief executive's department, a woman with personality, and willing to do any job to the best of her ability. She joined CBC in March 1980, as a word processor operator, although she would agree that she didn't know what the title meant when she applied for the job. Word processors had replaced typewriters, so the job would have been similar, and she made history by being the first word processor operator to work for the borough council.

I didn't know at the time, but in the course of a conversation, Maggie told me she was the wife of David Handson, who was a planning officer with Tewkesbury Borough Council (TBC). Maggie knew that I had been a councillor on TBC, which is why the matter came up. I had known David during my thirteen years as a TBC councillor. I had spent time with him when I was a member of the planning committee. Our paths crossed many times; he was good at his job; and he was always helpful and fair when discussing a planning issue. David left TBC in 1983 and became an independent planning consultant. This meant that I only saw him on the occasions when he visited the Tewkesbury Borough Council offices.

It came as a shock in later years to be told that David, who was only 57, had taken his own life.

It was sensible for the mayor-elect to keep in touch with the PA in the months leading up to the mayor-making ceremony. The PA would know the names of those who must be at the top of the invitation list, she would also need to know the mayor's choices – the family names and the names and addresses of friends, and of course, making sure no-one was omitted who should be there. One important part of a mayor's speech of acceptance is to inform the audience and the wider community of the mayor's charities, which he hoped they would support in the following year.

In the weeks leading up to the ceremony on 19th May 1997, I had several discussions with Maggie and other officers to make sure everything went well. I even took part in a dummy run of the procession to ensure that there were no hitches on the day – a final visit to the Town Hall with Simon Lee to see what he had achieved with the floral display; it was simply awesome. The matching colours and the designs to bring out the best possible display of the flowers were truly something to behold.

The invitations had been sent – and the final count showed just over 600 positive responses. One more thing before the ceremony was to decide the three charities that I would support and announce during my speech.

Maggie suggested a number of charities that I could consider, which I then whittled down to three: The 'Cheltenham Breast Cancer Care Fund', which raises money for patients undergoing treatment related to breast cancer and based at the Cheltenham General Hospital: the 'Senior Citizens Welfare Committee' which provides a range of assistance to elderly people in the town: and 'The Cheltenham Young Arts Centre', which provides a focal point for artistic activities for young people in the town.

In the next chapter we will see how well these choices worked out.

There is another side to local government, which is the position held by a mayor. This is seldom described in print, and its seems apposite to relate some of the events that occurred in 1997 and 1998.

CHAPTER 11

My Mayoral Year – 1997/98 (Part One)

It is the province of knowledge to speak and it is the privilege of wisdom to listen.
Oliver Wendell Holmes (1809 -94)

---

*There is another side to local government, which is the position held
by a mayor. This is seldom described in print, and it seems apposite to
relate some of the events that occured in 1997 and 1998.
Chapters 11, 12 and 13 cover aspects.*

The week prior to the mayor-making ceremony was hectic – there was an atmosphere of excitement in the lead up to the day of the ceremony on Monday 19 th May 1997.

On the previous Monday I had been introduced to those who would be receiving the council's Medals of Honour at the mayor-making ceremony, for their outstanding work in the community. Persons nominated for the Medal of Honour must have completed many years of exceptional service to the community, not necessarily continuous, but should have covered not less than 10 years continuous service, which had been publicly acknowledged by the community of Cheltenham. In 1997, there was a committee of high profile members of the community, headed by Malcolm Lomas JP. They met in March and selected three people to be presented with their medals at the mayor-making ceremony.

The people selected, Bob Attwood, Roma Naden and Ann Attwood, were pleased to have been nominated, but they were a little nervous at the prospect of standing on the stage at the Town Hall listening to the accolades that would be bestowed upon them, before I presented them with their awards.

Later that day, I had lunch with the Board of Directors of the Cheltenham Arts Festival Limited, who wanted to explain their plans for the current year. I was impressed with their programme of events, and I assured them I would lend my support to them whenever I could.

On Tuesday 14th May there was an Extraordinary Meeting of the Council when a proposal for the redevelopment of the former St. James' railway site was debated. The proposal included a Waitrose store on the site. The development plan had been controversial for some time because some of the land belonged to Cheltenham Borough Council (CBC), and it was unclear at the time how CBC were going to dispose of the land; what was its value; could the council taxpayer be assured that the council would get a good deal for the taxpayer. Further detail on this matter is explained in the CBC v Laird chapters.

I met my son Andrew and his fiancée Debbie at the Royal Well bus station on Wednesday; they had travelled from Bermuda to be at the ceremony. I did a radio interview on *Radio Gloucestershire* on Thursday morning because they were anxious to know what an independent councillor with no ties to a political party would do for the people of Cheltenham. In the evening, I met the volunteers who would become members of my future charity committee. They had experience in fund-raising; their ideas on the sort of events the committee should consider for the mayoral year were inspiring. They were an excellent group of individuals on whom I came to rely on more and more as the mayoral year proceeded. The committee, with Maggie Handson acting as the facilitator, met regularly. Maggie kept me informed of what the committee had been discussing, so that I was well-prepared whenever I met them. Jo Bailey was the lead member of the committee; she had more knowledge and expertise on the subjects we were going to pursue than anyone else.

Along with Jo was another expert, this time in the field of fashion, Pam Thomas, who had done fashion shows before and was keen to persuade the members of the committee to hold a 'Mayor's Fashion Show' at the Town Hall. Pam's ideas of what should be included in the fashion show were such that it would require a venue as big as the Town Hall to make it the major event in my mayoral year. The committee thought this a great idea, I did too, and I promptly gave it my backing. I had been told at the start of my mayoral year that I could have use of the Town Hall and the Pump Room in Pittville Park for up to two mayoral events free of charge. I had no doubt that one of the occasions would be to hold the fashion show in the Town Hall, and, in the capable hands of Pam Thomas, we all knew it would be a success. It would be the first time a mayor's fashion show had been held in Cheltenham, and it was a big enough incentive for the committee to start thinking about different things that could be included in the show in order to make it a success. Pam Thomas worked in a ladies clothes shop in town, and she later opened her own lingerie shop in The Strand, which has become very successful.

Other members of the mayor's committee included Anita Claridge, Maureen Claridge, Jo Davis, Celia Durk, Gill Bullock, Ann Creed and others whose names unfortunately I cannot remember. But, whoever they are, they all did an excellent job for me and the three charities I had chosen.

My last duty as deputy mayor was to attend a fund-raising function on behalf of the Gloucestershire Association for Mental Health on Friday 16th May. The event was held at Stanway House in the Cotswolds, the home of Lord and Lady Neidpath. Stanway House is an outstanding example of a Jacobean manor house; the formal garden, including the water garden, is delightful.

The evening was a most pleasurable occasion – Cllr Brian Jones, the newly elected Mayor of Tewkesbury was there, so too was Laurence Robertson MP who had recently won the Tewkesbury parliamentary seat.

Doug Grazier, the chairman of the PAB group and the chairman of the Gloucestershire Association for Mental Health, introduced me to the guests. I felt relaxed with Doug doing all the introductions.

John Edmonds was the organiser of the event. We had a long chat about the time when he and I were on the Cheltenham & District Community Health Council in the late 80's and early 90's. Mental health issues and the funding of them had always been an agenda item and a topic of great interest to both John and me during our time on the health council.

Basically, it was a fund raising event, but I dedicated my speech to all those who had worked so tirelessly for mental health sufferers in the county – giving their free time for the sake of others. The evening included a bumper draw in aid of the Mental Health Association and I was asked to take out the first lucky ticket; and as is often the case, I drew out my own ticket. As one would expect from a future mayor, I declined to take the first prize. It was a very good evening and a lot of money was raised for an excellent cause.

On Monday 19th May, a final rehearsal took place in the Town Hall in the morning with the main participants in attendance – nothing it seemed was being left to chance. Whether this is still done today, I do not know. Simon Lee was there, putting the final touches to the floral display, which hardly needed it.

The chief executive, Lawrence Davison, told me that the mayor-making event was going to be video recorded. By whom and for what purpose, I wasn't told, but the finished tape is something I have kept and shown to friends. It was supposed to be a serious occasion and it is, but some parts of it are hilarious, partly because of the humorous tales I told of my earlier years. The unsteady video recording is testament to the quality of the stories because the video-recording man couldn't stop laughing either. The news about the video recording was an unexpected surprise, but it seemed to me as though the whole of the afternoon was going to be a very special occasion for everyone.

Pam and I were driven to the town hall in the chauffeur-driven mayoral car, arriving some thirty minutes before the start of the ceremony, to enable last minute tips to be given to me by Maggie Handson and her colleague Tim Harman. Pam was taken to her position on the stage, where other guests were seated, including the local residents who would be receiving the Cheltenham Order of Merit.

The councillors who had assembled in the drawing room were donning their robes and there seemed to be an air of excitement that I had not experienced at previous mayoral ceremonies. I spoke to Cllr Andy Cornish and Cllr John Newman, my PAB colleagues, who were going to formally propose me to be Mayor of Cheltenham for 1997/98. Cllr Garth Barnes had been proposed by the Liberal Democrats to be the deputy mayor for 1997/98, so I had a last-minute chat with Garth so that we were completely 'switched on' regarding the ceremony.

Arthur Graham, the mayor's chauffer, helping with the robing at the
mayor-making ceremony

At the exact scheduled time of 2.25 p.m., the fanfare began and the parade of councillors, Honorary Aldermen and Honorary Freemen of the Borough, took their seats on the stage. I had followed the procession, a few feet behind the parade, just as I was told, presumably so that people in the hall could see the mayor-elect.

It was a memorable occasion indeed. The main hall was full of smiling people whom I acknowledged as I walked along the aisle leading to the steps of the stage. I was trembling – not with fear, but with the sheer joy of seeing so many people I knew; my family and friends; twinning friends from Annecy and Gottingen; business friends and members of the PAB group. On the stage, I turned round. A sea of faces greeted me. The attendance filled the Town Hall with a few people standing at the back of the hall.The ceremony went according to plan. Not a faux pas by anyone.

Cllr Andy Cornish formally proposed me as mayor, and Cllr John Newman seconded the proposal, and in doing so, gave what I thought was an admirable speech on why I should become the Mayor of Cheltenham for 1997/98. Cllr Newman had not been noted for making speeches in the council chamber, so I was a little apprehensive about what he was going to say. As it turned out, the speech received rapturous applause. He warned the audience that his speech would be longer than the shortest one on record last year when he formally seconded me for deputy mayor. This is an extract of what he said:

> "My pleasant task today is to second the motion that Les Godwin be elected Mayor and to say a few kind words about him, and Pam, his wife, the future Lady Mayoress.
>
> Les Godwin will make a good mayor. In the months leading up to this event, whenever the discussion turned to this ceremony, without exception, people have said to me 'Les Godwin will make a good mayor'.
>
> Not, I might add, how do you think Les Godwin will get on as mayor, or what sort of mayor will Les Godwin be, or whether he will make a good job of it. No, the message has been loud and clear that Les Godwin will make a good mayor.
>
> To his probable embarrassment, I shall now outline the qualities which lead us to make this assumption.
>
> Les Godwin has presence – you notice him. Maybe it is his years of service as a Borough councillor, or his duties on the bench, that has given him this air of confidence and self-assurance. He gives the impression of being able to cope with all eventualities. He is a good communicator and I am looking forward to his speech, which I am sure he will make with a lot less effort than me.
>
> But, above all he is able to get on well in all levels of society, which will be most important in the next twelve months.
>
> Having worked with Les since 1991, when I first became involved with PAB (it is more than something you join, members in the audience will know this and appreciate what I mean by involvement). He is a stickler for organisation and attention to detail, and whatever the subject, he always does his homework.
>
> Stamina – he has this in abundance. Anyone who has canvassed with Les will know this from first-hand experience, and to their cost, me included.
>
> Les believes in delegation of responsibility though he does check up on us a lot, but the PAB group are proud that Les is to become mayor. We have no illusions about the fact that we are going to be very busy on his behalf throughout the year. I sincerely hope that we will be up to it.
>
> I will now put an end to his embarrassment and say a few words about Pam, the long-suffering politician's wife.
>
> When Pam first heard about this impending honour, I gathered she was less than thrilled with the prospect, but the stint as deputy mayoress has obviously helped her get used to the idea. Les is fortunate to have Pam by his side this coming year. She is a lady to grace any occasion. I hope she enjoys the coming year.
>
> In conclusion, I am sure we can all look forward to a mayoral year to remember, and I am sure you will join me in wishing Les and Pam every success."

It was an excellent performance by Cllr John Newman; he had set the bar high and I was determined to achieve the goals I had set.

After the robing procedure and the signing of the 'office of acceptance' document, I delivered a fifteen minute speech in spite of a request from my family "To keep it short". However, judging from the laughter and applause from the audience, I think I hit all the right buttons. It is worth making a more permanent record of what my aspirations were at the time, and of the names of those who

One big happy family at the mayor-making ceremony. Andrew, Lorraine, Joanne, with Mum and Dad.

received special recognition in my speech. I gave a special "thank you" to Simon Lee and his staff for the wonderful display of flowers in the Town Hall (loud applause). I told of my delight at being asked to become Mayor. I explained that I was a local man: born and bred in the town: been through its educational system: worked for local employers. "Cheltenham for me" I told them, "was the best place on earth".

It is normal practice for the new mayor to announce his three chosen charities at some point in the speech, and early on I gave a little detail of each charity. They were certainly popular choices as far as the audience was concerned as the long applause showed.

One other routine matter that I needed to do before I got into the main thrust of my speech was to announce the name of my chaplain. Breaking with tradition, I announced that I would be having two chaplains – Father Stephen Gregory of St, Mary's Church, Prestbury, and Father Ross Northing, the vicar of St. Philip & St. James' Church, Up Hatherley. I couldn't see the eyebrows being raised behind me, but I learned later that some councillors were surprised at my decision. However, I lived in Up Hatherley, and I represented Prestbury on the council – so the decision made good sense.

I told the audience of the tremendous debt we owed to Honorary Alderman Douglas Grazier, who was sitting behind me, who with Terry Joyner had helped me to set up the PAB group in 1976. In remembrance of Terry, I told a story of how

Terry and I went out one evening to raise money for PAB funds from what he called
'a rich part of town'. One house we visited was large and grand with a long driveway
– I was nervous – I had not done this before, so Terry did the talking. He asked the
elderly lady if she would support an independent group of people who were against
party politics in local government. If she did, would she help the PAB group by
donating a small sum of money? At this point, the elderly lady produced an old
fashioned ear trumpet and asked Terry to repeat what he had just said. Terry did so,
but the elderly lady claimed she still couldn't hear what he wanted. Terry thanked
her and we went back down the drive.

"Don't forget to shut the gate" said the woman.

"She knows what she can do with her ruddy gate," Terry said to me loudly.

"And you can do the same with the PAB group," shouted the woman.

Much laughter came from the audience and I noticed Barbara Joyner, Terry's wife
in the audience who had travelled from the Isle of Wight to be at the ceremony,
laughing too.

"What are my hopes and aspirations for the coming year?" I asked the audience,
knowing that they couldn't give me the answer.

> "The answer is" I told them, "I want to promote Cheltenham – its unique setting in
> the Cotswold – its international standing as an educational, arts and cultural centre
> because they are all important to the future prosperity of the town. But in the
> process, I shall never forget that there are people, our people out there who need
> affordable homes, community projects, urban green spaces and rural escape
> hatches. Not only are they basic requirements, they are essential ingredients for a
> happy community.
>
> I would love to see the Royal Crescent restored to its former prestigious past,
> together with the transformation of the rear of the Municipal Offices. I dream about
> a new gym centre on the Midwinter allotment site of international standard, and I
> pray for the reinforcement of our planning policies, which will safeguard our green
> and open countryside for generations to come.
>
> These are my aspirations – I hope they are yours too."

My speech finished on a 'thank you' note and I wished safe journey home to those
who had travelled long distances: it was important I made this point because I knew
that several friends had travelled long distances to be at the ceremony. Friends from
Rochdale, Shrewsbury, London, Newbury and the Isle of Wight had made long
journeys just to be there for a very special occasion.

It gave me enormous pleasure to present the inscribed Cheltenham Medals of
Honour, and a framed citation to Mrs Anne Attwood of Up Hatherley, for her work
for the mentally handicapped, Mrs Roma Naden of Cambray Court, for her work in
relation to multiple sclerosis, and to Bob Attwood, of Arle, for his work as secretary
of the Cheltenham Saracens Sports Club.

I congratulated them for their work in the community and wished them well in
whatever they chose to do in the future.

With no more speeches the time had arrived for me to formally close the Annual Meeting of the Council for 1997. But before I let the audience go I invited everyone to stay for tea and light refreshments, and if my memory serves me well, most people did so.

I had previously arranged a private party for my family and close friends in the Mayor's parlour in the evening, and by the end of the day, Pam and I were exhausted and glad to go to bed. I never thought the mayoral year was going to be easy, and in some respects it wasn't, but at the same time, I never thought it was going to be so exciting and pleasurable as it turned out to be. This was all down to the fact that I wanted to open up the 'mysteries' of the mayoralty, including inviting as many local people as possible to visit the mayor's parlour, so that they felt as though they were sharing my year with me.

Apart from the official engagements, Pam and I agreed to invite as many local people as possible to the parlour for tea and cakes in the afternoon, and for others to join us for a glass of wine and canapés in the evening. We knew it would take care of a lot of the money allocated to the mayor for entertainment purposes, but we believed that local people were just as important as well-known dignitaries, and in my view they deserved the same consideration.

My first day in the Mayor's parlour

I think we succeeded; careful notes of the names of those who were invited to 'an evening in the parlour' during the mayoral year, show that over 1,600 people from all walks of life came to the parlour and learned something of its history and the background behind some of the artefacts in the room. I had made sure that I knew the history of every item in the parlour during my time as deputy mayor so that I could answer any question that might be asked during my twelve months as mayor.

But again, just as I noticed at the ceremony, the sheer joy on the faces of those who were invited to the parlour – just being there – seeing for the first time something that had been denied to them in the past, was something that pleased me more than anything else.

For some time after my time as mayor, people would stop me as I went about the town, to tell me how much they enjoyed their particular night in the parlour, and to thank me for letting them see the inside of the parlour that had always been a place of mystery to them. They had enjoyed learning something about the historical past of Cheltenham and the work of the Borough Council.

The *Gloucestershire Echo* captured my thoughts in their Tuesday night article on the mayor-making ceremony with a headline "Les in pledge to put people first."

My aspirations of protecting the green open spaces, and the pledge to get the Royal Well bus station revamped along with improvements to the Royal Crescent, were mentioned in the report. And I am sure that it helped to stir local people's imagination of what was possible; the will was there, but could I find the means of carrying it out?

It was a challenge I was determined to take on.

As a first step in my desire to open up the parlour and the mayoralty to the people, I invited all the deliverers of the PAB *Newsletters* and election material to a party in the parlour on Tuesday 20th May 1997. It was very much appreciated by everyone, because I had shown consideration to those who had done the hard work for the group so soon after the mayor-making ceremony. It was the forerunner of the style of the mayoralty that Pam and I would continue to do right to the end of the mayoral year.

On Wednesday, 21st May I took part in a 'photo-shoot' at the Cheltenham Race-course. I had never been invited to do a photo-shoot before, so I was intrigued to know what it was all about.

Ken Jennings, the CBC Tourist Manager in 1997 and Edward Gillespie, the director of Cheltenham Racecourse, had arranged to publicise the launch of the new tourist guide that included reference to the Network Q RAC rally. This would be staged at the Racecourse in November.

The photo-shoot consisted of shots of the Gold Cup winner Garrison Savannah, alongside the Subaru car that had won the 1996 World Championship. My job was to pat the racehorse, which I am glad to say was skilfully held by the reins by Julia Chandler, a manager at Eagle Star, who were the sponsors of the borough council tourist guide for 1997.

It was certainly something different for me to do, but like everything else so far – very enjoyable.

Cllr Jim Pennington was the Leader of the Labour group on the council.

Jim was a much travelled man with China being one of his favourite countries to visit. He had forged friendship links with the Weihai administration in North East China since 1987 and each year the bond had become stronger. Weihai is twinned with Sochi in Russia, and as Cheltenham is also twinned with Sochi, Jim used this as a lever to try to persuade CBC that Cheltenham should be twinned with Weihai too. He was a leading member of the Society for Anglo-Chinese Understanding, and was keen to set up cultural relationships between the two towns. In the early days of Cllr Pennington's efforts, CBC made it clear that whilst it was prepared to encourage the formation of the Weihai Link, they were not persuaded that it should lead to the two towns being twinned.

In 1991, Jim Pennington became the first Labour mayor of Cheltenham, and this honour gave Jim more impetus to his effort to make the twinning of Cheltenham with Weihai become a reality. Always ready to help Jim whenever I could, especially when it concerned his friends from Weihai, I agreed with Jim that I would meet an invited group of people from China who were visiting Cheltenham on Thursday 22nd May.

The visitors were delightful people; not only could they speak English, but they were knowledgeable about the history of Cheltenham. They were keen to hear from me whether their knowledge of the town was correct, which often it was, and several took the opportunity to mention to me that the Weihai council had agreed to create parks and open spaces similar to the ones in Cheltenham. This was nice to know and a credit to Simon Lee and his team for creating such attractive parks in the town. Following further representations from Cllr Pennington and others, CBC finally agreed in 1998 that Cheltenham should be formally twinned with Weihai.

Jim Pennington retired from the council and became an Honorary Alderman in 1999; later he became an Honorary Freeman of the town.

His services to the community included being the first chairman of The Keep Cheltenham Tidy Group and a long association with the Parklands Community Centre. He was awarded an MBE in 2001.

Later that same day, I was invited to the annual general meeting of the RSPCA in the Carlton Hotel, which was a non-speaking event for me. It was an enjoyable occasion and a chance to meet the people who do such important work in the protection and welfare of animals.

Friday 23rd May was the first time I did three official duties in one day.

At 11 o'clock, I was invited by the Cheltenham Civic Society to unveil a plaque in the Regent Arcade. This was a memorial to the Plough Hotel, which was demolished in 1983 to make way for the Arcade in the Cheltenham High Street. "The hotel had been the venue for banquets, home to aristocrats and some of Britain's greatest political minds" reported the *Gloucestershire Echo*. I knew that "The Plough", as it was affectionately known, was a famous coaching inn in the 17th century, and, because of its place in history, many local residents wanted the hotel to be kept, but it was a forlorn hope. It had been one of the town's landmarks for 240 years, and the Cheltenham Civic Society thought its past should be recorded for posterity. In my short speech I spoke about the times when The Plough Hotel was regarded as a focal point; a place where people met, especially on market days; a place for a quiet drink. "It's demolition" I said, "was to make way for the Regent Arcade – it was one historical fine building of the past, being replaced by an equally fine building for the future."

In the afternoon I was driven to Gloucester Cathedral for a thanksgiving service by the Archbishop of Canterbury.

The evening engagement was a dinner to mark the 50th anniversary of the Cheltenham Victory Club, which is a club for ex-servicemen. The dinner was held at the Pittville Pump Room where 150 former comrades shared their memories of the Second World War. The dinner was a special moment for me too, because I had been a long-standing member of the club, sharing its ups and downs and participating in its activities over many years. The celebration dinner of the club's 50 years was a golden opportunity for me to include in my speech a homily regarding the importance of its honorary secretary, Arthur Bailey. I told the guests:

> "We should all be grateful to Arthur, because it was he with his determination and love of the club that brought about its modernisation. The improvements he has made to the club are too many to mention, but we all know what they are. His tireless work as the unpaid secretary of the club now shows that the Victory Club is the best family club in Cheltenham."

Another guest of honour was Peter West, the well-known cricket commentator. He became the Life President of the newly formed Cheltenham Cricket Society (CCS), which Arthur Bailey and others had established in 1983.

Saturday and Sunday 24th/25th May were not days of rest and recovery; far from it, I was at Dean Close School at 10.15 a.m. on Saturday meeting the headmaster Christopher Bacon, who was keen to show me around the school, and more importantly, he wanted to know what my aspirations were during the next twelve months.

I liked Christopher Bacon because of his courteous and thoughtful manner; he wanted me to know that some of his plans would include helping me raise money for my charities. He had refurbished many parts of the school in previous years, and the theatre was the place that was closest to his heart. He wanted me to know that I could stage events there without charge providing the theatre was available.

It was all very interesting, but I couldn't help feeling that he was "running the rule over me" for some reason, or, perhaps, he was being exceptionally kind to me. Nevertheless, I did enjoy his friendship, and when he retired in 1998 to his farm in Monmouthshire, the theatre was renamed The Bacon Theatre.

There was an early call for me on Sunday morning – I was scheduled to "Flag Away" the RAC Classic cars from the Pittville Pump Room at 8.00 a.m. Then, according to Maggie Handson, the rest of day was mine.

It was even better the next day because it was a Bank Holiday, which enabled me, and to a lesser extent Pam, to recharge our batteries in readiness for the engagements already scheduled for the remainder of the week. I sat down to relax with the Bank Holiday issue of the *Gloucestershire Echo.* However, I was soon jolted out of my repose when my eye caught a headline

"Banish this blot, says new mayor."

I had forgotten temporarily that Alison Wade, a reporter from the *Echo*, had interviewed me a few days previously. This was to do with my pledge at the mayor-making ceremony, "to do something about the deplorable state of the Royal Well bus station in Royal Crescent".

Although it was a Bank Holiday, the *Echo* published its usual copy, which included an article by Alison Wade. The headline said:

"Cheltenham's unpopular bus station has made a powerful new enemy – town mayor Les Godwin"

The article read: "The first citizen has revealed he cannot stand the Royal Well bus station and nothing would give him greater pleasure than to see it demolished.

The founder member of the People Against Bureaucracy Group and Prestbury councillor said the borough council should look for alternative locations on the outskirts of town for the bus station. I would love to see Royal Well restored to its prestigious past when lords and ladies sat on benches in the open space and admired the view. In order to do this the bus station would have to come down."

The Echo editorial followed this up in the Opinion column with the heading "Mayor's pledge just the ticket." It opined: "The days of the Cheltenham bus station must surely be numbered. The few who had anything positive to say about it in the past are now distant memories. All that remains is that monstrous carbuncle and a growing will to see it raised to the ground.

The latest voice to join the cause is the town's new mayor Councillor Les Godwin. The people who have been against the bus station have been in search for a worthy and powerful champion for some time.

We must now hope that we have found one in Councillor Godwin."

A photograph accompanied the article showing me inside the graffiti covered concrete bus shelter, which truly was a blot on the landscape. A comment from the council's information officer Carol Merriman indicated that CBC were looking to relocate the bus station if a suitable alternative was available.

On Tuesday morning at 10.00 a.m., I presented a long-service award to Martin Bartram in the mayor's parlour, Then I visited The Body Shop in the Regent Arcade to launch a recycling campaign. The Body Shop, nationally, is a green-minded business, and the staff had always been in the forefront of recycling campaigns. It was a joy to be at their Cheltenham Branch and to meet such friendly people.

The *Gloucestershire Echo* covered the occasion, and the report that followed had an eye-catching headline:

> "Climb on yer bike and get recycling." Then followed: "Where the Mayor leads the rest of us follow – and that is exactly how it should be. Cheltenham Mayor Les Godwin is at the forefront of a special recycling campaign that involves us all.
>
> Organised by those environmentally friendly folk at The Body Shop, in the Regent Arcade, and The Keep Cheltenham Tidy Group, it aims to encourage us all to re-use, refill and recycle.
>
> This means not throwing things automatically in the bin when you've finished with them without first thinking if they can be recycled."

I enjoyed the visit and it was the first of many occasions when the staff in the Body Shop, and The Keep Cheltenham Tidy Group, came together to help me raise money for my three charities.

Whilst I would have loved to have stayed longer to talk to everyone involved, I had to get back to the parlour for the presentation of National Vocational Qualifications (NVQ's) to a number of council staff employees. The NVQ is a work-based award achieved through assessment and training, but in order to receive the NVQ a candidate must prove that he or she has the ability to carry out their job to the required standard. There are five levels of NVQ ranging from level 1, which focuses on basic work activities, to level 5 for senior management. They can be awarded to someone in a paid or a voluntary position, so they are an important acquisition for the recipients.

Wednesday 28th May marked the rehabilitation of a small enclave of Victorian houses in St. George's Street, which is in the centre of Cheltenham. I unveiled a plaque to commemorate the occasion. The unveiling was due to take place at noon, which gave me the opportunity to do some quick research about the work and the people who were responsible for the refurbishing.

I knew for a start that the commemoration was to celebrate the 10,000th tenancy of the Knightstone Housing Association. I also knew that the project would have been impossible for CBC to do on its own, which is why they went into a partnership with the Association, who provided the bulk of the funding. The large gathering of people who had been involved in the project; builders, architects, solicitors, the contractors, CBC housing staff, including the borough Valuer, were all there to mark the occasion. The following is an extract from my speech:

> "To those of us who have known St. George's Street over the years – the years when the street was an attractive and important part of Cheltenham – the following years when the area was in decline with one building after another becoming derelict, it is a marvellous moment now to see a further part of the street refurbished and transformed to provide seven family homes to let at affordable rents.

> The dwellings blend in well with the recently refurbished Wesleyan Chapel and adjoining former school buildings, and they have been renovated to a high standard by the Knightstone Housing Association – they are a great credit to all who have been involved with the project."

The ceremony took place in a very small area between two large buildings, so it must have been difficult for a number of people to hear the speeches.

At least the message that I had invited everyone to join me in the Municipal Offices for tea and cakes must have been heard, because we continued our conversations in one of the council offices for some time afterwards.

Thursday morning at 10 o'clock I was back in the Regent Arcade, this time to launch a St. John's Ambulance Competition – a three-day event to mark 75 years of service for the Cadets, and a decade for the Badgers. My task was to launch a "guess the number of coins that had been stuck to a giant roll of sticky tape", which was on display in the Regent Arcade.

The prize for the winner was a day at the Cheltenham races, and fund-raiser Jenny Blake, for St. John's Ambulance, told me, "The competition was proving to be a good money spinner." That was good to hear – I didn't hear how much money the St. John's Ambulance folk raised, and I didn't guess the right number of coins, but it was all good fun and for a very good cause.

In the afternoon I chaired my first council meeting. I took the opportunity to say a number of things, starting with my thanks to everyone for their support at the mayor-making ceremony; I told them I enjoyed it and hoped that they had enjoyed it too,

Apparently not, if the looks on the Liberal Democrat faces in the council chamber was anything to go by; no smiles, no nodding of heads, just sullen looks.

Undeterred, I soldiered on using another tack; I thanked Cllr Pat Thornton for her excellent year in office as the Mayor of Cheltenham. I looked around the council chamber, any smiles or nodding of heads, not a thing. Not even a little bit of hand-clapping to show their agreement that Cllr Thornton had done a good job the previous year.

Following one or two little homilies, I concluded my opening speech to tell the councillors:

> "Each new mayor brings his or her style and flair to the meeting, and I did not intend to be any different. I may insist on the right protocol being followed, but I will be fair and consistent.
>
> I hope our debates will be interesting and constructive – they should be if we remember that on most issues we have common goals, it is only the means of getting there which are different.
>
> On those things where there are differences of opinion, always remember that whilst we may be opponents – we should never be enemies.
>
> If we remember that then we shall do just fine."

As there were no responses, I took the first item on the agenda.

Throughout the following years there has been little improvement in the attitude of Lib/Dem councillors towards me. Doug Grazier had written to me a few days after the mayor-making ceremony saying how disgusting it was for a large number of Lib/Dem councillors not to have joined in with the applause at the end of my speech. Doug remarked: "You couldn't see what was going on behind your back, but I could and I feel I must make a public protest."

I wrote to Doug immediately and asked him not to go any further with the matter – in my view, it really didn't matter what the Lib/Dems did, or what their intentions had been. The ceremony had been a success in spite of them.

On Friday at 9.30 a.m., I met the Reverend Timothy Watson the vicar of St. Matthew's Church, Clarence Street, Cheltenham. The church is a short distance from the Municipal Offices, and each year the mayor, councillors, and other dignitaries walk in procession to St. Matthew's church for the traditional Mayoral Sunday Service. Timothy Watson and I discussed the arrangements for the service, which was scheduled to be held on 15th June. St. Matthew's church is a stone building which was consecrated in 1879. It lies in the heart of the town.

It was my first meeting with Timothy and I was immediately impressed with his friendly and courteous manner. He wanted the arrangements and the choice of hymns for the service to be shared with me, and of course, to let me know the passage in the Bible that I would be reading to the congregation. I welcomed the pre-service discussion with Timothy Watson because I knew from our conversation that on the day he would ensure that everything went well.

The following day turned out to be one of those days that will stay in my mind for ever; Pam and I had been invited to the Pittville School by the head teacher David Abbott. The school used to be the Pate's Grammar School for Girls (opened in 1905). It became a secondary school with 700 pupils when the grammar school moved to another part of town.

The school had a thriving tennis section, which was run by Terry Parker and his wife Pam; the school had arranged a tennis coaching session in the afternoon for adults and the children. The head teacher thought that having the mayor in attendance with his chain of office would add a little gravitas to the occasion. On our arrival we were met by David Abbott, who explained that he had also invited the colourful athlete Kris Akabusi to come to the school and help with the tennis coaching. He was unsure whether the athlete could make it.

However, it wasn't long before the sound of a helicopter filled the air and it got louder as it approached the Pittville School playing field. The blue helicopter circled overhead and finally landed a few yards from us. Within a few minutes, Kris Akabusi emerged from the aircraft, with the largest tennis racket I have ever seen, and, of course, complete with that broad grin and his famous 'over-the-top' laugh, which has always been his hallmark. We all laughed at what we were seeing – it was impossible not to.

After the introductions, I said to Kris Akabusi, "I thought you were an athlete, not

With Terry Parker and the Pittville School tennis section

Kris Akabusi and me at the launch of the Pittville School Tennis Day June 1997

a tennis player." His laugh was continuous as he answered "So did I, until this invitation came along." He was a wonderful character, and the children loved him. Kris Akabusi was a very good athlete specialising in the 400 metres until switching to the 400 metres hurdles in 1987. In the 1984 Olympic Games in Los Angeles, he won a silver medal as a member of the British 4 x 400 metres relay team. In 1992, he was awarded the MBE by the Queen, in recognition of his services to athletics.

It was a very enjoyable afternoon for several reasons – David and I seemed to hit it off immediately, and we became good friends. I went back to Pittville School several times during the mayoral year, and I have had a close association with the school ever since.

Throughout June 1997, I attended a number of different events visiting schools, local organisations and sports clubs. In the evenings, in keeping with my promise to invite local people to the parlour, Pam and I invited groups of 15 to 20 people to come to the parlour for drinks and canapés, whenever we had a 'free' night.

Few people declined the offer and those who came were overjoyed at being invited. Most of the guests brought their cameras to record the occasion, and those who were cheeky enough wanted their photographs taken in the mayor's chair. How could I refuse?

Halfway through the evening I would give a short speech about the history of the Coat of Arms and Insignia of the borough. I would explain the Crest which embodies and denotes the legend of the discovery of the mineral waters: the Coat of Arms of Edward the Confessor: the Open Book and the "Eruditio" in the Motto. I would explain that the badges were emblematic of the educational advantages that Cheltenham possesses, for which it is famous as an educational centre.

Another idea that occurred to me, probably a spin-off from the wine and canapé evenings, was to invite the council staff to join me for a cup of coffee in the mornings, or a cup of tea in the afternoons, whenever I was in the parlour.

Maggie, my PA, thought it was a good idea and set about preparing a list, but she did warn me not to be surprised if only a few took up the invitation. She was right – very few did come along for a chat, but I believe that those who did were glad they had accepted the invitation.

In answer to one of my questions, the staff admitted that they had never seen the inside of the mayor's parlour, even though they had worked for the borough council for a number of years. Like my guests in the evenings they were pleased to see the memorabilia, the mayor's mace and even have the chance to handle the mayor's chain of office.

Friday 13th June was a particularly busy day, which started with an early meeting with Julia Chandler regarding the Eagle Star sponsorship of the mayor's Fashion Show, plus another visit to St. Matthew's Church, to go through the final details of the mayoral parade and service.

I joined the Age Concern meeting in the council offices, and I presented golf awards to members of the council staff who had participated in a recent golfing competition.

Besides the mayoral engagements, there were council matters to attend to such as signing documents on behalf of the council.

My charity committee were meeting regularly and bringing forward ideas to make the fashion show in September a special occasion. Whilst they kept me informed of the programme of events, I was becoming increasingly concerned that they might be embarking on something that was perhaps too big for us. Pam Thomas, and the rest of the committee, were so enthusiastic to make the show a success, and the suggestions they made were always brilliant – I just hoped that it would all come together successfully on the night.

My worries were eased when Maggie Handson informed me that the Chelsea Building Society were interested in helping my charities, and that too turned out to be a blessing, which I will refer to later.

I was grateful to the Reverend Timothy Watson for being so helpful with regard to the Mayoral Sunday Service because it went very well. The *Gloucestershire Echo*, which thankfully was never far away from any of my engagements, was there to record the event.

Their report, complete with pictures, was published on Tuesday 17th June 1997. The headline above a photograph of the mayor leading a long line of councillors, aldermen and freemen of the town said, "Mayor leads way to make children's day at church service."

The article with a sub-heading "Les on parade" reported that more than 200 worshippers and their families filled St. Matthew's Church for the annual mayor's service. The mayor, Les Godwin, broke with tradition by greeting 30 children from the congregation. He said after the service *"The children were overjoyed to be greeted by the mayor in his red robes – some thought I was Father Christmas."*

Vicky Tuck, who was now the principal of the Cheltenham Ladies' College, invited me to lunch on Friday 20th June, which was followed by a concert by the junior girls in the Princess Hall.

Both were enjoyable events and it was the start of an association with the Ladies' College that still exists today.

The following day, Pam and I attended the annual RSPCA Fun Dog Show in the morning, and in the evening we were the guests of honour at the Soroptimists' 40th Anniversary Dinner at the Carlton Hotel (now called the Hotel du Vin). From the information I had been given, I was aware that the dinner was a special night for the Soroptimists, so I worked hard on my speech during the afternoon to make sure it was just right. Diana Sharpe, the Regional President, welcomed Pam and me as we entered the hotel. She then introduced Dame "Rennie" Fritchie, who I had met on other occasions when I was the chairman of the Cheltenham & District Community Health Council.

We were introduced to other guests before we sat at our dinner places. I was surprised to see so many faces I knew, so much so that I thought about making changes to my speech while I enjoyed the first two courses of the meal.

Having thanked the Soroptimists for inviting the mayoress and myself to the anniversary dinner, I turned my attention to all the familiar faces and explained to them that their presence had made me feel more comfortable than when I had first entered the hotel. " I know I am supposed to propose a toast" I said, "but Diana Sharpe has already made it clear to me that I should make the speech short, otherwise the guests glasses become empty too soon, and the guests anticipation is then lost."

The next part of my speech I knew was going to be tricky – having learned from Diana that fellow Soroptimists had travelled from our twin-town Annecy; I was keen to include them in my welcome.

This is what I said: *"To our visitors from Annecy, bienvenue a Cheltenham. j'espere que vous aimerez bien votre sejour dans notre ville."*

It received a round of applause whether or not the French grammar was good. If there had been any criticism, I would have replied that it had been a long time since I studied French at school. The following were the other main points of my speech:

"As you are probably aware, I have been mayor for only a short time, and so far I have found the job most interesting – even 'quirky' at times. For example, on my first day in the parlour, I was going through the names in the visitors' book, when I came across names like Mr B. Clinton from Washington, a Mrs D. Windsor from London, and even a signature that read L. Lucan of no fixed abode".

This brought a ripple of laughter from many in the room. "But the most fascinating thing about being mayor" I continued, "is the numerous opportunities it presents for meeting so many people who all play a different, but equally important part in life's great tapestry.

But different though they may well be, the majority of people I have met so far, appear to have one common aim – to do whatever they can to help people less fortunate than themselves.

I have been surprised at the number of people who willingly give up their time to help others – I often meet the same people at other functions working for different caring organisations. They work long hours, often unpaid, and are definitely unsung, but who are without any doubt, the backbone of support in many different charity organisations.

So madam chairman, when I heard about your annual programme of fund raising for worthwhile causes, together with your core charity, the Gloucestershire James Hopkins Trust for children in need of respite care, I felt quite humble, knowing that the work the mayor's charity committee is doing to raise money for three good causes is small in comparison.

The important point of course, is that we are all working for one common aim and for that we should all feel proud."

To conclude – I proposed a toast to the Cheltenham and District Soroptimists.

Sunday morning at 8.00 a.m., Pam and I were at the Cheltenham Racecourse to start the annual 26 mile Cheltenham Circular Challenge. There were dozens of walkers and runners [competitors can do either], waiting for me to 'fire' the starting gun, which, metaphorically speaking, I did, and off we all went clutching our route maps. The circular walk takes the walker along some of the most delightful paths around the Cheltenham boundary, and the walk is well worth doing at any time.

The *Gloucestershire Echo* had asked me to take part in a photo session concerning the circular walk a week before the event. The *Echo*, along with Eagle Star, Whitbread, and Design Solutions, were sponsoring the event, so it was important that the walk was given as much publicity as possible. The bus company, Stagecoach, provided coaches to take walkers back to their start point, should they be needed.

The headline in the *Echo* on Tuesday 17th June read: *"Join challenge – it's good to walk. Mayor urges all to take part."* "*Cheltenham Mayor Les Godwin is urging fellow councillors to get out and hit the trail – for a good cause"*, the article claimed.

It also made the point that the mayor and his wife Pam would be walking six miles of the Circular Challenge and although they had not sought any sponsors, they would be making a donation towards the charities. The sponsored walk was organised by the Cheltenham and Cleeve Vale Rotary Club and Rotaract, who distributed bottles of water to the participants along certain points of the walk. The organisers expected to raise thousands of pounds for several charities, including the Cheltenham-based YHP Community Projects, and the mobile counselling service Talk About. All were worthy causes.

Week commencing 23rd June turned out to be busier than the previous one.

My first engagement was to attend the Police Centre at Churchdown Lane, Hucclecote, to see how road traffic offenders, as the Police instructor told me, are 'taught to see the folly of their ways'. The site was a large complex containing several buildings, which, I recall, included a large and impressive library.

The display by the police officers was impressive too, but it seemed to be a large undertaking for the small number of road traffic offenders that were likely to choose to go through the 'training' programme rather than pay a fine. The Police Centre at Hucclecote is now closed and the property, which belongs to Gloucestershire County Council, is up for sale.

At 11.30 a.m., I held a reception for Annecy students in the Drawing Room at the Town Hall. Getting to know them was always going to be interesting, because it gave them an opportunity to practise their English and at the same time for me to practise some French.

I spent the afternoon on council business, and then, following an invitation from Lady Apsley, the charity patron of the Macmillan Cancer Relief Appeals, I cut the ribbon to celebrate the opening of a new Appeals and Information Centre in Wellington Street, Cheltenham.

I joined other guests that included the charity's Gloucestershire Head of Appeals, Barbara Hampel, and local Macmillan nurses, consultants and committee members. There were representatives from the NHS and local supporters of the Macmillan Cancer Support. I learned a lot about the work of the Macmillan Cancer Care Support charity that afternoon, and I have continued to support them.

On Friday morning at 10.30 a.m., I met Graham Sacker (a friend who served with me during my time on the Cheltenham Magistrates' Bench), together with his colleague Joe Devereux. They had co-written a book with accompanying photographs, charting the history of Cheltenham men who had fought and died during the 1914 to 1918 First World War.

Their research for the book had taken four years to complete, and it contained over 1,000 photographs, some of which had never been published before. Graham and Joe had taken the names of those on the Cheltenham War Memorial and then visited War Grave sites on the continent and taken the photographs.

It is an amazing 700 page book which contains the names and photographs of 1,600 servicemen from Cheltenham who gave their lives in the war. Details are given of each soldier; their short lives and in many cases their ordeals in the war, and in what part of France they were killed and buried.

It is called "Leaving All That Was Dear" and it is a brilliant reference document and a great credit to the authors. Graham and Joe asked me to accept a copy of the book for the council library, and to my surprise they presented a personal copy to me as well.

I attended the Gloucestershire Therapy Eye Trust open day on Saturday morning, and Pam and I were invited to listen to the Cheltenham Bach Choir in Tewkesbury Abbey in the evening.

The following day we welcomed the 22nd Vintage Motorcycle Club International to Cheltenham. I congratulated the Cotswold section of the vintage motorcycle club for their work in the area, and for bringing the 22nd International Assembly to Cheltenham. The array of different motorcycles was impressive, and while the noise of some of them would not be appreciated by everyone, it must have been an impressive display to those who came along to see what the Assembly was all about.

Later, Pam and I had lunch with the organisers of the event in the Town Hall.

In the evening we were invited to a reception at the Carlton Hotel with members of the Association of Anglican Musicians. It is an organisation of musicians and clergy serving in the worshiping communities of the Episcopal Church and the larger Anglican tradition. The members are organists, pianists, bishops, guitarists, presbyters and deacons, teachers of music, and friends of Anglicanism's musical tradition. I was not surprised to find that the majority of the members we met at the reception were Americans: they were in the United Kingdom for a number of days, and hoping to see as much of Cheltenham and the surrounding areas in spite of the weather, which was inclement to say the least. In my speech, I apologised for the awful weather they had been experiencing, and hoped that it hadn't curtailed their programme too much.

I told them that Pam and I had been to Tewkesbury Abbey the previous night to listen to a programme of English choral music; the programme had contained a piece about the famous Milton organ, which I knew they had seen during their visit to the Abbey that day. They were delighted to hear that I had obtained two copies of the programme, which I wanted to present to their President, John Hooker, and their chief organiser of this year's Convention in the United Kingdom. They were a delightful crowd of people and it was a most enjoyable evening.

I didn't hesitate when I was invited by Angie Rowlands to spend a morning in the Cheltenham Tourist and Information Centre in the Promenade. Angie was the manager of The Centre. She had charm and a bubbly personality. The ideal person to be manager. I spent the morning there, helping to welcome visitors to the town. You can imagine the surprise of many visitors being welcomed by the mayor.

Indeed, some visitors were put off by what they perceived to be a gimmick dreamt up by the Council. But as soon as I explained the situation to them, they began to see that it was an admirable novelty in the promotion of the town, and then all went well.

The *Gloucestershire Echo* was on hand once again to write an article, complete with photograph to claim: *"Mayor does his bit to boost town's tourist trade."*

I thoroughly enjoyed my morning in The Centre, and would have done more time there if other engagements had allowed. The Centre has always been a popular place for visitors to go, and Angie Rowlands was outstanding in her managerial role.

When Angie completed 30 years' service, in 2003, I sent her a message of congratulations. Ten years after that, she retired with 40 years' dedicated service behind her. She received her pension, but alas, no other form of recognition for her devoted service. Not good, in my opinion, not good at all.

The afternoon of 2nd July took an unexpected turn. I received a late request to meet 20 American and Canadian tourists who had walked from Stratford-upon-Avon to Cheltenham, visiting several Cotswold villages on the way. They told me they had covered over 100 miles in their walk.

They wanted to 'call in' on the mayor, so that they had something to take back home. It turned out to be a great pleasure – their conversations were interesting, and they told me they had taken similar walking holidays in the past. They loved the Cotswolds and they loved Cheltenham.

They were very pleased to have tea in the mayor's parlour, and like everyone else who had visited the parlour, were fascinated by the memorabilia. To commemorate their achievement, I presented them with certificates on behalf of Lord Winston's Walking Tours, and, to complete their day, a photograph of the group with me on the steps of the Municipal Offices.

My diary shows my attendance at a number of concerts and presentations in the week commencing 7th July, and, in between these events, there were visits to the Cheltenham General Hospital, the Art Gallery & Museum, and to attend St. Edward's School's Speech Day.

On Wednesday evening 10th July, Pam and I gave a short Civic Reception during the interval of a performance by the Sundsvall Chamber Orchestra (Sweden) in the Town Hall.

It was the sixth day of the Cheltenham Music Festival, and the town hall was buzzing: six days and already several top orchestras had played in one of Cheltenham's magnificent buildings. My duty was to thank all those who had made the Festivals such a success so far; the sponsors, the trusts, patrons, and of course, the Artistic Director of the Cheltenham Music Festival, Michael Berkeley. I thanked all the town hall staff, particularly people such as Jeremy Tyndall, Kim Sargeant and Anne Strathie. They had always worked tirelessly each year to make the Cheltenham Music Festival a success. The interval was short, so my allotted time was just seven minutes. I particularly wanted to say a few words about the education and community work that all three Festivals had undertaken (Jazz, Literature and Music).

> "Those of you who have been to any of the concerts will have seen a number of young people performing, but what you have probably not seen are the particular programmes and workshops that have been taking place in schools and local communities in Cheltenham – projects at Bishop's Cleeve, Hester's Way, and the World Music, who performed in front of 10,000 people at the Picnic in the Park event that launched the Cheltenham Festivals."

I also mentioned the Axiom Centre, which I thought was doing a great job for the arts and culture in the town, and by the applause, most people agreed with my comments.

Following the Speech Day and buffet at St. Edward's School on Friday 11th July, Pam and I attended The Cheltenham Ladies' College Summer Concert. The range of musical talents of some of the girls was amazing, and, of course, a pleasure to hear. The Ladies' College have continued to invite Pam and me to the annual summer concerts and we seldom miss this special occasion.

On Saturday morning 12th July, we were up early in order to be at the Gloucester-shire Warwickshire Railway (GWR) station situated at the Prestbury Racecourse. It was to celebrate the official opening of an extension of the GWR railway line to Gotherington. It was the first time Pam and I had been on the popular, voluntary-run GWR train service, although it had been officially opened by Nicholas Ridley MP as far back as 1984.

The GWR runs along a part of the former Great Western Railway's mainline from Birmingham to Cheltenham via Stratford-upon-Avon. The railway journey commands wonderful views of hamlets and villages through the Cotswold country-side.

Before the short journey to Gotherington, we were introduced to several people who were prominent in either radio or television. We also had the company of our new-found friend Brian Jones, the new mayor of Tewkesbury Borough Council, who attended the opening with his daughter. Brian and I had met on other joint mayoral engagements across our two areas. We got on well and we appreciated each other's company.

Sunday 13th July was the Cheltenham Lions Club Annual Fete on Cox's Meadow. The club had become famous over previous years due in the main to their successful family fun days.

The correct title of the club is "The Lions Club of Cheltenham" and it is affiliated to the International Association of Lions Clubs. Its brochure states *"The Lions are a friendly and active group of men and women who come from all walks of life. They are united to give some of their free time to help those less fortunate than themselves. Time that is given and money that is raised is spent largely in Cheltenham".*

John Grover, who was President of the Lions Club in 1997, and his close friend Des Cresswell, had contacted me some time earlier to explain in detail the Lions Club Summer Fete, which they hoped I would attend. When I agreed to do so, I detected a wry smile on their faces, which was either relief that I had accepted their invitation, or, they had something else up their sleeves. They explained to me that each year in the weeks running up to the Lion's fun day, they held a "Lions Day Princess" competition, which would require me to introduce the 'princess' at the appropriate time during the Summer Fete Day.

They also explained that the usual carnival parade with colourful floats would not take place in 1997, due to a lack of entries. I knew that the parade had become a popular event each year and was always well attended by Cheltenham people lining the route. I expressed my disappointment at the news, which I was sure would be shared by other people.

John and Des were equally disappointed because they had done a lot of work leading up to the event, but as Des Cresswell explained to me, the businesses and a few of the smaller organisations had lost interest in the parade.

It would also be a disappointment for the Lions Day Princess and her attendants, who would have looked forward to being on the most decorated float in the parade and enjoying their moment of glory.

It was clear from our conversation that every effort had been made to persuade the usual entrants to co-operate, so there was no point in my pursuing the matter any further. I expressed the hope that next year might see a return of the colourful parade.

The wry smile that I detected at the start of our meeting returned to their faces. They wanted me to know that for the very first time at their summer fete, a number of camel races would take place during the course of the afternoon. Apparently, they had arranged this by courtesy of a nearby circus. My jaw dropped, I knew what was going to come next – yes, and they wanted me to be a rider of one of the camels in the first race. I don't like camels at the best of times: they are usually smelly and most unpredictable. Expecting the mayor to actually get on the back of one and run a distance along the field without something dreadful happening, was asking a bit too much of the mayor, I thought.

John Grover and Des Cresswell are both splendid people, and Des, in particular, has that persuasive smile and 'gift of the gab' that makes one feel uncomfortable unless one agrees with his suggestion – so I agreed to do it. Naturally, they were both pleased: they promised to keep me updated with the programme of events and that would include the name of the camel I was expected to ride. The camels actually had names they said – I was beginning to regret my decision to participate in this

The Mayor leads the way in the camel race.

spectacle. They left the parlour smiling like cats that had just had a saucer of cream.

The *Gloucestershire Echo* contacted me the next day and asked me to write a letter to the *Echo* readers urging them to attend the Lions Club Fete. I agreed and they added that they would publish the letter together with a photograph of me in my mayoral robes outside the Cheltenham Town Hall. The headline said: "Let's make Lions' fete a real success." My letter said:

"Dear Friends,

Like many other people who have enjoyed previous Lions Club carnival parades, I am very disappointed that this year the parade of floats will not take place.

The spectacular parade of the colourful floats, with the music and the cheerful partici-pants, was part of the Cheltenham scene each year. I do hope this is a temporary 'blip' and that next year we shall see its return, better than ever.

Of course, the Lions Club Fete will still take place on Sunday 13th July and I shall be pleased to give it my full support, even to the extent of riding a camel, if I have to.

The Lions Club has always been in the forefront of raising funds for worthy causes, and those most in need have benefited from their efforts.

Please make it a bumper year for fund raising, and by our presence we may succeed in making the Lions Club think again about a carnival parade in 1998.

I hope to meet as many people as possible on Sunday, and I wish the summer fete every success."

The letter must have had some success because the fete had a record attendance in 1997.

A week before the Summer Fete, John and Des informed me that the winner of the competition to find a 'Lions Day Princess' was ten year old Nikita Iddles. She was a Greatfield Park (Up Hatherley) Primary School pupil. Her mother was delighted because when she was a teenager, she had only managed second place. Once again the *Echo* were on the phone to tell me the result, and also to tell me that Nikita's two attendants would be Sarah-Jayne Bourne from Rowanfield, Cheltenham, and eleven year old Abby Kinch who lived in Bishop's Cleeve.

The report in the *Echo* edition the following night, complete with photographs of the three girls, was excellent. The list of events to entertain the crowd at the fete included charity fun stalls, face painting, silent auctions, fun fair rides, Nelson's ladder, quad bikes, archery, a bouncy castle and many refreshment stalls including ice cream ones.

The main event was the camel races. The announcement came over the tannoy system that the mayor was about to ride a camel in the first race. No rush of people to witness the event. That was just as well, because first I had great difficulty getting on the camel, and then when I thought I had got it right, I fell off, much to everyone's amusement.

Eventually I managed to get on the camel, and with the help of a swift blow by the camel's handler, off we went. Camels are obstinate creatures and I tried really hard to get the camel to run faster, but to no avail – I came in third, which wasn't bad except there were only four runners.The crowd cheered me on, and several wanted photographs taken with them and me and the camel – I have no idea why, but there you go.

Council matters still had to be attended to, including several important planning applications. There were the usual individual problems of my constituents that also needed to be addressed.

On 11th July 1997, Galliard Developments Limited (Agent Mr N. C Tucker-Brown) submitted a planning application to construct a North West bypass on land to the north of Cheltenham from the A435 (Evesham Road) to the A4019 (Tewkesbury Road) adjacent to Sainsbury's.

The application included the construction of a new park and ride facility using the former Honeybourne (disused) railway line in Swindon Lane: a segregated bus route: a cycle way and a footpath between the new park and ride facility and the St. James's site in the centre of Cheltenham.

It was a mammoth proposal, and if it had been approved, it would have resulted in the loss of many hectares of green belt land. It was opposed by residents in the areas who would be affected, and rightly so, because the construction of a North West Distributor Road around Swindon Village and finishing at the Honeybourne line, would have resulted in hundreds of houses being built in order to pay for it.

What concerned me and the local residents at the time were the possible consequences that would flow from the development once it was completed. How would we be able stop further encroachment into the green belt, for example?

At the public local inquiry, where individuals and representatives of the County Highways, TBC, CBC and Mr Tucker-Brown expressed their views, it seemed that each representative had a different opinion of where any future bypass should be constructed. Some wanted the road to be close to the boundary of Swindon Village. Others took the opposite view and suggested it should be constructed in a wider arc some distance from the village and ending much further along the A435 than the planning application had indicated.

TBC made good points in stressing strongly their concerns about the future of the green belt, and particularly the development potential in the Swindon Village and Uckington areas. They preferred a road closer to the village, whereas Swindon parish council preferred it to be further out.

CBC preferred a bypass even further out than the other proposals, which must have been as confusing for the Inquiry inspector as it was for the listening public.

The road was never built, but the publication of the Joint Core Strategy (JCS) in August 2013 proposed 4,829 houses on land to the North West of Swindon Village. But, without a distributor road, or other additional road infrastructure improvements to accommodate the extra traffic, it was difficult to see how the number of extra dwellings could be accommodated.

Swindon parish council and the local residents were totally opposed to the JCS proposals: they formed a 'Save Our Countryside' group who became increasingly prominent with their intensive advertising and reports of their activities in the local press.

This had little effect on the planning strategists advising the JCS committee that the construction of 4,829 dwellings on the green belt around Swindon Village was an important part of the long term housing strategy for the area.

The JCS proposals and their impact will be included in a later chapter.

It came as no surprise to hear that an outline planning application had been submitted for residential development on 14.98 hectares of land at Swindon Farm, Swindon Village, following the public inquiry on the North West bypass. It was refused, just as a similar planning application had been refused in 1972.

Another visit to the Body Shop, an Art Exhibition, judging a junior school painting competition, attending the Cheltenham YMCA annual general meeting were typical events throughout the month.

On Wednesday 16th July, I met the Cheltenham in Bloom judges Stan Gardner and his colleague, who I was told "had both been garden judges for many years", with Simon Lee and Stella Fisher, the chairman of the Cheltenham in Bloom committee. Claire Everest, the national marketing services manager of sponsors, Bryant Homes, also joined us. We walked around the magnificent garden displays in the parks – all looking in tip-top condition. It was not difficult to feel proud to be showing off the gardens to the judges; they must have been impressed.

We came top of the 'regional heats for cities' for the 12th time, which meant that Cheltenham would automatically go forward to compete in the following year's national final in August. But the current success suggested that our prospects in the Heart of England Britain in Bloom contest in 1997 were also looking good.

Drinks and a concert in the evening and then it was time for bed, pondering about the events that Maggie Handson had arranged for me for the rest of the week and the speeches that I needed to prepare.

Some weeks earlier, Pam and I had accepted an invitation to attend the Fairford Air Show on Saturday 19th July. It was one of those rare occasions when an invitation arrived with the suggestion that there was no need for the mayor to attend wearing his chain of office. The letter politely explained that the intention of the invitation was for the VIP's to enjoy the Air Show.

I thought it was an excellent suggestion considering the Fairford Air Show was a very informal occasion for thousands of people.

We were issued with special passes which gave us a direct route to the VIP parking spaces and a directional map to the VIP lounge in the vast space of the airfield.

Arthur Graham, who had held the position of the mayor's chauffeur for a long time, arrived early as usual, smartly dressed, complete with his peaked cap, and off we went.

Everything went according to plan until we were about five miles from Fairford – the line of traffic heading in the same way, stretched as far as the eye could see. When we stopped, the number of cars behind us gradually increased.

Arthur always took his job of mayor's chauffeur very seriously; he didn't think the mayor of Cheltenham and his wife (with or without their chains of office) should have to queue to get into an event that they had been requested to attend. He decided to do what he thought a man in his position should do in such circumstances; he pulled out into the oncoming lane and headed for the Air Show entrance.

Arthur always drove at a very moderate speed, probably because he believed that others would be able to see clearly that it was the mayor's Daimler, complete with mayoral flags and a peaked cap driver, driving along with his very important passengers. But on this occasion, Arthur dispensed with the formalities and drove at a fairly high speed, with Pam and me holding firmly to the arm rests and praying that nothing would suddenly emerge from the opposite direction.

Thankfully, no traffic came along and we arrived at the gate set aside for the VIP guests, 'shaken but not stirred' I would say, as we stepped out to shake the hands of our hosts.

It was the first time Pam and I had been to an Air Show, so the number of planes on show was impressive – many belonging to continental air forces as well as planes with the famous red, white and blue circles.

Following lunch, we were informed by our host that the arrival, for the first time in the United Kingdom, of the semi-secret American F111 aircraft, was imminent. We were invited to go to the balcony to witness the arrival of the plane. We trained our eyes across the sky because we had been told that we would be unable to hear its approach to the airfield. And then came a voice from an official, with a finger pointing to the sky, saying "there it is", which prompted everyone to look in the same direction. There it was, a small black spot in the sky, and before anyone could say anything, this massive black aircraft came smoothly into sight without a sound being made, and landed perfectly on the runway.

We were lucky in one respect, because the aircraft, after the usual procedures, then taxied and came to rest just a few yards from the VIP lounge. The silent flight and the black aircraft were an awesome sight and well worth the unusually hectic drive to the Fairford Air Show.

Cheltenham Borough Council, with the support of the Cheltenham Chamber of Commerce, ran a competition for the local primary schools. The children were asked to let their imaginations 'run riot', and to come forward with ideas of environmentally friendly ways of travelling to school.

Children aged between five and eight had taken green transport as their theme for a "Walking to School Competition" and they designed posters showing new ways of getting to and from school.

Children between the ages of nine and eleven were invited to write stories or poems about why they liked walking to their school in the town.

The *Gloucestershire Echo* which covered the competition with a caption: "Taking Steps to be Greener", reported that "Leckhampton Primary School had swept the board in the awards, and six children have been invited to have tea with the mayor in the parlour." I looked forward to these occasions because they fitted in with my desire to open up the parlour to as many people as possible. Children always show an excitement that is unequalled by older visitors, so Monday 21st July was a special day for me and Pam.

I welcomed the children to the parlour and talked to them about the answers they had given in the competition. Six year old William Poll, who came second in the competition, said: *"I watched Newsround and they said that pigs are intelligent animals so I decided to do a pig. It could take you to school and then it could eat all the scraps from the canteen."*

Francesca Clarke, nine, who won joint first prize in her age group, said: *"I did a long poem about walking to school and how the driving of cars starts me coughing and the air gets dirty."*

It was a real pleasure having tea with three boys and three girl pupils – just listening to what they thought about their schools and the town in which they lived was both refreshing and interesting. Following the tea with the children, the *Echo* wanted a photograph of me with them "taking steps to be greener" along the road outside the Municipal Offices. We practised the walk until we got it right and they loved the attention that was being given to them.

As I said farewell, I reminded them to go on being 'as green as possible' and they all assured me that they would do so.

An early call from Arthur the chauffeur at 8.15 a.m. on Tuesday 22nd July was the start of a long day for Pam and me, and for our two fellow travellers.

Pupils William and James Poll, Alex and Laura Bilas, Sarah Hawkins and Frances Clark from Leckhamptom Primary Scool, join me in a 'Walk to School' campaign in July 1997

At a council meeting each year, the name of a councillor is drawn by the mayor, which entitles the councillor and spouse to accompany the Mayor and Mayoress to the Royal Garden Party in the grounds of Buckingham Palace.

In 1997, Councillor Chris Read was the successful councillor, and with his wife Ann accompanied us to London for this special event.

To make the day even more special, Nigel Jones MP, the Member of Parliament for Cheltenham, later to become Lord Jones, arranged to meet us outside the main door of the House of Commons in the morning, to show us around both Houses of Parliament.

Both the Commons and the House of Lords hold a fascination for most people; to be inside them is a wonderful feeling from the start. The history of the place becomes overwhelming – I didn't know, for example, that the first palace of Westminster was the home of the Kings of England until fire destroyed much of it in 1512. It was after the fire that it became the home of Parliament; around the corner are the Royal Courts of Justice and Westminster Hall.

The architecture and the paintings alone are worth a visit, and there are plenty of other interesting memorabilia to hold one's attention. According to the history books, another fire in 1834 did immense damage; the only buildings to survive were Westminster Hall, the Cloisters of St. Stephen's, the Chapel of St Mary Undercroft and the Jewel Tower. The rebuilding of the palaces did not start until 1840 and it

Chris Read, his wife Ann, Pam and me attending a Buckingham Palace garden party in 1998

took thirty years to complete: the reconstruction of the Commons Chamber following the bombing raid in 1941 took far less time.

The Palaces of Westminster and the Elizabeth Tower (Big Ben) in particular, are iconic landmarks of London – the seat of democracy.

When we arrived at the House of Commons, Arthur, who had done the trip many times before, drew up near the front of the building. The place was teeming with tourists, sightseers and London people going about their business. Before we had chance to open the doors, a burly policeman poked his head through the window of the limousine and said, "You can't park there", and told us to move on.

Arthur, unperturbed explained to the policeman in his most official voice that the Mayor of Cheltenham was visiting the House of Commons, and before he could say another word the policeman blurted out once more: "I don't care who you have in the car – you can't park here."

In the circumstances, we got out of the car as quickly as possible, and I gave Arthur a place to pick us up after the visit, and off he went before the policeman could come back again.

It wasn't a problem as far as I was concerned – the policeman was doing his job, which included keeping the road free of parked vehicles even for a short period of time.

The visit was a wonderful experience, and thanks to Nigel Jones, we enjoyed a pleasant lunch on the well-known terrace of the House of Commons.

Buckingham Palace in the afternoon was far less exciting; Arthur drove us to The Mall and parked some distance from the palace. In his most apologetic voice he explained that it was the best he could do. Apparently, it was more or less the same parking place where he had parked the Daimler when he had brought previous mayors to the Royal Garden Party.

I asked him what he was going to do whilst we were in the Palace, because our pick-up time was not until 6.30 p.m., but he told us not to worry, he would do what he always did, in other words, he would follow the same routine that he had always done, take a little walk, but always with the car in his sight.

As we walked along The Mall, there were dozens of people in smart clothes making the same journey. When we reached Buckingham Palace we saw two exceptionally long queues of smartly dressed people, waiting to enter the palace grounds through the two main gates. We chose the shorter of the two queues, which turned out to be the quickest route for getting into the palace grounds. Once inside, one is reminded that photographs are not allowed.

Guests are directed to walk through one of the ornate palace rooms that lead to French windows and into the palace garden. Once there, you become one of a thousand other invitees all herded together in a section of the garden, which had a fenced off area where we would be able to see Her Majesty walking to a very large marquee in a corner of the garden. There she would meet former prime ministers, high commissioners and other VIP's.

For the visitors –bishops, high sheriffs, mayors, councillors, and specially invited people who had done sterling voluntary work in their communities, there were smaller marquees, where tea and minute sandwiches were served.

It soon became clear that we were not going to have tea with the Queen.

It also became clear that the thirty or so seats that had been made available were totally inadequate for the number of people attending the garden party. Gentlemen, some with top hats, and their ladies in expensive dresses, soon succumbed to the tiredness brought on by standing too long, sat on the grass, in dread of spoiling their delightful outfits.

Thankfully, it was a beautiful summer's day, and apart from a few creased dresses, the visitors gave the impression that they were enjoying their day at Buckingham Palace.

The word went around that Her Majesty would be coming out of Buckingham Palace to meet her VIP's in the large marquee – did this mean she would walk across to meet her subjects? Some had travelled long journeys to be at the garden party. On reflection, it would have been a bit too much to expect.

Once the move to the fence started, I found myself along with others walking swiftly to the fence in anticipation that I might see the Queen.

Pam, Ann, Chris and I had a good view of the marquee and we saw the VIP's arrive, some recognisable, some not; the Queen emerged from the palace surrounded by her retinue, and walked to the marquee. A pair of binoculars would have come in useful, but no doubt these would have been included in the list of things banned before you entered the palace grounds. A three hour wait on uncomfortable grass, eating tiny cucumber sandwiches and drinking weak tea, is not usually my idea of a usefully spent afternoon – unless of course, one added that a glimpse of the Queen some 500 yards away, heading for a marquee entrance, was sufficient compensation for aching legs and a sore backside.

Around five o'clock in the evening people started to make for the entrances to go home; we had time to spare so Chris, Ann, Pam and I decided to walk around the nearby woodland area, where I noticed several picnic points. It was pleasant but not outstanding, and it did pass away the time.

We came across a policeman while we were walking along the woodland path, but when we made for one of the exits there was no-one to see us leave. I did wonder about the level of security on days with a Royal Garden Party, but I noticed the exit gates were one-way only, so the Palace grounds were reasonably secure.

We knew Arthur would be early, he was noted for it, and sure enough he was there by the limousine at the same point in The Mall where he had left us four hours earlier.

Arthur, always the perfect gentleman, asked us whether we had enjoyed the visit to Buckingham Palace, and showed no emotions and gave no comment when we said words such as: "It was all right, but we would not go again."

In answer to our questions, Arthur admitted he had not done a lot during the afternoon, other than a walk around the area where he had parked the car. We didn't press him, but Arthur's loyalty and his personal protection of the mayoral car meant that he would not have let the car out of his sight. He also looked very tired; perhaps he had been 'standing guard' over the car, which would have explained it.

Once we were settled in the car Arthur began the long journey back to Cheltenham. Getting across London and on to the A40 is a tortuous journey at the best of times – at 6.30 in the evening it is not good. However, as we came to the wide section of the road by Hyde Park, Arthur slowed down and then finally came to a halt. He reached across to the drinks cabinet and produced four glasses and a bottle of Merlot red wine and poured it gently into the glasses – what a gem of a chauffeur.

After the weak tea and cucumber sandwiches a few hours earlier, this could not have been more welcome. But before the first sip had been taken, a police car drove up behind us and two tough-looking policemen got out and went to the front of the car. They then took a look at the four passengers in their fine clothes, and started to put questions to Arthur.

Poor Arthur, he usually suffered from a ruddy complexion, but on this occasion it was even ruddier. We could hear him explaining the circumstances to the policemen as only Arthur could do; it worked and with a little salute from one of the policemen, we continued our journey back to Cheltenham.

As we approached Oxford along an open part of the countryside, the limousine suddenly swerved to the left and mounted the grass verge – "Arthur" I shouted as the car righted itself – "what are you doing?" I asked. Arthur was full of apology and assured me that everything was now all right. He had fallen asleep at the wheel, which had momentarily scared his four passengers; the consequences could have been more serious.

It had been a memorable day in more ways than one, but Pam and I were glad to get home safe and sound, and no doubt Arthur, after his sackcloth and ashes performance as we stepped out of the Daimler, slept well that night too.

I had received a letter from Penny Holton, the managing director of the local radio station *Severn Sound*, who wanted to meet me, as she put it, as a matter of urgency. I wondered what the 'urgency' could be about and invited Penny to the parlour. She told me that she and her *Severn Sound* colleagues liked what they had been reading in the local papers about me and the various events with which I had been involved. She told me that *Severn Sound* wanted to help raise money for my charities and to give me support whenever they could.

It was very good news indeed. Listening to Penny and the advice she was offering, I knew she would make sure that everything associated with my events and my public engagements would be aired on the *Severn Sound Radio*. But, more importantly, having Penny and members of her team helping my charity committee was an unexpected bonus for us.

We spoke about the impending 'Mayor's Charity Fashion Show' at the Town Hall, and Penny immediately indicated that she would like her radio station to get involved with this event. When I asked what she had in mind, she offered the services of her top radio presenter, who had recently joined *Severn Sound*, who would do the introductions and the interviews throughout the evening.

I could not believe what I was hearing; I knew my charity committee would be delighted at the prospect of such professional coverage of the Fashion Show from the popular local radio station. I reported the good news to my charity committee and just as I expected, they were delighted with the news.

The Cheltenham Fashion Show seemed to have taken on a new level of excite-ment with the charity committee members – but what was the *Severn Sound* input going to be. A further meeting with *Severn Sound* representatives was needed so that the committee, and particularly Pam Thomas, could arrange the programme of events including the opening ceremony introduced by the 'top radio presenter'.

Before she left the parlour, Penny Holton told me that I would be formally invited to attend the 'Severn Sound Cricket Day' at the Cheltenham Cricket Festival on Friday 25th July. She hoped I would be able to accept the invitation.

I had already accepted an invitation to visit the Gloucestershire Cricket Club marquee on Wednesday 23rd July to meet the players, as well as receiving an invita-tion from Cllr John Todman to host the Cheltenham Borough Council Cricket Day on the following day. Three days of cricket at the Cheltenham College was not going to be an ordeal by any means and I looked forward to the period of relaxation.

Even with the best of intentions I was never going to be able to watch three days of continuous cricket at the College ground. The usual schedule of meetings had been arranged by my PA, which included meeting the Board of Directors of the Cheltenham Arts Festival at 2.30 p.m. on 25th July.

Their enthusiasm at this meeting was not in short supply as they explained in minute detail their programme of events in the autumn. Their proposal that I should greet the main sponsors and performers before each event came as no surprise. It was a pleasure to be part of this national event, because that is what it was becoming, and in later years the Cheltenham Festival Week became internationally famous.

A quick lunch and back to the *Severn Sound* cricket day for a few more hours before going through the detail of the arrival plans for our guests from Gottingen.

Cheltenham has been twinned with Gottingen, a town in Lower Saxony, since 1951. The visits between the two towns started in 1976 and they take place every two years alternating between Cheltenham and Gottingen.

Music is an important part of the twinning exchange and it is often celebrated with a summer concert where singers and musicians from both towns perform throughout the festival week.

Annette Wight has been the CBC twinning officer for many years and she is exceptionally good at her job. Annette organises everything associated with a twinning visit; arranging accommodation; organising numerous visits around the Cotswolds; and making sure the mayor of Cheltenham is fully briefed with everything that is planned for the visit.

I met the leading members of the Gottingen council and we talked about many things of common interest as well as their schedule of events in and around Cheltenham. The following day I would be hosting a "Welcoming Lunch" in the Town Hall for our visitors, so it was important for me to try to learn from them a little bit about their backgrounds.

The Mayor of Gottingen, Herr Oberburgermeister Dr Rainer Kallman and his wife Frau Kallman were very friendly people and Pam and I enjoyed their company on several occasions during their visit. He was a prominent member in the German SPD party and I was anxious to know how he thought they would fare in the forthcoming German elections. He was confident the SPD would do well, but he thought the new Green Party would spoil their chances of an outright victory.

The lunch was held in the Pillar Room for the senior members of the Gottingen party so I had taken every care to ensure I said the right thing for the occasion. This is an extract from my speech:

> "Cheltenham is particularly proud of its links with Gottingen and there is a very significant and deep relationship between the two towns which does not end when the 'big party visit' ends; it continues in all kinds of ways throughout the year. The youth sports exchange and the exchanges between schools and other groups are in many ways the most valuable and tangible aspects of friendships which have grown up between our two towns.

Cheltenham is anxious to build on the existing link and to develop closer business and economic links, so I am pleased that the Cheltenham Chamber of Commerce is supporting your visit to the town. I know there will be an opportunity for some of the officers from Gottingen to meet with the Chamber of Commerce members and a number of local employers, and that is good to hear."

I ended my speech by thanking the host families for their generous hospitality.

Later that day there was the formal civic welcome to all our German guests, which was also an opportunity for the officers from both councils to exchange formal greetings, but also to learn about the running of each other's councils.

On Sunday 27th July, I started the Race for Life event at the Prince of Wales Stadium in Tommy Taylors Lane. The event had only been going for a few years so I was more than pleased to boost its long term ambitions to be one of Cheltenham's most sought after events each year.

In fact, it is not a race, because the participants can run, jog or even walk, providing they take the opportunity to get sponsorships and raise money for cancer relief. It was one of my easier tasks as mayor and a delight to be part of it. The Cheltenham Race for Life now attracts thousands of women to the Cheltenham Racecourse each year a more suitable venue for the event because of the large number of women who now participate.

Monday there was a special meeting in the council offices to discuss a report by Michael Smith, Head of Engineering Services, on the future of the Royal Well bus station. Mr Smith reported that there were several options to be considered including knocking it down. The committee was told that several thousand pounds of council taxpayers' money had already been spent on replacing smashed glass and painting over graffiti. They were also told that a further £3,000 would be spent on the shelter in the next three weeks. Mr Smith reported that he would be presenting a report to the Environment Committee on 15th September 1997 when a decision should be taken to demolish the bus station and landscape the area.

The *Gloucestershire Echo,* in their report of the meeting on August 1st, said that the mayor was delighted with the news and offered to "take a sledgehammer to it" adding, "he believes it should be removed as soon as possible and the Royal Crescent opened up."

The Echo also reported the three following comments:

"Cllr John Todman, Leader of the Conservative Group shared the mayor's view that the shelter was an eyesore and we should get rid of it."

Cllr Alistair Cameron, Leader of the Liberal Democrats said: "It detracts from the town. We've got to decide whether to knock it down, knock part of it down or improve it." (No change in the Lib/Dem thinking here).

Cllr Pat Thornton (Lib/Dem) mayor of Cheltenham in 1996, threatened "To ride naked (Lady Godiva style) through the town if Cllr Godwin succeeded in getting the Royal Well bus station demolished."

It seemed a rather drastic announcement to make, and if it was meant to be a serious threat to stop what many local people wanted, then I didn't think it would work. I only hoped that the spectacle of a councillor riding naked on the back of a horse wasn't a greater incentive for people to watch rather than watch the demolition of the dilapidated bus station.

Should the Environment Committee decide at the meeting in November to demolish the bus station in spite of the threat from Cllr Thornton, then the actual removal would not take place until 1998. I hoped the demolition would happen before my mayoral year ended.

Tuesday morning I visited the Whitbread Brewery site with senior members of the Gottingen party. From there we travelled to the Cheltenham public library where I opened the "People, Books and Libraries" Exhibition.

In my speech I welcomed Dr Kallman and his friends from Gottingen. This is an extract of my speech:

> "The exhibition is based on the important part which books and libraries play in our lives. Cheltenham is very proud of its library and this building is always one of the most significant features of the town centre. It is also the home of our art gallery and museum and the location of these two important facilities close together provide a focal point for many cultural activities in Cheltenham.
>
> Libraries play an essential part in the lives of so many people, not only providing reading for pleasure, but also for being an education and information centre. And ladies and gentlemen, the theme of the Exhibition, which we are opening today, follows very closely this role and emphasises its importance to everyone.
>
> There will be an opportunity for everyone in Cheltenham to visit the Exhibition, as well as our guests from Gottingen, throughout the coming week."

In the evening, Pam and I were invited to Hoopers Department Store in the Promenade for what the company called their "Summer Garden Party", which was a publicity occasion for the business community. It was a pleasant summer evening. The gardens to the rear of the premises were over-flowing with guests. It was an informal and convivial occasion.

On Wednesday morning I met a group of Japanese teachers and students in the parlour who were visiting the local education centres, including the Japanese colleges located in the town.

The visit of our friends from Gottingen was drawing to a close and on Thursday 31st July, I watched two teams from Cheltenham and Gottingen compete in an athletics challenge match at the Prince of Wales stadium.

In the evening the Borough Council gave a 'Farewell Dinner' for the German visitors at the Frogmill Inn, Andoversford, which is six miles from Cheltenham. It was a good choice of venue by Annette Wight the Twinning Officer, because the Frogmill Inn is quintessentially Cotswold, with a heritage dating as far back as the Domesday Book. The Inn is full of charm, and no doubt its log-fires in the winter, and the garden in the summer with a small stream trickling through it, attract many visitors throughout the year. The restaurant is well designed – modern but without losing its historical charm.

In many ways it was a sad occasion, because the week had been highly successful. The German party had visited several Cotswold villages, participated in council matters and made many new friends during their visit. Because the farewell dinner at the Frogmill Inn was special, in as much as I would probably never be asked to give a farewell speech to any twinning guests in the future; I took extra care when writing my speech.

The following is an extract from it:

"Herr Oberburgermeister Dr Kallman, friends from Gottingen, fellow councillors, ladies and gentlemen.

We have spent many days this week greeting each other, enjoying each other's company, enjoying our town and the beautiful surrounding countryside – and at times, we have had the most stimulating conversations about our respective towns.

As I recall, we have sorted out the problems of the European Community on more than one occasion, and put the problems of the world into its proper perspective within the space of one evening.

But the overriding theme for the Mayoress and me throughout this week, has been the warm friendship of the Gottingen 'Big Party' delegation, which has been extended not only to us, but to the Borough Council and to the people of Cheltenham.

I now speak for everyone on the Cheltenham side, the host families, all those who have been involved with your visit, how delighted we are that you have been our guests, how much we have enjoyed your company, and how much we look forward to seeing you all again in the not too distant future.

Have a safe and enjoyable journey back home to your loved ones in Deutschland – Meine Frau und ich sie aller vermissen."

I managed the German farewell with the help of Annette Wight, and it was well received.

The following day I was at the coach station to say goodbye to our German friends – it was not an easy time for most people, but the photographs of the week and the subsequent letters, will be a constant reminder to Pam and me of a memorable week in July 1997.

Saturday, 2nd August, Pam and I listened to an evening of music by the Church-down Male Voice Choir in Gloucester Cathedral.

Sunday morning we visited St. Mary's De Crypt Church in Southgate Street, Gloucester, to commemorate 300 years of the Gloucestershire Regiment. It is an Anglican church and it was first recorded in 1140, and played an important part in the history of Gloucester. The original Crypt School adjacent to the church, was founded in 1539, and the old school room still exists, but the school is now located in another part of the city.

Among the other information that was given to us during our tour of the church, was that during the siege of Gloucester in the First English Civil War

(1643), the church was used as an ammunition factory. There are many Norman features even though the church was rebuilt and extended in the latter part of the 14th century.

On Monday 4th August I paid a visit to the International Youth Camp where I met young people from Germany, Poland and the United Kingdom; on Tuesday Pam and I attended the Cheltenham Town Hall to hear the National Youth Orchestra of Wales playing to a packed hall.

My duties on Thursday 7th August took me to Bristol for an interview about a television programme: a rush back to Cheltenham for a visit to the King George V sports field to watch young sportsmen compete in a fun day; in the evening, Pam and I held a reception in the parlour for a group of Americans from the American Embassy in London.

The reception was memorable for a number of reasons. The Special United States Liaison Officer, Jim Neam, and his wife Pam, were the friendliest couple we had met for some time. They were kind and considerate, and we got on fine throughout the evening.

Jim in his 'thank you' speech admitted that he had done his research before coming to Cheltenham, and he was intrigued to meet the mayor of a town who was against bureaucracy. "He had spent some time looking at the PAB website", he told the other guests, "and it sounded like something he could be at ease with."

That was a relief, for me at least, and Jim had chosen just the right words to put everyone in the good mood that a drinks reception requires.

As I recall, it was one of those evenings where everyone wanted the evening to go on forever, but like all good things it had to come to an end, even though it was well into the night.

Within 24 hours, I received a hand-written letter from Jim Neam; this is what he wrote:

"Dear Mr Mayor,

Pam and I thoroughly enjoyed last night's social and the opportunity to talk to you and your wife and to deepen our knowledge of Cheltenham. The hospitality we experienced on this occasion is among the most cherished experiences of our forty months in this wonderful country.

As I mentioned to you last night (perhaps more than once) the Americans on my staff were delighted to be part of the occasion and, this morning, several told me how special they feel to have been included.

Pam and I wish you and Pam continuing success and enjoyment in your roles as Cheltenham's Mr Mayor and Mrs Mayor. It is a lovely town and its many wonderful attributes are surely enhanced by your gift of making people feel special and welcome.

Thank you again, from all of us, for a lovely evening.

Sincerely,

Jim Neam.

With all the good things that were happening during my mayoral year, it was inevitable that a tragedy of one sort or another would occur.

Maggie Hanson, my PA, informed me that Malcolm Brewer, a well-known Cheltenham & County Harriers athletics coach, who was the father of three children, had suffered a heart attack and died on Boxing Day 1996. Malcolm had been taking part in the Sue Ryder Fun day with his two children Jo and James.

Maggie told me that John Anderson, the chairman of the athletics club, wanted to talk to me about a memorial event for Malcolm, which he hoped would include a contribution from me.

It sounded very much as though it was something which a mayor should become involved with, and my PA arranged for John Anderson to come to the parlour for a discussion.

I had met John at other sporting events, but this was the first time we had met in what was a semi-formal occasion. John briefly explained to me that the Cheltenham & County Harriers was a long-standing athletics club. It was founded in 1880 with no established home until they were given a base at the Prince of Wales stadium in 1981. John told me that Malcolm Brewer had been the under-15's athletics coach and that he had intended to run in the London Marathon in 1997. The news of his death had shocked the Cheltenham Harriers Club and the club's management committee were anxious to provide a lasting memorial and tribute to Malcolm in the most appropriate way.

John explained that as Malcolm was training for the London Marathon when the tragedy happened, the committee thought they should arrange their own version of the world-famous event, where the runners would be sponsored and the money raised would go to Malcolm's favourite charity – Winston's Wish. That sounded fine to me.

Additionally, a silver birch tree would be planted in his honour, and a memorial plaque would be unveiled at a special event in the Prince of Wales stadium on Saturday 9th August when the last of the marathon runners had completed the course. I didn't hesitate in saying that I would be there even though I knew that it would mean altering my schedule for that day.

The *Gloucestershire Echo* had already published a splendid article with the headline "Marathon tribute to tragic Malcolm". The article written by Ken McCormick said "The event would attract 500 people to the charity run", and added, "that some of the runners would attempt to run the whole of the 26 miles and 385 yards, whilst others would do it in relays, and some would just do a few circuits of the Prince of Wales track."

Heather Brewer, Malcolm's widow said, *"The event has been done in his spirit. It is a fitting tribute. Our children are taking part in the run and they are trying to rope me in too. Malcolm would have approved of people who didn't usually take part in athletics being given a taste. He very much felt that athletics was for everybody."*

The *Echo* followed up their story by announcing a few nights later that I would be attending the marathon event, and I would be unveiling a plaque in memory of athletics coach Malcolm Brewer in the evening. The article urged as many people as possible to attend to pay tribute to Malcolm Brewer.

The weather on Saturday 9th August was very good – for those who came to watch, but a tad too warm for those who took part in the run. It was very much a family day out for many local people and a friendly atmosphere existed throughout the day. I met several of my sporting colleagues at the stadium, who tried their best to make me do a run around the track, but I resisted their persistent temptations.

When the last of the runners had returned to the stadium I was invited to unveil the plaque. In doing so I made the following comments:

> "It gives me great pleasure to be here today to pay tribute to a great sportsman as well as a good husband and a great family man. Whilst many people will remember Malcolm as an ordinary guy, interested in all kinds of sports, we all knew that his real passion was for athletics, and his particular passion for the sport was shown in his energetic zeal he put into the task of being club coach to the under-fifteen year old athletes.
>
> Malcolm knew that the successful coaching of young people was essential if the Cheltenham & County Harriers were to compete with the best in an ever-increasing popular sport. I think he did this exceedingly well and the proof of that is that the club now has over 450 members, and after 117 years is still in good shape for the years ahead.
>
> And ladies and gentlemen, I wouldn't be at all surprised if that famous Malcolm Brewer smile is still smiling down on us today and wondering what all the fuss is about – but if you are watching Malcolm – on behalf of all the people here, I have to tell you that we all miss you very much.
>
> Mr chairman, I applaud the Cheltenham & County Harriers for deciding to make the Cheltenham Games the Malcolm Brewer Games – it is a fitting tribute to a great man who sadly died early in his life, yet filled his short life with more commitment and dedication to the sport he loved than most people achieve in a lifetime.
>
> The effort that Malcolm put into his coaching of the under 15 year olds should be an inspiration to all you young athletes to go out and win for Malcolm.
>
> It gives me great pleasure and enormous pride to unveil this plaque in memory of a great man and a truly great sportsman."

The speech had been relayed outside to the stadium and it received a rapturous roar of approval, which was very satisfying.

I am pleased to record that having met a rather sad nine year old James Brewer that day in August 1997; he is now a successful local, national, and international athlete. Among his many successes, he won the World Indoor Champions Trials 800 metres in 2007; a silver medal at the European U23 Championships 1500 metres in 2009. He has been one of Cheltenham's most successful local athletes in recent times, and his father would have been mightily proud of him.

Cheltenham has always been a popular place for Japanese tourists to visit. During my mayoral year, Pam and I entertained several groups of visitors from Japan in the parlour, or in one of the council's committee rooms. They seemed to be interested in everything British, local government in particular.

I always took the opportunity to invite them to visit the council chamber, and it always excited them. I would invite them to sit in the councillors' seats and the more adventurous ones would take turns sitting in the mayor's seat. And, of course, the Japanese made their digital cameras work overtime, much to my fascination because they were not in common use in the United Kingdom in 1997. The visit to the council chamber always brought a nod of approval as each one left the chamber with a 'thank you' Japanese style.

I entertained two large groups on Monday and Tuesday 11th and 12th August, and at the end of the second day a very young Japanese girl whose name was Naoki Seki, asked me if I would mind receiving a letter from her when she returned to Japan. I told her that I would be delighted to hear from her, not believing for one moment that the occasion would be remembered, but I was wrong. Within two weeks I received a letter from Naoki telling me how much she enjoyed meeting me, and that she had written long accounts of her visit to Cheltenham and meeting the mayor in her class essays.

Later on, I learned that Naoki had qualified as a dentist.

Two other important meetings took place in mid-August: – I met Les Burgess the well-known teacher of music, and, shortly afterwards Darren Stevens, thePublic Relations Manager of the Chelsea Building Society (CBS). The *Echo* once described Les Burgess as "one of the finest trumpet and cornet soloists of his generation."

Les had been the Director of Music and conductor of the Cotswold Male Voice Choir for twenty years. His talents knew no bounds, he was in demand as a trumpeter and played in the Morris Motors Band, the Cheltenham Silver Band, and he formed a Brass Consort called the Cotswold Orchestra. Les also established the Cheltenham Youth Brass, which still thrives to this day. He was a lyricist and a versatile composer, and his creation of the Cotswold Song, which he dedicated to the Cotswold Choir, is still their signature tune to this day.

One of Les Burgess's many achievements was the formation of the link with the Band of the Life Guards, which led to an annual series of sell-out concerts in the Town Hall, raising thousands of pounds for local and national charities. Of course, Les had not come to see me about his past record of achievements, but to offer any help that he and the Cotswold Male Voice Choir could give to support my charities.

My good luck continued the following day when I met Darren Stevens. He explained to me that CBS had relocated their Head Office from London to Cheltenham in 1970 and since that time they had played an increasingly active role in the local community in and around Cheltenham. Darren was responsible for CBS's sponsorship programme and he was a firm believer in the value of businesses and their employees putting something back in the communities.

"Chelsea" he said "were impressed with the high profile events the mayor had supported, and 1997 was a particularly significant year for CBS because it marked the 25th anniversary of their move to Cheltenham."

With the Fashion Show fast approaching, Darren was anxious for CBS to become involved with this and other events that were being discussed and formulated with those who would play a large part in the events during the rest of the mayoral year.

To have so many people wanting to become part of my year in so many different ways never ceased to amaze me. Once again, I had met someone who was so full of enthusiasm and ready to support me and my charities, I really could not believe my good luck.

I visited the Art Gallery and Museum early on Thursday morning 14th August; I attended a party for Senior Citizens in the Women's Institute Hall, Prestbury, on Saturday, and in between these times, Pam and I met members of various local organisations engaged in local charity work.

My events programme prepared by Maggie Handson for the week commencing 18th August, looked, at first glance, to be lighter than usual, but I had forgotten that with my agreement, Maggie would arrange for different local people to come to the parlour for a coffee in the mornings, or tea and cakes in the afternoon.

I entertained the Annecy School Exchange students on Monday, and went over the details with Simon Lee regarding the Heart of England Awards event that was due to take place in the Town Hall on Friday, 5th September.

In the afternoon I met Chinese students who wanted to meet me, and look around the council building.

On Wednesday, I was invited to Silks of Cheltenham in the Montpellier Courtyard. They are specialists in providing high quality designer formal women's wear and they were celebrating their 10th anniversary in the fashion business. The owners of the shop were keen to have me there, complete with my mayoral chain of office, and although I felt a little trepidation about accepting the invitation, I thought it would be churlish for me not to accept it, particularly as I had been gaining a reputation in business circles for supporting small businesses across the town.

The visit turned out to be a repeat of what I had previously done during my day in the Tourist Office, except of course, the shop was open that day to sell ladies' fashion clothes, as well as for anyone wanting to wish the owners well on their 10th anniversary, and share a glass of wine with them. Many ladies came to me for a chat, not about the clothes I might add, but to ask me questions about my role as mayor and to wish me well. On 28th August, I received a lovely letter from Anne Forsyth, who with her business partner Susan Hayes, set up the shop in 1987.

This is an extract from Anne's letter:

"I would like to thank you once again for all your support and kindness when we celebrated our 10th Anniversary on Wednesday 20th August.

You made the day extremely special, not only by giving such a super speech, drawing the prizes, but also by spending so much of your precious time talking to our clients. Sue and I very much appreciated all your help and I must say that without you the day would not have been such a success."

Now in its 27th year, Silks of Cheltenham is still a thriving business in the town.

On Saturday 23rd August Pam and I were invited to the "Raise the Flag" celebration at the Indian Club in Cheltenham. It was a celebration by the local Indian community of their homelands 50 years of independence. The welcome was warm and friendly, and we enjoyed the Indian fun that was put on for our benefit, and the excellent food that was being provided. It was an informal occasion with many local families, both Indian and English, relishing the food, the music and the entertainment. With the invitation had come a request from the organiser that the mayor should say a few words when the 'raising of the flag' took place. It was not an unusual request and I said:

"I am delighted to be here today to celebrate with you 50 years of independence of the Indian sub-continent.

Whilst it is right and proper that we should be celebrating the actual day of independence 50 years ago today, we should never forget that independence is not the act of signing a treaty and expecting everything to be different the following day, for we all know it doesn't happen that way – independence is like a marriage, you have to work at it to make it successful and long-lasting.

50 years is a long time, and you have made it successful and long-lasting; the celebrations today should also be an occasion to remember those who gave their lives in order to achieve the independence of the Indian sub-continent.

It is a real pleasure for me as mayor of Cheltenham to join with Gloucester City Council, the Gloucestershire County Library, arts and museum service, together with the local communities from India, Pakistan and Bangladesh, to be part of the marvellous programme of events throughout Gloucestershire in support of the European year against racism, anti-Semitism and xenophobia.

Our world is shrinking all the time and we are becoming closer to each other, we must therefore, all of us, people of all nations across the globe, rid ourselves of all the xenophobic tendencies and work towards a long-lasting peace.

We must understand that all communities have their own way of life, their own language, their own religion and culture; nothing will change it.

Providing we understand that fundamental point, then we will all benefit from the many different cultures which have enriched not only local communities, but communities throughout the United Kingdom.

There is a special relationship between India, Pakistan, Bangladesh and the United Kingdom – may it long continue in a loving, peaceful and friendly way."

The following day, Pam and I were up early in order to attend the opening of the Cheltenham and Gloucester Blind Bowls Club Tournament. Unfortunately, the weather on that Sunday morning was awful. It had started raining the previous evening and it was non-stop for most of the day. When we arrived the ground was saturated; the organisers were doing their best to 'mop up' in case the rain relented and allowed play to take place.

In my speech I referred to it being the monsoon season and assured those present that it wasn't always like this in Cheltenham. I told them that Pam and I were delighted to be at the Bowls Club, not only to start the Blind Club's annual tournament, but also to be present among so many talented sports players from a wide area. I added:

"To be able to attract blind and visually handicapped bowls players from all over the West Country and from South Wales to a friendly bowls competition in Cheltenham, speaks volumes about the importance of such a club. It also indicates to me that all of you here today, by your presence, want to show your appreciation to Joy Jervis for starting this club 11 years ago, and making it the happy and successful club which it is today.

I have been involved with sport all my life and it saddens me to read that during the last 10 years over 5,000 sport and recreation grounds in the United Kingdom have been lost to developers.

How on earth can we hope to compete with the world's best if this trend is allowed to continue?

On behalf of Cheltenham Borough Council I warmly welcome you all to our town – enjoy your stay here – have a good and happy tournament, in spite of the weather, and I look forward to being with you again later when the prizes are awarded."

The Cheltenham Blind Club membership has dwindled over recent years, but in spite of the low numbers they continue to meet whenever they can.

Joy Jervis was awarded a MBE for her work with the disabled in 2004.

Bank Holiday Monday, 25th August, was a reasonably quiet day with only a visit to the Parklands Community Centre in Whaddon Road to attend their annual fete.

Wednesday, Pam and I enjoyed a friendly informal social evening at the Cheltenham Playhouse in Bath Road.

On Friday, I made another visit to the Prince of Wales stadium to support the Cheltenham and County Harriers Spar Track awards for young athletes.

During Sunday, 31st August 1997, the nation and the world heard that Diana, Princess of Wales, had died as a result of injuries sustained in a car crash in the Pont de l'Alma road tunnel in Paris the previous day. Her boyfriend, Dodi Fayed, and the driver of the car Henri Paul, had also died in the crash.

I was returning to Cheltenham following a visit to the Severn Sound studios in Gloucester when the news was broadcast to the nation.

My engagement at the Cirencester Park Polo Club in the afternoon was immediately cancelled, and the rest of the day, as I recall, was a period of shock for everyone.

Monday morning 1st September, I met reporters and radio interviewers who wanted my reaction to the death, and to know what steps I would be taking to enable local people to respond and to show their respects following the death of Diana. I told them that Tim Harman, the council's public relations officer, had arranged for a Book of Condolence to be made available in the Reception area of the Municipal

Offices that morning and the book would remain open until Monday 8th September. They were also told that a Memorial Service would be held in St. Matthew's Church as soon as it could be arranged.

With the help of the *Gloucestershire Echo* and the local radio stations, I invited everyone in the town to join me in bringing a candle to plant in the Promenade gardens on Saturday evening; I would also arrange for my chaplain, the Reverend Canon Stephen Gregory, to open proceedings from the steps of the Municipal Offices with prayers at 9.00 p.m.

After the prayers, I would invite members of the public to follow my example and plant their candles in the Long Garden in front of the Municipal Offices. I told the reporters that they could report in their newspapers that candles would be available free of charge for anyone unable to provide their own. The Press and radio reporters were satisfied with my short statement and they promised to cover the evening ceremony on Saturday 6th September.

Long before nine o'clock on the Saturday evening, hundreds of residents from all parts of the town started to gather in front of the Municipal Offices. They listened to Father Stephen Gregory lead the prayers for Diana, and for the families and friends of those who had died with her. This is what he said: *"Diana had touched the lives of so many, the sick, the dying, the needy, young and old, and those who are sometimes on the margin of society."*

Father Stephen then led the mourners in saying the Lord's Prayer before Elton John's poignant tribute song Candle in the Wind was played. I placed my candle in the garden and this was followed by an orderly procession of people who followed me to the garden. The council had arranged for solemn music to be relayed until 11.00 p.m.

"It was a sombre occasion and people wanted to be silent and think about everything that Diana represented. Clearly, she will be missed by everyone, and I think it was right that Cheltenham people should show their respects in this way", I told the reporters.

The *Gloucestershire Echo* covered the Promenade vigil, and the article by Paul Stimpson covered the occasion well. The headline said: "Light shines on". The photograph of the crowd around the memorial and along the Promenade was impressive, as were the photographs of the hundreds of lighted candles in the Long Gardens. (If only coloured photographs had been available in 1997).

Paul Stimpson wrote:

"Diana – you were the light of our lives." He reported "That was the moving message of a candlelit vigil for the Princess in Cheltenham. The Promenade became an ocean of light as thousands of flickering flames danced among the flowers laid out in her honour.

It was a time for tranquillity and reflection at the end of a harrowing week as Cheltonians paid their final respects."

On Monday 8th September, I issued the following statement to the people of Cheltenham:

> "I wanted to let everyone know that I have today written to His Royal Highness, the Prince of Wales, extending the heartfelt sympathy of everyone in our town to him, the Royal Family, and most particularly, Prince William and Prince Harry.
>
> The enormous reaction by people across the world to the death of Diana, Princess of Wales, is the finest tribute to her and to the special position she occupied in the hearts and minds of so many people.
>
> The Mayoress and I were saddened by the tragic news, and we would ask everyone in the town to remember the late Princess in their prayers, and pray that all her family will be given strength in the period which lies ahead."

The day before the candlelit vigil, another important event was due to take place in the Cheltenham Town Hall. It was the Heart of England Britain in Bloom Awards, and Cheltenham had cause to celebrate a double victory in the 1997 regional competition, and to win the trophy for the Most Outstanding City. Cheltenham would go forward to represent the area in the 1998 national final.

It was a very big occasion for the town, and for me; I welcomed 250 guests who were representing the competing cities, towns and villages from across the region who gathered in the Town Hall for the special awards ceremony.

The following is an extract from my speech:

> "When I have completed my mayoral year, and I reflect back on all the things I have done, hosting the Heart of England awards here in Cheltenham's Town Hall will rank as one of the highlights of my term of office.
>
> I am delighted and pleased to welcome you all to our lovely town – and like you, I am excited about the unfolding of today's events.
>
> It was George the third who changed Cheltenham from an ordinary market town to a spa of national importance when he visited Cheltenham in 1778.
>
> He had heard that the mineral waters in the spa wells were very good for one's health. The king had an incurable disease, as we all know, and he was anxious to see if the waters would do him any good; you must make your own judgment – he died eight weeks later.
>
> Cheltenham is a beautiful town; it has been described by one foreign visitor as 'A town within a park, in as far as the park is so much part of the town that the two are indivisible.' For me, Cheltenham is the garden town of England.
>
> Our parks, gardens and floral displays are indeed the glory of the town, and once again this summer, the council, with the support of the 'Cheltenham in Bloom' committee and 'The Keep Cheltenham Tidy Group', have ensured that the town looks a perfect picture.
>
> Many local businesses including the Kenco Coffee Company, Royscot Trust and Cavendish House have all supported this event – all demonstrating the importance of the Britain in Bloom competition, and the holding of the awards in the town.
>
> When I look out of the window and look at the beautiful display of flowers in the

Long Gardens, I am reminded of the story of the man who bought a derelict house with an equally sized piece of derelict land. He beavered away night and day to make it nice.

The overgrown garden eventually became a show-piece display of beautiful flowers. One day the local vicar was passing the garden as the man was toiling away, he stopped and said to the man, 'I see the good Lord has helped you with your garden, to which the man replied, yes vicar, but you should have seen it when he had it all to himself.'

On behalf of the people of Cheltenham and the council, I extend a warm welcome to you all – have a wonderful day."

Joining the organisers of the event, the Heart of England Tourist Board and the judges, was special guest Patti Boulaye, the star of many musicals and films, who handed out the prizes to the winners.

Sir William Lawrence, chairman of the Heart of England Tourist Board, said, *"Among the elements singled out for praise in Cheltenham by the judges were the impressive multitude of floral features in the town centre, the imaginative use of artwork in public places and the colourful displays on the Municipal buildings and business premises."*

It was a great day for Cheltenham, not only for its success in the regional heats, but it gained automatic entry into the national finals in August 1998.

On Sunday afternoon, Pam and I attended the quickly arranged memorial Service in St. Matthews Church at 3.00 p.m. It was a special multi-faith service for anyone wishing to attend the church to mourn the Princess's death.

The Reverend Timothy Watson assured me the service would be relayed over a sound system to those outside the church, if every seat in the church was taken. Nigel Jones MP, the local Member of Parliament, and I both read lessons during the service.

On Monday 8th September the final dress rehearsal for those taking part in the Fashion Show took place in the Town Hall. The previous week a large half-page advertisement appeared in the local newspaper, sponsored by the various companies who would be showing off their clothes and subscribing to the charity event. I was stunned by what I saw. The headline claimed "Cheltenham Festival of Fashion", a subheading stated: "Festival is a first for town". This is what the text said:

"Cheltenham rightly enjoys an international reputation for the sporting and arts festivals it hosts. Now the town has a new festival to add to the illustrious list – the Cheltenham Festival of Fashion – and what a glittering occasion it promises to be.

On Tuesday at 2.00 p.m. the Town Hall will open its doors for a mammoth arts and crafts fair featuring more than 40 exhibitors.

Then at 7.00 p.m. the Mayor, Councillor Les Godwin, raises the curtain on the main event of the day and hands over to Emma Reed of Severn Sound who will compere the show.

One of the biggest events staged at the Town Hall this year, the 700–seat show is an extravaganza of the best in fashion for all ages. More than 100 models, most of them locals, will 'strut the catwalk', backed by an army of hairdressers, make-up artists and more.

Advance bookings suggest that the Mayor's target of raising £4,000 for charity will easily be achieved. The money will go to the Cheltenham Breast Care Fund, the Cheltenham Senior Citizens' Welfare Committee and the Cheltenham Young Arts Centre. From the moment the Town Hall doors open, visitors can look forward to displays, demonstrations, plus the best in fashion and entertainment.

Get to the root of your hair problems at the Hair Care Question Time and catch up on the latest styles for everyone from infants to senior citizens.

Revel in nostalgia as Pittville School recalls the roaring 1920's and Charleston mania, or look to the future as Cleeve School presents Millennium.

The Cheltenham Tidy Group will re-create the famous 'black and white' Ascot scene from My Fair Lady with clothes made from recycled paper, and there will be a celebration of hats.

Also in the programme is singing by a Tewkesbury Abbey chorister, a raffle with prizes ranging from a music centre to a magnum of champagne .... and much, much more.

Councillor Godwin said: "I am delighted the first Cheltenham Festival of Fashion has been so warmly supported by retailers, crafts people and the many individuals of my charity committee, who have volunteered their time and energy. This is one of the major fundraising events for my appeal, which will raise much-needed resources for the three charities."

The advertisement was sponsored by Cavendish House, Philip Gomm (Hairdressing), Kaliko, Austin Reed, Toppit (Hats for Hire), Marks and Spencer, Headquarters (The Hairdressers) and Dash. The publicity material, including the stylish tickets and the immaculate programme of events was sponsored by Eagle Star.

The *Gloucestershire Echo* contributed by publishing an article claiming that I had said that *"I was hoping my Festival of Fashion will rival the catwalk shows of Milan and Paris."* I don't think I was, but it was all good stuff for the 9th September show.

The article went on to say, *"The mayor's 700–seat show in aid of the Mayor's Charities Appeal will involve 100 models and more than 30 back room staff. He originally planned a three-hour show but there was so much enthusiasm from High Street fashion stores to get involved, he extended it to four hours. The mayor admitted that when he came up with the idea he never thought it would end up so big."*

Ciro Citterio, New Look and Mothercare also participated in the fashion show.

Whilst I was extremely grateful to all the businesses for their support and sponsorships, I was acutely aware that someone in the mayor's team had arranged all this, which was quite a humbling feeling. The charity committee had arranged for a top class photographer to be present, and the whole of the fashion show was videoed by Compass Video.

The only setback was the announcement by Penny Holton (Severn Sound) a few days before the event took place that Emma Reed, the compere of the fashion show had withdrawn. Penny was clearly embarrassed by the situation because she had persuaded me to have Emma do the presentation of the show because of her

Last minute check by Rosemary Crouch before the young models do their stuff on the catwalk

previous experience. She had worked in the top people's store Harrods before moving into the world of journalism. She obtained a media degree and joined *GWR Radio* in Bristol. From there she went to 2CRFM Bournemouth before joining *Severn Sound* in May 1997.

Whether the prospect of compering a top event like the Festival of Fashion at the Town Hall so soon after joining *Severn Sound* was too much for Emma, will always remain a mystery. But with the programmes printed and a very good bibliography of Emma at the front of the programme, it was very disappointing. Hurried meetings with Penny Holton resulted in Helen Purcell, a senior broadcaster with *Severn Sound*, agreeing to compere the show.

As it happened, it could not have turned out better. Helen was a popular *Severn Sound* announcer, a co-presenter of the Breakfast Show and the star of the feature programme 'Hot 7 at 7'. Helen lived in Montpellier at the time, which meant she could come to the mayor's parlour or to a charity meeting very quickly, and we were grateful that she did.

The downside of the withdrawal by Emma Reed was that the organisers had to quickly produce a programme change notice to go inside the programme of events. Emma Reed did not stay at *Severn Sound*, by the way.

In spite of the setback, the Craft Fair and the Festival of Fashion was a total

Some of the ladies who volunteered to become models for the night. They did an excellent job and made it a memorable evening

Pam Thomas with some of her Fashion Show team

Pam Thomas receiving my grateful thanks at the end of the fashion show

success. Over 1,000 people had visited the Town Hall that day and it was standing room only throughout the four hour fashion show.

At the end of the show it was my turn to walk along the catwalk, not to show off any clothes, but to thank everyone from the bottom of my heart for bringing the fashion show to the Town Hall and making it such a fantastic success story. Of course, without the dedication and expert handling of the fashion show on the night, and the nights of rehearsal in the run-up to the show by Pam Thomas, none of it would have been possible.

I called for Pam to join me on the catwalk even though I knew she would feel embarrassed by being in the limelight, but the applause following my words of appreciation simply said it all. Pam Thomas now owns the successful Joyce Brooks Lingerie in in the centre of Cheltenham, and she still plays a large part in the mayor's fashion show each year.

At noon on Wednesday 10th September, a horse-drawn Landau carriage arrived at the Municipal Offices to take me to the Beaufort Homes Imperial Apartments in Imperial Square. The Landau, complete with livery dressed horseman, drove me along the Promenade to Imperial Square where a small crowd had assembled to watch me unveil a Napoleon Fountain in the Broad Walk.

The construction of the majestic Regency style apartments along the Broad Walk by Beaufort Homes was a credit to the town and they blended in well with the long-established Imperial Square.

The apartments and the restoration of the Napoleon fountain completed the whole concept of the original intention in 1834, and improved still further the elegance of Imperial Square.

> "The fountain had quite a chequered history", I told the listeners, "Apparently, it was brought over from Italy during the time that Bonaparte and his army robbed that country of some of its valued and important monuments.
>
> Historians tell us that the fountain was part of a cargo of a vessel on its way to France, which ended up being seized by one of Britain's cruisers in the Mediterranean. What happened after that is unclear, but the earliest reference to the fountain being in Cheltenham can be found in the Cheltenham Journal dated 19th June 1826.
>
> At first it was displayed at the Sherborne Spa, and then it was on display for a period of 68 years in the Montpellier Gardens.
>
> Monuments like the Napoleon Fountain gradually lost their popularity, and because doubts were cast about the fountain's originality, it remained hidden for a number of years until 1985/86, when it was restored in the Art Gallery and Museum's conservation workshops, before being put on display at Lloyds Bank. Now, it is here in the Broad Walk, which I believe is its rightful location."

Beaufort Homes and Ralph Guilor, the architect, deserve praise for their vision and effort to improve this part of the Cheltenham environment.

On Friday 12th September, I was asked by the Cheltenham Civic Society to attend another plaque unveiling ceremony in the Regent Arcade. This time it was to commemorate the raising of the first troop of Gloucestershire Yeomanry at the Plough Hotel in 1795, and it was my job to invite Lt. Colonel Ashford-Sandford to unveil the plaque.

I told everyone that this was the 24th Cheltenham Civic Society plaque to be unveiled in the town since 1982. Once again, the Civic Society had reminded us about the important moments in our history, and it was right that they should be recognised.

I was up early the following morning to attend the Business Men's Fellowship breakfast meeting in Hallory House Hotel, in Shurdington Road, Cheltenham.

Darren Stevens, the Public Relations and Corporate Affairs Manager (Chelsea Building Society) had invited Pam and me to the Gloucester versus Toulon rugby game at Kingsholm, Gloucester. Chelsea had a box on the ground and together with excellent company and a good game of rugby it was an occasion that will never be forgotten.

Sunday 14th September, Pam and I attended the Salvation Army Citadel in Bath Road, for their afternoon service.

Early on Monday, 15th September, Pam and I were at Bournside School to see their new classrooms. Then a dash back to the Municipal Offices to meet Dr Georg Gura from Sochi, our twin town in Russia. Through the interpreter, we extended fraternal greetings between our two towns, and although it was difficult at times, I do believe we enjoyed what each other had to say.

The Mayor of Sochi, Nikolay Karpov, had written to me on the 1st September to explain that Dr Gura would be representing him in Cheltenham. He wanted me to know that even though he could not make it, he wished 'all the staff of the municipality, and the citizens of your town, the best wishes of prosperity, peace and well-being.' I asked Dr Gura to take back the good wishes from the people of Cheltenham to the Mayor of Sochi.

At 4.30 p.m. the same day, I chaired a special council meeting, held to enable councillors to decide what to do with the Royal Well bus station. A quick summary of the current position by Michael Smith, the borough engineer, was followed by a robust debate on the issues facing the council. As I expected, PAB councillors fully supported my suggestion that the bus station should be demolished and replaced with something more in keeping with the setting of the Royal Crescent. Councillors from both sides of the political spectrum supported my proposal.

At 6.45 p.m. I attended a council seminar on the future development of the Art Gallery and Museum.

Tuesday morning I had coffee with Frederik Roder and his wife in the parlour. They had asked to meet me so that they could tell me about their creation of the Paradise Community in a large country house called Paradise House, which was situated in the village of Paradise, a few miles from Painswick. They explained that it was a centre and home for young adults with learning difficulties and those who needed special care. Frederik further explained that they had started the 'community' based on the educational and care principles that had been established by the Austrian philosopher and social reformer, Rudolf Steiner.

They were aware that they were asking the mayor from another local authority to visit their 'community'. They had read in the local press about my support for those with special needs, and they hoped that I would be able to visit Paradise House. I suggested to Frederik and his wife that they should be talking to the Stroud District Council rather than me, because the village of Paradise was beyond the Cheltenham boundary.

They were disappointed with my suggestion. They thought that a visit by Pam and I would boost the staff morale, and the residents would look forward to seeing us.

They were a charming couple, and they made their request sound 'special' so much so that it was difficult to refuse. I told them that I would go through the usual protocols with Stroud District Council, and I would overcome any Cheltenham problem by using my own car should a visit be arranged. It was clear from the look on their faces that they were pleased with my suggestion, and little did they know that I was as enthusiastic as they were to visit the Paradise Community, not least because I was curious to find out what the place was like and how it was organised.

Maggie Handson took on the task of 'clearing any obstacles' and a visit was arranged for October.

At 6.30 p.m. Pam and I attended a reception in the Officers' Mess at RAF Innsworth, along with mayors from other local authorities.

On Wednesday afternoon, the Blind Association held their Annual General Meeting in the Pump Room, which I attended. The evening was a special occasion for Pam and me as we welcomed every member of the Mayor's Charity Committee and their spouses, to a 'thank you' party in the parlour – for achieving a successful evening at the Town Hall on 9th September.

The Festival of Fashion raised over £4,250 for the mayor's charities.

Thursday evening was the occasion of the Cheltenham in Bloom awards, which was held in the Pump Room. It is a special evening for local people who have contributed and exhibited flowers, fruit, and allotment produce and entered the best garden competitions throughout the year.

I reminded the large crowd who came to the Pump Room that the recent Heart of England awards and the Cheltenham in Bloom awards go hand in hand towards fulfilling the meaning of the words by Dr Garrett, Cheltenham's Senior Health Officer in 1901, who wrote: "Whether you look at it as one great garden or a place where a garden is attached to almost every home, Cheltenham is the garden town of England." The following is an extract from my speech:

> "The parks, gardens and floral displays in Cheltenham are indeed the glory of the town; once again this summer the borough council, with the support of the Cheltenham in Bloom committee and The Keep Cheltenham Tidy Group, have ensured that the town looks a perfect picture.
>
> In the early 1980's, the Cheltenham in Bloom organisation was formed to foster links between the volunteers and local businesses with the aim of enhancing the beauty of the town. Today, Cheltenham in Bloom co-ordinates more than 20 competitions; promoting floral decorations of all sectors of the community, from hotels and public houses, to retail and commercial premises and private homes.
>
> The beauty of Cheltenham and its glorious gardens is that it plays a major part in attracting visitors and tourists to the town. And all of you receiving awards tonight, indeed everyone who makes their gardens and homes so attractive with floral displays, deserve all our thanks for making Cheltenham truly, the most pleasant town in the land."

It would be easy to believe that my charity committee had done nothing else but arrange the Fashion Show in the Town Hall, but this could not be further from the truth. Whilst the build-up to the Fashion Show was a concerted effort by the committee, there were other events planned throughout the mayoral year. A 'Race Nite' at the Victory Club, a 'Golf Day' at the Lilleybrook Golf Club, a 'Table Top Sale and Line Dancing' at the Hillview Community Centre, were just a few of the events that my energetic committee were working on.

To achieve total success with the events, the committee relied heavily on the 'behind the scenes' work of Maggie Handson, my PA, who made sure that all the logistics were in place, including the commitments by the various sponsors.

Understandably, I have looked back on my mayoral year many times; the effort and hard work of the charity committee and others, who for one reason or another, gave their all to make the year a success, still amazes me.

However, another event the charity committee had organised was an "Old Tyme Music Hall" at The Playhouse in Bath Road on Friday 19th September. How they did it, I will never know. They had to go through the legal complexities with Entertainments UK-Europe Limited, who agreed a 'One Performance Only' in association with The Mayor's Charities Appeal, including a clear reference to the fact that the proceeds were in aid of the stated charities. The committee arranged the programme, which included a novelty act by Vicki Lestor, a night of song by Caroline Fields, and two comedians, Baffle-O-Bill and George Saunders, plus the music of The Foundation Jazz Band. The notices and programmes were sponsored by Chelsea Building Society.

There was no let up on the following day for Pam and me with the presentation of tennis awards to junior tennis players at the Pittville School in the morning, followed by attendance at the Dean Close Theatre in the evening to listen to music by the BBC Big Band.

Sunday 21st September we attended the RAFA Battle of Britain Service, and in the afternoon we visited Gloucester Cathedral for a rededication service.

In the evening we attended All Saints Church for a Holst Birthday Concert.

Monday morning I had talks with Garth Barnes the deputy mayor and Tim Harman at 9.00 a.m. regarding extra mayoral engagements, which was followed by a quick trip to the Montpellier Gardens where I had promised Paul and Mette Larsen, the owners of the Storyteller Restaurant in North Place, Cheltenham, I would join them in their re-creation of a historic hot air balloon flight starting from the Gardens. Paul and Mette had made history six years earlier when they flew the first hot air balloon at the North Pole. On this occasion (1997), they donned period costumes to mark the 160th anniversary of the first ascent by a man and a woman together. Apparently, on September 22nd 1837, Mrs Graham and her friend Mr Garrett, the landlord of a pub called the White Lion, gained notoriety because they took off in their balloon without a chaperone. These Victorians caused a sensation at the time, and it is alleged that they took a monkey with them, which was later jettisoned from the basket so that the couple could test-fly one of the world's first parachutes.

The *Gloucestershire Echo* covered the story with a headline "All fired up for the big flight". The article with excellent photographs of the occasion read: "Cheltenham's mayor Councillor Les Godwin went up, up and away for a bird's eye view of his beloved town. The intrepid civic leader took off from Montpellier Gardens in a hot air balloon with restaurateurs Paul and Mette Larson. The flight lasted about three-quarters of an hour and the balloon came down safely just south of Prior's Norton, near Tewkesbury, close to the A38." What the article did not report was that there was a fourth person in the basket, a cameraman from one of the television companies, who wanted to film the whole event. I would love to see what he filmed because the take off from the Montpellier Gardens was not perfect by any means. When the balloon, which was difficult to hold by the handlers, finally took off, we must have missed the trees by inches before we soared over the town. The trip was a unique and lovely experience, but as Mette Larson told the

Take off from the Gardens.

Paul and Mette Larson with me in the balloon before take-off.

Western Daily Press reporter: "Unfortunately, strong winds took the balloon towards Gloucester and the Staverton Airport, and the hour-long flight ended in a field near the A38."

That wasn't quite the end of the adventure; the winds were taking us in the wrong direction and it was interesting to listen to the comments of the air traffic controller at the Airport, who was clearly keeping his eye on where the balloon was going. The decision was taken to descend into a freshly cut cornfield, alarmingly between power lines, and descending twice as fast as the take-off in the Montpellier Gardens. We were told to hang on tightly as the balloon careered towards the field. The poor cameraman was protecting his camera for all he was worth, and who could blame him. The basket hit the ground at an enormous speed, unceremoniously tipping me, the cameraman and Mr and Mrs Larson into the field of corn stalks, which can be very uncomfortable unless one is wearing thick clothing. The cameraman protected his camera, but at a cost to his face and arms, whilst Paul, Mette and me were shaken, but in one piece. If the paparazzi had been lurking behind the hedgerow, they would have had a field-day, no pun intended. Thankfully, our discomfort was felt only by us.

Paul was in constant touch by phone with his contact in a car, who quickly came to the spot where we had landed. We swopped our means of transport and we were driven back to Cheltenham, leaving our 'chaser' to take care of the balloon. There is often two sides to every story.

I was back in the Municipal Offices by 2.00 p.m. in time to meet Simon Lee, Paul Fry (Group Director) and Bob Attwood, to discuss the arrangements for the council's 'garden awards' in the Pump Room at 5.00 p.m.

At 7.00 p.m. Pam and I were in the Town Hall for a charity reception in aid of the Gloucestershire Association for Mental Health. I was asked to do the welcome speech and this is what I said:

> "Lord Neidpath, the Lord Lieutenant, Mr Robertson, honoured guests, fellow councillors, ladies and gentlemen.
>
> When I was deputy mayor, you kindly invited the mayoress and me to your supper evening at Stanway House, again to raise funds for the association; we enjoyed the evening immensely.
>
> It is nice to be among friends particularly those who do so much for others in a voluntary way; to listen to their views on how they see the work they do in the community, is a very humbling experience.
>
> I am sure the Lord Lieutenant and the mayors from other towns and cities, would agree with me that of all the duties we have to perform, none is more pleasurable than meeting members of voluntary bodies, who give so much of their time and energy to helping others less fortunate than themselves.
>
> I often wonder, and it is a frightening thought, that should all our wonderful volunteers in this country decide on the stroke of midnight one day, not to do any more voluntary work, what on earth would happen?
>
> Just think about it for a moment, the very fabric of society would crumble under

the weight of all the responsibilities suddenly thrust upon it, and of course, those in most need would be the ones who would suffer most of all.

We all know it will not happen, but the thought of it does make one realise, perhaps more than ever before, the important work that you do along with everyone else in the voluntary services.

The Gloucestershire Association for Mental Health was established in Cheltenham 33 years ago, and the 'Nearly New Shop' in the town was the second charity shop to be opened in the country. But time goes on and changes have to be made; since I last spoke to you in Stanway House, the 'Nearly New Shop' has closed, and there is bound to be pressure on the two other shops in Stroud and Gloucester when other voluntary organisations open their own outlets.

Money raising events are all important to any voluntary body, and whilst welcome changes have come about with the financial support of the Barnwood House Trust, I believe we should never forget the value of all the volunteers during the Association's 33 years in raising well over £300,000, which has ensured help, advice and support is always at hand for those and their families who are experiencing mental ill health. Congratulations to you all.

Without hurting others, I would like to mention the sterling work of your tireless director, Diane Dent, the praise for her work is richly deserved.

In conclusion, I would like to recite a little poetry, which I think is appropriate for the occasion. I have no idea who wrote it:
> 'May we strengthen the weak?
> Give light to the blind
> Clothe the naked
> And be friends to mankind.'

I welcome you all to the reception."

Although the public funeral of Diana, Princess of Wales had taken place on 6th September, the television news programmes rarely missed an opportunity to go back over the events leading up to her death; the flowers, the public outpouring and the funeral procession.

I launched the mayor's memorial appeal so that local residents could donate money towards a plaque, or a garden seat in one of the local parks. Within a few days, a trickle of small donations started to come in.

An important event took place in Cheltenham on Friday 26th September, when the Co-operative Funeral Service Managers' Association, held their annual three day conference at the Cheltenham Park Hotel. It was the first time the Conference had been held in Cheltenham. More than one hundred delegates attended the conference, and they came from all parts of the United Kingdom.

We were met by Graham Lymn, the President of the Association, who had a chain of office about his neck which sported around thirty different badges of past presidents, which made the mayoral chain of office poor by comparison. Graham Lymn invited Pam and me back to the hotel the following evening, to enjoy with the funeral managers their 'informal evening of entertainment'.

A quick look at the diary showed that we were due at the Albion Social Club to open an extension of the club and a new bar area at eight o'clock, but we promised to be back at the Cheltenham Park Hotel by 10.00 p.m.

Arthur, the chauffeur, was not too keen for the mayor to be attending an informal night, but we told him that he could have the night off as we would be using our own mode of transport on this occasion. Pam and I were pleased that we attended the informal night, because Graham, his daughter and a host of his friends made us most welcome. We left the hotel around midnight, and much to our surprise, Graham made a little speech before we left, thanking us for our attendance to their conference over the two days, and inviting us back again the following night to their banquet, which, as he said, was their normal way of bringing their conferences to a close.

Although Pam and I were surprised, we accepted the invitation. We made our way towards the hotel exit, and as Graham escorted us to the car he told me that he would be proposing a toast to "The Town of Cheltenham" at the banquet, and he would like me to respond. It would have been difficult to refuse, but I did remark that after two speeches already, did he not think that his colleagues and their wives would have heard enough from the mayor of Cheltenham? Graham rejected the notion, and assured me the managers and their wives would appreciate my response to the toast.

As I drove back to Up Hatherley, I could only think of the speech I would need to prepare – it had to be different, but what should I say. I had never given a response to a toast before, and what would the President be saying in his speech to the banquet guests?

My speech had to be a good mix of stories and several mentions about Cheltenham being the right place for conferences to take place; I needed to thank Graham, his daughter and the delegates for their company over the three days. I hope my response was suitable for the occasion.

Sunday afternoon, Pam and I were invited to an Asian Community celebration of 50 years of independence of the Indian sub-continent. The event was held in the Gas Green Chapel in Baker Street.

At six o'clock that evening, Arthur took Pam and me to the Cheltenham Park Hotel for the banquet. The delegates and their wives were in evening dress and the air was filled with soft music.

Arthur, thinking that there was a long night ahead for him, sidled up to me as we entered the foyer, "Sir", he said, "I hope you don't mind me saying so, but it is the usual practice for the mayor on these sort of occasions, to give the speech, and then at a convenient moment, to make his excuses and leave the room."

If Arthur had not had such a serious look on his face, I would have thought he was joking. He clearly had been thinking about the previous two nights of the conference, and his inward desire to be home early on that Sunday night, prompted him to make the suggestion. Graham overheard the chauffer's comments and quickly intervened. "The mayor and mayoress would be driven home by one of the delegates at the end of the evening's event, or whenever he felt the need to leave," he told Arthur. Arthur looked sheepishly towards me and I nodded approval of the arrangement.

My curiosity about where the banquet for so many people could be held was soon satisfied as Graham led the way to the French windows, which opened out into the largest marquee I had ever seen.

The President, Graham Lymn, in his toast to Cheltenham was very kind with his choice of words about the town. He was pleased that the Association had chosen Cheltenham as their venue for their conference, and in his words "they could not have made a better choice."

CHAPTER 12

My Mayoral Year – 1997/98 (Part Two)

I first met Peter Stone, one of my constituents in 1984. He had been a member of the Cheltenham and North Gloucester Branch of the Multiple Sclerosis Society for a number of years. He had been a professional musician before his illness, and this was not lost on other members of the society, who persuaded Peter to arrange musical concerts for local MS sufferers, their carers, families and supporters. Peter's MS had progressed to the stage where he had to take to a wheelchair in 1984, which was about the time he moved to Prestbury.

In 1989, he was contacted by a Gloucester based charity called ART SHAPE, who wanted Peter to organise a 'music appreciation society' at the Prestbury Day Centre in Prestbury Road.

Peter agreed and it turned out to be a change of direction for him, and something that would keep him occupied for the next twenty years. He persuaded a musician friend to play her harp to the staff and patients at the Day Centre, and she reported to him that she had received rapturous applause for her performances.

The news prompted Peter to contact ART SHAPE with an idea that he should organise a series of morning concerts at a convenient venue in Gloucestershire for MS sufferers and people with disabilities. The idea was attractive, and Peter was given the go-ahead.

He put his idea to the management at the Cheltenham Town Hall, which was accepted, and they offered to provide a three-year funding of the shows. After two years with ART SHAPE, Peter started the Cheltenham Connections' morning concerts in 1991, putting on shows in the Town Hall Pillar Room.

The first show featured the local singer and songwriter Johnny Coppin, which attracted 95 people, but the popularity of the shows increased and sometimes attracted up to 160 people, which was the capacity of the Pillar Room.

After twenty years, Peter passed the baton on to someone else, but he deserves every credit for the work he had done by creating an annual long-lasting musical event for disabled people, their Carers and the Society's supporters. All the work associated with the concerts had been done by Peter from his wheelchair.

Peter invited Pam and I to one of the tribute concerts at the Town Hall on Friday 3rd October 1997 to hear a group called "A Taste of Honey" who played the 'Songs of the Bee Gees', which was most entertaining.

In the evening we attended a Civic Reception given by the Forest of Dean District Council, which was hosted by the chairman of the council, Bill Hobden. The council offices are situated in Coleford. Pam and I had met Bill and his wife at other civic occasions. He was a down-to-earth man, who enjoyed his job as chairman, and was someone who could always keep the party going with stories of his past experiences.

On Saturday evening we enjoyed an evening of song by Churchdown Male Voice Choir at Cheltenham Town Hall. The blend of voices was very good, and as I listened I wondered whether they would be willing to join two other local choirs for a Three Choirs Charity Concert. I put it to Leslie Burgess who agreed with the idea and promised to come back to me with a programme of music.

On Monday 6th October I held a reception in the parlour for German teachers who taught English in their schools. They were visiting the United Kingdom to further their knowledge with visits to schools in the Cheltenham area.

In the evening, I visited the Cheltenham Sea Cadets at their headquarters in Stoneville Street.

The following day, Pam and I attended the Paradise Community, in the village of Paradise, which is near Painswick. We had met Frederik Roder and his wife in the parlour in September, and they were keen for Pam and me to visit their 'community'. I had received clearance from Stroud District Council.

The road map was not very helpful; apart from telling me that the village was located somewhere along the A46 between Brockworth and Painswick; there was no distinct marking of the road to the village. I drove slowly along the A46 so that I did not miss any sign post to Paradise. Eventually, Pam spotted a half concealed 'finger' sign, which, after closer examination, pointed to Paradise. The narrow lane to the village was only wide enough for one car. Two isolated houses were visible as I drove along the lane, and then came upon the entrance to Paradise House, which we assumed was the home of the Paradise Community, so I drove through.

A Cotswold stone wall surrounded the property, which had two large pillars either side of the entrance. I drove slowly along the driveway, and on either side we could see there were large tracts of land containing several piles of logs that had been recently cut. Most of the land was pasture, but there was no sign of cattle.

Several 'sleeping policemen' prevented a speed of more than five miles per hour, and the driveway was long. Paradise House was a large old building, in need of repair; there were several ancillary smaller buildings in the surrounding areas, and the sound of our car brought curious faces to the windows of the house to see who had arrived.

We were met by Frederik Roder and his wife who introduced us to members of the staff and a number of the residents. Frederik had arranged for coffee to be served in a separate room, which was just as well because my chain of office seemed to hold a certain amount of fascination for some of the residents.

It was not a long visit, although we did manage to have a look at the outside workshops, always closely followed by several inquisitive residents. Pam and I talked about the visit on our way back to Cheltenham. Frederik and his wife had explained to us the purpose of the "community", but there seemed to be so many unanswered questions about the place, not least about how it was funded and by whom. Nevertheless, we had enjoyed the visit and been impressed with the work of the Paradise Community. We came to the opinion that it was an unusual experience to find a community of adults, aged between 18 and 60 with learning difficulties, some needing special care, being cared for in such an isolated part of the beautiful Cotswold countryside, with no evidence of involvement by the local council. We agreed that the special care being provided by Friedrich and his wife appeared to be completely independent of the social care usually provided by the local authorities, so we left it at that. Perhaps future visits would reveal more information about the Paradise Community.

Wednesday 8th October was another special day for Pam and me because it was the Queen's Golden Wedding and Commemoration Party at the Pittville Pump Room. Earlier in the year, couples across the United Kingdom had been invited to apply to attend a golden wedding party at Buckingham Palace, to celebrate the Queen and Prince Philip's golden wedding celebrations. Not everyone, of course, would be successful with their applications.

Many local people had been unsuccessful and Henry Elwes, The Lord Lieutenant of Gloucestershire, who was the Queen's representative in Gloucestershire, contacted my PA, Maggie Handson, to see whether I would arrange a party for local couples who shared 1997 as their golden wedding year with Her Majesty the Queen and Prince Philip.

It sounded like a good idea to me and I agreed.

Arrangements were made inviting local couples to apply for tickets to attend the Pump Rooms for this special event – seventy couples applied. I knew it would not have the glamour of Buckingham Palace, but I thought it was something that would be appreciated and worth doing. Henry Elwes, Timothy Watson, the Rector of Cheltenham, and other dignitaries attended the event, and Timothy invited the couples to renew their marriage vows, which proved to be very popular. Pam and I knew several couples in the room as we went to each table to have a friendly chat with everyone. This is what I said in my speech of welcome:

"You will all have memories of your own wedding day, and perhaps many of you will find it hard to believe that half a century has passed, and like me, you will wonder where those fifty years have gone.

1947 was in the period of austerity just after the Second World War, and many commentators have observed that the marriage of the then Princess Elizabeth to the then Lieutenant Philip Mountbatten was the first flash of colour since the end of hostilities.

You will not need me to remind you that in 1947 rationing of many items was still in force and life was not easy by any means. But, it is often said that hard times are always the times most remembered, and strange though it may seem, they are often the most enjoyable times of one's life.

I am sure you will all have your own memories of those times, and that you have often shared them with others.

Her Majesty the Queen and His Royal Highness, the Duke of Edinburgh, were not to know at the time of their marriage that only five years later, Princess Elizabeth would be called upon to succeed her father following his untimely death.

Like all marriages, they have faced good times as well as bad times, and in recent years they have probably had more than their share of difficult times. But in spite of it all, they have remained a united and devoted couple, and I am sure that their relationship, like so many of yours, has been a great strength to them.

I am particularly pleased to welcome the Lord Lieutenant of Gloucestershire, Mr Henry Elwes, who will be reading a message to you shortly from Her Majesty the Queen."

The *Gloucestershire Echo* followed the event with a photograph of the couples filing into the Pump Room. The article reported: "70 couples who had missed out on the Queen and Prince Philip's golden wedding party made up for it in style yesterday." The article carried a headline that proclaimed "Golden couples party at the Pump Rooms". It reported: "The celebration was organised by Cheltenham mayor Les Godwin and the Lord Lieutenant of Gloucestershire, Henry Elwes, who wanted to ease their disappointment at having missed out on July's party at Buckingham Palace.

The couples, celebrating 50 years of wedded bliss this year, said yesterday's party had been just as special." Margaret and Eric Allen from Charlton Kings told the *Echo*: "It was a real honour to be there, and the re-taking of the marriage vows was a nice surprise." David and Betty Pennington from Benhall remarked: "It was lovely of the Mayor to invite us to the party", and Joan and Alan Bate remarked, "It would have been nice to have been invited to the Palace, but they have done ever so well today. We are thrilled to be here."

A number of letters appeared in the local newspaper, all thanking the Lord Lieutenant, the mayor and the mayoress, for putting on the celebration party. It was a very special day for everyone and I am sure it will not be forgotten.

Later in the evening, I presented the Arts Council awards in the Drawing Room at the Cheltenham Town Hall – a complete change from the afternoon's celebrations, but equally important and pleasurable.

Monday 13th October, Pam and I attended the 10th Anniversary Celebration of the 'Veronica Jones Photography' in the Regents Arcade.

In the evening we attended The Everyman Theatre as part of the Cheltenham Literary Festival.

The following day Pam and I attended the opening of the Mental Health Day Fair, which was held in the Cheltenham and Gloucester College of Higher Education.

Thursday 16th October, I presented the prizes at the Cheltenham Allotments Presentation Evening, which is held annually in the Pump Room.

Maggie Handson had given me early warning that the next big event in my diary was the Annual Conference of the National Council of Women of Great Britain, to be held in the Carlton Hotel on Friday 18th October. Although I had accepted the invitation, the thought of giving a speech of welcome to such a well-known organisation as the National Council of Women (NCW) filled me with trepidation. Thankfully, there was a reception for the NCW delegates the previous night, which gave me an opportunity to meet and talk to them, and hopefully to feel more comfortable when I delivered my speech the following morning. A suitable speech for most occasions is worrying. On this occasion, I came to the conclusion that as it was a first ever visit to Cheltenham of the NCW, I could safely use a combination of past speeches.

As in previous speeches, I took the opportunity to tell the visitors that when they were looking at the lovely floral displays around the town in their free time, they will understand why Cheltenham was the 'Britain in Bloom' winner in the 'City Class' for the twelfth time in fifteen years in 1997. The following is a précis of my speech of welcome to the delegates:

> "Madam President, the NCW was formed in 1895, although I am told that the Cheltenham branch was formed two years earlier in 1893, and to be still flourishing 104 years later shows that the NCW is truly a well-respected organisation.
>
> At the local level, I take great pleasure in thanking on your behalf, your recently retired regional chairman, Mrs Margaret Prentice, for all her hard work. I also congratulate Mrs Joan Jenkins who has taken on the task of guiding the NCW (at regional level, of course), into the next century.
>
> I know that my councillor colleague, Mrs Pat Thornton, is a valued member of your organisation, and I know you will be able to count on Pat's support in the years ahead.
>
> I am impressed with the wide range of issues you are going to discuss, and I am pleased to learn that Joan Ruddock MP, the Secretary of State for Women's Affairs, will be joining you later. I do hope you will take the opportunity to remind her of one of the aims of your organisation, which is "To Promote Equality of Opportunity for Women". And when you do, you should point out to her that the recent statistical information on the Local Government workforce shows a lamentable discrepancy in salaries between males and females doing similar work. This is in spite of the fact that the Equal Pay Act has been around for more than 30 years.
>
> Another of your aims is 'To improve the quality of life for all', which I know you are more capable than most of doing exactly that.
>
> There is a lovely quotation written by a man of a woman, and I would love to share it with you. 'Oh the shrewdness of their shrewdness when they're shrewd: and the rudeness of their rudeness when they're rude: But the shrewdness of their shrewdness and the rudeness of their rudeness, are nothing to their goodness when they're good.'"

Once the NCW conference was underway, Pam and I thanked our hosts and we made our way to the Regent Arcade to give our support to the Occupational Safety Exhibition. In the evening, the NCW were holding their Conference Dinner at the Pump Rooms, which Pam and I attended.

On Monday 20th October, we visited Betteridge School, which is adjacent to Bournside School in Warden Hill Road. It is a special school, which caters for pupils who have special educational needs due to severe learning difficulties, physical disabilities or behavioural problems. The head teacher, Mrs M. Saunders, showed Pam and me around the school where children of all ages were being taught and cared for by dedicated staff. We learned that the school also gave support to the parents of the children.

We enjoyed our visit; some of the pupils wanted to escort us around the classrooms, to hold our hands, urging us to stay longer than we had planned. A young girl called Lucy was particularly pleased to see us, and never strayed too far away throughout the visit. It was nice to see Lucy again when she and other pupils attended the musical events arranged by Peter Stone at the Town Hall. We often think about Lucy and the pupils of 1997, always hoping that they reached their potential.

In the evening I attended a wine and cheese evening at the Grove Street Neighbourhood Centre where I met the staff.

The Arle Court park & ride scheme started operating on 31st October and the *Gloucestershire Echo* reported on 7th November that the £750,000 service had "got off to a slow start on its first day with only four paying passengers all day." However, the *Echo* added: "Numbers started to build up on Monday with 10 passengers, followed by 25 by Thursday and by the end of the week an average of 30 a day have climbed aboard the Cheltenham Flyer." The cost of the service and the loss of large swathes of Green Belt land was still regretted by many local people – and still regretted today.

Tuesday 21st November was an important day for me and my PAB colleague Malcolm Stennett. A presentation by Michael Smith, the borough engineer, of the land drainage scheme for Prestbury, was unveiled.

The scheme was the second stage of a joint undertaking by Tewkesbury Borough Council (TBC) and Cheltenham Borough Council (CBC) to end the persistent flooding of local residents' homes in the parish over many years. I had raised the problem of surface water flooding in Prestbury on numerous occasions when I was a member of TBC in the early 1980's.

Persistence by PAB councillors had finally brought a commitment by TBC to fund the first stage of a scheme providing CBC were prepared to fund the remaining stages, albeit, after the boundary changes in 1991.

It had made good sense at the time, except, of course that it would mean that PAB councillors would have to start the long process of discussion and debate to secure future funding from CBC following the secondment of the parish.

Michael Smith went over the history of the flooding in the village, and reminded the meeting of the council's commitment to fund the second stage of a land drainage scheme.

He confirmed that TBC had funded and completed the first stage of the scheme and CBC had provided funds to carry out the next stage of the scheme.

Plans of the two stages were displayed and whilst they were impressive, it did reveal the need for the two stages to be connected before the problem of flooding would be overcome.

In answer to our questions, the borough engineer explained that the third stage was being devised that would link the two schemes. It would be up to CBC and Gloucestershire County Council to provide the funds to do the work. It sounded simple, but as later chapters will show, it took many more years of heartache for the residents and hard work for the local PAB councillors.

In the afternoon, I visited the *Severn Sound* Studios in Gloucester, where Penny Holton showed me the 'tricks of the trade', as she put it, which resulted in the popular broadcasts made each day from the studios.

A break for coffee with Penny and Helen Purcell gave me the chance to thank them for their involvement with the Fashion Show. Penny presented me with a video of the evening's performance; it is a family treasure.

On Wednesday, Pam and I visited the St. Vincent's Centre in Central Cross Drive for those with severe learning difficulties. It was an Open Morning for the parents and the volunteers. We were shown around the Centre and watched the carers doing their excellent work.

In the afternoon, I visited RAF Innsworth to meet the new Station Commander, Wing Commander Tony Spearpoint. He was replacing Wing Commander Mike Bullock who had been posted to another part of the country. Pam and I had found Mike very good company, and we were sad to hear that he had moved.

Because the official ceremony of handing over the command of RAF Innsworth had to be witnessed and recorded for posterity, an official photograph of the handover was taken in the presence of the three mayors from Gloucester, Tewkesbury and Cheltenham.

Friday, 24th October, was another special day in my calendar. Arthur Bailey and Les Williams, both keen golfers, had made arrangements for an 'AM/AM Golf Tournament to take place at the Lilleybrook Golf Club, in aid of my three charities. They had persuaded 38 teams to take part, and the Abbey Business Systems of Cheltenham offered to sponsor the event.

I agreed to be at the golf course at 9.00 a.m. to tee-off the first competitors.

I was pleased to learn that a team from the Municipal Offices comprising Ray Turner, Robin Hayward and Kevin Dawson had entered the competition, so I had more than a passing interest in who would win the tournament. Golf, as we all know, is a long process, so whilst the 38 teams battled it out, I returned to my other mayoral duties in the parlour.

Later in the day, I returned to the Lilleybrook Golf Club to welcome the last of the players back to the clubhouse, and to present the prizes. The team from the Municipal Offices did well, but they just failed to win one of the prizes. It had been an enjoyable day for the team players, and for the spectators.

On Monday 27th October, I met Mr Robert Gerhard and his wife Cindy from our twin town Cheltenham, Pennsylvania. The town is a small suburb of Philadelphia, and it has been twinned with its Cotswold namesake since the 1950's. Robert and Cindy were a lovely couple and delighted to be in the UK and especially Cheltenham in Gloucestershire.

They went to great lengths to tell me how they and their friends back home cherish the link between the two towns, and stressed the importance of retaining and expanding the close relationship. We exchanged framed citations in the parlour and repeated the procedure in the formal setting before the start of a Cheltenham Borough Council meeting.

Brian Jones, the Mayor of Tewkesbury, invited Pam and me to the Annual Remembrance Service at Churchdown School, on Saturday 1st November.

The following evening we were invited to the 60th Anniversary Gala Concert by the Cheltenham Silver Band, in the Pump Rooms.

On Monday morning, Maggie Handson with a look on her face I had seen before, told me that I was going to be busy in November because she had received a large number of invitations from organisations inviting me to their events during the next few weeks. She added, "That is apart from the official engagements on behalf of the Council you will be required to fill."

The first of those engagements was to attend the weekly tea dance at the Town Hall, which was more of a pleasure than a duty.

Tuesday 4th November, The Keep Cheltenham Tidy Group, run by Marjorie Fulford and Doreen Garland-Jones, asked me to take the Wedgewood Trophy Cheltenham had won in the Heart of England Competition, to Gloucester Road Primary

The Mayor of Cheltenham, Councillor Les Godwin, J.P. with Gloucester Road Primary School, Year 1 and Year 2 Pupils, participants in the award ceremony

School. Marjorie explained that the children had recently helped the group to 'clean up' the Churchill Gardens, and she reminded me that the children had sung in front of a large audience in the Town Hall when the trophy was presented to me on behalf of the town.

It seemed an excellent reason for the trophy to come out of the cabinet, and for me to take it to the school for the children to see. The children were very excited; everyone wanted to hold the trophy and to be the one holding the trophy when the official photographs were taken.

The *Gloucestershire Echo* covered the story with the photograph of the children and me, with the heading: "Pupils praised for helping town win prize". The article said: "Pupils share in the glory when Cheltenham mayor Les Godwin visited their school with the Britain in Bloom Wedgewood Trophy. The children sang at the Heart of England awards ceremony at the Town Hall in September, where Cheltenham claimed the best city award for the 12th time. Councillor Les Godwin called in to thank the pupils for their efforts at the ceremony, where they performed four songs, including 'Let it be' and 'Thank You Lord ', which contained a verse made up by the children especially for Cheltenham in Bloom."

According to the deputy head teacher Paul Maisey, "The children got very excited at the prospect of meeting the mayor".After the visit, I told the *Echo* reporter, *"Every association I have had with the children of Cheltenham has been simply brilliant. Their love for the things they do is great: I will return with the trophy full of sweets, that's a promise."*

On Wednesday afternoon, I attended the Award Ceremony for the students at the Cheltenham & Gloucester College of Higher Education (C&GCHE).

In the evening, Pam and I visited the Everyman Theatre to see a production of the 'Merry Widow' by the Cotswold Savoyards. The Savoyards was formed in 1962 to produce the works of Gilbert and Sullivan, and from that time they have gone from strength to strength. They have presented staged versions of all surviving operas and other operettas by Sullivan, usually at the Cheltenham amateur theatre, The Playhouse, or at the professional theatre, The Everyman.

6th November, Pam and I were back in the Pump Rooms to give support to the Fine Art Exhibition. In the evening, we welcomed to the parlour The Keep Cheltenham Tidy Group, where we enjoyed talking to the members about their work in keeping Cheltenham tidy, and their future plans.

I returned to the C&GCHE on Friday morning to present the Cheltenham Bowl to the most successful student at the Awards Ceremony.

On Saturday evening, Pam and I attended the official opening of the Dean Close School's £1.5 million state-of-the-art Music School by HRH Prince Michael of Kent. To celebrate the occasion, the School staged a spectacular Gala Concert featuring a host of scholars, past and present, who had a wide range of musical talents. Christopher Bacon, the headmaster said: "It has been a marvellous evening. I am delighted to see the new Music School open and extremely proud of the performance of our scholars."

*

Remembrance Day was marked on Sunday, 9th November with a service at the war memorial in the Cheltenham Long Gardens. The traditional two minutes silence is sounded at 11 o'clock, which is followed by the laying of wreaths by the mayor and other leaders in the community, as well as heads of the Armed Forces.

It is a very sombre occasion and the Promenade is usually crowded with people who have come to pay their respects to those who gave their lives in the cause of freedom in two world wars. The Festival of Remembrance, organised by the Royal British Legion was held at the Town Hall in the evening. I was invited by the organisers to give a speech of welcome. This is an extract of my speech:

"Every year at this time, we pause to remember those who gave their lives in two world wars, and those who have fought and died in other conflicts around the world.

I was honoured when asked to take part in the 'Dedication of the field of remembrance' ceremony on October 30th, which was an opportunity to raise the awareness of everyone to the act of remembrance this weekend.

Although the two world wars are part of the history lessons taught in schools and colleges today, for those who lived through those terrible times, and those who still witness the suffering of family members who were wounded in the wars, memories will always be with them.

But they know, just as we know, that the Royal British Legion is always there to help and offer advice whenever it is needed.

The work of the British Legion has become more important as the years have gone by. Former servicemen and women have become older, which means that more care and attention is needed, and those who sustained serious injuries in the war, often requires additional assistance.

The Legion knows that in order to sustain the work they do, they need the support of the British public. Each year the public give you their full support because they know that they owe you for the sacrifices you made so that all men and women could live in peace and freedom everywhere.

We will never forget you."

Monday, 10th November, I kept my promise to the children of Gloucester Road Primary School and returned with a framed photograph of me with the children; plus the Britain in Bloom Wedgewood Trophy full of sweets.

The children were delighted.

In the evening I attended the launch of the Music Festival sponsorships in the Pump Rooms.

There were no official engagements on Tuesday, which gave Maggie time to arrange a social gathering of former mayors and council officers at the Holst Suite (C&GCHE).

The mayor's chauffeur, Arthur Graham, who had been chauffeur and personal assistant to many mayors over the years, was due to retire on 30th November. The social evening was an opportunity for the mayors and other council officers to say 'thank you' to Arthur for his loyalty and length of service with the council.

The occasion was a complete surprise to Arthur, and I am sure he wondered why so many former mayors were there when he arrived, but my presentation of a clock to him with a kind word or two, soon put him at ease. A few days later I received a hand-written note from Arthur saying how surprised he was to find that the social evening had been arranged for him. He was delighted with the clock and assured me in his letter, "It will always take pride of place in my home."

Wednesday evening I returned to the Carlton Hotel to chair the Annual General Meeting of the Cheltenham branch of the Royal National Lifeboat Institution.

Thursday morning, Pam and I visited Darley House Nursery School in Carlton Street. The visit had been arranged by Doreen Garland-Jones and Marjorie Fulford as part of the Tidy Talks Road Show. Doreen and Marjorie were the founders of the 'road show', which was aimed at young children to educate them in tidiness, recycling and dog ownership responsibilities. The children were delighted to show us how seriously they take the matter, as only very young children can, but the laughter and the joy in the school that morning was something Pam and I talked about long after our visit.

In the evening, we visited the Prince of Wales Stadium, where a sponsored track marathon was taking place in aid of the Winston's Wish Charity.

Friday evening, I attended the Women in Business Charity Auction at the C&GCHE, and the following evening I went to the Stroud District Offices where a 'buffet and chat' occasion took place, followed by a Young Voice Concert.

The Town Hall was the venue for another charity fund raising event on Sunday 16th November, when the band of the Royal Air Force performed in aid of the Cheltenham Lions Club and Royal Air Forces Association (RAFA). The RAFA is the largest single Service Membership organisation, and the longest standing registered service charity that provides welfare support to the RAF family. It provides friendship, help and support to current and former members of the Royal Air Force and their dependants. Pam and I were pleased to be invited and to give it our support.

Monday, 17th November, I invited fourteen men and women from the Summer-field Nursing Home to the parlour. Arthur, my chauffeur and assistant, served coffee and biscuits to the visitors, and I gave my talk about the history of Cheltenham and the memorabilia in the parlour.

A few days later, I received a letter from Carole Dewhurst, the Nursing Home Matron, thanking me for my kindness and hospitality, which had been a great treat for her residents. She enclosed a donation for the Princess Diana Memorial Fund, which I had set up a few weeks earlier.

Early on Tuesday morning, Pam and I arrived at the Overton Lodge Hotel to attend the Rotary Club's breakfast meeting at 7.15 a.m. I knew very little about the Rotarians, other than to know that their purpose is to bring business and profes-sional organisations together in order to provide humanitarian help both locally and internationally.

I had been invited by the Rotary Club to talk about my personal life and my

*Matron Carole Dewhurst and residents from the Summerfield Nursing Home
visit the parlour.*

general opinions about the way I thought the town and the council were performing.

It was a wide brief and with so much time ahead of me, I thought I would make the most of it. The bibliography of my school days and my six years in the Royal Navy did not take too long, but my path in industry from the shop floor to the position of personnel manager, took a little longer.

This is an extract of my speech:

"When I was thinking about my speech to you this morning, I remembered a letter to the Gloucestershire Echo a few weeks ago, which was highly critical of CBC councillors. The writer thought our performance was poor, and we were doing immense damage to the town and the countryside. He said the electors, at election times, should not be looking at the candidate's party political credentials, but his or her job description.

The letter is pinned on the notice board in my office, next to a copy of the book by Timothy Mowl, 'Cheltenham Betrayed', which acts as a constant reminder to me that the people who care most about our town, are not necessarily those who sit on the seats in the council chamber."

When referring to my absence from the Cheltenham Magistrates' Court during my mayoral year, I told the Rotarians:

"I did miss the dour legal arguments and the breath-taking excitement of listening to defendants putting forward their reasons for snatching an old lady's handbag outside Marks and Spencer."

"There have been times" I added, "when it has been difficult to keep a straight face – like an occasion when a motorcyclist hobbled into court on crutches to give evidence against a charge of driving without due care and attention.

I asked the defendant what gear he was in when the accident occurred, to which he replied – a blue tee-shirt and matching jeans, sir.

Or, an occasion in the Crown Court when the barrister said to a witness, 'you say the defendant was drunk' and the witness replied, 'yes, sir, as drunk as a judge'.

Judge Gabriel Hutton said, 'You mean drunk as a Lord', to which the witness replied, Yes, my Lord'.

Two of my ambitions as a borough councillor have been 'to achieve a satisfactory conclusion of the St. James's site and the demolition of the bus shelter in Royal Well'.

It has been sheer incompetence on the part of the council to allow a prime site in the centre of Cheltenham to remain derelict for over 30 years, and the best example of a Regency Crescent in the country, obscured by a hideous and graffiti spoiled bus shelter in the heart of the town.

The PAB Group have always supported the idea of a multi-purpose two tier conference/exhibition centre, capable of easy conversion to a multi-use leisure centre, which would include all the suggestions put forward by the people of Cheltenham, such as an ice skating facility with an ability to convert to roller skating, five-a-side football, tennis tournaments – in fact, all the disciplines that one can think of. The provision of a focal point in the centre for families to come together should be included.

Our proposal also suggested a second storey for retail businesses, with two large restaurants at each end, where parents could book a meal and watch their children play in the leisure area below.

I sent a copy of the PAB proposal to all councillors several days before the meeting where it was scheduled to be debated.

Several councillors wrote to me from both political parties saying they thought the PAB suggestion was a good thing for the town and they would support it. However, in politics, life is never easy. Just when I thought we might be moving forward, I was told that the Liberal Democrats had called an urgent meeting to discuss the PAB proposal and they decided to oppose it.

My other ambition, as you are aware, is to bring about the demolition of the bus station; I despair when a councillor threatens to do a 'Godiva' act if the shelter comes down. It debases the debate on an important subject."

Terri Brewer, the President of the Rotary Club of Cheltenham, wrote to me on 1st December, to thank me for attending their breakfast meeting.

She wrote: "I know it is often quite a tall order to be 'compos mentis' at that time of the morning, let alone give an informative and amusing talk, so our grateful thanks for making it such a success."

Thursday 20th November, I attended the Airborne Security and Emergency Exhibition in the Town Hall.

The following day, I listened to a concert by the junior pupils at Cheltenham Ladies' College in the afternoon, and in the evening I hosted a Civic Dinner in aid of Network Q RAC Rally at the Queen's Hotel. The Dinner and the subsequent Rally that was to be staged at the Racecourse were important occasions for Cheltenham, not least because we had 'pipped' the competition from Manchester, Leeds and Chester, and we would be staging the event at the Racecourse for the next three years.

The following is a précis of my welcome speech to the RAC officials and other invited guests:

"Sir John and Lady Rogers, distinguished guests, ladies and gentlemen – a warm welcome to you all. My welcome is not just to you assembled here tonight, but to all our visitors, rally drivers, officials, media and spectators alike, who are going to make this the biggest sporting event Cheltenham has ever seen.

I feel proud and privileged to be the first mayor of Cheltenham to welcome the RAC and Network Q and the world famous rally to our town.

When I heard that Cheltenham had been chosen by you as the host for the event for the next three years, I was very pleased indeed. Furthermore, I am sure that Cheltenham people will consider it an honour that you have chosen our town as your base.

I know that the RAC is involved in many prestigious events, and its reputation as a world class organisation is well-known.

The support you get from Network Q is vital to the success and organisation of the event, and I would like to take this opportunity to add my thanks to them for their support to the Rally.

The support of the Cheltenham Racecourse Company in acting as host for the Rally cannot go unmentioned. The Racecourse is probably Cheltenham's most famous sporting venue, and it is certainly the home of the best in National Hunt racing, so we are delighted that Lord Vestey and Edward Gillespie have been so active in promoting the RAC Rally.

They have done it in such a way that they have attracted you all here for what will be an exciting weekend.

In a few moments we will be enjoying dinner; I would like to thank Michelle Norton from the RAC and Maggie Handson from the Borough Council, who have done most of the work in organising the evening's event, and Vicky Hickson and the staff of the Queen's Hotel for their help and service.

Do enjoy this weekend; I look forward to seeing and speaking to many of you during the course of the next few days.

A sincere welcome to you all."

At 7.15 a.m. on Sunday, Pam and I wrapped up as warm as we could be on a cold November day, and waved away the first cars in the Network Q RAC Rally 1997 from the Cheltenham Racecourse.

I was surprised by the number of people who had turned out for the start of the Rally, and the presence of reporters and photographers ensured that there would be good copy in the local and national newspapers the following day.

Paul Stimpson, the *Gloucestershire Echo* reporter, had written an article some days earlier with a heading: "Car rally stars roar into town". He wrote: "Britain's biggest sporting event is putting its foot down and steering straight for Cheltenham."

The reporter quoted Paul Fry, CBC's Director of Leisure: "The eyes of the world will be on us", and Ken Jennings, the Head of Tourism said: "It's a phenomenal tourism boost for the town. It will carry the name of Cheltenham across the world and gives us an unprecedented opportunity to raise the town's profile. It is the biggest event Cheltenham has ever bid for and won – now we have got to make it work."

During our time at the Racecourse, Pam and I were attended by Sir John Rogers who kept us informed of what was happening and what to expect next. This was just as well, because we had never been to a car rally before. The sight of two hundred cars going through what was clearly a well thought out procedure was spectacular; the roar of the engines and the colourful car bodies screeching away from the Racecourse was a rare but special occasion for us. We were told by Sir John that the Cheltenham stage of the rally was the final round of the 1997 World Rally Championship, so the final day, which was the following Tuesday, was going to be a very special occasion indeed

Later that day, Pam and I attended the 60th Anniversary Dinner of the Gloucestershire Contract Bridge Association (GCBA) at the Carlton Hotel.

I had been invited to propose a toast and to present prizes to the winners of the various competitions held throughout the year. Bridge, like car rallying events, had not attracted my attention over the years, but I was given valuable help, as you can see from the following précis of my speech:

> "My wife and I are delighted to be here tonight to celebrate with you the 60th Anniversary of the Gloucestershire Contract Bridge Association.
>
> In the short time we have been with you, some of you have been very kind in trying to explain to us the rudiments of the game of bridge. Personally, I am still baffled. Some of my friends, who are here tonight, have told me that the first thing you need to have if you want to play bridge is a strong constitution.
>
> I am told that one can quite easily lose lifelong friends at the end of the game, especially if you fail to spot the secretive glances or the idiosyncratic gestures of one's partner. Not a game for promoting friendships apparently.
>
> However, we are here to celebrate your 60 years as an association, which is a tremendous achievement. Your membership of over 400 members is proof that your association is respected and regarded as a club worthy of membership.
>
> Your anniversary celebrations today, which have attracted expert players and

dignitaries from the world of British bridge, are a tribute by them to you for your respected standing as a leading contract bridge association . . ."

Week commencing Monday 24th November, I met Paul Williams, the mayor's new driver and personal assistant, who would be replacing Arthur at the end of the month.

The Cheltenham Senior Citizens' Annual General Meeting took place in the council chamber at 2.30 p.m., and I was invited to act as the chairman. It was a privilege to do this because the Senior Citizens' Welfare Committee was one of my selected charities.

Tuesday afternoon, Pam and I returned to the Cheltenham Racecourse to watch the closing stages of the Network Q RAC Rally. The grandstands were full and there was a buzz of excitement about the place. Sir John Rogers had explained to me that the event was being beamed to 70 countries around the world, so Cheltenham, he said, "was well and truly on the map." I didn't disagree with him.

During the early evening, a hot-air balloon came over the Racecourse. It was so dangerously close to the Grandstand that one could almost touch it.

Once the last of the rally cars had arrived, I was invited to present the trophy to Colin McRae, the winner, which apparently was the third time he had won the event. For someone who had not taken too much interest in car rallying in the past, I found the atmosphere very exciting.

Thursday evening, Pam and I attended the annual prize giving ceremony at Pittville School. David Abbott had invited me to give what he called "A speech that would inspire the pupils."

It was a tall order – I hoped at the end of it, it would be what the pupils wanted to hear. This is a précis of the speech:

"My wife and I are delighted to be here tonight, to share with you the important occasion of the presentation of the GCSE certificates.

We celebrate with you the exam successes of all school leavers this year who have gone on to either sixth form schools, colleges, or those who have sampled the delights of a working life.

My wife and I are parents of children who have succeeded with their examinations, and made successful careers for themselves.

But we appreciate that we lived in a different era.

We remember the times when LSD meant pounds shillings and pence, when smack meant a clip round the ear, and coke was a bottle of Pepsi. When people mentioned speed, it was usually about a vehicle travelling too fast; weed and grass referred to the garden.

How times have changed?

But opportunities are there for everyone – providing they reach out and take them. The widest possible choice of sixth forms is now available to Pittville students; Bournside, Cleeve and Pate's School, as well as Gloscat and the Agriculture College at Hartpury.

All credit to Pittville School for retaining the link with the Richard Pate School.

The Pate's school as we all know was a 'girls only' school for almost 50 years, but in 1986 it became a co-education comprehensive school. But, throughout this time, there has been that important link with the Pate's sixth form.

The school's attitude regarding the importance of the natural environment is appreciated by the borough council. We were delighted by the response of the Heart of England judges to the school's exhibition stand in Pittville park in June, which portrayed the importance of environmental care along with your plans for a 'wild garden'.

I could not let the evening go by without saying a very big thank you to the pupils and staff of the school for the wonderful display of talent at the mayor's charity fashion show on September 9th.

Not only did you perform to a packed Town Hall, but you gave a lot of pleasure to the public and helped to raise money for local charities.

Headmaster, you have invited me to your school on more than one occasion – I seem to be a regular visitor. Not only have you made me most welcome, I am always impressed with the quality of teaching and the successes you have achieved.

I was delighted to learn of the academic success of last year's head boy, Joe Haines, who gained all passes this year at Grade A, or Grade A*. It is a tremendous achievement, of which I'm sure Joe and his parents can feel justly proud.

But a school is made up of pupils of all abilities. Each and every one of you plays an important part in the school's success, and in its future.

My message to you tonight is to remember always that Pittville School has given you all a good start in life – keep in touch with the school – go back when you need advice, and do build on the start the school has given you.

Good luck to you all."

Saturday, I turned my attention to my fund raising activities with a visit to the Cheltenham Victory Club, where my charity committee had arranged a 'Skittles Marathon'. I was invited to bowl the first ball to start the event. Eight teams from the Cheltenham Skittles League joined individual players in taking turns to floor as many pins as possible.

The *Gloucestershire Echo* followed the event and at the end of the marathon they interviewed Maureen Claridge, the chairman of the Victory Club Ladies' Committee. She said: "It was an excellent day, but one never knows with these events whether they will be a success or not."

She added: The mayor is a local man and a lot of people know him. We had a very good response – people were very generous." The *Echo* reported that the skittles marathon raised more than £600 with additional sponsorship money still to come in. I told the reporter: *"The Victory Club had played an important part in organising several events to raise money for the mayor's charities. They had been instrumental in raising large sums of money by way of a quiz night and a summer fete, and they still had plans to do other things."*

Later that morning I went to St. Michael's Church Hall in Whaddon, to judge paintings in a local exhibition.

In the evening, I switched on the Christmas lights in the usual annual event that always attracts a large number of people to the Promenade. It would be nice to think that they came along to see the Christmas illuminations and the visit of Father Christmas, but the usual entertainment provided by one the top groups is usually the main attraction. Pam and I could not stay long to enjoy the music, because we had been invited to the Scottish Society St. Andrew's Night Dinner at the White House Hotel at Staverton later that night.

Iain Willox, who lived near me, was President of the Society. He asked me to propose a toast to Cheltenham at the end of my speech. I agreed. He then told me, as a warning I believe, that the main part of the meal would be haggis, a traditional Scottish dish, which would be piped in by a couple of Scottish Pipers. "Prior to this", he added, "Pam and I would be given a small glass of whisky. At the given signal, the guests would be invited to drink the whisky in one gulp, and then we would all be free to drink whatever we liked." Whilst it was true that I had drunk a tot of whisky from time to time, I knew that Pam would be mortified at the thought of it, and even more concerned when I told her that haggis was the main course on the menu. However, the night went well, including the Scottish rituals.

In spite of my trepidation, my speech was well received, due no doubt to the amount of whisky that had been consumed.

Sunday, 30th November, we were invited to lunch, along with other guests, at Colesbourne Park, the home of Henry Elwes, the Lord Lieutenant of Gloucestershire and his wife Caroline. The Colesbourne Estate lies in the beautiful setting of the Churn Valley, halfway between Cirencester and Cheltenham, in the heart of the Cotswolds. Unfortunately, we didn't have the opportunity to walk around the vast estate, and I would have loved to have seen the large lake in the wooded valley, with its blue colour believed to be caused by the colloidal soil in the water.

Following a welcome break from mayoral engagements, Pam and I attended the Young Arts Centre on Wednesday, 3rd December, to watch a performance of "The Enchanted Nightingale" by the Centre's young people.

The following day, I had pleasure in presenting a Certificate of Retirement to Charles Badham, who had worked for Cheltenham Borough Council for 31 years.

Thursday, we enjoyed the W. I. Christmas Concert at the Town Hall. We were also invited to attend the Royal National Lifeboat Institution Christmas Concert at the Cheltenham College the following night. Saturday was a busy day with four mayoral visits. In the evening we listened to an excellent concert given by the Cotswold Male Voice Choir in the Town Hall.

Sunday morning, we visited the Severn Sound Studios to support the radio station's Money Mountain Auction. Cllr Brian Jones, mayor of TBC was there, and we were both interviewed by Helen Purcell about our time as the first citizen of our respective towns.

It was a quick visit for Pam and me; we had been invited along with mayors and their wives from other local authorities, to enjoy a Civic Lunch at the Ebley Mill offices of Stroud District Council.

Tuesday, 9th December, I attended the Charlton Kings Primary School for a performance of the children's Christmas School Play.

In the afternoon, I visited Gloucester Road Infants School to watch the children perform their Christmas Play 'Hosannah Rock'. It was a delight to see the very young children perform so enthusiastically.

Later, Pam and I attended the Senior Citizens' Christmas Party in the Town Hall. This has always been a special event in the Cheltenham calendar, and like all previous occasions, the Town Hall was full. Following a short speech of welcome, we went round the hall, chatting with everyone, which seemed to be appreciated.

Wednesday, Pam and I attended a Carol Service at St. Mary's Church, Lydney. It is a medieval church with a history going back to Saxon times, and very well maintained.

Thursday, I opened the new Laura Ashley fashion shop in the Promenade.

Friday 12th December, I opened the new Tempo Store, Tewkesbury Road, in the morning, and had lunch with the Mayor's Charity Committee at the Muffin Man, a cosy café/restaurant, in the basement of 3, Crescent Terrace, where we discussed our charity fund-raising plans for 1998.

At six o'clock, I opened the Christmas Fair at St. James' Church of England Primary School in Merestones Road, The Park.

In the evening, Pam and I attended the Cheltenham Ladies' College Christmas Concert.

Saturday evening, we watched a performance of the Young Gloucestershire Group of actors at The Everyman Theatre.

The week before Christmas was always going to be busy. Maggie Handson and I went carefully through the list of people who had invited me to their functions. I decided that I would carry out as many engagements as possible, even if it meant going quickly from one event to another. My PA thought I was doing too much.

Monday morning, 15th December, I went to Darley House Nursery School in Carlton Street to see a Nativity Play by the children in the Blue Class. And to be doing things fairly, I agreed to return to the school the following morning to watch the children in the Red Class perform a Christmas Concert, which I was told "was especially for the mayor".

In between those occasions, I attended a special Policy & Resources Committee meeting, to discuss the latest position on the park and ride scheme at Arle Court. Immediately following the meeting, I chaired the December Council Meeting in the council chamber.

In the traditional way, I invited the councillors present to join me in the parlour for "Christmas Drinks" and light refreshments.

Later that evening, Pam and I were invited by the Cheltenham Chamber of Commerce, to a Christmas Reception at Hoopers Department Store in the Promenade.

On Tuesday, following our second visit to Darley House, I needed to rush back to the parlour to meet the Radio Five reporter Zog Ziegler, who wanted to interview me for the Top Gear programme. "The interview would be different", he told me, and "it will be done as we do a test drive around the town in a new Daimler with a super-charged V8 engine." It would be different to other interviews, but it sounded great.

The difference between the mayor's 11 year old Daimler, and the one used for the interview, was enormous. The inside of the car was luxurious; fully air-conditioned with leather seats; electric sunroof; electrical adjustable seats; electric headrests; small wooden tables, and an 18–speaker stereo system. Zog Ziegler told me that the car also went from 0 to 60 mph in 5.5 seconds, but I asked him not to demonstrate it. Zog also told me that the cost of the new car would be £63,500, which I assured him would be out-of-the–reach of Cheltenham Borough Council.

Paul Williams, my chauffeur, who had only been in the job three weeks, was inter-viewed by the *Gloucestershire Echo*. This is what he said: "I would like one if I could afford it. I'm not keen on the old one – it's a great big thing. The new one would be a pleasure to drive, but there's no way Cheltenham Borough Council would buy one." Zog, who lives in Cheltenham, told the reporter, "I'm not too sure what kind of chauffeur I was, but I think the mayor enjoyed himself." I certainly did, and I wondered what Arthur Graham would have made of it all.

Later, Pam and I visited the Bethesda Church for their annual Christmas party. We could not stay long because an important 'de-briefing' of the recently held RAC Rally at the Racecourse, was to be held in the Municipal Offices, which required my attendance.

At 5.30 p.m. I welcomed the winners of the Golf Awards, and thanked them for their efforts in raising so much money for my charities at the Lilleybrook Golf Club event.

To end the day, Pam and I attended a Rotary Club Carol Concert at the Town Hall, which was most enjoyable.

Wednesday, 17th December, we visited Pate House, in Princess Elizabeth Way. It provides accommodation for people 60 or over, who are either single or widowed, and able to care for themselves in all the activities of daily life.

From Pate House, we visited the Caroline Strickland Homes at Naunton Park and the Hay Cottage Homes in Hales Road.

All the Homes are charitable housing; provided to enable people who can no longer afford to pay rent to continue living in the community. They are usually maintained by a charity or the trustees of a bequest.

After lunch, Pam and I attended the Christmas Draw at the Shop Mobility Centre in the Beechwood Shopping Centre in the centre of the town.

In the evening we visited the Pump Rooms where the Bournside School Sixth Form Awards Ceremony took place.

Thursday, The Shop Mobility Centre invited Pam and me to their Christmas Party, which was held in the Swindon Village Hall.

In the afternoon, we invited the CBC directors and their personal assistants to the parlour for a 'Christmas drink' and to thank them for their support during my term of office.

Later, we attended the Severn Sound Christmas Carol Service in Gloucester Cathedral.

Friday 19th December, I was invited to lunch in the Unemployed Centre, which was housed in the former Salem Church in Clarence Parade.

Sunday evening, Pam and I went to the Carols by Candlelight service in Christ Church, Malvern Road.

With Christmas approaching, I received Christmas and New Year greetings from our twin towns Annecy, Gottingen, Weihai and Sochi. Other Christmas greetings came from the Consulate of the Republic of Poland and Stampersgat (Netherlands). One of the two Christmas cards that Pam and I treasure came from the residents of the Paradise Community. It was a home-made card with a photograph on the front showing Frederik and his wife among the residents, and inside the handwritten names of everyone, some just about legible. The other card came from Noel and Sheila Telling, Cheltenham.They had written inside the card: "To the People's Mayor and his wife – Christmas greetings and thank you for the Christmas tea party." A lovely thought from two residents, which we appreciated.

Christmas week was less demanding than the previous weeks; a visit to the Leonard Cheshire Home in Charlton Lane, was my only engagement on Monday, 22nd December.

On Christmas Day, Pam and I visited Dowty House residential home in St. Margaret's Road which is a care home for the elderly, to wish everyone a Happy Christmas. From there we went to the Salvation Army Goodwill Hall in Swindon Road, where a Christmas party was underway.

The rest of Christmas was spent with the family, and a relaxing one it was too.

CHAPTER 13

My Mayoral Year – The Final Months

1st January 1998 began with a visit to the Cheltenham Racecourse. Pam and I had accepted an invitation from the local company Kraft Jacobs Suchard, to join other guests in their box for the first race meeting of the New Year. Raymond Savage, their Director of Trade Relations, was our host, and the day, although very cold, was enjoyable.

In the evening, we agreed with an organisation called "Time for Peace" to attend a Vigil in the Long Gardens outside the Municipal Offices.

Friday, 2nd January, Pam and I, with our children, Lorraine, Andrew and Joanne, attended the Veronica Jones Photography Studios for family photographs.

Monday, I spent an hour with the children of the Springbank Playgroup, which is held in the Ron Smith Pavilion, Spring Field Park.

The following morning I paid my second visit to the Charlton Kings Infants' School to see how the children were preparing for the new term, and to watch the variety of subjects they were undertaking.

I was very impressed. I wrote to the Head Teacher. This is a précis from my letter:

> "May I take this opportunity to say how much I enjoyed my visit to the Charlton Kings Infants' School last Tuesday morning. It was a joy and pleasure to be with such a happy group of young children who were clearly excited and impressed by the Mayor's visit to their school.
>
> Their enthusiasm in everything they did was there for all to see. You and your staff can be proud of the work you are doing; the close relationship between teacher and pupils in the different aspects of your work was impressive.
>
> Please tell the children how much I enjoyed my visit."

At midday, I attended the weekly luncheon meeting of the Rotary Club at the Carlton Hotel, where I was met by the President, Douglas Thomson.

I had researched the voluntary work that Rotary clubs do across the country and it formed the basis of my speech to the club members.

It was also an opportunity for me to remind them of my aspirations, which included inviting as many local people as possible to the parlour, and demolishing the concrete bus shelter at Royal Well.

On 16th January, I received a letter from Douglas Thomson. This is an extract from his letter:

> "On behalf of the Rotary Club of Cheltenham, please accept our warmest thanks for coming to our lunchtime meeting last Tuesday, and for giving us such an interesting and enjoyable address.

Several members to whom I have spoken since Tuesday have confirmed my own opinion that it was the best mayoral address we have had for many years. It was humorous, informative without submerging us in too much detail, eloquently delivered and beautifully timed. Altogether an excellent contribution which was greatly appreciated."

Pam and I visited the Cheltenham Stroke Club at the Delancey Hospital on Friday 16th January. It was an uplifting evening being among those who had suffered strokes, and still struggling to come to terms with it. In spite of this, they all joined in with the singing. The music was performed by a local group called 'The Cheltones'.

Derek Brown, a Stroke Club volunteer, wrote to me following the visit. He told me that the members and volunteers were delighted with our visit, and that we had made a very happy impression on everybody.

It was a lovely response, which we appreciated.

An early call on Wednesday 21st January was needed when I joined members of the Gloucestershire Business Breakfast Club at the Queen's Hotel, in the Promenade who were celebrating the 7th Anniversary of the club. The members meet every second Wednesday of the month to discuss business matters over breakfast. The chairman, Brian Chaplin, told me that the object of the Club has been to provide a monthly venue for business people to meet; to exchange views and information about business activities.

During breakfast a talk was given by Denise Livemore, regional fleet manager for Daewoo Cars, and in the background music was provided by the Alex Steele Jazz Band.

It was back to the Queen's Hotel on Friday where I hosted a dinner on behalf of Severn Sound Radio. The invited guests were the highest bidders in the Severn Sound Money Mountain Appeal.

Sunday, 25th January, Pam and I, together with mayors from other local authorities, attended the Tewkesbury Borough Council Civic Service at St. Andrew's Church, Churchdown.

On Wednesday, 28th January, we went to the grand opening of the Bay Tree Court Care Centre, Prestbury, by Lord Oaksey OBE.

Linda Buckland, the Care Centre general manager, explained to the guests that Bay Tree Court had been designed and purpose-built to provide health care services for elderly frail clients. She added: "Considerable thought and effort has been put in to ensure that clients enjoy all the comforts of home."

The High Sheriff of Gloucestershire, W.G.F. Meath Baker, Esq. also attended the opening ceremony.

Thursday, Pam and I attended the Annual General Meeting of the Cheltenham & District Samaritans, at Victoria House, Back Albert Place.

The following evening, we visited the Cheltenham Pregnancy Crisis Centre (CPCC) in Clarence Street, which offers support to women and families in crisis because of unplanned pregnancies.

The volunteers in the Centre had been working hard for months to get the Centre opened by the beginning of 1998, so it was a pleasure to be asked to officially open the Centre on Friday, 30th January.

"Among the 70 guests", according to the CPPC newsletter published in the Spring 1998 edition, "were church ministers, social and health workers, teachers, youth workers and counsellors who had assembled over cheese and wine to listen to various speeches informing them of the Centre's vision and objectives.

Both Nigel Jones and the Mayor, Councillor Les Godwin, spoke supportively of the Centre's work and welcomed our presence within the town."

Saturday morning, I gave support to the Salvation Army Red Shield Awareness Day in the Regent Arcade; the following day, Pam and I went to the finals of the Cotswold Table Tennis Championships at the Cheltenham Recreation Centre.

Monday, 2nd February was a special day. I had been invited by the head teacher, Mrs Ann Fitzpatrick, to visit St Mary's Infants School, Prestbury.

I thought it would be a good idea if I took along the civic mace, and the mayor's chain of office. I was right; the children were excited and wanted to wear the chain around their necks, and to hold the mace.

The *Gloucestershire Echo* came along to film the occasion, and to record for posterity what happened on the day.

The headline of the *Echo* report said: "First citizen sparks a chain reaction when he drops into school". With a photo and caption that read: "Mayor's mace has clout in the classroom". The *Echo* reported: "The mayor's chain of office caused a stir with youngsters at St Mary's Infants School in Prestbury. Cheltenham's first citizen Councillor Les Godwin took the chain and his civic mace along to the school and allowed the pupils to try it on."

The photograph showed pupils Poppy Smith and Charles Homer with the chain around their necks and me explaining the history of the mace, which they both wanted to hold.

Mrs Fitzpatrick told the reporter: "The children really loved it. We have been talking about promises in our morning assemblies, and Cllr Godwin, who is our ward councillor, told them about how, when he became mayor, he promised to do his best for the people of Cheltenham. A few of them tried his chain of office on and they couldn't believe how heavy it is. They guessed it was worth hundreds of pounds when of course it is worth thousands."

After lunch, I met solicitors acting for *Severn Sound* who were defending a claim by Emma Reed for unfair dismissal. Readers will recall that Emma was due to compere the Cheltenham Fashion Show on 9th September 1997, but pulled out at the last minute.

On Wednesday, I made a second visit to St. Mary's School, Prestbury, and this time to visit the Junior School. Although it was a repeat of my Monday visit, it was equally enjoyable.

Peter Vaus, the head teacher, showed me around the school and my talks to the children in the classrooms and in the assembly hall were welcomed. The children put several questions to me about the position of the mayor; the work the council did; who was responsible for various jobs. The questions were incisive and well thought out.

Thursday evening Pam and I were invited to the Royal National Lifeboat Institute Dinner at the Frogmill Inn, Andoversford.

Saturday, 14th February, The Church of St. Philip & St. James, Up Hatherley, arranged a Dinner and Cabaret in the Hatherley Social Centre, in aid of the Mayor's Charities. Pam and I were the guests of honour. It was a delightful evening. The cabaret acts performed by church members, were colourful and carried out skilfully.

Following discussions with my chaplain, Father Stephen Gregory, it was agreed that the traditional Civic Church Service should be held in the Parish Church of St. Mary, Prestbury on 15th February 1998. The occasion warrants the wearing of the ceremonial robes by the councillors, Honorary Aldermen and the Freemen of the Borough. They are required to walk in a formal procession to the church.

Bruce and Margaret Morris, who lived in The Priory adjacent to the church, kindly allowed me and the other councillors to robe in their house. The Civic Service was held within the Parish Family Eucharist. The First Reading was read by me, and the Second Reading by the chairman of Prestbury Parish Council, Malcolm Stennett. The church was full with family members and friends; excellently decorated with flowers; another memorable occasion.

Wednesday, 18th February, I visited the Cheltenham Breast Care Clinic at the General Hospital. I was to meet the clinical nurse specialist, Mrs Sue Kendall, and the staff of the Stoma/Breast Care Unit and to hear about the improvements that would be made to the unit with the money from my charities.

In the evening, Pam and I attended the Annual Dinner of The Insurance Institute of Cheltenham at the Racecourse. The evening went well, and I was pleasantly surprised to receive a letter from the President, Mr Paul Williams, on 24th April, enclosing a cheque for £720.45. Mr Williams, in his letter, said that the cheque represented the amount collected on the night of the Annual Dinner.

He also added: "I am delighted to confirm that this is the highest amount that has been collected on a single occasion, and I am very pleased to be able to offer our support to such worthy causes."

In the weeks leading up to Friday, 20th February, I had been working with my charity committee on several ideas regarding money- raising events.

One suggestion put forward was that I should talk to Vicky Tuck, the Principal of the Cheltenham Ladies' College, and Christopher Bacon, Headmaster of Dean Close School, to try to persuade them to allow a joint musical concert by their pupils, to be performed at Dean Close School's New Theatre.

I spoke to both and they agreed that it was a good idea, even though it had never been attempted before.

They also agreed that the heads of the two music departments would get together to arrange a programme of light classical music, and the practice sessions that would be needed before the performance.

Having set the wheels in motion, I told the charity committee that I would arrange the advertising and other programme details, whilst they had the responsibility of arranging the printing. Everything went according to plan.

The Knightsbridge Business Centre sponsored the event and the programmes and tickets were printed by Kall Kwik, Imperial Square, Cheltenham.

Because the joint musical evening by the pupils was new there was a feeling of trepidation amongst the charity committee members. As it turned out, the two schools put on an excellent programme of light classical music, ending the evening with a performance of jazz music by the newly formed Dean Close School Jazz Band.

The programme went down well with the audience. Some of the pupils from the Ladies' College, who were sitting in the same row as Pam and me, became excited at the performances by the jazz players; tapping their feet and applauding loudly at the end of it.

When the show ended, the girls politely asked me to use my influence with the Principal of the Ladies' College, to seek permission for the formation of a jazz band at the college. I did of course, how could I refuse after all they had done for me and my charities that night?

The Cheltenham Ladies' College eventually had its jazz band; it performs at both the summer and Christmas concerts, where it always receives a rapturous reception at the end of each performance.

I wrote to Christopher Bacon on 25th February, thanking him for the use of the school's facilities, which had enabled members of the public to listen to an evening of excellent music performed by talented young musicians. I also thanked him for the generous donation he had made to my charity appeal, and wished him well as he prepared for his retirement to his farm in Monmouthshire.

Monday, 9th February, *Gloucestershire Echo* had a front page article: "'Secret' plan 4 at GCHQ site", with a sub-heading: "No-one told us – residents". The article claimed: "A new set of plans have emerged for homes and a superstore on GCHQ's Oakley site. People who live near the base are furious and say the proposals have been brought in by the back door."

It added: "Until now, Cheltenham spy-base chiefs have said if it moved its whole operation to Oakley, they would leave half the site untouched because it is an area of outstanding natural beauty. Now, Bristol-based Symonds Group has tabled an application to build a superstore and an unspecified number of houses there."

The *Echo* further reported: "Cllr David Prince (Lib/Dem), whose house in Hillview Road borders the GCHQ site, hopes to arrange a public meeting for residents to discuss their concerns." The following night the local newspaper reported that the Cheltenham Liberal Democrats had suspended Cllr Prince for allegedly 'leaking' the new plans for the GCHQ site. It added that the allegations were being investigated.

When Cllr Prince was interviewed by the *Gloucestershire Echo*, he told the reporter that he had resigned from the Liberal Democrats in protest over the GCHQ plans, adding, "...the Liberal Democrat group was run like a dictatorship." He would now sit as an independent.

I was aware that Cllr Prince was spearheading a residents' campaign against plans to concentrate a GCHQ complex at Oakley, together with a supermarket and several hundred houses. But the cause of Cllr Prince and the local residents seemed to be lost at the CBC Policy & Resources committee meeting on the 9th February, when they 'agreed in private' that council land about the size of five football pitches next to the Oakley site could be built on if the proposed option was chosen.

Whilst the proposed option may not have been welcomed by everyone, it did ensure that GCHQ would remain in the town.

(*Meetings held in private are deemed to be confidential and the press and public are excluded*).

Prestbury Parish Council held an emergency meeting to discuss the Oakley development, which in their view would damage the local environment.

Week commencing 23rd February was varied. Cllr Prince contacted me to explain the problems associated with the GCHQ Oakley proposal, and invited me to be chairman of a public meeting, which was to be held in the Adult Opportunity Centre, Whaddon. "The purpose of the meeting" he told me, "is to give local residents the opportunity to air their views."

My immediate reaction was that he, Cllr Prince, should chair the meeting as he was the ward councillor. This was not accepted. To support his claim that I should chair the meeting, he added that "...having the mayor as chairman would give the meeting more gravitas ..."

I was not impressed, but agreed with his suggestion.

From the briefings I received, including one from the chief planning officer, it seemed that there were three original options for GCHQ.

1. To close the existing Oakley offices and transfer all 4,000 staff to Benhall, with the Oakley site becoming a mini-village of 500 homes with a supermarket, a take-away, video store and a doctor's surgery.
2. To close Benhall, moving all 4,000 staff to Oakley and construct 750 homes and an industrial park on the Benhall site.
3. Close both operations and move to a green field site somewhere between Cheltenham and Tewkesbury.

I also learned that there were four consortia interested in coming forward with plans to take GCHQ into the next millennium. It was all interesting stuff, but I came to the conclusion that the decision by the Policy & Resources Committee to agree to the possible sale of their land at Oakley was premature and it didn't help to move the situation forward.

*

Tuesday afternoon, 24th February, I met Darren Stevens, Chelsea Building Society, and Philip Bernay, chief executive of the Everyman, in the parlour. We discussed the forthcoming Gala Performance of *Talent* in the theatre on 26th March 1998, in aid of my three charities.

Philip explained that *Talent* was an hilarious comedy by Victoria Wood.

He further explained that following a national tour, Granada Television had made *Talent* into a one-hour television play with Julie Walters and Victoria Wood playing the main parts. He told Darren and me that the performers of *Talent* would be John Junkin, Meena Anwar (PC Habib from the BBC's The Thin Blue Line), Freddie(parrot-face) Davies, Sarah Moffett (Kelly from Granada TV's Coronation Street), David Holt and Oliver Beamish, with Rachel Bell taking the part of Kitty. It sounded great to me, and when Darren Stevens reported that Chelsea Building Society would sponsor the event, it was difficult not to get over-excited.

Philip further stated that the Everyman would organise the advertising contributions by writing to local companies. My contribution would be to write a message from the Mayor, which would go on the inside of the front page of the programme.

At 6.30 p.m. I attended the public meeting in Whaddon.

Before the start of the meeting, Cllr Prince introduced me to the committee members of the Oakley Development Residents' Action Group (Odrag).

Following the introductions, I made a final effort to persuade Cllr Prince that as the local ward councillor he should be the chairman of the meeting.

David didn't agree with me and I took my seat next to the secretary of Odrag, Diane Hibbert.

Cllr Prince stood at the back of the hall as though he wanted to be seen as a member of the public and not one of the principal players in the action group.

As the meeting got underway it was clear to me that Diane Hibbert knew the background to the proposal and she answered most of the questions from the audience. I kept my answers to the official facts as I knew them.

I made notes of what had been said during the meeting, which I passed on to the chief planning officer the following day.

In the evening of Wednesday 25th February, I held a reception in the main committee room, Municipal Offices, at 7.30 p.m. for senior members of the Cheltenham branch of the Gloucestershire Youth Council.

The newly launched Cheltenham branch would provide a support team with two centres operating in the town working with young people who need additional support in a variety of ways.

John Anderson, chairman of Cheltenham Harriers, had contacted me at the beginning of week commencing 23rd February, to tell me that Heather Brewer and her children had raised a lot of money for the charity Winston's Wish. John wanted me to agree to a ceremony in the parlour where he and the Brewer family could present a cheque to a representative from the charity. I agreed and arranged for the parlour to be available at six o'clock on 26th February, whilst John contacted the *Gloucestershire Echo* to ensure that a photographer was present to record the event.

On 5th March, the *Echo* published the photograph with a caption that read: "Wish comes true for pals". Winston's Wish, as readers will recall, was the favourite charity of Malcolm Brewer who had died suddenly on Boxing Day 1996. James Brewer (Malcolm's son who was the Great Britain International Indoor 1500m winner) is, at the time of writing, the organiser of the Winston's Wish annual charity run on Boxing Day.

It was another early morning call on Saturday; Brian Jones (Mayor of Tewkesbury Borough Council) and I did a *BBC Radio Gloucestershire* broadcast on our year as mayor.

In the evening I attended the Victory Club Charity Day in aid of my three charities.

Sunday, 1st March, Pam and I attended the Chapel Service at the Cheltenham College Junior School. The headmaster Nigel Archdale had invited me earlier in the year with a request for me to read one of the lessons. Following the service, Nigel and his wife invited Pam and me to their home for coffee and a chat about my mayoral year, which we enjoyed. A few days later I received a card from Nigel Archdale. In it he wrote: "Thank you very much indeed for coming to Chapel yesterday and for reading to us so well. Everyone enjoyed meeting you and your wife and we are most grateful to you both for finding time to spare with us all." The message also included a reminder that the collection during the next College Chapel Service would be for my charities.

In the evening, Pam and I went to David and Stella Prince's house in Hillview Road for a wine and cheese evening. Diane Hibbert and other members of Odrag attended.

Monday morning, Andy Peyton, Cheltenham Independent Insurers, made a visit to the parlour. I had known Andy for a long time. He was impressed with the memorabilia in the parlour, and I was even more impressed when he presented me with a cheque for £1,000 for my three charities.

Tuesday, 3rd March, I was invited by the Salvation Army to go to the Regents Arcade where they would be celebrating a record month for collecting donations in Cheltenham. I joined Nigel Jones MP in a musical programme of hymns that the Salvation Army do with such enthusiasm.

Some shoppers expressed surprise; others joined in.

The *Gloucestershire Echo* complete with photograph, reported: "Army drums up record donations". It added: "Thanks to the generosity of residents, the Salvation Army Corps raised £11,071.49 in February – the highest total in more than 100 years.

Major Harry Wilson said the money raised would go to the national fund and would be used for the charity's social work."

Tuesday evening, Pam and I attended the Severn Sound Money Mountain Presentation Evening at the Cheltenham & Gloucester Moat House, Shurdington Road, Brockworth.

I had the privilege of starting the awards to six charity organisations. There were eight charity groups of six and each group had a presenter who presented cheques to them. It was a tremendous night, which ended with 48 very happy charity organisers clutching their cheques as they went happily home.

In my speech, I thanked *Severn Sound*, its managing director Penny Holton, and all her staff for putting on the presentation, and especially their supreme effort in raising money for so many charitable causes.

Brian Jones the founder and original bandleader of the Rolling Stones was born in Cheltenham in February 1942, and he met an untimely and mysterious death on July 3rd 1969. Brian was a talented musician and an accomplished guitar, harmonica and keyboard player.

His gravestone in the council-owned cemetery in Bouncers Lane is in a prominent position and it is always lavishly adorned with flowers and messages from his fans. In the early part of 1998, a local group of loyal fans wanted Cheltenham Borough Council to formally recognise Brian Jones by erecting a statue in the Promenade to his memory.

I was asked for my opinion by the local press and the media. I told them that I could not support such a proposal, mainly because the reputation of Brian Jones in the local community was not good. His use of drugs during his short life was highly publicised and in my view, did not portray a good example for young people to follow. I also came to the conclusion that should the Borough council have ratepayers' money to spend on statues, then there were far better men and women in the community who had done a lot more for the people of the town than Brian Jones. The printed articles seemed to please a large section of the population, although my words had not been well received by the fans of the late Brian Jones. Although I didn't see the article at the time, I understand that a journalist who wrote in the *Sunday Telegraph* supported my stance against a statue for the pop singer. The article, prompted someone in Florence, Italy, to write me the following letter:

"Dear Mr Mayor,

I read in the Mandrake column of yesterday's Sunday Telegraph that you are opposed to the erection of a statue to a late rock guitarist with the Rolling Stones, Brian Jones – well done!

I absolutely agree with your reasons and your motives – I would like to have a mayor like you here in Florence, Italy.

If my family and I will ever come to live in Cheltenham, we will be proud to have such a sensible and good mayor. We visited Cheltenham last summer and we found your city lovely, beautiful, clean and full of nice and friendly people: a real nice place to visit and stay.

Yours sincerely, L. Gristina, Florence, Italy."

The letter was handwritten; I hoped my letter of reply reached the addressee in Florence safely. I am not sure that it did because I had difficulty understanding the postal address.

At 10.30 a.m. on Wednesday 4th March Pam and I met James J. Devine, Special United States Liaison Officer, and his wife Anne Marie, in the parlour.

I asked the deputy mayor Cllr Garth Barnes to join us. James and his wife were a delightful couple and we got on well.

James told us he was responsible to the Director, National Security Agency (NSA) in all crypto-logical relationships with United Kingdom policy authorities including GCHQ. He was also the principal U.S. advisor to the Director, GCHQ, with offices at the GCHQ complex. James and his wife had lived in Maryland before arriving in England on 20 August 1997. He told me that they were spending their time in London and in Cheltenham at the moment, which suited them.

Garth and I took them on a tour of the council chamber, pointed out the seating arrangements, and explained the protocol and the procedures.

This is a copy of the letter from James Devine dated 18th March 1998:

> *"Thank you for the warm hospitality which you extended to me and my wife during our recent visit to your office. We were delighted to meet you, your lovely wife Pamela, and deputy mayor Garth Barnes.*
>
> *The conversation was stimulating, the surroundings elegant, and the coffee and biscuits delicious! We very much appreciated the opportunity to see the council chamber and to hear you describe the proceedings.*
>
> *We are thoroughly enjoying our assignment in the United Kingdom, and one of the most pleasant aspects of it is the time we get to spend in Cheltenham. The city is a beautiful, friendly and interesting place, and we look forward to exploring it and the surrounding countryside in the months ahead.*
>
> *I welcome the opportunity to work with you, Garth Barnes and the other members of the Council in the days ahead. I hope to visit Cheltenham, Pennsylvania in April, and I will let you know how the visit goes.*
>
> *Best wishes for continued success in your mayoral tenure and very best regards to the Mayoress and Deputy Mayor.*
>
> *James J. Devine."*

At 3.30 p.m. Pam and I met a party of Senior Citizens in the parlour.

I have no idea who selected the names for the visit, but those who came to the parlour seemed to enjoy themselves.

Pam Phelps wrote me a letter which was typical of many I received from local residents who had been invited to the parlour on previous occasions.

This is what she wrote:

> *"Thank you so very much for giving of your time and providing us with the history of Cheltenham, and explaining the wonderful appliqué depicting Cheltenham.*
> *The 'Tea Party' was super; such scrumptious sandwiches and cakes.*
> *Thank you again; my husband enjoyed his cake that I brought home for him; you are really nice people.*
>
> *Pam Phelps."*

At 7.30 p.m. Pam and I attended the Annual General Meeting of the Cancer Research U.K. (Cheltenham) Branch. I was invited to take the chair at the meeting, which was held in Charlton House, Charlton Kings.

Thursday 5th March, Pam and I went to the Town Hall to listen to a concert given by the pupils of Bournside School. "Pupils offer rich mix", said the *Gloucestershire Echo*, and it certainly was that and excellently performed. The *Echo* added: "African drumbeats and a plague of rats were two of the more spectacular features in this wide-ranging concert performed by the pupils and staff of Bournside School and Sixth Form Centre.

The colourful display of African drumming by an ensemble from Year Eight included the African freedom song Siyahamba, sung with fervour and distinction.

Later a 200–strong choir from Year Seven wearing coloured rat masks cut a dash with some lively numbers from the Hesse-Browne musical based on the Pied Piper of Hamelin."

Along with other memorable pieces it was a musical treat, and Roger Jones concluded his *Echo* article with these words: "After a good rousing finale from the Jazz Band, the Mayor, Coun Les Godwin, paid tribute to the talents of Cheltenham's young people and expressed his confidence that the town's reputation for musical excellence was safe in their hands."

Friday morning 6th March, I met 34 Commonwealth MP's, Speakers and presiding Officers, who would be attending the 47th Commonwealth Parliamentary Seminar in London the following week. The delegates from Australia to Tanzania provided stimulating debate in the Pittville Room throughout the morning. Following a short tour of the council building, a visit to the council chamber and the Mayor's parlour, we made our way to the Rising Sun Hotel for lunch.

The occasion had been interesting and the delegates were gracious with their thanks for the time I had spent with them. They presented me with a Wedgewood plate, engraved on the back, which is one of my treasures.

They assured me they would enjoy their short stay in Cheltenham over the weekend before they travelled to the Seminar in London.

One of the most important dates in the mayor's calendar of engagements is the Mayor's Civic Ball. The very name always creates an air of excitement, and so it should, because it is the one occasion when the mayor shares the evening with local people as well as the local dignitaries. It is also an occasion when mayors can make a final appeal to everyone to support their local charities.

Maggie Handson, my PA, sent out invitations to a long list of people including mayors from other local authorities, the High Sheriff and the Lord Lieutenant of Gloucestershire.

The Mayor's Civic Ball on Friday 6th March, was a sell-out.

It was a very enjoyable and successful evening with lots of money pledged for my charities by several people. Much of the success was down to the hard work of people such as Maggie Handson and Tim Harman, who organised the programme of events.

Ken Brightwell, the Town Crier, was the Master of Ceremonies, and music was provided throughout the evening by the Gloucestershire Youth Jazz Orchestra: disco music was played by Mike Crawford from midnight until 1.00 a.m. Midway through the evening there was a Grand Raffle Draw, which proved to be very popular, raising lots of money.

The *Gloucestershire Echo* with a suitable photograph, reported: "Mayor's party is such a ball", with a sub-heading: "Dance the night away".

It added: "More than 300 people tripped the light fantastic to raise hundreds of pounds at the Mayor's Ball at Cheltenham Town Hall.

A party of MP'S from Canada, Australia, India, Pakistan and the Caribbean island Montserrat, attended the dance. They were part of the Commonwealth Parliamentary Association delegation who were visiting Cheltenham for the weekend.

Among those attending were former Labour Home Secretary Lord Merlin Rees, the Lord Lieutenant of Gloucestershire Henry Elwes and his wife Carolyn. The High Sheriff of Gloucestershire, W G F Meath Baker and his wife were also at the ball…"

A few days later, Henry Elwes wrote:

"Dear Les, Thank you so much for a most enjoyable party at the Town Hall. I am so sorry that we had to leave so early but my driver (or more correctly, his wife) was a bit 'iffy' about the late hour.

I do hope your charities did well. You certainly seem to have set a difficult target for your successor.

Henry."

Mr Meath Baker wrote: "Dear Cllr and Mrs Godwin, Thank you for your invitation to the Civic Charity Ball.

Mrs Meath Baker and myself had a most enjoyable time, and met a number of interesting people, particularly those members of the Commonwealth Parliamentary Association, some of whom subsequently came to tea with us the following day.

W G F Meath Baker"

It was certainly a night to remember.

In spite of the previous late night, I was up early the following morning to attend the National Schools' Cross-Country Championships at the Cheltenham Racecourse. The weather was appalling; torrents of water from the hill, washing away everything in its path. Thankfully, channels had been dug through the centre of the competitors' marquees allowing surface water to flow through them and out the other end. At least the areas either side of the channels were dry to allow the athletes to change with some degree of comfort. Notwithstanding the conditions, the runners went out and 'did their stuff' without a murmur of complaint, which I admired.

The mayor's weekly 'diary sheet' suggested warm clothing should be worn, but rainwear and a large brolly would have been more advisable.

In the evening, Pam and I attended the Cheltenham One Act Play Festival at the Playhouse Theatre. A number of amateur drama clubs from across the county performed one act plays throughout the evening.

At the end of the programme, the theatre staff took us back-stage to see 'what goes on behind the scenes' while the shows are being performed.

They told us about the theatre's history, including the fact that the site used to be the Montpellier Baths. It was converted to a swimming pool in 1898 and then to a theatre in 1945.

Cheltenham Borough Council still owns the site. It is on a long term lease to the Theatre Company, which means that a body of volunteers are needed to ensure that amateur drama groups in the county have somewhere to perform throughout the year.

It is self-supporting; dependent on the volunteers and those who have become associate members in a scheme called 'Partners of the Theatre'. I became a 'partner' once my mayoral year had ended.

Sunday 8th March, Pam and I attended St. Matthew's Church, Stroud, for the Stroud District Council's Annual Civic Service.

In the evening, we went to Cheltenham Town Hall to hear Verdi's Requiem Mass performed by Cheltenham Ladies' College.

Monday morning I met the Cultural Councillor of Weihai in the parlour, and with the assistance of Jim Pennington I managed to extend fraternal greetings to our Chinese friends.

Later, I met Darren Stevens (Chelsea Building Society) to put the finishing touches to the forthcoming Gala evening at the Everyman. We were joined by Les Burgess who had come to tell me that final arrangements had been made for the Three Choirs Charity Concert on Saturday 14th March. Darren confirmed that Beaufort Homes had agreed to sponsor the event and would provide the programmes and the tickets. It seemed that everything was in place, although Les Burgess did reveal that because the choirs had other commitments, they had been unable to rehearse together and would be unable to do so until the morning of the concert. Les assured me that everything would be all right on the night, because each choir had been rehearsing the songs under his watchful eye.

At 4.00 p.m. Pam and I enjoyed the company of senior citizens at a tea party in the parlour, which, like the previous ones, was enjoyable and appreciated by all who attended.

Monday 9th March, Cllr David Prince applied to join the PAB group, and his application was accepted.

The scheduled Prestbury Parish Council meeting met in the Prestbury Library at 7.30 p.m. when the main topic of discussion was a new option four for GCHQ. The option comprised the closure of the Benhall site and the housing of all 4,000 staff at Oakley, plus the construction of a supermarket and the an unspecified number of homes on land next to it.

Although the proposal was similar to the previous one, the additions to it would increase the pressures on the road infrastructure and other local facilities.

The *Gloucestershire Echo* reported: "Chairman Malcolm Stennett told the council that there was vital information missing from the plan. He believed that the additional information about the plan, which is yet to arrive, will not give the planning committee enough time to consider the proposal, let alone any public consultation." CBC planning committee were due to discuss the application on Thursday March 26th, but the parish council wanted the committee to defer the application until its next planning meeting on April 23rd to allow the parish council to call a public meeting of Prestbury residents.

At the same time, Charlton Kings Parish Council at its meeting said the new option four for GCHQ could mean a traffic hell in Charlton Kings should it go ahead.

In the Opinion column of the *Gloucestershire Echo* on March 10th, the editor wrote: "Say no to this Oakley plan. No, no, no, no and no again. That must be the only answer to GCHQ's outrageous proposals for its site at Oakley.

We accept that it makes sense for the spy-base to merge its two operations onto one site. We accepted (more or less) the initial outline proposals for each site. But the latest 'Option Four' which popped out of the woodwork after Cheltenham Borough Council had given GCHQ's other three options the go-ahead is beyond the pale. To move the WHOLE of GCHQ to Oakley AND to build houses in an area of outstanding natural beauty PLUS a superstore and heaven knows what else on parkland behind the base is madness"

The opposition to the GCHQ proposal was growing at a pace that I felt someone or something would have to give before the planning committee made its decision.

The local Member of Parliament Nigel Jones told the local newspaper that "… the GCHQ's Option Four was 'pie in the sky' and will not get off the drawing board."

This was followed by forty-five children of Whaddon Primary School writing letters against Option Four and presenting them to CBC via Cllr David Prince. Teacher Ainslie Evans told the *Echo*: "Some pupils don't go out of Whaddon in the summer and the hill is the only place they have to go for picnics or ride their bikes."

Odrag member Diane Hibbert said "….. the feelings expressed by the children are the most genuine one can find."

Wednesday, 11th March, Pam and I were pleased to accept an invitation to attend the Cloud Nine Charity Fashion Show at the Carlton Hotel. Cloud Nine is a local charity that provides holidays for children in Gloucestershire who suffer from acute and chronic illness.

I had promised the children at the Betteridge School that I would visit the school again, so the following day, after a chat with the Head Teacher, I made another visit to the school.

In the evening I attended a charity committee meeting. I outlined the final details of the Three Choirs Concert on 14th March; the committee told me of their plans for more money raising events in the following weeks.

Friday, I was invited to a tree-planting ceremony at Warden Hill Primary School. The event was of special interest for me because my grand-daughter, Charlotte Walker, would be among the children taking part in the ceremony.

Saturday, 14th March was a busy day. In the morning, with other spectators, I watched the Cheltenham & Gloucester College for Higher Education Rag Day procession.

In the afternoon, I opened the Spring Fayre at Pate's Grammar School in Princess Elizabeth Way. I shared the afternoon with Eddie the Eagle, the well-known British Olympic skier who in 1988 became the first competitor to represent Great Britain in Olympic ski jumping.

I received a letter from Karen Belcher, chairman of the Pate's Parents' Association in April. This is what she wrote:

> *"Thank you so much for coming along and opening our Spring Fayre on 14th March. It was most kind of you to fit us into your hectic schedule and we very much appreciated having Cheltenham's Mayor with us for the afternoon.*
>
> *I'm sure you will be pleased to know that we raised well over £3,000 at the fayre. All pupils at Pate's benefit from the extra funds we are able to raise and the school is most appreciative of our efforts. So thank you for contributing to our success.*
>
> *Karen Belcher (PA Chairman)"*

On 12th March, *Gloucestershire Echo* in their daily guide to what is on in Cheltenham, published an article with the headline: "Choirs tune up" with a photograph of me and the Police Male Voice Choir. It said: "Great songs and exciting music are on the cards for Saturday's Three Choirs Concert at the Town Hall. The event will bring together the male voice choirs from Churchdown, Gloucestershire Police and Cotswold for the first time. The choirs will be supported by the soprano Sue Black and the Centurion Brass Ensemble. Miss Black, from Malvern, last performed in Cheltenham in Tosca at the Playhouse Theatre.

Barry Woods, secretary of the Churchdown Male Voice Choir was looking forward to Saturday night. He said: 'It promises to be a very exciting night with lots of lovely music making.'"

The *Echo* article went on to report that the decision to bring the three choirs together was made 12 months ago following discussions with the organisers. It also informed the readers that there would be over 150 vocalists on stage performing a vast array of popular songs.

Apart from Sue Black and the Centurion Brass Ensemble, I should mention Greg Abrahams the organist and the two comperes of the show, Pete and Sue Wilson from *BBC Radio Gloucestershire*. It was a tremendous evening of song and music. Considering that the three choirs only sang together for the first time a few hours before the concert was due to start, they gave an excellent performance. Because it had never been done before, it was certainly a night to remember.

The *Echo* reporter Max Pilgrim wrote: "Three male choirs, a brass ensemble and the Town Hall organ all combined to give a full house a generous helping of entertainment. That it was all in aid of Mayor Les Godwin's charities added to the pleasure of the evening.

The Churchdown, Cotswold and Gloucestershire Police choirs were in robust voice with their selection of hymns and popular classics. This was the first time they had performed together and, judging from their enthusiastic reception, it may well not be the last. Kalinka was especially polished, with soloist Albert England to the fore.

Soprano Susan Black gave effective and contrasting items, including a fine version of 'Time to Say Goodbye'. The Centurion Brass Ensemble and organist Greg Abrahams also made their mark in an effectively presented programme.

Genial comperes Pete and Sue Wilson hinted that rehearsal time had been short for this event, but there was no sign of this in a relaxed and eminently enjoyable occasion." These sentiments were expressed in several letters I received.

> *Jo O'Shea wrote: "Well done! A marvellous evening of singing. Enjoyed it immensely. I hope they do it again."*
>
> *M. C. Donohue from Charlton Kings wrote: "My sincere thanks for a most enjoyable and entertaining choral evening at the Town Hall last Saturday. My wife and I thoroughly enjoyed ourselves and felt the Three Choirs, Brass Ensemble and Soprano acquitted themselves with distinction.*
>
> *I totally agree with the sentiments you expressed and do hope that this evening continues to feature as an annual contribution to the cultural calendar in Cheltenham.*
>
> *I apologise for not staying to express our thanks at the end of the concert; as it was you seemed to be swamped with well wishers.*
> *With very kind regards.*
>
> *M. C. Donohue."*

Monday 16th March, Sam Ilott and members of the Victory Club skittles section, came to the parlour to hand over a cheque for £300 for my three charities.

In the afternoon I attended the Board meeting of the Cheltenham Arts Festival. In the evening Pam and I went to the Reception (Set 98) at the Nuclear Electric Conference Centre in Barnwood, Gloucester, for the 1998 Chemical Engineering Awards Ceremony.

Wednesday morning, Pam and I were invited to the Annual Council Meeting of the Gloucestershire Federation of Women's Institutes (GFWI), at the Town Hall. In opening the annual meeting I gave the delegates a 'potted' history of Cheltenham and what it offers to people who come to stay or visit the town. I finished my speech with the following:

> "The GFWI was formed around 1919 and you now have 6,000 members. This means that you are still going strong, which can only mean that your organisation is greatly respected both in the county and in the country.
>
> You provide a forum for discussion and play a major part in the life of the community – may you continue to prosper in the years ahead.
>
> I am impressed with the wide range of issues you are going to discuss today, and

even more amazed that you can pack so much into one day. It would take the Borough council most of a day to discuss just one of your subjects.

I smiled when I read that a talk was to be given later by Severn Trent Water Authority on 'Water Economy'. Will we be told again by Mrs Bartlett how Severn Trent intends to plug or repair all the leaking water mains? Better still, it would be more interesting to learn how Severn Trent intends to conserve the rainwater and the snow that falls each year."

On Thursday, Pam and I were invited to Gold Cup day at the Cheltenham Race-course. At the end of the Grand Annual Steeplechase race, Edward Gillespie asked Pam to present the trophy to the winning jockey A. P. McCoy.

Later, we were invited to the Royal Suite to have tea with Her Majesty Queen Elizabeth, the Queen Mother – a regular visitor to the Cheltenham Racecourse.

The weather was exceptionally good for the March meeting, which tended to help make the day more than just a memorable experience.

Keeping a promise to the children of St. Mary's Junior School, I invited a party of them, together with their teachers, to come to the parlour on Friday, 20th March. I am sure, like other children who had visited the parlour, they enjoyed every moment.

I received a letter from Claire Price (Deputy Head) of the Junior School dated 30th March. This is what she wrote:

> "Dear Councillor Godwin, Just to tell you how much Class Y3P of St Mary's Junior School enjoyed their visit to the Mayor's parlour on Friday March 20th.
>
> I personally as well as enjoying the visit, was most impressed with your patience and kindness to the children.
>
> The Mace Bearer and yourself made them feel very privileged and important to have been invited into the parlour and the Council Chamber. You will see from their letters to you that they had listened well to the information you gave them. Thank you so much for inviting us.
> Kindest regards.
> Claire Price (Deputy Head)."

On Saturday afternoon, Pam and I attended the Cheltenham Horticultural Society Spring Show at Pittville Pump Room. All the displays were of a high standard. I was pleased that I only had to present the trophies to the winners, rather than choose the winners.

A few days later I received the following letter from R. W. Whorlow the Hon. Secretary of the Society:

> "At our recent committee meeting the Spring Show was discussed. I was asked to write to you to say how much we appreciated the presence of yourself and the mayoress.
>
> It was most kind of you to take such an interest in our event at what must be a very busy time for you.

We thank you very much for your interest and hope that things go well during the remainder of your term of office."

In the evening, we were guests at the Annual Reunion Dinner of the Royal Gloucestershire, Berkshire & Wiltshire Regiment at the Cheltenham Town Hall. The three regiments were amalgamated in April 1994.

Two close neighbours, Jill Robinson and Gwen Parratt, came to see me at my home on Monday 23rd March, to tell me of their concerns about a public open space in Caernarvon Road. They told me that the open space was attracting undesirable people because it was over-grown and uncared for. They believed that if it was equipped with children's play equipment and looked after by the parks department it would be used by the local children. Jill and Gwen wanted to know what they had to do to make sure that the public space was made an attractive area for members of the local community to use. They also wanted me to use whatever influence I had to get funds allocated for the provision of play equipment.

The answer to the first question was easy. All they had to do was to establish a group of like-minded residents and create a title such as 'Caernarvon Road Playing Field Action Group' and start raising funds to help them purchase the equipment. If they were seen to be succeeding with fund raising then the answer to the second question, I told them, would be easier. The Parks & Recreation Department would find it difficult not to support the local residents' aspirations and would enjoy the publicity that went with it, rather than bad press reports should they fail to respond.

I spoke to Martin Burford, a member of Up Hatherley Parish Council, who was keen to help, and immediately took on the task of urging the parks and landscape department to make the open space more usable as a playing field. Martin, Jill and Gwen did a first class job getting local residents interested in the project; I spoke to the Parks & Leisure Manager and the member of the council whose job was to allocate funds for environment improvements. Within a short space of time the open space became a recreation playing field. It was certainly not as easy as it may sound, but all credit is due to Jill, Gwen, Martin and others, for giving the local community a first-class open space for children and adults to use with safety. Sixteen years later it is used as much as ever and respected by the users.

Monday morning 23rd March I was told by a planning officer that there was a good chance that the GCHQ Option Four planning application may not receive a recommendation to permit at the forthcoming planning meeting. Listening to the reasons behind their report, it seemed that they had been surprised by the number of people and organisations who had written to the planning department expressing their concerns. Apart from local residents and two parish councils, letters had been received from architects, Friends of the Earth, the police and the local Member of Parliament.

In the early evening of 23rd March, Pam and I went to the Chelsea Building Society Administrative Headquarters in Thirlestaine Road, where we met Michael Bage the Society's Chief Executive and other guests in the reception area.

Mr Bage made a short address and then invited me to unveil a plaque that commemorated the official opening of the new West Wing and the 25th anniversary of Chelsea Building Society's location to Cheltenham.

We toured the new wing with 30 or 40 other people, mainly representatives of the firms involved with the construction.

Darren Stevens had written to me in February about the opening ceremony and their anniversary, with a request for me to write a message for inclusion in an eight page supplement to be published by the *Gloucestershire Echo* on 24th March.

With a photograph of me in my mayoral robes and a headline: *"Offering valuable support for Cheltenham"*, I wrote the following message:

"I was delighted to accept the invitation from Chelsea Building Society to perform the opening ceremony of the new West Wing at Thirlsestaine Hall, which coincides with the 25th anniversary of the Society's relocation to Cheltenham.

In recent years, the charities of my predecessors have benefited from the support of Chelsea Building Society in so many ways, and principally through its support for a major Charity Gala at the Everyman Theatre.

This year, it is being held on Thursday March 26th and features a performance of Victoria Wood's comedy *Talent*.

We are very proud to have the headquarters of Chelsea Building Society in Cheltenham. I would like to take this opportunity to place on record my thanks to the Building Society, not only in providing valuable employment in our town, but also for the considerable support it gives to so many good causes and charities. I was pleased to note the report in the Gloucestershire Echo (March 3rd 1998), this indicated that you have seen an increase in profits of 38 per cent and mortgage lending has risen to a new record.

This is an excellent result for the Society and is well-timed to coincide with the Anniversary and the opening of the new West Wing.

On behalf of everyone in Cheltenham, I would like to thank Chelsea Building Society for its support of our community."

At 7.30 p.m. I chaired a second meeting of Odrag in the Adult Opportunity Centre in Whaddon. The *Gloucestershire Echo* reported: "More than 50 people crammed into the Centre to hear Cheltenham Mayor Councillor Les Godwin (PAB, Prestbury) announce that a proposal for the controversial Option Four had been deferred.

A loud cheer greeted the news that the bid from the Oakley Partnership would now not be considered by the CBC planning committee on Thursday, when officers had recommended it for refusal."

I told the meeting that the decision, whilst welcome, was only a battle won and we will need to carry on protesting until the developers come to their senses and make Benhall the preferred site to relocate the GCHQ complex.

On Tuesday 24th March, I was invited to open the Bella Pasta Restaurant in the High Street, and later to sample some of the food that had been prepared.

The headline on the front page of the *Gloucestershire Echo* that night: "Park and ride loses fortune", with a sub-heading "Council plods on regardless", was a surprise. "Cheltenham's controversial park-and-ride scheme at Arle Court is losing £2,500 per week" said the article. "Despite the losses" it added, "county councillors are pressing ahead with plans to double the size of the 150–space car park to 300 places. They also want to build two more in Tewkesbury Road and Shurdington." According to the article the county council ploughed £550,000 into setting up the the Arle Court service on October 31st, and Cheltenham Borough Council paid £200,000."

The article concluded: The Mayor of Cheltenham Les Godwin, who stayed away from the opening ceremony, commented that "it didn't strike me as a successful operation, and it doesn't seem right that the facility is digging into the pockets of the local taxpayers in Cheltenham."

Wednesday morning I welcomed a party of Annecy students in the meeting room at the Cheltenham Art Gallery and Museum.

Later that morning Pam and I travelled to Paradise House to have coffee with Frederik Roder, his wife and the residents. Frederik was especially keen that Pam and I should extend our visit this time, taking in most of the workshops and the surrounding area, probably because he realised that the our visit could possibly be the last one we would be making.

Paradise Community, as it said in large print on its headed notepaper, was based on the principles of Rudolf Steiner, being unique it is difficult to describe. The peace and tranquillity that pervades was special, and the service that Frederik, his wife and staff provided for the residents was special too.

I wish Pam and I had made an effort to go back to the Paradise Community soon after the mayoral year had ended; we could have learned a lot more than we did when we visited in 1997 and 1998.

In 2013, I did go back to Paradise village. The one person I spoke to seemed vague about the 'Community', which upon reflection I found odd considering Paradise House was only a few hundred yards away from where we were standing. On another occasion, I was bolder and drove down the long drive to Paradise House. Nothing much had changed it seemed. The neat piles of sawn logs were still in the same places, the outbuildings were still there but there was no sign of human activity, so unlike the situation that Pam and I had experienced when we visited the house all those years ago. There was a small car park which was not there before, with a few parked cars and a few spaces. I parked the car and took a short walk to a reception office.

I knew from the web site that Paradise House was still a care home for people with special needs, but when I spoke to the receptionist about the Roders and the Paradise Community, (recalling the frequent visits that Pam and I had made when I was mayor of Cheltenham in 1997 and 1998), the receptionist could give no information and the conversation became one-sided. I was beginning to wonder whether the Paradise Community had existed in the late 1990's because the replies to my questions were so negative.

I wanted to refresh my memory of the place, but I was told most emphatically that I couldn't walk around the place unescorted. I wondered what Frederik Roder would have thought about such a rule.

I have since contacted Stroud District Council, spoken to villagers and local business people, but the answer has always been the same, "Sorry I cannot help you". The only information I have obtained is that Frederik Roder died a few years ago, and that his wife is alive and living in Painswick. But I have also been told that the records do not show the name Roder currently living in Painswick, so my research has come to an end.

Later that day I went to the Everyman Theatre to meet the cast of *Talent*. Bearing in mind I was in the presence of comedy performers, the visit was a big laugh from start to finish. Even the tour back stage, which Philip Bernay undertook at great risk to his reputation, was interspersed with jokes about things that could go wrong, and have gone wrong in previous shows.

Finally, we got around to the purpose of the visit, which was to allow official photographs to be taken.

Even this was a laugh – John Junkin got an easy chair (one of the props), made me sit in it whilst Freddie (parrot-face) Davies wanted to pose with him lifting my legs off the ground for some inexplicable reason. Apart from the usual banter from the cast, the photo-shoot went well.

The following morning I chaired the Annual General Meeting of the Senior Citizens' Club in the Montpellier Room. In the afternoon I took my place in the Planning Committee Meeting, and in the evening Pam and I attended the much anticipated Charity Gala Performance of *Talent* at the Everyman Theatre. It was an excellent show to a packed house with a standing ovation at the end.

The *Gloucestershire Echo*, with a photograph said: "Gala boosts appeal". The article went on to say: "Theatre-goers boosted the coffers of good causes when they turned out for Cheltenham mayor Les Godwin's gala evening. More than 550 people attended the Everyman Theatre for a special performance of Victoria Wood's comedy drama *Talent*, starring John Junkin and Freddie ('parrot-face') Davies. A total of more than £4,500 is expected to have been raised by the event, which was sponsored by Cheltenham-based Chelsea Building Society. The total raised by the mayor's charity appeal now stands at £26,000."

The following day I received a letter from Henry Elwes, Lord Lieutenant of Gloucestershire. This is what he wrote:

"Dear Les, Thank you very much for a lovely evening at the Everyman, we both enjoyed the way in which Victoria Wood had portrayed the hopelessness of the characters and thought she had probably seen it all for real.

Many thanks and best wishes for the last few weeks of your very successful term of office. Yours sincerely,

Henry."

On Friday 27th March, I took part in the appraisal of Andrew North, Chief Executive of Cheltenham Borough Council. Later Pam and I entertained another party of friends and guests to an evening in the parlour.

Saturday morning I was invited to a Service of Remembrance for those who served in HMS Legion between December 1940 and March 1942. Jim Swain, Cheltenham Branch Royal Naval Association (RNA), invited me to the dedication, which was held in the foyer of the Town Hall. It was, in Jim's words, "An opportunity to remember and to honour the civilian effort of Warship Week in Cheltenham in 1941 when a massive £1,046,960 was raised for the war effort."

Apparently, the Admiralty were so impressed that they allocated a new Fleet destroyer to be adopted by the town. HMS Legion was the chosen vessel. The ship played an important part in the Second World War, guarding convoys to and from Malta. Unfortunately, the ship did not survive a Stuka attack on March 26th when she suffered a direct hit on the forward magazine whilst she was at anchor in Valletta harbour.

In the evening, Pam and I went to the Town Hall to listen to the Spring Concert of the Cheltenham Bach Choir.

On Monday 30th March, I attended the Annual General Meeting of the Lillian Faithful House in Suffolk Square, and on Tuesday afternoon I attended the unveiling of the Sir Charles Irving bust in the Town Hall.

Cllr David Lawrence, chairman of the CBC civic sub-committee, unveiled the plaque commemorating the life of Sir Charles Irving, who had been the Conservative Member of Parliament for Cheltenham from 1974 until 1992.

He was elected to Cheltenham Borough Council in 1947 and the following year he was elected to Gloucestershire County Council. He had been mayor from 1958 to 1960 and again in 1971/72. He was knighted in 1990.

Wednesday, 1st April, I attended the official "Take-over Ceremony" of the Sports Hall at the Bournside School, Warden Hill Road.

Friday morning, I was invited by the Borough Council and the Cheltenham Civic Society, to tour the buildings in the town that had met the Civic award 'standards of excellence' in the restoration of historic buildings, and those that had made improvements in Cheltenham's built environment.

The annual Civic Awards Ceremony took place in the Town Hall and the awards were presented by Sasha Lubetkin. Later, I hosted lunch in the parlour. Karen Radford, the organiser of the Civic Awards, sent me a lovely card a few days later adding the following words:

"Dear Les and Pam, Just a brief note to thank you both on behalf of the Civic Society and the Civic Awards Adjudication panel, for not only attending the Civic Awards last Friday, but kindly hosting a lovely lunch.

I think it was a very enjoyable day for all those concerned and a very proud occasion for some enlightened building owners, architects and contractors.

Your words of praise for the Award recipients, and yet concern for the architectural future of Cheltenham was appropriate.
With many thanks and best wishes.
Karen."

George A J Mathers, Gloucestershire Architectural Association wrote:

"Dear Mr Mayor,
First I wish to thank you for the luncheon kindly offered to the Panel last Friday, a fine fitting to a worthy event.
Following your forthright remarks at the luncheon, I have prepared a menu, which I attach, to advise members of committees on which I serve of what seems to be a somewhat unsatisfactory state of affairs. I hope I have interpreted your remarks accurately.
All those on committees and panels offer their time and expertise in the expectation that it will be respected and will contribute towards a better, or at least a controlled environment for us all, and if, as you have inferred, we are all wasting our time, we feel the situation ought to be remedied.
Perhaps we could hope for your support in any action we find it possible to take. I would be glad to have your views.
George A J Mathers ARIBA"

I responded and this is an extract from my letter:

"Thank you for the copy of the memo and I hope it does some good in the right quarters so that future planning applications concerning the town are dealt with in a serious manner.
I would remind you that Karen Radford the Conservation Officer appeared to agree with the sentiments I expressed at the luncheon.
I thought it was noticeable at the Awards Ceremony that only one council officer was present and no other elected member attended. If they were invited and did not turn up then that is appalling. It also says a great deal about their attitude to safeguarding the town's most precious assets ."

Later that evening, we attended the Tewkesbury Borough Council Civic Ball at RAF Innsworth.

On Sunday, we went to the City of Gloucester Civic Service at the Hospital Chapel, Gloucester Royal Hospital.

Wednesday, I welcomed members of The Keep Cheltenham Tidy Group who had participated in the National Spring Clean Relay, to the parlour for lunch.

Paul Williams, the mayor's chauffer, was getting the hang of providing wine and serving lunch to my guests, and he seemed to be enjoying his role.

Doreen Garland-Jones, chairman of the group, wrote the following letter:

"On behalf of the members, I do want to express our appreciation for your support and interest at the National Spring Clean Relay.

It was a real boost for us to be able to meet in the Mayor's Parlour and to have lunch there thus providing a very happy start to the event. May I ask you to pass on our thanks to Paul, your officer, who was so helpful in so many ways?

Despite the inclement weather, I felt it was a happy occasion and went extremely well. It was good fun too. The success was due in no small measure to your presence, support and interest and we do thank you.

Dee Garland-Jones."

Jim Swain informed me that the Marinekameradschaft (German equivalent to the RNA), Gottingen, were visiting Cheltenham on Thursday 9th April 1998, for a three day visit.

Jim had been secretary, chairman, branch delegate and president during his lifetime with the RNA, and a fount of knowledge whenever it was needed. He told me that the two RNA's had been 'twinned' for many years with both Associations sharing hospitality and warmth whenever they met.

The RNA rented a room at the Victory Club where naval memorabilia and plaques adorn the walls. I met Jim there one evening; he told me that the Marinekameradschaft had formed a Shanty Choir in 1974 and they regularly performed in Germany. Jim had arranged for the choir to give a concert of shanty music at the Victory Club on Friday night, and invited Pam and me to be his guests.

Jim, as informative as usual, told us that it would be the first time they had performed in England, and he was hoping for a full house.

After the performance, the Shanty Choir presented me with a quartz clock. It is very special in as much as it has the Shanty Choir's emblem on the centre of the dial, and it serves as a constant reminder of Jim Swain, a most loyal member of the Cheltenham Branch of the RNA. Jim died on 26th May 2006. The clock hangs on my office wall and it keeps perfect time.

Saturday morning I was invited to join Cllr Dave Prince and other members of Odrag at the Imjin Road Playing Field. The purpose was to see the layout of the field and its importance as a community facility.

In the afternoon, Pam and I attended a performance of "Charlotte's Web" at the Everyman Theatre. It was a very special occasion for 200 bereaved children who were treated to an afternoon of fun and entertainment, whilst celebrating the fifth birthday of the Winston's Wish charity.

We enjoyed the show, and the children, as usual, showed their enthusiasm throughout by cheering almost everything that happened on stage. At the end of the performance, I was invited to give each of the 200 children an Easter egg.

Mrs Alison Broadbent (Assistant Fund-raising Co-ordinator) wrote to me a few days later, thanking me on behalf of the team at Winston's Wish, for attending the Everyman Theatre. She hoped "I was not too exhausted after giving out so many Easter eggs to the children."

She enclosed a "Certificate of Caring" signed by Julie Stokes, which is another of my prized possessions. There was an excellent article in the *Gloucestershire Echo* which captured the occasion. In the centre of several photographs of the children was a heading: "A wish comes true". The article explained: "E B White's children's classic deals with death, life and friendship, a subject which touches them all.

Many children met pals they had made during one of the charity's weekend camps in Mitcheldean. All carried the Winston teddy bears they were given to show they had at least one friend to turn to for a comforting cuddle. The theatre trip was paid for with £500 raised in the memory of former Cheltenham Harriers under-15's athletics coach Malcolm Brewer. Easter eggs were donated by Kraft Jacobs Suchard, who also sponsored the event. Winston candles were given to the children at the end of the party together with a cake which was supplied by the Swindon Village Ladies' Club."

Easter Monday, April 13th, Gill Bullock, a member of the mayor's charity committee, held a coffee morning at her home in order to raise money for the Breast Care Fund. Apart from the coffee and cake sales, Gill had arranged a number of bring and buy stalls, which proved to be very popular with the ladies who called in to give support to the charity.

In the afternoon, I joined a group of a hundred or more local residents on the Oakley playing field signing petitions calling on GCHQ "to leave our playing field alone." The *Gloucestershire Echo* photographer was there to record me signing the petition along with local residents from Prestbury and Pittville.

Tuesday morning, I welcomed a number of Council representatives from County Mayo, Ireland, to the parlour.

On Wednesday morning I met a group of 27 teachers from East and West Germany in the parlour. Mrs Gay Foster, Charlton Kings, had arranged the Reception through Maggie Handson my Personal Assistant. It was an annual event in the Cheltenham mayor's calendar. Mrs Foster, thankfully, was there to act as interpreter, although many of the German teachers spoke very good English. She explained to me that the teachers spend two weeks in Cheltenham with local families, visiting and observing classes in secondary schools in the town. When they return to Germany, they write a report to the Berlin Education Ministry, which, Gay revealed, had been glowing ones following past visits.

In the evening, Pam and I saw the Gloucester Gang Show at the Bacon Theatre, Dean Close School.

Thursday morning, we were among the guests at the Gloucester City Civic Luncheon in Gloucester Docks. The 'Docks' were undergoing a very large refurbishing project, which the guests were shown in detail by the Gloucester City mayor.

In the evening, Pam and I hosted a former mayors' Dinner at the Prestbury House Hotel.

Friday, 17th April, I accepted an invitation to record a programme for the *Cotswold Listener*. I met Paul Woodbridge at his home in Swanswell Drive,

Benhall. He explained that the *Cotswold Listener* was a 'talking newspaper' for the blind who lived in Cheltenham, Tewkesbury and the north Gloucestershire areas. "The purpose of the 'talking newspaper'," said Paul "is to help the visually impaired stay in touch with events that happen locally, and to be kept aware of the issues that interest them." The *Cotswold Listener* was established in 1978 and is run entirely by volunteers and funded solely by donation, and it is a registered charity. The *Cotswold Listener* had a recording studio at Ellerslie House in Albert Road, but there was sufficient recording apparatus at his home where the interview took place.

He explained that he would ask me questions about my earlier life, my experiences in the Royal Navy, and of course my mayoral year up to that time. It was a new experience for me; I hoped it would be a success.

I received a letter from Paul Woodbridge on 5th May. He wrote:

"Thank you so much for recording your most interesting story for our blind and partially sighted listeners. Please find enclosed a copy of our latest magazine tape, which includes your interview. Your year of office is soon ending, but it will be a year you will always remember with pride and satisfaction.
Paul Woodbridge."

At the Town Hall, Pam and I attended a Peter Stone 'musical tribute concert' for disabled people. It was a tribute to the music of Georgie Fame.

On Sunday morning, we went to the South Gloucestershire District Council's Civic Service at St. Mary's Church, Hawkesbury. The church dates back to the Saxon period.

Tuesday 21st April, I welcomed to the parlour a party of visitors from Hungary.

The visit had been arranged at short notice by the Gloucestershire Education Office, who explained that the visitors were local government officials who were visiting Cheltenham and were keen to establish good links with the town.

Later that day, I was asked to present a set of Ford Mondeo car keys to Mr Michael Halsted of Pittville, on behalf of the Arsenal Gunners Association. Apparently, he had won the first prize in a national raffle competition by the Gunners.

After the presentation ceremony, Mr Halsted told me that the 'Regimental Gunners' had held a dinner a few months earlier when the raffle tickets were drawn by the well-known Welsh comedian and singer, Harry Secombe. He added, "It was so long ago I had forgotten all about it."

A few days later I received a photograph from Michael Halsted showing me presenting the keys to him as he sat in the Mondeo. On the back of the photograph he wrote:

"To the Mayor, Les Godwin. Thank you: a memento of your 601st engagement from a grateful citizen, who is happy to make your acquaintance – and often.
All the very best. Michael Halsted."

It was very touching and I appreciated it.

At 7.30 p.m. I presided at the AGM of the Cheltenham Local History Society, which was held in the Council Chamber.

Jean Lacock wrote thanking me for being their President during my mayoral year and for chairing the AGM.

Wednesday evening Pam and I attended the Junior Final of the Rugby Combination Cup at the Prince of Wales Stadium. At the end of the game I presented the trophy and individual medals to the winners, the Old Patesians Rugby Football team.

In spite of dozens of letters; hundreds of names on a petition; demonstrations, and public meetings; outline planning permission was given for plans to move all 4,000 staff to Oakley at the 23rd April planning committee meeting.

The planning officer's report stated there were no "insuperable" planning objections to the development of the fields because none can be found in the Local Plan. This was a strange comment to make when only four weeks before the same officer recommended refusal on the grounds that it would ruin the Area of Outstanding Natural Beauty (AONB).

The only change in the April plan from the March plan was a reduction in the height of the main building, which would hardly save the AONB from ruination. Malcolm Stennett, Chairman of Prestbury Parish Council was furious. He claimed that nothing had changed since the last application. He told the local newspaper: "Once again the council have shown they will do nothing to protect the open countryside around the town." It was a statement that would be repeated many more times in the future as the countryside and the Green Belt became threatened by developers. Friends of the Earth and the local Member of Parliament sought a public inquiry on the GCHQ plans for the Oakley site. The Secretary of State rejected the application.

Thursday evening 23rd April, Pam and I went to Gloucester Cathedral for the St. George's Day Service.

Friday morning I attended the opening of the Academic Year at the Shukutoku Cheltenham College in Pittville Lawn. The Japanese students made me most welcome; they wanted to show me their work and to explain in minute detail what they were hoping to do during their time in Cheltenham. Mitsunori Dozono the College Principal wrote:

> *"Dear Cllr Godwin, On behalf of the students and staff at this college I would like to thank you very much for joining us on April 24th and officially opening our new college year.*
>
> *The students were excited and thrilled that you were able to visit our college and found you to be a very friendly 'head of our town'.*
>
> *We are enclosing some photographs taken on that day and we wondered if we could have copies of photographs taken by your chauffeur.*
> *With many thanks.*
> *Mitsunori Dozono."*

For the record, I did obtain photographs and negatives and they were passed on to the college Principal.

In July 1997, I had received a letter from John Lymbury, Press officer and Conference Convenor of The Law Society Sole Practitioners Group, asking me to open the business session of their Annual Conference at the Golden Valley Hotel on April 25th 1998.

I had accepted the invitation and John Lymbury sent me another letter setting out the arrangements of the conference. This is a précis:

> *"Dear Mr Mayor,*
>
> *Thank you for kindly agreeing to open the Conference, and thank you for your friendly letter, which will be published in the Conference brochures.*
>
> *After introducing you, my chairman, Tim Readman, will invite you to say a few words to our delegates.*
>
> *At the end of your address, which should be no longer than five minutes, my chairman will make a small donation to you on behalf of the Group; he will then invite you to stay as long as you may wish to listen to the deliberations.*
> *John Lymbury."*

My speech of welcome included the usual praise for the Cheltenham and Cotswold area, pointing out the shopping facilities and the parks and the villages on the outskirts of the town.

Once the applause had ended, the chairman presented me with a beautifully patterned glass jug as a thank you gift from the Sole Practitioners Group.

In the evening, Pam and I took part in a Quiz Night at the Hillview Community Centre in aid of my three charities.

Sunday 26th April, we attended the Cotswold District Council's Civic Service at St. Mary's Church, Fairford.

Monday morning, Maggie Handson told me that there had been a number of late requests from different organisations for me to attend their functions before my mayoral year came to an end.

"Apart from the invitations to the parlour in the evenings", Maggie said "it looks as though you still have 29 official engagements before you can call it a day."

We went through the list of engagements and the names of those who wanted to come to the parlour for a chat. One thing was clear, I would need to see as many people and organisations as possible each day so that no-one was turned away.

Maggie reminded me that the 29 engagements did include the Mayor's Farewell Party in the Pittville Pump Room on the 14th May, adding that most of the arrangements had been made. She intended to send out the invitations once I had agreed the final names in the list.

Pam and I had agreed that we would hold the 'thank you' farewell party as a mark of appreciation to all those who had played a part in my mayoral year. Names at the top of the list were my hard-working charity committee members; names of the representatives from local businesses who had donated or sponsored events, plus friends and members of several local groups who had made a contribution.

A large group of Japanese students visiting the Municipal Offices

A welcome speech to the Japanese students

PAB colleagues and their wives were also on the list. There were nearly two hundred names the last time I counted. Monday 27th April, I chaired my last Council meeting.

Wednesday evening, Pam and I went to the Prince of Wales Stadium to watch the final of the Cheltenham Senior Rugby Combination Cup. I presented the cup and trophies to the winning Cheltenham North RFC team.

Thursday morning, we visited the telecommunications and data cabling firm Krone (UK) plant in Runnings Road, Kingsditch Lane. Klaus Krone, chairman of Krone (AG), the German parent company, welcomed the Duke of Gloucester to the company; he had expressed an interest in visiting thriving companies during a whirlwind tour of the county. We were told that Krone had been selected by the Duke after winning the best factory award in the electronics and electrical sector from the *Management Today* magazine. The Duke of Gloucester spent 30 minutes touring the factory.

In the evening, Pam and I attended the Showcase Concert at The Hexagon Theatre, Kingsfield School, South Gloucestershire.

Friday 1st May, I was invited to open the Majestic Wine Store in Winchcombe Street, Cheltenham. Emma Davis, Public Relations Manager, wrote to me following my visit:

> *"Dear Mr Mayor, Thank you so much for sparing the time in your hectic schedule to open Majestic Wine's new branch in Cheltenham. It was lovely to meet you and I hope you enjoyed the event as much as we did.*
>
> *Once again may I take the opportunity to thank you for attending the opening and announcing the store open?*
> *I will forward a photograph of the event in due course.*
> *Emma Davis."*

I received a letter dated 30th April from Smith Robinson & Co, a Cheltenham firm of solicitors and advocates, enclosing a cheque for £300.

The letter said:

> *"Dear Les, I am sorry about the delay which has been caused by a bout of ill-health, but I enclose my cheque in the sum of £300 as promised, made payable to The Mayor's Charity Fund. The firm is pleased to assist.*
>
> *You are now coming to the end of your year in office and I think that I can truthfully say without letting any cats out of the bag, that you have been a wonderful Ambassador for the Town and have been the best Mayor of Cheltenham for ages.*
>
> *No doubt you are missing your other roles and perhaps we will have the pleasure of having you back at Court so that you resume your nasty habit of sending naughty boys down.*
> *Tim Robinson on behalf of Smith Robinson & Co."*

In the afternoon of May 1st I welcomed Rotarians and their wives from Chatellerault, France, on their arrival at Pittville Pump Room.

Dr Max Cranna had written to me in April to explain that the visit was a traditional one between the two Rotarian Clubs because they had been twinned for some time. "When the visitors arrive by coach" he wrote, "there would be a fifteen minute period when the guests would unload their luggage and then greet their Cheltenham Rotarian friends. Once they had reloaded their luggage in the backs of the waiting cars, we would go inside. During lunch, the President of the Cheltenham Rotarians Mr Douglas Thomson will introduce you and the President of the Chatellerault club, Dr Philippe Derouet, consultant cardiologist will reply – probably in English in which he is fluent."

In conclusion, Max Cranna asked me to send him a copy of my speech because he had the job of translator for the visit, which was a blessing in one respect, but can be difficult when it comes to the pauses in the speech one is supposed to make. However, the whole occasion was very friendly and it went well.

The following is an extract from my speech of welcome:

> "Mr President, ladies and gentlemen, on behalf of Cheltenham, your fellow Rotarians in Cheltenham, a very warm welcome to you all.
>
> Cheltenham on the first day of May is a lovely place to be; we have made special effort for the town and the parks to look especially nice for you so that your visit to Cheltenham in 1998 is a memorable one.
>
> Like Chatellerault, Cheltenham is a beautiful town. It was once described by a visitor as a 'town within a park, in as far as the park is so much part of the town that the two are indivisible'
>
> Those of you who have visited Cheltenham before will understand the meaning of the words, but visitors for the first time will have a lot to see, and I know you will enjoy your time here.
>
> It is fortuitous that we should be greeting each other here in the magnificent Pittville Pump Room 30 years on from the first occasion when contact was first made with Monsieur Albert Ludi, who was chairman of the affiliated company, Sarco S.A. in Chantellerault.
>
> The late Lionel Northcroft, chairman of Spirax Sarco Limited, who I knew well, was a respected leading figure in the life of Cheltenham. He was a great benefactor to many causes within the town; the chandeliers and the floor of this building were generously donated by him.
>
> The twinning of the two Rotarian clubs is an incredible story, and from what I have read and heard about your lasting friendships, it is very much on the cards that it will last another 30 years.
>
> I am a fervent believer in strengthening bonds between peoples from all countries; we must try to understand the reasons that often keep us apart. We should recognise and accept that other cultures have a different life to ourselves, and we are all entitled to share this beautiful planet. It is far better to share things in a loving and friendly way, and if we succeed in doing that then we can at least claim to have established the first step towards a lasting world peace.......
>
> Welcome and enjoy your time here, and may you establish many more new friendships before you return home."

Dr Max Cranna wrote to me a few days after the visitors returned to France. He wrote:

> *"Dear Mr Mayor, Here is another item for your scrap-book (photograph of me among the French Rotarians and their wives).*
>
> *Your warm welcome to the visiting Rotarians from Chatellerault was very much appreciated, as was your thoughtful speech. The President of the French club, Dr Philippe Derouet and his wife were greatly impressed.*
> *Many thanks from us all, and best wishes for your "retirement" on 18th May.*
> *Max Cranna."*

The evening of May 1st I attended the Annual Dinner of the Cheltenham Rugby Football Colts at the Prince of Wales Stadium.

Saturday afternoon, I was invited to visit the Cheltenham Town Football Club at Whaddon Road.

In the evening, Pam and I watched the Cheltenham Operatic Dramatic Society (CODS) production of *High Society* at The Playhouse Theatre.

Sunday 3rd May, we attended the service at the Highbury Congregational Church, Priory Walk, Cheltenham.

Tuesday morning I invited the winners of the Cheltenham in Bloom Spring Garden Competition to the parlour when I presented them with their prizes and trophies.

The *Gloucestershire Echo* covered the event with beautiful photographs of two of the winners in their colourful gardens. The captions: "Winners' gardens are growing just fine according to the competition judges" and "Ann's beds are top of the crop" were fitting for the article that had been written. This is an extract of the *Echo* article: "Gardening is a labour of love for midwife Ann Attwood. After a hard shift in the maternity wards, there is nothing she likes better than weeding the flower beds or mowing the lawn.

Now she has been awarded first prize in the Cheltenham in Bloom Spring Garden competition. Her award-winning display was made up of hundreds of pansies, tulips and daffodils.

Mrs Attwood, a recipient of the Cheltenham Medal of Honour for her 28 years' work with the town's branch of Mencap last May, received her prize of a framed certificate and a silver rose bowl from Mayor Councillor Les Godwin.

Contract cleaner Alex Lewis of Union Street, took second place in the competition at the first attempt. His garden is full of pots, tubs and baskets with just enough space to put up his deckchair.

Shelagh Hallaway, of Collum End Rise, Leckhampton, came third."

In the evening, I attended the 75th Anniversary of the Adoption of the Constitution – Gloucestershire Rural Community Council (GRCC) at College Green, Gloucester. GRCC offers professional advice and support for Gloucestershire's communities. It was established in 1923 with the aim of promoting education and alleviating poverty in rural communities in the aftermath of the First World War.

The Community Council was new to me yet its benefactors included the county council, the YMCA, the British Legion and others, with whom I had had dealings over many years.

Meeting the volunteers at College Green was a pleasure; trying to develop social life in the rural villages seemed to me to be a worthwhile cause. I was told that the Community Council was non-political, which pleased me. The mission of GRCC is "To enrich the lives of people living in Gloucestershire by supporting them through change and by enabling them to determine, shape and develop their own communities." If that was the case I asked myself as we travelled back to Cheltenham, why had I not heard of GRCC?

Wednesday 6th May, Pam and I hosted a reception in the parlour for the 13th Cheltenham Brownies (9 adults and 12 children). The brownies were so pleased to be with us; the look of excitement as Pam and I explained the memorabilia to them was unforgettable. They were no different to those who had visited the parlour before them; they wanted to sit at the mayor's desk, put on the Mayoral chain and, with a little help, hold the Civic mace.

It seemed as though they had all brought a camera to the parlour to record the visit. On 13th May, I received the following handwritten note from Brownie Hayley Dadge:

> *"Dear Mr Godwin, Thank you very much for letting us come and see what you and your lovely wife the Mayoress do. I also thank you very much for giving us refreshments. You're very lucky to be a Mayor.*
>
> *I really loved holding the golden mace but it's very heavy. We would all love to come and visit you again.*
>
> *Yours sincerely, Hayley Dadge and the 13th Cheltenham Brownies."*

Cheltenham Borough Council elections were held on Thursday 7th May.

I held my Prestbury seat, polling 1,153 votes against 504 votes for John Walker (Conservative), 202 votes for Jennifer Jones (Liberal Democrats) and 66 votes for the Labour candidate Philip Greening.

It was a bad night for Liberal Democrat candidates; many lost their seats, including the deputy mayor, Cllr Garth Barnes. The Lib/Dems lost overall control of the council.

The Conservatives were cock-a-hoop; they won most seats and would now run the council. Conservative Les Freeman regained the seat he lost whilst he was mayor two years previously. "I'm chuffed to death" he told The *Gloucestershire Echo*. He added "I want to support all the people who want to get rid of the Noddy Train."

Alan Stone, a former Liberal Democrat who stood for PAB, was blamed for the loss of the deputy mayor's seat in College ward, and "was treated with shouts of traitor by the party faithful when the result was announced. Newcomer Duncan Smith (Con) turned The Park ward blue with a 500 vote majority over Yvonne Nichols (Lib/Dem)", said the *Echo*.

Sally Stringer, who had defected from Lib/Dem to PAB mid-term, failed to hold

her seat, whereas David Prince who had defected to PAB a few months earlier, won
the Pittville seat for PAB with the Lib/Dem candidate finishing in third place.

The local newspaper was kind enough to report: "The mayor, Les Godwin, not
only retained his seat, but with the biggest ever percentage majority in his 21–year
career in local politics."

The day before the election, I received a letter from Darren Stevens, Prestbury. It
had a heading "Liberal Democrat 'Focus' Prestbury Ward."

He wrote:

> "Dear Councillor Godwin,
>   Please find enclosed a copy of a letter that I have sent to Cllr Andrew Pennington
> today." (The letter concerned an 'Election Special' delivered to every home in the
> Prestbury Ward by the Liberal Democrat party; Cllr Pennington was the Lib/Dem
> election agent at the time).
>   "I have not written this letter because of our connection through my work. I have
> written it because we know from our own experiences that their statements are grossly
> unfair.
>   I also think it is quite unnecessary and unprofessional for such tactics to be deployed in
> local government elections.
>   Such tactics do not work and there is no substitute for a good honest and common
> sense approach to local problems.
> Yours sincerely
> Darren Stevens."

The 'Election Special' that Darren Stevens referred to was sent to me by several
Prestbury residents who like Darren were offended by the wording.

It said:

> **"Don't YOU deserve a councillor who lives in the area, rather than the man
> from the PAB who lives miles away in Hatherley?**
>   **The Liberal Democrats don't just appear at election time like other parties do."**

Darren's letter to Cllr Pennington spelled out that he and his wife did not think it
necessary for the Liberal candidate to 'knock' an opponent in such a manner at
election time.

He added: "Whilst my wife and I have only lived in Prestbury for seven months
we have been greatly impressed by Councillor Les Godwin. Despite the 'burden' of
the office of Mayor, Cllr Godwin was forthcoming with both his support and advice
when we approached him to support us regarding a planning issue. Whilst we are
not aligned to any party, or for that matter PAB, we cannot fail to be impressed by
the work it undertakes and the manner in which it communicates through its
Newsletters. Cllr Godwin has also done an excellent job in ensuring that the
dangers of the Oakley development are at the top of the local agenda.

The timing of our move means that on this occasion we will be voting elsewhere
in Cheltenham. I am confident that the people of Prestbury Ward will judge Cllr
Godwin by his actions and duly re-elect him.

As for future elections and your campaigning style, I hope you will consider adopting a more intelligent and mature approach.

Darren Stevens."

The Lib/Dem leaflet did more harm than good for their candidate– yes, she was a local resident, but Prestbury people also knew that her husband was a Borough councillor for the Lansdown ward.

Friday evening Pam and I were guests at a film night at the Cheltenham & Gloucester College of Higher Education. The evening ended with a buffet supper.

Saturday 9th May, in Gloucester Cathedral, we witnessed the Ceremony for the Induction as Archdeacon of the Reverend Canon Hedley Ringrose.

Because my term of office was coming to a close, Wing Commander Tony Spearpoint and his wife Pat invited Pam and me to a private dinner at their house in Innsworth.

It was an evening of joy and regrets; going over the occasions when we had met at official ceremonies and functions; sad, because we knew we were going to miss each other's friendship.

Maggie Handson had received a fax from Reg Carpenter, Winchcombe Street on 3rd April inviting me to a coffee morning on May 11th. This is what it said:

"I wonder if the Mayor might be able to call in for a coffee on Monday May 11th at 10.00 a.m. at the above address with the Neighbourhood Watch members.

We would love to see him before the changeover. The best Mayor for many a year."

Later at 5.30 p.m. I welcomed to the parlour Michael Bage and Darren Stevens, Chelsea Building Society, who presented me with a cheque for £4,276 for my three charities.

This was the proceeds from the Mayor's Charity Gala Performance of *Talent* at The Everyman theatre on 26th March.

Following the presentation, I attended the Annual General Meeting of the Cheltenham Chamber of Commerce in the Municipal Offices at 6.30 p.m.

Tuesday morning, I met the nominated recipients of the Cheltenham Medal of Honour, who would be presented with their awards at the mayor-making ceremony on 18th May.

In the evening, Pam and I went to the Tewkesbury Borough Council annual meeting and mayor-making ceremony at the Churchdown School, whilst my deputy, Cllr Garth Barnes, attended a concert given by pupils of Chosen Hill School in Gloucester Cathedral.

Thursday 14th May, Pam and I attended the Gloucester City Annual Council Meeting, which is held in Gloucester Cathedral, and in the evening we were at the Pittville Pump Room to greet our friends and many volunteers at my 'Thank you and Farewell Party'. During the interval I said:

> "Although I still have a few more days to go before I hand over my chain of office, I want you all to know that Pam and I are extremely grateful for the important part you have all played in making 1997 and 1998 a most successful mayoral year.

We appreciate your kindness and friendships, and the excellent way that you have supported my three worthwhile charities. Of course, and I am sure you will agree with me, that without the hard work put in by my charity committee, the numerous events you and everyone else have enjoyed during the past twelve months, would not have taken place.

And lastly, without the generous sponsorships of so many Cheltenham businesses and organisations, the anticipated record of money-raising would not have happened.

Please enjoy your evening and our grateful thanks to you all."

It was a short speech, but interspersed with cheering and clapping throughout, and it ended with loud applause and stamping of feet. In the days that followed I received several kind letters from many different quarters.

Audrey Stevens, Swindon Village Society, who attended the 'farewell party' with Stephen Brewer (who had a special interest in saving the Green Belt), enjoyed the party. She wrote: "My husband had a hospital appointment so Stephen Brewer, a committee member came in his stead. We both enjoyed it.

We have been proud to have Les Godwin as Mayor during the past year and we would like you to accept the small donation enclosed towards the Mayor's Charities."

Darren Stevens (Chelsea Building Society) wrote: "On behalf of Alan, myself, Gail and Jennifer, I would like to thank you for inviting us to your party last night. We all thoroughly enjoyed ourselves and thought the atmosphere and spirit amongst everyone present was excellent.

I am delighted that you and your committee have been successful in raising such a large sum and I am sure this record will stand for many years to come. I and everyone at Chelsea Building Society are delighted that we were able to play a part in such a successful year, and we appreciate your very kind comments."

Joan Ashley wrote: "Just a little note to thank you for your kind invitation to the Party on the 14th May – it was very much appreciated. Both Elizabeth (daughter) and I enjoyed it immensely.

I suppose your term of office is now at a close, but I would hazard a guess that you have been the most popular and efficient Mayor the town has had for many years – if ever. Everyone I have spoken to is of the same opinion."

Godfrey Bodenham Up Hatherley wrote: "On behalf of Marcia and myself may I thank you for the invitation to your farewell party. It was a huge success which we enjoyed.

Congratulations too on your superb year in office – you've certainly set a splendid example for others to follow. Many people have commented on your tireless efforts in the execution of your duty.

Also thanks to your wife. We appreciate the amount of time and effort she must have expended in supporting and aiding this very successful mayoral year."

Apart from the letters there were numerous cards from friends and supporters, all gracious in their thanks for a good mayoral year, which they had enjoyed just as much as Pam and I. The party went on until the early hours, so Friday morning was "a morning after the night before" occasion, which thankfully was a relaxing one. That is to say, apart from the numerous telephone calls from people who had enjoyed the party and just wanted to tell me so.

In the afternoon I attended the Community Development Review Conference in the Municipal Offices.

Saturday morning, Pam and I attended the official opening of new premises for the homeless in Grosvenor Street.

Mrs Flip Thornett-Roston, the founder of the local charity Open Door, introduced us to Sharron Davies, the Olympic Swimmer, who had been invited to officially open the new centre.

The *Gloucestershire Echo*, with a headline above a photograph of Sharron with Flip Thornett-Roston said: "Sharron launches project", adding, "Olympic swimming star Sharron Davies helped open the door to a new centre for the homeless in Cheltenham. The expectant mum joined guests including Nigel Jones MP and Mayor Les Godwin, at the unveiling of Open Door's centre in Grosvenor Street." The new centre, which was formally a WRVS office, had been converted to provide shelter, meals, clothing and much-needed company for the homeless. "It was converted with the help of donations including £16,000 from Kraft Jacobs Suchard UK", added the *Echo*, "and will open on Mondays, Wednesday and Sundays, and later to six days a week." "A lot of the time" said Sharron Davies, "the homeless seem to be people who have fallen on hard times and just need a hand to make fresh start."

Early that evening, I presented the Gold Cup to the winner at the Competitive Festival of Performing Arts at the Town Hall.

Later Pam and I attended the production of "Auntie's Glow" at the Church of St. Philip & St. James, Leckhampton.

The penultimate engagement for us was to attend the Diamond Celebration of the WRVS at Gloucester Cathedral.

Although our final engagement was to attend Wembley Stadium on Sunday 17th May 1998, to watch Cheltenham Town Football Club versus Southport F C in the F A Trophy final, it did not happen without controversy. I had been a fan of the "Robins" for as long as I could remember, although it has to be said that my own playing days, which went on until I was 47, meant that the number of times I could watch the 'Robins' play was limited.

In my playing days, Arch Anderson, a former Scottish League player, became manager of the Robins, which was long before Paul Baker became chairman of Cheltenham Town FC. Arch Anderson during his time with Cheltenham, was noted for bringing footballers down from Scotland to play for Cheltenham. The club became better known for having so many Scotsmen playing for it than its ability to win any football trophies.

The *Gloucestershire Echo* telephoned the council to enquire whether the mayor would be attending the FA Trophy Final. They wanted to know what arrangements had been made with Southport council for the two mayors to meet and exchange fraternal greetings.

In spite of the fact that it had always been good practice for the offices of mayors to be in touch with each other when arrangements are made for joint visits to public events, it didn't happen on this occasion.

It did prompt CBC to contact the football club to enquire about the mayoral visit to the Cup Final; Maggie Handson my PA was told that Paul Baker would be contacting her about the details of the day. Nothing was forthcoming.

It appeared that Pam and I were not to be part of the Cheltenham FC's plans when the players ran onto the turf at the Wembley Stadium. I was not aware of the telephone calls and other activities going on behind the scenes, but a few days before the final, two tickets were delivered to the parlour, presumably by Cheltenham AFC.

Although the whole business was embarrassing, at least Pam and I had tickets for two Wembley seats. They were in Block PS, row C and seats numbered one and two. There was no official welcome in the VIP lounge for us when we arrived; we found our own way to our seats. Later we witnessed the arrival of the Mayor of Southport and other VIP's who took their seats in the front row.

Someone must have drawn the Southport Mayor's attention to the fact that Pam and I were in our seats; he turned around and waved to us.

As for the game – it was interesting. Southport had most of the play, missing several scoring chances, but Cheltenham scored the only goal and we won the F A Umbro Trophy Final in May1998.

CHAPTER 14

Back To The Day Job

In friendship false, implacable in hate: Resolved to ruin or to rule the state.
Dryden – Absalom and Achitophel (1681)

On 7th January, 1998, there was a meeting of the CBC Environment Committee which I was unable to attend due to a mayoral engagement.

I wrote to Clifford Ride, Director of Environment Services, explaining my situation and offering my apologies for being absent. I added,

> "I have no doubt that agenda item 8 will generate a good deal of debate, and should I have been there it would have been my intention to express the importance to Cheltenham of the demolition of the Royal Well bus shelter and it's replacement with a modern design. Until we know where a centrally located bus station should go, we should wait until road infrastructure changes are agreed, and traffic flows assessed.
>
> ….Cheltenham has experienced a lot of good things this mayoral year, including major events taking place in the town for the very first time. Other organisations who used to come here and have been conspicuous by their absence, have come back to Cheltenham during my year in office.
>
> Talking to business and other influential people at civic functions has been encouraging for the town's future, but almost without exception, they express disappointment in the fact that we allow the centre of the town to be spoilt by a hideous and outdated bus shelter.
>
> …The bulk of my mail consistently calls on me to press the Council to remove the bus shelter. Letters come from people who live in other parts of the United Kingdom, and even from foreign tourists who visit Cheltenham.
>
> The weight of opinion expressed in the *Gloucestershire Echo* by the Editor and the 'letters to the press' page shows overwhelming support in favour of the demolition of the bus shelter."

The following evening the *Echo* published a report of the meeting: "Bus shelter – it *will* be demolished". These were the main points.

"The bus shelter in Cheltenham's Royal Well will definitely be demolished next year, councillors have decided. The committee decided to go ahead with the demolition of the 50–year old shelter at a cost of £50,000.

The town mayor, Cllr Les Godwin who led a campaign to demolish the shelter, sent a letter to the Environment Committee. In it he said that the bulk of his mail in the last seven months had called on him to press the council to remove the bus shelter. The new shelter will ensure that visitors can see the Royal Well Regency

Crescent." I was delighted with the news, and having received so many telephone calls that night, it was clear that other people shared my pleasure too.

If I thought that the next few months were going to be plain-sailing for the demolition of the Royal Well bus shelters, I was soon to be disillusioned.

The matter of financing the demolition was always going to be difficult with other capital projects in the pipeline. In addition, the Cheltenham Member of Parliament Nigel Jones was raising objections to my proposals.

Gloucestershire Echo reporter Simon Freeman wrote: "MP Nigel Jones has whipped up a storm by saying Cheltenham's biggest eyesore, the Royal Well bus shelter, should stay put for the time being. He says getting the town's park-and-ride and Spa Shuttle service running smoothly is more important than bulldozing the bus station."

He also suggests: "... parking charges should be increased to pay for the Spa Shuttle and the loss-making park-and-ride – and spending on the bus shelter can wait."

According to the reporter, Nigel Jones suggested that the demolition "should be delayed until the traffic pollution problems are solved."

When Simon Freeman interviewed bus users, several claimed "The MP had lost touch with the people of the town." One user, Mrs Mary Oldmeadow from Stow-on-the-Wold, said: "The bus station should be top of the list. It's a disgrace to such a beautiful town. If your MP thinks otherwise, he needs his head looking at."

Pensioner Anne Whittaker said: I dread to think what visitors think." The article concluded: "Next week the borough council is spending another £120,000 on the third Spa Shuttle, the prototype for which was nicknamed the 'Noddy' train by Mr Jones.

Incoming mayor Cllr Jeremy Whales supports replacing it." [the bus shelter]

Clearly, public opinion supported the removal of the old bus shelter and its replacement with something modern that enhanced rather than detracted the elegance of the Royal Crescent.

Patience had to be a virtue as to the date when the work would be done.

In the meanwhile, I was disappointed to learn that the Dowty Arle Court complex in Hatherley Lane had been sold, which included the Arle Court cricket ground. Many local cricket clubs had played there, including Gloucestershire County Cricket Club.

The news of the plans prompted me to write to the *Gloucestershire Echo* on February 19th. This is a small extract:

"... Before Christmas I was asked to attend a presentation of plans for the film studios. I was shocked to find that while the plans for the studios and the Arle Court grounds (to be opened to the public) were admirable, there was a sting in the tail this time with additional plans submitted to build 50 or more houses on the edge of the cricket ground. This will result in the removal of the copse, the row of laburnum and maple trees, all of which have made the Arle Court cricket ground a place to visit since the turn of the century.

Many famous players have played cricket at Arle Court; hundreds, if not thousands have given their time and energy to preserve the ground and its setting now and for future generations.

I hate planning applications that say 'if you allow this – we will give you something in return'. It never works out very well and we should not fall for this.

Since 1987 more than 5,500 sports and recreation grounds have been lost to development. Isn't it time we took stock of the damage we are doing to our environment and say 'enough is enough'?"

Unfortunately, my plea for refusing houses on part of the cricket ground fell on deaf ears and the development was approved.

The playing of senior cricket at Arle Court soon ended due to the reduced size of the playing area. Once residents in the new houses started to complain about the damage to their properties, it was only a matter of time before the sports field ceased to be used for cricket.

Mayor-making ceremonies in towns and cities across the UK are usually formal occasions, often with dull speeches, although I did try to make my inaugural speech last year as informal as possible.

This year, it was my duty to hand over the chain of office to the new mayor Councillor Jeremy Whales at the annual mayor-making ceremony. Before I did this I was expected to give a report of my previous twelve months in office. This is what I said:

"This is the part of the proceedings when the past mayor talks about his year in office, and it always brings a twinkle to my eyes when I think of the numerous speech days I attended when the head teacher gave his or her annual report. Each form waiting with bated breath for an individual mention, or better still praise for the work they had done.

For me of course, I can write my own annual report. It has, without doubt, been an exciting and outstanding year both for me and for Cheltenham.

We saw the first ever RAC Rally at the Racecourse, the first ever conferences of the Co-operative Funeral Service Managers, the Law Society and the return of the National Council of Women to the Town Hall after an absence of thirty years.

Many conferences, too many to mention, took place at various venues in the town, where each and every one played an important part in emphasising the importance of Cheltenham, not only as a beautiful and historic town, but also as a conference centre as well.

When I stood here last year, I pledged three things: I would reach out to the people of Cheltenham because I believed then and I still do now, that if people are given the chance to share the mayoralty with you, then they will respond back in such a way that it will astound you.

They certainly did and they were magnificent.

From the youngest to the oldest, from the richest to the poorest, they contributed in such way I never thought possible. From it many lasting friendships have been established and they will continue to flourish in the years ahead.

Secondly, I pledged I would open up the mayoralty to Cheltenham people to enable them to see and understand what the mayoralty was all about. It had always seemed to me that the mayor's parlour and all the historical memorabilia within it should be made available to everyone.

The parlour contains a lot of history about our town, with gifts presented to the town from countries across the world, which should be seen by as many townspeople as possible. It gives me pride and pleasure that during my year in office, my wife and I invited over 1600 Cheltenham people to a reception in the parlour in the evening, and over 350 people came to the parlour for tea and cakes in the afternoon.

I think you will agree that it was quite an achievement.

Thirdly, I pledged to the people of Cheltenham that I would do everything I could to rid the town of the awful bus shelter at Royal Well.

What an eyesore it is in what should be one of the most attractive parts of our town? But the news is good; the money is there and the volunteers are waiting to swing into action. Soon, the relic of the past will go, which I believe should have happened many years ago.

Last year, the parks and landscape department, The Keep Cheltenham Tidy Group, individuals and businesses, all contributed towards Cheltenham winning the 'Britain in Bloom' competition for the twelfth time in fifteen years.

What an achievement and what a record? And what a proud moment is was for me to receive the coveted Wedgewood Trophy on behalf of the town?

But whilst we give richly deserved praise to those who make our town so beautiful, we must never forget that our elegant Regency buildings play an important part too in making the town so special and attractive.

We have a priceless asset here in Cheltenham – its fabric is precious and we should never harm it, not even in the name of expediency. The wrong sort of street furniture for example, can do untold harm to our town.

Throughout my year in office, I have often been asked to comment about the highlight of my year. There have been so memorable occasions it would be difficult to choose just one.

To visit places like Betteridge School, St. Vincent's Centre, the Paradise Community and many other similar establishments has been sheer delight for Pam and me. We have visited several infant, junior and six form schools, as well as several colleges. On every occasion we have been amazed at the talent of Cheltenham's young people whether it is academic or music, sport or drama, our young people take some beating.

I only wish the press would write more about the good things our children do, rather than constantly highlighting single bad things that happen in which there is often very little interest.

It is always a good time during a speech to say 'thank you' to special people. To Stephen Gregory, my Chaplain, who has been a tower of strength to Pam and me, and from what I can gather, a friend to everyone.

It is often said that behind a good man there is a good woman; some people will say 'a better woman'. But on this occasion, it was not just one person to whom I owed a great deal but sixteen of them. Two daughters who often gave me advice, Pam who always gave me advice, Maggie Handson who never stopped giving me advice, and thirteen ladies on my charity committee who worked tirelessly for me and my three local charities non-stop throughout the year.

A special word about my wife Pam; at the beginning of my year she had great trepidation about taking on the role of mayoress, simply because she had never been in the public eye before, and she didn't believe she could do the job. I don't know about you, but I think she brought grace and style to the job of mayoress and was a great credit to our town.

At this point I would like one member from each of the charities to come on stage when I shall reveal to everyone the amount of money we have raised for three worthwhile Cheltenham charities.

Ladies and gentlemen, with still a few more cheques to arrive, the sum has reached £36,000.

Finally, I couldn't end my annual report to you without saying something about the marvellous victory yesterday of Cheltenham Town Football Club.

Pam and I were there supporting the team and also supporting the large party of Cheltenham supporters who had made the long journey to Wembley.

Well done the Robins – you have put the icing on the cake of a very successful year for me. Thank you and good luck for the future."

As I helped the Reverend Jeremy Whales, the new Mayor of Cheltenham, put on the robes that I had proudly worn the previous year, I could not but feel relieved that tomorrow I would not be up early to prepare a speech, or have the mayor's chauffeur waiting patiently outside the front door with that anxious look on his face indicating that if the mayor and his wife didn't hurry up we would be late for a mayoral engagement.

Even though I knew that I would miss meeting new faces at conferences and dinners, I also knew that it would take a few days, if not weeks, to recover from the glamour and excitement of it all.

At the mayor-making ceremony on Monday, 18th May 1998, I shook Cllr Whales' hand firmly and wished him well in the year ahead. I had known Jeremy and his wife Joyce for a long time, and I knew he would carry out his mayoral duties with diligence and dignity.

I had invited friends and PAB members to the mayor-making ceremony, and at the end of proceedings Pam and I enjoyed their company as well as the tea and cakes provided by the Borough Council.

Hon. Alderman Douglas Grazier, the PAB Group Chairman, joined us and it soon became apparent that Douglas had not been happy with the way the ceremony had gone. Apparently, he thought it had been too political: too long and disrespectful to me as the successful outgoing mayor of the town.

I was surprised to hear Doug's comments, but other people in our small group agreed with what he had said and some added to it.

Because of my position at the front of the stage, I was unaware of what was, allegedly, going on behind me. I listened intently to what was being said. It seemed that some councillors were chatting amongst themselves whilst I was delivering my 'end of year' speech; giving an air of disinterest in what I was saying. Some councillors did not join in with the applause when I announced that the charity committee had raised the record sum of £36,022.41 for my three charities, nor did some of the councillors join in with the applause at the end of my speech. If it was correct, then Doug was right, it was very disrespectful.

My opinion at the time was that the ceremony was over and my year had ended on a successful note: it was best not to worry about it. Douglas clearly didn't agree with me and it took some time before I could get our small group to talk about something else.

When Pam and I returned home we talked about the events that took place during the ceremony, the long speeches from the proposers; the appointments of the Honorary Aldermen, and the awards of merit to the recipients, and we wondered whether the audience had been bored by the whole procedure.

I reminded Pam that my speech was my annual report to the council and to the town, and was full of interesting points that the audience must have enjoyed because they applauded several times during the speech.

Pam agreed, and for the first time throughout the previous twelve months, she made an adverse comment about the mayoral event that surprised me. "Yes", she said, "but you didn't see what was going on behind you. There was applause but not by all the Liberal Democrat councillors."

Pam seldom made political comments, and when she did they were never personal ones, but on this occasion, she looked and sounded annoyed, and took the same stance that Douglas Grazier had taken a few hours earlier.

Whilst I felt disappointed with what I had heard, not least because Pam was usually loath to make an adverse comment about anyone, it was clear she had been upset with what had gone on during the ceremony. She thought that what was supposed to have been a pleasant afternoon had been spoilt.

My immediate response to Pam's comments was to 'let it go' – the glamour and hard work of the previous twelve months had ended, and it was far more important for me to get on with the council and constituency work than fret about the discourtesy of a few Liberal Democrat councillors at the mayor-making ceremony.

Douglas Grazier, however, was not going to 'let it go'; the following day I received a copy of a letter he had sent to Jeremy Whales, the new mayor; this is a précis:

"Dear Mr Mayor, I convey best wishes for your term of office trusting you and the Mayoress enjoy a memorable year as leading citizens of our town. To be chosen Mayor of a Borough is a great honour and the mayor-making ceremony should reflect the dignity of the office, not a political meeting as sadly the occasion on Monday 18th May became.

I was first elected in May 1955. So I have attended the majority of mayor-making ceremonies over the last forty three years, and I was disgusted with the occasion on Monday May 18th.

My recollection of past ceremonies was a memorable day for the new Mayor and Mayoress and the retiring Mayor, who would make a fitting tribute on past achievements and a welcome to the new mayor. This was their hour, not cluttered with disconsolate individuals sullying the waters following the recent election results.

Just because the electorate had made their choice, which was not to the liking of some of your members, was no reason to behave in the manner they did"

Not until I read Doug Grazier's letter concerning the poor election results for the Liberal Democrats, did I conclude that perhaps this was the reason why Cllr Barnes lost his College ward seat, not because of a PAB candidate's name on the ballot paper.

In any event, the selection of PAB candidates for local council elections is the responsibility of the PAB management committee, not mine. Even so, I agreed with the comments that had been expressed, using the mayor-making ceremony to vent their disappointment was not the occasion to express their feelings. I replied as follows:

"Dear Douglas, Pam and I agree with your comments about the mayor-making ceremony. It seemed such a shame that a traditional and important system should be so abused by people who have the nerve to call themselves politicians. They should have learned by now that a ceremony is one thing and a political platform is something quite different. One should not expect too much from political opportunists, whose only aim seems to be to promote the cause of the Liberal Democrats and not the town and its people.

I was particularly sorry for Pam who told me afterwards that she was embarrassed by the Lib/Dem councillors not applauding when I had finished my speech. We had a rough time from the Lib/Dem councillors throughout our mayoral year. They refused to support anything we did to raise funds for our three charities and made us as uncomfortable as they possibly could at the Civic functions.

We will not forget their attitude towards us. But you can rest assured that I will have the last laugh ..."

In his reply to my letter, Douglas Grazier wrote:

"I convey my thanks to you both for the excellent manner in which you carried out your Mayoral duties in the past year. I believe you set a standard that enhanced the PAB Group in the eyes of many people. Well done!

It is a long way back to those days when we were fighting Tewkesbury Borough Council over their financial policies, yet the Group has survived and made headway under your leadership beyond our wildest dreams.

It is a shame that Monday's ceremony was spoilt by disgruntled ex-councillors who could not accept the wishes of the electorate.

Best wishes for further PAB successes and thank you both for the fine example you set in your distinguished term of office."

A week later, I met the members of my charity committee to thank them for their hard work and to make arrangements for the presentation of the three cheques to the officials of the three charities.

Meanwhile, I answered the letters and cards I received from well-wishers.

A card from Simon and Karen Radford thanked me for inviting them "... to a really lovely farewell party", adding "Your fund raising efforts have been truly fantastic, and it was nice to be present when the grand total was announced. You have both worked hard and have been an excellent Mayor and Mayoress."

John Todman, the Conservative Party Group Leader wrote: "Just a note to congratulate both you and Pam for the excellent year which you had as our Mayor and Mayoress. You were first class ambassadors for the town in every way and very much admired for the way you spoke out on issues which concern us all – not least the coach station.

I shall welcome you back on the Council benches for the interesting year that lies ahead. Thank you both again for all that you have done for Cheltenham in the last year."

A letter from Bunty and Cllr Rob Wilson dated 19th May said: "Well done! What a good year you have had. Many congratulations for raising such a wonderful sum of money for your charities – it is going to be difficult to beat that one. Thank you for inviting us to your party last Thursday- it was a lovely idea, and much appreciated by all.

Keep at it Les, and keep in touch- don't let those Liberals get you down!!"

Bunty and Rob were present at the recent mayor-making ceremony and their letter was short and to the point – a telling point, in my view.

It was a pleasant surprise to receive a letter from the Cheltenham Association of Wrens inviting me to "...start their 50th Anniversary week in the Municipal Offices on Friday 5th June 1998." The invitation included Pam and we both enjoyed a superb evening with sixty former Wrens who were excellent company throughout the evening. Nigel Jones MP was there but there was no mayor or deputy mayor present.

The *Gloucestershire Echo* published a lovely picture several nights later with a heading: "They've sailed the seven seas". Underneath the photograph it read: "Reunited – ex-Wrens with Chairman Mary Hawthornthwaite, MP Nigel Jones and ex-mayor Les Godwin."

On 12th June I received the following letter:

"Dear Les, Very many thanks for hosting our Reception in the Pittville Room last Friday. Your presence made it a very special event. It was kind of you and your wife to give up your time for us and I know I speak on behalf of all the former Wrens when I say how much we appreciated it."

Another invitation followed two weeks later from a group who were campaigning to stop the development of the former St. James' railway site.

In an earlier chapter I explained why I was against the development of the site and the circumstances surrounding the alleged 'give away' of the land that eventually became the home of the Waitrose store.

When I arrived at the St. James' site I was met by Rob Wilson, Chairman of the Cheltenham Civic Society and Jo Grimster of the Cheltenham branch of the Friends of the Earth.

There were around fifty people present; pensioners as well as young children. We were invited to sit in a circle and the leader of the campaign invited certain speakers to go to the centre of the circle and give their reasons why they were opposed to the development.

In the *Gloucestershire Echo* article on July 27th, Steve Jones wrote: "Eco-army is 'here to stay'". More than 50 people turned up to a family picnic in support of the protesters campaign to stop developers building there.

Councillor Godwin was first to speak, saying 'The people of Cheltenham need another supermarket like they need a hole in the head. This green and pleasant land must be preserved against all the odds ...'

He concluded his article by stating that the protesters intended to stay on the site until the application is withdrawn."

Meanwhile, GSL, another consortium group comprising Tarmac, Broadway based Group Four and British Telecom, came forward with plans for what they called a futuristic 'Millennium doughnut' for GCHQ Benhall.

They also revealed plans for the Oakley site.

GSL made it clear that should they be chosen by the council to build the consolidated base at Benhall. Oakley would become an estate of 525 homes, with a supermarket, doctors' surgery, video shop and takeaway. GSL would also demolish the six-story office block at the rear of the site.

The proposal seemed to be nearer to the objectives of the council than those who supported the Option Four proposal submitted by The Oakley Partnership.

There was still some time to go before a council decision would be made; GCHQ and Central Government would decide in October which bid to accept.

On Friday 19th June, the East Gloucestershire NHS Trust invited Pam, me and members of my charity committee, to visit the Breast Care Clinic at the Cheltenham General Hospital. With the money from our fund raising efforts, we had been able to refurbish the quiet room for women coming out of surgery, and the transformation of the room was truly amazing. There was an air of satisfaction amongst all who were there, and rightly, everyone felt a sense of pride in what they had achieved.

Mrs Sue Kendall, Clinical Nurse Specialist Breast/Stoma Care, wrote to me on 29th June:

"Dear Les, I would like to thank you, Pam and your team for visiting the Breast Clinic the other Friday.

We are extremely grateful to you for choosing the clinic as one of your charities and are overwhelmed at the huge amount of money you have raised.

I hope you feel that the money has been put to good use. From our perspective the new quiet room will be, and has already proved to be, invaluable. We could not have hoped to have such a facility without your support.

I think you and the team should be very proud of your efforts. I am certain it will be a long time before any of your successors achieve such a target.
Sue Kendall."

On 24th June, I received the following letter from Mrs Gillian Shipton:

> *"Dear Mr Godwin, I know it is over a month since your term of being mayor ended, and I had meant to write then, but did not get round to it. Seeing in the Echo tonight how well you did for the three charities, it has made me put pen to paper to say 'thank you' for the year you spent in mayoral duties.*
>
> *I read reports of the places you had been to, and saw photos in various poses and with all sorts of people, and I felt that you were an excellent ambassador for the town, and always smiling.*
>
> *At your mayor-making ceremony your sponsor said 'you had presence' and he was right. I hope you have been able to settle back into a normal existence now – perhaps with a sigh of relief. Again, my thanks and best wishes.*
> *Gillian Shipton."*

It was a nice feeling to think that someone wanted to write to me four weeks after my term of office had ended, just to say 'thank you'.

Although I had not been involved in any more Odrag meetings in June or July, it came to my notice that Odrag intended to hold talks with the GSL consortium behind closed doors at the Municipal Offices.

I was not invited to the meeting in spite of the fact that I had 'chaired' two Odrag meetings in their early formation, and no reason was given. It could have been the fact that my membership of the PAB group would have prevented me from attending a 'secret' meeting and I would have understood this if it had been explained to me. I was not briefed following the meeting so I have no idea what was discussed and whether any agreements or compromises had been reached.

However, the more I became involved as a local councillor for Prestbury, and my study of several reports on the two GCHQ proposals, the more I came to the conclusion that the GSL option was more sensible and would have the least impact on both the Oakley and Benhall areas.

The Oakley Partnership, led by the Symonds Group, allegedly wanted to build an H-shaped office block and parking for 1,750 cars at Oakley. There would also be around 40 homes, three shops on land owned by CBC at the foot of Cleeve Hill. Benhall would have an industrial park and 750 homes.

Even though the Oakley Partnership had been given outline planning permission for its scheme the previous April, I believed the GSL proposal made better sense.

Because of this I was surprised to read a letter in the *Gloucestershire Echo* on August 6th from an Odrag member, praising the Oakley Partnership proposals. It was the first time I had read an Odrag opinion on the two options and as Odrag members had met with GSL, albeit secretly, only a few days earlier, I came to the conclusion that perhaps the meeting had not been seen as a success story by all those present.

The letter went on to indicate that a decision to support the Oakley Partnership proposal had been made. The letter concluded: "We believe that if GSL is given the green light to build 500 houses and a supermarket at Oakley, it will open the floodgates to urban sprawl from Oakley to Prestbury."

Apart from the misuse of the words 'urban sprawl', the letter was alarmist to say the least. It also misunderstood the importance of land ownership and the inevitable additional traffic problems the development would produce over a large area of the town.

The opinions of Odrag didn't have the support of everyone.

Malcolm Stennett, Chairman of Prestbury Parish Council (PPC), wrote to the *Gloucestershire Echo* on August 7th "…advising readers that PPC no longer shares the views of this organisation (Odrag)."

He added: "By invitation, I and a number of other parish councillors spoke at earlier meetings organised by Odrag against the proposed development of the green fields to the north of the GCHQ Oakley site. We are most disappointed that Odrag has capitulated to the Oakley Partnership and is supporting the outrageous development proposals." He continued, "The Odrag letter suggests they have won significant concessions from the developer. In reality, this amounts to a 'promise' not to build on two of the 16 acres of public land they want to place under concrete, to retain some chain link fencing at the bottom of a few gardens and to provide a community centre, which will be a replacement for the old pavilion, which stands in the way of the access road the developer now wants to cut through the existing playing field."

The letter concluded, "If people are really interested in continuing to preserve the green fields then their only option is to support GSL in its bid to develop GCHQ at Benhall, plus a new village on the old existing Oakley site."

For the next few weeks the GCHQ development became the main topic in the local press and the local radio. The themes were always prefaced with a "Will it be Benhall or will it be Oakley for GCHQ?" The subject provided good copy for the *Echo*, who throughout the discussion period supported the complex being developed at Benhall.

Meanwhile, whilst the discussions about the future of GCHQ were going on, Michael Smith, the Borough Engineer, was doing his best to promote the advantages of the Spa Shuttle, which had been approved by a majority of councillors several months earlier.

It soon became known as the "Noddy" train by local residents (the name given to it by the local MP), because it looked very much like a children's 'toy-town' train seen at the seaside or in leisure playgrounds.

Mr Smith, it was alleged, had been sent by the council to Italy where 'shuttle services' by similar trains were popular.

He had reported to the council that they were used in Italy, not as a tourist attraction, but to enable people to travel from one part of the town to another. He thought it was worth trying in Cheltenham and he proposed that it should operate on a short route from the centre of Cheltenham to the Montpellier area before any expansion of the service was undertaken.

I did not support the idea for two reasons; it would look out of place in the centre of the town; the cost of purchase of three 'trains' and future maintenance costs would be too much for the local council taxpayers to bear.

The Liberal Democrat administration voted for it and the strange-looking 'toy train service' was underway. Whether it would become a permanent feature in the town, we had to wait and see.

In August 1998 CBC announced that the Royal Well bus shelters would be demolished on Sunday September 20th. They also confirmed that £26,000 would be put into the revamp project; advertising firm Adshel would provide another £40,000 as part of a new 15–year deal with the council.

The news was well-received by residents across the town and my telephone line was busy for several days after the announcement.

On 8th August the *Gloucestershire Echo* published an article saying: "Shelter: demolition day is set" It added: "September 20th is demolition day. That is when the concrete shelter which sprawls before Cheltenham's Royal Crescent finally starts to come down.

In a five-week project the eyesore will be replaced with three all-glass shelters similar to the ones used by the Spa Shuttle.

Former Cheltenham mayor Les Godwin has vowed to be there with a sledgehammer to help out. He made it his mission to get rid of the shelters in his mayoral year last year."

The local newspaper interviewed Cllr Pat Thornton regarding the demolition of the bus shelters, asking her whether she would be carrying out her threat to "ride naked through the streets of Cheltenham should the bus shelters be demolished." An article was published in the *Gloucestershire Echo* which said:

"… but you won't catch me stripping, says Pat."

The article went on to say: "Former mayor Pat Thornton, who vowed to do a Lady Godiva to save the town's bus shelter, has changed her mind."

It added that Cllr Thornton had made her threat after it was suggested that the shelter in Royal Well would be replaced with a memorial garden for Diana, Princess of Wales. She told the reporter: "I was so angry by the comment from the former mayor Cllr Les Godwin that he intended to use the money from the Princess Diana fund to knock down the bus shelter."

The comment was a ridiculous untruth; the demolition of a council owned bus shelter is the responsibility of the council; the cost of demolition would be far in excess of any amount raised for a Diana memorial.

It was a clear case of a councillor 'opening mouth before engaging brain'.

In conclusion, the *Echo* article ended with a final comment from Cllr Thornton: "At least the comments provoked a debate. I agree it is dilapidated and has to go. That doesn't bother me at all. You can find me a horse and cart and I will ride it up there to see the shelter go but I don't think I will be naked. It's too cold!"

As Cllr Thornton said, it "provoked debate". There were numerous letters to the letters column in the local press. Shirley Bloom wrote: "Nothing further from the truth" adding, "I was horrified to read the interview with ex-mayor Pat Thornton (*Echo* 5th September). Not content with her U-turn on 'doing a Lady Godiva' (for which heaven be praised), this lady had the temerity to state, not suggest, that Cllr

Les Godwin "intended to use money from the Princess Diana fund to knock down the bus shelter".

Nothing could be further from the truth. I trust that Cllr Godwin will take the appropriate action to expose this distortion of the truth."

Another letter from Tim Bacon with a headline: "Fund suggestion is outrageous" went on to say: "Cllr Les Godwin, during his year as mayor, repeatedly called for the demolition of the Royal Well bus shelter.

The death of Diana, Princess of Wales, led to the setting up of a public fund to create or enhance a memorial garden.

It is outrageous of Cllr Thornton to suggest that Mr Godwin would seek to use or switch money away from the memorial fund to finance a project for which such money was not prescribed. Meeting the cost of demolishing the bus shelter is clearly the responsibility of Cheltenham Borough Council."

Another letter from Mrs Bullock along similar lines and with a headline: "Ex-mayor should eat her words", concluded with the following: "May I suggest that Mrs Thornton now publicly eats her words with a plate of humble pie made from sour grapes."

Whilst I welcomed the letters in the local newspaper, it seemed to me that Cllr Thornton had made a public statement that I was intending to use money donated by the public to establish a Princess Diana Memorial for the purpose of demolishing the bus shelter. This was not only untrue, but should I let it go unchallenged then the general public could, quite rightly, think it was true.

I contacted my solicitor who agreed with me.

A letter was sent to Cllr Thornton demanding an apology; a few days later a letter from Cllr Thornton's solicitors arrived saying: "... she was happy to confirm that she did not intend to suggest that Cllr Godwin had sought to misappropriate monies donated for the Princess Diana Memorial Fund." A suitable letter from my solicitor was sent to the *Echo* for publication which put the record straight, but I could not help thinking that the possible outcome of the publicity might mean that people would stop donating to the fund.

Demolition day was approaching and Health and Safety officials had already scuppered the idea of me wielding the first sledgehammer blow on September 20th. A compromise had been reached: the day before demolition day, the mayor, Cllr Jeremy Whales, I and two other former mayors, Les Freeman and Jim Pennington, were allowed to enter the bus shelter suitably dressed and with our hard hats and sledgehammers, to pose for the *Gloucestershire Echo* photographer.

Two days later, *Echo* reporters Jason Chare and Ben Hurst wrote: "Timber! Bus shelter is bulldozed at last." It continued: "Four of Cheltenham's elder statesmen could not wait to get to grips with the Royal Well bus shelter. They armed themselves with sledgehammers to pave the way for the demolition of the eyesore, which starts in earnest on Monday."

It was a great relief to know that my dream of wanting to rid the town of the appalling bus shelter in the centre of the town had actually happened.

Former mayors Les Freeman, Jim Pennington and Jeremy Whales, join me in the demolition of the Royal Well bus shelters

I wrote to Marjorie Fulford on 13th September, thanking her and The Keep Cheltenham Tidy Group for their help during my mayoral year. I particularly mentioned the part they played in the 'Britain in Bloom' competition and the 'Mayor's Fashion Show'.

Marjorie replied on 4th October saying:

> *"Thank you for your most welcome letter. It was so kind of you to congratulate all of us for our part in the 'Bloom' awards.*
>
> *It was a worthwhile job of work involving so many people in the communities – and didn't we do well!*
>
> *Doreen Garland –Jones and I enjoyed and appreciated the amount of support you gave (and still do) to the work we do. I look forward to seeing you again.*
> *Best wishes Marjorie."*

The message was written in the usual style of Marjorie; she seldom used the first person singular; it was always what "we" have done and never seeking self-praise.

She was a most charming lady with a wonderful personality, and the ideal person to be the Projects Officer of Cheltenham Borough Council. She retired from the council in October 2000 due to ill-health.

I received a letter from Alex Bryce, Honorary Treasurer of the Cheltenham Senior Citizens' Welfare Committee on 28th November, thanking me for the cheque. It said: "I have just received a second cheque from Jo Bailey which comes from your record-breaking amount for a year of Mayor's Charities Appeals in Cheltenham. Together with the interim payment we have received £12,008.46 for which we offer our sincere and grateful thanks. We are very much closer to replacing our minibus following your support and Cheltenham townspeople's enormous generosity.

We hope that you enjoyed your year in office and will continue to reap the benefits from your unstinting work. Congratulations for the outstanding results of you and your charity team in raising so much money during your mayoral year."

Greg Smith, Principal, Gloucestershire College of Arts & Technology (Gloscat) invited Pam and me to their Higher Awards Ceremony in Gloucester Cathedral on Friday November 27th which we were pleased to accept.

By the end of the first week of October there was speculation that the GCHQ base would be located at Benhall although there was still the possibility that it might be located at the Business Park at Brockworth.

The GSL consortium had drawn up plans for what they called a space-age futuristic circular 'doughnut' shaped block, to house the 4,000 listening post staff.

Although the site was still to be chosen by the Foreign Office, it was clear that the choice of Benhall or Brockworth meant the end of the road for the controversial proposal to build on publicly owned fields next to GCHQ Oakley.

The campaigners hailed it a victory in their battle to save the fields, but some members of Odrag were disappointed with the outcome.

I was pleased with the announcement because good sense had prevailed and the fields had been saved. There was still a good case to be made for the 'doughnut' to be located at Benhall and the possible creation of 1,000 jobs.

CHAPTER 15

Investing In The Money Markets

You may fool all the people some of the time; you can even fool some of the people all the time;
but you can't fool all of the people all the time.

Attributed to Abraham Lincoln (1809 – 1865)
and Phineas Barnum (1810 – 1891)

It came as a shock to most people to learn in January 1999 that Cheltenham Borough Council (CBC) had borrowed £22.5 million in 1996 at a fixed rate of interest over 15 years and re-invested it in the belief that it would make a profit from soaring interest rates. Unfortunately for the council the interest rates fell and the council had made a huge loss.

The decision to go ahead with the investment had been taken at a CBC Policy & Resources Committee (P&R) meeting on 15th April 1996.

Five days earlier, all members of the council had been invited to a treasury management seminar to hear a report from the Director of Resources, Lawrence Davison, on treasury management. He was supported by senior officers of the council, plus representatives from the council's specialist financial advisers, Butler Asset Finance Limited.

We listened to Mr Davison's report on the "Review of Treasury Management Strategy", and debated the document at length. It sounded good, and with the words from the council's financial advisers still fresh in their minds, the P&R committee approved the report.

However, the economic period between 1996 and 1999 had been worse than expected; interest rates were low and the council incurred a loss of around £500,000.

None of this would have been known to the Cheltenham ratepayers if it had not been for the 17 page audit report by the District Auditor, Elizabeth Cave in February 1999. Once the audit report was published, the *Gloucestershire Echo* printed extracts from it which was soon followed by a spate of letters to the editor from very cross members of the public.

The following day and with a photograph of Elizabeth Cave, the *Echo* printed an article: "What the auditor's report says", and then went on to record some of the principal points in the report, including: "The borrowing of £22.5 million was not within the council's powers and was possibly unlawful. The council was badly advised financially. The council did not take out its own legal advice. The council may have needed to borrow some money but not £22.5 million. It would be very expensive to pull out at this stage; it has exposed itself to unnecessary risk. It would not be in the public interest to take the matter to court since it would cost even more tax-payers' money."

The auditor's report concluded: "We recognise that the arrangement was not motivated primarily by a wish to speculate but by a desire to stabilise the council's future borrowing costs."

Lawrence Davison responded by issuing a report on the auditor's findings. He claimed: "Borrowing the £22.5 million was well inside the council's powers. Expert advice was sought before the loan was taken. So far, no costs have been incurred to the council. The cost of pulling out would be £6 million. Interest rates are likely to go up in the future."

More and more letters were sent to the *Gloucestershire Echo*. The writers' criticisms of the council intensified against those whom the letter-writers deemed were responsible.

On 4th February, the *Local Government Chronicle* (LGC) reported: "Cheltenham to reschedule debts after damning audit" adding, "... the district auditor insisted the council did not need the amount involved to finance its capital programme. Councils are not allowed to borrow purely to make a profit on the money markets."

There were two important quotes in the LGC, one from Cllr John Todman, the leader of the council in 1999 who said: "The council acted in good faith at the time following advice from specialist consultants and believing what it did was lawful."

The other question was from Cllr Steve Jordan, leader of the council at the time the loan was taken out, who said: "The council's opinion on the legality of it has always been at odds with that of the district auditor."

It seemed that whatever the response from the borough council, the mood of the public would not change. The letters to the local newspaper all carried similar headlines such as: "Loan excuses do not wash", or "bring forward the local elections" and, "are we stuck with this council?"

A letter from Anthony Davies contained the following comment: "... judging by the reported comments of Cllr Todman and Cllr Jordan, no-one seems responsible for anything at the borough council, particularly when things go wrong; it seems prepared to maintain its original position in the face of irrefutable evidence ... It is not as if this is the only financial fiasco that has occurred in the past decade. There was misleading financial analysis of the various options for the St James' station site. There was the 1998 budget crisis when the council suddenly discovered a £1.5 million shortfall requiring savage cuts to services. And then there was the Noddy Train.

It is time the borough council was prepared to admit error and hold those responsible accountable for their actions to the taxpayer who continues to pay the price."

Liberal Democrat councillor Andrew McKinlay wrote to the *Echo* on January 30th claiming "the public had got it all wrong". He said "Your readers would be forgiven for thinking that the District Auditor had criticised the council", and then having put his interpretation on the main points of the audit report, ended his letter with the following: "This is the second time that an article has appeared in the *Echo* which gives an interpretation of the District Auditor's report with which I disagree ..."

Phil Newcombe, a well-known member of the Cheltenham Civic Society, answered the letter. He wrote: "I was interested to read Cllr McKinlay's attempt to explain his council's financial problems (*Echo* January 30). Your readers may recall that last year when it was reported that the existence of the waste tip and repair of the leisure centre were under threat, he implied that to pay for them and cancel the 'Noddy' train contract would double the council tax we pay – which was not correct as, according to the council's own figures, most of the tax goes to the county's police authority. How naïve does he think we are?"

Mrs Seton-Smith wrote: "I thought borough councillors had reached the height of stupidity with the Spa Shuttle and the purchase of land at Charlton Kings. I was wrong. The news that councillors have borrowed £22.5 million for investment and cannot pay it back leaves me almost speechless (*Echo* January 26). It is useless to say that although they did not take legal advice in 1996 the council has taken it now. Rather like shutting the door after the horse has bolted. Councillors are not elected to play the money markets – they are there to look after the affairs of the taxpayers"

On 1st February 1999 the P&R committee met to discuss the position and the implications contained in the District Auditor's 17 page report.

The following night the editor of the *Gloucestershire Echo* wrote a strong Opinion in her column. This is an extract: "There were dozens of disgruntled members of the public in the public gallery. And we would not mind betting that there are thousands more tutting with disapproval at Cheltenham Borough Council's disastrous foray into the money markets.

The idea to borrow £22.5 million and reinvest it may have seemed jolly clever in 1996. Nearly three years on, it looks pretty daft, some might say scandalous, given that it has already cost the council taxpayers £500,000 and is set to be a financial burden for the next 15 years.

At the meeting of the P&R committee last night, there was a mood of outright anger in the public gallery. On the council benches, there was an air of quiet contrition. Those responsible for agreeing the deal in 1996 did not get up and protest that they were right. The leading Lib Dems held their hands up and agreed they were ill-advised.

Even the Conservatives in opposition did not point the finger of blame at their opponents. And no-one took the District Auditor Elizabeth Cave to task as she stood by her guns and insisted that the council had gone beyond their powers."

Although the editor included all councillors in her scathing Opinion column, I thought it was a good article and one that councillors should respect.

The editor concluded her column with the following: "What a disaster. What a shambles. We repeat what we said a week ago: heads must roll for this monstrous mistake. The trouble is who will wield the axe when officers and councillors are all in it together?"

It was powerful stuff: I could fill the next few pages of this book with letters from local residents following the editor's comments. Among the letters was one from Cllr McKinlay refuting everything that had been written and published on the subject. It claimed: "No crisis, just technical speak" adding "... the council has in no way acted improperly in borrowing £22.5 million."

The letter went on to say: "The loans for £22.5 million allowed the council to pay off a number of more expensive loans and is common financial management practice ...."

Having then justified everything the council had done over the previous three years regarding loans and borrowing, the letter concluded with the following: "In short, this is a technical financial matter common to a number of councils and not the financial crisis your article suggests."

Clearly, Cllr McKinlay believed that Elizabeth Cave, the district auditor, had got it all wrong. His letter did not make me feel relieved; to the contrary, it disillusioned me about local politics and the way certain councillors saw their role.

Whilst the £22.5 million fiasco was rumbling on, money was still being sent to the Princess Diana Memorial Fund. They were small amounts, and the officer keeping the memorial fund account told me that the number of contributors had become fewer and the amounts of money had become smaller.

Whether the publicity surrounding the fund and the demolition had been detrimental to the falling-off of contributions or not, I felt it was time I closed the account. I wrote to Lawrence Davison, Chief Executive, on May 5th 1999 suggesting to him that the account should be closed. I also asked for a meeting to discuss the purchase of a bench seat with an appropriate plaque; landscaping of the Royal Well area and the planting of twelve silver birch trees around the edge of Royal Crescent.

At the meeting, together with the accountant and Simon Lee, Head of Parks & Landscape, in attendance, we discussed how much could be achieved with the public donations supplemented with money from the borough council's 'environment improvement fund'.

Apart from the memorial seat, which we agreed had to be securely fixed, we agreed that the landscaping work would be carried out by Simon Lee's department. Simon would come forward with his proposals for the area in July.

The council formally announced that the Diana Memorial Fund was closed.

I met Lawrence Davison and Simon Lee at the Royal Well bus station a few days later and we took stock of what was available with the money. We selected what we thought would be the best location for the commemorative seat.

Simon Lee wrote to me on 22nd July saying: "Further to our meeting with Lawrence Davison at the Royal Well bus station to discuss proposals for incorporating a commemorative bench as part of the proposed refurbishment project for this site. The proposals, shown on the attached plan, include the removal of the existing shrubbery, planting up of a Beech hedge at the Crescent side of the former shrubbery, to hide cars: the planting of 12 Silver Birch trees and laying of the site to turf.

This should recreate the original landscape which I am sure the designer of the Crescent had in mind when it was first laid out.

As we discussed, there are numerous positions for a new ornamental park seat to be sited within this new landscaped area. What I would be very grateful for in order to progress the project, would be the exact wording to be put on the small plaque which is attached to the seat.

I anticipate the refurbishment work starting in November 1999 at the earliest."

On 20th August, the *Gloucestershire Echo* printed an article stating "Work to start on Diana's garden soon". It said: "Shrubs at the Royal Well bus station are to be ripped up to reveal the Royal Crescent and replaced with a 4ft hedge. The work will be part of a facelift of the area using money donated at the time of Princess Diana's death. A line of new silver birch trees will also be planted.

When the Royal Well enhancement project is complete, people will not be able to cut through the new line of trees to get from Royal Crescent to the bus station. They will have to walk round.

The existing shrubbery is high and obscures the façade of Royal Crescent. It will be pulled out and replaced with 12 silver birches following the curve of the crescent. A sycamore and a chestnut tree will be kept. Now that the work on the bus shelters has finished the memorial garden scheme can go ahead."

All I needed to do now was to write a suitable inscription for the plaque that would be attached to the seat. This was my suggestion: "In memory of Diana, Princess of Wales – 1961 to 1997. She touched the hearts of many and will always be remembered."

CBC issued a press release in December 1999 headed: "Rediscovering our Regency Landscape" It reported that work on the landscaping etc. would begin on 12th December, adding: "Until recently the concrete bus shelters and the shrubbery have acted to conceal the splendour of the Royal Crescent, which in terms of urban landscape is a magnificent and precious part of the town's heritage. The removal of the existing shrubs will open up the view into the Royal Crescent and at the same time recreate the link with the adjoining open space. The landscaping is part of improvements to the bus station which include the recent installation of three modern shelters."

Cllr Duncan Smith, chairman of the council's Leisure Committee remarked, "For many years the importance of our Green Heritage – our parks, gardens and trees – has been undervalued. I am delighted that we are now able to start addressing the neglect of the past and hope that this will be the first of many schemes aimed at restoring our green landscapes to their former glory."

The press release also mentioned that new black railings would be installed plus a bench seat dedicated to Diana, Princess of Wales.

The comment from Cllr Smith that the Royal Well scheme would result in 'other green landscapes being restored to their former glory' must have been a pipe-dream. No other schemes have come along, as far as I know, but if they do, they will have my full backing.

On the 15th September, Grahame Lewis, Head of Development Services, reported that the "Cheltenham Spa Railway Station Development Brief" had been approved by the planning committee and should be sent to all relevant interest groups and the general public for their comments.

Following public consultation the council announced that it intended to adopt the document in the form of a Supplementary Planning Guidance (SPD), which would be taken into account by the council in the determination of planning applications for development within the area covered by the development brief.

For reasons known only to council officers, a SPD was never presented to councillors for their approval. In 2012 the council published a Concept Statement on the Cheltenham Spa Railway Station, which was similar, but different from the earlier development brief.

The purpose of the Concept Statement issued by the Local Planning Authority (LPA) is to encourage and influence owners of land and potential developers. It also sets down what the LPA would find acceptable in planning terms, but not, of course, in the process of delivery. There was a strong belief at the time that the council through its Local Development Task Force were prompting Network Rail to invest money in upgrading of the Cheltenham station to make it more user friendly.

In 1999, central government decided that all 'parties' whether they were political or non-political should register with the Electoral Commission. The Register of Political Parties Act 1998 required political parties to register, and in spite of our non-political status, the PAB group at its October management meeting decided to register with the Commission.

The big advantage of registration was the inclusion on the ballot paper of the PAB emblem next to the name of the candidate. This enabled voters who could not remember the name of the candidate, to look for the PAB emblem when casting their vote.

The registration also required the group to provide names of its senior officers, including the name of the person who would become the group's Nomination Officer and would be the named contact during the local election period.

Most of the information required by the Commission is about financial matters such as campaign expenditure, donations, and information regarding the accounts of a political party. This wasn't, and still isn't, as straightforward as it may sound, but thankfully PAB had, and still has, a very capable treasurer in David Hyett who has kept the Electoral Commission satisfied with the complex information they require.

We have made frequent representations to the Commission about the inclusion of minor parties such as PAB in the mainstream political arena. We have repeatedly expressed the view that should a 'non-political' group's interest only cover local elections then a different set of rules should apply to them. We were informed at the end of 2000 that central government intended to introduce Regulations that would exempt minor parties and groups who only contested local elections, from having to supply the same information as that required from the mainstream political organisations.

I gave a report to members of the PAB management committee on 3rd October 1999 on the District Auditor's report concerning the £22.5 million loan and rein-vestment on the money markets by the council.

It was not easy for me because I had been a member of the P&R committee in 1996 when the decision was taken to support the loan and the investment. I had no other defence than to say that I had been a fairly new member of the committee in 1996 and that I had followed the flow of the more experienced councillors when the vote was taken to proceed.

My colleagues were sympathetic but not impressed with my excuse. I told them that I should have asked questions, particularly those of a legal nature, but I didn't.

By the time I had finished my explanation, I could only promise that at the first opportunity when the council debated the issue, I would formally apologise to the people of Cheltenham for having let them down.

Rumours were rife at the time that a number of Cheltenham residents had formed a "Concerned Cheltenham Electors' Group" and it was reported that they would be challenging the decisions taken by the officers and members regarding the £22.5 million loan.

Whilst the circumstances regarding the "loan" were being argued and discussed on a daily basis, I was also having discussions with the local highway authority about the increasing traffic volumes in New Barn Lane, Prestbury.

I knew there was money available for traffic management use in the Prestbury area, so I requested that some of it should be used to construct a Pelican Crossing in New Barn Lane near Seven Posts Alley.

On 30th November, I received a letter from Michael Smith, Head of Engineering Services, confirming that a crossing would be installed, which would contribute to the future "Safe Routes to School" initiative.

In answer to further questions, Mr Smith confirmed that the project would cost £34,000, adding that more funding would be needed in order to improve the path through Seven Posts Alley.

The PAB management committee ended the year by presenting a cheque for £555.00 to the Cotswold Hospital Radio, which helps them to keep in touch with patients at the Cheltenham General and Gloucester Royal Hospitals.

The committee also announced that PAB members would raise money for the Winston's Wish Charity during the year 2000.

It was a bitter blow for the PAB group in January 2000 when Cllr John Newman and his partner Cllr Lesley Silvester announced they were leaving the PAB group and joining the Conservative group.

The reasons for their defection were unclear; his interview with the local newspaper claimed that I had undermined his position as a councillor following my suggestion at the Prestbury Parish Council meeting that "maintaining good relations between parish and borough councillors was a two-way process".

If anyone can fall out with a colleague over such an inoffensive comment, then I could only feel that there was more to the defection than met the eye.

Had they left PAB and sat as independent councillors that would have been understandable, but to join a mainstream political party simply did not make sense unless it had been planned over a period of time.

Cllr John Todman, Leader of the Conservative group, was delighted with the defection because it strengthened their fragile overall majority of one, which had then become three.

I told the local newspaper that I was shocked by the defection as they had applied to join the PAB group about ten years earlier, because they believed that party politics in local government worked against the best interests of the electors.

I added: "The pair is letting the people of Prestbury down."

At the time, it was touch and go whether the letters of anger from Prestbury residents published in the *Gloucestershire Echo* were going to exceed those that had been sent to the newspaper about the £22.5 million loan.

Headlines to some of the letters said: "Defection has left us amazed": "We did not vote for Tories": "Pair have betrayed us voters".

G R Guest, Prestbury, suggested in his letter that 'as the defectors had resigned from the parish council, they should also resign from the borough council'.

One letter to the editor that particularly pleased me read:

> *"It was with disbelief that we read the letter from Cllr Silvester expressing her views about the traffic problems in Swindon Lane. The letter gave the impression that the problems had just occurred.*
>
> *The residents of Swindon Lane, with the help of Cllr Les Godwin and Cllr Andy Cornish, have been battling away for years to reduce the speed, volume and size of vehicles using Swindon Lane. We can remember when the bridge over the old Honeybourne railway line had no footpath and pedestrians were forced to walk in the road in the face of the traffic, because there was no other way to get to the other side.*
>
> *It was Cllrs Godwin and Cornish who argued the case for us to have a footbridge built to enable us to walk in safety. It is Cllr Godwin who, with his team of local residents, is constantly monitoring the use of the lane by heavy goods vehicles.*
> *Mr and Mrs Harris, Cheltenham."*

The proposed development of land at the University & College Admissions Service (UCAS) in New Barn Lane, Cheltenham, prompted me to write to the local highway authority about highway safety should the planning application be approved.

The proposed access to serve the 15 dwellings was opposite the entrance to the Racecourse park& ride facility, and it was my view that only a substantial round-about would prevent accidents from occurring.

I also wanted the highway authority to construct pedestrian islands away from the roundabout to ensure pedestrian safety when crossing the road.

Gloucestershire County Council (GCC) commissioned Halcrow Fox "To carry out a Northwest Cheltenham Traffic Study to consider the traffic situation to the northwest of Cheltenham and in particular the corridor between the A4019 and the A435."

The traffic consultants would also carry out a review of the current traffic movements in the area using available data and analysis.

GCC believed a review of traffic was necessary because of the continued interest being shown in the possible construction of a northwest bypass. They were also aware that the road had been included in the Gloucestershire Structure Plan (First Alteration) which had been the subject of an Examination in Public in 1989.

Halcrow Fox published their report in March 2000. Their concluding remarks revealed that the analysis of traffic movement in the study area had shown a complex pattern of movement with a diverse range of trip origins and destinations. They came to the conclusion that the only clear pattern to emerge was "a significant proportion of the trips to Hyde Lane, Wymans Lane and Kingsditch Lane were local."

The consultants also concluded: "… The construction of a bypass would be a major undertaking, including the need to cross a major railway line" adding, "Whilst not wishing to prejudge studies to assess the impact and effectiveness of the other alternative measures and initiatives suggested above, the analysis of the previous work undertaken on the bypass alternatives shows that it performs poorly on traffic and economic assessments. This would suggest that the implementation of a bypass scheme may not provide sufficient advantages to the study area to outweigh its disadvantages."

One can only guess what the reaction was to the Halcrow Fox report behind the doors of the council offices. As far as PAB councillors were concerned, we decided, after studying the report, that we could not support the construction of a northwest bypass for two important reasons.

1) The construction of the road would result in the loss of many hectares of important Green Belt land, and
2) We believed that its construction could not take place without large-scale housing developments being approved by the councils in order to pay for it.

We arranged a meeting with the CBC chief executive on Thursday 6th April to express our reasons why we could not support the construction of a northwest bypass. It was also an opportunity for us to give notice to the chief executive that should the bypass be included in a future Cheltenham Transport Plan proposal, we would vote against it.

As with other major happenings in the local authority area, the news about a possible northwest bypass brought dozens of letters to the local newspaper. Most of them were written in angry tones and often directed against councillors from the Conservative party, who had expressed a view of being supportive of the proposal.

John Durrows wrote: "Common sense must take over", adding, "Cllr Todman (Conservative), suggests the new road will be an application of common sense. Is it really common sense to destroy more green belt? Surely it is common sense to use the nearby M5. Is it really common sense for the council leader to support this road-building plan when recent literature from CBC tells us to leave the car at home and become more environmentally-friendly?"

There were other letters on the same theme, often adding the importance for Junction 10 on the M5 to be upgraded to cater for traffic in both directions. Fourteen years later, the same people are still making the same request to the Gloucestershire County Council Highways Department, but the upgrade of Junction 10 is still as far away now as it was then.

The only hope for changes to the junction hangs on the success of the Joint Core Strategy, where designated employment land adjacent to the M5 would require improvements to Junction 10 and possibly Junction 11.

Central government is being pressed for financial support in 2014, but even if the funding is forthcoming the improvements to the junctions would not take place for several years.

Because the letters to the local newspaper constantly referred to the north west bypass, I wrote to them explaining that 'the bypass had been removed from the County Structure Plan, and should now be referred to as the north west distributor road.'

In my letter, I said:

> "The re-invented 'distributor road' will cut into several hectares of green belt land around Springbank and an even greater loss of green belt around Swindon Village.
>
> Surely the local residents and their elected representatives should be consulted? And why is it that whenever there is talk about roads and development, it is always at the Gloucester end of the town.
>
> On the Charlton Kings side of the town, the worst they have to endure is talk about the possible de-trunking of the A40."

In March 2000, the Civic Awards Adjudication Panel, under the umbrella of the Cheltenham Civic Society, agreed that the replacement bus shelters in Royal Well, and the adjoining automatic public conveniences, should be recognised by a commendation in the category "Improvements to the Built Environment".

The awards took place in June.

The debate and investigation into the council's £22.5 million loan continued within and outside the Municipal Offices throughout the year.

The history of events show that Butler Asset Finance (BAF) had contacted Desmond Knight, Head of Accountancy Services (CBC) in November 1995, explaining its views on the advantages of externalising debt.

It was further alleged that Mr Knight followed this up in February 1996 by writing to BAF asking that progress be made on the report on externalisation of investments referring, inter alia, to integer and Audit Commission work then being conducted on "Debt Performance Index Survey Report".

Following further correspondence between the Head of Accountancy Services and BAF, (as we learned earlier) a seminar and a meeting of the P&R committee took place in April 1996 when the decision to adopt the BAF 'course of action' (the externalisation of the council's internal investments) was taken.

It became general knowledge in January 1997 that Mr John Howell QC gave general advice to the Audit Commission on, inter alia, the use of provision for credit liabilities to fund expenditure. Apparently, it was made clear at the time that the Advice did not specifically relate to Cheltenham, but in December that year, the District Auditor's Management Letter for the period 1996/97 to the council, was seeking clarification of the reasons why the council had externalised £22.5 million on internal debt.

Clearly, the request for clarification must have started alarm bells ringing, because in January 1998, Mr Gerald Ford, Head of Legal Services (CBC), instructed Mr Mark Lowe QC and sought Advice on Treasury Management.

Mr Lowe QC advised that in his opinion the council had acted lawfully, and I am told that a copy of the Advice was sent to the District Auditor (DA).

I have no record of being informed of the above activity between the council and the legal advisors, but I had been made aware that Elizabeth Cave, the DA, in her Management Letter to the council in February 1998 had written that "…she was satisfied that the arrangements the council had made were for reasons other than unlawful financial speculation."

As a result of the DA's letter, Des Knight wrote to her in February 1998 seeking her views on the rescheduling of £22.5 million of loans. The alleged written reply from the DA confirmed "… there were no problems rescheduling the loans".

The change of emphasis over the arrangements became known through a further communication from the DA in July 1998 when allegedly she wrote to the Head of Accountancy Services explaining her view on the lawfulness of the borrowing, which apparently, "… depended on whether there had been, or could have been, a loss to the council as a result of [the] transaction", and it seemed," … wanted information about certain projected figures".

The borrowing costs and 'fund managers returns' were supplied to the DA.

I do not have any record of the exchange of letters between the council and the DA during the above period – the information above is the result of requests to the council for information during the writing of this book.

The information supplied to me certainly showed that the DA had either changed her view, or she had received other legal advice that conflicted with her earlier opinion of the situation.

There was a flurry of legal communication between Mr Ford and Mark Lowe QC following a meeting between the DA and Lawrence Davison in September 1998.

In December, the DA issued an opinion report on the 1997/98 accounts for inclusion in the Statement of Accounts drawing attention to the council's treasury management arrangements, which apparently, were to be reconsidered in February 1999.

Just before Christmas 1998, the DA's management letter (1997/1998) arrived in which she expressed the view that the external borrowing and the reinvestment of £22.5 million was not within the council's powers.

Upon receipt of the letter, Mr Ford sought further Advice from Mark Lowe QC in January 1999 enclosing inter alia the report that was going to the P&R committee on 1st February.

It was following this meeting that the local newspaper and the general public expressed their anger at the council for what they perceived to be an "illegal" expenditure of public money.

There were seven members of the Concerned Cheltenham Electors Group who were determined to get to the bottom of what they thought was maladministration by officers and councillors of Cheltenham Borough Council.

Two members of the group, Mr A P Davies and Mr C J Smith, wrote to Des Knight in February seeking background information about the £22.5 million loan. They subsequently sent a 'Notice of Objection' to the DA in April 1999 who agreed to meet the two objectors in May to discuss their notice of objection.

Once the DA had received the full details of the evidence from the objectors, she was obliged to make a statement of facts, which would summarise the various steps taken that had brought the matter to a head, including what she believed to be the basis of the council's reasons for going ahead with the borrowing.

One can only guess that there was a lot of activity going on behind the doors of the Municipal Offices: C J Smith wrote to the DA in July requesting an update on the progress of his formal objection. There were more exchanges of letters and endless meetings between officers, legal advisors and the DA.

In December 1999 the DA wrote to the chief executive informing him that she had received preliminary legal advice on the objection by Mr Smith to the 1996/97 accounts of the council, which was that "... the arrangement entered into by the council to borrow £22.5 million was unlawful."

Once this information became public knowledge, the Concerned Cheltenham Electors Group increased their pressure on the council and the DA for further information. They urged the DA to take the council to court.

Throughout the first four months of 2000, there seemed to be nothing else discussed in the council offices or the local newspaper but the £22.5 million loan, but of course, scheduled meetings had taken place and decisions made.

In July, the news broke that Elizabeth Cave had decided not to take legal action against the borough council, because as she said "... it would not be in the best interests of the people of Cheltenham to 'saddle' them with more costs."

The news inevitably brought an angry response from the objectors and many local townspeople. Those who contacted me couldn't understand why the borrowing was at first declared 'lawful' then 'unlawful' and now in July the alleged illegality would not be taken any further. Most, if not all of those who contacted me, took the view "to hell with the expense, let's bring those responsible to book".

I was sympathetic with the views that had been expressed: having been a member of the P&R committee in 1996 made me more uncomfortable as I listened to their complaints.

Time had come for PAB councillors to discuss the changing situation: we agreed that a statement on behalf of the PAB Group should be made immediately. The statement dated 1st September 2000 made the following points:

> "The issue is no longer about recrimination. The District Auditor has decided that the matter of lawfulness will not be pursued through the High Court. The important issue now is whether Cheltenham Borough Councillors were misled into believing that there were no legal implications concerning the Treasury Management Strategy document presented to the council in 1996.
>
> From the Auditor's report, which has been supported by the Advice presented by Mr A A Child, we are of the opinion that the officers' recommendation to the CBC Policy & Resources Committee in 1996 was unlawful and contrary to the spirit and meaning of Section 17(1) of the Audit Act 1998.
>
> We are of the view that had the councillors been made aware of all the facts in 1996 that are available today, we believe they would come to a different conclusion.
>
> We accept that we are amateurs in what has become a very complex business in the world of commerce and finance: we rely on sound professional advice from officers, including legal advice, whenever we are asked to make such important decisions..."
>
> The statement concluded with the following: "...A very grave mistake was made in 1996; the people of Cheltenham at the very least have every right to expect someone from the council to say they are sorry.
>
> Whether councillors were misled, given bad advice, or incorrect advice, we believe that that was incompetence and should be treated as such.
>
> We also believe with the general comments of Mr A A Child on page 6 of his Advice that 'local authorities are not entitled to engage in a trade or business (whether of borrowing and investment or otherwise) for the purpose of deriving a profit therefrom: see Att Gen v Smethwick Corporation (1932) 1 Ch 562; Hazell v Hammersmith & Fulham LBC (1990) 2 QB 697 at p779.
>
> It is up to those responsible to consider whether they should resign from the council."

The borough council gave notice that a 'Special Council Meeting' would be held in the council chamber on Thursday 28th September to discuss the £22.5 million loan.

The *Gloucestershire Echo* published a full page article the previous night with a headline "Don't whitewash £22.5 million loan farce". The article written by Jason Chare reported: "A pressure group concerned about CBC's £22.5 million loan, fears tomorrow's crunch meeting will be a whitewash. They believe that the 122–page report giving the senior officers' account of what happened when the loan was taken out in 1996 is aimed to blind people with waffle."

C J Smith, one of the objectors, when interviewed said: "There is one question missing in the report, where does the buck stop?"

The council meeting on 28th September, as expected, attracted more than 100 people to the public gallery. The meeting lasted six hours with a fifteen minute break at 8.00 p.m. It was a noisy meeting and the protestors heckled the councillors throughout the meeting.

The mayor 'suspended standing orders' so that councillors could speak more than once during the debate and without a time limit.

The following night Jason Chare wrote:

"The £22.5 million loan saga was debated in a marathon session at an extraordinary meeting of Cheltenham Borough Council last night.

For almost six hours, the debate raged. It was punctuated by heckling from the 100 people who listened in the public gallery.

It began at 5.30 p.m. when head of legal services Gerald Ford and head of accountancy Des Knight presented their report on District Auditor Elizabeth Cave's 18–month investigation.

In her statement of reasons published in July, Mrs Cave deemed the borrowing in 1996 was unlawful because she felt the money was used to speculate on movements in interest rates for a profit.

Mr Ford denied there was any speculation and said the money had been used to reinstate capital reserves after four years of internal borrowing."

The words from Mr Ford did not find favour with people in the gallery. Shouts of "It is our money" could be heard amongst other comments.

I gave my longest speech since I had become a borough councillor. There were two issues for me,

1. whether the loan was lawful or not, it was not our money and
2. the possible consequences for the taxpayer if the borrowing had been lawful.

I told the council:

"... PAB councillors have spent countless hours discussing the detail and the background of the council's decision to borrow £22.5 million and then re-invest it for profit in 1996. We are also aware that recent reports imply that the money was not re-invested or speculated, even though these claims fly in the face of the Auditor's report.

One could argue that if the strong case put forward by the two legal advisers to the District Auditor was no more than the required answer one should expect from a paid professional, then the same logic should be applied to the Advice given to the council by Mr Mark Lowe ..."

I ended my speech saying: "... Let us assume for one moment that the council's decision to borrow £22.5 million was done in good faith; then stretch the imagination to believe that the council's actions were legal; the facts of the matter show that the events of 1996 caused the council to reschedule its loans at different rates of interest. Huge penalty charges have been incurred and at the end of the day, whether it is this day, tomorrow or another day in the future, the people of Cheltenham will have to foot the bill.

PAB councillors believe that someone should be honest enough to admit that the decision was wrong and at the very least to say sorry to the local taxpayer for the events that occurred in 1996... If as some people allege, 'the borrowing was lawful' then the council presumably, if it felt like a 'flutter on the money markets' tomorrow, could do it all over again. What a frightening thought that is?"

In the Opinion column of the *Echo* the following night, the editor wrote: "Why didn't they own up before?" She added: "Last night's marathon six-hour debate draws to an end one of the sorriest episodes in the history of Cheltenham Borough Council.

On the agenda was that £22.5 million loan which the council took out to invest in the money markets. In the process, however, they cost council tax payers an unnecessary fortune. They were also acting illegally.

We feared last night's extraordinary meeting would be a whitewash – and it nearly was. At the end of the day, however, councillors did have the decency to admit the incident should never have taken place, and that no such borrowing will ever be allowed again.

They also rapped council officers for not informing the committee properly when they agreed to the loan in 1996.

It is a pity only one councillor – PAB leader Les Godwin – had the courage to apologise.

However, given their insistence in the past that all was hunky dory and that they did nothing wrong, perhaps we should be grateful that the other members did not do as much ducking and diving as expected.

At least members spent six hours chewing over the affair and did not try to brush it under the carpet in five minutes.

As they consign the fiasco to the borough history books, officers and members must realise that the most precious thing that the council has lost in this sorry affair is the respect of the public.

Until last night, they refused to admit the district auditor was right, and refused to accept any blame. Why? That attitude has done them absolutely no good. And it means they will have to live with that tarnished reputation for decades to come."

The extraordinary meeting brought to a close a scandal which had rocked the borough since January 2000. The meeting ended with councillors agreeing that the officers did not carry out adequate investigations before they advised councillors in 1996.

The councillors also agreed that leading Liberal Democrats did not adequately challenge the officers' report. They regretted the auditor's report. The council unanimously agreed that it will not do the same again.

In spite of the admissions and the assurances, I could not believe that it was the last time we would hear mention of the £22.5 million loan fiasco. I was equally sure that the seven members of the Concerned Cheltenham Electors Group would not be packing their files and folders away for a little while.

I believed the year 2001 was going to be just as interesting as the previous one.

CHAPTER 16

Silver Jubilee

When to the sessions of sweet silent thought I summon up remembrance of things past, I sigh the lack of many things I sought, and with old woes new wail my dear times' waste.
Sonnet 30 William Shakespeare 1564 – 1616

With reference to chapter one when I wrote about the inaugural meeting at Lakeside School in February 1976, it was nice to read an article in the *Gloucestershire Echo* by Simon Freeman on May 26th 2001, who wrote: "They said we'd never make it". The articled continued: "When a disgruntled band of activists set up their own action group to take on the might of the Town Hall, many said they would not last six months.

Now, 25 years down the line, the People Against Bureaucracy party has 400 members and councillors holding six seats in Cheltenham. The group has celebrated its silver jubilee in its spiritual home of Prestbury – where all three councillors are PAB – with an AGM and a trip to the local pub.

Andy Cornish, Dave Prince, Malcolm Stennett, Joanna McVeagh and me, celebrating the PAB successes at the May 2000 local elections

PAB was born in 1976 when Les Godwin, then a personnel manager with a local company, placed a £5 advert in the *Echo*, reading 'If you are as fed up with Tewkesbury Borough Council as I am then come to a meeting at Lakeside Junior School.'

Mr Godwin said: 'I couldn't believe it. I thought 20 people might turn up, but in fact 89 did. We were certainly unhappy with the way the council was behaving and felt we needed to get someone in there to represent our views.'

For the record, Mr Godwin won a majority of 200 when he stood in a by-election in Prestbury two years later. It is a seat he has held ever since."

Concluding his article, Simon Freeman wrote: "...another of the achievements of which Mr Godwin is proud is the party's desire to keep local politics local. Members are now gearing up for the 2002 elections where they hope to field more candidates than ever before."

Reflecting on the past Mr Godwin said: "At first many people wrote us off as irritants and claimed we would not last a week, but we have proved them all wrong. We represent the people and not a party political machine. That is why we have succeeded."

Because of my interest in defending the Green Belt around Cheltenham, the council invited me to attend a one-day course at Oxford Brookes University on Wednesday 13th June 2001.

The title of the course was "Green Belts: The Future".

It was an interesting course mainly because the tutors took great pains to inform the students that the Green Belts across the country were an important asset and should be protected from predator developers. In my case, they were talking to the converted: Green Belts and the countryside go together and they are a tremendous asset to any community.

Whether the council sent me on the course at Oxford in the hope that I might change my view about the proposed northwest bypass and the potential loss of the Green Belt land around Swindon Village, I know not. But if they did, then they had been misinformed about the content of the course. If anything, I was more convinced than ever that the Green Belt should not be sacrificed in order to provide a road that may or may not be used in the future.

On Saturday June 16th, there was a lengthy article in the *Gloucestershire Echo* asking the question: "Why is bypass still in plan?"

The article by Peter Gavan said: "The controversial northwest bypass for Cheltenham still features in the area's transport plan – despite mass protests and petitions against the idea from residents.

But according to the Project Nexus Group (PNG), 79 per cent of people were supportive of the scheme when it was put out for public consultation."

This figure however, was disputed by the newly formed Greenbelt Protection Society (GPS), who claimed that of the 5,200 PNG responses; only 119 explicitly supported the bypass plan.

According to the *Echo*, John Ruane, the founder of the GPS, reported "...4,900 replies specifically objected to the concept and, out of more than 40 organisations asked; only three supported the road plan. To ignore such overwhelming objections is a measure of the ignorance of those who are determined to force Cheltenham to accept the road that so few people support."

On Wednesday July 4th, *Gloucestershire Echo* published an article by Jonathon Porritt, which included his view on the Cheltenham Local Transport Plan.

The article had a headline: "Road planners taking us for a ride". It read: "On Monday [2nd July 2001] as expected, Cheltenham Borough Council voted to incorporate the Local Transport Plan into the Local Plan.

This basically means councillors are minded to proceed with the Local Transport Plan, including the highly-controversial North West Distributor Road (NWDR), subject to further "consultation" in October.

I put consultation in quotes because one has to ask exactly what this means. The level of opposition to this backward-looking and hugely destructive road scheme is overwhelming.

Gloucestershire County Council think it's rubbish, both local MP's think it's rubbish, 37 of the 40 organisations that made a formal submission in response to the Local Transport Plan think it's rubbish, and nearly 5,000 people have expressed their own personal opinion that it's rubbish – against the tiny minority in favour. And, for what it's worth, I think its rubbish too.

One is hard put to understand the kind of thinking that lies behind such a process, with the vote on Monday being driven through by the Conservative majority on a three-line whip.

It's all the more astonishing as many other aspects of the Local Transport Plan are really rather good.

It's only this throwback to our road building past that sticks out like some developers' self-interested fantasy, dreaming of all the new houses on Green Belt land that the road will serve."

Jonathon Porritt had made some very strong points in the article.

A letter written to the local newspaper, but unsigned read: "The tally of Cheltenham Borough councillors' votes after the debate over the controversial NWDR was a disturbing revelation.

The former mayor, Cllr Daphne Pennell, who had publicly stated her opposition to the construction of this new road when she received a weighty petition from objectors, did a complete volte-face and voted for it.

Cllr Rob Garnham, when on the Westminster campaign trail a month ago, expressed his objection to the proposed road. Surprise, surprise, he voted for it. I leave it to others to draw their own conclusions.

Is it any wonder that politicians as a whole are regarded with such disdain? As for Cllr Todman's comments, 'over my dead body will 5,000 houses be built'- I am digging out my black tie."

The year 2001 was also the year when Gloucestershire County Council (GCC) renewed their interest in developing land at Starvehall Farm in New Barn Lane.

The GCC interest was supported by Conservative members of the borough council. At the meeting on July 3rd they proposed a motion which endorsed a scheme for a road to be constructed from the Prestbury Road Day Centre, across the playing fields and the land at Starvehall Farm, exiting at the farm gate in New Barn Lane.

They claimed it would relieve congestion at the double mini-roundabout at the junction of Tatchley Lane, Deep Street and Prestbury Road.

The *Echo* report on the council motion, which was passed by 20 votes to 15, said: "Cllr Les Godwin reported there had been no consultation on the scheme, or any discussions about a possible housing development at Starvehall Farm.

He warned the council that it would have a tough time with a planning proposal until there was proper consultation with the local residents."

We now had the possibility of two unwanted roads being constructed in Swindon Village and Prestbury. Both would swallow up valuable countryside and in the Swindon Village case, would result in the loss of many hectares of Green Belt.

Mrs J M Smith of Swindon Village summed up the situation in a letter to the the local newspaper on July 11th. This is a précis of her letter: "As a mother of three young children and a resident of Swindon Village, it is not surprising that I am concerned about a road plan that will spoil my village and threaten the future environment for my children.

I object most strongly to the disparaging words used by Cllr Jacky Fletcher (Conservative) at the recent council meeting, which I attended along with many others.

Your headline 'Yes to bypass' was totally wrong and misleading – a bypass is usually built many miles from the town it is aiming to bypass. It is for vehicle drivers who do not wish to enter the town.

The North West Distributor Road would need to be drawn tightly inside the Cheltenham borough boundary otherwise the adjoining authority would almost certainly object to its presence and the inevitable loss of greenbelt land . . ."

Mrs Smith ended her letter thus: "The Conservative councillors' weak excuse for swapping the Tatchley Lane link road in Prestbury for another road without prior consultation with the local people was another example of the way they intend to proceed.

It is obvious to me and I am sure many other local people that other roads and costly initiatives will continue to be pushed through against the wishes of the people . . ."

The editor of the *Echo* added weight to the letter in the Opinion column with a heading: "Developers on the prowl". It continued: "Look out Prestbury and Leckhampton. And hold on to your hats in Swindon Village. Because if the green fields in those areas don't get pounced on by developers in the next five years, it will be a miracle.

The people of Swindon Village face double trouble: the prospect of a distributor road winging its way across the Green Belt that surrounds them, as well as the threat of housing developments which would bring in enough cash to pay for the road. . ."

The Opinion concluded: "As for our councillors, they will have to listen. They cannot ride roughshod over every local protest. If there is really no alternative but to build on Green Belt, they will have to prove it. And they haven't done that yet."

It is often said that 'history repeats itself' and the words in the letter by Mrs Smith in 2001 and the editor's Opinion, have been written and uttered by protesters again and again as proposals for residential development on Green Belt land in Swindon Village, Up Hatherley and Prestbury continued during the following years.

In spite of the protests from local residents, CBC seemed determined to press ahead with the NWDR and support for the road came strongest from the Conservative members of the administration.

John Ruane told me that he had received a letter from Lawrence Davison stating that in spite of public opinion, the council believed that the road would play an important role in relieving current and future traffic problems in the northwest part of Cheltenham.

John was not impressed, mainly because the independent examination of traffic flows in the Princess Elizabeth Way/Tewkesbury Road junction area did not concur with any of the data that had been put forward by the council.

It was around this time that central government were addressing a new approach to transport problems in towns and cities and CBC were hoping that central government would support their view that a new road was necessary.

When the appraisal was published by central government, it showed that the plan for a distributor road, including the cost and the loss of Green Belt land, was not a sustainable option.

This did not deter CBC and the Conservative administration; they continued to support the inclusion of the NWDR in a future Cheltenham Transport Plan.

GPS condemned this decision and promptly delivered over 2,000 letters to CBC in an attempt to get the council to change its mind.

A breakdown of the letters revealed 633 letters came from residents living in the areas that would be affected, namely Swindon Village, Fiddler's Green, Arle Farm, Springbank and Brockhampton. More than 900 letters came from other parts of Cheltenham who were against the Cheltenham Transport Plan for other reasons.

The *Echo* Opinion column on October 13th read: "On the road to costly inquiry".

It said: "Cheltenham Borough Council now has 2001 reasons not to ignore the claims of the Green Belt Protection Society.

John Ruane, one of the campaign's prime movers, is rightly pleased with yesterday's stunt outside the Municipal Offices where these symbolic numbers of letters of objection were delivered to the mayor. . ."

It continued: "And what has got the folk of Cheltenham all fired up? It's the thought of a not-so-super highway tearing through Green Belt land at the back of Hester's Way and Swindon Village. They pose some powerful arguments to make their case: The so-called NWDR – as included in the Cheltenham draft Local Plan – has already been discredited by Gloucestershire County Council.

Support for the anti-bypass campaign would appear to range from all corners of Cheltenham.

It is a hard task to find many people willing to speak up in favour of the proposed road. And, most crucially, it might open the door to massive development on the Green Belt bordering Cheltenham…"

The *Echo* Opinion ended: "The words which struck a real chord are Mr Ruane's when he intimates that his campaign and the borough council are on a collision course with a very costly public inquiry. With forces like this ranged against the road, it isn't worth it."

However, in spite of all the activity by the GBPS, there was no support from the Conservative administration. Cllr John Todman continued with his claim that unless the NWDR was built the traffic congestion on the western side of Cheltenham will only worsen.

Thirteen years have passed and the road congestion that Cllr Todman was so concerned about has only marginally worsened, because highway infrastructure improvements have been undertaken over the years; and the Green Belt land that would have been lost, is still there.

I attended the GBPS November meeting to explain the public inquiry procedure, which I forecast would begin around October 2002. And because Lawrence Davison had written to GBPS exhorting the importance of the road, I advised that GBPS should seek a copy of the government publication "New Approach to Transport Appraisal" from Mr Davison so that both sides had equal access to the information.

I also informed the meeting that GCC had commissioned Halcrow Group Limited (HGL) to carry out a second survey on the feasibility of a distributor road, in spite of the fact that CBC had commissioned HGL in March 2000 to carry out an appraisal. They had already concluded that it was not feasible and as the land and the environment had not changed since 2000, it seemed to be a waste of council taxpayers' money.

The purpose of the study in February 2002 was to 'undertake a traffic assessment of the principal corridor of orbital traffic movement in the North West Cheltenham area (North West Corridor). The overarching objective of the study was to "assess solutions to transport issues in North West Cheltenham".

The study was to look at all possible travel plans for the area in order to reduce highway capacity for motor vehicles; but the study did reveal issues that raised concerns, principal amongst them being the possible diversion of traffic from the North West Corridor into surrounding, less suitable residential streets.

HGL published a final report in September 2002.

The large expanse of Green Belt surrounding Swindon Village was not the only land that attracted the attention of CBC; land to the rear of existing houses in New Barn

Lane which extended to the boundary of Cheltenham Racecourse, was also receiving attention.

A planning inspector dismissed an appeal in 1984 [see chapter 8] for 46 dwellings on the land because in his view, *"... the possible impact of the proposed development on the character and environmental setting of the Racecourse is a prime consideration irrespective of the green belt boundary. This site provides an attractive grassland buffer between the New Barn Lane housing and the Racecourse..."*

The decision, which emphasised the importance of the open land to the setting of the Racecourse, also established beyond any doubt that the land from the rear of the properties in New Barn Lane to the Racecourse perimeter was Green Belt.

In 2001, a New Barn Lane resident applied for outline planning permission to build a large detached dwelling on land to the rear of his property.

I wrote to the planning department warning them that the land in question was Green belt and the application should not be supported. Having been a member of Tewkesbury Borough Council (TBC) planning committee for 13 years, I was well aware of the TBC Environs Plan (EP), which clearly delineated the boundaries of green belt, the AONB and other features.

Further discussions with council officers made little difference to their position; even the production of the TBC maps and drawings of the area failed to impress them.

Residents adjoining the application site who would be most affected by the development should it be approved, contacted me for advice; we put together a sound case to oppose the application should it eventually receive a recommendation to permit by the planning officers.

I also held meetings with other residents in New Barn Lane who were equally concerned that should the application be approved, it might be the thin end of the wedge which would open the door to more development.

In January 2002 I had meetings with the case officer when highway issues related to the New Barn Lane proposal were discussed. I reminded the planning officer that the land was shown as Green Belt on the EP, which had been the appropriate document used by TBC planning officers in resisting other planning applications since its approval and publication in 1974.

For a while it looked as though the planning application may have been withdrawn, or perhaps put on the 'back burner', as they say. But in April 2002 I was informed that CBC were seeking advice from Queen's Counsel (QC) on whether it was "safe" to allow the planning application to proceed.

It seemed to me to be a drastic and expensive step for the council to take for the sake of one detached dwelling. But did they have other applications in the pipeline, or did they have longer-term plans for the future development of the land on the south side of the Racecourse?

The local residents did not sit back and allow changes to be made without taking any action. They sought legal advice too once they heard that CBC had altered the Green Belt boundary in new plans (1995) following the transfer of Prestbury and other peripheral parishes to Cheltenham in 1991.

Because I questioned some of the points in the QC's Opinion at the planning committee meeting, I received a letter from a solicitor in July 2002, acting on behalf of the QC, explaining what he thought "I did not understand about the status of the land to the rear of the houses in New Barn Lane".

The solicitor wanted me to accept the premise that because the borough council had incorrectly redrawn the Green Belt boundary line when the parish was transferred from Tewkesbury to Cheltenham in 1991, it had now become the new boundary line. In other words, he was condoning the error and wanted me to go along with it. I didn't, and in 2006 a new Cheltenham Borough Council Proposals Map was published showing the Green Belt boundary line close to the properties in New Barn Lane.

In spite of all the evidence that was produced by me as the ward councillor and the main objector to the proposal, the planning case officer recommended the application should be permitted. On 27th June 2002, the planning committee considered the application and by a majority of votes the application was approved subject to what is called a Section 106 Agreement.

Residents who would be adversely affected by the development received a letter from the planning department telling them of the planning committee's decision.

To add insult to injury, the letter suggested to them that 'should they want a copy of the planning officer's report, and/or a copy of the Decision Notice, they were welcome to seek copies of them, but there would be a fee'.

The decision by the planning committee to breach the Green Belt was bad and irresponsible; the professional advice of the officers was poor, especially as they had been made aware of where the Green Belt line was drawn.

They had chosen to ignore the advice, knowing that by doing so, they would be breaching their own policies and opening up the area to possible further planning applications.

Rightly, in my view, a resident who would be most affected by the decision, formally complained to the Local Government Ombudsman (LGO) in August 2002 on the grounds of maladministration by the council when dealing with the planning application.

In his submission to the LGO, the resident quoted the paragraph in the Planning Policy Guidance (PPG2) (Green Belts) which states: "The essential characteristic of Green Belts is their permanence." This was an important point and one that the Planning Inspector had used in his decision to dismiss the planning appeal to develop land to the rear of New Barn Lane in June 1984.

The LGO followed the usual procedure of checking whether the complaint was one that the law allowed him to investigate; to inform the council of the complaint; to invite them to comment; to examine council's files and to visit the site during the investigation.

The complaint by the resident was as follows:

"The council failed to correctly identify the boundary of the land designated as Green Belt land adjacent/to the rear of 83B New Barn Lane; that the council has admitted there was a drafting error; and the error led to the planning application being approved to the detriment of the amenity of the occupiers of 83B."

Cheltenham Borough Council (CBC) did not respond to the LGO's correspondence, which required him to make further representations to CBC in November 2002.

On 15th January 2003, Richard Levett, Head of Audit and Assurance Services (CBC), wrote to Mr P E Warren the Investigator on behalf of the LGO, apologising for the delay in responding to the letters of complaint, and enclosing a five-page "note" from Mr Bob Wills the council's Strategic Land Use Manager.

Included in the "Note" was a reference about the enlargement of Cheltenham Borough in 1991 and the fact that the council had "revised their Local Plan to cover the whole of its new area".

Mr Wills's note went on to claim: "... The revised Local Plan incorporated, as appropriate, policies and designations from the Cheltenham Environs Local Plan [a Tewkesbury Borough Council document]. This included the Green Belt boundary in the New Barn Lane area. There was no explicit intention on CBC's part to amend the designated Green Belt boundary at this point, but there was a drafting error on the Proposals Map, which led to a change to the previous boundary at the rear of 81 and 83 New Barn Lane. The change was first published in October 1991 in a Consultation Draft of the revised Local Plan, and subsequently in the Deposit draft in April 1992. The Local Plan was finally adopted in December 1997..."

The note from Mr Wills concluded: "... The council accepts that there was an error in the drafting of the Proposals Map which led to permission being granted for a dwelling on land where otherwise it might not ..."

It was a disappointment to me and to the complainant that the LGO subsequently determined in January 2003 that "... the complaint by the resident was not one the LGO could pursue and that he was minded to discontinue the investigation..."

The LGO was looking at the decision by the planning committee who had made their decision on the facts before them at the time and the drafting error of the drawing was not a matter for the planning committee.

However, there was a ray of hope. The use of the words 'minded to discontinue the investigation' in the letter from Mr Warren, and his reference to the council admitting that it had inadvertently altered the boundary of the Green Belt designation, meant that the matter was not closed.

His letter also referred to the fact that the issue of Green Belt designation is one of legal fact. Green Belt boundaries are set by the Local Plan and therefore any changes in the Local Plan meant that there could be changes in the boundaries.

The planning officers had decided before recommending planning approval for a dwelling in the Green Belt that they should seek Counsel's advice. The Advice that was subsequently given was that 'it was safe for planning permission to be granted because it was outside the designated Green Belt area'.

The LGO could not change the planning decision, but he could make some important remarks about the 'drafting error' and the inordinate amount of time it took the council to respond to his enquiries.

Because of the planning decision, the Investigator would assess the impact the 'new house' would have on the neighbour's property and the loss of privacy and loss of amenities caused by the council's administrative faults.

It was unfortunate that the cartographic error was not discovered earlier, which would have prevented the 'new house' being built. The council, in spite of their admission, are responsible to ensure that council plans should reflect what is on the ground, and should be checked for accuracy before they are published.

In March 2003, Mr Warren made a further assessment of the complaint against the council for maladministration and he wrote to the complainant as follows:

> "...When I decided that the Local Plan process did include an option for you and others to raise objections to the change in the boundary of the Green Belt, and had the council intended to make those changes, it would have been required to put forward detailed reasons. They would have given you the additional alerts to the fact that a change was proposed.
>
> There was clearly an error and it has been the result of that error which has exercised my judgement during the investigation. You clearly suffered an injustice as a result because you were denied the protection you might reasonably have expected from the designation of this land as Green Belt. You could also have reasonably expected that if the designation was going to change that it would be changed through the proper process i.e. through a deliberate change using the procedures set out in the Local Plan, giving reasons why the change was necessary ..."

The LGO does not have the power of rescinding a planning permission, but he does have the power to ask councils to apologise to complainants for their mistakes and to instruct a council to award compensation in certain cases.

In this case, it took until April 2010 before a full and final payment of compensation recommended by the Ombudsman was made by the council to the complainant, which was accepted. In his letter to the LGO on 9th April 2010 the complainant wrote: "... This brings to a close a process started in August 2002 when we sought your help in fighting our case against a council which totally ignored clear evidence that the land behind our property was Green Belt and, apparently, in the belief they could walk rough shod over our concerns, granted planning permission..."

The moral of this unfortunate story is not to give up your fight when you believe you have right on your side.

Not that it had anything to do with the planning application at 81 New Barn Lane, but PAB councillors were successful in persuading the Head of Engineering Services to agree to reduce the speed limit from 40 to 30 mph along the whole length of New Barn Lane.

At the same time, we requested a mini-roundabout at the junction of Albert Road with New Barn Lane, which was approved and installed at the beginning of the 2003 financial year.

Mr A Davies, a Cheltenham resident and a member of the 'Concerned Cheltenham Electors' Group', had made a formal complaint to the Chartered Institute of Public Finance and Accountancy (CIPFA), regarding the behaviour of two of its members, Lawrence Davison and Desmond Knight.

Readers will recall that Mr Davison was the Director of Resources in 1996 when a decision was made to invest £22.5 million on the money markets in the hope that a large profit would be made. Desmond Knight was Head of Accountancy Services. [See chapter 15]

After hearing the representations, the CIPFA investigating committee found that Mr Davison "... did not ensure that all relevant risks and possible financial implications of the proposal were identified and analysed to the council's Policy & Resources Committee."

A report of the proceedings was published in June 2002.

The local newspaper reported that the two officials at the centre of Cheltenham Borough Council's £22.5 million loan fiasco have been criticised by the accountancy's official body. It also reported that both members would have a black mark against their names and this would be for a period of two years.

It was the end of another costly experience for the council and for the electors who would have to pay for the mistake in the years to come.

CHAPTER 17

Cheltenham Borough Council Versus Laird

"If you can keep your head when all about you are losing theirs and blaming it on you ..."
Extract from Rudyard Kipling's 'If' (1910)

Lawrence Davison, the chief executive, decided to seek early retirement in 2001 which meant that the council's Structural Review Committee would be required to start a recruitment process in order to advertise, recruit and appoint a new Head of Paid Service.

After the saga of investing £22.5 million of council taxpayers' money in 1996 it had been only a question of time before the request for early retirement came from Lawrence Davison. No-one on the council was opposed to the idea.

The fact that it took as long as it did was probably a means of defraying the blame over a reasonable period and at the same time diverting all the blame away from the two principal officers who were at the centre of the financial storm.

Nevertheless, and perhaps in anticipation of what was likely to happen, Desmond Knight the Chief Finance Officer, decided to emigrate to Australia. The Chartered Institute of Public Finance and Accountancy (CIPFA) found in his absence that he had not conducted himself within the rules of CIPFA's financial management and he was censured.

However, I didn't think along with other councillors at the time that we were about to embark on a recruitment process that would lead to the appointment of a very capable replacement and, at the same time, plunge Cheltenham Borough Council into a period of administration that turned out to be so spiteful and vicious that it was regarded nationally as unique in the history of local government.

The recruitment process including the presentation of successful candidates to council members was concluded in January 2002. This was one occasion in my local government career that I was not in attendance for a most important council meeting. I was out of the country visiting my son and his family who reside in Sydney, Australia.

On my return, I was told that Mrs Christine Laird had been the winning candidate securing 18 votes against a total of 17 votes for the second candidate.

I was also told that other councillors had been absent from the council chamber, although their absence was different to mine. I understand from my PAB councillor colleagues that several councillors did not participate in the final vote. It would be pure conjecture to anticipate what the final vote would have been if all members of the council had been in attendance.

Even though the voting was close, my colleagues informed me that there had been no indication of any trouble ahead whilst I had been away. When I returned from holiday I had the pleasure of meeting Mrs Laird in the early part of February and immediately came to the conclusion that she was someone with intelligence and positive ideas that were needed if councillors were to restore the reputation of Cheltenham after the disastrous years of the mid 1990's.

She was totally different from her predecessor in many ways and I was confident from my first meeting with her that she would do everything that was needed to put Cheltenham back on the local government map. Unaware of the course of the debate in the council chamber and the subsequent closeness of the vote I was as unbiased as anyone could be in making an early judgement.

As Leader of the PAB Group I was contacted by Cllr Duncan Smith, Leader of the Council, on my return from holiday. He updated me regarding the council matters that had taken place during my absence. The most important of these concerned the details of the modernisation programme that the Structural Review Committee had presented to council. This included a requirement to reduce the Base Budget together with a complete review of the senior management posts with the aim of producing a cost effective slimmed-down management structure.

The selection process for the post of managing director was explained to me, which included details of the council's future programme.

All the short-listed candidates had been briefed about the structural review that the council would require the successful candidate to carry out. Each applicant had to confirm whether they thought they had the ability and the enthusiasm to carry out such an unpopular and demanding exercise which could, they were told, turn out to be a very difficult exercise.

Each of the candidates had the option to pull out of the final selection if they felt the restructuring would be too much for them, but to their credit, I was told, they all accepted the terms on offer and said that if they were successful, they would be keen to start the process.

I congratulated Cllr Smith on the positive interview process that he and his panel had carried out, which seemed to me to allay any fears I may have had that the successful candidate might claim she didn't know what she had agreed to do.

Mrs Christine Laird took up her post as Managing Director (MD) of Cheltenham Borough Council on 4th February 2002 and she immediately set about the task of reorganising the management structure and achieving the objectives set by the Structural Review Committee. The structure had been approved by the full council in January.

As in all local government systems the council boss is also recognised as the Head of Paid Service, which is a legally protected job and as we shall hear later is a powerful protective tool for the post holder when termination of employment is under discussion, or even threatened.

Having taken up her post, Mrs Laird was entitled like any other employee to a

Christine Laird arriving for the first day as managing director of Cheltenham Borough Council, February 2002

A troubled Christine Larid after twelve months in the job

Contract of Employment. The Employment Relations Act, 1999 required all employers to issue their employees with either a detailed statement of particulars, or a contract of employment, within 8 weeks of the start of their employment.

In Mrs Laird's case, a contract should have been issued no later than 1st April 2002. On Tuesday 23rd April Mrs Laird wrote to Miss Jo Pitman, Assistant Director Human Resources (AD/HR) and also to Gerald Ford the Monitoring Officer (MO), advising them that she had not received a statement or a contract of employment within the required time and *'requested that the matter be expedited'*. Mrs Laird was informed that her contract would be issued on Thursday of that week, but in spite of the promise no contract of employment was issued.

Whether the Leader of the Council had been made aware of the problem is not known, but there was evidence at the time that he had made representations to the Human Resources Department about the matter. What the representations were is unclear.

It was not until Thursday 16th May that Mrs Laird received a draft copy of a contract of employment from the MO. It differed significantly from the terms offered to her when she was offered the post of managing director on 4th January 2002. It did not comply with the Joint Negotiating Committee (JNC) conditions, which are explained in a later chapter.

On Friday 17th May in my capacity as PAB Group Leader, I received a telephone call from the MD inviting me to her office.

The MD told me that she had received a draft copy of her Contract of Employment (CE) from the MO, and knowing that I had spent part of my working life heading up a Personnel and Industrial Relations Department, she asked me to read the contract and give an opinion before she signed it.

The first thing I looked at was the date of issue of the contract of employment, which was outside the legal time period. Secondly, she was right to question the content of the document.

I read the draft copy carefully and I was surprised how little detail it contained, I came to the view that it fell a long way short of the necessary requirements and I advised Mrs Laird not to sign it.

Having told the MO she was not prepared to sign the draft contract, a second draft was sent to Mrs Laird on Friday, 31st May. This too was lacking in detail and, in my view, did not conform to the JNC conditions approved by the Local Government Employers' Association (LGE).

It was not until the first week in August that another CE containing the additional details of Mrs Laird's offer of employment was received. This time it contained information which conformed to the JNC conditions and was acceptable to Mrs Laird.

This was an extraordinary state of affairs – here we have the Head of Paid Service, who would be obliged to take action against a member of staff who had failed to give a new employee a proper contract of employment, having difficulty securing a statutory CE for herself.

It is also worth noting that Mrs Laird would have been in a difficult position if she had taken disciplinary action against the MO for failing to provide her with a satisfactory contract of employment, because he reported directly to her.

Considering that the MO has the benefit of statutory protection from dismissal like the MD, it was incredible that Mrs Laird was the person affected by his lack of action. The standard elements of a contract of employment would have been the same for both the MO and the MD.

It is commendable that Mrs Laird, knowing that she could have gone to an Industrial Tribunal, decided against taking action because she knew that if she had done so and won her case, the reputation of the council would have been tarnished.

Mrs Laird was between a 'rock and a hard place' because she had a duty to protect the name of Cheltenham Borough Council, but at the same time she was keen to receive her own contract of employment.

At the Group Leaders' meeting with the Managing Director on 6th November 2002, I reported that the MO had failed to comply with a council resolution, namely that he had failed to issue a satisfactory contract of employment to the MD in the prescribed time. I reminded them that the cross-party Appointments Panel had issued instructions via the former Leader of the Council (Cllr Duncan Smith) to the MO to deal with the final details of the contract on their behalf.

I asked what action was being taken to address the situation with the officer concerned so that a repetition could be avoided in the future.

Cllr Smith said he would support any action taken because during the latter part of his leadership, he had tried to resolve the current situation without success.

He also told the meeting that he had been concerned about the performance of the MO over a long period of time and he highlighted a number of areas where he believed the MO had failed.

The MD acknowledged the concerns of the two group leaders but advised members that there were specific terms of reference for progressing complaints against the council's statutory officers.

Cllr Andrew McKinlay, the new Leader of the Council following the May elections, advised that if the issues raised were legitimate then they should be investigated in accordance with the guidelines. He also suggested that to try to solve the situation by informal means would not be appropriate.

The MD suggested that she should make contact with the joint secretaries of the Joint Negotiating Committee (JNC) for Chief Officers, and to advise them, in confidence, of the concerns that had been expressed at the Group Leaders' meeting. This was agreed. The meeting also agreed that the matter should be treated as confidential.

On 9th December 2002 a council meeting was held and the MD gave a detailed report on the process and governance requirements of the forthcoming Comprehensive Performance Assessment (CPA). She urged councillors to be ready and prepared for the assessment.

Addressing the council, she expressed the view that the Leader of the Council, the opposition group leaders, and the chairmen of all the scrutiny committees, must be fully aware of the governance arrangements and what is required from them.

At the same council meeting the Leader of the Council presented a report of the review carried out of the council's new Management Structure Plan, which was discussed and debated and finally accepted by members of the council.

Cllr McKinlay further announced that the Cabinet had given consideration to Phase 2 of the management restructuring process and a further report would be made in the New Year.

Even to the uninformed it would have been easy to believe that there was nothing seriously wrong taking place in the council offices if the usual agenda business of the council was taking place – formal but in a friendly manner.

However, the outside world and junior members of the council staff who were not directly involved with the executive control of the council, were probably not aware that the MD had been subject to unpleasant pressures by members of the Cabinet.

Yet in spite of this, and I have no doubt that the good citizens of Cheltenham were pleased to read the article in the *Gloucestershire Echo* the following evening stating that the council were making changes to its management structure, resulting in financial savings for the council.

As she promised, the MD made arrangements to meet Adam Barker, Head of Consultancy, Local Government Employers' Association (LGE) on 12th December 2002, to discuss the complaints that had been made by two opposition group leaders.

Mr Barker wrote to Mrs Laird on December 18th confirming the written advice she had received from him.

On the principal point, he confirmed that in his view there had been a failure of Mr Ford the MO, in spite of several reminders, to issue the MD with an accurate statement of particulars within the legal time period.

Mr Barker also acknowledged the second matter concerning the complaints of Cllr Smith, who had questioned the overall performance of Mr Ford and the general quality of his legal advice.

He set out in his letter the requirements of the Local Authorities (Standing Orders) Regulations 2001 concerning the statutory protection of chief officers that included Monitoring Officers.

He advised that the effect of the Standing Orders Regulations meant that any disciplinary action against a chief officer could only be taken following a recommendation in a report made by a Designated Independent Person (DIP).

The letter also reminded Mrs Laird about the principles set out at paragraph 16 of the JNC for chief officers containing within it the disciplinary and capability procedures.

The letter contained other technical information, but it ended with advice or perhaps a warning from Mr Barker when he wrote 'most local authorities prefer to negotiate a solution with the officer concerned'.

[When I consider the treatment that the managing director had to endure during the years 2002 to 2004, I am surprised that no-one from the council took the trouble to negotiate a compromise solution along similar lines].

Perhaps the council didn't want to try in case a way forward was found.

On 8th January 2003 the MD wrote to all four group leaders informing them that the National Employers' Organisation (Local Government Services) had written to her explaining the potential options and processes the council would be obliged to follow if the complaints against the MO were pursued. She also indicated that she had invited Mr Barker to attend the next meeting of the Group Leaders in case there were specific questions they wished to ask him.

She concluded by asking her Personal Assistant (PA) Karen Watson to arrange a meeting as quickly as possible.

The meeting took place on January 29th and Mr Barker was in attendance.

Unfortunately, Cllr Smith was unable to attend for business reasons, but he sent an email to the MD with copies to the other group leaders, confirming his position regarding his concerns 'about the ability of Gerald Ford to undertake the role of Monitoring Officer and chief legal advisor to the Council'.

He was also concerned about Mr Ford's 'ability to provide accurate advice, his organisational ability and his technical ability'.

The most damning paragraph in Cllr Smith's email, in my view, was the following:

"I still believe that while he remains in place and without a major change to the way he performs, the Council and the Board of Directors remain seriously exposed on all matters legal."

Cllr Smith suggested that in fairness to Mr Ford "... he must be given the opportunity to put his side of the case before any formal action is taken."

He also requested that the MD should read his email to the meeting because he was concerned that copies of the email to the group leaders may not have reached them in time.

This was a clear indication that Cllr Smith wanted his views known.

The minutes of the Group Leaders' meeting record that the MD introduced Adam Barker who then reiterated the detail contained in his earlier advice notes to the MD. He emphasised it was not his role, or that of the JNC, to determine whether or not the issues raised in connection with the council's MO were valid. His role was to advise members on the process should the complaints be investigated.

He also took the opportunity to remind the Group Leaders that they needed to appreciate that most local authorities try to avoid pursuing an investigation of the kind being discussed as the process was lengthy, disruptive and often damaging to both the individual and to the employer. He added that it often generated negative publicity and was often very costly.

Having listened intently to everyone's comments, Mr Barker thought that in the light of the concerns raised, the only alternative would be to pursue the possibility of securing improvements in the MO's performance.

To do this, he suggested that the council would need to devise an 'improvement plan'. This is what he told the Group Leaders:

"The purpose of the plan would be to set performance targets for the individual to reach and to put in place agreed monitoring mechanisms to assess the extent to which the individual was reaching those standards."

Cllr Martin Hale, the Labour Group Leader, agreed with the line of approach that was being suggested. He thought an informal resolution of the problem was better than any formal investigation.

Cllr McKinlay disagreed with this view. He did not accept the main substance of the complaints that had been made against the MO and he questioned whether there was a case to be answered.

Cllr McKinlay also stated that he was not in favour of 'behind the scene deals' and he thought the meeting was suggesting that the MO was guilty before an investigation had been carried out. He questioned whether the complaints made by me and Cllr Smith were justified because we had not produced any evidence.

These comments were unnecessary. Either Cllr McKinlay had not paid heed to the fact that the MD had not received a Contract of Employment within the timescale required by legislation, or he had a different agenda to the rest of us.

He obviously dismissed the content of the email that Cllr Smith had sent to the meeting. There was certainly no suggestion of a meeting behind closed doors, as he had indicated, but if there had been and a solution had been found, surely that would have been better than the existing situation.

On that point alone, the Contract of Employment which was a legal matter for which Mr Ford was responsible, should have been sufficient evidence for the Leader of the Council to have similar concerns as the other Group Leaders. The very fact that the council's chief legal officer had been found wanting, should have raised alarm bells for him now that he was the Leader of the Council.

His comments and attitude indicated that there may have been a close relationship between him and the MO, and if that assumption was correct then it was not a healthy situation for the council.

I also wondered whether the comments from Cllr McKinlay were a result of earlier discussions with his colleagues prior to the Group Leaders' meeting.

In any event, Cllr McKinlay should have remembered the words in the email from Cllr Smith, which suggested that the MO 'should be given the opportunity to put his side of the case before any action was taken'.

The conclusion from the meeting was that we should be helpful and considerate to Mr Ford. This was in spite of his failures and poor advice he had given Group Leaders and council members over a period of time.

Cllr McKinlay did not support the decision.

The MD, in spite of her personal situation, was supportive of an Improvement Plan because she too had genuine concerns about the administrative skills of the MO and she thought an Improvement Plan (as suggested by Mr Barker) could focus on these failures. She told the meeting that Mr Ford had been trying to improve his performance in these areas, but she thought that he did not seem to recognise that his role was also akin to the role of an 'internal policeman'.

In spite of Cllr McKinlay's comments, it was my view that the Group Leaders had a responsibility to find a way forward on this important issue before it became a bigger problem.

Following further discussion, it was agreed that the MD and Jo Pitman the AD/HR, should arrange a meeting with the MO to acquaint him with the concerns expressed at the Group Leaders' meeting. They would also jointly develop an 'Improvement Plan' to secure an improvement in the MO's performance over the next six months.

Monitoring the situation was important and it was agreed that a follow-up meeting should take place after three months.

Cllr McKinlay voted against the decision.

My purpose of recording the discussions that took place on January 29th in such detail is that it was not easy for me to grasp at the time what was actually going on in the corridors of power in the council offices. But writing this book has enabled me to search archives for facts both internally and externally and the results have been quite revealing.

It was important for me to search for minutes, reports, letters and emails that were printed and sent during the period 2002 to 2009.

For this and for other help I am indebted and grateful to several people who have sent me copies of useful information; not all of it usable, but interesting just the same.

Much of it filled the gaps in my memory; without it the story could not be told.

Having studied the material, together with the information I had already researched, I was able to look in closer detail at earlier minutes and reports that contained useful information that had long been forgotten and had probably not been seen by members of the general public.

Far too much information was concealed from the public eye – too many debates held behind closed doors and to the exclusion of the press and public. It is not a healthy situation in a democratic system, in my view the events might have turned out differently had the public been aware of what was going on and the dispute avoided.

Putting the information into some chronological order has enabled me to look at the whole picture of that disastrous period in the history of Cheltenham Borough Council.

During the period in question [2002 to 2004] it was only possible to see parts of the jigsaw, never the total picture. I had sympathy with the local residents who often contacted me to tell me that they had read the latest instalment of the Laird dispute in the *Gloucestershire Echo*, but they couldn't follow what had been happening because the story was fragmented and there was no continuity that made it easy to follow.

They were right of course and the eventual discovery and availability of important information about the dispute was not only the glue that held the jigsaw together, but it also provided the means for making the story intelligible.

The facts were there, all that was needed was for the facts to be sorted and put in some semblance of order.

I did not realise at the time that the constant diversions from one set of circumstances to another may have distracted the councillors' attention from other matters that were going on which also needed investigation.

I have no doubt that many councillors were at fault for not understanding what was going on before, during and after each meeting on the subject of the dispute. Even though most of the meetings were behind closed doors, we all needed to know what was going on, not just those who were intimately involved.

In March 2003 I received a telephone call from the MD asking me to attend a meeting at 6.00 p.m. in her office on 19th March.

Upon arrival, the Leader of the Conservative Group, Cllr Duncan Smith, and the Leader of the Labour Group, Cllr Martin Hale, and the MD were already there. We sat chatting to one another about generalities whilst we awaited the arrival of the Leader of the Council, Cllr Andrew McKinlay.

By 6.15 p.m. Cllr McKinlay had still not arrived and Cllr Smith, the principal opposition leader, invited the MD to start the meeting and to explain the reason why she had called for a 'special' meeting with the Group Leaders.

She reported that since the change of administration from Conservative to Liberal Democrat she had been subject to hostile and abusive comments from the Leader of the Council and hostile and intimidating comments from several members of the council Cabinet.

She alleged that the day following the election the new Leader had called in to see her; his purpose, apparently, was to tell the MD that "things were going to change".

The MD also alleged that Cllr McKinlay had told her that a number of council officers had suggested to him that "she was no more than a Tory nark and on that point alone he didn't trust her".

Although the MD appeared to be upset just going through the detail, I didn't consider this to be a contentious matter; I would have expected any new Leader to put his 'marker' down as quickly as possible. I may not have used the same sort of language that he was alleged to have used, but he was entitled to say what he did.

His comments may also have suggested that he thought the MD had more than a working interest with Cllr Smith and his Conservative administration that he thought was unhealthy.

He may also have thought that she was a supporter of the Conservative Party.

The fact that the Leader used the words 'things were going to change' could have been his way of saying that a new broom was now in place and she should be aware of this. Of course, when they are spoken in an aggressive manner it is only natural that the recipient would feel uncomfortable about the underlying content of the statement.

Cllr McKinlay was also alleged to have said "As he had not been involved in the recruitment and selection process of the managing director, nor attended the council meeting when she was selected, he considered that he had no obligation to honour her appointment."

According to the MD,' he then left the office slamming the door behind him'.

I could understand the MD's feelings because the words used must have been hurtful and she probably did not expect that kind of language from the Leader of the Council so soon after the change in the administration.

It did strike me at the time that the comment from Cllr McKinlay about not being 'obliged to honour her appointment' was rather disturbing for a new leader to make. I always believed that whatever one's personal views might be it was part of our democratic system to accept a collective decision.

If that was his view, was he going to be too dictatorial?

The MD, continuing her report, told us that following the visit from Cllr McKinlay she received a visit from the Deputy Leader of the Council, Cllr Steve Jordan who proceeded to complain about the proposed restructuring programme.

She said that even though he came across in a forthright manner with his criticisms, when she asked him to explain the parts of the restructuring programme he did not like or agree with, he declined to comment.

It was then alleged that he told the MD that he shared Cllr McKinlay's view about her and revealed that he too had not been involved with her appointment and therefore, on that point alone, he didn't feel obliged to recognise her appointment either.

So now we had the two top men in the council's Cabinet, not willing to accept the collective decision of the council members.

For the Leader and the Deputy Leader to make similar comments about the appointment of the MD, if they were correct, showed that there had been collusion on this point and had probably been in the making for some time.

Would I have been presumptuous to think at the time that this was the moment when the Liberal Democrat councillors launched their campaign to get rid of the newly appointed managing director?

If I was right then it certainly got off to an inglorious start.

There was still more to come; the MD informed the opposition group leaders that during a meeting with the council's Press Officer on the evening of 3rd March 2003, the Cabinet Deputy (Exchequer) Cllr James Stuart-Smith knocked on the door of the P.A's office, entered and demanded an urgent meeting with the MD.

Once the Press Officer had gone Cllr Stuart-Smith was invited into the MD's office and almost immediately said to her *"what would it take for you to go?"*

Not surprisingly, the MD told us that she had been stunned by the question, but recalled that when the question was put a second time she said something along the lines that 'Cheltenham Borough Council could not afford her value which she put at £1 million'.

I remember looking at the other group leaders sitting around the table and I was relieved to see that they too were open-mouthed at what they had just been told.

It was the question from Cllr Stuart-Smith, not the MD's reply that had stunned us. I remember Cllr Smith asking the MD to repeat again what she had just said so that he was sure he had heard the information correctly. I was busy writing a note on my pad but I am sure it was with a very shaky hand.

All three group leaders simply could not believe that a councillor, irrespective of the position he held in the hierarchy, would have confronted the most senior officer in the council and ask her to name a price for the termination of her employment. Incredible and unbelievable readers may think, but that is what happened.

I don't think it was made clear to us what the sequence of events had been in the MD's office, it was alleged that Cllr Stuart-Smith had revealed at another meeting that "... the Cabinet had spent more than fifty per cent of its time discussing the MD and the ongoing problem involving the Leader of the Council ..."

On this matter too, according to the MD, he appeared to be unhappy when she asked him to explain why he thought a rift existed between them. *"It was because you are perceived by the members to be the obstacle to the Cabinet working effectively together."* He is alleged to have replied.

In response, the MD asked Cllr Stuart-Smith to take back to the Cabinet "She was not looking to be difficult, in spite of what they were alleged to have said, but she had a job to do as Head of Paid Service and she intended to carry on doing it."

Cllr Smith broke the inevitable silence following the revelations by the MD, suggesting to those present that in his opinion, there had been a clear breach of the members' Code of Conduct by Cllr Stuart-Smith.

He also believed there had been an intended breach of the statutory requirements associated with the employment of the MD.

The MD in response told us that even though she knew that a serious offence in employment terms had been committed, she was quick to point out that she had no axes to grind with Cllr Stuart-Smith.

She said she had always found him reasonable and he had always treated her in a courteous manner whenever they met to discuss the financial matters of the council.

The MD admitted that she had been intrigued to know from Cllr Stuart-Smith why the Cabinet members and the Leader in particular, had resented her presence and why they had embarked upon such a bitter course of dialogue with her.

His reply, we were told, was that the Cabinet did not like her style of administration and the majority of his party were of the view that her appointment was a Conservative led decision and they resented it.

During the previous ten months the MD told us, she had taken the opportunity to speak to senior council officers about the impending changes in the management structure. She wanted to know from them what they felt about the changes and whether they believed the changes would have an adverse effect in the various departments. It was not a matter of imposing something for the sake of it, but a genuine desire by her to seek their opinions.

She said the general response from officers was positive, many admitted it was something that needed to be done and that she was doing the right thing. The MD was also 'warned' that some senior officers had noticed a change in the mood of the councillors, particularly those belonging to the Liberal Democrat group.

Other officers informed the MD that they had been concerned at the way leading councillors in the authority had been visiting their departments unannounced, and within a short space of time would suggest to staff different ways of dealing with problems or procedures.

This was unusual to say the least, but was there an underlying reason for this behaviour?

Apparently, the officers told the MD they had not experienced this sort of behaviour before – mentioning the protocol that should be observed by councillors.

It was revealed to the MD by some of the office managers that they had received visits from Cabinet members allegedly to talk about their respective portfolios. But the discussions soon changed to questions from the Cabinet deputies about how the staff viewed the MD and what they thought about her style and conduct as a managing director.

It was alleged that during the discussions and at the slightest indication of disapproval of her from a member of staff, the Cabinet deputy would immediately suggest that a formal complaint should be made about her if the officer thought there was a case, or if the officer thought there had been a problem. Was this another breach of the members' Code of Conduct?

The meeting on the 19th March 2003 concluded around 7.15 p.m. and as we went downstairs to the car park, still in a state of shock at the revelations by the MD, I suggested to the other two group leaders that we should not be too hasty in our actions, but to carefully consider our options, although I added that our options were very limited.

I also remember commenting to my colleagues that if only 50 per cent of what we had just heard from the MD was correct then we had very serious problems on our hands.

It was my view that a letter should go in the first instance to Cllr McKinlay signed by the senior opposition group leader Cllr Duncan Smith. The letter should stress how disappointed we were that he could not attend the meeting and suggest to him that another meeting should be convened with a time and a day to suit his diary. This was agreed by all of us.

Later that evening Cllr Smith sent an email to Cllr McKinlay with copies to me, Cllr Martin Hale and Karen Watson (Mrs Laird's P A). The recorded time when the email was sent was 11:39 p.m., the subject heading was 'urgent meeting'.

The email read as follows:

> "Further to the message I left on your answer phone this evening, Les, Martin and I would like an urgent meeting with you.
> Can you make 6 pm tomorrow (Thursday)? If not, we can all spare some time on Saturday afternoon. It should only take 15 minutes.
> Thanks.
> Karen – can you co-ordinate this for us and leave phone messages as appropriate?"

There is no doubt that contact with Cllr McKinlay was made by Cllr Smith, albeit by telephone rather than by letter, which was followed up by the email sent by Cllr Smith a few minutes before midnight.

The following day March 20th, an email from Becky Robinson, an Administration & Support Services Assistant (recorded time 2.39 pm) to Cllr Duncan Smith, Cllr Martin Hale and me, subject: Meeting of Group Leaders.

The email read as follows:

> "Dear Cllr, please note, the meeting scheduled for either this evening at 6pm, or Saturday afternoon with the Leader will not be going ahead. Cllr McKinlay has taken advice and he feels it would be inappropriate for him to meet with you at this time. Regards, Becky".

What was this advice he alleged he had been given? Was it negative, perhaps suggesting that if the Leader attended the meeting, it would weaken his opportunity to terminate the employment of the MD? Was it from someone in the legal department, the Monitoring Officer perhaps, or was it advice from senior members of Cllr McKinlay's own political party?

It was something that was not revealed at the time and it is still a mystery, but it does reinforce the belief that has been put forward by me and others for some time that there were forces at work who were planning the demise of the MD.

At 11:00 pm on March 20th, Cllr Smith sent an email to Cllr McKinlay with copies to all members of the Cabinet with copies to Cllr Hale and me.

The message read as follows:

> "Andrew,
> There is no excuse for not meeting with us to discuss this matter.
> Given that members of the Cabinet have briefed the press in detail, there is no valid reason for you to refuse to extend the same courtesy to the group leaders.
> From what we understand the collective actions of the Cabinet, and you in particular, have breached our own council's code of conduct, the national code of conduct for members, JNC employment provisions, Local Government Act 1989 requirements and the Employment Rights Act 1996 regulations.
> You have exposed the Council to the risk of a litigation claim against it and your actions if they become public will bring the Council into disrepute.
> This is a matter for the whole council and not just the Cabinet. If there has been a breach of contract or a disciplinary matter that needs dealing with, then we need to deal with it openly and by the book.
> Your Cabinet's stand on the rights of the Council employees has been a firm one, particularly in respect of the restructuring and latterly with regard to the Monitoring Officer. We cannot understand why in this case you appear to be abandoning your position.
> Personally, I cannot believe that members of your Cabinet who have distinguished records within the Magistracy and Trades Unions can be party to such actions.
> We would like to give you the opportunity to put your side of the story.
> If there is a case to be answered you will have our support for action to be taken

correctly, legally and within the terms of the JNC employment provisions.

If you continue to refuse to discuss this matter properly, we will have no alternative than to believe that there is no evidence against Mrs Laird and that the actions of you and your Cabinet members are no more than a concerted effort to intimidate and undermine her.

I will also have no hesitation in making an immediate complaint to the National Standards Board.

Mrs Laird has the full confidence of all 3 group leaders and the 19 members of council that we represent.

I do hope on reflection you will consider your refusal to meet with us. As you know, Les is due to go into hospital on Sunday but we are willing to meet you on Saturday afternoon at a venue and time of your choosing.

Duncan".

Strong and appropriate words from Cllr Smith that needed a reply, but no reply came. [In the summary and conclusion at the end of the High Court trial, I will examine whether the email was read out in court.]

I should explain to readers that the Joint Negotiating Committee (JNC) for Chief Officers referred to in the email above is provided by the Local Government Employers Association (LGE).

The LGE offers advice and support to local authorities on national agreements, pay structures, job evaluations and assistance in tackling conduct and capability issues.

In April 2003 the *Gloucestershire Echo* was able to publish details of the events occurring behind the council's doors. When some of the alleged events were revealed it must have raised a few eyebrows and even left a nasty taste in the mouths of some of the *Echo* readers.

On another occasion in April 2003, the *Gloucestershire Echo* published a story about the tensions that had been evident at a Cabinet meeting between the MD and the Leader of the Council. The *Echo* report caused even further tensions between them and as the matter was getting out of hand they both agreed to publish a joint statement dismissing claims of disunity between them.

The statement was subsequently published in the local newspaper.

Considering the MD's ordeals at the hands of the Leader and the Cabinet were not revealed to the group leaders until the meeting on 19th March 2003, I am still mystified when I recall that not one member of the Cabinet, or the Leader of the Council, took the trouble to call me or any other group leader to explain their dissatisfaction with the performance of the managing director.

They could have done so at the annual appraisal of her performance, because that was the place and the opportunity for any problems to be discussed. They could have told the group leaders about any operational problems if any existed, and they could have been resolved there and then enabling the council to move on.

Was the MD incompetent? Not as far as the opposition group leaders were concerned, and certainly not if the changes and innovations she was making during the first twelve months of her employment was anything to go by.

The email from Cllr Smith confirmed that she had the confidence of his members and she certainly had the confidence of mine.

Were the structural changes not going according to the approved plan? Not if the Leader's report to the council meeting in December 2002 was correct.

Remember that Phase 2 of the review had been introduced and presented to the council by the Leader; his recommendations were approved by councillors so it begs the question – what could the problem be?

Reading previous council minutes and the minutes of Group Leaders' meetings from March 2002 to March 2003 I could find no references to complaints from Cabinet members, the Leader of the Council or any senior member of staff that the MD was not performing to her job description.

She had been accused of bullying officers and councillors. (This will be examined in detail later). But in spite of these alleged accusations I wanted to find out whether she had breached her Contract of Employment, or had failed in her duty of care to any member of the council staff. Both were important issues.

I wanted to know if she had failed in any other areas that I did not know about. Had she been guilty of any offences, if so I would have been able to find evidence of this by reading the minutes or documents that were available.

But, and this is a crucial point, there was no suggestion from the Human Resources Department or the Legal Department during the early part of the MD's employment that she had breached her Contract of Employment, or had been dishonest by incorrectly filling in the medical questionnaire after her appointment.

It is also worth recalling that at no time during the early years of the MD's employment did the Liberal Democrat administration, or the senior officers of the council, hold discussions with me or any other opposition group leader reporting that they had concerns about the MD's health or had cause for concern from the references they had received from previous employers.

[One of the early innovations that the MD introduced was the creation of a new committee called the Staff & Support Services Committee (S&SSC) whose main business was to discuss all staff problems as well as wider employment issues that Cheltenham Borough Council may face in the future].

Ironically, it was the S&SSC that played a major part in the termination of the MD's employment with the council; it was instrumental in agreeing and spending large sums of council taxpayers' money in order to take the case to the High Court in 2009.

This will be examined in detail in chapter 24.

Even to this day I find the CBC versus Laird story incredible. When I reflect on the events at the time, I can understand why Cllr Stuart-Smith appeared cross and uncomfortable when he was instructed to gate-crash the meeting that was taking place in the MD's office to deliver a message of such incriminating importance.

It would also incriminate him as the Cabinet Deputy (Exchequer) unless he could depend on his colleagues to confirm that his message to the MD was a collective decision of the Cabinet members; otherwise he was virtually 'up the proverbial creek without a paddle'. (I referred to collective decisions earlier).

Cllr Stuart-Smith was a good councillor, straightforward and knowledgeable and always a pleasure to talk to. I could only believe that he could not have been happy with the task of confronting the MD in her office suggesting to her that she should go and inviting her to name a sum of money that would be acceptable to the council executive. It just was not the councillor that I knew.

He had been handed the poisoned chalice by his colleagues and my guess was that he knew in his heart that such a request to the managing director could only be made if it had the approval of the full council.

But the story that went around afterwards appeared to suggest that he had no choice in the matter. After all, he was the council's 'chancellor of the exchequer' and any matter concerning the council's finances had to be dealt with by him.

I had no other reason but to believe that Mrs Laird's first fourteen months of employment with the council had gone well; the council was making steady and reasonable progress and was moving in the right direction.

Apparently, the steady progress I had seen had been achieved despite the intolerable pressures the MD had been under.

Not until my research in 2011, was I aware that Mrs Laird had had an appraisal after the first six months of her employment with the council. This was normal practice.

However, it came as a complete surprise to me to learn this fact because I had not been informed that it had taken place in 2002 until I had read the associated papers of the appraisal in 2011. The reason I was surprised to learn this was because the appraisal of a MD is normally undertaken by the Group Leaders. My research revealed several interesting points regarding the appraisal. Some papers supplied to me are undated, but whilst this is a failure on the part of the sender, I believe it is possible to get the right sequence of events by studying the documents.

The Conservative Group Leader Cllr Smith received a letter dated 26th July 2002 from the Monitoring Officer (MO) inviting him to sit on the appraisal panel.

Cllr Smith in his reply said:

"I am happy to sit on the review panel for the managing director. However, I cannot see how any appraisal can take place until the Council has produced a Contract of Employment that is in accordance with the offer made in January including the standard terms and conditions for Heads of Departments.

I understand that the latest draft of the document is still not in accordance with the offer made.

Please can you explain what the issue is holding this up?

No instructions were given to you or Miss Jo Pitman (Human Resources) to vary the offer prior to May 3rd. Have you been given instructions to do so post May 3rd?

I look forward to your reply so that I can confirm to Cllr McKinlay my availability".

This exchange of letters between the main opposition group leader and the MO is important because it confirms the point I have made throughout the previous pages that there was an undercurrent of mischief and deviousness from the day Christine Laird took up her post in 2002.

Another copy of a Contract of Employment was provided, which enabled Cllr Smith to participate in the appraisal.

I have no evidence that the new document was not accepted by Mrs Laird.

The six month interim appraisal took place on 11th September 2002. The appraisers were Cllr McKinlay, Cllr Smith and Cllr Mrs Hay (Liberal Democrat).

[I was not invited to be on the panel even though I was available]

Mr Russell Symons from the South West Regional Assembly (SWRA) attended as the independent facilitator.

Cllr McKinlay outlined the format of the appraisal, and reminded the appraisers of the objectives determined by the members of the Structural Review Committee when they met on 8th April 2002.

The record of the appraisal shows the MD was given nine questions by the Leader of the Council prior to the appraisal. The object of this was to enable the appraisers to discuss the answers that the MD would subsequently provide.

The questions were the type that appraisers would put to someone who had completed their first six months employment in a senior council post.

According to the record of the appraisal provided by Russell Symons, Cllr Smith asked the MD how she felt about her personal relationships with the council staff. She replied that *"She had contacted some of the key players and following discussions with them felt she had made progress and some of the feedback had been very positive."*

Cllr Smith commented *"Yes, I have picked up similar feedback too and it has been very positive and complimentary."*

In answer to a question about managing pressures, the MD admitted that her personal workload was very high in the early part of her employment; she readily admitted that she probably did far too much at the beginning, but by increasing the strategic capacity of senior officers her personal workload had reduced.

In answers to questions about working relationships, the MD replied that she saw members and officers as two different sets of people, and because of this she accepted that her job was to act as a broker between the two.

Cllr Smith asked the MD whether she thought she had received support from members and whether she felt that they trusted her.

She replied *"Not always"*.

Cllr Smith then asked whether 'he and the Leader of the Council could do something about this'?

The MD answered the question by stating that in any local authority there are political factions. Each one believes the other group is being favoured, but she explained that she would always support the group whichever was in power.

Cllr Hay thought that 'relationships had improved significantly' and Cllr McKinlay accepted that the MD's comments about the changeover from Conservative to Liberal Democrat was 'absolutely fair'.

He added *"I think relationships have improved markedly."*

The second part of the appraisal dealt with the review of the management structure.

The management restructuring programme had been the cause of many unpleasant meetings between staff members, the Leader, his Cabinet and the MD. The matter was discussed carefully during the appraisal without any harsh words being spoken.

According to the notes made at the time, Cllr Smith suggested that 'motivation and morale' was a big issue and asked the MD 'How she could keep the staff on side?'

In reply, the MD thought that a development route for the staff rather than a 'competitive interview process' would be a good thing for officers. She also thought that there was a need to develop 'corporate capacity' and to design a 'performance management system to ensure things are delivered'.

She was also keen to bring the new Assistant Directors (AD's) into the picture, which prompted the question from Cllr McKinlay *"Are there problems with Stage 3"?*

According to the record, Stage 3 of the restructuring programme involved the AD's and some of their section managers.

The MD agreed there had been problems, which she put down to a learning experience for the AD's. She also revealed that some of the section managers were having more problems with the new system than others.

The record also showed that there had been discussions on a range of other issues in which the MD had been involved and she explained her views on each; where necessary, she indicated to the appraisers her programme for dealing with them.

The appraisal finally discussed the 'development needs' for the MD covering the next twelve months, which were approved.

The appraisers adjourned for a short break.

Upon resumption, Cllr McKinlay told the MD *"We have looked at all the hard targets and agree that you have met them very successfully."*

It was praise indeed from the Leader of the Council, and he concluded by saying *"We have acknowledged the difficulties that we had with relationships, with me, and with some of the other members, and we believe that you have taken the appropriate steps to improve this. It has moved on with a new method of doing things and hopefully we can carry this on in the future.*

We also need to tell you that we will be recommending to the Salary Review Board that when your salary is reviewed you should be receiving your pay award and the appropriate increment."

The meeting then ended.

Many people when reading these pages will ask themselves a simple question, 'whatever went wrong between the appraisal of the MD in September 2002 and January 2003?' I have asked myself the same question over and over again and I come up repeatedly with the same answer.

Either something of great significance happened between these dates, or the fate of the MD had been decided from the day she took up her employment, or perhaps, even before. Perhaps the appraisal was a bizarre part of the plan.

What if something of significant importance had taken place, the question would still remain – where was the evidence to show what had happened during this time? I have scanned the available documents between September 2002 and March 2003 and nothing came to light. Were there other documents not available to me?

So, if significant matters had occurred during this important period, other than the discourteous behaviour we had already learned about, where is the record of it?

Furthermore, you can rest assured that if any documents existed, they would have been produced at the High Court hearing in 2009. Lots of documents were produced in evidence, but none revealed the answer to the question above.

The only thing the court judgment (15 June 2009) had to say on the interim appraisal was that 'it took place in September and a pay rise was agreed; and Mrs Laird agreed to undergo personal skills training.'

But what about the 'glowing terms' expressed by Cllr McKinlay and the other appraisers? Was this outlined to the judge? I checked – it is not in the judgment.

According to the official record of the appraisal, Mrs Laird suggested to the panel that when her development needs were discussed, she would be pleased to develop her coaching skills to enable her to 'bring on the amiables' in the hope they would develop more pragmatic skills to their jobs.

Why was that part of the appraisal not known to the judge?

Whichever way one looks at the appraisal exercise, it was good for Mrs Laird: the words used by the principle participants were very interesting, and they posed more questions that needed answers.

I have tried throughout the previous pages to show evidence that a great deal of animosity existed between the Leader of the Council, his Cabinet and the Managing Director. But did the interim appraisal show that there was some hope for the future, or was it a part of a charade that had been carefully crafted?

Was the management restructuring programme just a convenient excuse to cover a more serious contempt of Mrs Laird? It was certainly used to great effect in the early months of her employment.

And the other claim that the restructuring programme was solely the work of the previous Conservative administration and nothing to do with the Liberal Democrats could also be regarded as a complete 'red herring'.

The Cabinet knew, as did everyone else in the council offices, that the Structural Review Committee was a cross-party committee. The minutes of the committee meeting held on 8th April 2002 records that Cllr McKinlay was in attendance as a Liberal Democrat nominee.

The minutes also show that the MD presented a comprehensive report on the progress of the management structure. She proposed the establishment of a new middle management structure, which she promised would be presented to the committee for discussion and approval at the end of May 2002.

The minutes do not indicate that there was a comment from Cllr McKinlay or anyone else, nor do they report that the MD's proposals were not acceptable. I think it can be safely assumed that the constant excuse that the restructuring programme was the root cause of the problem was a ruse to divert attention away from the real problem, the removal of Mrs Laird as the council's managing director.

My view, and it is only a view, is that Cllr McKinlay found himself in a difficult position. We know from minutes of meetings that he had been supportive of a review of the management structure, even though he had reservations about the way it was being implemented. At the same time, he was receiving adverse comments from several council officers who believed their jobs were being put at risk if the structural review went ahead.

One middle manager who had been vociferous in his opposition to the review worked for the Commercial and Support Services Department (C&SS).

His name was John Webster.

The duties of Mr Webster brought him into contact with members of the general public and he carried out his duties in an efficient manner. Sometimes he was accused of carrying them out too robustly and it has been alleged that he had upset council staff, elected members and local residents in the process.

Occasionally, our respective responsibilities brought us together, but I had no regular contact with him. I do remember that John Webster was what I would call a 'busy' person, because he always seemed to be in a hurry with whatever it was he was aiming to do. A long conversation with him was a rare occasion.

However, the Structural Review Committee that met on 8th April 2002 received a report from Mr Chris Huckle, the Director of Commercial and Support Services, setting out his reasons why he was recommending to the committee that they should allow a member of his staff to take early retirement in the interest of efficiency.

In support of his recommendation, he meticulously took the members of the committee through the document. It was certainly needed because the report outlined where the officer, in Mr Huckle's opinion, had breached the council's disciplinary Code of Conduct, which, it was alleged, involved members of the public.

It was the most damning report of an employee I had ever read.

On the basis of what was contained in the report, it was clear to me that the officer concerned should have been disciplined some time back; and as far as the report went there was clear evidence that there had been a serious breach of the disciplinary code and it was still not too late for the council to take action along the lines that are set out in its Code of Conduct.

Mr Huckle concluded his report by telling the meeting that although the charges against the officer were bad he was proposing that the officer should be allowed to leave under the council's early retirement scheme. This meant that he would leave with a substantial lump sum as well as a healthy pension to take him through his future years.

The officer named in the report was John Webster.

The report was bad, but to my surprise some members of the committee seemed to be untroubled by the facts and were quite prepared to accept the recommendation. I could not believe that with such damning evidence before them the committee were not going to discipline the officer, but were prepared to let him take early retirement.

"The reason for not taking disciplinary action against the officer," reported Mr Huckle, was that "it would be easier for the council to let him leave rather than use the disciplinary process against him." This meant, in my opinion, that there were probably more about the day-to-day activities of the officer than was being revealed to the committee.

I spoke against the Director's proposal and suggested that proper disciplinary action should be taken as laid down in the Code of Conduct with dismissal being the ultimate sanction if necessary.

My proposal was not received too kindly by the Director or the MD, and each spoke against it. Their reasons, or excuses, seemed to be that they knew John Webster better than me, which was true, and they anticipated that he would make life difficult for the council in the future if he was not allowed to go in the way that had been proposed.

It was not an argument I could support and I repeatedly said so.

It was then decided, in order to give the council protection in the future, that a Compromise Agreement would need to be signed by the officer if the early retirement proposal was to be taken forward.

After what can only be described as a 'sparse' debate I asked for the matter to be put to the vote; only one other member supported me and another member abstained.

It was not a unanimous decision, but it left a nasty taste in my mouth for some time afterwards.

On 8th June 2002 I received a letter from John Webster, so did others, in which he raised several points regarding the meeting on April 8 including a request for a copy of the minutes of the meeting. There was no doubt in my mind that he had been told the result of the meeting following Chris Huckle's report. He had also acquired the names of the members of the committee.

The letter was also copied to Gerald Ford the MO.

I wrote to Mr Ford on June 13 suggesting that the points raised by John Webster should be addressed. I also confirmed that I had no objection to a copy of the minutes of the meeting being sent to him.

The concluding part of my letter said:

"You will recall that I was totally opposed to the early retirement, not least because the report by the Director begged more questions than it answered, I hope it is suitably noted in the minutes that I proposed that the report should not be accepted and that the usual disciplinary steps should be applied."

My conscience was clear – it was others who had to look closely in their mirrors.

It was ironic that the proposal was supposed to be a 'soft way' of preventing the officer from causing trouble for the council. As we shall see later, he proved to be one of the biggest thorns in Mrs Laird's side in the months and years that followed.

It was also ironic that at the meeting on April 8th, it was Mrs Laird who put forward a robust defence of John Webster; she played a large part in ensuring his early retirement was approved, yet in spite of this, he turned out to be her most serious critic.

Talk about 'biting the hand that feeds you'.

Quicker than anyone could have imagined, John Webster wrote to Cllr McKinlay on June 15 making various allegations against Mrs Laird. The court judgment refers to this and records that one of the allegations was a claim that she had accused him of leaking information to the press about the council's restructuring proposals.

Cllr McKinlay asked the MO to investigate this, although as Mrs Laird mentioned at the time, John Webster was no longer an officer of the council.

Expanding on the view I expressed earlier, I believe it was at this point that Cllr McKinlay found a 'soul mate' in John Webster; a disgruntled council officer who hated the managing director and someone who would be a willing ally in the fight to remove her from her post.

In May 2004 John Webster became a Liberal Democrat councillor.

Evidence shows that the early months of the MD's employment were demanding. The work programme contained several objectives, several identified as urgent.

Opposition group leaders had been asked by the MO, even before Mrs Laird had taken up her post, to set out a list of targets, which they expected her to achieve in her first year with the council.

This was new to me; I had never come across a situation previously where I was expected to detail a list of objectives for a newly appointed Head of Paid Service prior to him or her taking up the appointment.

On behalf of the PAB Group I responded to the MO letter on 4th February 2002 setting out my group's concerns.

Only now, as I write these pages, the thought is occurring to me that I may have unwittingly played a part in making life hard for the new managing director, or even perhaps, been set up to play a part in some Machiavellian plot.

Innocently, my letter to the MO suggested that the MD should establish good relationships with staff at the council offices and the outlying council sites because the new management structure had affected staff morale. I wanted to know how she intended to tackle this problem. I also asked how she would bring about changes to the town's traffic problems.

What was her opinion and how would she approach the 'Arms Length Housing' proposals, which would change the concept of council housing for the town.

There were other questions of equal importance to the PAB Group, which were included in my letter; to her credit the MD dealt with them in her usual robust way. This was soon to become her hallmark in the months ahead.

Were the questions a set up? It is difficult to say; whether the other group leaders were asked to do a similar exercise, I honestly do not know.

What I do know is that I wasn't asked to compose questions for the next Head of Paid Service prior to his appointment in 2006.

Apart from the 'hard targets' the MD was directed to achieve, she set about creating a permanent committee to deal with all future staff issues. This was to be called the Staff & Support Services Committee (S&SSC) which I referred to earlier, which would also replace the Structural Review Committee.

The terms of reference for the S&SSC were vague and over time other matters only loosely connected to staff problems started to appear on the agenda. In its early days it served a useful purpose and was used to great effect when the dispute between the MD and Cllr McKinlay was most active in 2003.

The S&SSC was used by the legal department to win support for their decisions, including the use of external legal sources, which will be included in later chapters.

One decision made by the committee that proved to be a disaster was the decision to go down the path of litigation rather than using the services of the Advisory, Conciliation and Arbitration Service (ACAS). It was the S&SSC that decided to spend thousands of pounds of council taxpayers' money on external legal advice that in the end turned out to be poor.

The mounting costs of the dispute, which was being highlighted regularly by the press, brought anger from Cheltenham residents who eventually wrote to the independent auditors KPMG in 2009 demanding an investigation into the council's financial affairs, including expenditure on the dispute. Clearly, they were concerned about the way the MD had been treated, but they were also aware that significant expenditure had occurred, which warranted an investigation and the publication of what is called a Public Interest Report (PIR).

A later chapter will describe in detail how KPMG were appointed by the Audit Commission to audit the Cheltenham Borough Council accounts and their eventual conclusions. Because of the scale of the financial costs and the level of interest shown by the general public a PIR was published in March 2010.

As the management review process continued, Mrs Laird introduced twelve thematic service portfolios to assist four newly formed support and service groups.

The Structural Review Committee supported the suggestion by the MD that each 'portfolio' should comprise a small number of functional business units headed by a Business Unit Manager.

In order for the management teams to understand and work with the new systems, the MD reported that she had arranged 'away days' to take place on 12th February and 12th March 2002. They were held in two local conference centres and enabled senior officers to openly discuss the proposals with the councillors.

Workshops were held in the venues and exchanges of views were expressed.

As far as I can recall, I do not remember Cllr McKinlay raising any objections to the proposed way forward; when the 'away days' took place it was generally accepted by all sides that they were more than just useful exercises, but informative and successful as well.

PAB councillors referred to their importance on several occasions at subsequent council committee meetings, but in spite of requests for more 'away-days' they have never been repeated.

What puzzled me when I read the High Court judgment is the recorded comment that Cllr McKinlay and Cllr Stuart-Smith visited Mrs Laird *'on or about the 25th February 2002 to raise certain concerns that the Liberal Democrats had in relation to the restructuring plan'.*

If this was true then the minutes of meetings when the restructuring programme was discussed should show this to be the case? The problems, if there were any, could have been raised at any of the 'away' days.

The judgment also states *"Although the Liberal Democrats were not opposed to restructuring, they did have concerns about how it was to be implemented."*

Did they? And where are those concerns recorded?

At least there was now a record from a High Court judge that the Liberal Democrats were not opposed to the restructuring, but the court should have known that this had already been confirmed in the minutes of the Structural Review Committee meeting held on 8th April 2002.

Were these minutes presented to the court? I am not aware that they were.

Further confirmation of the Liberal Democrat position on the new management proposals is also evident in two sets of minutes of the S&SSC. The first dated 7th August 2002 and approved by council on 30th September 2002. The second dated 19th November was approved by council on 9th December 2002.

Like all minutes, they make better reading later than they do at the time: an examination of the August 7th minutes reveals that the first phase of the restructuring had affected staff morale, but Cllr McKinlay, Leader of the Council reported that changes to the new structure, involving members of staff, meant that the management structure was now workable and it met the criteria laid down by council.

He also confirmed that savings of £170, 000 as a result of the new structure had been referred to the District Auditor (DA) for his comments.

The minutes further show that the Leader was quoted as saying "he accepted full responsibility for the principle and proposals, which were considered by S&SSC, and confirmed the implementation of the restructure beneath the level of Assistant Director, which would be based on 'robust performance assessments'.

Liberal Democrat councillor John Morris indicated that although he was a new member of the council 'he recognised the need for a new structure and also recognised that staff morale was low but it had improved recently'.

He supported the changes, but in his opinion, "they needed to be implemented quickly".

Questions from members of the Conservative Group brought swift responses from Cabinet members and the Leader of the Council. The Leader claimed that 'the Cabinet had acted for the benefit of the authority and the new management structure was sustainable and met the criteria'. He confirmed "the proposals would be supported by the Cabinet".

Council approved the S&SSC report by 19 votes to 3 with 10 abstentions.

The S&SSC minutes dated 19th November 2002 recorded that a review of the council's management structure had taken place, including a report from the Board of Directors setting out their proposals for the second stage of the restructuring programme.

The Board had developed their proposals jointly with the newly appointed Assistant Directors.

The MD reported progress on the roles of the three thematic divisions that had been established, namely the Corporate Services, Social & Community, the Environment and their subdivisions.

She recommended that a permanent Democratic Services Department should be established in order to provide a service to both councillors and officers.

All these groups, subdivisions and services are still in operation today.

At the same November meeting, Cllr McKinlay, in his role of chairman of the Appraisal Panel, presented a report setting out the objectives for the MD as part of her recent appraisal, which included thirteen additional objectives. Cllr McKinlay reported that the appraisal had been conducted by appraisers drawn from the S&SSC [I was a member of the committee] and the process had been facilitated by Russell Symons, a senior member of the South West Regional Assembly.

According to both sets of minutes and in spite of political differences of opinion, the management structure was approved after a 'tweak' or two here and there; it was not a unanimous decision, but the Lib/Dems with its three-line whip, plus the support of PAB councillors, ensured it would get council approval.

It was a strange situation to read the record as it is today, that the new management structure was eventually approved even though it was constantly used by the Liberal Democrats as the main reason for the dispute between the Leader, the Cabinet and the MD?

The fact remains that not because of it, but in spite of it, the new management structure virtually dragged the council from its outdated system of governance to a modern system of management. It was a successful exercise because of the determination of the MD and the principles she projected that are still there today.

It is necessary to remind readers that local elections took place on 2nd May 2002 and the Liberal Democrats regained control of the council from the Conservatives.

In spite of the fact that the count of the votes dragged on until the early hours of the morning, it did not stop Cllr McKinlay calling on Mrs Laird at 11.00 a.m. the following day. It was not a social call.

Mrs Laird claimed in her evidence to the High Court in March 2009 that Cllr McKinlay had warned her that morning, she should expect a very different approach to the way the council was run to the one she had been used to.

She also claimed that Cllr McKinlay had accused her of being a 'Tory nark' and that she was too closely associated with members of the Conservative group.

Malcom Stennett, Diane Hibbert, Dave Prince and me following the PAB election victories in May 2002

I had heard similar sarcastic expressions by officers and members in the council building after the May elections so I had a genuine interest to read what the judge had to say about them.

The paragraph in the judgment says: *"Whilst it is possibly true that Cllr McKinlay regarded Mrs Laird as being too closely associated with the Conservatives and he may well have indicated this at the meeting, I do not accept that he used these words."*

Did Mrs Laird make up the 'Tory nark' story? If she did then she also misled the Group Leaders on 19th March 2003. But is the comment worthy of further consideration? I don't think so.

It is a known fact that a MD in any local authority would be required to work closely with the political party that formed the administration. It would not be unusual for the incoming political party to presume that the outgoing party had worked closely with the managing director. I would also suggest and readers will not need me to remind them that political parties rarely 'love each other'.

I believe the words 'Tory nark' was a throwaway remark by Cllr McKinlay, still enthralled by the fact that he had won an election and that his 'party' was now in control after several years of a Conservative administration.

Readers must make what they will of the judge's comments.

In spite of the alleged claims and counter-claims by both sides during 2002 the running of the council continued as it always had done; policies discussed and decisions taken.

And as we know, the interim appraisal was satisfactory and the recorded minutes of the appraisal written by Russell Symons (SWRA) show this to be the case.

Cllr McKinlay received a copy of the minutes and asked the MD 'to look at the transcript and to comment on it if she so wished'.

On 16th October 2002, Becky Robinson, the MD's Admin and Support Assistant, replied to Cllr McKinlay by email informing him that the MD had looked at the minutes and she held the same view as Cllr Rowena Hay that *'there were bits missing in the record and they were in a strange order'*. She concluded by adding: *"You may wish to speak to Bryony or Russell"*. (SWRA) [Bryony Houlden is the chief executive of the SWRA]

Not unexpectedly, the MD assumed that her concerns would be passed back to the SWRA by the Leader of the Council, but there is no record that this was done.

In the meanwhile, Cllr Stuart-Smith the Cabinet Deputy (Exchequer) is alleged to have had an off-the-record chat with the MD in her office. He suggested to the MD that it appeared to him that the relationship between her and Cllr McKinlay had deteriorated. If it was true, he wanted to know why it had happened.

The MD told him she was of the same opinion and in answer to a further question about the cause of the deterioration; she suggested that it could be because of the matter concerning John Webster and his early retirement.

The matter was not pursued and Cllr Stuart-Smith then talked about improving relationships with the Leader, but the MD reminded him that it took both sides to want a relationship to succeed. However, for her part she was 'willing to give it a go' she told him.

Cllr Stuart-Smith then commented, I am told, that he had heard that the MD had taken leave of absence because of a migraine, which she admitted was correct, adding that it had been the worst attack of migraine she had suffered for four years.

Why didn't the MD see the pattern of events, including the visit by Cllr Stuart-Smith and others, as the possible 'trap', or 'campaign plan' to oust her from her job?

Was it, for example, the forerunner before questions about medical questionnaires and sickness absence became the topic the council eventually pursued?

I mention the matter concerning the migraine only because I think more of this will be made in later chapters when the question of the MD's medical history is put under scrutiny.

I am told that during the afternoon of 6th November 2002 Cllr Mrs Hay called into the MD's office to discuss the setting of performance objectives for the following twelve month period. But, once the performance objectives were agreed the conversation changed to a discussion about the MD's relationship problems with the Leader of the Council.

Another part of the pattern, perhaps!

Cllr Hay admitted to the MD that it was a difficult situation and asked her whether she had any suggestions on how to improve the situation.

The MD took the same line as she had done with Cllr Stuart-Smith adding that she was making a real effort to improve the situation, but it also required an effort on the part of Cllr McKinlay too.

Apparently, the MD had suggested earlier to Cllr McKinlay that a social evening away from the office environment might ease the tension, but he had rejected it.

The MD had also suggested mediation as a way forward but this too had been rejected by him.

Cllr Hay then suggested that she should set up regular Friday meetings between the MD and the Leader to discuss council business, which would perhaps generate a mutual respect for each other and help the existing situation. This was agreed.

The importance of mentioning these alleged discussions is that if they did take place, and the gist of the conversations was centred round the points I have mentioned, then it was a step in the right direction, if nothing else.

The underlying thread of what was going on seemed to be a need by members of the Cabinet to constantly refer to the strained relationship between the MD and the Leader of the Council, so that perhaps, if it was repeated often enough then officers, members and the general public would believe it. It is called propaganda, often used successfully in wartime and a weapon used by politicians to gain support.

Everyone knew there were tensions, but I found no evidence that the MD was having difficulties with other elected members of the council.

I questioned my PAB councillor colleagues about their relationship with the MD and they had nothing but praise for the way she had set about her responsibilities.

They told me that if they had problems with office staff or their managers they knew they could talk to the MD who would quickly investigate the matter and more often than not, would get the problem resolved in a short space of time.

Another thread in this difficult puzzle was the possibility that the Leader of the Council might have had difficulty in dealing with people of the opposite sex.

This is another subject I will explore later.

Meanwhile, I make the following observations. I can find no evidence of any incident recorded in any document or council minute where Cllr McKinlay had working relationship problems with male members of the council.

An appraisal after six months employment is not uncommon for senior local authority officers, but all other employees are entitled to an annual appraisal.

For senior officers, the person responsible for arranging the appraisal of the MD is normally the Leader of the Council.

The MD informed me a few weeks after her anniversary of employment date that she had not been given a date for her annual appraisal. I suggested to her that she should write to the Leader of the Council reminding him that it was overdue.

On 9th April 2003, The MD sent an email to Cllr McKinlay, with copies to the opposition group leaders and a copy to Cllr Mrs Rowena Hay, concerning the failure of the council to hold her annual appraisal.

The MD explained in her email that she had been with Cheltenham Borough Council for more that twelve months and was entitled to an annual appraisal in accordance with JNC procedures.

The appraisal should have taken place on 4th February 2003, her anniversary of employment date, and this would have been the time to question her competence and any other matters pertaining to her employment with the council.

In spite of her request no appraisal was forthcoming, which meant that she had been unable to discuss the restructuring programme she had been set during the previous twelve months. She also needed to agree her work programme with the group leaders for the next twelve months and if necessary, to agree a future training schedule with members of the appraisal panel.

But, wait a minute, wasn't this part of the six month appraisal, and didn't Cllr Hay call on the MD on 6th November 'to set her performance objectives with her?'

The pattern of what was going on had suddenly become clearer.

The appraisal of the Head of Paid Service (MD) is normally carried out by all the group leaders with an independent facilitator present to ensure that the interview is carried out correctly. It is not the practice for someone other than a group leader to be invited to be an appraiser of the Head of Paid Service.

The South West Regional Assembly (SWRA) is usually invited to supply a qualified person to facilitate the appraisal.

The fact that the MD was not appraised on the due date may have been deliberate, because the appraisal would have been an ideal opportunity to discuss the outstanding problems with the Leader of the Council. It would have been done in the presence of the group leaders and the independent representative from the SWRA, and it would have been the moment when Cllr McKinlay came face to face with his alleged adversary and he would have been obliged to openly discuss his alleged problems in front of independent witnesses.

If the appraisal had taken place it would have turned out to be a satisfactory exercise, embarrassing though it may have been for the Leader for a short while, but in the long-term the gains would have been enormous.

A crystal ball would have been helpful; and hindsight is always a wonderful thing.

Nevertheless, the facts were there; dubious disagreements about the restructuring, the impact on staff morale and the way the changes should be carried out. All these things and many others could have been discussed.

I had no doubt in my mind that staff who believed they might lose their jobs as a result of the restructuring had made early representations to the Leader of the Council and probably to other Liberal Democrat councillors as well.

That situation is quite normal in a large organisation and sometimes it creates a tension between those who don't like the proposals and those who do.

Even accepting this, there was no reason for the bitterness to continue.

Writing about the past events today, leads me to believe that had the appraisal taken place in February 2003, then the dispute between the Leader and the MD would have been resolved. The Liberal Democrats, with all their posturing, would have found it difficult to continue their antipathy towards the MD if the appraisal had taken place in the presence of the SWRA facilitator, and was as successful as the interim appraisal that had taken place on 11th September 2002.

The fact that it didn't take place is a criticism of all the councillors; we should have seen the impending writing on the wall, but we didn't.

There are still questions today that need answers. First, why did the Leader of the Council not set up the appraisal of the MD at the appointed time?

Second, was the appraisal not carried out because the first twelve months of the MD's employment had been successful and she had achieved her objectives?

Third, the successful interim six month appraisal was still fresh in their minds and they didn't relish the thought of having to further congratulate the MD again for her achievements.

And fourth, was the delay deliberate because there was a feeling brewing that some of the pressures on the MD was having the desired effect in so far as a resignation might not be too long forthcoming?

During the first year of the MD's employment it was normal to be in close communication with the Leader of the Council, more than with the group leaders representing the opposition parties. From my perspective I was more than pleased to be 'kept in the picture' about the progress of the management changes being made and I offered support whenever it was needed.

There was no reason for me to assume that the same discussions were not taking place with the other opposition group leaders and on occasions there were meetings between the MD and all the group leaders to discuss the operational matters of the council, including the management restructuring programme.

In the early months of the MD's employment I was impressed with the way she mastered the various subjects under discussion at committee meetings. This was most evident when she attended a meeting of officers and councillors; on more than one occasion she would be given a report at the meeting concerning an agenda item and in no time at all she would participate in the discussion just as easily as though she had been studying the report for a week prior to the meeting.

This new style of management became very noticeable in the early part of the MD's employment and it quickly made its mark.

The MD was clever with overtones of astuteness. She quickly understood the thrust of a document put before her and she could turn the doubters around the table into staunch supporters of the proposals before the end of the meeting.

My private discussions with officers and councillors revealed a satisfaction with the MD that was good to hear especially as the council was about to enter a difficult period with the management changes.

This was the time and the opportunity for both officers and elected members to express any contrary views to the purpose of the proposed management structure, or indeed, any adverse comments about the new MD if any existed.

None were made to me during the first fifteen months of the MD's employment, and if the MD had been as bad as the Liberal Democrat councillors had constantly been claiming, then why on earth did the Leader of the Council not raise the matter with the Board of Directors? The appraisal too would have been the proper place to express their dissatisfaction, if of course, the appraisal had taken place.

In normal situations, representations can be made at any time. Complaints about an officer or a councillor can be assessed against the council's disciplinary code. Any complaints can be formally made to the MO, the chief legal officer.

That would have been the correct way to proceed, but the situation at Cheltenham Borough Council (CBC) was not normal for several reasons. For example, how can it be normal when officers who are supposed to be neutral, appear to be taking sides in a dispute between two people – one a senior officer, the other a senior councillor?

CBC, like other local authorities, has a Standards Committee (SC). It consists of local councillors, parish councillors and individual members of the public. They are trained to look at all kinds of complaints about member behaviour and their brief is far-reaching. The Leader of the Council could have asked the SC to investigate his allegations, but he failed to do so. It could not have been because he did not have faith in the ability of the SC to come up with an answer, because the legal officer who advised the SC at the time was Mr Ford, the MO.

In addition, there had been a change in the council structure from a previously non-executive arrangement consisting of several committees, to an executive system with a Leader and up to seven Cabinet deputies.

The Leader would appoint the Cabinet deputies who would then be responsible for the portfolios covering the various sections of the council's responsibilities.

The new system seemed to work well, with non-cabinet members expected to volunteer for the Overview & Scrutiny meetings whose job would be to hold the executive to account.

Even with these changes and the possible loss of jobs, there was no inkling that the attitude of staff and elected members would rise up against the restructuring programme.

Some opposition councillors who were 'close' to the Liberal Democrats told me that there had been "mumblings of dissatisfaction about the way the structural changes were taking place" even before the local elections took place in May 2002.

If this was true then it beggars belief that no-one proposed that the structural changes should be debated in the council chamber where opinions could have been aired and changes made.

Some junior officers too had expressed similar feelings, but I put this down to the possible apprehension by officers who may have been worried about their future employment. At the time, I was not sure whether these were just strong opinions being expressed, or if there was a genuine dissatisfaction amongst the council staff about the changes.

But again, if staff affected by the changes had strong views about them, formal approaches to me or any other group leader would have resulted in arrangements being made to discuss the matter in committee.

Changes to a management structure occur regularly in the business and commercial world in order to keep up to date with changes in the markets, the cost of raw materials and the labour market.

There is always a need to streamline the way things are done; that is the only way to succeed in the commercial world.

So why are changes always a big problem when proposed in local government?

Local councillors are a broad mix of individuals, some I call 'rhino skinned' and difficult to get through. And at the other extreme there are those who are so 'soft skinned' that they will believe anything and everything that is said or proposed to them, especially if the subject is uttered by council officers.

The councillors I prefer most are those in the middle who are neither 'hard' nor 'soft skinned' who look at every issue on its merits and speak and vote according to the way their conscience dictates.

Unfortunately, there are some 'middle of the road' councillors, who because they belong to a main stream political party, will not express a contrary view on any subject in committee or the council chamber in case they upset their political hierarchy.

Thankfully, PAB councillors are not bound by such political nonsense and can express themselves freely and vote accordingly.

Would local authorities be better run if the councillors nominated by a main stream political party were prevented from operating a three-line 'whip' system of voting?

I think it would.

There would still be those who would continue to put the 'party' first rather than the needs of their communities, but at least for those who were brave enough not to follow a 'party line' they would not be reprimanded.

The reason that the 'party line' issue is so controversial in the eyes of the voter is the knowledge that any issue coming before the council has already been discussed by the political party in a closed room before the start of the meeting.

This means that the decision about whether to support or to oppose a proposal has already been taken, and the members of that political party will vote accordingly irrespective of their personal views. This is the 'three-line whip' system I refer to.

Currently, if anyone breaks the rules and speaks against the 'party line' then they know they will be censured or even suspended from the political party by the hierarchy.

Even a decision to abstain from voting would be regarded as an act of disloyalty by other members of the same political party.

On rare occasions it has been known for a member of the Conservative party to break ranks, but rarely by Liberal Democrats.

If PAB challenged main stream political councillors to vote as their conscience dictated, a senior member of the Lib/Dems would claim that the three-line vote was a measure of political discipline, but PAB would argue that it is the stifling of free independent-thinking voices.

What a sad state of affairs for local government when the needs of the political party are put above the needs of the townspeople and their local communities?

Thankfully, PAB councillors are independents in every sense of the word; they speak and vote on matters freely having listened to the merits of each case.

When a 'middle of the road' councillor informs me after a council debate on an important community issue that the PAB group's position on the issue was the correct one, I would immediately challenge the councillor to explain why he didn't speak and support the PAB position during the debate?

The answers to my challenges have always been the same, "...they are all bound by party political dogma and the 'three-line whip' regime has to be obeyed."

Towards the end of 2002 it became clear that the dissatisfaction being expressed by some members of the Liberal Democrat group about the restructuring programme was a pretext to undermine the MD. Unfortunately, the expressions were often accompanied with adverse personal comments about the MD.

What the Lib/Dems couldn't understand, or perhaps didn't want to accept, was the fact that the MD was not the architect of the proposals, only the messenger.

The decision to change the management structure was not hers, but the decision of everyone on Cheltenham Borough Council.

As the momentum grew it was obvious to me that the person leading these personal attacks during a committee meeting was the new Leader of the Council.

It was disconcerting to hear audible comments being made by Liberal Democrat councillors during meetings, which were clearly aimed at the MD and usually disrespectful. The comments were certainly not in accordance with the provisions of the members' Code of Conduct, but in every case they were allowed to continue.

On one occasion when the MD was reading an update report on the progress of the management changes, Cllr McKinlay could clearly be heard making rude comments about her. She would pause and give the councillor a long hard look and then continue reading the report.

Surprisingly, when it happened, the chairman would allow the incident to go by without reprimanding the individual. The chairman should have referred the culprit to the paragraph in the Code of Conduct about 'respect for others'.

Not sufficient by any means, but at least it would have been helpful.

On each occasion it was appalling behaviour, and in my opinion the chairman should have dealt with the situation immediately.

In spite of these unfortunate breaches of the code of conduct, which happened on several occasions, normal business continued each week with the MD guiding through the Best Performance Plan, establishing new committees and improving the format of others.

She was very strong on council governance and made many useful suggestions on ways to improve the way Scrutiny Committees (SC's) performed. She explained in detail how important it was for the SC's to hold the Cabinet and Executive to account.

Following representations from the Leader of the Council, the MD agreed to establish regular meetings with the four Group Leaders, when problems and new ideas could be discussed before they became general knowledge, or as occasionally happened, appeared in the local newspaper.

Suffice to say at this point, that throughout the period February 2002 to April

2003, the matter of performance, or lack of it by the MD, was never referred to the S&SSC. Neither did the Human Resources Department (HRD) make a request during this period for 'a new employee's medical questionnaire' to be placed on the agenda for the committee to consider.

The S&SSC, introduced by the MD to deal with staff matters, was silent on both these two important points in 2002 and 2003.

The terms of reference for the S&SCC required a member of HRD and the legal department to be present at all meetings in order to deal with any complex or legal matters affecting council staff.

Ironically, the council's Constitution was amended with an added clause requiring the S&SSC to be chaired by the Leader of the Council.

The facts surrounding the creation of the S&SSC and the two points mentioned above should have been placed before the judge at the trial in 2009. In my view, it carried weight because of its importance.

The council made much of the fact that the S&SSC played a major part in dealing with what they called 'An Employment Matter', yet the committee's perceived effectiveness of acting as a staff protection committee was poor. If it had been effective, it would have discussed the allegations about the MD's perform-ance and the tardy allegation about the false medical questionnaire long before it did in 2004.

For the record, the composition of the S&SSC had to be by political proportion-ality and as the Liberal Democrats were the largest political group on the council they occupied most seats on the committee. The PAB group had just one seat.

Local authorities are legally required to appoint three statutory officers, namely a Head of Paid Service, a Monitoring Officer and a Section 151 officer who is usually the council's chief finance officer and/or the chief accountant.

All three appointments are protected by law, which means that unless the individ-ual post holder commits an act of gross misconduct or a serious criminal offence then the employment of the individual is secure until he or she leaves the council by mutual consent.

I explained earlier that the Head of Paid Service is the most senior council officer and is usually employed with the title of chief executive or managing director.

The Head of Paid service is responsible for the efficient operation of the council, its legal responsibilities and the duty of care of all council employees.

To use a well-used phrase – the buck stops with the Head of Paid Service (MD).

The Monitoring Officer (MO) is usually the senior legal officer employed by the council and is responsible for all legal matters including the composition and main-tenance of the council's Constitution.

The MO reports to the Head of Paid Service.

The Constitution is a council approved document that gives clear details of the functions and rules of procedure as well as codes of conduct and protocols.

The Constitution is an important document; it requires to be regularly updated because there is a continuous requirement by both officers and councillors to carry out their various functions in accordance with the Articles and Rules of Procedure contained within the document.

The Section 151 officer is responsible for the sound financial management of the council's income and expenditure, which of course, is public money.

As this chapter will reveal the amount of public money spent on the dispute between the Leader of the Council and the MD in the early months ran into thousands of pounds; by the time the dispute found its way to the High Court it had reached a figure in excess of £2 million.

The Section 151 officer reports to the Head of Paid Service.

The council (CBC) decided to take Mrs Laird the MD, to the High Court in 2008 on the flimsiest of charges, in order to try to reclaim some of the money that had previously been spent on internal and external legal advice. A second action by CBC against Rhondda Cynon Taff Borough Council (RCT) the former employer of Mrs Laird, in respect of supplying the council with a *faulty* employee reference (my italics) was also lodged, but the claim was later withdrawn before the trial began.

An explanation of this will appear in Chapter 22.

It will be seen that all three statutory council positions played an overarching part in the ongoing dispute between the MD and the Leader of the Council. However, readers should also take into account the possibility that the Leader's antagonism towards Mrs Laird may not have been sustainable unless he knew and was confident of the support from his Cabinet colleagues, senior officers and the council's legal department.

It is inevitable for the council's legal department to give expert advice whenever it is required and generally to be supportive of the Leader of the Council.

During April 2003, in spite of attempts by opposition group leaders and officers of the council to end the disagreement between the MD and Cllr McKinlay, it became clear that committee meetings had become more difficult and embarrassing for those not directly involved in the ongoing dispute.

From both sides there was increasing evidence that things had become so bad that the MD and the Leader of the Council would only communicate with each other by letter and they would only meet when a third party was present.

It was an unsatisfactory way of running the business of the council.

Following a joint statement to the editor of the *Gloucestershire Echo* dismissing claims of disunity, under a heading *"Rift? We just thrash out issues"* the *Echo* reported on April 4th *"The tensions were so evident between Mrs Laird and Mr McKinlay at a meeting of the Cabinet that they failed to greet each other and a gap emerges between the two at the head of the Cabinet table".*

The statement to the local press suggesting there was no rift was always doomed to failure, because the situation between them had been built on hate, malice and a total dislike of each other.

No-one in the council offices, officers or councillors had the slightest hope that things would change, or get better overnight. They were right.

Councillor John Melville-Smith, a solicitor working for a local firm of solicitors, sent an email to his Group Leader Cllr Duncan Smith on 22nd April 2003 asking him to make contact "... *as things have progressed dramatically regarding Christine.*"

John informed Duncan that Christine Laird had sought his legal advice 'hence my involvement'.

He also explained in his email that Mrs Laird "*had received a letter from the South West Regional Assembly who had been instructed by the Cabinet on behalf of the Council to negotiate severance terms.*" The letter also explained that she had received a telephone call offering her £63,000 if she would leave Cheltenham Borough Council, but she had to make her decision by Tuesday 22nd April.

"*In default*", his email went on, "*she would face a press campaign to oust her.*"

John Melville-Smith's final comment was "*...it is all turning very nasty.*"

The advice that anyone could give Christine Laird at the time had to be that the offer of £63,000 by the Liberal Democrat executive was probably unlawful.

An offer of this kind needed the authority of the full council.

The Section 151 officer (Chief Financial Officer) could not have been aware of the offer because he was on leave at the time; and the District Auditor, I am sure, would not have been impressed had he heard news that an individual councillor, either acting alone or on behalf of a small group, had been offering public money to the most senior member of the council, as a means of terminating the employment.

This was an act of maladministration, and far as I am concerned the matter should have been investigated by the Local Government Ombudsman.

I was not privy to any advice that may have been offered to Christine Laird by Cllr John Melville-Smith, but I was made aware of a letter from Mrs Laird to the MO and the Section 151 officer dated 25th April 2003, which suggested she was acting on legal advice that had been given to her. The letter to the two senior officers was long. It expressed Mrs Laird's concerns about the way corporate governance was being handled, including the way in which certain councillors had been conducting themselves.

She suggested in her letter that they should initiate an independent inquiry into the conduct of the Cabinet members and produce a Section 5 report to be tabled at the next meeting of Cheltenham Borough Council.

The letter also expressed concerns that the Leader of the Council and Cllr Stuart-Smith, without the authority of the council, had invited the MD to consider her continuing employment with the local authority.

I would have been surprised if the two councillors had not sought approval from the other Cabinet members before they embarked on such an approach, and I would have been equally surprised if advice had not been sought from the legal department. If they acted together without the approval of the Cabinet, or if the Cabinet had approved their actions, the requirements of the Functions and Responsibilities Regulations 2000 had not been observed by the individuals or the Cabinet collectively and therefore their actions were unlawful.

I explained earlier that the Head of Paid Service and the other two statutory officers are protected from unlawful dismissal and any alteration to the terms of their employment rests solely with the council. In other words, neither the Leader nor any member of the Cabinet has the power to initiate such an action on their own.

Also, to involve the South West Regional Assembly (SWRA) in a possible 'negotiation' with Mrs Laird about the termination of her employment seems rather perverse to me.

What on earth was the SWRA thinking about?

Officers employed by the SWRA are usually regarded as independent people who can be relied upon to give sound independent advice.

That is why they are invited by the Leader of the Council to facilitate an annual appraisal of the senior officer of the council. I have explained the mechanics of the procedure and the difficulty that Mrs Laird experienced when she requested a legitimate appraisal, which was due after twelve months in the job of managing director.

The SWRA chief executive must have been aware of the legal position regarding the MD's statutory protection and should have made this abundantly clear to the Leader of the Council. The SWRA should only advise, not be involved in any negotiation.

Not only did they fail to do this, but they contacted Mr Richard Penn the MD's trade union, the Association of Local Authorities Chief Executives (ALACE), with details of the offer of the severance payment (£63,000) on condition that the MD did not return to work 'on the following Tuesday'.

I have no doubt that if such a 'deal' had been accepted then the council would have required Mrs Laird to accept and to sign a 'Compromise Agreement' before her departure from office. This would have limited what Mrs Laird could have said and done after she left the council's employment.

Not only was this episode a breach of the Regulations but, in my view, it would have been contrary to the provisions in Section 101 of the Local Government Act 1972.

The SWRA would have been aware of the legal position and should have made it clear to the Leader of the Council and his Cabinet colleagues that if they continued down this path they would be acting illegally. If the SWRA was unaware of the legal requirements, which I doubt, it could have sought external legal advice.

Clearly, this attempt to hasten the end of the MD's employment only made matters worse; as the dispute continued the personal abuse also became worse and more intense.

It seemed that only the deliverance of Mrs Laird's head on a plate was going to satisfy the Liberal Democrats; even if it meant the continuing expenditure of large sums of public money to achieve it. In the end it did.

It is worth recording at this point that Richard Penn (ALACE) wrote to Mrs Laird about the offer that had been made and reminded her, if she needed reminding, that the offer of £63,000 by the Cabinet represented a sum equivalent to nine months salary. He believed that the Cabinet members thought it was a reasonable offer in the circumstances, but Mr Penn had made it clear to them that in his opinion, their offer would be unacceptable.

Mr Penn also held the view, following discussions with the council, that if the offer was not accepted by Mrs Laird, then he believed the council's 'imminent intention' would be to go down the 'disciplinary route' leading to possible termination.

Of course, if this had turned out to be the case at the time, then Mrs Laird's statutory protection would have required the council, not the Cabinet, to follow the process set out in paragraph 16 of the Joint Negotiating Committee (JNC).

This would mean that the council would need to appoint a panel of members to hear the allegations made against her.

Cllr Melville-Smith had warned in his email to Duncan Smith that *"things are becoming very nasty"* and he was right, but there was worse to come.

The MD faced a choice – she could, through her trade union representative, negotiate a better 'deal' than the one on offer, or she could face up to the fact that she would be required in the future to defend any allegations of disciplinary misconduct to a Disciplinary Panel.

If the council had come to the decision of 'accept the offer or else' then it begs the question of who knew about the decision other than the Leader and his Cabinet colleagues?

We know Bryony Houlden the chief executive of the SWRA, was party to the offer, but were senior officers of the council also involved?

Then there was the question of the 'allegations'. What allegations, and if there were any, why had the opposition group leaders not been made aware of them.

The PAB Group had not been informed that discussions had taken place about an 'offer' and I was certainly not aware that accusations of a disciplinary nature had been discussed by the Cabinet, or by other members of the council.

The opposition group leaders, had they been told, would have informed their members, sought meetings with senior officers, followed by a motion to council so that the problem could have been discussed in open debate.

That is the normal way for council business to be conducted.

Further investigation has revealed that the decision was not recorded in any minutes so the facts of what went on were known only by those who had been called to the meeting. Nothing was ever put into the public domain.

When I made this point to the Standards Board for England (SBE), I was told that the Investigating Officer did not think it improper for there not to have been any publicity or reported discussions with other members of the council. Unbelievable!

This was the comment of the SBE – the independent watchdog of public servants.

It was not until the transcript of the High Court judgment was published in June 2009 that we learned that on 6th November 2002 a meeting took place between the MD and Cllr Rowena Hay at which issues between the MD and Cllr McKinlay were discussed. As we know, the MD agreed to hold regular Friday meetings with Cllr McKinlay and Cllr Hay in an effort to resolve the ongoing difficulties.

Cllr McKinlay, according to the judgment, decided to contact Mrs Bryony Houlden, at the office of the SWRA for advice.

Mrs Houlden advised Cllr McKinlay to be open-minded and honest. There are different versions about what happened at the meetings, but whichever version one chooses to believe, the face-to-face meetings between the two didn't resolve anything. In fact, they only made matters worse with more unpleasant exchanges between them.

There is good evidence available that the MD, on more than one occasion, offered the hand of friendship and conciliation to Cllr McKinlay and his Cabinet, but each time it was offered it was rejected.

So, attempts by individual Cabinet members to set up meetings between the two sides can now be dismissed as nothing more than a 'smokescreen' because the real evidence shows that the Leader and his Cabinet had no intention of coming to any kind of agreement with Mrs Laird.

The High Court judgment further revealed that towards the end of 2002 and the early part of 2003 rumours had circulated that the Cabinet were seeking advice on the ways and means of terminating the MD's employment.

Once again, Mrs Houlden had been consulted and she advised that there should be a private conversation between the MD and Cllr McKinlay about how they saw the future, particularly the working arrangements for the longer term.

The court judgment further revealed that the advice given by Mrs Houlden included an opinion that if the MD thought that the problems were soluble, but the Cabinet disagreed, the Cabinet could then pursue a disciplinary action against her providing they had evidence of the MD's misconduct.

The alternative to this, according to Bryony Houlden, was for the Cabinet to consider another restructuring exercise that would delete the managing director post from the management structure.

Strange advice, in my opinion, considering the whole problem and perhaps the cause of the dispute, was the management restructuring programme in the first place.

Nevertheless, the advice must have had a considerable impact on the Cabinet members because it resulted in Mrs Houlden being invited to Cllr Hay's house on 5th February 2003 together with invitations to Cllr McKinlay and other prominent Liberal Democrat members. It was here, says the court judgment, that various options were further discussed.

This clandestine meeting seemed to attract nothing more than confirmation from the judge that a group of Liberal Democrat councillors, plus the chief executive of the SWRA, met in a private house to discuss the 'options' of terminating the employment of the council's managing director.

A meeting of politicians in a private house would, however, not be open to the local press so there would be less likelihood of the discussion ever getting to the ears of the general public.

The fact that the dismissal of the council's most senior officer is the sole responsibility of the full council seems to have been ignored by those who were anxious for Mrs Laird to go. Did they seek legal advice before they met in a private house?

In June 2009 I received a copy of a letter from Bryony Houlden addressed to Cllr Rowena Hay and dated 8th January 2003. The letter came by royal mail.

The date of the letter is important for two reasons.

1. The meeting that took place in Cllr Hay's house four weeks later was a reaffirmation of the content of the letter.
2. Some of the content of the letter coincides with the judge's comments in the court transcript published 15th June 2009, but what is missing in the judgment are the other points raised in the letter from Ms Houlden; the scribbled notes in the margins, for instance, were of great importance.

From someone who attended the High Court on the day that Ms Houlden gave her witness evidence about the letter and the subsequent meeting in the councillor's house, I was told that the judge asked the witness to 'read the letter and the comments in the margin'. This she did and admitted that the comments in the margins were hers.

Having studied the letter and the scribbled notes, I am still at a loss to understand why the content of the letter was not taken more seriously in the court hearing.

It did not even attract a comment in the judgment.

Towards the end of April 2003 the opposition group leaders decided that "they would be failing in their duty if they did not write to the Standards Board for England (SBE) outlining their concerns and formally registering complaints against the Leader of the Council and the members of his Cabinet".

On 28th April 2003, the opposition group leaders formally submitted a letter of complaint to the SBE detailing alleged failures by the Leader of the Council and his Cabinet colleagues.

The allegations included their failure to comply with the Code of Conduct of Cheltenham Borough Council.

The crux of the allegations centred on the Cabinet's illegal attempt to remove the managing director from her post, involving themselves with staffing matters and incurring expenditure without authority from the council.

The SBE acknowledged receipt of our complaint on 8th May 2003. They informed the group leaders that their complaints had been considered by the Board and would be referred to an Ethical Standards Officer (ESO) for investigation.

Once the complaint to the SBE became public knowledge a letter was posted to members and officers of the council by Cllr McKinlay and his Cabinet.

The letter was dated 29th April 2003 and it criticised the opposition group leaders for making their complaints known to the public.

The opposition group leaders found this unbelievable considering they had done everything possible to avoid such a situation. They had used every device possible to get the Leader of the Council to sit round the table and talk to them in an effort to resolve the dispute between him and the MD.

They also found it hypocritical for the Liberal Democrats, who prided themselves on being open and honest with the general public, to want to keep the scrutiny of its behaviour from them.

When one compares the opposition parties' approach to the problem with the one that they had undertaken in Cllr Hay's house, I think their approach, in the eyes of the public, would be regarded to be more akin to openness and transparency than that shown by the Lib/Dems.

According to the letter, the Monitoring Officer (MO) had been instructed to conduct an internal investigation into the allegations made by the opposition group leaders; after due consideration, he found that the Cabinet had not acted unlawfully or unconstitutionally.

From such legal advice, it must be presumed that if an offer of £63,000 is made by a Cabinet member to a senior officer to leave the council's employment it should be regarded as an 'informal proposal and therefore not unlawful'.

If that advice is to be regarded as sound then Cabinet members would be free to do whatever they liked, which would be an unsatisfactory situation for any local authority.

It should be understood that during this period of the dispute the MO was advising the Leader and his Cabinet members, so it was hardly a surprise to find that his conclusions on the offer turned out the way they did.

It did not help towards improving the relationships between the MD, the Leader and the members of his Cabinet.

Meanwhile, the *Gloucestershire Echo* was having a field day. On 1st May 2003 they carried a headline *'Pay-off offer causes uproar"* with a sub headline asking the question *'Has Council's MD been asked to go?'*

The report stated that the opposition group leaders had complained to the Standards Board for England (SBE) because proper council procedures had not been followed.

On 7th May 2003, the MO wrote the following letter to the opposition group leaders:

> *"The Leader of the Council had raised a question of discipline with him in connection with the managing director. Therefore, this required him to appoint a politically balanced group of members to sit on a JNC Disciplinary Panel.*
>
> *The appointments would be carried out in accordance with the provisions of the JNC Conditions incorporated into the managing director's contract, which would then require the appointees to consider the allegations.*
>
> *Councillor McKinlay has expressed the view that group leaders and members of the Cabinet should be excluded from serving on the JNC Panel".*

The MO had already decided that other councillors should not serve on the Panel because of their involvement in the ongoing dispute, including members of the council's Standard Committee (SC). But if he believed this to be the right course of action, then he must have been of the opinion that members of the SC did have a role to play in resolving the dispute.

If I am right, then why was no attempt made by the MO or the Cabinet members, to consult and involve the SC about the dispute throughout the period 2002 to 2004? The reasons are obvious, in my view, The SC is the watchdog of the council and contained in its terms of reference is a duty to ensure that the Code of Conduct is followed by members of the council at all times.

Even without notification by the MO, the chairman of the SC knew it had the power to investigate a known problem if the committee thought it was needed without waiting for someone else to initiate the procedure.

I am not aware that the MO explained this important matter to them.

Complaints received during the period of the dispute were forwarded directly to the SBE for consideration and action. The SBE was abolished in 2011 and local authorities can now appoint a SC with powers to deal with all complaints in-house.

The SC continues to be advised by the MO.

In response to the proposal to set up a JNC panel, the MD wrote to the MO on 20th May 2003 expressing her disappointment with his adherence to the request of the Leader of the Council.

In her letter, she reminded the MO that the council's Constitution did not provide the Leader with delegated authority to implement the JNC procedure on the council's behalf.

No allegations of indiscipline had been placed before the MD or to the opposition group leaders, so it was difficult to know what the allegations were.

But surely, in the interests of natural justice, the allegations should have been published in detail so that adequate responses could have been made by the MD?

Even at this point in the unhappy saga, the MD suggested in her letter to the MO that she was prepared to meet him and representatives from the council in order to resolve the situation.

Throughout the period of the dispute I found there was ample evidence to show that elected members, other than Liberal Democrat members, had tried hard to get the two sides together to talk through the problems: to agree an accepted method of conciliation, which would allow the council to move forward. Unfortunately, every-attempt by those who wanted to see an end to the dispute, was thwarted by the Liberal Democrat administration.

It was said at the time that some Lib/Dem councillors and some officers, were trying to achieve a resolution to the dispute, but if they were then all I can say is that they were certainly going about it in a very strange way.

On two occasions at Staff & Support Services Committee meetings – long before the council decided to sue Mrs Laird in the High Court at the end of 2008, I suggested that the dispute had gone on long enough and that the estimated cost of the dispute was already too much for council taxpayers to bear.

Not once, but twice I asked the committee to draw a line under the matter to allow the local authority to move forward.

As with all other attempts – my plea not only fell on deaf ears, it provoked a rebuke from Cllr McKinlay for making the suggestions.

Prior to the Bank Holiday on 5th May 2003, the opposition group leaders were informed that the MD had registered complaints with the SBE against the Leader of the Council and members of the Cabinet.

She had submitted thirty six allegations of failure to comply with the Code of Conduct and Sections of the Local Government Act 2000. The allegations covered the period from 1st April 2002 to 27th October 2003.

Many of the allegations were trivial and should have been dealt with within the council offices by the Personnel Department, but the climate was never right for this to happen.

As the events started to unfold, it became clear that the department was not up to the job. It didn't help to know that it was led by a director who had been less than friendly towards the MD from the early days of her appointment.

Some of the MD's complaints to the SBE against the Leader of the Council and Cllr Stuart-Smith, referred to threatening and intimidating behaviour during discussions on the restructuring programme.

More than one complaint centred around the Leader's wish to 'stop the restructuring' or on other occasions to 'slow down' the restructuring programme.

It is worth remembering that in December 2002 the council approved the progress report of the restructuring programme and the Leader of the Council had introduced Phase 2 as the next step towards a new management structure.

Other complaints included the offer of money as an inducement for Mrs Laird to leave the council, and another allegation that Cabinet members had refused to declare 'personal and prejudicial' interests when the managing director's employment position was being discussed.

These were by far the most important complaints, but they were all treated with the same disdain by the SBE. Readers should take into account that the SBE relied heavily on the briefings it had received from the council's MO.

When the records of the events are studied it raises the question of whether he should have been told to step down and relieved of his duties by the council's Board of Directors.

By not doing so it begs the question whether the Board too had failed in their duty of care by allowing the MO to continue in his advisory post.

The records also show that the MO failed to declare an interest at meetings when the matter of the MD's employment was being discussed. The fact that he later declared an interest at meetings allowing another member of the legal team to take over his responsibilities indicated that the MO did have an interest.

It also proves that the 'interest' should have been declared from day one.

It was not a surprise, therefore, to hear that many people from within and outside the council thought that the SBE decisions were flawed. The council taxpayers had based their opinions on the belief that the Code of Conduct was a reliable document and that councillors were obliged to work within it. They believed it gave them confidence as council taxpayers that everything done and said by their elected representatives on their behalf was honest and reliable, and in accord with the council's code of conduct.

The Ethical Standards Officer (ESO) dismissed the first three of Mrs Laird's complaints because they occurred before Cheltenham Borough Council adopted its Code of Conduct document on 22nd April 2002.

The majority of the other complaints were dismissed by the ESO because, in his opinion, the Cabinet members had not failed to comply with the Code of Conduct. Therefore, it is safe to assume that the first three allegations would have ended in dismissal if they had occurred after April 22nd.

The allegation that Cllr McKinlay and his Cabinet colleagues had failed to 'declare personal and prejudicial interests and should have withdrawn from the meeting of the council on 27th October 2003', (the meeting at which Christine Laird's alleged misconduct was to be discussed), the ESO said: "... *even though they had failed to comply their actions were not wilful because they had sought advice from the Monitoring Officer*". A MO who at the time was himself harbouring a grudge against the person who was being hauled in front of the council to answer questions about her alleged misconduct.

If the SBE had checked out this important detail, they may have come to different conclusions.

It seemed to me and many others that one either complied with the council's Code of Conduct, or one was in danger of breaching it. There could not possibly be a 'half-way house' on such an important matter.

According to the code, the declaration of an interest is the responsibility of the individual. If that is the case, then surely individuals who have been in a long dispute with a member of staff, including offering a 'bribe' to get her to leave, in Mrs Laird's case, must seriously consider whether staying in a meeting room when the subject is being discussed, is either ethical or 'legal'.

The test for any councillor is written in the Code of Conduct – '*A member will have a personal and prejudicial interest in a matter if the interest is one which a member of the public with knowledge of the relevant facts would reasonably regard as so significant that it is likely to prejudice the member's judgement of the public interest*'.

Considering the extensive reporting by the *Gloucestershire Echo* on the unpleasant difficulties that existed between the MD and the Cabinet for more than a year, it could hardly be said that the criteria for declaring an interest did not apply to the Leader of the Council or any members of his Cabinet.

The MO's advice on this occasion was poor, but he had other pressing matters on his mind at the time such as his own employment position to consider.

On two other allegations in the MD's complaints, the ESO was unable to find corroborative evidence, but he declared that even if the allegations were 'proved' he would not consider the allegations as breaches of the Code of Conduct.

Knowing all the details, I did wonder what the council taxpayer made of it all.

After all, the Code of Conduct, by its title alone, would conjure up in the mind of the public that elected members, when carrying out their duties, would need to conduct themselves in a responsible and respectful manner.

The code says that a member must treat others with respect; in another part it states: *"A member must not in his official capacity, or any other circumstance, conduct himself in a manner which could reasonably be regarded as bringing his office or the local authority into disrepute."*

From the responses it must be assumed that 'non-declarations of interest'; the 'offering of severance payments to a senior officer'; the 'patterns of behaviour' by certain elected members, were quite in order during the long period of the dispute.

The ESO may have thought so, but many people would disagree with him.

The most interesting point that emerged from the SBE was the ESO's comment when dismissing the allegations. He wrote that he had made his findings under the terms expressed in Section 59 (4) (a) or (b) of the Local Government Act 2000.

A finding under paragraph

(a)   is 'no evidence of any failure to comply with the Code of Conduct' and

(b)   implies that where a breach has occurred then 'no action needs to be taken in respect of the matters which are the subject of the investigation'.

In other words – case closed.

But, even more bizarre as far as the CBC versus Laird dispute is concerned is paragraph (c) of the Act. This states that if a breach of the code is proved by the ESO he could recommend 'that the matter which is the subject of the investigation be referred to the Monitoring Officer of the relevant local authority'.

Thankfully, the MO didn't have to deal with such an embarrassing situation, but to say the least the investigation report by the MO would have made interesting reading.

There was a period at the start of the New Year 2003, albeit prior to the allegations by Mrs Laird to the SBE in May 2003 that is worth recording.

Apparently, an email was sent by Cllr McKinlay to Mrs Laird on 25th January 2003, with a copy to Cllr Mrs Hay, written in the friendliest of terms about her future annual appraisal and seeking a mutually agreed date for the appraisal.

Bearing in mind the minutes of the six month interim appraisal had still to be approved, the email read as follows *"Dear Christine, Just to let you know I intend to set your appraisal date for the 28th February. Can you confirm that you are available so that I can let the other panel members know?"* Signed *"Andrew"*

Considering what had gone before, the email sounded courteous and civilised.

On 5th February 2003 Mrs Laird received an email from Cllr Mrs Hay in the following terms *"Dear Christine, in preparation for your appraisal, I would appreciate it if you could confirm that the notes of your six month review, which confirmed your current salary, are acceptable. Rowena".*

My earlier comments explained that I was unaware of the interim appraisal, so it was 'mind-boggling' to read the email about the 'confirmation of notes of your six month review'. But why had they taken so long?

However, Mrs Laird replied to the email saying she could not accept the 'notes' as they were 'incomplete and inaccurate'. She reminded Cllr Hay that she too had been of the same opinion when the notes had been discussed.

Mrs Laird also made the point that because of the muddled way the notes had been set out and the fact that some of her 'expressed concerns' at the appraisal were not included in the notes, she would be reluctant to use the SWRA as facilitators at any future MD appraisal.

In response, Cllr Hay wrote that she *"agreed the notes were unclear, but not that they were inaccurate"*.

She added *"... in order to move forward to your annual appraisal we need to have an agreed set of notes"*.

Where was this all leading? The answer was soon to be revealed. On 19th February 2003, Mrs Laird received an email from Miss Jo Pitman; Assistant Director Human Resources (AD/HR) headed Personal/Your Appraisal. This is what it said:

> *"Christine, Firstly, I hope you are feeling much better now? Secondly, although we spoke about this briefly the other day, I thought I would take the opportunity to confirm to you that your annual appraisal will not now be held on 28th February, as first thought. As you know from our conversation the Leader has recognised that it would be sensible to arrange training for all those elected members who will be involved in your appraisal before it actually takes place (I hope that you agree that it seems eminently sensible too?). I have therefore asked Emma to undertake some research to identify a suitable trainer, who can deliver the work for us reasonably quickly, and so that we do not go too far outside of your year here.*
>
> *At the moment I am unable to confirm which elected members will be involved in your appraisal but as soon as I am in a position to do so I will. I should also confirm that I have notified the Leader and the Leader of the Opposition that it is your express wish that we do not use the South West Regional Assembly to facilitate/chair your annual appraisal. I hope you find this update helpful?*
> *Jo"*

I have quoted the email in full because it is important for readers to try to get into the minds of those who, allegedly, were either neutral, or antagonistic towards Mrs Laird, and also so to enable them to carefully examine the words used in the email.

My conclusion, once I had analysed the content of the email, was that it was a deliberate attempt to delay and then prevent the appraisal from taking place.

The talk about training individuals for the appraisal was a diversion and probably not the individual opinion of Jo Pitman, but based on a command from others in the anti-Laird circle.

Take a look at the facts – the Leader, as we know, set up the appraisal for 28th

February. A few weeks later the Leader, using the AD/HR as his spokesperson, cancels the arranged date and uses the spurious reason that the appointed appraisers needed training. His reason that the appraisers would need training is laughable considering he had conducted the interim appraisal with the assistance of the Leader of the Opposition and Cllr Hay, a Cabinet member. What training did they receive? If they did receive training then there would be a record in the training department.

The common practice is for all group leaders to appraise the MD in a local authority, not a Cabinet member.

The AD/HR referred to 'those elected members who will be involved in your appraisal'. She is talking about councillors who would not have had day to day dealings with the Head of Paid Service, being asked to appraise her. From her previous experience in the HR job she would have known that chief executives and managing directors are normally appraised by all the Group Leaders because of their day-to-day working.

Similarly, chairmen of committees are normally appraised by their Group Directors or Managers. It is a procedure adopted by all local authorities.

It was noticeable too that the AD/HR referred to the Leader of the Opposition only and not the other two opposition group leaders.

In more than thirty years service as a councillor and a group leader, the interim appraisal of Mrs Laird was the only appraisal that I had not been invited to participate in as a member of an appraisal panel. The reason was obvious – I did not support the 'vendetta' against Mrs Laird and I said so on more than one occasion in S&SSC meetings, and I certainly did not support the excessive expenditure of council taxpayers' money in order to terminate the MD's employment with the council.

Remembering the date of the email from Jo Pitman (February 19th) I was surprised to be given a copy of an email dated 3rd March from Cllr Hay to Christine Laird. This is the text: *"Christine, I would like you to identify where you consider the notes to be inaccurate. I would suggest if you are happy to do so that we postpone your appraisal for a month or so until these issues are sorted out. Rowena."*

The plot was obvious – even to a blind man.

Mrs Laird had unwittingly, given the anti-Laird group the opportunity to prevent another appraisal taking place, by complaining about the minutes of the interim appraisal. It was an ideal reason for the Leader, aided and abetted by Cllr Mrs Hay, to prevent the twelve month appraisal taking place, particularly as they knew that the twelve month appraisal was likely to be just as positive as the last one had been.

Two weeks went by and it appeared as though the left hand didn't know what the right hand was doing. Or, maybe it did, and it was probably part of the plan to bring more pressure to bear on the MD.

But, there was more to come. On 5th March, Cllr Hay wrote again to Mrs Laird thanking her for the reply and reminding her that she had not responded to the suggestion about postponing the appraisal.

Agreement by Mrs Laird would have been perfect.

One could assume from the words of Cllr Hay that the council Cabinet, including an officer or two, were not overly keen for a second appraisal to take place so soon after the successful interim appraisal, which had been held in the previous September, even though the MD was entitled to one.

It is interesting to read the hand written notes of Russell Symons (SWRA), which made it clear that Mrs Laird had been able to go through each of the stages of the interim appraisal, highlighting those parts of the discussions and the decisions that had been agreed.

But these 'highlights' were missing from the final minutes.

In a letter from Mrs Laird to Cllr Hay dated 12th March 2003, she respectfully asks that she accepts her updated version of the minutes as 'a more accurate picture of the review processes than the SWRA ones'.

The final paragraph read as follows:

> "I would be grateful if you could let me have a revised date for my appraisal as I am conscious of the fact that I cannot progress the appraisals of the Group Directors who in turn need to initiate appraisals with the Assistant Directors until my operational targets are set. In consequence, I would be most grateful if arrangements for my appraisal could be put in hand and take place before the end of March."

In reply, Cllr Hay wrote: *"I recall the SWRA sent us copies of the notes on 25th September 2002, asking for our comments."*

Cllr Hay then suggested in her letter 'that no-one had taken advantage of the offer by the SWRA, so it was a bit late to start referring to them'.

But upon examination, it appears that the letter from the SWRA, containing the notes of the appraisal and dated 25th September, had been routinely sent to Cllr McKinlay as the chairman of the appraisal panel.

Did he send copies of the notes to the panel members immediately on receipt, or was there a deliberate delay?

Becky Robinson, Admin Assistant to the MD, wrote to Cllr McKinlay on 16th October 2002 informing him that the managing director had looked at the notes and she was of the same opinion as Cllr Mrs Hay in that there were 'bits missing' and 'they had been compiled in a strange order'.

On my reckoning, a quick response from the MD, possibly within fourteen days of receiving a copy of the notes, was more than reasonable.

Local government moves slowly at the best of times, but bearing in mind the surreptitious activities that were going on at the time and with Christmas approaching, I was not at all surprised to read that Cllr Hay had written to Mrs Laird on 5th February 2003 asking her to confirm the notes of the six month review in preparation for her annual appraisal.

Although she was right to believe at the time that it would all be sorted out in the end, it is clear now, having read the letters and emails, the annual appraisal was never

ever going to take place, and it didn't. Obviously, for the reasons I have explained above.

Whatever one's view regarding the strange exchanges surrounding the annual appraisal, it appears that with all the fight and robustness that the MD showed in carrying out her duties, she was slowly becoming demoralised.

In all my years working at a top level in industry, or working in the local government environment for more than thirty years, I found nothing in my experiences that equalled the treatment that had been meted out to Mrs Laird.

In looking for comparisons, I would match it alongside the incessant warring by Gordon Brown and his team to oust Tony Blair from his position of prime minister in the period 2005 to 2008.

Thankfully, Tony Blair was able to walk away and do other things, but Mrs Laird, having borne the brunt of a most hateful campaign against her for several years, had her glittering career being brought to an early end by a group of individuals who clearly had no concern for the suffering they were inflicting on her. The grim legacy of the dispute for Mrs Laird is having to battle continually against debilitating bouts of depression now, and probably for the rest of her life.

Later in the book, I will write about the suffering she has been through, but in the meantime, it is helpful to remember once again the constant visits from various members of the Cabinet to Mrs Laird's office throughout the period of the dispute.

From the evidence given to me it seems that it was an orchestrated action taken in turns, it seems, by different councillors.

Few of the visits could be called genuine and certainly not friendly. The visitor usually carried a message about her expected departure, or more often the case, the visitor moaned about the way she was carrying out her duties. The unqualified complaints were alleged to have come from her council colleagues.

Debilitating stuff to say the least and medically harmful in the long run.

"How much will it take for you to go" (March 5th 2003) is hardly 'friendly' and "your style of management of always wanting to do things constitutionally right" is not a basis for working together. In fact, the last comment could imply that the managing director should do things 'illegally', which would have put the council at risk.

What a dysfunctional state the council was in; and the people of Cheltenham were completely unaware of what was going on.

As the situation was getting progressively worse, Mrs Laird wrote to Cllr McKinlay on 17th March 2003. The content is significant and I reproduce the major points of the letter for your consideration.

> *"Dear Councillor McKinlay,*
>
> *I refer to your letter of 13th March. In responding to your letter I am afraid I must disagree with the assertion that I have not previously raised with you my concerns about how you sometimes treat me. Specifically, on at least three separate occasions I can recall telling you that your conduct towards me, and especially on May 3rd following the elections, frightened me very much.*

I can also clearly recall a number of conversations with you when I have indicated that I was unhappy at the way in which you were treating me and how this made me feel – two conversations on 16th and 17th September specifically spring to mind.

I can also recall advising you that reported comments and discussions you have had about me with other members of staff placed me in a difficult position and made me feel uncomfortable and undermined. It is also the case in November of this year I raised with Councillor Rowena Hay, during discussion about my performance objectives for 2003/04, my concerns about our working relationship and how I sometimes felt in your presence.

I can recall also, several conversations with at least one Cabinet Deputy, none of which I investigated, during which I have been told you "loathe me", which inevitably has spilt over into our working relationship. Indeed, on several occasions you have told me, during 1–2–1 meetings, you feel physically sick in my presence or at the prospect of seeing me.

In consequence, I cannot accept that you are not aware that on occasions I have felt intimidated in your presence or that you have sometimes distressed me by the things that you have said to me during meetings, whether or not it was intention to do so. Equally, you cannot be unaware of the efforts that I have made to try and improve our working relationship in an effort to address this particular issue, which for the most part you have chosen to rebuff.

In the meantime, I suggest our personal assistant, Karen Watson or Becky Robinson in her absence, accompanies us at future meetings to ensure the work of the Council continues to progress.

May I respectfully request that if it is your intention to write to me in such terms again, that you at least mark your letters 'personal' or 'private and confidential' for two reasons. First, it is not appropriate that members of our secretariat, or the Council's post room staff should be aware of such letters. Second, I am entitled to the same rights of privacy and courtesy as any other member of staff working for the Council.

Finally, can I repeat my previous request to you that we find a way of working amicably together for the good of the Borough and my willingness to discuss with you how this can be achieved?
Yours sincerely,
Christine Laird.

The letter does not require any comment from me because it puts the whole problem of the CBC versus Laird matter into perspective. Whilst there is ample evidence of Mrs Laird pleading with Cllr McKinlay to find a solution to their problem, I have no evidence of Cllr McKinlay writing to Mrs Laird in the same vein.

The reference in the letter to 'our personal assistant Karen Watson' can be explained by stating that it has been a long-held practice in Cheltenham Borough Council for the Managing Director (MD) and the Leader of the Council to share a personal assistant.

Later this arrangement created further problems for Mrs Laird.

From a good start to the year 2003 matters went disastrously wrong by the end of March. Because of this a 'private' meeting was arranged in the splendid setting of the Cheltenham Town Hall to discuss and to 'clear the air' regarding the alleged problems between the MD and the Leader of the Council.

Cheltenham Town Hall was built in 1902–03 in order to provide a venue for social events. The main hall, with its Corinthian columns and coved ceiling has a seating capacity for 1,000 people. There are a number of smaller rooms and to the left of the main entrance hall the Central Spa dispenses the waters from all the pump rooms of the famous Cheltenham Spa.

Would the soothing spa waters help to create the right atmosphere? Only time would tell.

The meeting had been arranged at the request of the Association of Local Authority Chief Executives (ALACE) so that the alleged concerns of the Leader of the Council could be explained to Richard Penn (ALACE) and the managing director.

Russell Symons represented the SWRA and the Cabinet was represented by Cllrs David Fidgeon and Rowena Hay.

Originally, it had been suggested that the whole Cabinet should attend the meeting so that it could be established whether or not the Leader's concerns were shared by all of them.

Mrs Laird thought that this arrangement would be unfair to her and it was agreed that only two members of the Cabinet should attend the meeting.

Cllr Fidgeon opened the meeting by emphasising "... the meeting should not be confrontational and it should not be used to apportion blame; and the discussion should not overshadow Christine Laird's good points."

The thrust of Cllr Fidgeon's contribution was centred on the tension in member and officer relationships and he thought that this had been 'greatly exaggerated as a result of the Cabinet system'.

He also thought that it had been further exaggerated in Cheltenham circles following the recent council elections.

"Cabinet members were constantly being told that the relationship between the MD and staff was difficult and some members of staff had claimed that they could not work with the MD", he said.

Cllr Fidgeon also remarked: "Some officers claimed that the MD had been openly critical of the new Liberal Democrat administration", but he added: "This must be regarded as hearsay."

The MD's response was an admittance that relationships could have been better, but she claimed that this wasn't helped in the knowledge that soon after the council elections she learned that the Leader of the Council 'wanted her out'.

She had no problems with the new administration's manifesto, but she thought that when 'some of the things in the manifesto could not be done' she was entitled to give her view. She had no problem with implementing the policies of the administration providing they conformed to the standard regulations.

On the question of relationship problems with members of staff, Mrs Laird pointed out that this was not borne out by the evidence. She referred to the evidence contained in the Performance Appraisals and 360 degree assessments that showed a completely different picture to the one being portrayed.

Mrs Laird further claimed that because of her good relationships with the staff, there had been a decline in the days of sickness absence at all levels of staff.

Anyone listening to the opening comments of Cllr Fidgeon in the Town Hall would have thought that everyone who worked in the council offices had the same opinion of Mrs Laird as that portrayed by him. But his comments were far from the truth. Several officers had contacted me during 2002 and 2003 to express support for Mrs Laird, although now it seems for various reasons, they wish to remain anonymous.

An email from an officer to Mrs Laird was copied to me. This is what it said.

> "December 2003
> Christine, I would like to say how brave and considerate for you to come to our office and issue those sentiments and words of encouragement. As you stated, it is vitally important to pull together in order to work towards a common goal and in doing so maximise the benefits to the Borough as a whole. With this in mind, I look forward to continuing to provide a first rate service under your directorship. Finally, as I did not get the opportunity to say it, welcome back and good wishes for a super Christmas and a prosperous New Year.
> Adrian".

Undoubtedly, there was no difficulty with operating a good working relationship in that particular department, and what is more, the senior officer was not afraid to go into print on behalf of his staff.

If the email is taken as an example, then there is reason to believe that the alleged problems were more to do with Cllr McKinlay than with Mrs Laird.

If one senior officer felt so supportive of the MD, then it is possible that there were others who may have felt the same, but were not prepared to come forward.

It also raises the question again of how one small group of people could spend the bulk of their time, spending council taxpayers' money pursuing a female employee to the highest court in the land on the premise that they couldn't establish a working relationship with her.

The answer to this question is still the same as it was earlier, too many people saw an opportunity to 'jump on a bandwagon' that once it started to roll it was difficult to stop, and equally as hard to get off it.

As for the legal fraternity – they couldn't believe their luck.

The only outcome that came out of the Town Hall meeting was the SWRA advising the Leader of the Council that should he remain determined to go ahead, then he should appoint a Panel of Members to conduct a Preliminary Investigation into the allegations that had been made by both sides.

CHAPTER 18

The Long Journey To The High Court

'Curiouser and curiouser!' cried Alice.
Alice's Adventures in Wonderland (1865) ch2

By Lewis Carroll

I found it curious, to say the least, that during the period of the dispute between the Managing Director (MD) and the Leader of the Council, the Monitoring Officer (MO) appeared to be representing both the MD and the Leader of the Council at the same time. One could argue that on a point of principle the MO was obliged to do this. On the other hand, it is hard to visualise a solicitor in a court of law representing both the accused and the accuser. However, this is what he was doing, although at a later stage in the dispute he withdrew from some of the meetings on the basis that he had a prejudicial interest.

He subsequently issued a formal complaint against the MD.

Meanwhile on Monday 31st March 2003 a report appeared in the *Gloucestershire Echo* claiming that a "massive rift" existed between the MD and Cllr McKinlay. The MD in a letter to the editor Anita Syvret on April 3rd refuted the claim, but she acknowledged that political leaders and their staff often had differences of opinion about conflicting viewpoints. Mrs Laird also made it clear to the editor that in spite of this 'they were both working for the benefit of Cheltenham and its residents'.

The local press report clearly had local people talking, not least because most people in Cheltenham were unaware of the animosity that existed behind the closed doors of Cheltenham Borough Council.

The report claimed that the MD had suggested to the Leader of the Council that they should issue a joint statement in the *Echo* 'admitting that there were difficulties that had to be resolved, but at the same time, point out that they were both prepared to resolve the difficulties and to protect the council's good name'.

The matter was of such importance that the MD invited Messrs Wiggins & Co, a firm of local solicitors, to prepare a possible joint letter to the *Gloucestershire Echo* that would be acceptable to both parties.

From the letters I have read, the MD was willing to accept the solicitor's suggested letter, but Cllr McKinlay, as wary as ever not to give the impression to anyone in the outside world that he was ready to accept any compromise with the MD, insisted that the following text should be included.

"I am prepared to sign the joint letter in order to reduce the risk of further damage to the Council being caused by the report in Monday's newspaper, but on the condition that my doing so indicates no further intention. The 'difficulties' to which the Echo report refers must be resolved soon. The letter must not be used, or referred to, in any way in connection with the resolution of those difficulties".

Considering the difficulties the council were experiencing, the letter could hardly be regarded as a first step in the march towards reconciliation.

In fact, the opposite was the truth. By looking at correspondence between the MD and the MO during April 2003 it could be seen that the MD had learned from a third party that the Leader of the Council and Cabinet members had 'appointed the South West Regional Assembly (SWRA) with a remit to initiate negotiations to terminate the MD's employment on behalf of the council'.

Another curious situation; if this unusual arrangement with the SWRA had been set up on behalf of the council, then surely the council members should have debated it in the normal way, and if in agreement, would have approved it. They did not do so, therefore, it was either a bogus attempt to put further pressure on the MD to leave, or to make her position even more untenable than it had already become.

Were the SWRA aware of the letter prepared by the firm of solicitors: more importantly, had they been made aware of the inclusion of the text by the Leader of the Council? If they were aware of these facts, surely they should have taken them into consideration before they decided to accede to the council's proposals?

A local authority has rules and procedures, a Constitution and a Code of Conduct, which ensures that the elected members conform at all times to the correct procedures when dealing with council business. For good measure, Parliament has passed several Local Government Acts that 'make provision with respect to the functions and procedures of local authorities' and these are legally binding on the council and its members.

Why, you may ask, did the Leader and the Cabinet not go through the proper procedures, or even involve the opposition group leaders, or seek advice from other statutory officers of the council, before embarking on such a madcap proposal?

I certainly had not been approached by the Leader or any member of his Cabinet.

Nonetheless, I did try to find out the reasons for the Cabinet wanting to terminate the MD's contract of employment. Not surprisingly, it turned out to be an impossible task, probably because the Cabinet members didn't know themselves. In my opinion, it was important for the allegations to be made known so that the charges were clear in everyone's minds.

I also needed to discuss with my PAB group colleagues the details of the allegations and whether they were based on facts and could be supported. I also wanted my councillor colleagues to know that any attempt to terminate the employment of a statutory officer, including an offer of a financial settlement, could possibly be illegal.

The Cabinet were treading a dangerous path, but who was advising them?

When trying to tease out what the allegations were, I was told that the Leader of the Council and the Cabinet had concerns about the MD's ability to do the job she had been engaged to do. This was absurd: the appraisal panel, chaired by Cllr McKinlay, had recently undertaken a six month appraisal of the MD and had come to the conclusion that she had done an excellent job.

This is well documented in an earlier chapter.

When I reminded my informer of the appraisal, I was told in what only could be described as an afterthought, 'the Cabinet also had concerns about the MD's conduct'.

This was getting more curious as time went on – this was the first occasion I had heard anyone mention that there was something unacceptable with the conduct of the MD. Was this something to do with the way she was managing the day-to-day business of the council, or did they have evidence that the MD's conduct was such that it was contrary to the officer and members' Code of Conduct?

Either way, it was a serious charge and one that should have been relayed to council members so that the allegation could be investigated.

Once again, it seemed that the anti-Laird 'brigade' were 'clutching at straws', looking for any excuse that might be used to terminate the employment of the managing director. What was more frightening; it was the same people who had been in control of Cheltenham Borough Council during other 'dark periods' for the town. [The investment of £22.5 million of council taxpayers' money on the Stock Market in 1991 in the hope that it would produce a profit is just one example]. More about this and other disastrous events attributed to them will appear in a later chapter; and now, like the 'Gadarene swine', the same people appeared to be in another headlong rush to go over yet another cliff.

It would almost certainly end in the same dire result for Cheltenham, the council and the townspeople, just as it had done before.

Unfortunately, I had not been able to see all the letters that had passed between the MD and her correspondents. Those I did see proved to be extremely useful.

She referred to the same question that I had posed about the strange connection that appeared to exist between the MO, the Leader of the Council and the MD.

In reply to a letter from the MO dated 8th April 2003, she made it clear at the beginning of her letter that she was fully committed to ensuring that the council acted properly and in accordance with procedures and the statutory regulations at all times.

The next paragraph of the MD's letter reads as follows *"In your letter you ask whether I have recently sought external legal advice regarding my personal and legal position"*.

Why had the MO posed the question?

Had he heard that a 'grievance procedure' was being undertaken and in his usual roundabout fashion he was 'hinting' about legal advice, but his question was incomplete? He had not named the person in his letter who was the subject of a grievance procedure, but why not.

If the letter had identified it was the managing director then I am sure she would have reminded the MO in her reply that there was no provision in the council's

Constitution that allowed a grievance procedure to be pursued against the Head of Paid Service.

If the MO's letter had made it clear that it was the MD who was the subject of a grievance procedure, then she would have wasted no time in getting 'legal advice', either from her trade union or from some other source.

April 2003 was turning out to be a memorable month for the MD – the threat of termination, a possible 'illegal' financial offer to leave the council, a number of allegations about her conduct and now the threat of a grievance procedure against her. What else could be drummed up against her?

For anyone in a managerial role it is difficult to combat all these things at the same time, but in the top position of managing director of a large organisation, it must be almost impossible. The situation for Mrs Laird must have been unbearable, not least because she knew that in the early years of her employment she had been a successful holder of the post, yet as time went on it was clear that in spite of her early successes, she was under extreme pressure from forces that were ranged against her.

If she expected the Board of Directors to support her then she was disappointed; as the dispute continued, the support she should have expected from them was not forthcoming.

Even the Human Resources (HR) department, who had a duty of care towards the MD, should have been taking a leading role in the disorder that was prevailing, yet they failed to measure up to the standard of care that a personnel department would be expected to deliver.

Whether this failure was deliberate and part of the 'plot' we shall never know, but it probably encouraged some of the council's senior and middle managers to endorse the actions of the Executive Cabinet. It was the same managers who had been supportive of her assertive style of management in the early part of her employment; some managers had even referred to it at the time, as being a 'breath of fresh air'.

Not surprisingly, in April 2003 Mrs Laird decided to lodge a formal complaint with The Standards Board for England (SBE) on the failure of the Leader of the Council to treat people with respect, of damaging the reputation of the office of Leader, and using his position improperly and misusing the resources of the local authority.

On Thursday 1st May 2003, the *Gloucestershire Echo* printed a headline "Pay-off offer causes uproar. Has council's MD been asked to go?"

The local newspaper claimed "they had been made aware that a six-figure pay-off offer had been made to Mrs Laird although the opposition group leaders revealed that the offer had been made without their knowledge".

When Cllr McKinlay was asked to comment the *Echo* reported that he said "the claims were poppycock". But, history and evidence has confirmed that a 'pay-off' offer was made, which raises the question about his truthfulness and the validity of other statements made by him during the period of the dispute.

The Conservative, Labour and PAB Group Leaders were in no doubt that the offer had been made and promptly complained to the SBE. They followed this up by writing an open letter to the people of Cheltenham, which was published by the local newspaper.

The *Gloucestershire Echo* report took up nearly two pages of print. It concentrated on the news that the opposition group leaders had complained to the SBE about the Cabinet members making decisions behind closed doors and involving themselves in 'staffing issues'. The *Echo* also reported that the letter to the SBE also claimed that a severance payment had been made to a member of staff without consulting the appropriate officers or having any regards to the legality or financial implications of their actions.

The local newspaper contacted each opposition group leader once the letter had been sent to the SBE. I told the reporter that I had listened very carefully to the words of Cllr Duncan Smith, who had been chairman of the Structural Review Committee, and also to Mrs Laird's catalogue of complaints about the Cabinet members' behaviour. I told the reporter 'if I had been a radio or TV scriptwriter, it would have been impossible to have written the script because it was so unbelievable'.

Cllr Smith, in his press interview, stressed the point that 'senior officers had complained to him about pressures and bullying from members of the Executive and because of this and the alleged financial irregularities, he felt obliged to inform the SBE'.

Cllr McKinlay on the other hand, when approached by the local press, informed them that 'he was entirely confident that any inquiry by the SBE will vindicate his actions and the actions of his Cabinet members'.

The comment should be carefully considered and examined; 'his actions and the actions of his Cabinet members will be vindicated'.

He was not saying that the reported abuse and the illegal offer of cash to end the employment of the managing director did not take place; he was saying that when the time comes his actions and those of his colleagues would be seen to be of such little importance that they would be rejected by the SBE.

The comments were not a denial so they should be regarded as confirmation that the actions of abuse and the misuse of public money did actually take place.

The *Gloucestershire Echo*, as fair as always, finished the article by reminding its readers that Cllr McKinlay had been elected to the council in 1991. They added that it was one of the council's most controversial periods.

The *Echo* claimed that Cllr McKinlay "was a leading light in the Liberal Democrat team responsible for the 'Noddy Train' fiasco and the decision to invest £22.5 million on the stock market, which ended up costing the council a fortune".

The *Echo* also told its readers that his achievements included the regeneration of the St James railway station site and that "he pioneered the Arle Court park & ride scheme".

But who gained most from the St James development? Waitrose certainly did, but a former Liberal Democrat councillor Sally Stringer, wrote to me in February 2011 to reveal that the Waitrose store "...was a done deal before it ever got to the Liberal Democrat group". The former councillor alleged that the Liberal Democrats set up a working group in 2000, which included Cllr McKinlay and Cllr Jordan, to look at the possibility of regenerating the former town centre railway station site; it became the Waitrose store.

Sally Stringer's email to me revealed another facet of the way the Liberal Democrats conducted their business during this period of office. 'First, set up a working group, do any deals that are necessary and then call the rest of the political party together and report to them the detail of the agreement reached between the developer, senior officers and members of the working group'.

At what point in the negotiations could the other elected members of the council expect to be consulted? In this case, not at all; as Sally Stringer suggested – it was a 'done deal'.

Colin Nye, the chief executive at the time, had engaged a well-known town centre development expert by the name of Reg Ward to reach a deal with representatives from the John Lewis organisation.

My source tells me that after the 'deal' was done, the chairman of the Economic Development & Regeneration Committee, Cllr Barry Anderson, briefed the Liberal Democrat members about the 'deal', which included transferring council-owned land to Waitrose. Some members were unhappy about this.

According to Sally Stringer one or two members objected to the way the 'deal' had been undertaken, accusing the senior members of the party of acting undemocratically and threatened to vote against the proposal should it go before the full council.

On the last point, according to Sally Stringer, the chairman reminded the committee that Liberal Democrat members would be expected to follow the 'party line' when it went before the council and there should be no dissenters. Thinking that everyone was of the same mind, he posed the question – "We all want John Lewis to come to Cheltenham, don't we?"

Not everyone agreed; she claimed, there was unease amongst members and there was a whiff of deceit pervading the atmosphere because an important 'deal' for the town had been done without all the members of the committee being involved.

Not only had members of the committee been excluded, but none of the opposition group leaders had been made aware that clandestine meetings had taken place and decisions taken by just a few senior Liberal Democrat members of the council.

Cllr John Todman a Conservative member and a local solicitor, tried hard to forestall the 'deal' until all details of the discussions between John Lewis and the council had been examined. John had a strong opinion there was something wrong with the deal, but any questions put by him in the council chamber, or by any other member of the council for that matter, were either deflected by officers, or given negative answers by the Cabinet member.

In support of John Todman's line of questioning, I wanted to know on behalf of the PAB Group, who had been responsible for the engagement of Reg Ward and how much were the council paying him; who would benefit from this so-called 'deal' when Waitrose constructed their superstore on high value council-owned development land?

Mr Nye told councillors that Reg Ward was an expert in town centre development and the town were lucky to have acquired his services. He also told councillors that the benefits that a John Lewis store would bring to Cheltenham would far outweigh the employment costs of Mr Reg Ward.

I didn't get an answer to my question about the appointment of Mr Ward, and Cheltenham didn't get a John Lewis store; all it got was a Waitrose supermarket. At the end of the day, although it was some time later, councillors were eventually told that the high value development land had been seconded to John Lewis as part of the so-called 'deal'.

We were told that not a penny changed hands.

Waitrose was constructed in 2001 and opened in 2002.

According to the former councillor Sally Stringer, there was much disquiet in the Liberal Democrat party. Even the local Member of Parliament got involved by giving the deal his approval. He even went further with his involvement; prior to the council meeting he ordered the former councillor and others to stop bickering and to follow the 'party line'. He supported disciplinary action against anyone who refused to do so.

Liberal Democrats boast about their belief in local democracy, but on this occasion the senior members and the local MP showed very little of it towards their own members when they expressed a different point of view.

Before the council meeting took place, Cllrs Sally Stringer and Deborah Griggs were summoned to attend a disciplinary hearing, which paradoxically, was held in the council chamber.

Both had expressed a view that when the council members debated the proposal they would object and vote against it. Their reason being the proposal was not in the best interests of Cheltenham people.

According to Sally Stringer, the whole hearing was a farce. It was conducted by Cllr Alexis Cassin, a senior member of the party, who asked each of the dissidents whether they had anything to say for themselves. They repeated that they would vote against the 'party line' because the interests of Cheltenham would not be best served. Furthermore, they objected to the original decision being taken by a few members of the party behind closed doors.

Cllr Surgenor, a member of the disciplinary team, took it upon himself to be particularly nasty to the two councillors, accusing them of disloyalty to the political party and reminded them of their duties as Liberal Democrat councillors and what it entailed.

Another member of the 'disciplinary team' according to Sally Stringer 'who was simply vile', was Cllr McKinlay.

She wrote in her email to me dated 19th February 2011, that after listening to Cllr

McKinlay's outburst at the hearing, she came to the conclusion "he was arrogant, pig ignorant and a bully".

Apparently, both councillors stood their ground and in spite of the way they had been treated, they repeated that they were going to vote against the proposal for all the reasons they had previously mentioned.

Both councillors were then formally reprimanded.

Whilst the principle of park and ride is a sound one, the facility at the out-of-town site called Arle Court ran at an average loss of around £75,000 per annum for the first ten years of its operation.

The site was constructed on green belt land against local opposition; and in spite of questions about the initial construction costs, none were ever revealed.

It was not a financial asset for Cheltenham Borough Council or the County Council as was first proclaimed in order to get planning approval.

So the achievements of the Leader of the Council expressed by the *Gloucestershire Echo* on 1st May 2003, (the construction of Waitrose and the establishment of the park & ride facility), when set against the cost of the 'Noddy Train' and the loss of £22.5 million spent in a gamble on the stock markets, would indicate that the excesses of the Liberal Democrat administration at that particular time far outweighed the advantages of its alleged achievements.

A letter from the MD dated 25th April 2003 to the council's MO expressed her concerns about the conduct of Cabinet members.

In the letter, she asked the MO in his capacity as Monitoring Officer to investigate her complaint and report back to her. She informed him *"There have been three separate occasions when members of the Cabinet, namely Cllr McKinlay and the Cabinet Deputy Cllr Stuart-Smith, have invited me to consider my employment position with the local authority".*

Whatever the opinions expressed at the time and subsequently, the powers to suspend or dismiss a managing director rests with the full council.

This fact is repeated in the letter of 25th April 2003 when the MD informed the MO that she had sought the advice of Mr Peter Keith-Lucas, a specialist local government partner with solicitors Wragg & Co, who had confirmed this point. He qualified his advice by referring Mrs Laird to Section 101 of the Local Government Act, 1972, which allows a council "to discharge any of its functions to a committee, sub-committee or an officer, but not to the Executive (Cabinet) or to an elected member of the council".

Based on the advice, Mrs Laird believed that "the offer of £63,000 by the Cabinet executive members on condition that she did not return to work on the following Tuesday, could have been unlawful".

The MD's letter to the MO was long and detailed and it is right that the salient points are made. It appears that David Perry, the Section 151 Officer (Head of Financial Services) was unaware of the £63,000 offer to the managing director.

This fact leads to three important points.

*

1. Had he been consulted about the size of the payment?
2. How had the figure of £63,000 been arrived at?
3. Had the figure been plucked out of the air and by whom?

But, as the MD mentioned in her letter,

"It is difficult to understand how the Section 151 Officer could lawfully meet his statutory responsibility in approving such an offer retrospectively. It also begs the question of how members of the Cabinet intended to secure making such a payment had I accepted it. In consequence, I am of the view that in authorising or otherwise agreeing that the SWRA could offer the Head of Paid Service a severance payment in the absence of any prior knowledge on the part of the Section 151 Officer, then the Cabinet were, presumably, proposing to require the Section 151 Officer to commit an unlawful act.

I am forced to conclude that the Cabinet has exposed the Council to an unacceptable degree of risk and in so doing you have a responsibility to report unlawful acts reported in this letter to the Council as a matter of urgency.

I am concerned about the way I am and continue to be treated by the Cabinet, and in particular by their decision to instruct you to convene a politically balanced investigation panel, to hear unspecified charges against me, which my trade union representative, Richard Penn, advised me would be the case if I did not agree to accept the Cabinet's offer of £63,000 in return for my agreement that the Council could terminate my contract of employment.

I am firmly of the view that senior members of the council have misused their office and repeatedly breached the national code of conduct."

The letter was copied to the District Auditor (DA) and the Section 151 Officer.

I was not aware of the letter until 2010 and I was surprised to read that the opposition group leaders had not been included in the distribution of the letter. In spite of this, the letter clearly showed that the MD was having serious difficulties with Cabinet members. Remember too, at the same time she was managing to run a local authority, which had become embroiled in changes brought about by the new Leader and Cabinet system.

The MO was told by the MD that if she did not receive confirmation from him that the council would be informed of her concerns, she would have no alternative but to seek the assistance of the DA.

[The DA has the power to investigate a local authority and upon its conclusion can carry out and publish what is called a Public Interest Report (PIR)]

In April 2003, in spite of what was going on around them in the council offices, no-one working there or members of the public would have thought for one moment that a PIR was remotely possible as a result of the dispute between the MD and the Cabinet.

They certainly would not have thought at the time, that in March 2010 the world renowned independent auditors KPMG, would be asked to carry out an audit of the accounts of Cheltenham Borough Council? And the reason for the investigation would be the sheer scale of the financial costs incurred as a result of the dispute; and the level of interest being expressed by members of the general public who had become more than just inquisitive bystanders.

But that is what happened and there will be more of this in a later chapter.

Because the MO took external legal advice from Counsel, (more cost to the taxpayers) it took seven days before the MD received a reply to her letter.

The letter dated 2nd May 2003 rejected most of the content of MD's letter dated 25th April with one exception: Counsel confirmed that the dismissal of the managing director was a matter for the full council and no-one else.

Counsel also advised that the actions of the Leader and Cabinet involving the SWRA in discussions about the possible termination of employment of the managing director did not mean they were acting improperly.

The Advice from Counsel was based on the requirements of the various Local Government Acts, which then begs the question why was this cost for external advice needed when the council's own legal department should have been competent enough to provide the same answers. It also begs the question on whose authority was the advice sought by the MO and how much did it cost?

As the dispute progressed steadily towards a showdown at the High Court, the Cabinet and the MO became more reliant on advice from external legal sources. We will also learn that the advice, which started from a low level ended up with a visit to the council by Queen's Counsel (QC) who wanted to be assured that the advice he had given was being heeded.

Advice from a QC is not cheap. And knowing that external advice whether good or poor, was going to be expensive, it is worth repeating the question on whose authority was the external legal advice sought. Was it an individual or a council department responsible for the authorisation? Did anyone have any idea how much external legal advice was needed and how much it would eventually cost? Were the council members involved and if they were, did they have any idea, or even care what the final cost of legal advice would be?

These were important questions at the time, and answers should have been demanded.

On reflection, I still find it hard to believe that a council of grown men and women couldn't deal with a simple situation of two people not liking each other at their place of work. A common occurrence at a place of work, but it became increasingly obvious that the most vociferous members of the S&SSC did not want to find a solution to the problem.

Instead of doing what was required, both officers and members of the council took sides, which only helped to make a bad situation become even worse.

In spite of this, evidence shows there was common ground on a number of issues and a compromise could have been reached without too much trouble, but for reasons which are becoming clearer, the Leader of the Council was not prepared to concede, neither was he prepared to stand down from his post.

The inevitable result was a stalemate.

It would have been so much easier for the two sides to have drawn a line under the dispute, shaken hands and agreed that the work of the council was more important than the hard positions they had created. But that was not to be.

> "He never wants anything but what's right and fair; only when you come to settle what's right and fair, it's everything that he wants and nothing that you want. And that's his idea of a compromise".
>
> Tom Brown's Schooldays by Thomas Hughes (1857)

Thomas Hughes was a lawyer, politician and writer.

If anyone thought that the month of July 2003 was going to be easier than the earlier months then they were going to be disappointed.

The MO was dealing with two major issues, the possible dismissal of the MD and a possible disciplinary procedure that could be used against her should the council agree.

Members of the S&SSC were well aware of the external legal advice that had been sought by the MO, but the seeking of a Counsel's Opinion was a further extension of the need to obtain legal advice on a matter associated with the dispute.

Anyone would know that obtaining Counsel's Opinion is costly and is, as the title suggests, an opinion of an individual on facts presented to him for consideration. Counsel opinion is usually sought by legal officers who are unsure of their own opinions. Sometimes it is sought on the basis that there is a certain amount of inevitability of a case finishing up in a High Court, so the need for a barrister's involvement is taken early. Both scenarios were evident in the CBC v Laird case.

Following questions from Cllr Duncan Smith, the councillor received a letter dated 3rd July 2003, informing him that the MO had sought Counsel's advice on 'a number of important matters touching on the present difficulties between the MD and the Cabinet'.

Cllr Smith was told that Counsel had provided a Legal Opinion on the instructions of the MO concerning discipline and dismissal.

The letter was addressed to Cllr Smith and not copied to me or the Labour Group Leader.

However, Counsel explained that the appointment and dismissal of a managing director of a local authority was a matter of public law and quoted the appropriate local government legislation.

He further explained that whilst the appointment and dismissal of a Head of Paid Service was the responsibility of the full council, the Executive must be involved and their approval sought before any appointment or dismissal is made.

Regarding a disciplinary matter, Counsel stated that 'no disciplinary action could be taken against the Head of Paid Service except in accordance with the recommendation and report of a Designated Independent Person' (DIP).

Considering the importance of the content contained in Counsel's Opinion, it is difficult to understand why the MO decided not to send a copy of the information to the PAB Group, or to the Labour Group. It would have ensured that we were all given the same information and would be 'singing from the same hymn sheet'.

On 15th July 2003, the MD informed the opposition group leaders by email that the Leader of the Council had spoken to the MO and informed him that he intended to take a report to the July council meeting proposing the establishment of an investigatory panel with powers to suspend the Head of Paid Service.

The report would include the Leader's intention to appoint an independent investigator to investigate alleged 'concerns' relating to the MD's conduct.

Unfortunately, no contact had been made with the other group leaders by the Leader of the Council before he had spoken to the MO, so there was no opportunity for the group leaders to set up a meeting to discuss the background of the report with him.

If we had been given the opportunity to discuss it, I am sure the opposition group leaders would have wanted to know the reasons that caused the Leader to take such a drastic step: and they would certainly have wanted to see evidence based information regarding the alleged 'concerns' relating to the MD's conduct in order to come to a sensible conclusion.

I have no doubt in my mind that had we been given the opportunity to discuss these matters with the Leader, we may have persuaded him to take a step back and to consider other options before he went down a possibly long and tortuous path.

So once again, the opposition group leaders had been ignored and denied the opportunity to talk through what was clearly a crisis looming, just as we tried desperately to do so on 19th March 2003, albeit without success.

Readers will recall that the Leader of the Council did not attend an arranged meeting with opposition group leaders in March 2003, to discuss the serious problem between him and the MD. We will never know whether this would have averted the crisis that followed, but just four months later, history it seemed was repeating itself. This time, it was the Leader of the Council who had the opportunity to avert a possible crisis, but he did not even bother to tell the opposition leaders of his ill-judged intentions.

Was it not the Leader of the Council in the early part of the new Liberal Democrat administration in 2002 who wanted to re-establish the Group Leaders/Managing Director meetings so that problems and difficulties could be ironed out before they became serious matters?

This fact was recorded in an earlier chapter.

Another email from the MO to the MD on 18th July 2003 informed her that the Leader and the Cabinet had two 'concerns' about the MD's conduct. The letter said that she had "misinformed the Leader and other members of the Cabinet" and had "intentionally sought to undermine the Leader's position, members of the Cabinet and some of your fellow officers".

A vague statement giving no information to support the alleged 'concerns' or when any of the occasions had taken place.

Once again, the opposition group leaders were not included in the distribution of the email so it came as a shock when I first read it in 2010.

So this was what all the fuss was about – the Cabinet had "concerns" about the words and actions of the MD – not earth shattering stuff, nor quite on the same level as the alleged Zinoviev Letter that was largely responsible for the overthrow of the first Labour Government, but it was sufficient to start a long drawn out series of legal and non-legal wrangles that cost the taxpayers of Cheltenham in excess of £2 million by the time the trial ended in 2009.

Because the MD was not in the same financial position as the council, she was unable to seek expensive legal advice and she relied heavily on whatever advice her trade union, the Association of Local Authority Chief Executives (ALACE), could provide for her.

On 18th July 2003, Mr Richard Penn the Association's consultant wrote to Mr Gerald Ford, the council's Monitoring Officer refuting his claim that she was in dispute with Cheltenham Borough Council.

Mr Penn reminded the MO that from the beginning of the dispute she had been unhappy about the conduct of some members of the Cabinet and, as a result, had made a formal complaint to the Standards Board for England (SBE).

He further reminded the MO he was well aware that Mrs Laird's views are shared by other members of your council.

On the matter of the disciplinary action to be taken against the MD, Mr Penn criticised the MO 'for remaining silent on the alleged grounds for any proposed action'. In Mr Penn's opinion, 'to talk about disciplinary action whilst withholding information to justify such an assertion, flies in the face of natural justice: it was also contrary to the council's own standard practices in dealing with such cases'.

Continuing, Mr Penn told the MO that from ALACE's perspective, the matter now raised doubts about the MO's own role in the dispute. Why had he sought Counsel's Opinion regarding a disciplinary matter, yet appeared to deny the MD access to the same best practice? "This is discriminatory and certainly not what ALACE would expect from any local authority", he wrote.

Readers will know that I had raised the same matter earlier in the dispute, so it was gratifying to know that someone in such a high position in a respected trade union held the same view.

Mr Penn's letter to the MO consisted of four pages of criticism of him, the council and Counsel's Opinion. It is important to quote some of the content of the letter in order to show how one-sided the dispute had become: it also showed that there was a great deal wrong with the way the council appeared to be pursuing their 'prey' aided and abetted, it seemed, by the MO.

This is an extract:

> "ALACE is also concerned that you do not appear to consider the alleged breach of Mrs Laird's employment contract by the Leader of your Council to be a matter of significance. It is totally unacceptable that the clear breach of her contract of employment by the Leader of your Council is being ignored and that the Council has not been informed of the Leader's failure in this regard.
>
> Counsel's Opinion also suggests that he has been requested to comment on whether he considers the Leader's breach of the contract to be of 'any relevance to a dismissal on disciplinary grounds'. This suggests that Counsel have been asked to respond to you in the context of a very specific brief, which again implies that attempts are being made to deny Christine Laird the usual rights afforded to a Head of Paid Service. It is difficult not to infer that the outcome of any independent investigation into her conduct is irrelevant as her fate has been politically pre-determined and that you are aware that this is the case.
>
> ALACE is extremely concerned that Counsel's Opinion appears to reflect a brief that implies that Christine Laird's dismissal is a desired outcome. This is wholly contrary to the principles of natural justice, best practice or national guidelines for dealing with the Head of Paid Service.
>
> ALACE also objects to the fact that you have stated that you intend treating the Leader's alleged 'concerns' about the Managing Director as an entirely separate issue to the current investigation by the Standards Board for England into his conduct and that of his Cabinet colleagues towards our member".

On 24th July 2003, Mr Penn wrote directly to each member of the council on behalf of ALACE stating he wanted to put on record *"… its concerns about the treatment of your Head of Paid Service by the Leader of the Council and other members of his Cabinet"*.

Members were informed by Mr Penn that he was still waiting for a reply to his letter dated 18th July from the MO and enclosed a copy of his letter for information.

The letter also referred to the fact that Mr Penn had seen the report the Leader is submitting to Council on 28th July for its consideration. Having read the report he wanted the members

> "… to be aware of a number of relevant matters, which have a very important bearing on the decision you are being asked to take as Christine Laird's employers. Over recent months the Leader and a number of his Cabinet colleagues have been 'encouraging' Mrs Laird to leave the employment of the Council. On March 5th 2003, with no prior warning, the Deputy Leader asked her what it would take and cost for Mrs Laird to leave the Council's employment. When asked to justify his request he claimed that the Cabinet believed the Liberal Democrats would not win the next election if she remained as the Head of Paid Service, and the Leader 'did not like her.'"

When I read the letter from Richard Penn, together with the copy of the letter he had written to the MO on 18th July, I felt elated. I was sure that councillors, or at least some of them, having read for the first time about the serious issues that had been going on without their knowledge, would respond in a positive manner.

There was no reaction – their lack of response was symptomatic of what had gone on before – minds made up by one-sided information.

Another letter from Richard Penn to members dated 24th July was just as descriptive as his letter to the MO on the 18th July. I have quoted parts of it so that readers can understand the petty issues that had been deployed, long before the decision was made to go to the High Court.

Mr Penn wrote:

"At a meeting with me on March 25th 2003, Councillors Mrs Hay and David Fidgeon claimed that the Cabinet had concerns about 'staff morale' and Mrs Laird's 'management style'. These claims were addressed in a letter from me on 27th March that demonstrated that there was no objective evidence for this and that the incident on the 5th March was contrary to employment law and a specific breach of Mrs Laird's contract of employment and statutory rights. No more was then heard until 15th April 2003 when the Cabinet alleged that it had concerns about her conduct, but refused to specify the nature of those concerns.

On Friday 18th April 2003 I was contacted by a representative of the South West Regional Assembly (SWRA) who made an 'off the record' suggestion on behalf of the Cabinet of a payment of £63,000 to the Managing Director if she left sooner rather than later and signed a Compromise Agreement.

I was left in no doubt that if she was not prepared to negotiate around this opening 'offer' then the Leader intended to convene a politically balanced Panel to investigate concerns about her conduct. Not surprisingly, Mrs Laird has notified the Standards Board for England of these events.

I have to remind each of you as Mrs Laird's employers that the appointment and dismissal of the Head of Paid Service of a local authority is not simply a matter of contract, but also a matter of public law.

Mrs Laird believes that throughout this period, the majority of Council members have not been aware of or party to these events. She wishes to stress that she does not consider she is in dispute with the Council, but she is concerned at how she has been treated by the Leader and a number of Cabinet colleagues.

Embarking on a disciplinary process in respect of the Head of Paid Service should not be contemplated lightly and must be a decision taken by the whole Council.

ALACE considers that the Cabinet has usurped the authority of the Council in its approaches to Mrs Laird and that its actions could potentially bring the Council as a whole into disrepute. It has failed to comply with the requirement to demonstrate fairness in decision-making and ALACE is forced to conclude that the Cabinet's actions are either politically motivated (an unlawful act) or are the consequence of a personal vendetta by individual members of the Council. Such actions, if intended to achieve a party political purpose, contravene the Code of Conduct as well as the Local Government Housing Act 1989".

A powerful letter and to the point, but did it have any effect on the Liberal Democrat councillors? The evidence shows that it did not. They had a reasonable majority in the council chamber and they could have changed the course of events, but they had no desire to do so.

The senior members of the party, with advice from the MO, could have developed an exit strategy as a fall back should anything go wrong, but I found no evidence of this in any official papers. Of course, if determination to succeed whatever the cost is uppermost in the minds of a determined group, then an exit strategy would have been the last thing the Liberal Democrats would have considered.

My suggestion earlier that July 2003 was not going to be an easy month was turning out to be true. More people had become involved, which indicated to me that the point of no return had already been reached.

On 25th July 2003 Mr Chris Huckle (Group Director, Social & Community) sent an email to Cllr McKinlay on behalf of the Board of Directors.

The email was a criticism of the Leader of the Council for sending out a letter on 17th July to all members of staff via the email system.

Mr Huckle said in his email that the Board had no desire to comment on the content of Cllr McKinlay's letter, but they did have concerns that the email involved the MO and as such 'you may have inadvertently breached the members' Code of Conduct or the Protocol for Member/Officer relations. As a result, the Board of Directors was seeking legal advice on both issues'.

The final paragraph of Mr Huckle's email read as follows:

"We have received copies recently of several emails from you to the Managing Director. We feel that it is inappropriate to copy us in on these communications. We would not wish to find ourselves in a position where we receive confidential information related to the Managing Director's employment with this Council."

Although I was not aware that the letter had been sent to council staff, the email from Chris Huckle did highlight a possible breach of the Code of Conduct, which was the main reason for the opposition group leaders complaining to the SBE in March 2003. Secondly, the fact that the Board of Directors were concerned that the MO had been mentioned by the Leader of the Council could indicate that there was after all, a close relationship going on between the Leader and the MO that was unhealthy for both sides; it was certainly questionable considering it involved the employment of the council's Head of Paid Service.

CHAPTER 19

The Cost Of Human Suffering

*'Our deeds determine us, as much as we determine our deeds; and until we know what
has been or will be the peculiar combination of outward with inward facts, which
constitute a man's critical actions, it will be better not to think ourselves
wise about his character.'*
Adam Bede (1859) chapter 29 By George Eliot

Monday 28th July 2003 was a warm and pleasant day with people going about their business unaware of the drama that was about to unfold in the debating chamber of Cheltenham Borough Council.

Councillors getting ready for the meeting knew, but they viewed the forthcoming session with trepidation. They knew that they were about to discuss the alleged misconduct of the very person they had appointed to the top job of managing director the previous year.

Prior to the meeting, councillors had been informed by the Democratic Services Manager (DSM) that the report concerning agenda item 21 headed 'Staffing Matters' was not available 'as certain professional advice on its implications is being obtained'.

The reason behind the communication from the DSM was that councillors had received a copy of the letter from Berwin Leighton Paisner, a legal firm representing the MD, to the MO, warning him that "if the Council was to adopt the Leader's proposal we have no doubt that our client's rights will have been infringed".

And the solicitors went further, they warned the MO that "legal action would be taken in the event that the Leader's unlawful and misconceived proposal is adopted by the Council".

So the scene was set for a difficult afternoon, but in truth no-one had the faintest idea what would happen other than the fear that something may happen that might, just might, put everyone in a very difficult legal position.

The council meeting got underway and the previous minutes of 9th and 19th May and 23rd June 2003 were all read and approved by council members. If there had been problems during those previous two months, or any underlying problems between the Leader and the MD that needed addressing, they were not mentioned in any of the May and June minutes.

If any problems had been discussed then a report of those discussions would have been recorded in the appropriate minutes.

But the July 28th meeting turned out to be something quite different after all. Prior to any discussion of Item 21 the mayor, Cllr Barnes, adjourned the meeting to allow a private and lengthy discussion to take place between Mr David Fletcher of Counsel, the Group Leaders, the MO and the Section 151 Officer.

It was some time later before the mayor reconvened the meeting and discussion on item 21 began.

I should explain to readers that agenda item 21 was held under what is called in local government terms, 'an exempt matter', which means it can only be heard once the press and public have been excluded from the meeting. The jargon usually associated with it is the meeting took place 'behind closed doors'.

The minutes are not for publication (Local Government Act 1972) and are usually not very descriptive, and for reasons which have always baffled me, the committee and council members resist any proposals to change them, even when they are glaringly incorrect, or woolly. This fact was highlighted by KPMG in their Public Interest Report, which will appear in a later chapter.

Whilst I cannot reveal the content of the minutes of that meeting, even though eleven years have passed, I can summarise the main points of the discussion that took place.

Several members expressed a view that it was difficult to come to a reasonable decision when they had not been told the substance of the allegations against the MD until late on the previous Thursday night.

Whilst this was an important point, it was made known to them that the MD had not received a copy of the 'allegations' until earlier that day.

Some councillors complained to the mayor that if the information was correct then it was totally unacceptable.

The councillors received a long report detailing the various problems and a legal explanation about each one, but they had little time to study it.

Not surprisingly, some councillors expressed their concerns about the lack of justice and fairness, some quoted the Human Rights Act and the contravention of natural justice, but none of it had any effect on the outcome of the meeting.

The Section 151 Officer added to the debate by stating that he was unable to bring to the councillors' attention the financial implications of some of the issues: the MO claimed he was unable to give proper legal advice and supported a move put forward by a councillor that due to the lack of information, the matter should be deferred to the council meeting on 27th October 2003.

The MD showing signs of strain agreed that members should take notice of the advice from the senior officers and asked them to support the deferment.

From my point of view, it was a bit of a shambles and a non-event, but in supporting the proposal I did not lose sight of the fact that the drama we had participated in would be rehearsed and gone over again and again before we all re-assembled on October 27th to make a considered judgement on the facts presented to us.

There were those of course, who knew exactly where they wanted to go and nothing was going to stop them. Councillors with similar views to mine saw the early signs of trouble; with all the legal advice and visits by a prominent QC the odds on it all ending in a court of law was becoming greater. The rhetoric, which unfortunately you will not be able to read in the minutes, was quite appalling from some councillors, but I can assure readers that every attempt was made to stop the madness before any final decision was taken.

How the MD managed to cope with the strain and pressures put on her in the months leading up to the council meeting will remain a mystery. But as I have written above, the signs were beginning to appear, which in the circumstances was not surprising.

But, I write with anger as I tell the reader that even as the council meeting was taking place, anonymous letters were being put in the post room for members and on the council notice boards, making a series of unpleasant allegations about the MD and the job she had previously held at the Chartered Institute of Housing in 1997/98.

Fortunately, the letters and notices were discovered by officers and members before too much damage had been done, and the offensive material was removed.

But what kind of people are they that would do such a despicable thing?

When the inevitable investigation began one member of staff alleged that Cllr Lloyd Surgenor (Cabinet member) had been seen entering the post room with what appeared to be a full plastic carrier bag. And when he left the post room the bag was clearly empty.

The question is – did the bag contain the offending material, or did it contain something else? That is the question which unfortunately will never be answered.

Later that night the same anonymous letters that had been removed earlier were sent to all councillors via their email addresses under the name of Daphne Townsend. But, who was this person?

There was no-one named Daphne Townsend on the council's employment roll, so who was she, and who put her up to carrying out such a dirty trick?

We didn't have long to wait for an explanation. Cllr Paul McClain contacted the MD to explain that the Daphne Townsend email address was a name used by Nigel Jones, the Liberal Democrat Member of Parliament for Cheltenham.

Paul had previously worked in the M.P.'s office and claimed that he had seen the name used in email correspondence. This was an important fact.

What is equally important is that Cllrs David Fidgeon and Zoe Forbes also worked in the local M.P.'s office and it is not inconceivable that they too could have been involved in this unpleasant and sneaky business.

The revelation prompted Mrs Laird to take the letter and copies of the emails to the Central Police Station where a domain name search confirmed it was a name used by the office of Nigel Jones M.P. The Police contacted the Standards Board for England (SBE) who requested that the offending material should be sent to them and they would take the appropriate steps needed to deal with the matter.

What did the SBE do – absolutely nothing?

They had a duty of care, which they failed to exercise, they had evidence from the Police that showed that there was an attempt by some Liberal Democrat councillors to discredit the MD and they may have breached the council's Code of Conduct, yet they did absolutely nothing.

The SBE's incompetence in dealing with this important matter did not go by without comment during the CBC v Laird trial in 2009, which will be detailed in a later chapter.

The High Court judge ordered the council's Q.C. to contact the SBE and ask for the emails and letters to be released. The judge made it clear that if the SBE failed to do so he would issue a court order for their disclosure if they were not forthcoming.

The message came back from the SBE that all the documents relating to the complaints against the Leader and his Cabinet members had been destroyed because the investigation had been completed.

It is incredible that valuable documents concerning an important 'legal' matter and barely six years old had been destroyed by a Government department. This incompetence by the SBE and other flaws in their assessments will be examined later.

The sly and underhand attempt to plant false information about the MD on notice boards and in emails caused Cllr Duncan Smith, the Leader of the Conservative Group, to send an email to the MO and the Section 151 Officer on 30th July 2003, which was brief and to the point.

Referring to the anonymous letters, Cllr Smith said "... it was harassment and intimidation tactics and not relevant to Cheltenham Borough Council.

He also claimed "... the tactics only added weight to the claims by the MD and increased the exposure of the Borough Council".

The harassment and intimidation that Cllr Smith referred to, plus the ordeal of having to face the elected members whilst they discussed her possible suspension, was clearly too much for Christine Laird and it was taking its toll.

A visit to her doctor the following day resulted in Mrs Laird being signed off work for a period of two weeks on the grounds of stress reaction following the council meeting.

Coincidentally, the MD had pre-booked two weeks annual leave, which would take place following her sickness absence. Was it a holiday that she could enjoy, or did it turn out to be nothing more than a period of convalescence in order to overcome the stress and personal vilification heaped on her by those who did not like the way she was carrying out her job?

On 1st August 2003, the Group Director Marie Fallon, who was also a Board member, wrote to all group leaders informing them of the MD's sickness absence. She suggested that the group leaders or any of their members should not contact the MD at home in a working capacity during her sickness absence.

It was clear from the letter that the council took the MD's sickness absence seriously and we were told that Jo Pitman, Assistant Director Human Resources (AD/HR) would have regular contact with her.

August is the traditional month when council staff takes annual holiday, leaving a skeleton of staff to deal with the usual day-to-day matters. Nevertheless, it did not go unnoticed that the MD would be away from her place of work until the beginning of September.

Two other important points in the letter from Marie Fallon need to be mentioned. It was claimed that as a result of the outcome of the council meeting on July 28th, the MO had decided to seek the advice of Counsel on certain outstanding key issues.

He would instruct Queen's Counsel accordingly.

We were not told what the 'outstanding key issues' were and I do not recall them being mentioned in the council meeting.

But, instructing Queen's Counsel does not come cheap and the question that needed to be asked was 'on whose authority?'

The answer was found in another part of Marie Fallon's letter when she wrote that the council did not determine the recommendation in relation to financial matters contained in the 'implications report'. And further wrote that "it will be necessary to incur additional expenditure on further external legal and human resource advice in order to progress the matter." David Perry, the Section 151 Officer under his delegated powers, agreed to the expenditure of a further £20,000 from the contingency reserves in order to fund this external legal advice and to provide additional officer support.

This £20,000 was additional to what had already been spent on external legal advice, but opposition councillors had no idea what the total expenditure had been up to that point. What was clear was the expenditure was solely for legal advice, and what councillors should have realised at the time, was their determination to go to litigation would inevitably mean that the financial costs would soar. They knew this but they had no intention of letting it deter them from getting rid of the managing director. After all, it wasn't their money.

From the previous pages, readers would think that the only matter of any consequence debated at the July 28th council meeting was the agenda item 'staffing matters'. This was not the case; there were debates on the Financial Outturn for the period 2002 to 2003, communications by the mayor and the Leader of the Council, plus a joint report by the MD and the Group Director (Economy & Business Improvement) concerning Treasury Management.

Other items debated were the Housing Investment Programme, a Homelessness Strategy and the desilting of the town's popular Pittville Park Lake.

David Perry, Group Director (Economy & Business Improvement) gave a detailed report on the latest position regarding the Comprehensive Performance Assessment (CPA) and the process that Cheltenham Borough Council would need to follow.

On Corporate Governance there was a Statement of Assurance, which began with a reminder to councillors that *Cheltenham Borough Council was responsible for ensuring that its business is conducted in accordance with the law and proper standards, and that public money is safeguarded and properly accounted for, and used economically, efficiently and effectively'.*

The Statement further read: *'During the year, Cheltenham Borough Council has started to put in place appropriate management and reporting arrangements to enable it to satisfy itself that its approach to corporate governance is both adequate and effective in practice. Specifically, it is developing a risk management strategy, which will be implemented over the coming period.'*

Whilst the Statement reported on what had been achieved so far, it also stated that there were several aspects of the code of governance that still needed to be put in place, The Statement concluded with these words.

'We propose over the coming year to take steps to address the above matters to further enhance our corporate governance arrangements. We are satisfied that these steps will address the need for improvements that were identified in our initial review and we will review their implementation and operation as part of our first annual review.'

The Statement of Assurance was signed by Cllr Andrew McKinlay, the Leader of the Council and Christine Laird, Managing Director.

The extracts from the Statement of Assurance are significant. They show that important meetings had taken place over the year that involved senior officers of the council, including the MD and the Leader.

No doubt there were differences of opinion on the different issues when they were debated in committee, and, no doubt, heated discussions took place before the content of the various reports were agreed. So, what's new? This is what happens on a daily basis in other councils and it certainly happens in a more ferocious way in the world of industry and commerce.

There is no denying that the Leader didn't like the MD, but if the evidence of a well-run council meeting, plus written accounts of the various reports in the minutes are anything to go by, then it is incredible that the council, as a whole, had to take such extreme and costly steps simply because two people in a council building didn't like each other.

Furthermore, a member of the general public, having read the minutes of the council meeting of 28th July 2003, could be excused for thinking that such a harmonious council did exist and that the town's affairs were in good hands.

But, if they had been given the opportunity to read the exempt minutes on the 'staffing matter', they might well have thought that there was something strange going on in the council chamber that looked like a sinister plot to get rid of someone, not for incompetence, but solely for political reasons.

On 1st August 2003 a letter was sent by Cllr David Hall, Chairman of Up Hatherley Parish Council to the mayor Cllr Garth Barnes. It was to inform him that a representative from the five parish councils in the Borough had met to discuss the Quality Parish Councils' Partnership Scheme promulgated by the Office of the Deputy Prime Minister.

Cllr Hall reported that the meeting had been arranged by the MD and had resulted in a 'very useful exchange of views' ending with a working party being established to carry the project forward.

Cllr Hall wanted the mayor to know that the parish councils were appreciative of the work the MD had done in managing the council's Parish Boundary Review and the interest she had always shown in the work of the parishes.

He added that the parish representatives had expressed concerns that the trust established between the MD and parish councils had been clouded by recent events, mainly through revelations in the local press about the MD's strained relationships with certain members of the council.

In his view, the news had brought the council into disrepute, and casts doubts in the minds of the public about the way in which the council was conducting its business. He wrote: *"Because of this pall of distrust hovering around the council, you will sympathise with parish councillors who may be reticent about entering into important partnerships with the local authority."*

Cllr Hall was expressing the views of the parish councils and wanted the mayor to give him an assurance that the Partnership Scheme had the full support of the council.

The letter suggested that the Leader of the Council should address a meeting of the parish council representatives and explain *'what may have led to the alleged breakdown in relations between elected members and the leadership of the executive. Such a meeting would enable the Leader to tell us (and through us, of course, a much wider audience), what the perceived problems are all about and what he and the Borough Council intend doing to resolve them.'*

Cllr Hall suggested that the meeting should be under the chairmanship of the mayor and that the other Group Leaders should be invited to attend.

In Cllr Hall's words "it would be an opportunity to clear the air and put the record straight."

The reply from the mayor, according to Cllr Hall, was that there was not a problem and therefore no need for him to call a meeting.

Once again, evidence shows that if there was a problem, it was not sufficiently important to even prompt the mayor into any sort of action.

The council meeting on 28th July 2003 ended at 5.40 p.m., excellent debates had taken place and sensible decisions had been made; the 'staffing matter' was postponed until 27th October.

An 'away day' for councillors and officers to get together and discuss matters of mutual interest on Tuesday 29th July was cancelled. A scheduled Gloucestershire Airport working group meeting was cancelled on Wednesday 30th July, but the scheduled Planning Meeting went ahead as scheduled the next day.

I had an early morning radio interview at 7.00 a.m., on Thursday morning with *Gloucestershire Radio* who wanted to ask me questions about bureaucracy and how the PAB Group could reduce it in a local authority. I was relieved the questions put to me were easy to answer, but I was nervous that the interviewer might stray a little and ask me why the personal animosity at Cheltenham Borough Council had gone on for so long and proved so difficult to overcome. On the other hand, the local radio station and its listeners might have lost a golden opportunity to hear a few facts that hitherto had not been known, if the questions had been put to me.

Apart from routine matters the weekend went quietly for me. It was looking to be a typical August month when the majority of council staff took their annual leave and there would be a welcome pause from the emails and the telephone calls.

The MD would be away for two weeks as a result of her stress problem, plus another two weeks annual leave, spent recuperating from the sickness and the drama of the events leading up to the 28th July council meeting.

However, the peaceful period did not last long. Early Friday morning 8th August, I received a briefing note from the *Gloucestershire Echo* warning me that the *Echo* intended printing a substantial article on the CBC v Laird dispute.

The briefing note was headed 'Crisis Looming at Municipal Offices' and spoke about a 'huge rift at the heart of Cheltenham Borough Council being blown sky high today.'

The note also mentioned that the Leader of the Council had told them 'the whole council was grinding to a halt.'

My immediate reaction to the 'huge rift' claim was to ask myself what had happened since the council meeting on July 28th. The council offices were closed for day-to-day business with only a handful of staff on hand to deal with emergencies. The MD had been signed off work by her doctor the day following the council meeting, so what and who had found cause during those ten days to inform the *Gloucestershire Echo* that a 'huge rift' existed in the council offices?

I found it hard to believe what the briefing note was claiming. Only ten days earlier the whole council had been told in joint reports of the work undertaken by the Leader of the Council and the MD, including the introduction of a robust programme of measures for the future, which the council members had approved.

This hardly matched with the claim from the Leader that 'the council was grinding to a halt.'

Was this a question of 'when the cats away etc., etc?'

Whatever one's view about the dispute at the time, there were some very pertinent questions that needed to be asked, not least the question of what and who was behind the constant and vindictive accusations being levelled against the MD.

In previous chapters evidence has been shown where Mrs Laird had offered to sit down with the Leader and Cabinet members to sort out the difficulties.

Why didn't this happen? It was Robert Burns who said that people should talk about a problem rather than "nursing your wrath to keep it warm."

The opposition group leaders tried on more than one occasion to bring the two sides together, arbitration had been suggested, but all to no avail. So, when an olive branch is repeatedly offered and rejected, what conclusion can anyone draw?

The Friday night edition of the *Gloucestershire Echo* was excellent. It did not take sides and it portrayed the dispute even-handedly. The report covered four pages and it made good reading for anyone remotely interested in, as the *Echo* put it, 'A Tale of Two Personalities.'

The question the *Echo* should have posed is why two intelligent people whose responsibilities first and foremost was to the town, couldn't sit round a table and behave like two sensible adults and sort out their problems.

The four pages of the *Gloucestershire Echo* were divided into four sections. The front page claimed that 'breaking point had been reached' with photographs of a cheerful looking MD and a solemn looking Leader of the Council. The text told its readers that Christine Laird had been given sick leave and the Leader claimed 'the council is grinding to a halt'.

Momentous things must have happened between the period July 28th and 8th August 2003. But, just suppose, the Leader of the Council in his report to council on July 28th had announced that in spite of the year's good work, plus the schedule of measures he had proposed for the future, the council was actually 'grinding to a halt?' Uproar, possibly! But there is no doubt the Leader's words would have prompted a raft of questions from councillors, and answers would have been demanded of him. But of course, that wasn't the case; it had taken ten days whilst the MD was away on sick leave for the Leader to make a statement to the local press, which simply did not make sense.

Was it any wonder when residents read their local newspaper that they wondered what on earth was going on?

The second page of the *Echo* covered the transcript of a telephone conversation between a woman and the Leader of the Council. Whilst parts of the conversation were omitted on the advice of the newspaper's legal officer, the rest of the conversation is reported.

It seems that an *Echo* reporter dialled Cllr McKinlay on his mobile phone on Monday 4th August and although a connection had been made no conversation took place. The reporter realised that the mobile phone had been left on and to his surprise a conversation was taking place between the Leader and a woman. The reporter grabbed a notepad and took a shorthand note of the conversation.

It seems that Cllr McKinlay took 58 minutes to spell out to a female colleague, or was it a member of staff, his woes and tribulations brought about by the managing director. Apparently, he felt that the whole process of democracy was being undermined by the actions of the MD and his Cabinet members were beyond themselves because their decision-making powers were constantly being undermined.

The reported phone conversation came from Cllr McKinlay, because the *Echo* reported that the woman's words were muffled and therefore inaudible. Did she have her hand or a handkerchief over the phone, because it seems strange that for most of the 58 minutes the female voice was 'muffled'?

There were two important points that Cllr McKinlay is alleged to have said in the reported one-sided telephone conversation that should be noted. He suggested to the woman that he thought the point had been reached where we need an external Monitoring Officer. Perhaps it was because he thought the council's MO was under pressure because of his involvement in the dispute. Perhaps he believed a new or additional MO would add weight to his desire to get rid of Christine Laird.

The other point he made towards the end of the conversation "When this blows, it will blow big. So many people know about this, the Local Government Association (LGA), the employers know about it and SOLACE knows about it. I'm amazed it has stayed as quiet as it has. It affects so many areas of local government."

No-one knows if it impressed the woman on the other end of the telephone because the *Echo* reporter wrote "Woman (*muffled*) sound."

It seemed to me that the blue touch-paper was about to be lit, but when the Leader was approached by the *Echo* about the conversation, he declined to comment.

On page three of the evening newspaper the headline suggested that there was a crisis looming at the Municipal Offices. The report concentrated on the telephone conversation and the comments from opposition group leaders.

All three group leaders, the *Echo* reported, said that unless the dispute was resolved it would damage the local authority.

The Labour Group Leader, Cllr Martin Hale said 'the public had a right to know what had gone on.' He also believed 'the dispute should be sorted out as quickly as possible and when it was, there should be an indication of what had been going on.'

Cllr Hale was also reported to have said *"I do believe that when this is sorted out the public deserve some explanation as to what has gone on. At the moment, it's not the right time and I am sure that I probably don't know all that is going on."*

The Conservative Group Leader for some inexplicable reason was reported as being 'tight lipped' about the dispute.

When I was asked to comment I stated that the dispute had received a large amount of public exposure and had not done the town any good, but I disputed the claim that senior officers were running the council.

I told the *Echo* that "All the evidence suggests to me that the Liberal Democrats want to run the council their way and as far as I can see that is exactly what they are doing. With regard to the relationship issue between the managing director and the Leader of the Council, that was something for them to sort out."

On the fourth page the *Echo* printed profiles of the two main protagonists of the dispute. It highlighted the achievements of the Leader of the Council, which I have already mentioned, and a headline claiming that 'Christine was like a new broom.'

The article referred to her previous employment as chief executive of the Chartered Institute of Housing (CIH) in March 1998 and also as the director of housing at Rhondda Cynon Taff Borough Council (RCT) in July 1999.

The article further claimed that she was the driving force behind the restructuring at Cheltenham Borough Council, following the switch from the old committee style to what became known as the Cabinet style, which put decision-making powers in the hands of just eight councillors.

The restructuring meant that the heads of the main departments were no longer required and they were made redundant: it also meant that as a result of this a board of directors would be needed to oversee the running of the council.

The board consisted of three group directors, Chris Huckle, David Perry and Marie Fallon plus the MD Christine Laird.

This is what the Structural Review Committee wanted the new managing director to do when she was appointed in 2002 and the expression used by the local newspaper that 'she was like a new broom' was not out of place.

On 20th August 2003, members of staff and councillors received an email from the Leader of the Council. He wrote that he was concerned that everyone may be worried about the continuing coverage in the media of the dispute and particularly his quote that the "council was grinding to a halt."

He wanted to assure everyone that he did not mean that the day-to-day business of the council was not happening because this was not the case.

The final sentence in the Leader's email also caused a few eyebrows to be raised when he wrote that he was 'doing his best to bring about the earliest possible resolution of the internal management problem.'

Really! If that was the case then why on earth didn't he arrange a meeting with the MD that very day and talk through the problems, if any genuine problems existed? If arranging a meeting and talking to the MD proved to be a difficult task for the Leader, then all he had to do was to invite the opposition group leaders to make the arrangements and act as facilitators. He could have contacted the SWRA, who he had dealings with before, and they could have acted as 'independent' advisers.

I know the opposition group leaders would have been more than willing to act as facilitators and we would have made progress. This was exactly what we had tried to do on 19th March 2003, but unfortunately without success for the reasons already explained.

Both the Leader and the Group Leaders know that all internal problems can be resolved because there are mechanisms written into the council's Constitution which allows this to happen.

What isn't written in the Constitution is a mechanism to make two people like each other – that requires a modicum of common sense and the will to do so.

In spite of repeated statements by the Leader of the Council that he was 'trying his best to resolve the internal issues', there was too much evidence that suggested the opposite to be the truth. Notwithstanding the various attempts to get the two sides to talk to each other and the content of the email from the Leader to staff and councillors on the 20th August, the Leader decided to write to the editor of the *Gloucestershire Echo* just five days later complaining that the MD was blocking and delaying the hearing of complaints against her.

Did he really believe that such charges against the most senior officer of the council would go unchallenged?

The letter also accused the opposition group leaders of airing 'various grievances against the Cabinet in public rather than in a formal manner'. This was quite ridiculous considering we had tried hard to get the Cabinet to explain in a private meeting why they had made a decision to offer the MD a sum of £63,000 to leave the council's employment.

In any event, this information had been public knowledge once the Standards Board for England received the formal letter of complaint from the opposition group leaders regarding the behaviour of the Leader and the Cabinet members.

However, the letter from the Leader to the local newspaper on 25th August 2003 concluded with information to the readers that 'legal advice had been sought from the Government and a number of organisations and legal sources.'

What did it mean? I have no idea.

The report also claimed that the council 'had employed an experienced former officer in an attempt to set in place a procedure whereby the allegations against the MD can be considered within the framework of the law.'

Whether the Leader of the Council thought the letter, or parts of it, might be published in the local newspaper or not, it did suggest that the council's Human Resources and Legal departments were incapable of dealing with a simple and basic problem of two people unable to work together.

It was becoming clearer to me, and I am sure to many others, that the original 'political' excuse that it was all to do with the Conservative Group appointing Mrs Laird to the post of managing director in the first place, was no longer acceptable. There was clearly a feud between two people who had differences of opinion about the way the council should be run. From the written evidence that was available it was also clear that the MD had tried repeatedly to get the problems out into the open, to talk about the issues and to be prepared to reach a sensible compromise.

The Leader, for his part, talked about finding solutions on more than one occasion, but signally failed to put his words into action. On the contrary, his words in the email to everyone on the 20th August 2003 and the letter to the press on 25th August, copies of which had been sent to the MD, only drove her to a point of more stress and caused a 'panic attack' which had to be dealt with by her doctor.

The doctor concluded that the events of July 28th followed by the distribution of emails and the letter to the press in August had contributed to Mrs Laird's breakdown. He further diagnosed that she was suffering from acute anxiety and depression and signed her off work immediately.

At the same time as the emails went out to councillors and staff, the MD received a copy of the draft legal instructions from Gerald Ford the MO setting out the council's legal case.

Not surprisingly, the receipt of the charges brought on another panic attack.

Hugh Laird, responded to the letter and legal documents by reminding the MO about his wife's health and suggested to him that 'unless the council is able to give an undertaking that it would observe its duty of care towards his wife then the chances of the doctor allowing his wife to return to work would be slim.'

He also alleged 'his wife had been subject to harassment by a small group of politically motivated individuals who appear not to care about the possible consequences of their actions for the council, the taxpayer or the impact on his wife's health.'

Mr Laird reminded the MO 'the distribution of the anonymous letters at the time of the July 28th council meeting defaming his wife was deplorable. He suggested to him that Counsel, acting for the council, should be made aware of his letter so that he could see the appalling acts to which his wife has been subject.'

Mr Laird also suggested to the MO 'as the council, through him and the Leader, had started a legal process against his wife, further correspondence between the council's legal team and his wife should in future be done through his wife's solicitor.'

His letter concluded by asking the MO to pass on the following message to the Leader of the Council: *"If my wife's well-being continues to deteriorate as a consequence of his actions or his political associates, I am going to hold him personally responsible."*

Strong words from Christine Laird's husband, but he didn't know at the time that the long journey to the High Court had only just begun. He was yet to learn that the cost of human suffering in the shape of his wife's health would be enormous.

Her health would deteriorate and the people of Cheltenham would eventually be faced with legal costs amounting to more than £2 million before sanity in the council chamber prevailed again.

But has sanity now returned? Later chapters should answer this question.

Around this time and for reasons that still escape me, although it had been hinted at by the Leader and the MO, the council decided to engage the services of Mr Patrick Brady, a former retired Chief Executive and Monitoring Officer of a local authority in Derbyshire, to deal with the dispute.

He was paid £600 per day on the days he worked, which the judge remarked in his judgment 'was a reasonable cost that could be recovered.'

However, the question that was often posed at the time was whether Mr Brady in his former job of a Monitoring Officer could bring something new to bear in the dispute that the council's own MO was unable to do. We knew what the council were going to pay Mr Brady, but what were his terms of reference?

The answer was simple, no-one knew: it would have made more sense if Mr Brady had taken total control of the dispute immediately following the allegations and the early comments that Mr Ford appeared to be too close to the Leader of the Council.

In his defence, he did send out a letter on 29th August 2003 to all Group Leaders informing them that he had received a copy of a further anonymous letter, which had been sent to 'certain councillors concerning Mrs Laird'.

Mr Ford wrote that 'the letters are totally unacceptable'. He had declined from informing all the other councillors about it because he thought 'the letter might find its way to the *Gloucestershire Echo* and give the document publicity that presumably the sender was seeking.' The reason was accepted at the time, but now upon reflection, I think it was wrong not to have informed all councillors. The so-called fear of publicity would have been 'a price worth paying' because it would have given the public a further insight to the behaviour of certain people.

Whilst the letter from the MO was encouraging, we had not been made aware that he had engaged Queen's Counsel prior to the 27th August 2003, which caused the MD to take the protective action that she did. She sought representation from her professional association SOLACE and they wrote to the MO on 2nd September 2003 thanking him for sending them a copy of the draft instructions to Queen's Counsel and the Opinion of Mr David Fletcher of Counsel.

Once the news came out, it looked as though we were about to embark on something big although the scale of it took a few weeks to unfold.

Meanwhile, Mr Simon Collingridge of Davies and Partners (solicitors) had written to Mr Ford the MO on 2nd September 2003 informing him that he had been engaged to represent Mrs Laird and he wrote that 'he already had grave concerns about the way the council were dealing with complaints against Mrs Laird by the Leader of the Council.'

Mr Collingridge, in his letter, referred to the council's proposal to retain Senior Counsel in order to provide an Opinion to sit side by side with the Opinions that had already been provided by Mr David Fletcher.' Once again this fact had not been reported to the opposition group leaders.

The Senior Counsel appointed was Mr Timothy Kerr, QC.

Mr Collingridge said 'he had grave concerns about the document and its likely effect on the future financial health and reputation of Cheltenham Borough Council if the advice contained therein can be relied upon.'

The letter also stated that SOLACE was also concerned the council was receiving inaccurate and potentially damaging advice from Mr Fletcher of Counsel.

The most revealing part in the letter from Mr Collingridge was the setting out of three faults in the document provided by Mr Fletcher, which in the words of Mr Collingridge contained 'three blatant errors.' He also claimed that 'the usefulness of Mr Fletcher's Opinion must be seriously called into question.'

Mrs Laird, in her capacity as Head of Paid Service had stated that she was extremely concerned that if the council relied on the Opinion of Mr Fletcher, it was allowing itself to be poorly advised, thereby exposing itself to serious financial risk and future public criticism.

These words and the warnings they contained were not taken seriously enough by the council or the Cabinet members. They were words that came home to roost at the end of the trial.

Because SOLACE was so concerned about the legal advice that Mr Fletcher had provided, Mr Collingridge suggested in his letter to Mr Ford that 'the advice should be discarded and that Mr Kerr, QC should be invited to review the whole of the matter plus the supplementary instructions to Learned Counsel prepared by Mr Brady, and the twenty two additional questions that had been prepared by SOLACE and Mrs Laird.'

The point was clearly made by Mr Collingridge that the council had been poorly advised by Mr Fletcher and urged the council, through Mr Ford, to accept his proposal.

The concluding points in the letter suggested that Mrs Laird 'vigorously disputes both the veracity and timing of the allegations being made by the Leader of the Council and if she is made subject of a disciplinary investigation and further subjected to the indignity of suspension then she will make an interim application to the Employment Tribunal for immediate reinstatement'.

He who rides a tiger is afraid to dismount. (Proverb: late 19th century)

Having mounted the tiger's back the task now was to make sure that the rider stayed on it. By producing more documents, seeking the support of the MO and with the supplementary presence of Mr Patrick Brady, how could the Cabinet members not stay safely aboard the beast?

Add to that the steady trickle of external legal advice, irrespective of how much it cost, must have given the Leader and his colleagues all the encouragement they needed to ensure the tiger followed the route they had planned for it.

On 15th September 2003 the opposition group leaders received a memorandum from the MD enclosing a copy of a report written by the Leader of the Council, which had been used as a briefing paper when he addressed his Liberal Democrat colleagues. The report was dated 6th May 2003.

The date is important because much of this chapter concentrated on the events between the month of May and the council meeting on 28th July 2003.

It is interesting, therefore, to read the content of the report. The first paragraph reads "I have become increasingly concerned at the Managing Director's conduct in her dealings with me and with other members of the Cabinet."

This opening paragraph is both interesting and significant. The period in question is prior to 6th May 2003 and presumably it goes back to February 2002 when the MD took up her post. As we know from earlier events, the council operated quite normally throughout this period with important local authority business being undertaken by the MD on a daily basis and duly approved by either the Cabinet or the council members.

And it is interesting to note that the word used in the report was 'conduct' and not 'misconduct', so how serious was it?

Not saying good morning to the Leader and his colleagues, or questioning some of the decisions is hardly questionable 'conduct': and if it was so unbearable, the matter could have been raised on any number of occasions including the council meeting on 28th July 2003.

Similarly, it could be argued that if it wasn't misconduct, and there was no evidence to suggest that there had been, then could it have been instances of misde-meanours, which in legal terms, is an offence of less gravity than a felony?

Of course, none of it was serious, and as we learned in the report by the Leader of the Council to his party members, his complaint was that the MD had intentionally misinformed his Cabinet colleagues and she had also sought to undermine him and his colleagues. Those were the charges, and unbelievable as they may seem, they were the substance of the report.

In Cheltenham, we had a Leader of the Council who with six male and one female members of his Cabinet, could not manage the alleged intentions of one senior council officer. It was the same senior officer who had been engaged by the council to carry through some important changes to the management structure. And it was the same Cabinet members who had supported the changes when the

Structural Review Committee announced its recommendations to full council in 2002.

In the commercial and industrial world, should a similar situation exist then a member of the Board of Directors would bring the two people together and in the jargon often used, would hypothetically, 'knock their heads together and tell them to get on with doing the job the company had employed them to do'.

Perhaps, that is what Mr Brady should have done rather than spend so much time trying to find a resolution to what had become an impossible situation.

The council was now firmly astride the 'tiger's back' with both sides having briefed their Counsels of their accounts of the situation. Even though a critical stage in the dispute had been reached, it was difficult for the PAB Group and Conservative Group members to acknowledge that the council had a legal case against the MD.

On 16th September 2003 the disclosure of relevant matters between the two sides was beginning to create more friction between the MO and Mr Collingridge.

It appeared from a letter dated 16th September 2003 from Mr Collingridge that the MO expected the MD to pass over to him every piece of documentation in her possession.

Mr Collingridge wrote: "This is an unacceptable stance for the council's Monitoring Officer to take. I think it fair to say that your duties in this capacity include a close monitoring of information, whether it is documentary or otherwise. To suggest, therefore, that my client has somehow done herself a disservice in not handing to you certain documents casts something of a question mark over the function that you are retained to perform in this matter".

Mr Collingridge reminded the MO that Mrs Laird's complaint to the Standards Board pre-dated the Leader of the Council's own complaint about Mrs Laird's behaviour.

He went on to say, "As Monitoring Officer you are not performing your duties properly if you do not take a pro-active approach to the resolution of Mrs Laird's difficulties. In waiting for her to provide you with all the answers you are opening yourself to criticism".

Another paragraph in the letter is significant because it concerns a brief conversation between Mrs Laird and Cabinet member Cllr Mrs Hay.

Mr Collingridge wrote: "It is difficult to understand why my client's words to Cllr Hay were interpreted as anything other than a formal disclosure. Cllr Hay is the only female member of the Cabinet and a local magistrate. In her Cabinet capacity she was informed by my client on 6th November 2002 that she considered her gender was an issue for the Leader of the Council and that other women in the organisation were uncomfortable in the Leader's presence. The fact that my client approached her with this information ought to have sent alarm bells ringing".

He also reminded the MO that he was 'wearing two hats in this process and as such it is appropriate that you recognise this and waive the right to see the complaint she has made to the Standards Board.'

Mrs Laird's complaint to the Standards Board was based on her claim that she had been and continued to be victimised by the Leader and some of his Cabinet members, which was totally different to the complaints made by the Leader of the Council. The MO appeared to be comparing the complaints of the Leader and Mrs Laird as if they were of equal merit, which of course they were not.

To suggest that there was any parity between the alleged conduct of Mrs Laird and the defamatory treatment she had received at the hands of the Leader over a period of time was ludicrous. If the Leader had been advised to curtail or stop his defamatory comments against Mrs Laird then there was no evidence that he had taken heed of the warnings.

It is questionable whether the MO had reminded the Leader that the members' Code of Conduct clearly states at paragraph 2 (a) General Obligations, members should treat others with respect. If the MO had reminded the Leader of the Council, or any other member of the Cabinet of paragraph 2 (a) then from the evidence available, the Leader and some members of the Cabinet were in breach of the Code of Conduct.

On this point alone, it is worth questioning the conclusions of the Standards Board for England (SBE) following their investigations into the complaints made by Mrs Laird against the Leader of the Council. More on this in a later chapter.

The judge in his High Court ruling relied heavily on the report from the SBE when assessing the part played by the Leader in the dispute.

However, from the above comments and letters passed on to me, a different picture has now emerged.

For the record, Mr Fletcher was replaced by Mr Timothy Kerr, QC and it seemed that the council was in a completely different ball game as the next chapters will reveal.

The passing of the alleged complaints by the Leader in a document to Mrs Laird on the morning of the council meeting on July 28th was probably done deliberately. I have no doubt that Liberal Democrat councillors were aware of the content, but the PAB Group had not been informed of its existence prior to the meeting and listening to the comments made during the debate the Conservative Group had not been informed either.

On 16th September 2003, I wrote to Mr Brady informing him that I had seen a copy of the document and suggested to him that there were references in the document to letters and emails that could seriously prejudice the views of the Disciplinary Panel members.

I reminded Mr Brady that the MO had already declared the Panel would sit in a semi-quasi-judicial capacity and it concerned me that members who may be selected and appointed to the Panel may have already been privy to the detail of the alleged accusations. This would be undemocratic and contrary to the rules of natural justice.

The PAB Group was quite clear on this point and implored Mr Brady to constitute a Panel that was made up entirely of independent members.

Everyone knew that the scheduled council meeting on 27th October would include the postponed matter of the allegations made against the MD by the Leader of the Council at the July 28th meeting. It therefore came as a surprise to learn that on 3rd October a letter had been sent to the mayor signed by Cllrs McKinlay, Fidgeon, Jordan, Franklin and Thornton requesting an Extraordinary Meeting of the Council to be held on Monday 27th October 2003 at 5.30 p.m.

As far as I can recall the only item on the agenda was 'An Employment Matter – The Report of the Leader of the Council'. The item also stated that the report would be accompanied by relevant officer reports and advice.

Because the Liberal Democrats kept this letter to themselves, it was some time before the opposition groups became aware of this special meeting.

Allegations and counter allegations were being thrown around like confetti so it was no surprise to me to receive a call from Cllr Duncan Smith on Wednesday 15th October telling me that his Conservative Group were mindful to request an Extraordinary Meeting of the council on Thursday 23rd October 2003 at 5.00 p.m., to consider the employment grievance by the MD against certain members of the council.

I was not sure that PAB would want to be part of this proposal because the whole business was getting more confusing each day. Cllr Smith assured me that if the matter is debated there was a chance that the Advisory, Conciliation & Arbitration Service (ACAS) would become involved and the dispute could be settled.

That was certainly a step in the right direction and worthy of consideration.

Cllr Smith also confirmed that the Labour Party Group Leader was supportive and he wanted the PAB Group to be included in the request, which would show cross-party support from the opposition side. My members, persuaded by the possible intervention of ACAS, agreed that I should support the request for the meeting and I should sign the letter.

To conform to the rules in the Constitution a letter must go to the mayor quoting Paragraph 3 (schedule 12) of the Local Government Act 1972 requesting the meeting, giving the date and time and the reasons for the Extraordinary Meeting.

The letter stated that following the lodging of an employment grievance by Mrs Laird MD, the Council should i) consider the grievance against the named members of council, ii) suspend all action in relation to the dispute between the Leader and Cabinet and the MD and iii) refer the matter to ACAS to seek a resolution.

The letter was signed by the three opposition group leaders and two Conservative councillors.

In order to support our request to the mayor we explained in the letter that the MD's contract of employment contained no formal grievance process and it would be inappropriate for any grievance to be heard by officers who report directly to her or Board members.

We also reminded the mayor that Mrs Laird's employer is Cheltenham Borough Council and quoting a sentence in the Opinion provided by Mr Timothy Kerr, 'it is elected members not officers who exercise the function as employer'.

The letter further stated that Mrs Laird's contract did not contain a reference to the ACAS code of practice, but it did specify that 5 days notice was reasonable notice of a hearing of a grievance.

Procedural meetings and extraordinary meetings seemed to be commonplace in October and after the tit-for-tat palaver of previous weeks it was a relief to attend the first of the extraordinary meetings on 23rd October 2003.

There were four apologies for absence; Cllrs Fidgeon, McKinlay, Jordan, Lloyd, Stuart-Smith, Surgenor, Franklin, Hay and Thornton declared a prejudicial interest in the proceedings and left the chamber.

Mrs Laird was accompanied by her solicitor Mr Simon Collingridge.

Members of the Press and the public were not allowed in the council chamber and any subsequent minutes would be confidential and exempt.

The mayor Cllr Barnes outlined the procedure he intended to follow and announced that a stenographer would be present throughout the proceedings, this would allow councillors to refer back to any point that another member had made.

Mrs Laird reported her grievances to the councillors and placed a letter dated 23rd October before council, which contained comments on the officers' report.

She also presented a bundle of documents in support of her grievance claim.

After prolonged discussions and several adjournments, Cllr Duncan Smith proposed that the council formally receive the MD's grievance, which was seconded by Cllr Melville-Smith, put to the vote and was agreed unanimously.

Following the vote, Cllr Smith proposed that 'a politically proportionate panel of seven members should be convened, comprising four Liberal Democrats and one each from the other political parties'.

Cllr Smith further proposed that the Panel should adopt the usual procedural processes and they should convene within two weeks of the 24th October and report back to a meeting of the council by the end of November with recommendations on dealing with the grievances.

My colleague Cllr Diane Hibbert was unhappy with the membership of the Panel and thought that they should consist of one councillor from each of the four parties. She proposed this as an amendment, but it was defeated when the vote was taken.

The Liberal Democrats plus some Conservative councillors voted against the amendment.

The mayor then took a vote on the substantive motion proposed by Cllr Smith and it was passed with one vote against and six abstentions.

All votes were recorded following a request by seven members of the council.

For the record, the MD and Mr Collingridge left the council chamber during the debate.

It was reported by Cllr Smith that because all sides in the dispute could not agree with the suggestion that ACAS should be asked to intervene, the four week truce proposed earlier by the MD to enable ACAS to look at the problem would not be progressed.

At the conclusion of the meeting, councillors accepted that any additional costs arising from the recommendations should be met from the general fund balances.

It had been a long night and the mayor finally declared the meeting closed at 12.20 a.m. Councillors left the chamber looking tired and weary and as someone remarked to me as we went through the door – at the end of the day, will it prove anything and the answer it seemed was written on the faces of those who went home to their beds.

Surprisingly, the general topic amongst councillors following the long sitting of the council meeting into the early hours of the morning was not about the quality of the decisions taken, but the fact that the late sitting had created a new record for lengthy sittings of the council.

Equally, most councillors were concerned about the possibility of another long evening when the next scheduled council meeting took place in four days' time.

We were aware that the council meeting on 27th October 2003 was to discuss the deferred matters from the council meeting on 28th July, and the matter of the increasing legal costs had also been listed.

Later it became known that the Leader of the Council wanted amendments by the MO to his report to be debated under item 7 'An Employment Matter'. This was not relevant to the agenda item because the council had already accepted in principal that a disciplinary matter had been raised and that a politically balanced committee should be established and be known as the JNC Members' Panel.

It was widely known that since July 28th additional legal advice had been sought from external sources, albeit with the approval of councillors, but this item in the opinion of most councillors, should have been the sole item on the agenda to be discussed because it was linked to the 'employment matter'.

The late request by the Leader for his motion to be debated under item 7 seemed to be an attempt to distract members' attention away from the escalating legal costs in order to confuse those in attendance.

At the July 28th council meeting councillors were informed that the MD had only received a copy of the allegations that very morning: we were also told that the process that was being followed that day was fraught with inaccuracies, unfairness and concerns that the rules of natural justice were not being applied.

Because of these concerns the matter was deferred.

The Leader's report to council on 27th October 2003 started with an admission that there had been difficulties between himself and the MD over a period of time and he had come to the conclusion in April 2003 that the differences needed to be resolved.

Members of the opposition groups looked across the chamber at each other; some shook their heads in dismay listening to such a claim when for eighteen months a number of attempts had been made by opposition councillors, officers and the MD herself to resolve the dispute, but all to no avail.

What was behind the Leader's statement? Was it an attempt to publicly inform his Liberal Democrat councillors, at least those not in his inner circle, that he had been having a 'tough time' with the managing director? Or was it said in the hope that the opposition councillors would believe his statement and take a different line? Maybe he thought it was a good opportunity to open up another avenue of discussion that would make it easier for him and the council to dismiss its MD when the time came?

The questions still remain unanswered.

To justify the position he had taken he reported that he had asked the MO 'to assist him in putting in place the steps necessary to enable his concerns about the MD to be considered'.

It seemed to me that the wording of his request was woolly. Councillors were unsure what the words actually meant – 'putting in place the steps necessary' did not mean anything. It could have been a move to put more of the blame on the MD and thus diverting the blame away from himself.

But there was more to come.

Astonishingly, but obviously well-rehearsed, the Leader expressed his concerns about the well-being of the MD because he believed that recent events may have placed a considerable strain on her. He added that he had no intention of making her situation worse. Did that mean that the bullying of Mrs Laird was to stop?

Having wiped a tear or two away from my eyes, I wrote on my notepad – whose fault is this? He could have ended the dispute at any time of his choosing: a suggestion put to him on more than one occasion but repeatedly ignored. Enlightened staff and councillors knew this to be the case throughout 2002 and 2003.

The Leader continued reading his report and in an effort to convince those present, he pleaded that he had to balance the duty of care to the MD against the duty he had to the council. 'The correct balance' he said 'would ensure effective governance of Cheltenham'.

A chicken and egg situation – but which came first?

After more references to situations in which he had played a major part, he eventually referred to the matter of the two complaints he had made against the MD, which were

a. the MD had intentionally misinformed him and his Cabinet colleagues on occasions and
b. she appears to deliberately seek to undermine his position as Leader of the Council.

No details of the complaints were given as far as I can remember and as the report did not include any detail we sat there and listened in silence to the unsubstantiated charges being made.

The Leader then referred to the MO's report, which included legal advice concerning the Joint Negotiating Committee (JNC) procedure, which is incorporated in the contract of employment of local authority chief officers. This procedure enables the council to appoint a panel of members to undertake an initial investigation of complaints against a chief officer.

The feeling in the council chamber was becoming more intense because councillors knew that if a Panel was going to be established it would be obliged to examine the expressed concerns of the Leader, which had been presented to the council.

Subsequently, the Panel would require the MD to respond to the alleged complaints.

My worry at the time was the matter of consistency or lack of it, in the words used by the Leader – one minute he had talked about 'his complaints' and the next sentence he talked about 'his concerns'. There is a difference between the two and it seemed to me that we were spending a great deal of time and energy on something that was trivial and should have been dealt with through the council's internal grievance procedures.

Another worry was the Panel of members would not be balanced. Many councillors had, over the course of the previous two years, been involved in the dispute in one way or another and they would be deemed to have acquired a prejudicial interest, which normally would be declared.

However, assuming that an independent Panel could be formed and they had come to the conclusion that the Leader's allegations were not trivial or groundless, but required further 'legal' examination, the Panel could appoint what is called 'an independent person'. If they could not agree with this then the next stage in the JNC procedure is to contact the Secretary of State requesting the appointment of a 'Designated Independent Person' (DIP) whose job would be to investigate the 'complaints' in depth.

The person appointed would be from the legal profession, usually a Barrister.

Listening to the process being spelled out by the Leader of the Council, it did cross my mind that if a Panel decided the MD had been at fault, then before involving the Secretary of State, it would have been more sensible to ask all four group leaders to hear all the evidence before any other action was taken.

This was not an issue that required legal expertise, or the decision of a court, but a simple matter that could be dealt with internally by the group leaders, albeit with added guidance from the council's legal department.

Instead of trying to find a way forward on the evening of 27th October all we were unwittingly doing was preparing the way for the long road to the High Court. Inevitably, this would mean filling the pockets of the legal profession, and all expenses would fall on the shoulders of the local council taxpayer.

The reason being that Councillor McKinlay claimed he had a problem with the MD.

Everyone knew the MD had made official complaints to the Standards Board for England (SBE) against the Leader of the Council and his Cabinet members, the MD meanwhile urged the council not to go down the JNC route until after the SBE had announced their findings.

The opposition group leaders made a similar suggestion. This was rejected.

The Leader, however, reported there were a number of legal issues set out in the officers' report that prevented him from accepting the suggestion by the MD and the other group leaders to delay the procedure until the SBE made their findings known.

In order to validate his position he outlined a hypothetical example of a Chief Officer being in difficulty with elected councillors concerning his lack of performance or questionable behaviour, going to the SBE and by simply making a complaint against the councillors could hold up any internal procedure.

The example used by the Leader was received in silence by councillors.

But, to use such an example showed the temerity of the Leader in defending what he thought was his right to get his side of the story in first before the SBE published their decisions.

It would be difficult to imagine a situation in other councils where serious accusations of the kind made by Mrs Laird to the SBE, were allowed to be side-stepped by a council, based purely on a hypothetical example that had been posed by its Leader.

This is what the councillors were asked to believe and they went along with it.

PAB councillors were not impressed with the Leader's hypothetical comparison with the situation that currently existed between the MD and himself. Conservative and PAB councillors knew that the complaints made by Mrs Laird to the SBE were made as far back as April 2003, months before the Leader came forward with his allegations. The Leader's fictional character only added to the general opinion that he intended to continue his tit-for-tat behaviour in the belief that he would get the benefit of any doubt and it would work in his favour in the end.

He was even bold enough to state that whatever the conclusions of the SBE it would not be sufficient reason for the council not to implement the JNC procedure. As far as the powers of the panel were concerned he thought they should have the power to suspend the MD if they thought it necessary.

My understanding of procedures for investigation panels or similar bodies is for the members to look solely at the charges and then hear evidence from both sides. Once that procedure had been completed the panel would come to a decision similar to that in a magistrates' court; if the charges were proved then it would be at that point the legal adviser to the panel or to the magistrates, would set out the actions or remedies that the panel or magistrates had the power to impose.

For the Leader to tell the councillors, some of whom would be appointed to the panel, that they had the power to suspend the MD before the panel had been appointed was unfair, or to be cynical, he could have been indicating in a subtle way what he expected the panel to do.

On that assumption, how independent would the panel be?

On the same subject, I had written to Mr Patrick Brady on 16th September 2003 suggesting that the council meeting on July 28th required a study and examination of the papers appertaining to the dispute to establish whether they seriously prejudiced the views of would-be Panel members.

I reminded Mr Brady that according to the MO the Panel would be sitting in a semi-quasi judicial capacity and they had been acquainted with all the documentation.

I was aware that the Panel had already been constituted. This led me to suggest to him that it was not a democratic way of setting up a Panel and the method used could be contrary to the rules of natural justice. I repeated my earlier claim that the Panel should be selected from entirely independent people and not politically motivated councillors.

It is also interesting to note that throughout the long drawn out diatribe of the Leader and his written report to council, he did not mention once the council's Standards Committee; this committee, which includes independent people from parish councils and the wider community, often deal with complaints from the public about local councillors.

With their experience they would have been ideally suited to look at all aspects of the dispute before the council embarked on establishing a disciplinary panel. The Leader could have instructed the MO to convene a special meeting of the Standards Committee at any time in 2002 or 2003 so that his complaints could be heard – the question that continues to be asked is why did he not do this?

It seemed farcical to opposition councillors when the Leader suggested that 'it may be necessary to introduce interim working arrangements with the MD until such times as the present difficulties are resolved'.

In spite of questions, we were not told what the 'present difficulties' were and as far as we were concerned they had been ongoing since the day the Liberal Democrats took power in May 2002.

The other part of the sentence that needs to be examined is 'until the present difficulties are resolved'. How did the Leader intend to resolve the difficulties?

Surely, not by appointing a Grievance Panel, which would only exacerbate the situation further, and he had not mentioned the Standards Committee, so what magic wand-waving scheme did he have in mind?

The answer to this question was a suggestion from him that the Staff & Support Services Committee (S&SSC) 'be given the appropriate powers to deal with the situation'.

So, after thirty minutes of filibustering, the answer to this growing problem was to 'pass the buck' to the S&SSC, which had a majority of Liberal Democrat councillors, and was chaired by the Leader of the Council.

Councillors also agreed the 'terms of reference' of the Panel which included 'acting as a preliminary investigating committee' and 'reporting back to council with its findings'. Controversially, after taking legal advice, the Panel could also 'exercise the council's power of suspension of the MD, if they thought it appropriate'.

Once again the councillors were made aware that the additional costs of the JNC process would be met out of General Fund balances and the Group Director (Economy and Business Improvement) would have delegated power to approve the expenditure.

The Council was asked to note the names of the Panel, set out in the Officers' Report. They were Councillors Britter, Coleman, Holliday and Young representing the Liberal Democrats, Councillor D. Hale (Labour), Councillor Melville-Smith (Conservative) and Councillor Prince (PAB).

It would have been excusable if council members had been confused by the debate and the conclusions reached. It seemed that the council now had a Grievance Panel and a JNC Panel; one panel looking at the grievances by the MD and the other one the 'concerns' of the Leader of the Council – what a mess!

There was still a lot of mumblings going on in the council chamber as the mayor tried to move on to the next item on the agenda.

Once calm had been restored the mayor reminded members that the meeting on 23rd October agreed to set up a panel of members to consider the grievances put forward by the MD.

Having approved the Leader's Report, the council were then invited to consider the report by the MO which included an addendum to the earlier report of the Leader. The addendum proposed that if the JNC Members' Panel decided that an investigation should be undertaken, then it should agree and establish the procedures with the MD as a first step. If the MD agreed, then it should delegate its powers under S101 of the Local Government Act 1972 to the committee which had been set up by council members at the meeting on 23rd October 2003.

The MO further proposed that the question of the health and safety of the MD and its duty of care towards her should be the responsibility of the Board of Directors, the MO and the Assistant Director (Human Resources).

This acceptance of their duty of care by officers and members of the council was a step in the right direction, but their future actions needed to be carefully watched if the current signs of the MD's health was anything to go by.

The MO, in his report to council, suggested that there was likelihood that the complaints made by the Leader in his report would cover the same events and background as those covered by the MD's grievances. It did raise the issue of whether the same panel could consider all matters but only, he suggested, if agreement could be reached with the MD.

It all sounded very straightforward, but I could not help wondering what the 'politically balanced' panel could achieve that the opposition group leaders, or the Standards Committee could not. The legal department, equally confused it seemed, asked Mr Brady to try to find a way through the problem, but neither he nor the department came up with a satisfactory solution.

The JNC Procedure is complex and needs to be treated with the utmost care. It provides statutory protection of contracts of employment for senior officers of a local authority. These are normally the Head of Paid Service, the Monitoring Officer and its Section 151 Officer.

It was established as a result of the Widdicombe Report, which formed the basis of the Local Government & Housing Act 1989.

The Act and its subsequent Regulations, requires all councils to include in their Constitutions, a provision that disciplinary action cannot be taken against any of the statutory officers except following the report of a Designated Independent Person (DIP).

The law allows for suspension on full pay for up to two months, but the decision taken to suspend must be taken fairly and the reasons given in writing.

Unfair suspension in some circumstances could be grounds for justifying a claim against the council for unfair dismissal.

According to the JNC Procedure, the members' Panel can be appointed by the Leader of the Council. As the PAB Group Leader, I questioned whether this was lawful and my question was put to Counsel who advised that the members' Panel was, in effect, a committee, and as such could only be established by council.

Counsel, accordingly, advised that the council rather than the Leader should be the body to establish the Panel.

Whilst a good point had been established, it still troubled me to think that a Panel of members should be regarded as a committee, when their sole role was to carry out an investigation. Normally, a committee has powers that a panel, or working group do not have.

It also concerned me that a panel or working group established to look into any other aspect of council work should be 'politically balanced' and not proportionately balanced in favour of one political party.

The S&SSC meeting on 20th November 2003 will be remembered for the number of important agenda items. The subsequent minutes of the meeting were unclear and failed to identify who said what and who challenged the content of the various reports. It was officers' comments and their reports that monopolised the minutes.

In a later chapter the quality of the S&SSC minutes will be discussed at length and the chapter will include some of the criticisms made by the auditors (KPMG) on the accuracy and reliability of the S&SSC minutes in their Public Interest Report (March 2010).

The items on the agenda included corporate governance, a change to the terms of reference of the S&SSC, risk assessment, sickness benefits and employment and grievance matters.

Whether it was to consolidate their position, or for some other reason, the Group Directors presented a report to the meeting which proposed amendments to the Terms of Reference of the committee.

They wanted to clarify the role of the S&SSC with day-to-day responsibility for all staffing decisions, with the exception of those that fell to the Cabinet or the council.

Their report proposed in the interests of fairness and natural justice, that committees and panels considering staff matters should comprise members who had not had previous involvement in the matters under consideration.

In their opinion, it would widen the existing terms of reference so that members other than those on the S&SSC could be appointed to panels.

Whilst this point was acceptable, the opposition members were not happy with the rest of the proposal because it seemed as though the panel would have the power to vary the terms of a contract of employment of an officer; if this was to be the case it would be wrong in principle especially in the current circumstances.

Patrick Brady argued that this was not the case although he stated that the 'proposed mechanism would clarify how future decisions regarding staff matters were to be made.'

Those who had expressed a contrary view were not impressed with Mr Brady's explanation; they were even more concerned when it was suggested and agreed for additional clarity, that the position of the Head of Paid Service (Managing Director) should be included in the appropriate terms of reference.

Skulduggery in my view, and all the opposition members could do was to vote against the report or abstain.

Before the debate on Corporate Governance, Chris Huckle, Group Director (Social & Community) declared an interest in this item and left the room. Cllr Duncan Smith suggested that Cllr McKinlay should also declare an interest and not take part in the discussion.

I seconded Cllr Smith's proposal.

However, Gerald Ford, the MO, quickly intervened and advised the committee that the chairman (Cllr McKinlay) did not have a personal or prejudicial interest under the Code of Conduct and was entitled to take part in the debate.

Both Cllr Smith and I were surprised by the MO's advice.

As a result of the MO's advice, Cllr McKinlay introduced the report that would, he said, "Ensure clear corporate governance in the continuing absence of the Managing Director due to sickness."

He then proposed: "In the absence of the MD, Mr Chris Huckle should assume the role of Acting Managing Director with power to exercise any function normally delegated to the MD."

The report went on to say that if the committee agreed with the appointment then Mr Huckle would be paid a salary commensurate with that of the MD.

I was not happy with the proposal because my understanding of the job description for the Group Director (Social & Community) was a requirement for the post holder to act for the MD during holidays and absence. If this was the case, why should the council increase the salary of Mr Huckle when he was already required to stand in for the MD when she was absent?

Furthermore, it seemed to me that with the approval of the amendments to the terms of reference of the S&SSC, plus the appointment of Chris Huckle as Acting Managing Director, the decision had already been taken to suspend the MD; if it was legally possible.

I thought the proposal had all the signs of being the next stage in the process of replacing the MD with a ready-made member of the Board of Directors.

As expected, the discussion on the agenda item 'Employment and Grievance' was difficult. Jo Pitman, AD/HR reported the receipt of communications from two Group Directors, the MO and the PA to the MD regarding the behaviour and actions of the MD in recent weeks.

Although nothing was said at the time, it is worth noting that the 'communications' referred to above came from only two of the three Group Directors.

Cllr Duncan Smith queried the appropriateness of the MO participating in the discussion and advising the committee in relation to the MD's grievance as he had registered his own grievance against her.

He also expressed his concerns that the Cabinet members and two other councillors named in the grievance against the MD had a prejudicial interest in the matter and should not be allowed to participate in the debate.

He was aware that the Cabinet and the two councillors had been given advice by the MO who had indicated 'there was no interest to declare', but he wanted the minute to show that the opinions of the MO did not alter his personal view on the matter.

Cllr Fidgeon, adding to the discussion, confirmed that Cllr Smith had raised the same point at every meeting he had attended, even though the advice was not solely from the MO, but was also the opinion of Leading Counsel.

Mr Patrick Brady, the external expert brought in by the council, sought to reassure Cllr Smith that Mr Ford was not acting as the council's legal adviser in the matter of the MD's grievance. This role, he said "was being fulfilled by the Head of Legal Services, Mr Peter Lewis, and Cllr Smith had no need to be concerned about this particular matter."

How many other people were reassured by Mr Brady's claim we will never know because the minutes of the meeting were silent on this point, including comments by councillors on other aspects of the reports made at the S&SSC meeting.

Whilst it was clear that we were not going to win the argument, at least we had made our points.

Continuing with her report, the AD/HR reminded members that the MD had been absent from work for almost four months due to illness arising from circumstances at work. She said the MD had been due to see her doctor again on 17th November, which was the date the MD's current medical certificate expired.

The committee was also advised that discretionary powers existed to extend occupational sickness benefits to the MD; the present contractual rights meant that she was entitled to five months full pay and to five months absence on half pay.

The AD/HR confirmed that the MD's full pay benefits expired on 23rd December 2003 and the half pay benefits would expire on 22nd May 2004 if she remained absent through sickness.

Referring again to the letters she had received from the senior officers, the AD/HR suggested that the letters should be directed to the recently established JNC Members' Panel and this was agreed by the committee.

But if these senior officers of the council, three of them members of the Board, had been nursing complaints about the MD for several months, would it not have been sensible for them to confront the MD directly? I am sure an additional item on the Board agenda would have been the most appropriate way for the members to discuss their alleged grievances.

By not taking the initiative, it can only be presumed that these senior officers didn't think their complaints were serious enough, or if they did, they didn't have the courage to raise them in the usual 'time-honoured way'.

The final item to be discussed at the November 20th meeting was the receipt and acceptance of the Standards Committee (SC) minutes dated 31st October 2003.

The minutes, not surprisingly, contained no record of the complaints made by the Group Directors that the AD/HR had referred to earlier, nor did they contain any reference to the alleged concerns of the Leader of the Council.

The SC is an important committee. The chairman of the committee in 2003 was Mrs Pamela Hudson-Benderskey J.P., an independent member appointed by the council. As well as being chairman of the SC she was also the Chairman of the Cheltenham Magistrates' Court and her expertise in chairmanship and court procedures was invaluable.

Membership of the committee consists of volunteers from the community, a parish council representative and three Borough councillors. According to the council's Constitution, the person elected to the position of chairman of the SC must be one of the independent members. Members of the committee receive training in dealing with complaints and would have been capable of listening to the alleged complaints from the Group Directors or the alleged 'concerns' expressed by the Leader of the Council. So why were the SC minutes silent on these important matters?

The answer was simple; the SC had not been invited to look at these complaints or the Leader's concerns, or indeed any other matters throughout the period of the dispute in 2002, 2003 and 2004.

The legal adviser to the SC during this period was Gerald Ford the MO.

For the record, the Grievance Panel met on 13th, 14th and 27th November and 2nd December 2003. The MD returned to work on December 10th.

The Panel completed their report and this was presented to council on 18th December 2003. I was unable to attend the council meeting, but PAB colleagues updated me when I returned from holiday.

They reported to me that councillors asked for separate votes to be taken on several proposed addendums to the Panel's report.

The most relevant of these were as follows:

1. A proposal to delay any consideration of disciplinary action until the Standards Board announced their decisions was defeated by one vote.
2. A proposal requesting the mayor (Cllr Barnes) to write a letter to the MD regretting the council's failure to hold an annual appraisal was agreed by all except the mayor himself, who abstained from voting.
3. A proposal instructing the Section 151 officer to settle the claim for legal costs by the MD was agreed by 11 votes to 10.
4. A proposal asking council to note with concern the lack of clarity that existed in the contract of employment of the MD and asked the S&SSC to look into the matter. This was carried unanimously.

There were other less important addendums, which were approved and when the substantive motion was put by the Chairman (Cllr Melville-Smith) it was agreed unanimously.

It would be correct to say that council members had followed the set plan with each of the addendums and I don't think anyone was surprised by their decisions.

CHAPTER 20

2004 – A Year To Remember

Court Injunctions And Appearances

'Injustice anywhere is a threat to justice everywhere'.
Martin Luther King (1929–68)

The month of January 2004 started cold and changeable, a biting wind at times reminding everyone that winter was with us, but we hoped that things would improve as the month went on.

As I looked out of my window at the snow-capped Cotswold Hills, a little light rain started to fall and I wondered how long it would be before the snow would gradually disappear.

My daydreaming soon ended and I reflected on events of the past two years, which had been dominated by the dispute between the MD, Mrs Laird, and the Leader of the Council.

I went over the facts several times and I came to the same conclusion each time.

The MD had been engaged by the council in 2002 after the formal rules of recruitment and selection had been applied. At the time, she was well and enjoyed good health. She had been made aware that the job would require a tough assignment of reducing and reshaping the management structure of the council, and once in post, she set about her task with enthusiasm.

Unfortunately for Mrs Laird, the Liberal Democrats regained control of the Borough Council in May 2002 and in spite of their support for the restructuring programme when in opposition, they blamed the MD for carrying out the council's instruction now they were in charge. What was she supposed to do?

When reminded of their earlier support, they responded by saying that it was the previous Conservative administration that introduced it and therefore it was not incumbent on the new Lib/Dem administration to accept the policy in its entirety.

For reasons best known to the Liberal Democrats, they combined the disapproval of the policy they had inherited with a personal dislike of Mrs Laird and used it as a reason to start a campaign of hate, which they hoped would eventually bring about the termination of her employment.

I could not believe that a group of people with the responsibility of dealing with the affairs of the local authority could seriously believe that this was the right course of action to take.

It surprised me to such an extent that I sought the views of a friend who was knowledgeable about the science of the mind and he told me that the behaviour of such people often comes down to a number of factors. The first one could be the winning of the election and then having to implement their opponents' policies. This would be anathema to them.

Secondly, he thought that winning by a large majority could give them a belief that they were now 'all powerful' and they could do whatever they thought was right for them and the town.

And thirdly, he believed the personal dislike of the MD could be put down to misogyny.

What was immediately obvious was the determination of certain Lib/Dem councillors to remove this all-action Managing Director and replace her with someone of their choice.

That is how I saw it in 2004 and I still see it that way today.

The tactics used by Lib/Dem councillors have been well documented and I believe the method used was carefully chosen by them. It had been clear to most people for some time, and particularly to those with experience in such matters, that the perpetrators of such a campaign knew that should the method chosen be challenged in a court of law or a tribunal, their defence would be denial in the first instance, followed by a counter accusation that it was the other side in the dispute who had been responsible for the problems.

The tactics used were not new, and if my prognosis was correct then the MD stood no chance of winning the argument – she was not only up against the power of the Leader of the Council, but also the members of his Cabinet too.

I knew that certain senior officers had made allegations against the MD, so there was no support there either.

In other words, her case was hopeless.

My thoughts then turned to what could have been an alternative scenario; the Leader of the Council could have embraced the restructuring proposals and given the MD his full support. If he had done so then the council would have moved forward and the town would have benefitted from it.

If this had been too difficult for him to do because he had already 'nailed his colours to the mast' then he could have resigned as Leader of the Council and given the job to another member of the Lib/Dem team.

We know from previous chapters that senior officers of the council, who once thought the new MD was doing a good job, changed their stance and joined in the campaign of criticising the MD for the way the restructuring was being carried out. They professed unhappiness with the operation of the executive department, but were always careful not to go into detail.

They may have thought they were justified in their actions, but it had been suggested to me from several different quarters that it could have been a case of self-preservation which helped them to decide which side of the argument they should support. It may have been a question of 'sour grapes' on the part of some officers.

I do not think for one moment that they considered the available facts, few though they were, before they took sides in the dispute. And I have no doubt that they didn't think for one moment that the claims of the Leader and his Cabinet would ultimately drive them and everyone else along the road to the High Court in London, or the final cost that would be borne by the council taxpayer at the end of the dispute.

The sound of rain, gaining in intensity as it struck my window, broke my train of thought about the reasons for the dispute; about those involved and the complete failure of everyone in the council to bring the two sides together.

I looked across to the hills and my earlier thoughts were right, the snow on the top had almost gone as a result of the warm rain. However pleasant it might be looking out towards the hills, it was short-lived as my thoughts turned back to the task of sorting out in my mind the pros and cons of what had happened during 2002 and 2003.

In my view, the first mistake made by Cllr McKinlay was to believe that everyone outside his own political party had similar thoughts to his own. He also made the classic error of not seeking legal advice about the status of contracts of employment for senior officers before he embarked on what he thought would be an easy task of terminating the employment of the council's managing director.

If he had sought and been given the correct legal advice and still went ahead with his intention of ending the MD's contract of employment, then this error of judgement should have been investigated. Similarly, council officers and particularly officers from the legal department, who had failed to explain the important points about a contract of employment, had also failed in their duties.

And thirdly, the Leader probably believed and persuaded others to believe that a campaign of hate and abuse would be 'the straw that would eventually break the camel's back'. He probably believed that if the pressure on the MD was strong and effective enough, it would not be long before the MD begged the Cabinet to accept her resignation and to let her go.

Of course, as we learned from the events of the early years of her employment, she was made of sterner stuff and she fought her corner; she also had a better grasp of employment law and local authority regulations than those who were trying to get rid of her.

There was ample evidence in 2002 and 2003 that the MD had tried to find a way of resolving the dispute. Other members of the council too had tried to set up 'reconciliation meetings' in a genuine effort to resolve whatever it was that was troubling Cllr McKinlay and his Cabinet colleagues.

We had heard limp reasons in the past why he could not get on with Mrs Laird, although the detail of the reasons had never been fully revealed and it had been obvious for a very long time that nothing and no-one could make him change his mind about his feelings towards the MD.

Even though we knew this to be the case, it did not stop the opposition group leaders from trying to find a way through the situation.

In November 2003 the opposition group leaders met the mayor Cllr Garth Barnes and senior officers of the council, Chris Huckle and Marie Fallon (Group

Directors), to discuss the situation that existed between the MD and the Leader of the Council.

The opposition group leaders were anxious to see the dispute resolved and supported an arrangement that would allow the MD access to the council offices whilst she was officially signed off as unfit for work. If this 'arrangement' could be achieved then it would enable her to collect papers and documents during her sickness absence, which would help to keep her up to date with the business of the council.

Unfortunately, the two Group Directors took the opportunity to tell the meeting of their concerns regarding the MD; they criticised recent visits she had made to her offices. They alleged that the visits had been disruptive and not welcomed by the staff.

This prompted the opposition group leaders to ask questions about the visits and a request for more details and explanations regarding the complaints. They were particularly concerned about the claim that the MD had been disruptive, conduct which would have been unacceptable, but no substantive evidence was submitted by the Group Directors.

Not for the first time, allegations had been made that were lacking in detail and one could only classify them as trivial even though they seemed to be of great concern to those who had made them.

However, following a frank discussion about the situation, it was agreed that a meeting should be arranged between the opposition group leaders and the MD to discuss the problems that had been raised by the Group Directors.

It was suggested and agreed by those present that with the MD still on sick leave the meeting should be held at a neutral venue with the mayor acting as chairman and facilitator.

The mayor agreed to this suggestion and he offered to contact the vicar of St Luke's Church, which was in his ward, to see if the vestry could be made available for the meeting.

The mayor's offer was accepted and we all agreed it was possibly the last chance that anyone would have to resolve the long-running dispute. And with the mayor acting as the lynch-pin between the two sides, everyone was optimistic that a solution would be found.

It seemed a good idea to involve Cllr Barnes because apart from being the mayor of the town, he was also a senior Liberal Democrat councillor. And without over-stating the case, it would have been good for the standing of the Liberal Democrats as well as the town's reputation, if the dispute could be settled as a result of the meeting.

Accordingly, the meeting was arranged for Saturday afternoon 15th November 2003, in the vestry of St Luke's Church at 2.30 p.m.

We knew it was a clandestine meeting, which could do more harm than good if news of it was leaked, but we took a chance and those involved agreed not to divulge the details of the arrangement.

It was important too that Mrs Laird should attend the meeting and Cllr Duncan Smith agreed to contact her. There was a lot at stake on that Saturday afternoon and those attending had no idea how or if, the scheme of things would work out to the benefit of the council or Mrs Laird.

Therefore, it was of extreme importance to succeed in getting the two issues discussed and to find an acceptable compromise to end the dispute. It was equally important to agree a system that would enable the MD to enter the council offices, to visit her office and to access appropriate paperwork, which would keep her up to date with the day-to-day business of the local authority.

We arrived separately at St Luke's Church entering by a side-door where the vicar made us welcome. Mrs Laird was asked to arrive thirty minutes later, which gave the group leaders and the mayor the chance to go over the problems and the alleged difficulties that existed between the two sides.

We were looking for a solution.

As we discussed the ongoing dispute, the mayor gave me the impression that he was not overly enthusiastic for a settlement; other opposition group leaders may have felt the same because they pressed the mayor to talk to Cllr McKinlay and to resolve the problem.

Perhaps the mayor felt the pressure, because I noted that he did say on more than one occasion how bad the situation was for the town and its reputation; he also mentioned the escalating cost that was being incurred, which would be borne by the local taxpayers. This was true, but it was only a small amount at the time compared to the final cost that would exceed £2 million.

We didn't need to be reminded of this as it had been at the forefront of our minds in our attempts to bring the two sides together for a very long time.

The pressure put on the mayor by the opposition group leaders was going to be obvious because he was a member of the same political party as the Leader. This gave him an advantage of speaking privately to Cllr McKinlay, which might produce a dividend, and we expected him to put across a convincing argument that would end the dispute.

We were made aware that Mrs Laird had arrived at the church and she joined the meeting in the vestry. In normal circumstances she was ebullient and raring to go, but not on this occasion. I noticed that she had a look on her face that indicated to me that she was unhappy about something, or perhaps it was due to the fact that she had been unwell for some time. We soon found out what it was.

Following the usual courtesies, the mayor opened the meeting and outlined the following issues that needed to be discussed; i) was a reconciliation possible, ii) if so, would Mrs Laird be willing to play her part, and iii) the need for a structured system to allow the MD to visit the council offices.

It seemed to me to be a good way to start the meeting.

Unfortunately, we didn't get too far into the meeting before the mayor referred to a letter that had been sent to the MD a few days earlier, signed by the three Group Directors. (Chris Huckle, Marie Fallon, David Perry)

I also recall that he presented a lengthy document, which set out the concerns of the Group Directors regarding the previous visits the MD had made to the council offices, which according to the document, had not been without trouble.

It suggested that if the MD was prepared to sign the document, which contained a number of conditions, the matter of access would be granted.

The document also referred to the question of 'long-term' sickness absence and the steps that would need to be taken if the MD was absent for a prolonged period of time. The Group Director's letter also alleged that the MD had attended the council offices during her sickness absence and claimed she had criticised senior officers in front of junior members of staff.

It seemed a provocative move by the mayor to bring the letter and the document to our notice considering we were there to find a way through a difficult problem and to decide a strategy that would enable the MD to visit the council offices. On reflection, perhaps the Group Directors were as unsure about the outcome of the meeting as we were and wanted to be satisfied that the MD was aware of their concerns and she would follow the rules of access by signing the document.

There is nothing in my memory bank that tells me the course of action the mayor had taken with both the letter and document had been agreed with us at the earlier meeting.

Had the mayor agreed with the Group Directors to take the opportunity to discuss the letter and document before we agreed to the meeting in the church?

The fact that the mayor had put forward the document on behalf of the Group Directors (not the group leaders) was sufficient evidence for me to believe that was more likely to be the answer to my question.

Mrs Laird listened intently to what the mayor said and she confirmed that the letter and document had been sent to her a few days before the meeting so she was well prepared for what was forthcoming. She informed the meeting that she had contacted her solicitor Simon Collingridge, and he advised her to attend the meeting in St. Luke's Church, but to take emails from her computer that would show the allegations in the letter were false.

Mr Collingridge would write to the MO complaining about the content of the letter and the attempt by the council to get his client to sign what he considered to be an illegal document.

Mrs Laird's response, albeit through clenched teeth, was that the document was not about a system to enable her to enter the council offices, but an unlawful attempt to secure her voluntary suspension from the council.

My thoughts about the look on the MD's face as she entered the vestry had been answered in full; she was seething because she had a good idea of what was going to be said and she knew that the mayor would want the document to be signed.

She made it abundantly clear that she would not sign the document and she would provide a comprehensive reply to the charges, which she would send to the mayor within the next seven days.

She then gathered up her papers, said she intended taking further legal advice on the matter and left the room.

It took some time for things to settle down after she had gone, but it seemed to me that the well-intentioned 'secret meeting' had been hijacked by three senior officers who had been in cahoots with the mayor.

I was rather grateful that the Group Directors were not at the meeting; if they had been I cannot imagine what might have happened.

There was no point in any of the opposition group leaders running after the MD and persuading her to return to the vestry. For a while, we sat there ruminating on what had happened and wondered what kind of repercussions there might be.

The fact that we had tried to find a solution to end the dispute and found ourselves in an embarrassing situation was not what we had expected.

We left the church with a promise from the mayor that he would reconvene the meeting in the parlour in a few days' time to carry out a debriefing of the situation.

I was unable to attend the debriefing, even though I had pleaded with the mayor to choose a date and time when I could be there to enable me to make a suitable contribution.

The mayor chose not to comply with my request so I can make no comment on what took place at the meeting; as far as I am aware, there are no minutes of any of the meetings that took place in the vestry or the mayor's parlour.

Cllr Smith informed me later that the same people who had attended the first meeting were invited to attend the 'debriefing' meeting. He told me that the MD, not unexpectedly, would not sign any document and the mayor had informed the meeting that he had not been successful in persuading the Leader to move from his entrenched position. No surprises there either.

The MD had responded to the Group Directors' letter and copies were sent to the Group Leaders and the mayor, yet it was not discussed at the debriefing meeting.

In my email to the mayor on 19th November 2003 I reminded him that it was my suggestion at the church meeting that Mrs Laird should be invited to prepare a response to the document so that we could discuss it at the debriefing meeting. This was not done.

There was little doubt that the document the MD had been asked to sign was the work of Patrick Brady the former Chief Executive and Monitoring Officer of a local authority in Derbyshire, who was an expert on these matters. He had been engaged to smooth over the difficulties between the Leader of the Council and the MD, but whether he was an expert or not, it seemed a strange way to go about achieving an end to the long running dispute.

The MD had promised that she would respond within seven days to the allegations made in the letter by the Group Directors. She responded robustly to the charges. Simon Collingridge wrote to the MO asking him to make the content of the letter known to all councillors, so that they were totally aware of her response to the allegations made against her.

The request by the solicitor was not carried out and I can confirm that members of the PAB Group had not received a copy of the MD's response, nor had members of the other political parties.

Mr Brady, meanwhile, made several attempts to devise a document that would be acceptable to the MD, but in every case the wording of the document was such that it was contrary to the statutory protection that the MD was entitled to.

No-one in their right mind would sign a document that took away their statutory rights and I was surprised that he tried to do so. In the end, the MD became so fed up with the whole business that she kept away from the council offices until she was signed off as being 'fit for work' on 10th December 2003.

As far as I can remember, and having looked at past minutes, there is no record that the MD's responses to the allegations were even put before the JNC Panel.

The matter of an access agreement allowing the MD to enter the council offices and access her office was still something that the opposition group leaders felt would be useful. We had agreed that the wording in the agreement should be simple because we were mindful that the MD was reluctant to sign any 'woolly' document in the climate that existed at the time.

In an attempt to secure an agreement we agreed that an email should go from Cllr Smith to the MD asking her to draw up her own form of words for the access agreement, so that any interpretation problems could be overcome.

The email was sent on 18th November 2003 and it included a reference to the fact that the MD had previously agreed in principle to an agreement, which would protect the interests of everyone concerned.

In spite of this there was no response; Cllr Smith sent another email on 21st November to the MD explaining there had been no response from her solicitor in spite of earlier promises. There was no point in pursuing the matter further and we agreed that the matter should be considered closed.

In another of my reflective moments, I wondered if the position of the Leader of the Council would have become weaker if the MD had received continued support from her senior colleagues, similar to what she had enjoyed in the early months of her employment.

I am sure it would have helped, but then again, the call of self-preservation for some of the senior officers was too strong to gamble against the alternative.

It was a better option than being on the side of the MD.

Again, if Mr Ford the MO had been stronger, would it have prevented the Leader from being in the driving seat throughout the period of the dispute?

As opposition group leaders, we never knew whether our communications with the MO were in safe hands; there was always the feeling of being in a triangular web of competing forces.

I recall too the Group Leaders' meeting with the Board of Directors on 22nd October 2003 when Chris Huckle (Group Director, Social & Community) informed the meeting that the public service union had complained to him about certain councillors 'who had over-stepped the mark when dealing with officers'. This had been the second time the union had complained about 'councillor behaviour' and the Board were particularly concerned because the officers affected were those below the position of Assistant Directors. If this was the case then it was a matter for the council's Standards Committee to investigate, but there is no record that this happened.

Mr Huckle, when challenged, would not reveal the names of the councillors, but Cllr McKinlay revealed that he knew a Liberal Democrat member who was responsible for the allegation and he would deal with the matter.

Other Group Leaders confirmed they would talk to their members.

I make this point simply to inform readers that allegations were made by both sides during the stressful period of the dispute.

My position of PAB Group Leader did not entitle me to be privy to what was going on in the back rooms at the council offices so I found the month of January 2004 comparatively quiet.

My diary reminds me that I attended a Local Plan seminar, spoke to my orthopaedic surgeon about a possible knee replacement, met my solicitor about signing my will and attended a Gloucestershire Airport Working Group meeting.

There were meetings on Best Value and Comprehensive Performance Appraisals; long sessions on an Integrated Service Planning system, and the usual scheduled meetings such as planning and housing. Of course, this flurry of activity was due in no small part to the fact that Mrs Laird had been back in her office since December 10th and she took on the jobs with her usual enthusiasm.

I make no secret of the fact that when the occasion demanded it I held discussions with the MD about council business and matters of common interest. On 5th January 2004 she told me that she had formally waived her right to a 2003 appraisal. At the same meeting she had been told that her next appraisal would be in February 2004 with a focus on setting objectives for the coming year rather than reviewing events of the past year.

Whilst I was disappointed to learn that the MD had 'waived her right to an appraisal', I did wonder whether it was the beginning of a new dawn?

It was certainly good news and she was pleased that a positive decision on her appraisal in February had been made, although she was well aware that the underlying problems of the dispute were still lingering just below the surface.

When the JNC Panel met on 5th January they discussed the possibility of the MD undertaking an independent medical examination. The question it posed was whether this was a genuine concern about the health of the MD, or was it a way of finding a route for terminating her employment.

Mrs Laird thought it was the latter and I believe she was right to have concerns about it. However, the Panel members were informed that she had arranged an appointment with her GP on 13th January taking with her a list of questions relating to the purpose of the proposed medical examination.

On 16th January the GP wrote to Miss Pitman, the AD/HR, reminding her that his patient, Christine Laird, had been certified as unfit for work for periods between March and December 2003 due to reactive anxiety depression, precipitated by stress at work.

He expressed his concerns that 'since her return to work on December 10th she was still being subjected to many of the stressors that precipitated her illnesses. In his opinion, the imminent disciplinary hearing is causing a significant risk of a relapse and resultant long-term health problems.'

The doctor concluded his letter by informing Miss Pitman that Mrs Laird's treatment was ongoing, but he thought that with support and the right work environment she would cope with her demanding job. He asked the AD/HR to review the causes that had brought on the acute physical and mental illness of his patient and to provide an indication that the council would protect her well-being.

The AD/HR informed the members of the S&SSC about the letter; they received it with little sympathy and made it clear that they were determined to see the JNC Panel conclude what it was set up to do.

Any suggestion of a temporary suspension was quickly rejected by the committee, who wanted the council to operate in a normal way for a set period of time.

The intention of the S&SSC was to continue to talk about the duty of care towards the MD, giving the impression of being the 'guardian angel' but then later in the meeting insisting that the investigation will go on in spite of the warnings from her doctor that it would have an adverse effect on her health.

It had not gone unnoticed that following the MD's return to work from sickness absence, the JNC Panel had been convened

If there were green shoots of recovery a few weeks ago, then they had withered very quickly in the early part of January 2004.

I was unaware until later in the month that the JNC Members' Panel had met on 15th January 2004 to discuss a preliminary report on behalf of the MO. There had been an addendum to the report, presented to the committee by Patrick Brady.

The report before the Panel itemised a list of 96 complaints from the Leader, the Group Directors and others against the MD, most of which were trivia. The fact that they had gone to such lengths in their pursuit of the MD confirmed my long-held view that the situation had got to a stage where these so-called grown-up people, holding responsible positions in the council, continued to act like children rather than adults, just as they had done for the past two years. It was obvious to most informed watchers of the dispute, the accusers were quite oblivious of where their accusations might end, and showed little regard to the ongoing and ever increasing expenditure of council taxpayers' money, or the standing of the council.

These important issues appeared to be the least of their considerations.

A few examples here of the 96 complaints should give the reader some idea of what had been going on in the council offices. I have selected the following: *obstructive tactics, (presumably not physical), misinforming a councillor that the Leader was dealing with a report, informing the Leader that a conference centre could not hold entertainments, not advising the Leader of forthcoming meetings, not keeping the Leader informed and therefore undermining him, misrepresenting the Leaders' comments, ignoring the views of a councillor over a local matter, making inappropriate remarks about the Cabinet as they entered her office.* Interesting no doubt to the curious, but where did it lead us?

One can only think that officers and councillors must have spent a great deal of time jotting down every spoken word of the MD, noting her body language and anything else she said or did in order to make the report to the JNC members plausible.

Personally, I think the whole business was shameful and a complete waste of time.

The addendum, which I referred to above, informed the JNC members that the MD and her solicitor had responded to the charges and questioned procedural issues.

Although the MO has been a signatory to the complaints against the MD, it was still claimed that the MO did not have an interest that disqualified him from offering advice contained in the JNC report.

The let-out apparently, was that the MO had not put his name to the report and it had been submitted by someone else on his behalf; defending the indefensible it seemed.

Opposition group leaders found the excuse unbelievable – not least because the recent grievance letter from the MO, accusing the MD of certain practices, ought to have been of sufficient importance to warrant a declaration of interest. Even if the rules allowed him not to declare an interest, most people would have thought that in the interest of appearing neutral, the MO should have kept well wide of any official debates into the process of the dispute.

The most worrying aspect of the JNC report was the possibility that the Panel had the power to appoint a Designated Independent Person (DIP), and if they decided to do so, the report made it clear that the financial cost would be substantial.

It would be up to the council members to decide whether the allegations (some of them referred to above) were sufficiently serious enough to justify the expenditure.

On 2nd February 2004, David Perry (Group Director, Economy & Business Improvement) presented a report to the S&SSC on the financial implications of the dispute for the period 2004 and 2005.

In declaring a potential conflict of interest because of the requirements of his job, he reminded the committee that as a senior member of the council he had a duty to report his views and to offer advice on matters relating to the duty of care that he and the council owed to the MD and other staff members.

His report had already been given to Group Leaders in accordance with the requirements of the 27th October 2003 council meeting. It was an update of the expenditure to date, the projected expenditure for the remainder of the current financial year, and the possible financial implications for 2004 and 2005.

The report also sought the approval by the S&SSC of current and future use of consultants to support the council during the dispute.

Agreement was also sought for the on-going use of external consultants to support the council, including the back-filling of posts where required, in order to support members of staff involved in the dispute.

David Perry reminded the committee that the council had been incurring costs in relation to the dispute since April 2003, and while it had been hoped that the costs could be managed within current resources, it was unlikely this would be the case.

In May 2003 after consultations with the Group Leaders he had set aside £20,000 from an earmarked reserve held for contingencies.

After further consultation with the Group Leaders, David Perry reported that another £33,000 had been made available from the contingency reserve fund.

He had also recommended to council on October 27th that 'the council should *determine* a suitable source for the future funding of the dispute, *provide* details of general fund balances, and *set out* the implications of the decision taken by council on 21st February 2003 to set balances between £1 million and £1.5 million'.

It was no consolation to be reminded by David Perry that the Group Leaders had been given a breakdown of the financial costs of the dispute, but the burden of responsibility now lay on the shoulders of those members of the S&SSC who had favoured being in the driving seat along the road to the High Court for some time.

The Group Leaders were also told that the council had already incurred significant expenditure in dealing with the dispute a) as a result of obtaining external legal advice on how to process it, b) in obtaining external advice in response to issues raised by the MD, including protecting the council's interests against threats of legal action and c) through the use and appointment of external consultants to support the council during the current process.

David Perry further reported that very significant internal costs had also been incurred by several departments, not least in dealing with the Standards Board for England Inquiry.

The report by David Perry was depressing to say the least, and it was heard in silence. No-one challenged the figures, probably because they knew there was a lot more expenditure still to come. And, of course, there was.

He reported that the MD had ruled out negotiation and attempts at mediation had also failed, but he said there were still options such as a negotiated settlement on the grounds of ill-health, but any settlement would need to be detailed more fully at the time, should it be considered.

The District Auditor (DA) had been kept informed throughout the period and he had been regularly updated. The DA's concerns would be centred on the expenditure being balanced against the benefits that may be obtained.

David Perry reminded the committee that the DA would be concerned if General Fund balances fell below £1 million with the level of risk that it carried.

Turning to the internal costs, he said that costs associated with the appointment of Mr Brady were high and could be the largest item in the accounts in the immediate future. He had been appointed by SOLACE and the cost to date was £6,000 to £11,000 per month.

Added to this was the additional cost associated with the JNC Members' Panel, including the cost of legal support from the council. It all sounded so very depressing.

What was needed was a realisation that the report by David Perry was a warning that significant cost had already been incurred and there was no indication from any quarter as to how long the period of expenditure would go on.

He asked the committee to consider its position in relation to the continued use of consultants in order to advise senior officers because of the increasing costs.

He suggested that should the committee not wish to continue to outsource this work, they should advise the council what action they wish to take in relation to the work the consultants currently provide.

On the personnel side of things, David Perry warned that it was not possible to be specific about the extra human resource related costs that were likely to be incurred as the dispute continued.

The report was a warning shot from Mr Perry, albeit heard in silence, given out of courtesy and nothing else, but it was a message that the committee were unlikely to act upon. It had been delivered with clarity and the potential cost factor could not be ignored.

This was all strong stuff from David Perry and I was not alone in quietly being grateful to him for setting out the situation clearly and explaining what the possible costs might be. He concluded his report by setting out his final conclusions, which turned out to be a reiteration of all the points he had made in his presentation.

It would have been a breach of the members' code of conduct if I had applauded the Group Director for his report, but there was no doubt in my mind that he had spelled out in easy to understand language that the council, if it insisted on continuing down the path they had chosen, would have a heavy cost to pay.

No-one on the S&SSC could be under any misapprehension about the cost of the dispute and the unfolding consequences of their actions, but as we shall learn later, it was 'like water off a duck's back'.

Whichever side of the dispute the councillors or officers took, it was clear that a point of no return had been reached that evening. There was not going to be a truce or a reconcilliation between the Leader and the MD and by the sound of David Perry, he believed that too, although he did say more than once that if the committee intended to continue with the dispute they had better tell him how the future expenditure would be funded.

In August 2004 David Perry resigned and joined the South Gloucestershire Unitary Authority. He was appointed their Section 151 Officer and Deputy Chief Executive.

Although his report to the S&SSC had covered the period 2004 and 2005 he did not intend to stay to see whether his warnings and forecasts would turn out to be correct.

There was no doubt in my mind that Cheltenham Borough Council had lost a good and efficient officer and one that faced up to the reality of the situation.

Marie Fallon joined Cheltenham Borough Council on 1st July 2002 as Group Director (Environment). She was another new member of the MD's management team who was going to take Cheltenham Borough Council forward in 2002 and 2003, in accordance with the policy decisions of the Structural Review Committee.

Just prior to Marie's appointment, Jo Pitman had been successful in applying for the post of Assistant Director/Human Resources and she started working for Cheltenham Borough Council on 11th February 2002.

I was one of three councillors on the Recruitment Interview Panel when the applicants for the post of Group Director were interviewed and Marie Fallon was one of the applicants.

The Panel was chaired by the MD, although she did not have a vote.

Marie was up against other strong candidates and there was no doubt that she was a front runner for the job. Her curriculum vitae (CV) included references to employment with other councils and at the present time she was the head of a large department in Birmingham City Council. Although the panel were impressed with Marie Fallon's CV, I remember asking her about the size of her departmental budget in Birmingham City Council. She replied it was around £30 million, which was more than twice the budget for the whole of Cheltenham Borough Council.

Members of the panel had smiles of satisfaction on their faces, including the MD, but I was not as overawed with Marie's interview performance as the others appeared to be.

I asked Marie why she wanted to become the Group Director in a small council like Cheltenham Borough, when she clearly had a very responsible job in Birmingham City Council with far more power.

The answer she gave was not convincing; she thought the job offered a new challenge and she liked the thought of living in the Cotswold area. I recollect a comment about her daughter's school being not too far from Cheltenham, adding that if she was successful, she would be closer to her daughter.

However, I had not been convinced she was the right person for the job based on the replies she had given to the questions put to her; although it is true to say that other members of the panel were impressed. My main concern was that if we were minded to appoint Marie, it could turn out to be a temporary placement and we may not get what we were looking for – a long-term Group Director with ambitions to become the next managing director of Cheltenham Borough Council.

During the lunch break, the panel discussed the candidates' responses to the questions we had put to them and their suitability for the job. Whilst Marie was the favourite for the post I plugged for a male candidate from Swindon who had excellent credentials on highway improvements in urban areas. If appointed, he would have been a useful acquisition to improve the difficult traffic systems that prevailed in Cheltenham at the time.

Each candidate was told during the interview of a potential 'civic pride' project that would be undertaken in the town as part of new traffic arrangements for the centre of Cheltenham.

Before the interview panel resumed, the MD asked me to have a word with her in private. We did and the essence of Mrs Laird's approach to me was that she hoped the panel would be unanimous in its decision to appoint Marie Fallon. This seemed a strange request to make, not least because the voting by individual members of the panel was not recorded. It was also an unusual request from the MD, probably based on the questions I had put to Mrs Fallon during the interview; my view has always been that individual members of a panel should express an honest opinion about each candidate based on what they had heard, not because of the opinions of other members of the panel. The fact that I didn't vote for Marie Fallon at interview did not mean that I would not give her my full support during her time with the council.

It was clear that Mrs Laird had been impressed with the answers given by Marie Fallon, but I still voted for the man from Swindon for the reasons I have given. Marie Fallon duly took up her post and I have to say that in the early months of her employment she and the MD worked well together.

The fact that they worked well together may have been the cause for some of the sarcastic criticism levelled at the MD during the early part of the dispute when some councillors and others suggested that the appointment of Marie Fallon and Jo Pitman was a calculated desire on the part of the MD to replace all senior male officers with members of the opposite sex.

Marie Fallon and Jo Pitman were selected on merit, but that was how bitter and silly the dispute had become.

There was nothing to suggest to me that a good working relationship did not exist between Marie Fallon and the MD, but I am mindful of the fact that Marie was a signatory on the letter of complaint from the Group Directors regarding the MD's visits to the council offices that I referred to earlier.

It is worth noting that Marie Fallon left the council on 4th June 2006 and Jo Pitman left on 30th June 2006. With David Perry (Group Director-Finance) leaving in August 2004, it raised questions amongst staff and councillors about the reasons behind the exit of such prominent senior people.

Neither Marie, Jo or David gave evidence in the High Court proceedings, which is a significant factor too, and rumour has it that some, if not all three, were asked to give evidence on behalf of the council and they declined.

Members of the S&SSC were informed by the MO that a special meeting of the committee would take place on 26th February 2004. The main item was 'An Employment Matter'.

Every committee member knew that the 'employment matter' concerned the MD, so it seemed rather churlish not to report this on the agenda paper.

At least it would have given members of the committee a chance before the item was discussed to declare any interest that might prejudice their position. We knew from previous meetings that there were councillors and officers who had made allegations against the MD so why all the secrecy with the agenda item?

I wrote to Gerald Ford on 23rd February 2004 stating my concerns about the lack of clarity in the agenda item 'employment matter'. This is an extract from my letter:

> "The Managing Director has made serious allegations against the Cabinet, the majority of who sit on the S&SSC and have been reported to the Standards Board for England. They have repeatedly refused to declare a prejudicial interest, albeit on the advice from yourself and Mr Patrick Brady (Consultant Legal Adviser) and, as a result, they have remained in the room and participated in the discussion.
>
> If the Cabinet members had left the room there was, on each of the previous occasions, enough expertise in the committee to discuss the 'employment matter'.
>
> However, I have to inform you that I have written to the Standards Board for England expressing my concerns and the reply I have received leaves me in no doubt that the five members of the Cabinet should have declared a prejudicial interest and should not have taken part in the debates because they would have had a significant personal stake in the outcome in the decision of the committee.
>
> It is also clear that in a general situation where a member makes a serious allegation of misconduct, the Board believes that a member should not be sitting in judgement in any situation where the member is unlikely to be impartial and able to consider the merits without considering his or her own position.
>
> In the light of the above I shall not be attending the S&SSC meeting on Thursday February 26th 2004 or any others unless there is a change in the declaration of interest procedure and recognition of the requirements of the Code of Conduct.
>
> I would also like to know what you propose to do as the Council's Monitoring Officer to ensure that this committee operates properly."

I have no record of a reply to my letter.

Following the MD's return to work from sickness absence on 10th December 2003, visits by the Leader of the Council to her office increased. They were impromptu visits, usually about trivial matters and probably designed to put further pressure on the MD following her return to work from work-related stress.

It was not difficult to put two and two together to see why this pressure was taking place. After all, the Leader knew that the JNC Panel were progressing with their investigation and there was an air of anticipation in the Liberal Democrat ranks that the end result of the Panel's deliberations would probably be the departure of the MD, or at least her suspension from the council offices.

The random visits could have been made to frighten the MD: when bullies believe they are winning, it gives them additional delight to suddenly appear at their victim's door with some spurious reasons why they needed to be there.

The layout of the MD's department consisted of three offices.

In order to reach the MD's office, a visitor would need to pass through an outer office where three or more female members of the MD's staff were working.

Another small office for Mrs Karen Watson, the Personal Assistant (PA) was situated immediately adjacent to the office of the MD.

The female staff employed in the outer office witnessed the frequent visits of the Leader and the tense situations it was causing, while at the same time trying hard not to appear to be taking sides in the dispute.

The pressure of these visits by Cllr McKinlay and his presence in the outer office soon became too much for the MD and on 26th February 2004 Mrs Laird submitted an application to the Cheltenham County Court asking for an injunction to prevent the Leader from entering the first floor of the council offices so that the confrontations would stop.

On 31st March 2004, Mrs Laird withdrew her application for an interim injunction, which was due to be heard in Bristol County Court on 1st April 2004, and she was ordered to pay the costs of the application.

In the statement explaining why she had done this, Mrs Laird claimed she had advised the court that Cllr McKinlay had complied with her request to refrain from visiting her office or contacting her in any manner.

Mrs Laird in her statement reported that the successful application for costs by Cllr McKinlay, following the withdrawal of the interim application, had been overturned by the Bristol County Court on 7th June 2004.

In a further attempt to prevent Cllr McKinlay from entering the first floor of the council offices, together with another claim by Mrs Laird she had been systematically harassed by him, the Bristol County Court gave summary judgement on 26th October 2004 in Cllr McKinlay's favour, with costs.

It is important to mention the court proceedings if only to remind readers of the enormous animosity that existed between two leading members of the council and the extent to which each individual would go in order to make their point.

It also shows that while the council was spending large sums of money to defend and promote their position against the MD, she too was prepared to spend a large sum of money to defend her rights as she saw them.

The old saying that 'it is only lawyers who gain from this kind of dispute' is true. The money that went into the pockets of the legal advisors by the time the dispute ended at the Royal Courts of Justice was substantial, as we shall find out in a later chapter.

Whilst the squabbles in the county court were taking place, the JNC Members' Panel continued to meet regularly, looking at all the possibilities to suspend the MD. It was not difficult to get the impression that nothing else was happening in the council offices, but that was far from the truth.

In the early part of March 2004 the JNC Panel published an interim report, which was considered by councillors at the council meeting on March 19th.

The purpose of the report was to update councillors on the progress of the JNC Members' Panel, the proposed actions they intended to take and a timetable for the Panel to follow over the next month. Bearing in mind that the Panel was established by the council on 27th October 2003, it could be said that little progress had been made, although much had been written and spoken about the investigation since the Panel had been formed.

An hour before the March 19th meeting was due to start, Mrs Laird received an impromptu visit from two Conservative councillors, Cllr Garnham and Cllr Melville-Smith, who advised the MD that regardless of the recommendations of the JNC Panel, they 'intended to move a resolution to suspend her from the Council'.

Not unexpectedly, the MD accused them of prejudging the matter, which, as she explained, was a breach of the Code of Conduct. She then informed them that because of their comments, she would be obliged to make a report to the MO stating what had happened and what they had said and suggested to them that they should do the same.

I have been unable to find any evidence that shows that the MO brought the matter to the attention of the Standards Committee, which confirms again that its purpose in the local authority was of little value.

Apparently, Cllrs Garnham and Melville-Smith in their response indicated to the MD that 'they had no intention to report their comments to the MO, and in any case, it would be a case of their word against hers'.

Not a case of one person's word against the other one, but one against two. Remember it was Cllr Melville-Smith who wrote to his Group Leader in April 2003 asking him to make contact with him because in his words "things were turning nasty" regarding the dispute. Remember too he was, allegedly, giving Christine Laird legal advice at the time regarding her situation with the Leader of the Council.

How more bizarre could this situation become?

So, this was the reaction of some members of the political party that Mrs Laird was accused of being too close to; she had been accused of being a 'Tory nark' doing their bidding, although this was never substantiated.

But the words of the two Conservative councillors were significant, not least because throughout the dispute and beyond, Mrs Laird always found herself defending her position, not against one, but against several people at the same time. It was easy for officers and elected members to call in on the MD to express a point of view, often with others in support and then they would depart. It is called 'corroborative witnessing' and very effective it is too.

This had been a feature throughout the dispute.

Since the establishment of the JNC Members' Panel in October 2003, the chief legal adviser to the Panel was Miss Sarah Farooqi (solicitor) who also acted as its clerk.

At the first meeting she reminded members of their obligations with regard to the Code of Conduct and declarations of interest and then introduced Mr Alistair McGregor, Q.C., who had been retained to advise the council.

Several councillors who had been directly involved in the dispute did not respond to Miss Farooqi's reminder and I expressed a view that the councillors concerned should declare a prejudicial interest regarding the matter about to be discussed.

Mr McGregor also indicated that he had concerns regarding the position of some members and he had communicated his view to the Deputy MO (Miss Farooqi).

One or two other members expressed similar thoughts to mine and some even offered the view that 'it was inevitable that some members would be biased'.

At this point, I rose to my feet and walked to the exit door, followed by Cllrs Hibbert and Stennett (PAB), Cllrs McDonald, McLain, Mrs Driver and Mrs Regan (Conservatives). It was noticeable that no Liberal Democrats followed our example.

By not remaining in the council chamber, I am unable to go into the detail of any of the proceedings. I have relied, therefore, on the generosity of others who right-fully remained in the chamber and heard the debate.

The chairman of the Panel, Cllr Diggory Seacome (Conservative), presented the report and reminded council that the purpose of the Panel was not to judge, but to establish whether the facts presented to them required an independent investiga-tion to determine whether there was a case to answer.

If and only if there was a case to answer, the council would then be able to appoint a Designated Independent Person (DIP). A DIP is usually a barrister or Queen's Counsel (QC) and the appointment would need approval from the Secretary of State.

The chairman also advised council that the Panel had met the MD on 24th February and 15th March 2004 and on each occasion the MD had expressed a lack of confidence in the process. He also reported that the MD's legal representatives had previously put forward proposals to ensure that her concerns would be taken into account. By accepting the point, the Panel set a provisional timetable assuming that a DIP would be appointed by 29th March 2004.

Council was told that a final report would be available in the early part of May.

Mr McGregor Q.C., explained to the councillors the various regulations that would apply should the council proceed to suspend the MD; and not for the first time, the councillors were reminded that the post of Managing Director was one of the council's three statutory posts protected by the Local Government Act 2000.

The Q.C. then outlined in considerable depth the implications for Cheltenham Borough Council if it was minded to take a decision of suspending the MD. He also advised that if such a decision was taken then it was likely an injunction would be raised immediately, which would introduce further potential for a much longer delay in the next stage of the JNC process.

Cllr Melville-Smith claimed that the MD had put every possible obstacle in the way of the process. "This led to the dispute being longer than it needed to be," he claimed.

Another strange comment from someone who had been advising the MD in the early stages of the dispute; there was overwhelming evidence to show that every effort had been made by individuals, including Mrs Laird, the opposition group leaders and others to try and settle the dispute.

Every attempt had been vigorously rejected.

Mr McGregor was not convinced by the comment. He responded to Cllr

Melville-Smith by indicating that the councillor would need to produce evidence to show the MD had been interfering with the procedure before he could make a judgement on whether sufficient interference had taken place.

Miss Farooqi supported the comments of the Q.C. confirming that the MD had not interfered with the work of the JNC Panel. She believed the MD had responded in a way she would have expected from a named person facing an action.

Questions put to Mr McGregor centred round the question of suspension and the power of the DIP if one should be appointed. He replied that the DIP would only have power to extend or remove suspension, but not to impose suspension. The JNC Panel could suspend, in accordance with the council's Standing Orders, but only for the purpose of the investigation.

Cllr Garnham, deputy mayor and a member of the Conservative Group, was not satisfied with the answer. He claimed the MD had caused stress amongst staff, had threatened Group Directors with legal action, and had criticised officers in various meetings. Grave charges indeed. Mr McGregor's response was to repeat again his earlier comments that such allegations had to be supported by evidence.

Such claims by Cllr Garnham came as a surprise, not least because there is no record that such accusations had been made to me, or to those engaged in trying to find a solution to the dispute during the previous two years.

Readers would have gathered by now that he and any other councillor would have had ample opportunity to make representations to their Group Leader, or to mention the facts at their group's political meetings; it was well-known that the opposition group leaders had been trying hard for reconciliation throughout the period of the dispute.

Cllr Stuart-Smith (Lib/Dem), who did not declare an interest in the proceedings, and yet was someone who had played a significant part in the initial stages of the dispute, suggested 'the MD might interfere with the investigation once it got underway'.

He then referred the council to an email he had received from the MD reminding him that he should declare an interest at the council meeting. He responded to the request by informing council that a declaration of interest was the responsibility of the individual, and as such he had declined to declare any interest in the debate that was about to take place. Even if Cllr Stuart-Smith was right about not declaring his interest in the proceedings, he had pre-determined his position on what was about to be debated and he could hardly say as a result of his direct involvement in the dispute that he had 'an open mind'.

Readers should make their own judgement on this, but isn't the whole problem with the code of conduct and the particular clause about declaring an interest flawed, if it is simply up to the individual to declare it?

It is obvious from what had gone on previously, that the council's legal advisors were unsure about the position and as we shall learn in the next chapter, the Standards Board for England (SBE) appeared to be equally unsure.

[By not declaring an interest, an individual is open to accusations that he/she could be biased in that he she/has a closed mind and has already pre-determined the outcome of the matter to be discussed or decided].

There is a test in law in relation to the appearance of bias, which was laid down by the House of Lords in *Porter v Magill* [2002] 2 AC 357, at paragraph 103 per Lord Hope: *"the question is whether the fair-minded and informed observer, having considered the facts, would conclude that there was a real possibility that the tribunal was biased"*.

In spite of this ruling by the House of Lords, the in-house legal advice to the councillors involved in the dispute, was not to declare an interest. I took the opposite view; I ignored the advice, declared an interest and left the room.

My strong opinion is that any contribution in a meeting by a councillor or an officer, who had failed to declare an interest, should be disregarded.

But, as readers will see, unless 'the fair-minded man in the street' formally objects to the non-declaration by a councillor to the Standards Board, then nothing regarding breaches of the code of conduct is ever revealed. And, as we shall learn in the next chapter, the SBE was inept even when a breach of the code of conduct had been brought to their attention.

Following a brief adjournment the council reconvened, whereupon Cllr Melville-Smith proposed that the MD should be suspended from her post whilst the investigation took place.

Cllr Brian Chaplin (Conservative) was concerned that the proposal flew in the face of the advice given by Mr McGregor that suspension was not an option. He argued that the council chamber was not the place to discuss and question the individual allegations.

In Cllr Chaplin's view 'suspension would not speed up the present processes.'

There were repeated claims by both Conservative and Lib/Dem councillors that the MD would interfere in the investigation, but they were basing their assumptions on what had taken place regarding previous events in the council offices, which was quite irrelevant.

Mr McGregor reminded the councillors again that the council could not rely on past instances to support their allegations that the MD might interfere with the investigation and they should dismiss this from their minds.

Having listened to the legal advice, Cllr Garnham decided not to second the proposal by his colleague Cllr Melville-Smith. He did not think the council would be best served by suspending the MD and if, as a result of a suspension, the MD served an injunction on the council, how would the general public respond to such a decision?

No doubt, Cllr Garnham was also mindful of the fact that the way things were going there could be further legal costs incurred on top of the growing bill for the external legal advice.

The meeting went over the same points again with Mr McGregor giving the same advice about unsupported evidence in the allegations. He reminded members that in his view the JNC process was one month away from completion and that the MD had indicated she now had confidence in the process. On that basis, he advised the council members to accept the recommendation in the interim report of the JNC Panel.

Although it was getting late, the mayor adjourned the council meeting to allow Cllr Garnham, with the help of his Conservative colleagues, to formulate an alternative motion.

When this was done, the mayor reconvened the meeting at 8.35 p.m.

At the start of the resumed meeting, Cllr Melville-Smith stated that he wanted to withdraw his proposal to suspend the MD, but he added that he would seek to reintroduce it later, if he thought it was necessary.

The motion proposed by Cllr Garnham contained the following points:-
The council should

1. Adopt the interim report of the JNC Panel.
2. Issue a clear statement to the MD that the Council would not tolerate any delay or interference in the remaining currency of the investigation process. Failure on the MD's part could result in suspension.
3. Reassure staff that the Council had a duty of care to all employees and will endeavour to conclude the investigation as quickly as possible.

The motion was seconded by Cllr Melville-Smith. When the motion was put, 23 councillors supported the motion with one councillor against. (If there had been a recorded vote, it would have shown the name of the dissident councillor).

Before councillors were allowed to go home to their families they were updated on the risks associated with the dispute between the MD and certain members of the council. They were also made aware that the MD had issued injunctive proceedings against the Leader of the Council and they were told that the council's current insurance provisions protected them should they be sued by a third party.

Of course, the cost of insurance cover and the impending legal challenge would require further funding, and with more legal advice and court attendances in the offing, more council taxpayers' money would be spent to cover this.

In spite of the comments made at the council meeting, I continued the task with the help of others, to try to find a solution to what had become an almost impossible situation. It was not easy.

It does not enhance one's position in the popularity stakes either; it was a lonesome task at times, trying to seek out the truth when so many people held fixed views that were opposite to mine.

On 27th April 2004, Sarah Farooqi, the clerk to the JNC Panel, wrote to me regarding the meeting that had taken place between the MD and the Group Leaders on 19th March 2003. (Remember the meeting had taken place without the Leader of the Council being present) Why were the Panel members interested in what had happened at the meeting on 19th March 2003 when no-one believed it had ever taken place? The Leader of the Council claimed he had not been invited.

However, Miss Farooqi asked me to confirm whether the MD had made a comment at the meeting alleging that Cllr Stuart-Smith had told her that 'the PAB Group did not have confidence in the Managing Director'.

My reply on April 29th confirmed that the MD had made the comment at the March 19th meeting and I had immediately refuted it. I told Miss Farooqi that I had not met Cllr Stuart-Smith on any occasion during the period of the dispute, nor exchanged correspondence with him during this period.

Having answered the question, it seemed a good opportunity for me to restate in my letter that the MD had also reported to the meeting that Cllr Stuart-Smith had asked her to leave the council's employment with the offer of a financial inducement. The MD had also reported that discourteous comments had been made to her by various members of the Cabinet, including a claim that the Leader of the Council had said to her "The very sight of you makes me feel sick."

This alleged comment was to be repeated in the High Court, but the reader will hear in a later chapter that whilst the comment by Cllr McKinlay that "he told Mrs Laird that he often felt physically sick as a result of the stress she put him under" the judge claimed that this comment 'had been interpreted by Mrs Laird as an insult rather than a statement of fact'.

But wait a minute; isn't the use of insulting words by a councillor to another councillor or to a member of staff a breach of the council's Code of Conduct?

Readers will soon gather that all the events recorded in the previous pages would ultimately play an important part in the High Court proceedings. Having failed to dismiss Mrs Laird from her position as Managing Director, due to her statutory protection, the council needed to find other ways and means of terminating her employment. But the way the council had treated her in the past two years had already started to affect her health.

The stress of the job and the verbal abuse she had suffered had resulted in a long period of sickness absence and now she was back at work and the whole business of stress and worry had started again.

Readers will learn that with the setting up of the JNC Panel, the possibility of suspension and the appointment of a qualified DIP to investigate the alleged complaints against her were too much and she succumbed to the pressure.

She sought medical advice and the prognosis was dire. She was considered to be too sick to work by her doctor and she was signed off from work on 24th May 2004 never to return to Cheltenham Borough Council. A life ruined by the actions of others.

On 4th June 2004 Mrs Laird suffered a severe panic attack and as a result could not control her limbs, or control her speech; a situation she was to endure in the weeks and months ahead, and perhaps forever.

The story, of course, didn't end there. The conspiracy, led by Liberal Democrat councillors and supported by certain officers, to apply psychological pressure on the Managing Director who they did not want, had finally been successful.

But at what cost?

Who was going to pay the financial bill, which had by then reached over £1,000,000? The answer, of course, is the council taxpayer.

The next chapter will reveal how easy it is to spend other people's money and have nothing to show for it at the end.

CHAPTER 21

The Standards Board For England, Was It An Ineffective Quango?

If a thing's worth doing, it's worth doing well.

Proverbs (mid eighteenth century)

One of the first actions of the new Coalition Government in 2010 was to scrap the Standards Board for England (SBE) because they believed it was an expensive body that had very little to show for its efforts. The debate in the House of Commons preceding the eventual scrapping of the SBE was highly critical of the way it had dealt with cases of alleged impropriety since it was introduced in 2000.

In the words of one Member of Parliament, who was at great pains to explain to the members of the House of Commons why he sought its demise, 'it is an inefficient, expensive and woefully unfair outfit that should be confined to the history books as quickly as possible'.

Anyone listening to the debate would have found it interesting, because the language used by the MP's had been flowery at times, to say the least; the examples given by various MP's from both sides of the House were either bizarre, if they were true, or a clear indication that the SBE had failed miserably to carry out its proper functions.

To me, and I suspect to other local people who listened to the debate, it was a vivid reminder of the times when help and advice was sought from the SBE during the CBC v Laird dispute, which were not forthcoming (as referred to in earlier chapters).

There were a few Members of Parliament who wanted the SBE to continue, but most MP's agreed that it should be scrapped.

One MP suggested that the SBE 'was guaranteed to malfunction because it was designed by idiots'. Sharp words indeed.

Un-parliamentary language maybe, but he supported his belief by claiming that there were councillors in Devon under investigation because 'they wanted to scrap prayers before meetings to save time'.

In another example he quoted a case where a Liberal Democrat councillor had been reported to the SBE for 'removing a petition from a local post office'.

Apparently, in 2008, there had been 3,500 different complaints to the SBE, which only emphasised that the system of complaints had become a laughing stock rather than a useful tool in seeking a fairer system of justice in the code of conduct for people in local government.

The examples of wasteful complaints given during the debate on the future of the SBE were not confined to certain parts of the United Kingdom; they were endemic across the whole country.

In my time as a planning committee member, I was reported three times to the SBE. Once, when I voted for a Tree Preservation Order on a sturdy oak tree in someone's garden, having claimed some months earlier to a member of the public that 'I was against forest trees being planted by developers in new residential estates'. The complaint was rejected.

On another occasion I was reported to the SBE by an applicant for stating in a planning meeting that his garden, which he wanted to develop, 'had been such a delight for local residents that it had been open to the general public at weekends over a period of many years'.

I told the planning committee that the owner had raised thousands of pounds for various local charities and, in my opinion,' it would be a loss to the local community'.

Subsequently, the applicant told the SBE that his garden had not been open to the general public for the previous two years, so I had misled the planning committee members.

Of course, I was unaware of this fact, but even if I had been, it would not have altered my view that the garden still contributed greatly to the local community, and when it was open to the public, it had raised money for local charities for many years prior to its closure.

Like the previous complaint this was also rejected by the SBE.

The third complaint against me was the most interesting one of all because it was made by Gerald Ford, the Borough Council's Monitoring Officer (MO).

Unknown to me, and just prior to his retirement from the council on 31st May 2005, he wrote to the SBE complaining amongst other things, that I had 'acted as an Agent Provocateur on behalf of Mrs Laird during the period of the dispute'.

This came as a complete shock to me, because at no time during the dispute did he contact me with his concerns about me acting on behalf of the MD. One would have expected a senior legal officer to do so, not least because we were in contact with each other most days on various issues concerning the council.

I will go into more detail later in this chapter.

The SBE and the Code of Conduct were introduced in the Local Government Act 2000, in response to the Nolan Report concerning high profile failings in local government.

The thinking behind the 2000 Act was to promote high ethical standards in local democracy; it set out rules to oversee the Code of Conduct, which covered both elected and co-opted members who served on local authorities.

It also required councils to establish a Standards Committee (SC) as part of the ethical framework.

For the Act to be seen as fair, it should have covered the behaviour of council officers as well as members, but it didn't, which in my opinion, was a grave omission at the time.

Part lll, Chapter IV of the 2000 Act established The Adjudication Panel for England.

The Panel, a non-departmental public body, ruled on complaints referred to it by the Ethical Standards Officer (ESO), an independent investigating officer working for the SBE.

The ESO has two options at his disposal when dealing with complaints; he can refer the complaints to the Adjudication Panel (AP) or he can refer them back to the MO of the relevant local authority for further investigation.

So his decision on the Laird complaints against Cllr McKinlay and his Cabinet colleagues that no further action was necessary, or the code of conduct had not been breached by them was baffling, to say the least.

It raised inevitable questions by members of the public at the time, as to why the ESO did not refer Mrs Laird's allegations to the AP, or pass them back to the MO for submission to the local SC for further investigation.

The answers to these questions could have been any one of the following reasons. Firstly, the ESO may have come to the conclusion that the allegations were more to do with 'employment matters' rather than 'issues of conduct' and therefore did not come within the remit of the SBE, which would have been a way out for him.

Secondly, passing the complaints back to the MO would have brought a challenge from Mrs Laird that the SC would not be able to come to a fair conclusion when the legal adviser to the committee was the MO, who had a personal grievance against her.

The third and most likely reason was the overwhelming corroboration of the suspect evidence provided by Cabinet member colleagues of Cllr McKinlay.

Added to this was the ESO's reliance on the evidence of Karen Watson, the Personal Assistant to Mrs Laird, who claimed, allegedly, that 'as she sat at her desk in an outer office she would have known if Mrs Laird had been bullied by the Leader of the Council'. But the question that remains unanswered is whether the ESO would have given this evidence much weight, if he had been aware at the time, that Mrs Watson was having an affair with Cllr McKinlay? And was he also aware that to ensure better security of Mrs Laird's day-to-day decision-making duties, it had become necessary to transfer Mrs Watson to another office?

They are now poignant reminders of the past.

One thing was certain that neither the Cabinet members, nor Mrs Watson, were ever likely to confirm to the ESO, or anyone else, that the allegations made by Mrs Laird were true.

Another interesting point that needs to be made is Mr Justice Hamblen, the High Court judge, ordered the disclosure of all evidence considered by the SBE and the ESO to assist him in his considerations. He was told that the files relating to the investigation had been destroyed. How very convenient!

With such a high profile case, discussed nationally and raised in the House of Commons, one would have thought that all evidence associated with the dispute should have been kept on file until it had been established that it was no longer required.

The Local Government Act 2007 brought in a remodelled local standards framework, which should have resulted in a greater number of complaints being dealt with by local authority's standards committees. But, as we know from the debate in Parliament, over 3,500 complaints had been made to the Board in 2008, the Act having received Royal Assent in late 2007.

The name of the SBE was changed to Standards for England in July 2009, in order to emphasise that the role of the organisation had changed. It was now able to investigate allegations itself, but it could not impose sanctions on members. However, if it considered that further action was necessary, it could refer cases to the Adjudication Panel for England, or refer the cases back for determination by the relevant local SC. One can only assume that the complaints made to the SBE in 2003 would have had a better hearing in 2007 and perhaps a more just result.

It is interesting to note that SC's had the power to suspend members for up to six months, yet throughout the period of the Laird dispute, the council's SC was never asked to even consider whether the behaviour of the Cabinet members towards the managing director was contrary to the ethical standards one would expect in a local democracy.

On 18th May 2004, I wrote to Mrs Hudson-Bendersky, chairman of the council's Standards Committee, reminding her that the opposition group leaders had made serious allegations against the behaviour of the Leader of the Council and the Cabinet deputies. I informed her that the allegations had been submitted to the Standards Board for England (SBE) the previous month.

The letter also informed the chairman that complaints had been lodged against the MD by several members of staff, including the council's MO.

Of particular concern to the PAB Group was that councillors on the Staff & Support Services Committee (S&SSC), who had been involved in the CBC v Laird dispute had been told by the MO that they had no obligation to declare prejudicial interests when matters concerning the MD were to be discussed.

The letter also informed Mrs Hudson-Bendersky that the advice had been given in spite of external legal advice showing that prejudicial interests should be declared: the advice from the MO seemed rather odd coming from a legal officer, who had himself had lodged a complaint against the MD.

I told the chairman that in order to ensure my views were not at odds with the Code of Conduct, I had written to the SBE for advice and guidance. I explained to her that I had received a reply from Michael Toft, the policy adviser in the Policy and Guidance Department, who supported my view on the interpretation of declarations of interest.

I concluded my letter by asking the chairman for the views of the SC, particularly on the matter of the advice given by the MO to members of the committee.

I copied my letter to the co-opted independent members of the SC.

David Hall, Chairman of Up Hatherley Parish Council, an independent member of the SC, wrote to Mrs Hudson-Bendersky on 19th May 2004 concerning the matters I had raised in my letter to her.

Cllr Hall repeated the same points, but added that if the assertions made by me were substantiated, then as a member of the SC he would find the situation unacceptable.

I have no record that Cllr Hall received a reply to his letter, but on the 4th June 2004 I received a letter from Mr Ford the MO, who was replying to my letter of the 18th May on behalf of Mrs Hudson-Bendersky.

The letter claimed that the matter was receiving attention and she had requested him to arrange a special meeting of the SC on the 16th July.

The chairman wrote to me following the meeting stating that "...the committee discussed your letter in some detail in open session".

She further explained that some parts of the discussion had also taken place with the press and public excluded.

Mrs Hudson-Bendersky claimed in her letter that the SC had received regular reports from the MO, who had updated members on various issues concerning the dispute. She also wanted me to know that the committee had no role to play in connection with the complaints made to the SBE.

This information was unhelpful and seemed to have missed the point. The recorded minutes of the SC show that the MO 'had nothing to report on the dispute'. Considering the number of allegations made during the previous two years, including the complaints to the SBE, it seemed odd that the MO had nothing to report to the SC.

The second point explaining that the committee couldn't become involved once complaints had been registered with the SBE was irrelevant. The point is made clear in the Local Government Act.

In any event, SC members knew that the MD had been appointed to her post in February 2002. So, whatever excuses had been made in the past, the chairman and committee members should have been informed by the MO that a dispute between the MD and the Leader of the Council existed and it was resulting in a malfunction of the council.

He could have been more specific and told the committee that claims of abuse and intimidation of the MD should be investigated. This was not done and we learned from the minutes that the ongoing problem was not included in his report to the committee.

In retrospect, most people would agree now that if a councillor or a number of councillors had been accused of 'not treating others with respect' and were actively engaged in an unprofessional manner of trying to oust an officer from his or her post, the matter should have been referred to the SC.

The alternative option would have been for the MO to submit the complaints directly to the SBE, who, after consultation with the MO, would decide whether to carry out an investigation, or refer it back to the local SC for resolution.

Even if the MO didn't want to reveal what was going on, the councillors on the

SC could have requested an extraordinary meeting of the committee so that the complaints could have been discussed.

As readers will know from an earlier chapter, the opposition group leaders decided to write directly to the SBE in April 2003, and they could only presume that the SBE would collaborate with the MO on the findings of facts and other details, and then come to a decision on whether an investigation should take place or not.

Of course, as Mrs Hudson-Bendersky pointed out in her letter, once it became known that complaints had been registered with the SBE by the opposition group leaders, the committee had no power to discuss the dispute. That was true, but they had ample opportunity to do something about the constant breaches of the Code of Conduct long before the SBE became involved.

The next question that needed an answer, but was probably not even considered at the time, was whether it was right, or in the interests of natural justice, that the MO, whilst harbouring a grievance, should have been advising the SC, the Leader of the Council and the MD, all at the same time?

The PAB Group certainly did not think so.

The claims of abuse by the MD and the claims of breaches of the code of conduct by the opposition group leaders against the Leader of the Council and his Cabinet colleagues had always been hotly denied.

Even Judge Hamblen had doubts about the veracity of the claims, according to his judgement of 15th June 2009. But a study of the judgment, when it was published, left one with the view that perhaps too much attention was given by the judge to the reports by the Ethical Standards Officer.

By contrast, the First Tier Tribunal Judge Martha Street, in a disability claim by Mrs Laird in 2010, found that "Mrs Laird had been subject to an incessant stream of inappropriate and bullying behaviour towards her since the outset of her appointment".

Tribunal Judge Street also commented on the matter of the anonymous letters, which had been circulated by email in July 2003 and referred to in Chapter 19.

She commented that they were 'malicious and unpleasant, calculated to cause personal distress and to damage Mrs Laird's reputation'.

The anonymous letters and their circulation by email was bad enough, but who was the individual, or were there several, who had felt it necessary to write and publish these appalling letters, if their case against Mrs Laird was so good?

The Police had become involved and although they could not identify any one individual, they did trace the emails back to the office of the local Member of Parliament Mr Nigel Jones, where Cllr David Fidgeon worked as a political assistant. [Reference Chapter 19]

When the matter was raised during the High Court hearing in 2009, Cllr Fidgeon was not called to give evidence, so the matter was never properly examined.

However, the comments by the Tribunal Judge in 2010 were not only welcome news, but they vindicated the words and actions made by opposition group leaders in 2003 and 2004. We had alleged on several occasions that 'inappropriate behaviour' had been undertaken by the Leader of the Council and members of his Cabinet towards Mrs Laird since the beginning of her employment in 2002. So the comments made by the judge now, give a greater weight, albeit in retrospect, to the allegations made by Mrs Laird in her submission to the SBE in March 2003.

The Tribunal assessment and its findings of fact covered the period of employment of Mrs Laird from the date of her appointment in 2002 until she was diagnosed as too ill to work in June 2004.

The finding of facts stated that it was common knowledge that the council Leader was trying to terminate her employment. And it also found that when the Cabinet deputy offered her a financial inducement to leave immediately, it was considered to be unlawful and 'a repudiatory breach of her contract'.

If everyone in the council building knew what was happening to Mrs Laird, was it not strange that no-one in authority asked the SC to investigate the matter?

If they had done so, then an investigation would have established whether there had been a breach of the code of conduct or not.

The fact that they didn't do this suggests that the SC was ineffective during the crucial period of the dispute, or it acted on poor advice, or that no substantive advice was given.

The Tribunal findings established that inappropriate behaviour had taken place, and whatever excuses are given to the contrary, it is more than clear that there had been serious breaches of the code of conduct during the dispute period.

[Readers will not be surprised to know that reports of similar examples from other councils across the country led Central Government to announce in 2011 that Standards Committees would be replaced as a matter of urgency during the parliamentary session 2012/13].

The matter of compensation and the disability allowance, which resulted from the Tribunal case, will be included in a later chapter.

The month of June 2004 turned out to be an important month.

On June 2nd Mrs Laird received an interim copy of the long-awaited draft report from the SBE, dismissing most of the complaints she had made in April 2003.

On Thursday 3rd June 2004, an Extraordinary Council Meeting took place in the council chamber, which was not open to the press or general public.

The purpose of the meeting was to receive the report of the JNC Members' Panel, which had considered the charges made by the Leader of the Council that 'the MD had intentionally misinformed Cabinet members and some of her fellow officers' and that 'she appears to be deliberately seeking to undermine the leader's own position as council leader, as well as his Cabinet members and some of her fellow officers'.

On the face of it, the claims did not appear to have much substance. There was a feeling that if this was the best the Leader and his Cabinet colleagues could come up with to counteract the more serious charges that had been made to the SBE by the MD, then the dispute would soon be over.

The JNC Panel had no option but to consider the charges and respond accordingly.

The Panel consisted of one Conservative, one Labour member and three Liberal Democrats. The People Against Bureaucracy Group (PAB) was not represented.

The matter of whether the JNC Panel and the Grievance Panel should be 'politically balanced' was hotly disputed by Mrs Laird leading up to and during the trial at the High Court.

During the hearing the judge ruled that both Panels were deemed to be 'ordinary committees' and therefore subject to the rules contained in Section 15 of the Local Government and Housing Act 1989. Other opinions suggested that if a Panel or working group was not a 'decision-making' committee, then for purposes of fairness, it should be 'politically balanced'.

The Panel's report revealed that in order to come to a conclusion, the Panel had sought assistance and received advice from Mr Tim Rothwell, a Human Resources (HR) consultant and Mr Coopey, another HR consultant who had experience of operating the JNC procedure.

External legal advice was also given by Mr Timothy Kerr, QC.

Because of a paragraph in Section 12A of the Local Government Act, 1972 I am prevented from listing the sixty six allegations made by the Panel, although it is worth mentioning that some of the allegations were repeated to the judge and they are referred to in the judgment, which is now in the public domain.

It is hoped that there will be an occasion in the future for these sixty six charges to be brought out into the open – not least because the public have a right to know how much of the £2 million was spent on such trivial matters. Each one of the charges would make a good story and a compilation of them would probably turn out to be a best seller.

Here are a few of the charges brought forward by Cllr McKinlay against the MD that may raise your curiosity, or make you wonder why it needed expensive consultants, a solicitor and a QC to advise the Panel about such minor issues.

1. *The MD had misinformed a councillor that his questions were out of order because they had been submitted too late.*
2. *The MD had stated at a meeting that Cheltenham Borough Council was a 'hung council' when clearly, it was not.*
3. *In November 2002 the MD had improperly lobbied opposition members to support a proposal for a post to be created for a Democratic Support Officer, knowing this was contrary to the will of the Cabinet.* (This came as news to me as one of the opposition group leaders, but the facts show that the council needed officers to run the Democratic Services Department, which today covers the daily administrative duties of the council).
4. *In 2003 she had written a letter to a Member of Parliament and had unfairly singled out members of the Liberal Democrat Group for criticism.*
5. *She caused a misleading story to circulate that the Leader had said to her that he made her sick.*
6. *The MD had discriminated against her Personal Assistant (PA) because she was a*

mother with young children and bullied and harassed her.

   Also, in the presence of her PA, the MD had accused the leader of being a bully, unreasonable and difficult to deal with. (Later the PA became the wife of the Leader of the Council following the High Court case. The judge in his summing up stated that he did not hear evidence from the PA so he did not put any weight on the allegations made by her)

7. *The MD attempted improperly to influence and amend the reports of officers.*
8. *She bullied, intimidated and undermined the senior officers and junior officers as well.*
9. *At a meeting in 2003 the MD had appeared to be critical of an officer causing him considerable distress.*

If there had been a charge that the MD had failed to say 'good morning' to the Leader as she passed him in the corridor, or failed to smile at her senior officers when they attended a meeting, it will not be a surprise to find them included in the sixty six charges if they are ever placed in the public domain.

But, in all seriousness, these written charges had been made by intelligent adults, employed by the council and who, apparently, spent part of their working day composing trivial charges against the MD.

Instead of spending time and money racking their brains on what they should complain about, it would have been more worthwhile for these intelligent people to have sat down with the MD and come to compromises that would have allowed the council to do its work and to move forward.

In their report, the JNC Panel members recommended that 'despite the inevitable cost, the council should appoint a Designated Independent Person (DIP) to hear the charges that had been made against the MD'.

They also recommended that 'all assistance necessary to enable the DIP to carry out his investigation should be given, including the appointment of Counsel and other advisers'.

An easy recommendation to make to their council colleagues; as the report said 'in spite of the inevitable cost' they made their recommendation knowing the cost might be an open-ended cheque for the legal profession.

Unfortunately, there was no-one on the Panel, or in the council chamber, who was wise enough to say 'whoa, let's take a step back and consider the inevitable consequences of what we are proposing'.

The councillors knew that the cost of what they were doing would be enormous and they also knew that the council's reputation could be further damaged: we could also finish up not being any further forward in resolving the dispute.

Any sensible council would have taken a step back and reconsidered the options, but unfortunately, as so often was the case in this matter, there was no-one willing to find a sensible solution.

On 4th June 2004 Mrs Laird issued a claim in the High Court challenging the JNC Panel and sought an injunction to prevent the council from implementing its recommendations. On the same day, Peter Lewis wrote to Mrs Laird informing her that the council would be meeting on June 11th to consider her possible suspension.

It was on the morning of June 4th that Mrs Laird suffered a severe panic attack and was signed off from work by her GP.

Mrs Laird's interim injunction was heard on the 11th June and it was dismissed.

She was ordered to pay the costs of Cheltenham Borough Council on an indemnity basis.

On the same day, the council held an emergency meeting and decided to suspend the MD following evidence reported to them that she had instructed someone to remove certain emails from her computer. It was not revealed until much later that upon recovery of the emails by an IT specialist, they turned out to be of little or no importance in any event.

That was the excuse the council used to suspend the MD.

Peter Lewis telephoned Mrs Laird at her home and informed her about the suspension, which brought on a severe panic attack, causing her to collapse on the floor, hurting her shoulder. Her husband found her unconscious and hyperventilating: the emergency services were called.

There is no doubt that the panic attack was not unexpected because of the number of important decisions that had gone against Mrs Laird during the early part of June 2004. There was also the daily stress from the dispute, and not least the telephone call from Mr Lewis.

The *Gloucestershire Echo* on Monday 14th June 2004 captured the moment of suspension with a front page headline 'MD suspended by councillors'. The sub-heading reported: 'Laird out following meeting'.

The *Echo* reported that it was a 'secret meeting' and the matter of irregularities surrounding the email account of Mrs Laird would be investigated by the Police.

Andrew Pierce in *The Times* got it right when he reported 'A local difficulty gets out of hand'. A subtle comment that was absolutely true.

It was a unanimous decision by the council on 11th June 2004 to suspend the managing director and all but four of the forty councillors attended the meeting. Because I do not agree with secret meetings I did not attend.

Several interesting comments were made by councillors following the meeting, which are worth noting.

Cllr Barbara Driver for example, was reported to have admitted that 'she had distanced herself from the Laird issue, but felt impelled to attend the meeting'. She also added 'I haven't been backing one or the other, but this has hurt Cheltenham, this is why we decided to suspend Christine Laird. That is not to say she is wrong, it is because we have got to get the council working again'.

So, which was going to come first, the chicken or the egg?

Cllr Brian Chaplin on the other hand, said 'the whole affair is ridiculous'. He added 'it has taken far too long to get to any stage of resolving the problem and should have been knocked on the head months and months ago'.

The old saying 'you can lead a horse to water, but you cannot make him drink' was very apt here.

Cllr Gerry Gearing, apparently left the meeting before the end, because members would not agree to his proposal to have a recorded vote on the recommendation so that the public could see which way the councillors had voted.

Cllr Martin Hale, the Leader of the Labour Party group thought it was the right decision and claimed 'everybody wants it to end as soon as possible'.

If that was the case, why was the dispute continuing?

Cllr Duncan Smith for the Conservative Group declined to comment.

On behalf of the PAB Group, I told the *Echo* that 'I thought the decision was inevitable. If it was a question of getting the council moving again, then the decision could have been made 14 months ago when the opposition group leaders had asked Cllr McKinlay to meet us. He declined the invitation and the situation inevitably dragged on. It should have been nipped in the bud then'.

For the Liberal Democrats, Cllr John Rawson was reported as saying 'there was an overwhelming desire for the issue to be resolved. There is a desire among the public and the council staff, so the sooner the matter is resolved the better'.

But was it 'to resolve it to the satisfaction of both sides' or was it to resolve it by one side taking the other side to the High Court?

With all this desire and bonhomie, how come no-one wanted to do anything along the lines suggested throughout the period 2002 to 2004?

Did anyone really believe that by publishing 66 charges against the MD and appointing a DIP to investigate them, it would resolve the dispute?

What is more, did the councillors really believe that by suspending Mrs Laird it would bring about the resolution that everyone had allegedly desired?

Had they been advised that suspension did not mean termination? And the way things were going, did they not realise that it would be some time before the council would be in a position to appoint another person to the post of MD.

And if there was an overwhelming desire to resolve the issue, as Cllr Rawson and others had suggested, then instead of suspension, surely it needed both sides to sit around the table and settle their differences.

But after two long and bitter years of wrangling, this had become impossible to achieve, so in order to 'resolve the issue' a legal course of action would still be required to terminate the statutory contract of employment of the MD, which so far had proved to be impossible.

Although he was unsuccessful in his bid to be short-listed for the post of Managing Director in 2001 (Conservative administration), Chris Huckle was made Acting Managing Director on 11th June 2004 (Lib/Dem administration) and acted as Mrs Laird's deputy throughout the dispute.

In July 2004 in an attempt to gauge whether Mrs Laird was medically fit to continue in her role as managing director, the council instructed a consultant Occupational Health Physician to assess whether she was medically fit to continue in her job.

The consultant was Dr Phillip.

The council also wanted to know whether Mrs Laird was permanently unfit for work, and whether she should be considered for retirement by reason of being incapable of discharging her duties as Head of Paid Service.

After efforts made by Jo Pitman (HR/AD) and Mr Rothwell (Consultant HR) to reach an arrangement with Mrs Laird, an appointment was made for her to see the Occupational Health consultant.

A session with Dr Phillip eventually took place on 17th July 2004.

He did not produce a report on the examination until 24th September.

In his letter to the council Dr Phillip wrote that he was not prepared to certify that Mrs Laird was entitled to ill-health retirement. He thought that if the legal issues could be dealt with and Mrs Laird had clinical support for six months, then, in his opinion, she could soon be fit and able to resume her work.

This came as a surprise to senior members.

It was natural for Dr Phillip to believe that any legal issues could be resolved, but for the people engaged in the task of trying to achieve this, they only saw the seemingly intractable problem of Mrs Laird winning the hearts and minds of her opponents being as far away as ever.

On 3rd August 2004, councillors were informed by Peter Lewis that Mr Adrian Lynch QC had been appointed the DIP to investigate the allegations made against the MD.

His first duty was to extend the period of suspension of the MD until 1st September; a further extension of the suspension was granted by the DIP until 1st October 2004. Following the first oral hearing before the DIP on 29th September, he ordered that the suspension should be extended until 1st November 2004.

I was not privy to any communications between the council and Mrs Laird following the appointment of the DIP, but I was aware that Mrs Laird had become seriously ill, which may have been due to the news that a DIP had been appointed.

The stress of everything had resulted in Mrs Laird seeking psychiatric advice from specialists at The Priory Hospital in Bristol, following visits to her general practitioner.

At the same time, and in order to defend her position, Mrs Laird was advised by her legal team to commence court proceedings against the council.

The allegations that had been made by elected members and officers of the council about her had taken their toll, and her medical condition was steadily getting worse.

Relying again on the Findings of Fact in the First Tier Tribunal case in 2010, it alleges on 27th August 2004, the council copied Mrs Laird into a letter, which accused her of faking her illness, before seeking medical advice. The letter was unexpected and it brought on another panic attack during which Mrs Laird lost consciousness.

According to the report, the allegations continued. It would be interesting to know what the allegations were.

It was around this time that Mrs Laird was referred to the Mental Health Trust in

Gloucestershire by her GP. She was assessed by consultant physician Dr Ram who diagnosed severe depressive disorder, panic disorder and trauma.

Matters were not helped when Mrs Laird learned that a letter dated 8th October 2004 had been sent to Doctor Paul Dedman, the consultant psychiatrist at the Priory Hospital, Bristol, asking him to consider two affidavits before he completed his report on Mrs Laird's fitness to attend court.

The letter, allegedly, was from Miss Farooqi on behalf of the JNC Panel.

The letter caused a flurry of letters to go between the two legal practices and the medical profession. Simon Collingridge, solicitor acting on behalf of Mrs Laird, wrote to Miss Farooqi explaining that Doctor Dedman could not assist the court by providing a report, because it was not the policy of a doctor to provide opinions on legal documents.

Mr Collingridge did not help the situation and probably made an error of judgement, by suggesting to Miss Farooqi that if she thought Dr Dedman should see the affidavits she should put copies of the affidavits in the post to him.

In due course, Dr Dedman received a letter from the council and a bundle of confidential affidavits in the names of Gerald Ford, the MO, and Peter Lewis the council's solicitor.

He responded by writing to Peter Lewis on 12th October 2004 stating that he had seen Mrs Laird, following a referral from her GP. He went on to say that whilst he had agreed to provide a brief report to the court, in which he would comment about her fitness to attend, he had not at any time agreed to be an expert witness in a civil litigation case.

Having looked at the legal documents sent to him, Dr Dedman informed Mr Lewis that "… it would be inappropriate for him to be engaged as an expert witness in what is clearly a complex case."

He commented further by confirming that it would be inappropriate for him to take on an expert witness role where some degree of impartiality was needed.

It was correct for Dr Dedman not to become involved in the legal considerations and he recommended that both sides should agree to instruct Dr Paul Aylard, a consultant colleague who specialised in medico-legal reports relating to work related issues, for advice.

Dr Dedman copied his letter to Davies and Partners, solicitors acting for Mrs Laird, who immediately wrote to Miss Farooqi expressing concerns on behalf of their client.

The solicitors were instructed to make a formal complaint against the council based on its intention to influence Dr Dedman in the preparation of his report.

The council had erred on this occasion because the principal reason for Dr Dedman's report was solely to provide the treatment necessary for Mrs Laird's recovery.

Davies and Partners ended their letter by reminding Miss Farooqi "… it was further proof that the council had failed to have proper regard to the welfare of Mrs Laird who was also their client."

The final report and summary from Stephen Kingston the Ethical Standards Officer (ESO) was published and printed on18th November 2004, nineteen months after the allegations were made. His findings were a blow to Mrs Laird and only added salt into a widening wound as the ESO rejected nearly all the 36 allegations she had made in April 2003.

For the record, the first two of the allegations made by Mrs Laird took place before Cheltenham Borough Council had adopted its Code of Conduct on 22nd April 2002.

Therefore, these allegations were not considered.

The ESO found that in one allegation there was a breach of the Code of Conduct, but recommended no action should be taken against the named councillors.

The remaining allegations were deemed to be either 'employment matters' or the allegations were not supported by evidence and did not require any further action.

The method of interviews carried out by the SBE of the applicant and those accused was by telephone or face-to-face across a table. It wasn't until sometime after the interview sessions had taken place that I learned that two different systems had been used. In the interests of fairness, one would have thought the SBE would have wanted to treat everyone concerned in a like manner.

All three opposition group leaders were interviewed over the telephone, in each case for up to an hour or more, whereas, Cabinet members and officers were treated to face-to-face meetings with SBE representatives. This indicates that the system of interviews was irregular and unfair and, therefore, could have been flawed.

In a magistrates' court any evidence provided is given under oath and carries more weight than any other submissions that are made.

This was not a run-of-the-mill case that the SBE was dealing with but a case of serious charges being made by a chief officer of a local authority. Similar charges had also been made by the leaders of the opposition groups against a group of councillors belonging to the same political party. There was no way that any member of the political party was going to speak in support of the allegations made against them, so in order to get to the truth the questions and the answers needed to be carried out under oath.

It may be too much to ask, but if legal representations had been made and a cross-examination of those giving evidence undertaken, perhaps the results may have been different. Cross-examination by people experienced in these matters, may have produced a fairer result in this particular case, but unfortunately, this did not happen.

The ESO when investigating complaints is required to work closely with the local authority Monitoring Officer (MO). But how much collaboration took place between the two of them, and how big a part did the MO play in the final decisions of the ESO? It is unfortunate that the meetings and the discussions that took place between them are not on record.

What is on record is the ESO's final report showing detail for each of the allegations, which also appears in several paragraphs in the High Court judgment.

In previous chapters I have referred to the complaints made to the SBE by the three opposition group leaders against the Leader of the Council, Cllr McKinlay and members of his Cabinet.

The letter containing the complaints was made to the SBE on 3rd April 2003.

On April 28th the opposition group leaders also wrote 'an open letter to the people of Cheltenham' indicating amongst other things their intention to lodge complaints with the SBE against all the members of the Cabinet for allegedly meeting in secret and acting unlawfully in staffing matters.

The allegations against five members of the Cabinet were that they had been:

> "Involved in an illegal and unconstitutional attempt to remove the local authority's Managing Director from her post."

The allegation against the Leader of the Council was as follows:

"He was at the forefront of an illegal and unconstitutional attempt by the Cabinet to remove the local authority's Managing Director from her post. Cllr McKinlay is also alleged to have been verbally abusive to the Managing Director over a period of nine months, commenting amongst other things that 'I feel physically sick every time I see you.'"

The allegation against the Cabinet deputy Cllr Stuart-Smith was as follows:

"He was at the forefront of an illegal and unconstitutional attempt by the Cabinet to remove the local authority's Managing Director from her post. In addition, Cllr Stuart-Smith is alleged to have told the Managing Director on the 5th March 2003 that she was 'loathed by her staff and that if she did not leave, her life would be made difficult'.

The essence of the first and second allegations was that the Leader and the Cabinet were meeting in private and taking decisions that related to staffing matters. This was not the normal procedure and it raised a fundamental question of whether it was lawful for members of the Cabinet to be involved in staffing matters. The Local Government Act 2000 places the responsibility for all local authority functions operating executive arrangements on the executive other than those excluded by regulations made under the Act.

Two such regulations have been made and they are:

The Local Authorities (Functions & Responsibilities) Regulations (Enclosure D/9) 2000 and The Local Authorities (Functions & Responsibilities) (Amendment) Regulations 2001 D/10, yet the ESO found that there had not been a breach of the Code of Conduct.

Whether the Executive meets in private or not, decisions concerning members of staff should in the first instance, be discussed by the Staff & Support Services Committee. This is followed with examination by the appropriate scrutiny committee and any decision taken finally approved by council.

To support this view, Counsel had already advised the council that the appointment and dismissal of the Head of Paid Service can only be done by the full council (Paragraph 5 of the 2001 Regulations).

Yet, with this allegation too, the ESO found there was no breach of the relevant provisions of the Code of Conduct.

To the 'man-in-the-street' however, the decision would seem odd and could be forgiven for thinking that the Code of Conduct is nothing more than a worthless document if the Executive cannot be called to account.

Some of the allegations made against the Leader and his Cabinet could not be investigated because they occurred before the council had adopted the new Code of Conduct in May 2003.

With rejection of the remainder of the 36 allegations, it was not surprising that a new Code of Conduct was eventually introduced in 2012.

It would be impossible for councillors to behave today in a similar fashion without breaching the new Code of Conduct.

I doubt too whether the Standards Committee would be allowed to remain silent for so long as they did during 2003 and 2004 with the new system in place.

I do not suggest for one moment that the incoming Coalition Government in May 2010 were aware of the *Cheltenham Borough Council v Laird (2009)* case; although it is on record that several questions were tabled during the period of the dispute in the House of Commons.

The new government decided to change the name of the SBE to Standards for England, but the change was only to be a temporary measure, because the incoming government was determined that this particular quango, whatever it was called, was going to be scrapped as quickly as possible.

Arrangements were made for its abolition under the standards provision of the Localism Act 2011 and Standards for England was abolished on 31st March 2012.

CHAPTER 22

Trials And Tribulations

In the world ye shall have tribulation; but be of good cheer; I have overcome the world.
St John ch17, v 12

The period March 2005 to March 2006 was very much a continuation of what had gone before – claims and counter claims which resulted in one delay after another.

A claim by the council that Mrs Laird had deliberately failed to complete a medical questionnaire properly, and a counter claim by Mrs Laird that the council had unreasonably delayed agreeing to her ill health retirement, are just samples of the issues that will be explained in this chapter.

Both sides were responsible for the delays during this period. Any reason to delay the process was used, such as the need for further legal advice, people on holiday, or one side or the other waiting for an important report to be delivered.

Mr Adrian Lynch QC, the Designated Independent Person (DIP), started his investigation into the disciplinary allegations that had been made against Mrs Laird, but it was not easy because he was hampered by her ill health.

He directed Dr Aylard, the consultant psychiatrist, to interview Mrs Laird and to prepare a report on the state of her health for him to consider. Dr Aylard carried out his interview with Mrs Laird on 13th April 2005 and reported in writing to the DIP on May 4th that she was unfit to undergo a DIP investigation.

The report was comprehensive and included information from Mrs Laird's doctor about the anti-depressant drug she had been taking at times of stress since 1997.

After a period of three months, the DIP decided on 4th August 2005 that he could not continue his investigation into the complaints because of the state of Mrs Laird's health.

Five days later, the council wrote to Mrs Laird's solicitor claiming it regarded her contract of employment to be frustrated as a result of the DIP's decision that there was no reasonable prospect of the disciplinary allegations being investigated due to her state of health.

In plain words, Mrs Laird had now been dismissed from her position of managing director; she was now unemployed and would probably never be able to work again.

It had taken two and a half years of bullying, malicious dealings, attempts to suspend her, illegal inducements to leave the council and many other things that made her life unbearable, before the conspirators had managed to terminate her employment.

They had achieved what they had set out to do in 2002, but at what cost, both personal and financial?

The financial cost had reached £1million, but the cost in human suffering and a life destroyed had been a heavier price to pay.

In other similar cases that one can recall, having secured their victory, the successful party would have settled for that and drawn a line under the past events and set about moving the council forward in the best interests of the town and its population. There was a temporary lull, as one would expect following the DIP's decision, but in June 2006 the council applied for a third party disclosure against Gloucestershire Partnership NHS Trust because of their involvement with the assessment of Mrs Laird's medical fitness. The application for pre-action disclosure was opposed by Mrs Laird, but the judge who heard the applications in July 2006 made the order for disclosure.

As a result of the hearing, the council obtained a copy of Mrs Laird's pre-employment medical questionnaire on 31st August 2006 and discovered that it contained no mention of depression, depressive illness, stress related illness, or any anti-depressant medication. The council were disappointed.

But instead of looking carefully at the wording of their own medical questionnaire, to see whether the questions asked were sufficiently robust, in order to get an accurate picture of an applicant's medical history, the council immediately went off on another 'hare chasing escapade'.

They should have reminded themselves that the council had asked Mrs Laird upon appointment, to 'complete the medical questionnaire and return it to the Gloucestershire County Occupational Health Services (GCOHS), which she did. Subsequently a GCOHS representative sent a signed form to the council confirming that Mrs Laird had answered all the questions on the questionnaire, and from the answers given concluded that 'the applicant was found to be fit for the job'.

The council wrote to Mrs Laird in January 2002 informing her that 'the medical clearance certificate had been received and the council could now proceed with her appointment'.

It was hardly Mrs Laird's fault if there were no questions in the medical questionnaire that covered her previous bouts of depression that had warranted the use of anti-depressants.

This matter was a key element in the High Court case in 2009, which will be recorded in the next chapter.

Now officially dismissed from her employment, Mrs Laird made an application to the council on 6th September 2005 for immediate payment of ill health benefits. The council conceded the point after taking legal advice on the grounds of permanent incapacity, and her pension was backdated to the 10th August 2005.

Meanwhile, the council hierarchy worked on the basis that they had found a flaw in the Laird appointment, and started to look at other possibilities that might help them in their efforts to further undermine the appointment procedure.

The legal view taken at the time was that if the council could find other flaws in Mrs Laird's appointment, they could seriously consider the prospects of suing Mrs

Laird for damages for making fraudulent or negligent misrepresentations in her job application form.

Believing they had discovered a serious flaw in the completion of the medical questionnaire by Mrs Laird, they began looking at other paperwork associated with the job application, which led them to believe that the job reference provided by her previous employer might have been misleading, or at best questionable.

Rhondda Cynon Taf County Borough Council (RCT) was Mrs Laird's previous employer and the council had been engaged in a comprehensive restructure of their corporate governance in order to provide a functional corporate identity, and improve the council's day-by-day performance. In order to achieve this objective it was necessary to establish a new Corporate Management Team, which included the appointment of a Group Director for Community Services.

Mrs Laird applied and was appointed to this post, and according to reports 'carried out her tasks diligently and successfully'. Later, Mrs Laird sought to advance her career and applied for the vacant post of Managing Director at Cheltenham Borough Council (CBC).

The usual practice in most organisations once an appointment is made, is to ask the former employer to provide a reference. The request was made and the Chief Executive of RCT at the time provided a positive reference regarding Mrs Laird's previous employment with them.

However, in their pursuit for evidence that they believed would be strong enough to win a high court case, senior CBC officers came to the almost unbelievable conclusion that RCT had provided a reference that amounted to a negligent misstatement about Mrs Laird's time at RCT.

CBC alleged that the reference had 'failed to mention a number of features relevant to Mrs Laird's employment, including an alleged conflict with the then Chief Executive of RCT and other matters pertinent to Mrs Laird's state of health'.

In the allegations against RCT, CBC relied upon perceived omissions in the reference rather than the positive comments made; this may have been a mistake.

But in any event, there is ample case law on the giving of references and negligent misstatements, which should have registered highly in the minds of the senior members of the legal team.

The issuing of a reference in any circumstances should always be honest containing accurate information. Reasonable care should also be taken to ensure that the information given is not misleading. My previous experience as a Personnel Manager led me to ensure that any references sent on behalf of my company, included a disclaimer to avoid a possible action from the recipient.

I would have been surprised if RCT had not included such a disclaimer in their initial reply to CBC.

Not surprisingly, the claim attracted significant media attention with regular reports in the national and local press both in Gloucestershire and South Wales. The BBC made a programme about references, and it featured in the BBC 2 television programme, *Dragon's Eye*.

It is also interesting to record that it was possibly the first time that a local authority had pursued another local authority about a negligent reference in respect of a chief officer.

The claim had been brought under the Local Government Act 1999.

Undoubtedly advised by their legal advisors, CBC took unprecedented action against RCT, which we will see had serious and disastrous consequences for the council and its taxpayers.

But what was the legal advice that CBC had been receiving? There was no case law to rely on concerning chief officers, and as far as I could see there was no precedent for an action for damages along the lines that CBC was pursuing.

Long before the judge mentioned the matter in his High Court judgment, the PAB Group had made proposals to the Staff & Support Services Committee (S&SSC) asking members:

a. To put a ceiling on expenditure, and
b. To draw a line under the dispute.

Regular briefings on both legal cases were made to the S&SSC during 2006/07, including advice from CBC's external legal advisors, who always gave a favourable chance to the prospects of succeeding against both RCT and Mrs Laird.

It was towards the end of 2006 that the cost of the two claims being made against Mrs Laird and RCT started to ratchet up towards the £1 million mark.

There was no doubt in the minds of most councillors at the time that the two claims based on the legal advice they had been given, would easily pay for all the expenditure that had been incurred by CBC during the period of the dispute.

What they didn't consider deeply enough was that success is never guaranteed and sometimes the cost of success can turn out to be substantial.

In September 2006 it was reported that CBC had been successful in their pre-action disclosure cases against Mrs Laird, RCT and the Gloucestershire Partnership NHS Trust in the Bristol High Court on 21st July 2006.

It was also reported that Leading Counsel had advised recovery of damages from RCT had 'a reasonable chance of success', although he added 'the amount of damages claimed may only cover legal fees, management and disruption costs'.

Personally, I didn't think the report was very encouraging – a reasonable chance of success in a matter such as this would be regarded by the betting fraternity as little more than 'an outside chance' of winning.

Similarly, regarding the claim against Mrs Laird, Leading Counsel advised that there was a reasonable prospect of a successful claim, but he was not able to say whether all the costs incurred by the council were recoverable, which didn't fill me with much confidence.

The Public Interest Report (PIR) referred to earlier, was published by the external auditors KPMG in March 2010. They reported that the council had "acted through-out [the dispute] as if it expected to win and this had influenced its decisions."

KPMG is a leading provider of audit, tax and advisory services in the UK and they were appointed by the Audit Commission to audit the accounts of Cheltenham Borough Council under the provisions of Section 8 of the Audit Commission Act 1988.

KPMG reported that the Council *"throughout the development of the case received consistent legal advice that the prospects of winning were 60:40 in its favour. It was consistently told it had 'a strong case'. This clear message, combined with other factors, furthered the Council's resolve to pursue the case. It did not, however, give sufficient attention to the flip-side of the legal advice; that there was a 40 per cent chance it would lose."*

The (PIR) will be discussed in detail in a later chapter.

As expected, the allegations by CBC against RCT were rebutted with vigour by the Welsh council, and it was reported that they had spent a significant amount of time and money in defending the good name of the Rhondda Cynon Taff County Borough Council, and who could blame them on the flimsy allegations that had been made against them?

It was in the early part of 2008 that the legal advice concerning the claim against RCT began to be less than positive. Leading Counsel had moved considerably from his earlier advice that CBC would win both claims, to one of caution that the chance of success against RCT was no better than odds of 30:70.

A critical legal position had been reached by the CBC; the next meeting of the S&SSC would require them to make two important decisions that would determine whether further expensive litigation should be undertaken in the hope that the council would be able to recoup some, if not all, of the money invested, plus the additional costs of any high court cases.

It is important to record here the names of the S&SSC who finally made the ultimate decision to support either

   a. fight both cases,
   b. withdraw from them, or
   c. withdraw from one and fight the other.

In a report by Cllr Hall who was a member of the S&SSC, the committee met on 24th November 2008 and was attended by the following councillors: Councillors Steve Jordan, Nigel Britter, Andrew McKinlay, Garth Barnes, Colin Hay, David Hall, Stuart Hutton, Jacky Fletcher, and Tina Franklin. [None of the names were officially recorded in the minutes – a point picked up by KPMG in their PIR].

Cllr Jordan was chairman and Cllr Hall recorded that Cllr Duncan Smith and Cllr Godwin declared personal and prejudicial interests and left the meeting.

According to Cllr Hall a verbal report was given by Sarah Farooqi, the Borough Solicitor. Peter Lewis recently appointed acting Monitoring Officer, updated the position regarding the council's claims against RCT and Mrs Laird.

Members of the committee had not been provided with a written paper, but they were told that Leading Counsel's latest advice was that the chance of winning against RCT was, in his opinion, only 30 per cent. The chance of CBC winning its case against Mrs Laird however was put at 60 per cent.

The chairman put the question to members whether or not the cases should be continued; probably the most important decision they would ever make in their lives.

The legal officers explained that following discussions with Counsel the best advice available was that the prospect of success for the council in respect of the RCT case was 30–70. They advised that with only a 30 per cent chance of success the action should be discontinued.

The case against Christine Laird however, with a 60 per cent chance of success, meant there was legal justification for taking the case forward.

Miss Farooqi who was leading the court action, suggested that the 60–40 odds were favourable and then outlined to the councillors the risks involved should the Laird case go forward. What those risks were are unknown because there is no record of these in the minutes of the meeting.

But no-one it seems, apart from Cllr Hall, took sufficient notice of the serious fact that there was a 40 per cent possibility of losing the case. And with such poor odds of success, the case effectively became little more than a gamble. But it was a gamble with other people's money.

Miss Farooqi explained that the Laird case centred on the former managing director's failure to include in her pre-medical questionnaire the fact that she was on medication and that she had suffered from ill-health. We shall learn later that she had occasionally been treated for stress-related work problems, which is not unknown for anyone who works in a high-powered working environment.

Miss Farooqi reported that she was aware Mrs Laird had also suffered personal problems although she told members that Mrs Laird thought they were irrelevant to her job application. Most people would agree with that.

In answer to questions about the recovery of costs, Miss Farooqi said that it depended on what happened in court, such as the performance of witnesses and the nature of the judge. It would have made interesting reading to know exactly what Miss Farooqi meant by these words.

There was little debate about the RCT case. But Cllr Hall in his report said that Cllr Colin Hay spoke on the subject matter and also 'bad-mouthed RCT by intimating that they should have let CBC know that Laird was a problem'. After a short discussion the committee decided that the council should not continue with its claim against RCT, even though several members were disappointed with the advice they had been given.

It was the right decision, but it had taken one and a half years since the claim for damages against RCT had been issued, for common sense to prevail.

But we should not forget that had the odds been similar to those given against Mrs Laird, then one can only assume that CBC would have been facing not one but two high court gambles that would have been even more expensive and attracted more nationwide coverage too.

It is easy to determine who pays for the wild gambles of a council, but it also begs the question about who the real beneficiaries are at the end of the day.

After the decision of the committee not to pursue a legal case against RCT, the committee then turned its attention to the CBC case against Mrs Laird.

"It was clear" reports Cllr Hall, "from the body language of most people around the table they wanted to 'nail' Mrs Laird."

This is an extract from his report:

> "I entered the debate making the point that odds of 6–4 were not attractive and I was unhappy about risking tax payers' money on such a gamble, on such scanty evidence. This was immediately countered by Councillor McKinlay who said they were good odds, and he was convinced that the council had a good case and should proceed. He embellished his statement by a derogatory and highly defamatory rant against Mrs Laird, her history of bad behaviour, lies and deceitful actions and a number of other things. This theme was picked up by other Liberal Democrat councillors Barnes and Hay, who both came across with the mantra that Laird had 'damaged lots of people and made their lives hell', and they were in favour of proceeding.
>
> When the question was put, all members voted in favour of proceeding with the exception of myself. I abstained."

Cllr Hall was new to the council and to the S&SSC. He was elected in May 2006, and therefore had not been involved in the early days of the dispute between CBC and the former managing director during the period 2002 and 2005.

He was concerned that the sequence of events, referred to in previous pages, was mainly the work of the Leader of the Council and his Cabinet colleagues; he was also acutely aware of the escalating costs to be borne by the local taxpayers if the claims against the managing director proceeded to the High Court.

Considering the legal costs already accrued and the fact that litigation in the court would make the final cost even higher, it was extraordinarily odd to read in the minutes that were finally published in March 2009, that the S&SSC members, having chosen to 'withdraw from one and fight the other', option c) believed 'it was their duty to the taxpayers of Cheltenham to pursue the claim as far as possible'.

I repeat what I said in an earlier chapter, 'when you mount the back of a tiger, it is very difficult to get off'. Even at this point it would have been difficult to estimate the likely costs to each side should the case proceed to trial, but it had been suggested by the legal advisors that £200,000 was a realistic figure.

But that turned out to be a long way short of the actual figure.

Litigation is never an exact science and in my view, this case was a gamble too far with disastrous consequences for individuals and for the local taxpayers.

I was not surprised to learn that following the S&SSC meeting on November 24th, Cllr Hall sought a face-to-face meeting with Andrew North the Chief Executive (C/Ex). He wanted him to know of his concerns about the conduct of the case against Mrs Laird as he saw it, and he wanted to know more about the events leading up to her suspension, which had occurred long before he had become a councillor.

This meeting took place on Wednesday 26th November 2008.

Cllr Hall asked the C/Ex for more information about the background of the case and this information was given to him. But, and no doubt by a previous arrangement, the C/Ex then invited other members of the council staff to join the discussion, which was done to support the point that Mrs Laird had been 'difficult to work with'.

Becky Robinson, who had become the PA to Mrs Laird following the transfer of Mrs Watson to another department, was asked to corroborate this claim.

Cllr Hall on the other hand, expressed his concern to the C/Ex regarding the part played by Cllr McKinlay at the S&SSC meeting the previous Monday. His concern was that Cllr McKinlay had not declared a personal and prejudicial interest regarding the debate on the legal action against Mrs Laird, in spite of the fact he was the major protagonist in the council's dispute against her.

Whilst Andrew North agreed with the complaint, he referred Cllr Hall to the fact that 'it is up to the individual councillor whether he declares an interest or not'.

It may have been legally correct, but as a general principle – common sense should have prevailed.

Other matters were discussed ending with Cllr Hall complaining strongly to Andrew North that on such an important matter for both the council and the taxpayer, the legal officers' verbal briefing should have been supported with a written report setting out the details of their briefing. He told the C/Ex that he did not vote to continue the court case against Mrs Laird because the odds were too slender for the case to succeed in the High Court, and the risk assessment was unconvincing.

After the meeting, Cllr Hall wrote an email to Cllr Duncan Smith suggesting to him that the Conservative Group should withdraw its support from the case against Mrs Laird 'because he believed it was a losing battle'.

Cllr Hall made useful contributions to the events during and after the S&SSC meeting in November 2008: he also makes further comments later about the 'special' meeting of the S&SSC in January 2009.

Following the November meeting Cheltenham Borough Council announced that it had suspended its action against RCT because it was in the public interest.

RCT announced that 'whilst they were delighted with the outcome, they had consistently argued that there had been no case to answer'. RCT also stated "Unfortunately, the extremely disappointing stance taken by Cheltenham in this matter left Rhondda Cynon Taf with no alternative other than to conduct a vigorous defence." The reputation of RCT was of paramount importance and they intended to safeguard it at all costs.

In a statement to justify its position, CBC stated 'the parties had recently exchanged their witness evidence, which had allowed the council to fully review its overall approach'.

"It has been decided," the statement said "with the support of Counsel that the public interest would be best served, both economically and in terms of enhancing the prospects of success, for the council to concentrate its efforts in pursuing the claim against Mrs Laird alone."

The statement also announced that 'a full hearing in the Royal Courts of Justice had been set for 26th January 2009 and the proceedings were estimated to last 38 days. The council meanwhile was currently preparing for that hearing and added that in the RCT case each council had agreed to pay its own costs'.

The estimated cost of the RCT claim amounted to £60,000 but if the case had proceeded to a court hearing then it would have been nearer £200,000.

In spite of Cllr Hall's insistence that the risk of proceeding was too great, the Liberal Democrats were in no mood to concede defeat at the meeting. His interesting report states that 'In order to persuade the committee to continue with its claim, Cllr McKinlay, aided by Cllrs Barnes and Hay, led a vicious attack against the former managing director, raking over past misdemeanours and even went to the extent of calling Mrs Laird a liar'.

However, when the question was finally put to the members they all agreed that the case against Mrs Laird should continue, with the exception of Cllr Hall who abstained.

The minutes of the November meeting were not presented for approval until the 16th March 2009 meeting at which Cllr Hall asked for a number of amendments to be made to them, but not surprisingly none of his proposals were accepted by the committee.

Cllr Hall included this and other matters in a Written Statement to the High Court judge in March 2009, but it was thought that the statement had been received too late to be taken into consideration by the court.

On 18th February 2009, my wife and I returned from a two month's holiday in Australia. We had spent a glorious time with our son Andrew and his family in Sydney, enjoying hot but pleasant weather and completely oblivious to what had been going on in Cheltenham.

However, as we all know from past experiences, it is not long before the call of duty takes over and one is soon back in the old routine of responding to telephone calls, looking at the countless number of emails and of course, opening and reading the numerous letters that have dropped on the doormat during an absence.

A conversation with my PAB councillor colleague Malcolm Stennett, who had been my deputy during my stay in Australia, informed me that following the decision to discontinue the action against RCT, a special meeting of the S&SSC had been called for 15th January 2009.

The meeting had been called to give the committee members an update on the court action and also to discuss and support a resolution that was on the agenda authorising the Chief Executive to meet with Mrs Laird or her legal representative, to propose and agree an out-of-court settlement before the proceedings commenced. He was also asked to consult with the Group Leaders, the Chief Finance Officer and the Head of Legal Services before any meeting with Mrs Laird took place.

The resolution was approved, but it was reported to me that as the chief executive left to attend another meeting, Cllr Hay shouted after him that he should 'drive a hard bargain'.

Forever the eternal optimist, the resolution seemed to me to have been an excellent proposal: an opportunity to find a settlement of the dispute before it reached the High Court; an opportunity for Andrew North, who had been appointed to the post of chief executive in 2006, to meet for the first time the former managing director; and it would have been anyone's guess as to what may have come out of such a meeting.

Alas, it was not to be, perhaps it was the words of the Liberal Democrat councillor ringing in his ears as he left the meeting, or some other reason that prevented the meeting from taking place.

The information given to me showed that the task of speaking to Mrs Laird was turned over to a member of the legal department, which was not part of the approved resolution: to talk to them yes, but not to 'pass the buck' over to a member of the legal team.

On 16th January 2009, Mrs Laird received a letter from Miss Farooqi inviting her 'to make an offer to settle the claim for fraud with costs'. Mrs Laird discussed the letter with her legal advisor and not surprisingly she was advised to refuse the request. Again, this was not in accord with the 'spirit and intention' of the approved resolution; and for the record, the PAB deputy Group Leader was not consulted before, during or after the letter was sent to Mrs Laird.

The whole business was a farce – nobody it seems even bothered to ask why the resolution wasn't carried out as agreed by those who had previously approved it.

Was it just another example from those who wanted to go through the motions of sounding keen to resolve the dispute, but deep down they had no intention of doing so?

But, there was another opportunity on the first day of the High Court hearing when Andrew North visited the courtroom to listen to the opening exchanges of the trial. At any time throughout the day he could have spoken to Mrs Laird's solicitor and arranged a meeting between the two parties; he could have made an offer to settle, even at that late stage, but no conversation took place at any time during the day. And after all, he did have the S&SSC approved resolution in his back pocket, so he was on safe grounds.

Are the occasions reported above important, yes, I think they are. When taken together with other issues they become even more important, not least because it confirms that genuine attempts had been made to settle the dispute, and it shows that it could have been attempted even up to and including the first day of the trial.

The resolution approved by the S&SSC on 15th January 2009 reads:

"To authorise the Chief Executive to agree any terms proposed for settlement of proceedings after consultation with Group Leaders (or appropriate deputies), the Chief Finance Officer and the Head of Legal Services".

In spite of all the good intentions – it wasn't worth the paper it was written on.

On 6th February 2009 I received a letter from Mrs Laird's solicitor informing me that Mr John Dagnall, Counsel acting for Mrs Laird, would like me to give oral evidence on her behalf at the trial brought by Cheltenham Borough Council.

My presence would be required during the last week of March and the first week of April.

The High Court hearing was well under way by this time, and although it would be some time before I could give my account of the events between 2002 and 2004, I was determined to speak about the facts as they were and not as I would have wanted them to be.

I was filled with quiet anticipation of an experience that would stay with me for the rest of my life.

CHAPTER 23

The Royal Courts Of Justice
Cheltenham Borough Council V Christine Laird

The price of justice is eternal publicity
Arnold Bennett (1867–1931)

The Royal Courts of Justice are situated in The Strand, in the City of Westminster. They are usually referred to as the Law Courts and they house several courts including the Court of Appeal and the High Court of Justice of England and Wales.

Work on the building was started in 1873 and it took eight years to complete. Queen Victoria opened the building in December 1882.

It is a fine building and one is impressed from the moment one passes through the main gates in The Strand. There are carved heads of eminent judges and lawyers and other historical figures. At the north front, over the judges' entrance are a stone cat and dog representing fighting litigants in court.

There are numerous gateways leading to different courts, jury and witness rooms and separate staircases are provided to reach the appropriate boxes. The courts are panelled in oak, and in Court 4, the Lord Chief Justice's court, there is an elaborately carved wooden Royal Coat of Arms, and I was told that each of the small court-rooms has a unique interior.

In order to accommodate work in the Chancery Division and the Court of Appeal, 12 courts were added in 1968, and 25 courts were added in 1995.

Court 36, like most of the other courts in the building, is small with only a few rows of seats for witnesses and observers, and these are set immediately behind or adjacent to the defendant. The presence and closeness of the witnesses is discernible before and throughout the proceedings, which is not a particularly good arrangement.

Day 1

On 26th January 2009 in Court 36 Mr Justice Hamblen opened the case, which he described as 'novel', between Cheltenham Borough Council (CBC) and its former managing director, Mrs Christine Laird.

He said the basis of the claim was for substantial damages amounting to nearly £1 million by CBC. They claimed that as a consequence of employing Mrs Laird they "had incurred extraordinary expenses that would not have been incurred had some other managing director been employed".

The judge explained that because of the "differences which arose between Mrs Laird and the Leader of the Council, Cllr McKinlay, and other members and officers, much time and expense was spent by CBC in dealing with the resulting disputes, which arose rather than the normal running of CBC's business".

"Mrs Laird" he said "not only denies liability but disputes every element of the damages claimed. In essence she alleges that all the disputes and ensuing problems which arose during her employment were caused by CBC's own breaches of duty or fault. She also seeks to set off against the claim her own claim for damages for stress and ill-health. She also seeks to bring into account benefits which she says accrued to CBC only as a result of CBC employing her when they did."

So the scene was set, the gladiators were in the ring, but was the balance fair in the circumstances? CBC had lined up numerous officers and councillors to defend their position; they had employed a Queen's Counsel and a Barrister plus the services of Miss Sarah Farooqi, the council's solicitor, who was in attendance throughout the trial.

Mrs Laird's defence team consisted of John Dagnall, a Barrister, assisted by a Solicitor plus volunteers who would provide evidence on her behalf.

In the opening exchanges between the two sides, Mr Timothy Kerr QC for the council claimed that Cheltenham Borough Council was suing Mrs Laird for £982,000 plus interest in damages for the costs it had incurred as a result of making her its managing director in February 2002.

He said she had not informed the council of a history of depressive illness on her job application form and therefore, the amount of money being claimed was due to the non-disclosure by Mrs Laird.

He claimed she was already suffering from a depressive illness when she was appointed to the top job in February 2002.

Mr Kerr called Miss Farooqi as his first witness. She was invited to explain to the court why the council had decided to take legal action against Mrs Laird, and to give the court details of the expenditure to support the council's action.

Miss Farooqi went through the various costs that had occurred in minute detail. She itemised each individual cost and listed the legal companies who had provided a service to the council.

I am told that Mr Justice Hamblen, previously a Queen's Counsel specialising in commercial law, questioned Miss Farooqi about the costs incurred and whether those claimed were recoverable. It appears some were and some were not.

Following questions from Mr Dagnall about 'double-counting' it appears that some of the financial claims had been duplicated, which raised the question about the reliability of the facts that Miss Farooqi had provided.

I am also told that due to the complexity of the financial aspects of the council's claim and the endless questions and answers, plus the cross-examination of Miss Farooqi by Mr Dagnall, her evidence took several days to complete.

Notwithstanding the financial questions, she also gave details of the whole processes undertaken by the council during the dispute, which have been explained in earlier chapters, but it all had to be spelt out in detail to the judge including a breakdown of each individual cost.

The court heard about the bitter disputes between Mrs Laird and the Leader of the Council during her time at Cheltenham Borough Council. Their differences of opinion about the running of the council had turned into personal attacks by the Leader, and there were allegations of inappropriate and bullying behaviour by the Leader and his Cabinet colleagues towards Mrs Laird.

John Dagnall told the court that the conduct and behaviour of elected members and certain officers of the council had resulted in the current state of health of his client. He added she was no longer able to work.

He explained to the court that Mrs Laird still suffered from depression, and as his client was tearful at this early stage of the hearing, he told the judge that he was very doubtful whether his client would be able to take the witness stand.

Mr Kerr interjected and told the judge that his intention was to question Mrs Laird for two to three days in the early part of the trial.

With the preliminary stages over the court adjourned, but when Mrs Laird tried to get up to leave the court, her knees buckled beneath her. Thankfully, her husband was close to her and saved her from falling to the ground, but it was clear that the pressures of the first day were already having their effects on Mrs Laird – and there were 30 days of the same mixture still to come.

With the wide publicity of the first day of the trial and particularly where the sensitive matter of disclosure of someone's medical history in relation to a job application is concerned, it is almost inevitable that an employment law expert will come to the surface and make a comment.

In this case, Mr Selwyn Blyth, a leading lawyer in employment law, did so. Writing in *Personnel Today* in March 2009, he made a very percipient comment. This is what he wrote:

> "The council appears to be saying that if it had known about her bouts of depressive illness, this would have swung the vote against her and she wouldn't have been appointed. This sounds like an adverse decision based on the fact she had been ill, that is direct disability discrimination, which cannot be justified and is therefore, an unlawful basis for making a decision.
>
> Even though she had been ill beforehand, Mrs Laird may have been well enough to work when she applied for and took the job in Cheltenham, and the fact she had been working for two years before she took it suggested she was.
>
> Employers should not see this case as a green light to disciplining or dismissing employees who have not revealed information about their health at recruitment."

These were powerful words and the message soon reverberated around the commercial and industrial centres bringing changes to, or at least a revision of, employment practices in most of them.

Andrew North, who attended the first day of the trial as an observer, told the *Gloucestershire Echo* in a report of the proceedings "We don't really want to be here.

Coming to the court was the last resort. But we feel we need to protect the interests of Cheltenham council taxpayers."

Like many people who read their local paper I found the comment odd to say the least, because there had been ample opportunity to 'draw a line under the dispute' throughout its time, yet it had never been taken. If the council, assuming Mr North meant both officers and members, really did not want to be at the High Court, why didn't they draw that all important line?

If the local council taxpayers, whose interests Mr North was protecting, had known that only twelve days before the start of the 30 day trial a special meeting of councillors had instructed him to meet with Mrs Laird to negotiate a settlement and stop the case from proceeding, they may have wondered why the alleged opportunity had never been taken.

It was not until after the trial had concluded that I learned that the District Auditor (DA) had tried to facilitate a settlement between the two sides only days before the trial started.

Whether it was the enormous sum of money being claimed by the council, or the prospect that the cost of the trial may spiral, it was revealed to me after the trial that the DA had written to Mr John Dagnall two days before the case was due to start about the matter.

In his letter the DA indicated that should his client ask the council to settle the dispute on the basis of both parties bearing their own costs and Mrs Laird waiving her right to an injury allowance, then he would urge the council to accept the proposal.

The letter also indicated that the DA was aware councillors had previously ruled out a settlement and because of this, he could not guarantee that they would now agree.

However, the DA made it clear in his letter that he was taking this initiative himself in order to try and persuade the council to settle the dispute.

He gave two reasons for his suggestions,

1. He had been made aware that the Barrister's client did not have the assets to support the council's claim, and
2. He was concerned about the mental health implications of Mrs Laird's case if it proceeded.

It may be cynical to think that something may have happened between the 'emergency' resolution that had been approved at the special meeting of the S&SSC on 15th January and the start of the case on 26th January, or was it a complete coincidence? (Reference pages 429 and 430 Chapter 22)

However, the offer was turned down by Mr Dagnall on the basis that his client did not have the financial wherewithal to bear the costs already incurred. He was also aware that his client had been granted approval to enter into a Conditional Fee Agreement (CFA) by the Bar Council, which is for people with little money to fight expected costly court cases. The CFA is a contract whereby a barrister represents a client for free, but if the client is successful then an uplifted fee rate is payable.

As I understand the position, a CFA is usually granted if the Bar Council thinks the applicant has a reasonable chance of winning the case.

Even more surprisingly, I learned that an email had been received during the trial by John Dagnall from Timothy Kerr QC saying 'he was willing to suggest both parties walk away from the trial and each bear their own costs on condition that Mrs Laird made the first move'. First the District Auditor and then the council's QC – was there going to be a third proposal?

However, it came as no surprise to me to learn that Mr Dagnall had advised his client not to accept either of the two offers.

Let's assume for one moment that Mrs Laird had accepted the offer to 'make the first move'. She would have been saddled with enormous legal costs in defending herself from the claims made against her. Those who had brought the claims and brought the reputation of the council into disrepute, would have walked away unblemished. Would they have had any regrets about the cost to the local taxpayers, and would they have apologised for the distress they had caused by their behaviour?

In my opinion Mrs Laird was right to reject the offer, her defence was strong and the council's 6–4 odds-on chance of being successful with their claim was beginning to look a bit shaky, otherwise the offer would not have been made.

The fact that Mrs Laird had no money to fight a costly court case, let alone pay large sums of money in compensation should she lose, was emphasised by Mrs Yvonne Atkinson in an article by Aled Thomas, a political reporter, and featured on the front page of the *Gloucestershire Echo* on 21st January 2009, a few days before the start of the trial.

She claimed in the article that 'CBC would not receive a penny from Christine Laird even if it wins its legal case against her because she has no assets'.

Mrs Atkinson thought it would turn out to be a waste of council taxpayers' money, but she added that in spite of what Christine Laird had been through 'She wants to demonstrate to the court that she is not the person the council is making her out to be'.

Mrs Atkinson told the *Echo* reporter that Mrs Laird had 'mortgaged herself to the hilt, exhausted her savings and committed her entire pension for years to come in order to fund her defence costs'. She added, 'Mrs Laird thought it was worth it to clear her name, which was important to her, and if she lost then the council would get nothing because she would have nothing left to give'.

When asked for their comments a CBC spokeswoman stated "The council had not received full disclosure of Mrs Laird's financial situation and their claim relates to the completion of the pre-employment medical questionnaire."

Hugh Laird, Christine Laird's husband, in response said: "The form asked her if she had any illnesses or medical conditions that affected her ability to work, she answered no, which was completely accurate."

Council chief Andrew North, when asked by the *Echo* for his views on what had been said, commented that 'he thought it would be unhelpful to discuss in detail the issues raised on behalf of Mrs Laird with the case starting in a few days time'.

From these early comments and the statement by Selwyn Blyth, it looked as though the case would be determined on the validity or otherwise of the medical questionnaire, but why it should take 30 days for the court to decide, I shall never know.

The first four days of the trial had been taken up with financial matters and the alleged undisclosed sickness of Mrs Laird and the medical questionnaire.

Whatever the merits of the council's claim, I can categorically state that from my perspective as a Group Leader and being able to recall the first fifteen months of Mrs Laird's employment, I was not aware that she was unfit to do the job through ill-health. As a Group Leader I had regular contact with the managing director through normal group meetings, committee meetings and occasional briefings. Throughout this time, not one meeting was postponed because Mrs Laird had become ill, on the contrary, she was always 'on top of the job' and raring to go. It was only at times during a committee meeting when she could hear snide comments being uttered by those who disliked her that she looked a little forlorn, but having to put up with such rudeness, who could blame her?

Furthermore, I was unaware of any sickness absence by Mrs Laird during the first two years of her employment, which prompted me to ask for information about Mrs Laird's sickness record at an Extraordinary Council Meeting on 22nd March 2010. This special meeting of the council had been called by members of the public to enable them to put questions to the council about the Public Interest Report (PIR) carried out by the auditors KPMG after the court case. This will be the subject of a later chapter.

For the record, my questions at the council meeting were deemed to be unacceptable by Sara Freckleton the council's Monitoring Officer, even though I had sought and been given permission by Mrs Laird for her record to be made public.

More about this later.

Day 5

Mr Patrick Brady, a solicitor and former chief executive of a Derbyshire council, who had been brought in by CBC to give independent advice on the dispute, told the court that he couldn't remember details of every interview, but he could remember that Cllr McKinlay had told him that 'Mrs Laird made him sick'.

He also remembered that Mrs Laird had told him that Cllr McKinlay 'had a problem with women' but he couldn't remember the details of this or the complaint by Mrs Laird about Cllr McKinlay bullying her.

Selective amnesia is commonplace when important details implicate others and Mr Brady, a former professional in the business of dealing with people, couldn't remember the important detail of the alleged behaviour by Cllr McKinlay.

Mr Dagnall pressed Mr Brady about the alleged relationships with women, but nothing more was forthcoming. But, towards the end of the trial, a young woman, Melissa Neil, told the court that she had previously worked as a senior officer in the public relations department of Cheltenham Borough Council. Her position in the department and the nature of her work, she told the court, meant that she often had to spend long hours dealing with the press and other agencies after the offices had closed. It was not unusual for practically everyone else to have gone home and the light in her office to be the only one on in the building, so the presence of Cllr McKinlay loitering outside the office unnerved the young woman.

She told the court this had occurred on more than one occasion, usually accompanied with an offer of a lift home by the councillor.

A coincidence, maybe! Did it have any significance at the time? If he had been asked, no doubt he would have said he was only being friendly, like the occasion when he was in the outer office of Mrs Laird's department and when challenged claimed he was only wishing Bronwen Ball 'a happy birthday'. Bronwen was one of four females working as executive assistants in the outer office working under the direction of Karen Watson, the PA to Mrs Laird in 2002.

Day 6

The question about confidentiality was also raised by John Dagnall; it seemed whenever the matter of Mrs Laird's health was discussed in committee, it would promptly appear in the local press.

He asked Mr Brady whether it was correct that on various occasions in the past information which the council would normally wish to keep confidential, such as meetings held to discuss Mrs Laird, had a tendency to end up in the press.

Was this not a clear breach of the rules of confidentiality?

Mr Brady agreed it was.

Pressing Mr Brady further, Mr Dagnall suggested to him whether the possibility of someone leaking to the press the medical state of Mrs Laird would be a matter of legitimate concern to him, he answered 'yes'.

Reports in the local and national press about 'discrimination' or allegations of 'bullying' and 'misogyny' at the trial, usually prompted people to contact me.

Some are just inquisitive and others usually have something positive to offer.

The former Liberal Democrat councillor Sally Stringer, who had written to me by email on 19th February 2011, alleged that a young female councillor colleague by the name of Debbie Hall had become the girlfriend of Cllr McKinlay and she subsequently moved in with him. Unfortunately, the relationship didn't last and it ended, according to Sally Stringer, with the young female being 'thrown out of the house, which was situated in the St Pauls district of the town during the night effectively making her homeless'.

Apparently, the young woman walked to a hotel in a nearby square, which was owned by another Liberal Democrat councillor, carrying her few belongings with her and pleading for refuge until she could find other accommodation.

The experience was shattering for Debbie Hall and her brief career in politics came to a swift halt and she went back home to the north of England.

Day 7

The early days of the trial centred round the state of Mrs Laird's health both before and after her appointment as managing director. But on the seventh day of the trial there was a change: Mr Christopher Huckle, the deputy chief executive of CBC, told the court that Mrs Laird had a close relationship with Cllr Duncan Smith, the Conservative Group Leader, who was also the Leader of the Council in 2002.

So close, according to Mr Huckle, the *Gloucestershire Echo* reported him as saying, "As to allow her almost to act as his mouthpiece".

When asked for his opinions about the two sides in the dispute he alleged that Mrs Laird thought the cabinet under Cllr McKinlay was 'incompetent and dysfunctional' and that Cllr McKinlay 'did not trust Mrs Laird because he believed she was misrepresenting the views of his cabinet'.

He then told the judge that Mrs Laird had used 'delaying tactics' in order to delay the hearing into her conduct because "she anticipated the return of a Conservative administration at the council elections in June 2004, which she considered to be sympathetic to her cause."

For someone who always gave me the impression that he was completely neutral regarding the dispute, [earlier chapters confirm this] his evidence to the court recorded a bitterness that surprised me.

Political and non-political neutrality by officers is usually observed even after retirement from the council, but it seems when used in a court situation it does not apply. Maybe, a bit of deep-seated bias suddenly came to the fore.

Chris Huckle also referred to a long list of alleged offences committed by Mrs Laird, including the 'mistreatment' of staff and officers at all levels, from the junior clerk in an office to the most senior legal officer in the council offices. But what were the alleged 'mistreatments' of colleagues?

It has been difficult to find out, and no record can be found.

So, I do not place too much weight on the words uttered by Chris Huckle in the High Court, and after all, as the reader knows, he was in a prime position to take over the job of managing director should Mrs Laird be dismissed.

I have no idea what weight the judge put on the comments from Mr Huckle, and unless the court heard in detail what the 'mistreatments' were, there being no direct reference to them in the judgment, it is difficult to come to any reasonable conclusion.

When someone says they have been 'mistreated' by another person it very often means different things to different people.

I had made it my business to question some of the various comments alleged to have been made by members of the staff and passed on to me by other councillors. My questions were always of a general nature, but aimed to 'tease out' their opinions of the managing director. Not everyone wanted to be questioned, those that did often answered by claiming that Mrs Laird was 'aloof and unfriendly'; constantly chasing staff 'to carry out her instructions'; had 'an air of superiority' was a phrase often used, particularly when, it seemed, 'she walked around the council offices'.

But when I suggested that perhaps that was the way Mrs Laird saw her job and thought it was necessary in order to progress the council forward, the tone towards her changed. Although there was general agreement that the managing director was a woman with determination, several thought she came across too strongly, repeating that she should have been friendlier towards the office staff. This was fair comment, but the answers given on all the questions were nothing like the picture that had been constantly painted by her critics.

Perhaps it was a case that the officers at all levels soon realised in 2002 that their 'comfort zone' was not going to be as comfortable in the future as it had been in the past. Lawrence Davison, the previous chief executive, was a friendly individual, who relied a lot on other people and was seldom seen walking around the council offices. If in Lawrence Davison's view things were going reasonably well then Lawrence was more than happy to leave things to his executive staff.

The council office is situated in the centre of Cheltenham's famous Promenade. Officers and staff had no requirement to 'clock-in' and 'clock-out' in the early 2000's and the shops across the road were handy whenever they felt it necessary to 'nip out' and obtain a quick purchase – who would know, and did anyone care?

That situation is little different today than it was then.

Prior to Lawrence Davison there was another chief executive with a similar determination to that of Christine Laird. His name was Colin Nye.

Colin was not a man to turn a blind-eye to a 'comfort zone'; the staff was there to work and he expected total commitment from them and he usually got it. He was a man I admired because he was determined to make Cheltenham an even better place than its national image portrayed.

He didn't suffer fools gladly, and if a member of staff failed to come up to the standard he expected of them, he would quietly say to me "He's not one of us, you know". And the presence of Colin Nye walking around the corridors of the council offices, coat off and bright coloured braces prominent against his white shirt, was a sight to behold. Groups of people, even those who were genuinely talking about a work problem, quickly moved away when they saw him coming.

This leads me to suggest, and it is only a long shot, that the officers had become too comfortable during the Davison period and they would not welcome a return to the Nye days under the direction of a woman in the top job. A woman in the top job – that too must have been a sour taste in the mouths for some officers and staff to swallow.

In earlier chapters I repeatedly suggested that if there had been the will to end the bad behaviour then that could have happened at any time. If the undefined accusations made were serious then they could have been dealt with by the Standards Committee. If the charges were instances of 'gross misconduct' and subsequently proved, then suspension and/or dismissal would have been appropriate.

When Mrs Laird was finally dismissed because of 'frustration of contract' a local resident wrote to Cllr McKinlay on 3rd November 2005 asking "When will the taxpayers be told the reasons for and the reasoning behind the dismissal of Mrs Laird?"

A reply from Cllr McKinlay on 8th November 2005 stated: "Due to legal restrictions I am afraid I cannot tell you the reasons behind the dismissal of Mrs Laird at this time. We have tried to bring elements of this into the public domain but were prevented from doing so by the Conservatives and PAB parties by a vote at full council. As much as I personally would be extremely pleased to make people fully aware of the facts, I regret I am unable to do so."

The local resident was clearly not satisfied with the reply and wrote further to Cllr McKinlay on 11th November and this is what he said in his letter:

"We know why the opposition parties could not agree to your attempts to partially explain to the taxpayers the reasons for Mrs Laird's dismissal, but you have not answered my question. When will you explain to the taxpayers, fully and clearly, why Mrs Laird was dismissed?"

I am not aware that any further answer was given, but to seek an answer to that question was one of the reasons why I felt the need to set down all the facts as I knew them, assisted by the receipt of letters and emails, together with the reports from sources that were not available to me in the early days of the dispute.

Dismissal is a final act, but if instead of using a 'trumped-up' charge against the Rhondda Cynon Taf District Council about a job reference, or the incorrect filling in of a medical questionnaire, CBC had pursued the disciplinary route from the start, and then that course of action would have been more honest.

The reason the council didn't choose the disciplinary route was simply that it had no substantive evidence to prove its case; what became abundantly clear as facts became available was that the Leader of the Council, Andrew McKinlay, disliked Mrs Laird to such an extent that he would do and say anything in order to terminate her employment as managing director of Cheltenham Borough Council.

But, in order to succeed in his task, he needed the support of others who could and would be prepared to go to London to bear witness to his alleged accusations of Mrs Laird's conduct during her short time with the council.

He was not disappointed: a number of councillors and officers volunteered to make the trip to the Royal Courts of Justice, and some of them made more than one trip, with over-night stays in an imposing London hotel, all paid for no doubt by the council taxpayers.

Day 9

On day nine of the trial, Gerald Ford, the head of legal services and Monitoring Officer at the time, told the court that the reason he lodged a complaint against Mrs Laird was that 'she undermined me professionally'.

According to the report of the proceedings in the *Gloucestershire Echo* he was asked by John Dagnall whether that was the only reason he lodged a complaint. When challenged further, it is alleged that he said "he did not want to cause her any trouble or harm of any sort". He was not trying to implement a 'disciplinary process against her, but he did want an apology'.

John Dagnall pressed him to explain what he meant by 'undermining' him, Mr Ford replied 'endeavouring to reduce or lower his professional standing'.

Asked to explain how his professional standing had been reduced, Mr Ford was reported as saying "I am an experienced solicitor. I have worked in local government for more years than I care to work out. I have a certain reputation, which I believe was being undermined by Mrs Laird's actions. My standing was being lowered in the eyes of others."

His reply to the suggestion by John Dagnall that Mrs Laird 'was only trying to defend herself in an extremely difficult situation' was answered negatively.

It is interesting to note that the High Court judgment refers to the fact that both Cllrs Smith and Godwin, together with Mrs Laird and others, 'had long had concerns about his competence'. The judge referred to the meeting of Group Leaders to discuss this matter, but they were thwarted from taking any action against Mr Ford, because Cllr McKinlay, who the judge said was a supporter of Mr Ford, 'prevented the matter being taken forward'.

Although the judge did not accept that 'Mr Ford was biased against her in the dispute', he qualified this by adding that 'Mr Ford may have been disorganised, indecisive and slow in responding on certain issues, but he was scrupulously honest and at all times sought to perform his job to the best of his ability'.

This was a fair assessment of the man and I am sure Cllr Duncan Smith would agree with it. However, there were occasions when the quality of Mr Ford's advice was either wrong or at best questionable. Perhaps it was because he relied too often on the external advice he had sought from Counsel.

I have previously mentioned the arguments that took place about the responsibility for appointing the JNC Panel. There was a procedure to follow and it needlessly became controversial due to the poor advice given by Counsel, which Mr Ford did not challenge.

On another occasion, acting on further advice, Mr Ford announced that the Cabinet members were not obliged to declare a prejudicial interest at the full council meeting on 27th October 2003.

I remember the arguments that were put forward at the time by me and other members of the council that the Cabinet members should not be allowed to participate in an issue concerning the dispute, because of their deeply held views. But because of Mr Ford's advice they did participate in the debate, although they withdrew from the chamber before the vote was taken.

The protests and subsequent complaints to the Standards Board for England (SBE) by the opposition group leaders were vindicated by the Ethical Standards Officer (ESO) when he considered the complaint regarding 'failure to declare an interest' and accepted that it was a breach of the Code of Conduct. Unfortunately, the ESO regarded it as a minor factor and recommended that no action should be taken against the individuals concerned.

Gerald Ford retired from Cheltenham Borough Council on 20th May 2005.

Three days before he left on 17th May and without any prior discussion with me, he wrote to inform me that he had made a number of complaints about me to the SBE.

On the 20th May I wrote to Mr Ford expressing my concerns and disappointment that he found it necessary to report me to the SBE and requested details of the complaints. I reminded him that Mrs Laird had been suspended from the council for more than six months and the dispute had dragged on for more than four years, yet no discussions had taken place between us regarding anything I had said during this time. I also reminded him that if he had contacted me about his concerns I could have explained why I thought the appalling comments from other council members needed to be rebutted, if that was the substance of his concerns.

It was true that I had raised the question on more than one occasion about the distribution of minutes and reports and I had insisted that copies should be sent to the managing director because she was still employed by the council.

Whether this was the root cause of his concerns, I know not, but it did seem to me that if we were discussing Mrs Laird in her absence, the least we should do was to send a copy of the official minutes of the meeting to her.

Of course, I did not receive a reply to my letter because Gerald Ford had gone – lock stock and barrel and with no forwarding address.

It was not until 31st May 2005 that I received a letter from the SBE stating that they had received complaints from Mr Ford alleging

1. "The managing director allied herself with the minority group leaders on the council: Councillor Godwin is the leader of the People Against Bureaucracy Group. In particular it is alleged that the managing director tried to use Councillor Godwin to get rid of the complainant",
2. "It is alleged that Councillor Godwin gave the impression of exceeding the normal expectations of an opposition group leader by acting on the managing director's behalf: in particular that he
    a) Played games with senior officers with the aim of making them 'sweat a bit',
    b) Compromised the managing director's impartiality, and
    c) Breached confidentiality and failed to acknowledge the extent to which he was working for the managing director, acting as informant, advocate and *agent provocateur*".

Mr Ford's letter of complaint to the SBE further suggested that "Councillor Godwin and the managing director may have been 'friends' within the scope of the Code of Conduct, which could give rise to a personal interest".

I was not too sure what he meant by this comment, because I always declared a personal and prejudicial interest whenever the dispute or the MD's employment was on an agenda, unlike certain officers and councillors on the council. Nevertheless, I was surprised to read the full text of his complaints against me and particularly the terms in which they had been couched.

I had been a councillor for 27 years and Leader of the People Against Bureaucracy Group throughout this time; no-one had ever mentioned that I had powers such as those expounded by Gerald Ford to the SBE.

My thoughts on this were soon shattered when I heard from Cllr Duncan Smith that he too had received a similar letter from the SBE, so the power that Mr Ford thought I had was a shared power with another group leader.

Needless to say, the ultimate decision of the SBE was 'that these allegations against Cllr Smith and Cllr Godwin should NOT BE INVESTIGATED'.

Needless to say, the sequence of events where the head of the council's legal department writes a letter of complaint to the SBE just three days before he retires still rankles with me. It was underhanded to say the least.

On reflection, I wish the SBE had investigated the complaint. It would have been a good opportunity for me to 'tell the world' about people like Gerald Ford who had been working for the local authority throughout the period of the dispute and a council who had saddled the town with a debt in excess of £2 million.

Is it any wonder that the dispute went on for so long?

On 6th June 2005 I wrote to Peter Lewis asking him to respond to my letter dated 20th May. He sent the letter to Mr Ford and I received a letter from him on council headed paper also dated 6th June simply confirming that the complaints had been made and were in the hands of the SBE.

It informed me that I should be hearing from them shortly.

The letter was duly signed by Mr Ford above his title Assistant Director (Legal & Democratic Services) which seemed rather odd considering he had left the council's employment, but perhaps it was done to impress me.

It is anyone's guess whether the comments made by the judge regarding Mr Ford would have been different, had he known that Mr Ford had lodged complaints to the SBE against Cllr Smith and me.

Day 10

On day ten of the trial, Cllr Diggory Seacome, a Conservative councillor, told the court, according to a report in the *Gloucestershire Echo,* "he had voted in favour of the appointment of Christine Laird to the top job in 2002 because he believed she had the qualities needed to push through major changes in the culture of the local authority. But had he known of the circumstances in which she had left a previous employment, he might have taken a different view and not voted in her favour."

Mr Dagnall suggested that Cllr Seacome was adopting an extreme attitude to boost what he was saying, and to support the council's case against Mrs Laird. In response to Mr Dagnall's claim, the *Echo* reported that Cllr Seacome rejected his view and added "I might have changed my mind had I known, but I don't regard that as an extreme attitude".

Mr Dagnall reminded Cllr Seacome that Mrs Laird was described during the selection process as someone who 'doesn't suffer fools gladly, gives the appearance that she is abrasive, has energy, talent and overall performance'. When asked whether he agreed, Cllr Seacome told the judge that he would have used the word 'positive' rather than 'abrasive'.

Day 11

The council challenged the claim by Mrs Laird that she had played a major part in securing nearly £1.5 million for the local authority in social housing grants.

Mrs Laird was responding to the council's claim for £1 million damages, should they win the case. Credit, she claimed, should be given to her for all benefits received or derived by the authority as a result of her employment as their managing director.

A reasonable suggestion, but the council were having none of it. Mr Michael Redman, who was the assistant director, neighbourhood regeneration at the time, told the court that he was unaware that Mrs Laird had used any specialist knowledge or experience to secure any benefits.

Day 12

This was the day that observers from both sides of the dispute had been waiting for. The *Gloucestershire Echo* reported on 25th February 2009 that the Leader of Cheltenham Borough Council, Cllr Andrew McKinlay, told the court 'how his confidence was undermined by an aggressive and bullying managing director to the point where he felt physically sick every time he entered the council offices'.

He claimed that Christine Laird refused to discuss his concerns, and her attitude 'intimated that I was weak, incompetent and had a problem with women'.

Cllr McKinlay told the judge 'he felt increasingly isolated and alone and powerless'. He stated that 'his contact with Mrs Laird towards the end of 2003 was minimal', although he claimed, 'he refused her request to stay away from the council secretariat's office, because he sometimes needed to use its facilities'.

Day 13

Cllr McKinlay was cross-examined by John Dagnall.

In answer to questions, the court heard that he had started a relationship with Mrs Karen Watson, Mrs Laird's PA, but he claimed that the relationship only happened after Mrs Laird had left the council in 2005.

According to the *Gloucestershire Echo* on 26th February 2009, Cllr McKinlay admitted in cross-examination that he had been taking Mrs Watson to lunch as early as 2003, but he disagreed with John Dagnall that he was 'romantically linked to her at that time' suggesting it was more a 'boss-and-employee' situation. However, by the time the relationship had 'blossomed' they reported their situation to Gerald Ford the Monitoring Officer.

The *Echo* further reported that Cllr McKinlay and Karen Watson had a child and Mrs Watson had now become Mrs McKinlay.

When challenged by Mr Dagnall about his reputation for sexually harassing women, he denied he had approached other females and asked them out on dates. According to the *Echo* report, he admitted that he had taken a female employee to a concert because she was an opera fan, and on another occasion 'had invited another woman for a drink while they were talking'.

John Dagnall pressed Cllr McKinlay on Mrs Laird's claim that some female staff members were upset by his conduct, which had concerned her.

Cllr McKinlay denied any impropriety.

When asked by John Dagnall whether 'he was aware of making a pass at Lydia Bishop, a councillor colleague' he replied saying 'she had accompanied him on a couple of events, but he was not aware of making a pass at her'.

The *Echo* reported that Mr Kerr QC, acting for the council, objected to the line of cross-examination by John Dagnall, because it was based on 'anonymous hearsay', but in reply, Mr Dagnall claimed he was 'responding to the charge made against Mrs Laird that she had undermined Andrew McKinlay by criticising him in an improper fashion'.

Day 14

Further cross-examination of Cllr McKinlay took place on Day 14 of the trial, and at last, by kind permission of the *Gloucestershire Echo*, readers had the opportunity to read about an admission in court by Cllr McKinlay, that "he wanted to get rid of Mrs Laird". This desire to 'get rid of the managing director' was because he could not establish a lasting working relationship with her.

Mr Dagnall suggested to Cllr McKinlay that "He had tried to present his breakdown in relationship with Mrs Laird as a disciplinary offence on her part, which would lead to her removal."

Cllr McKinlay disagreed.

He was asked 'whether there came a time in 2003 when despite her request that they should get together and discuss their respective roles, he remained determined to get rid of her'.

Cllr McKinlay replied saying the Cabinet's relationship with Mrs Laird was by that time 'very difficult'.

When Mr Dagnall asked him whether it was his desire for Mrs Laird to depart from Cheltenham Borough Council, Cllr McKinlay replied that it was. He also admitted 'there were ongoing negotiations about her future'.

It was during the hearing on Day 14 that Mrs Laird, who was sitting behind her Barrister, collapsed and Mr Justice Hamblen adjourned the court to allow Mrs Laird to be treated by a first aid officer in the court corridor.

If a disciplinary offence was not the reason for trying to get rid of the MD, as claimed by Cllr McKinlay in the court, then surely a full and proper explanation should have been given to the court about the actual reasons the Leader and Cabinet members had in mind during the period 2002 to 2004?

Large sums of taxpayers' money had been used to set up a JNC Panel, a Grievance Panel and the appointment of a legally qualified Designated Independent Person. All spent in order to try and establish that the managing director was a not a fit and proper person to run the council, and was the sole cause of the council's problems.

So why did the Liberal Democrat administration, assisted by senior officers of the council, go to costly lengths to prove that Mrs Laird had committed 'disciplinary

Christine showing signs of the stress as she leaves the High Court with her barrister John Dagnall and her legal team

offences' before the trial, yet Cllr McKinlay told the court they were not the reasons for wanting her to leave.

And why, readers may ask, was Mrs Laird's interim appraisal in 2003 regarded so highly by Cllr McKinlay that it warranted a bonus payment, yet he prevented a second appraisal taking place six months later?

Day 15

Cllr Duncan Smith gave his evidence to the court on this day. He stated, according to the *Gloucestershire Echo,* that if Mrs Laird had disclosed her history of depressive illness at the time of selection she would not have been offered the job. However, in his witness statement to the court, Cllr Smith stated that Mrs Laird was a strong contender, and his initial reaction at the interview stage was that 'she came across as quite cold and clinical'.

Cllr Smith told the court 'the council had an ambitious programme for the future in 2002 and he knew it would be met with resistance, although most members of the council agreed with the principle that change was necessary'.

It was on the issue of how the change could be brought about that Cllr Smith thought there would be differences between the two main political parties.

'Mrs Laird expressed confidence that she was able to handle the sensitivities around staff restructuring' said Cllr Smith adding, 'she also had experience in managing change'.

Cllr Smith said *'it required a managing director who was mentally and physically fit for the job'.* He stressed that *'the council had a challenging programme and it would inevitably become stressful. In spite of this, during the first year of her employment, Mrs Laird had exceeded my expectations of her and she had delivered considerable change within the council. I was impressed by the skills she demonstrated in dealing with complicated technical issues and communicating them to her staff and members'.*

According to a summary of the day's proceedings given to me by Hugh Laird, Cllr Smith told the court that things were bad before Christine Laird arrived to take up her post.

The judge asked him to give some examples; Cllr Smith replied that the Monitoring Officer, Gerald Ford, never gave a straight answer to a question. He then listed a number of instances where he believed bad advice had been given to councillors, and there were instances when Mr Ford didn't stand by his own advice.

He was critical of the Liberal Democrat group for failing to admit there was a problem, and then failed to involve the council when Cllr McKinlay alleged that he was having 'difficulties' with the managing director.

According to the summary, he accused Cllr McKinlay of being offensive, threatening and aggressive with anybody who disagreed with him.

Setting aside for now the belated comments about Mrs Laird's previous bouts of work-related depression when working for previous employers, the judge would have noted,

a. that in spite of this tardy information, she was on top of the job in her first year, and

b. it was only when the abuse and the malicious and unpleasant behaviour began that Mrs Laird's health deteriorated.

In his witness statement Cllr Smith stated that he was unaware of any problems with Mrs Laird, her style of management or her health issues that may have been manifest at that point. It was not until later that year that Mrs Laird's behaviour became more irrational and emotional.

He admitted in cross-examination by John Dagnall, "that if Mrs Laird was innocent of any wrong, complaints made against her by the Liberal Democrats must have been extremely stressful".

Day 17

Cllr Robert Garnham was another member who went to London on behalf of the council, to tell the judge that he would not have voted for Mrs Laird if he had known about her history of stress-related illness. He admitted that at the selection interview Mrs Laird came across as 'an assertive and confident person who was not afraid of making and taking a decision; she was proactive and would take the council forward'.

He added that 'Mrs Laird's assertiveness and confidence at interview left him with the impression that she was a strong person, and there was no sign of illnesses'.

In his witness statement, according to the *Gloucestershire Echo*, he said 'The council would not have been fulfilling its duty of care to place a person with a history of stress into one of the most challenging roles within local government'.

In cross-examination, according to the summary of proceedings, Cllr Garnham agreed that 'a medical had not been discussed at the recruitment meeting'. He was then pressed by Mr Dagnall to explain whether there had been a move to suspend Mrs Laird in March 2003. He could only vaguely remember this, he told Mr Dagnall, who then produced damning evidence to prove that he and another councillor (Melville-Smith) had gone to Mrs Laird's office, one hour before the start of a council meeting, and 'threatened the managing director with suspension'. [Previously mentioned in an earlier chapter]

Days 18 and 19

These days were taken up by two members of the council's legal department.

Peter Lewis, solicitor and acting monitoring officer for the council, told the court that in his opinion the council's Grievance Panel was politically balanced.

The Panel was set up, he said, following complaints lodged by Mrs Laird against certain councillors. He did not think the panel was biased against Mrs Laird, and in his opinion, the panel operated fairly.

Jonathan Noel (Solicitor) told the court that he disputed the figure of £250,000 that Mrs Laird claimed she had saved in a planning appeal matter against Salmon Harvester. Even if the appeal had gone ahead, he said, the developer's costs were unlikely to have been awarded against the council.

Day 20

The court heard from Bryony Houlden, chief executive South West Regional Assembly (SWRA), a specialist in staff recruitment, who told the court she attended council committee interviews with all the candidates, including Mrs Laird, for the post of managing director.

She told the court "Although some panel members thought Mrs Laird might have too strong a personality, others felt this would be a real asset in delivering the changes they felt were required in Cheltenham. Also, it is normally the case with public sector recruitment that material supplied by the council would have made it clear that the appointment was subject to a satisfactory medical report from the council's medical adviser."

She added "It was normal practice for councils to make any job offer subject to medical clearance and they would ask prospective employees to complete a medical questionnaire: Mrs Laird did not indicate that she had any mental health issues".

[In Cllr Smith's witness statement there was a reference to an issue raised by Mrs Laird with Bryony Houlden about her departure from the Chartered Institute of Housing (CIH). Mrs Laird had produced a copy of a Compromise Agreement she had entered into on her departure from the CIH, which included and related to a one off incident while she was there.
Committee members asked Bryony Houlden to investigate the matter.
In due course, according to the witness statement, nothing came up in the investigation suggesting there were any concerns regarding Mrs Laird's conduct while she was employed by the CIH.
The committee decided that with what Mrs Laird had told them, plus the references from other employers, 'they were happy to put Mrs Laird forward as one of the final short-listed candidates.']

Day 21

Christine Laird was the victim of a malicious 'dirty tricks campaign' which contributed to the wrecking of her health and her career prospects, said her husband on this day in the High Court.

According to the *Echo* report on the day's proceedings (March 20th 2009), Hugh Laird told the judge "In 2003, when Liberal Democrat Andrew McKinlay and his Cabinet were in charge of Cheltenham Borough Council, offensive and libellous material about her was placed in council members' post room pigeon holes. It had been put there to influence members and disadvantage his wife Christine. It was pathetic and disgusting" he said.

Hugh Laird, a management consultant, told Mr Justice Hamblen "When he met Christine, age 18, she was rising through the ranks at a council. At no stage, until recently, did it occur to him she was suffering from a permanent mental health problem."

He told the court "His wife had been a successful chief executive at the CIH; she took on the job at Cheltenham, knowing that the job would entail a massive restructuring with personnel changes. This was something she was good at.

Even before his wife took up the post of MD she received a request from the *Gloucestershire Echo* for an interview. She was told by the editor, Anita Syvret, that the *Echo* had received an anonymous package of information on Christine's 'past'. She was embarrassed having to explain her past history to the editor. The package of information was malicious and untrue."

[A statement issued by the CIH president in May 1998, confirmed that Mrs Laird had worked as chief executive of the CIH. It gave a glowing assessment of the growth it had achieved under the leadership of its chief executive. It recognised the good work she had done whilst she was there. The statement went on to say that the CIH 'recognised Mrs Laird's energy, dedication and contribution in expanding the whole of our activity base'. It listed nine achievements since she was appointed, including a 60 per cent growth in net worth and increases in membership and revenue'.]

Continuing his evidence, Mr Laird told the judge, "My wife had a brilliant time in the job at Cheltenham; she enjoyed it and got on well with the then council leader, Cllr Duncan Smith until May 2002. The Liberal Democrats won control of the Borough Council and it was then that things started to change."

"On 5th March 2003, disaster struck" he told the court "the council's deputy leader walked in on a meeting and asked her to resign."

From then on, claimed Mr Laird, 'my wife came under daily attack from the Leader of the Council and was threatened with a disciplinary panel'.

According to the *Echo* report, he told the judge "One shockingly bad and desperate trick was when Cllr McKinlay during a meeting with a group director, left his mobile phone on after talking to an *Echo* reporter, so that the journalist could hear everything he was saying about my wife. By March 2004, she was having panic attacks of astonishing intensity, constant crying, vomiting and a level of depression he had never seen before. It was obvious his wife was in danger of becoming mentally ill. Doctors warned me that there was a risk of a suicide attempt".

Day 22

Timothy Kerr QC for the council suggested to Hugh Laird in cross-examination that medical reports in March 2004 painted a different picture to the one he had described. He said "Mrs Laird, although fragile, was coping well, and suggested he was exaggerating the situation and was playing it up because reports did not support his evidence".

A quick response came from Mr Laird saying "You weren't living with her and I was. I don't see how you can say that. I was seeing a very different side of Christine's health".

It was clear to everyone in the court room that Hugh Laird was becoming very emotional having to respond to questions about his wife's health, and following a brief pause in order for him to recover, he told the judge that his wife had been determined to carry on working, and had told colleagues that 'it was business as usual with council work needed to be done'.

It was sad to see and listen to him give his evidence, but he stood up well to the cross-examination. Christine, with head bowed, shoulders arched, looked nothing like the person I saw in full control of Cheltenham Borough Council.

I felt sad for both of them, it should never have come to this, but I hoped my evidence would help their cause.

Earlier in the day's proceedings, Mr Kerr stated "He understood that the judge might have received a communication from a councillor who was present at a professionally privileged meeting in January, during which he, as the council's QC, assessed the authority's prospects of success in the court action."

The communication from the councillor- Mr Kerr did not name him – "sought to disclose what happened at that meeting, even though neither side in the case had invited it".

John Dagnall, in response, said the defence team had been approached by the councillor, who was asking to be called as a witness to what happened at various meetings, but in his view, "the evidence would not be relevant to this trial."

The judge adjourned the court until Monday 23rd March 2009.

[The communication to the High Court was mentioned in the previous chapter and is referenced in Appendix 1]

The day's proceedings had been interesting for me. I had travelled to London the previous night, (Thursday 19th March), booked in at The Shaftesbury Hotel in Earls Court, and prepared myself for my day in court the following day.

I was scheduled to give evidence in support of Mrs Laird at the start of the morning's proceedings. I had been to the Royal Courts of Justice before on other matters, but it was still a daunting prospect having to give evidence in such a famous court room. I was told on arrival at the courts that Mr Laird would continue giving his evidence at the start of proceedings, and then he would be cross-examined by Timothy Kerr QC; my evidence would be taken after Mr Laird had completed the cross-examination.

This gave me time to prepare my thoughts and go over the points I wanted to make. It also gave me the opportunity to listen to the questions put by Mr Kerr, to weigh up the court procedures, and to watch the two legal teams at work. The judge appeared to be making copious notes of what was going on, but he rarely intervened unless it was for the purpose of clarification.

I found Court 36 claustrophobic due to its smallness.

Everyone seemed to be cramped for space, with witnesses and members of the public occupying the few seats available behind the appellants (the Council) and the defendant (Mrs Laird). I was seated two rows behind Christine Laird, her husband and her barrister, but there was no difficulty in hearing what was being said.

The working areas of both legal teams were covered with papers and files, and time was taken up whilst they searched for appropriate documents, but it all seemed to work out fairly well.

The court witness box was set up in a way I had not been used to in previous visits to the London Courts, or in magistrates' courts. A cardboard box construction had been made, divided into four compartments. Each compartment contained several lever arch files, each labelled with a reference letter and a number; probably twenty four files altogether.

It looked odd, but it was there as a ready access for each witness to the hundreds of letters, reports and emails that had been used during the dispute.

With this large cardboard structure, it was difficult to see someone in the witness box, especially if the person was short in stature. However, from my position in the court room, I could see Hugh Laid when he was giving his evidence, but anyone sitting on the other side of the court, I imagined, would only see his head and shoulders.

The important thing was that the witnesses could be clearly seen by the judge and the legal representatives, and this was certainly the case.

The break for lunch was welcome, but it did indicate that even if I was called to give evidence in the afternoon, I would probably be asked to return to the courts on Monday morning. As it turned out, the cross-examination of Mr Laird continued throughout the afternoon; I was told to return to the courts on the following Monday morning to give my evidence.

Fortunately for me, Hugh Laird's brother John and his wife, who lived in the London suburbs, offered to show me the way to the Underground station and to make sure I got on the right train. They were travelling in the same direction and they pointed out the station I needed to transfer to another line. I am sure I would have missed the connection if they had not been there.

Day 23

I arrived back at The Royal Courts of Justice just before 10.00 a.m., on Monday 23rd March 2009.

Outside court 36 the two legal teams were discussing issues with their clients, so

I thought it was in order for me to have words with Mrs Laird's barrister. I needed to have some idea how my evidence should be presented, and hopefully to get some idea of the questions I was likely to be asked.

However, before I could even put my questions to him, he told me it was not permissible for me to be seen talking to him and moved away from me quickly. This rather unnerved me. It certainly set me back because I didn't expect it.

I was there voluntarily and not because I had been summoned to attend.

Within a few minutes of entering the courtroom, I was called to the witness box and read the oath. I stared long and hard at the two dozen files in the cardboard structure, wondering what they all contained. I was soon to find out.

Mr Justice Hamblen opened the session with courteous comments, and with the judge's permission, I made a short statement.

I told the judge I had now travelled twice to London at my own expense, in order to speak the truth about the events leading up to and during the period of the dispute between the Leader of the Council and the managing director.

I know I said more and it was probably to enlarge on my first sentence hoping the court would sort out the lies from the truth.

Having said my piece I then waited for John Dagnall to ask me questions about my witness statement, signed by me as a Statement of Truth on 20th October 2008. To my surprise it was Timothy Kerr QC for the council who began putting questions to me. I remembered thinking that this was the wrong way round – surely it should be Mr Dagnall asking the questions and a cross-examination by Mr Kerr should come later.

It seemed odd to me, and I didn't have time to dwell on the point, because the questions soon started to flow.

The early questions from Mr Kerr covered my previous employment, my public duties and my position in the council and so on.

Then the questioning started in real earnest with Mr Kerr asking me to take a file from the cardboard compartment marked with a particular letter and to turn to a document in the file marked with a specific number. It was unnerving to say the least, because I had to check with Mr Kerr on several occasions whether I had heard his requests correctly, and whether I was reading the correct document from the appropriate file.

Without a copy of the transcript, I would not be able to tell readers what the questions were, and I would be even more doubtful whether the answers I had given were of sufficient value to help my efforts to tell the truth about the distressful events during the 'dark days' of the dispute.

I remember telling Mr Kerr about the 'bullying tactics' of Cllr McKinlay and his colleagues towards Mrs Laird, and I referred to the 'snide comments' about Mrs Laird made by them during several committee meetings.

Turning to the judge, I told him that long before the attempt to have a MD/Group Leaders' meeting on 19th March 2003, Cllr Smith had spoken to me on several occasions to talk about his concerns at the lack of information from the

Leader concerning the running of the council. From these conversations there was no doubt in my mind that Cllr McKinlay was deliberately excluding us.

Mr Kerr then asked me to refer to a specific file and to turn to a particular document, only to find it was a copy of an email from me to Cllr Smith, expressing my concerns about the situation that was developing. Counsel then asked me to explain to the court why Cllr McKinlay had not been included in the email. A strange question considering I had just indicated to the judge that the opposition group leaders, because of their position in the council, would talk and write to each other whenever it was necessary.

It was a normal daily practice of communication.

I told Mr Kerr that opposition political parties write to each other on many occasions regarding tactics about council business. 'It was our job' I told him 'that is what opposition members do'.

It would have been absurd to include Cllr McKinlay in the exchange of emails about matters to which the opposition groups were not in accord with the Liberal Democrats. They would not include Cllr Smith or me in the distribution of their emails, neither would we expect it.

This led to another question about the invitation from the managing director to all four group leaders to meet and discuss the behaviour of the Leader of the Council towards her in March 2003. Mr Kerr suggested to me that Cllr McKinlay had not been invited to the special meeting in the managing director's office, which I strongly refuted.

If Mr Kerr was correct in his assumption, then why did Cllr Smith send Cllr McKinlay an email later that same night, [referred to in an earlier chapter], enquiring why he hadn't attended the meeting?

Cllr McKinlay could have replied that he had not been invited, but he didn't, so who is telling the truth here?

Why, in fact, did Mr Kerr not recognise that the three opposition group leaders had subsequently tried to set up another meeting with Cllr McKinlay, in order to talk about the difficult situation?

Readers know from earlier chapters that he had been advised not to attend any meetings with the opposition group leaders regarding his disagreement with the managing director.

Who gave the advice and what was the purpose of it? Even now, that information should be revealed in full.

Without the benefit of the transcript, I have no knowledge whether similar questions had been put to Cllr Smith, by either Mr Kerr or Mr Dagnall. If in the light of their importance the questions were not asked, then in my opinion they should have been – it would have dispelled the notion that he had been deliberately excluded from the meeting by Mrs Laird.

In my witness statement to the High Court dated 20th October 2008, I stated that I had a meeting with Christine Laird regarding general council business matters on 12th March 2003. She had told me about the difficulties she was having with the

Leader of the Council. She wanted a meeting with all the Group Leaders to explain what was going on. Following the meeting, I received an email from her inviting me to a 'special meeting of all Group Leaders on 19th March'.

[The events surrounding this meeting have been well aired in an earlier chapter]

In the judgment at the end of the trial, the judge came to the conclusion that Cllr McKinlay had not been invited to the meeting. This means

a) he didn't believe my account of the situation, and
b) Duncan Smith had probably not been questioned about the email or the subsequent communications sent by him to Cllr McKinlay, by either the prosecution or the defence lawyers.

Meanwhile, the questions to me and the endless searching of the files continued throughout the morning. The theme deployed by Mr Kerr it seemed, was to try and undermine the importance of group leader meetings, or their significance to the operation of the Borough Council.

I cannot recall whether Mr Kerr asked me about the first part of my witness statement where I described Christine Laird as a very competent managing director; someone with a sharp mind and a determination to take the council forward. I hope he did.

The question and search process continued until lunchtime, I was warned by the judge not to talk to anyone during the recess.

The court resumed at 2.00 p.m.

I had already been in the witness box for three hours and the thought of further questioning was depressing, with cross-examination by John Dagnall still to come.

I learned there was no point in getting back to the court too early because the door to the court is locked until the two o'clock time is reached; a court usher comes along and the door is unlocked.

Apart from contact between barrister and client, there is no opportunity, even if it was allowed, to chat with anyone else involved in the court hearing.

Mr Kerr's questions continued inexorably after lunch, often about trivial matters, or to confirm the obvious detail. I was relieved when it drew to a close.

In my witness statement, I had confirmed that Mrs Laird had told me that the Leader of the Council had 'accused her of being a 'Tory nark'. It also stated that the expression had been used by Cllr McKinlay to justify his reason for not accepting Mrs Laird's appointment as the new managing director in 2002.

My statement also confirmed that after the March 19th meeting, the opposition group leaders agreed that a letter, reported above, should go to Cllr McKinlay, asking him to attend a meeting, leaving the date and time for him to decide. It contained all our signatures; we were desperate to speak to him in order to sort out the problems that obviously existed.

I expected to be questioned on this but it didn't happen.

In my view, the events leading up to March 19th should have been examined more closely during my cross-examination. It would have given me the opportunity to explain in detail the events leading up to the 19th March 2003 meeting, and of course, the meeting itself.

It was a crucial moment in the dispute, because the meeting had been deliberately thwarted by Cllr McKinlay; honest observers would have concluded that nothing would have been lost if he had attended the meeting.

The failure of Cllr McKinlay to attend the meeting in March 2003 had brought both sides to the London High Court, and a thirty day trial. Unforgiveable!

As the cross-examination went on, it appeared that Mrs Laird was becoming more stressful; she looked unwell and I worried for her. I hoped that any inadequacy in my answers to the questions was not the reason for Christine Laird looking so ill; the sheer strain of another day of listening to matters that evoked such awful memories for her, was more likely to be the answer.

It was the time when John Dagnall asked me my final question about the JNC process, about which incidentally, I had nothing to add, that Mrs Laird collapsed and was sprawled across the gangway. Although her husband was close by, he couldn't prevent his wife from falling. It was sudden and it was frightening, and other people soon came to assist her.

The judge asked me to leave the witness box and I had to step over Mrs Laird to return to my seat. Medical help had been called and she was helped outside, and in a matter-of-fact way the judge called the next witness.

Day 24

Christine Laird took the witness stand on 26th March 2009. She was supported by a NHS psychiatric aide because of her fragile mental condition as she gave her evidence in support of her long and detailed witness statement.

The *Gloucestershire Echo* reported that Mrs Laird told the judge "Cheltenham Borough Council's boast to job candidates that it was an open, forward thinking local authority was misleading; the entire appointment process was shambolic."

Mr Kerr suggested that "Mrs Laird's criticism of the recruitment package was an elaborate edifice".

In a defiant response, according to the *Echo*, Mrs Laird said "That's fine. It is my contention that this entire case is an edifice of deceit."

She continued, "The 'Introduction to Cheltenham' brochure, enclosed with the recruitment literature, referred to the town's Regency architecture, but failed to mention that outside the town centre, there was some dreadful public sector housing, and pockets of deprivation, about which the council had done nothing for years."

In answer to cross-examination by Mr Kerr, she said "The statement to applicants that the council embraced the values of being honest, truthful, of wanting to work together in partnership with other organisations, and provide quality service at the right price, was absolute bunkum."

She told the court "I was unlawfully removed from my post after a politically orchestrated hate campaign of bullying and harassment by council members in order to secure my removal from my statutory appointment.

I was subjected to anonymous letters and malicious press briefings, because they objected to me implementing the restructuring programme, which they had placed in my hands when I took the job."

According to the *Echo* report, Mrs Laird also said "She believed it entirely possible the current legal action is simply a continuation of that hate campaign."

She then turned her attention to those who had given evidence to the court on behalf of the council. The *Echo* further reported that "... she claimed that not only had they misled the court, they were, to be frank, incompetent."

This prompted Mr Kerr to ask whether Mrs Laird thought she had done enough to promote harmonious relationships between council members and council officers. In reply, Mrs Laird said that considering the extremely difficult working conditions she was under, she did her best to promote harmonious relationships within the council.

In a final comment before the end of the day's proceedings, Mrs Laird referred to the evening of 11th June 2004, when she suffered a seizure after being told by telephone she had been suspended from work with immediate effect.

Mrs Laird described in detail what the seizure feeling was like – 'it felt as though a bomb had gone off inside my head. There was a screaming noise in my head and I was unable to breathe. Yet when I was assessed as a suicide risk by a NHS consultant following my suspension, the council claimed I was not ill but a very good actress'.

Day 26

Dr Aylard, an independent psychiatrist, gave evidence to the court that he had interviewed Mrs Laird on 13th April 2005. His job was to assess whether Mrs Laird was fit to go through the DIP process.

In answer to a question, Dr Aylard agreed that 'anyone going through what Mrs Laird had gone through (if the claims were true) would have become very ill'. He also agreed, according to a summary provided to me by Mr Laird, that 'Christine Laird would not have realised she had a bad problem, especially as her GP was consistently telling her that she had a reactive problem and not a permanent one'.

Dr Aylard was then taken through the questions on the medical questionnaire form, and agreed that most of them had been answered properly.

Mr Dagnall referred Dr Aylard to the question "what was your last medical treatment" on the questionnaire; Mrs Laird had listed a back injury sustained on an outward bound course. This had resulted in her GP prescribing a course of anti-anxiety pills, which Mrs Laird took until the course was completed.

The court heard that she didn't regard this as a treatment for the purposes of the questionnaire, and more like finishing a normal course of antibiotics.

Dr Aylard, however, would not accept this.

The court heard that the independent psychiatric report was accepted by the council, and none of the points had been challenged by them. In the judgment at paragraph 446 (5) it records that 'once the report had been received there was no further suggestion by the council that Mrs Laird was feigning or exaggerating her symptoms'.

Day 27

Continuing her evidence to the High Court, Mrs Laird told the judge "I was so frightened by the presence of Cllr McKinlay that I had asked Cheltenham Borough Council in 2004, not to allow him near my office. He was the principle cause of my stress-induced illness, which had kept me away from my place of work."

"In spite of this," she told the court, "Cllr McKinlay visited my P.A's outer office in what I contended was an act of harassment."

"That man frightens me, he frightened me then and he frightens me now."

Day 28

This was the day when John Dagnall made his final submission to the court on behalf of Mrs Laird. This is what he said.

> "Cheltenham Borough Council agreed to employ Christine Laird as its managing director, which was binding and unconditional from the word go. She was asked to start getting prepared for the job straight away; there was no question of medical reports being required.
>
> The shaking of hands, an agreement on salary, a decision without opposition, to publicise the matter, to start immediately in getting Mrs Laird up-to-speed in the job, all pointed to an intention to create legal relations there and then.
>
> This was wholly inconsistent with the idea that the whole matter was conditional."

In response to the council's claim that Mrs Laird was guilty of deceit in fraudulently or negligently withholding details of her history of depressive illness when she applied for the job, he said she had answered the medical questionnaire correctly.

The Barrister said the council had accused Mrs Laird of lying, but the fact was that the questions on the questionnaire were so imprecise as to be capable of various interpretations. His client had answered 'no' to the question: 'Do you have a physical or mental impairment', because she thought it referred to learning difficulties, which had been confirmed by an expert psychiatric witness.

"It all comes down to the problems with this particular medical questionnaire form. It has so many possible answers, and I say she gave the right answers" said Mr Dagnall.

Day 29

The final day of the trial: the *Gloucestershire Echo* reported Mr Timothy Kerr QC saying in his parting shot on behalf of the council, that "money expended on Christine Laird because of her dishonesty could have been used for the people of Cheltenham."

An odd comment, in a way, because those opposed to the dispute and all its ramifications, were pleading the same cause throughout 2003 to 2005, but their pleas had fallen on deaf ears.

The High Court reserved its judgment on the £1million plus lawsuit brought by Cheltenham Borough Council against its former managing director.

Mr Justice Hamblen informed the court that he hoped to hand down his judgment by the middle of June 2009.

Following the High Court case, *Gloucestershire Echo* reporter Robin Jenkins interviewed Andrew North, the new chief executive, after the end of the trial.

In answer to a question by the reporter he said "Christine Laird's dispute with the council echoes the highly-publicised case of Sir Fred Goodwin. There are similarities between the case of the authority's former managing director and that of the disgraced ex-boss of the Royal Bank of Scotland".

Like many local people I was astounded by the comments of Andrew North.

He was equally ungracious about Mrs Laird's financial circumstances, complaining strongly that her pension 'was more than most people's average earnings'. Will he not be in the same wealthy position himself when he seeks retirement?

In answer to further questions by the reporter, he claimed that "Mrs Laird had, quite frankly, failed in her job. The period she was here was a disaster."

He then told the *Echo* "Both Mrs Laird and Sir Fred Goodwin took early retirement after presiding over a period of failure at their institutions."

[Mrs Laird was first suspended and then dismissed on inaccurate information]

As an afterthought, Mr North added "There is no doubt that the period when Mrs Laird was the managing director of Cheltenham Borough Council, was a hugely difficult one. Sir Fred presided over a period that got the bank into huge difficulty."

Most people who contacted me following the *Echo* publication were of the view that Mr North had made a terrible mistake by making the comparison between Mrs Laird and Sir Fred Goodwin. They thought it was a hasty comment from someone who had come from outside the county, long after the dispute had ended. And was the information given to him of the detail of the dispute supplied by someone who had a grievance, or a person who was totally neutral? An interesting point.

I received comments from my constituents along similar lines. I asked Mr North why he thought his predecessor had 'failed in her job when her first appraisal had been a success, with all targets achieved and a bonus payment had been awarded to her'.

I also asked him 'why he was of the opinion that Mrs Laird's period as the CBC managing director was a disaster' bearing in mind he didn't join Cheltenham Borough until 2006, and as far as I knew, he had not met her?

His reply to both questions was that he had had conversations with members of his staff and this is what they had told him.

The staff he referred to consisted of those who gave evidence in the High Court on behalf of the council; several had retired between 2005 and the start of the trial in January 2009. Hardly people who could be relied upon to be neutral.

It is not unusual for anyone to jump to wrong conclusions based on one-sided facts. If he had spoken to me and some of the other people I have mentioned in previous chapters, including former officers and councillors, he may have been a little less eager to condemn his predecessor so hastily.

Hugh Laird, when he read the *Echo* article said: "This has been a horrible time for Christine and I am disappointed the council is continuing its media campaign to insult and defame her, even before Mr Justice Hamblen has given his judgment."

The judgment was published on 15th June 2009.

CHAPTER 24

The High Court Judgment And Conclusions

It is a capital mistake to theorize before you have all the evidence.
It biases the judgement.

A Study in Scarlet (1888) Ch 3
Arthur Conan Doyle

To his credit, Mr Justice Hamblen wasted no time in delivering his judgment on 15th June 2009, just over two months following the end of the hearing on 8th April 2009.

The judgment consisted of more than sixty double-sided pages and included 628 separate paragraphs.

The point to remember when reading this chapter is that it was Cheltenham Borough Council who were suing Christine Laird and not the other way round: in simple terms she was 'defending, not claiming'.

The arguments and counter-arguments about the behaviour of the two main protagonists were put by both sides over the thirty eight day period; many were complex and to the ordinary citizen probably appeared to be irrelevant. However, the council had sued Mrs Laird for damages amounting to more than £1million and their claim was to show that it was mainly due to her behaviour during the period of the dispute.

In the words of Timothy Kerr Q.C. in his summing up, 'the money spent on dealing with the causes of the dispute, could have been spent on the town'. But in the judgment, some of the claims by the council were dismissed.

It would be impossible to make a valuable comment on the majority of issues that the judge had to consider, because only the lawyers have the detail of each matter that was considered during the hearing.

But, as I have tried to explain in the previous chapters, there were matters that the council portrayed during the trial that were a long way short of what actually occurred between 2002 and 2004.

In the previous chapters I have written about the conversations I had with numerous people, the receipt of unexpected emails that were useful and revealing, minutes of meetings often supported by officers' reports, and the helpful reports and articles about the dispute that appeared regularly in the *Gloucestershire Echo*.

Separately and sometimes together, they presented a different picture to the one portrayed to the judge in the High Court. I can refer to emails and documents, which have been approved for publication by the contributors; contrast this against the hearsay evidence provided to the court.

Of course, it is up to the reader to decide which version of events to believe. But the reader, like me, will wonder why the trouble taken by the opposition group leaders, particularly the efforts of Cllr Duncan Smith to make contact with Cllr McKinlay late in the night following the now 'legendary' meeting with Christine Laird on 19th March 2003, was not believed by the judge.

Cllr McKinlay told the court 'he hadn't been invited' and that was that.

But, was the judge aware of the exchange of emails following the meeting?

Did the judge know about the email from Becky Robinson stating that the Leader had been advised not to attend any meeting with the opposition group leaders?

Was it all a dream, or a figment of my imagination?

There is no reference in the judgment about the emails from Sally Stringer, a former colleague of Cllr McKinlay, which revealed much about the rude behaviour of the Leader of the Council towards members of his own political party; yet according to some parts of the judgment he had not been rude, or abusive towards Christine Laird. At best, it had been misinterpreted.

Was it really permissible for the council's most senior politician to utter snide comments in a meeting about the most senior officer in the council? And where was the contrary evidence that Mrs Laird had, at any time, resorted to such unacceptable behaviour?

How reasonable is it for the most senior legal officer to be advising both the Leader of the Council and the managing director (MD) at the same time when both are in dispute about the running of the council?

Is it right for the chief legal officer to advise councillors that 'they don't have to declare an interest' when an item on the agenda is about the future employment position of the council's MD?

What weight should be put on any advice by the chief legal officer allegedly given to elected members when he too had registered a grievance about the MD?

The evidence given by Melissa Neil, the former public relations officer, was given little weight by the judge, but if the content of the email from Sally Stringer, plus the treatment of Debbie Hall, another political colleague of Cllr McKinlay, meant anything at all, then it takes little or no thinking as to who was more likely to be rude, abusive and aggressive towards other people.

Certainly First Tier Tribunal Judge Martha Street had no doubts about where the responsibility lay once she heard about the abusive and malicious behaviour that had been meted out to the appellant Christine Laird.

(More about this in a later chapter)

Of course, the words from Judge Martha Street, like the emails from Sally Stringer and others, came after the trial had ended. The Tribunal judge was dealing with an 'industrial injury claim' by Christine Laird, and Sally Stringer had moved away from the area. But, powerful stuff, nonetheless.

Some of the issues contained in the judgment are complex, so I will deal with those that I have managed to understand and make the following comments.

The matter of the contract of employment and whether or not it included the completion of a 'medical questionnaire' was never going to be agreed, and at the end of the day it was the 'quality' of the questions that were contained in the questionnaire that became the determining factor.

The council claimed that Mrs Laird had 'fraudulently completed the questionnaire'. The court had to decide whether the 'construction of the wording' of the medical questionnaire was acceptable, and whether it was 'seeking only statements of subjective and honestly held beliefs'.

As we know from an earlier chapter, Hugh Laird claimed that his wife answered the questions honestly and truthfully. The declaration on the form includes a statement warning the applicant that 'the answers must be true'. if they are not, then the contract of service would be terminated. It also asks the applicant to agree to the council's medical advisor seeking information from the applicant's own doctor.

At paragraph 305 the judge commented, "In such circumstances there would have been no point in lying in the questionnaire, even if she had been inclined so to do, which I find she was not."

After all the arguments, the court decided that 'it was common ground that this was a poorly drafted questionnaire'. Dr McNamara, the council's occupational health expert claimed the form was 'very poorly drafted' and 'quite inadequate'.

Dr McNamara also acknowledged that 'a lay person would be likely to interpret the questions differently to a doctor and people might interpret the not particularly well-phrased questions in different ways'.

The judge stated at paragraph 317 "Given the ambiguity of the questions asked and Mrs Laird's reasonable understanding of her medical history, as I have found it to be, it was not negligent of her to answer the questions as she did."

There is ample case law concerning the wording of questionnaires and there is nothing I can see that allows for additional questions to be posed which are outside the questions asked on the form.

The judge found at paragraph 298 "... that the representations made by Mrs Laird in answer to the medical questionnaire were not false, nor, given the terms of the questions asked, were they misleading."

The important issue at paragraph 335 (h) "If no representation had been made and Mrs Laird had disclosed her full medical history, whether Cheltenham Borough Council would have been in breach of duty under the Disability Discrimination Act 1995 (DDA) had it refused to employ her" was also considered by the judge.

The person would have to be disabled within the meaning of the DDA and the judge referred to Mrs Laird's witness statement in which she said "I first became disabled and therefore entitled to the protection of the DDA [sic] in March 2004 during my employment with the claimant."

This, the judge concluded, confirmed in her own evidence that she was not disabled within the meaning of the DDA in early 2002, which accords with the views of the experts on both sides.

This was an important point especially in the light of the comments made by Mr

Selwyn Blyth, an employment law expert, which are quoted on page 434 (Chapter 23).

It is clear that Mrs Laird was not disabled within the meaning of the DDA in the early part of her employment and both sides accepted the fact; subsequent industrial injury claims were made by Mrs Laird in 2010 and dealt with by the Bristol Tribunal. These related to her state of health in March 2004.

On the issue of whether Mrs Laird "fraudulently misrepresented her medical history in her answers to the medical questionnaire" paragraph 341 of the judgment says "the council could with reasonable diligence have discovered the fraud by 16th December 2002, six years before the fraud claim was issued on 15th December 2008."

The court spent a lot of time listening to the claims and counterclaims about the behaviour of the two main participants – Mrs Laird and the Leader of the Council.

In spite of what has been written in the previous chapters of this book, it was disappointing to read that the harassment and the inappropriate behaviour by the Leader and members of his Cabinet did not constitute an alleged breach of duty by the council. The judge came to the conclusion that the numerous events and unpleasantness were not as bad as Mrs Laird and her supporters had described. The snide comments, it seems, were quite acceptable, and the efforts to bring about a reconciliation either did not happen, or at best would not have served a useful purpose.

I often wonder what the judge would have made of the attempt to end the dispute in the vestry of a church, if he had been made aware of the detail.

It would seem that all the references to the bad behaviour in the previous chapters, including the numerous attempts to end the dispute, are only believable providing each and every incident is backed up with expert evidence.

Whilst the judge accepted that the Leader spoke to Mrs Laird forcefully from time to time, and that on occasion he overstepped the mark, he did not find there was any campaign of bullying or harassment, or a sufficient course of conduct to constitute a breach of the trust and confidence. See paragraph 398 of the judgment.

The conclusion on the breach of duty can be found at paragraph 457 which states: "The only breach of duty by the council found to be established concerns the meeting at which Cllr Stuart-Smith asked 'What will it take for you to go.'" However, the judge further ruled that 'no loss has been proven as a consequence of this breach and accordingly the claim for damages by Mrs Laird fails'.

There is no doubt that the council put up a strong case against Mrs Laird in order to claim back some of the enormous cost that had been spiralling upwards from 2002 until the trial in January 2009.

Having experienced the dispute period and seen at first hand some of the irresponsible behaviour of grown-up people I found it difficult to accept some of the findings in the judgment.

Only by searching through a countless number of documents and emails could I come to any sort of conclusions. The numerous conversations I had with those who had more first-hand experience of the abuse than me, led me to the conclusion that there must have been a strange working environment in the council offices throughout the dispute period.

I had only experienced the occasional bad behaviour, but if I had not regularly registered my 'declarations of interest' perhaps I would have witnessed, as David Hall did, a great deal more.

However, the opinions of those who were more close to the events were invaluable. They helped me by writing down their views and opinions which in turn gave me the confidence to write the book.

Is this the total picture, not by any means; I have set the events down as near as I can in the same chronological order as they happened.

Having read the script several times I still ask myself the same questions. Who were these people and why did they persist in behaving in such a strange manner? I wondered too what the judge had in mind when he claimed that 'it was a novel case' did he mean 'new' or 'fanciful' or simply a 'vagary' of local government?

As it turned out, the judge dismissed the claim of Cheltenham Borough Council for the reasons outlined above. He concluded by hoping that after a long period of time and at personal and financial cost "...a line can now finally be drawn allowing Mrs Laird to get on with her life and CBC to get on with the business of governing Cheltenham."

We'll say sorry over Laird case 'errors', vows council

Fine and heartfelt words, but the financial costs to which the judge referred still had to be met by Mrs Laird. She subsequently made claims to the Bristol Tribunal and the Secretary of State and these will be discussed in a later chapter.

There were the feelings of the general public to be taken into account resulting from the tardy disclosures of the court case, together with the revelations that the council taxpayers would have to foot the enormous bill.

They wanted answers to questions from the council and they wanted the debate to be held in a public forum. It was public pressure that brought about the investigation by the auditors KPMG, and their subsequent conclusions, which were published in a Public Interest Report and will be explained in the next chapter.

CHAPTER 25

KPMG – The Public Interest Report (PIR)

The power to act according to discretion for the public good, without the prescription of the law, and sometimes even against it, is that which is called prerogative.

Second Treatise of Civil Government
(1690) ch. 14 sect. 160

KPMG was formed in 1987 with the merger of Peat Marwick International (PMI) and Klynveld Main Goerdeler (KMG) and their individual firms. Spanning three centuries, the organisation's history can be traced through the names of its principal founding members – whose initials form the name "KPMG".

KPMG is an international company providing, Audit, Tax and Advisory services in 153 countries worldwide. They were appointed by the Audit Commission to audit the accounts of Cheltenham Borough Council and to issue a report under the Audit Commission Act 1998.

Before moving on to their report, which took a number of months to produce, we can delve into the mounting interest and agitation in the intervening period.

Following the end of the High Court trial and the judgment of Mr Justice Hamblen on 15th June 2009, there was speculation by the public about what was likely to happen following the High Court decision. Not surprisingly, there were corridor chats by members of the staff in the council offices, seemingly because there had been great expectations that the council would win its case against its former managing director.

The mayor, Cllr Lloyd Surgenor, sent an email to all councillors the following day, urging them to take note of the words of the judge, and asking for "cross-party unity in order to do our best for the Cheltenham ratepayers."

I responded immediately and this was my reply:

"Dear Mr Mayor,

In response to your email dated 16th June 2009. The words of the judge in paragraph 628 of his judgment are identical to the words I used at the Staff & Support Services Committee several years back, when I proposed that 'a line should be drawn under the whole sorry affair'. Unfortunately, your colleagues did not back my suggestion and the process of litigation continued.

It seems odd to me to ask members of my group to support 'cross-party unity' in order to do our best for the Cheltenham ratepayers, when that was exactly what I was asking the political parties to do all those years ago, and it was rejected.

It will take some time to heal the wounds that have been caused by the dispute and not least the health of one of our former employees.

Additionally, there is no way we can compensate the council taxpayer of Cheltenham for the large payment they will have to make for a high profile case that few of them supported.

As for the future, yes, we will continue to do our best for the people of Cheltenham, which will not include the pursuit of lost causes that unfortunately have been the hallmark of the council in past years.

Councillor Les Godwin."

I did not receive a response from the mayor – the silence probably spoke for itself.

Nonetheless, there was an enormous amount of speculation in the air following the high court decision, and in order to end the speculation, a group of concerned councillors sent a petition to the mayor, which followed the rules of the council's Constitution, requesting an Extraordinary Council Meeting (ECM) to be held on Monday 3rd August 2009.

[*The Constitution rules for calling an Extraordinary Meeting of the Council can only be made by a minimum of six councillors signing a petition requesting the meeting, which must be presented to the mayor. The petition will explain the reasons for the meeting, and also set down the items to be discussed in the agenda. No other items can be added to the agenda by a councillor or an officer*]

The meeting would enable a discussion to take place on the outcome of the CBC v Laird case, and to receive a report from the council's Chief Executive (CE) Andrew North.

The petition was signed by Cllrs Malcolm Stennett, Diane Hibbert, Les Godwin (PAB Group) and Cllrs Stuart Hutton, Duncan Smith and David Hall (Conservative Group).

Following consultation with the CE, the mayor agreed to the ECM.

The following items were included on the agenda:

1. A motion proposed by the Conservative Group Leader, Cllr Stuart Hutton and seconded by Cllr Diane Hibbert, a member of the PAB Group.
2. A report from the chief executive on the financial implications of the High Court proceedings in the CBC v Laird case.
3. A letter from Mr Laurence Robertson MP. (Mrs Laird was one of his constituents)

The motion to council (item 1) read as follows:

"Following the failure of the council to win the recent legal action against Mrs Christine Laird, and the loss to the ratepayers of at least £750,000 in legal fees, the council

a) Acknowledges the anger and disappointment of many of the residents of Cheltenham at the financial cost and the damage to the reputation of the town.
b) Endorses the decision of the chief executive not to appeal the decision.

Whilst members and officers may wish to draw a line under this matter, council recognises that a situation like this should not be allowed to arise again. Therefore council resolves to appoint a working group of three members to review the lessons that must be learned from this long running litigation. The group will have the power to co-opt up to two independent members who are not councillors or officers of the council.

The working group should

1. Review the decision making processes in relation to the litigation against Mrs Laird, the legal and officer advice provided to members, and review members' own actions in the light of the Members' Code of Conduct.
2. Review current recruitment and appointment processes to ensure that best practice is now followed, and that the risk to the council in future appointments is minimised.
3. Review internal processes for handling dispute procedures with particular focus on the roles of officers and members in those processes.
4. Recommend changes to the Constitution, working practices and the code of conduct that arise out of their review.
5. That members of the working group should consist of one member from each of the political groups.
6. That the working group aims to report back to full council by December 2009.
7. Instructs all officers of the council to co-operate fully with the investigation and to make available to the group all and any information it requires.

Council agreed that Cllrs Cooper, Hibbert and Massey be appointed members of the Review Working Group (RWG).

The report by the CE (agenda item 2) was in response to an earlier request by Cllr Smith for details of the costs incurred by council during the period of the dispute. The petitioners agreed that the item should be included in the ECM agenda and to read as follows:

> "To receive a report from the chief executive, identifying the costs incurred by the council in relation to the disputes with Mrs Christine Laird. This should cover the period from April 23rd 2003 to July 1st 2009 and should include amongst other costs, all staff time, legal/professional fees, consultant time/fees, IT costs and the cost of temporary staff."

In his report, the CE referred to a 'thorough review' by the council's auditors, KPMG, which would be undertaken following the request for an investigation by Mr Laurence Robertson MP.

Regarding the matter of costs, the CE reported: "The net costs incurred during the 2003 to 2009 period were £1.639 million." He added that the cost of the review by KPMG plus any additional costs would be met from the General Reserve Fund. Needless to say, whether it comes out of any reserve fund, or some other council account, it is still part of the total money that will be paid by the local council taxpayers. The estimated costs of the review by the auditors were put at between £30,000 and £50,000.

The CE expressed his concerns about the proposal to establish a working group, contained in the motion to council. He thought it may divert officers from doing other important work; the council might suffer as a result of 'a blame culture' developing; the disclosure of information that might be covered by 'legal professional privilege'; and he was concerned that the council's Standards Committee (SC) might be undermined.

This last point was laughable considering how much effort had been made by opposition councillors to use the SC to resolve the dispute.

Regarding the letter from the Member of Parliament, The CE told councillors that (item 3) concerned the letter from Mr Robertson to KPMG on 6th July 2009 asking questions about the role of the auditors during the dispute. This included a question about their advice to the council at the crucial point when the council made the decision to proceed with the court action. He also requested that a review of the council's decision-making process should be undertaken.

KPMG, in their reply to Mr Robertson on 17th July 2009 reminded him that "Auditors can only intervene where it believes the council has acted unlawfully."

The letter confirmed that KPMG had been aware of the Laird case since 2007 and although they had not carried out any detailed work leading to a report, they had been having regular discussions with senior officers of the council.

The letter also assured Mr Robertson that KPMG had commenced a thorough review of the decision making process carried out by officers and members of the council.

The review had included an investigation about 'who made the decision to proceed with the legal action, their authority to do so, and the reasonableness of the processes'.

KPMG would also look at the 'completeness of the information presented to the decision makers regarding the potential financial implications'.

The review would also include an investigation about the risk assessment, including an assessment of Mrs Laird's ability to pay any award against her, had the council been successful in the legal action.

Two other important points that would be included in the KPMG investigation, according to their reply to Mr Robertson, would be to look at 'the legal advice obtained by the council on the merits of the case, and the likelihood of the council being successful'. They would also be interested in 'how this advice was used in order to inform the decision makers and to hear how the council responded to the advice and suggestions that were given by advisers and others, including the auditors'.

The letter concluded that it was KPMG's intention to report the outcome of its review to the council's audit committee in September 2009.

Although the letter stated that the audit report would be made public, it did not mention that it would be a Public Interest Report (PIR), which was going to be crucial once the general public learned that a PIR had not been mentioned.

Even before the content of the KPMG letter was known, there had been a call for a PIR by several members of the public, and as the time went by, the clamour for this type of report grew louder and louder.

It is common practice for local councils to allow members of the public to ask questions on any matter that is of concern to them. Cheltenham Borough Council is a council that allows public questions, and as with other councils there is a protocol to be followed, which if correctly adhered to, will result in the questions being answered by a leading member of the council.

At the 3rd August 2009 council meeting, four important questions were put by two members of the public concerning KPMG and the Christine Laird case.

Ken Pollock is a local man with a wealth of knowledge about the history of Gloucestershire, and he is particularly knowledgeable about the history of Cheltenham. He is a member of the Cheltenham Local History Society, and contributes to various publications such as the Bristol and Gloucestershire Archaeological Society. He was a founder member of the Leckhampton pressure group, known locally as LEGLAG.

There were several parts to Ken Pollock's first question, but his main concern was the appointment of KPMG to investigate the Laird dispute, when it was generally known that KPMG were the council's own external auditors. He quoted the admission by KPMG that they had been aware of the case since 2007 and had regular discussions with council officers.

In his view, he doubted whether KPMG could be regarded as 'independent' investigators, and asked why they did not act at the time to prevent the serious potential financial losses.

In reply to the question, the Leader of the Council, Cllr Steve Jordan, said that the appointment of the auditors KPMG was the duty of the Audit Commission and not the council. In any event, KPMG had decided to carry out a review of the processes following the receipt of the letter from Laurence Robertson MP.

Mr Pollock's second question took a different line and referred to the minutes of March 2006 S&SSC meeting where it was reported that Cllrs McKinlay, Hay and Jordan had left the meeting, which had made the decision to proceed to the High Court, yet minutes of subsequent meetings do not show that there were further 'declarations of interests' when the same subject was on the agenda.

He asked whether there had been a breach of the members' code of conduct.

The Leader responded by saying that it was the individual responsibility of members to consider whether they should 'declare an interest' on a particular agenda item. He added that the three councillors were members of the Cabinet and they followed the legal advice that was given by Mr Ford the Monitoring Officer.

(Readers will remember that this has been a constant theme throughout the pages of the book dealing with the CBC v Laird dispute).

Mary Nelson, like her partner Ken Pollock, is a member of the Cheltenham Local History Society. She was also a keen photographer and a campaigner for the preservation of historic buildings and public gardens.

She asked the Leader of the Council whether the council had a written record of details of the risks raised by KPMG, and whether officers had communicated the risks to the Staff & Support Services Committee (S&SSC).

In reply, Cllr Jordan said 'The quarterly meetings with KPMG were not recorded, but KPMG had indicated that they would expect the report to the S&SSC in January 2009 to clearly articulate the risks associated in continuing or ceasing the court action'. He said the report was considered by the committee at the January 2009 meeting.

Following the public questions, councillors debated the chief executive's report.

Cllr Rob Garnham referred to the KPMG letter and contradicted the passage where they claimed that the review had been agreed with the council. He disagreed by claiming that the council had not agreed to the review and that it was done entirely by the officers. He pleaded for the working group to be set up as soon as possible and suggested that a meeting should be arranged with the auditors in order to agree the scope of the work to be carried out.

Cllr Duncan Smith welcomed the new Monitoring Officer, Sara Freckleton, to her first council meeting. He referred to the letter from Laurence Robertson MP and explained that Mrs Laird was one of his constituents. He added that members should also be aware that Mr Robertson also represented a large number of Cheltenham residents, who were equally concerned that their council tax was being used to pay for the costs of the court action.

Cllr Smith was disappointed that the full costs requested in the requisition for the meeting "were not discernible in the table provided and asked when the detailed costs would be available for scrutiny by councillors and the public."

He added that the public must have confidence that the review was not a whitewash and that any evidence or conclusions, however critical of members or officers, should be made public.

The chief executive replied as follows:

"A wealth of detail was now in the public domain including the costs for the period 2003 to 2005 which had been included in the court claim. The detailed information regarding lawyers costs, expenses for hotel bills, meals etc., had been the subject of a Freedom of Information (FOI) request. All this information had been published on the council's website."

Cllr Malcolm Stennett (PAB) took issue with some of the wording in the chief executive's report; reference to internal officer costs as 'notional only' was negative and saying 'the costs would come from general reserves was misleading'. The money could have been used for the benefit of the town.

The *Gloucestershire Echo*, as expected on 4th August 2009, made the events of the Extraordinary Council Meeting its lead article. It reported on the general thrust of the meeting and particularly the report of the chief executive.

It reported that Mr North agreed the council would co-operate fully with KPMG, and that he was concerned about the amount of officer time that might be taken up, costing the authority more cash. He said he wanted to avoid any 'blame culture' developing within the authority while the review was carried out, and he added that once KPMG had requested a review there was no other choice but to agree.

Cllr Barbara Driver was reported as saying the whole Laird dispute had been nothing more than a "fiasco" for the council.

Most people within and outside the council probably agreed with those sentiments.

Cllr Rob Garnham, who readers will recall in the previous chapters, played no small part in the continuing progress of the dispute, was reported as saying "We have got to find out where we went wrong, what happened and how we can avoid it in the future." The answer was always there, but no-one, not even Cllr Garnham, was prepared to listen to the voices of those who had tried to end the dispute.

The *Echo* reported that Cllr Smith insisted the review must involve councillors as well as officers so the public would not think it was a "whitewash".

As for my contribution, the *Echo* reported me as saying: "Cllr Godwin said that it is the people of this town who will have to foot the bill, and they deserve to know what went on."

For the record, more than thirty people attended the Extraordinary Council Meeting.

The council issued a media statement on the 4th August 2009, claiming that councillors had agreed to a review of the Laird case. It stated that the council had addressed the costs incurred, and acknowledged the anger and disappointment of many Cheltenham residents at the huge financial cost and the damage to the reputation of the town. As a result, a working group would be established to 'review any lessons learned'. They would also commence their work immediately.

I have no doubt in my mind that KPMG waited to see what would come out of the Extraordinary Council Meeting before sending out letters to the principal players in the CBC v Laird dispute. I received my letter from Ian Pennington of KPMG on 7th August 2009 asking me to contribute to the review that KPMG would be undertaking of the council's financial situation, related, of course, to the dispute.

I replied on 19th August, setting out a 'potted history' of my time as a councillor on both Tewkesbury Borough and Cheltenham Borough Councils which covered a span of thirty years.

If I was to make a useful contribution to the review I believed my efforts would be best served by asking KPMG a number of questions seeking to find out whether they had been made aware of what had been going on during the dispute period.

My first question to Ian Pennington was as follows:

"In a number of minutes of the Staff & Support Services Committee, the record shows the spiralling costs of the council's two disputes with RCT and Mrs Laird, including external legal costs, staff costs and other external costs.

The records also show that 'the District Auditor has been kept informed of the financial situation."

I asked if this was correct.

My letter to KPMG contained nine questions, mostly about financial matters including whether the auditor was aware that Mrs Laird did not have the resources to pay damages or costs if she had lost the High Court case.

I asked whether the auditor was aware I had proposed at an S&SSC meeting that all options should be considered to end the dispute including retirement on the grounds of ill-health.

Another question along similar lines, concerned an S&SSC meeting on 13th May 2004, when I proposed that a ceiling should be set on the amount of money to be spent on the dispute. I had suggested a ceiling of £250,000.

Copy of my letter and the questions can be seen at Appendix 2.

Other councillors, as well as members of the public, were invited by KPMG to submit questions to them, and I became aware that there were other members of the public who thought they might not be invited to ask questions, took the initiative and sent off letters to KPMG.

I received a reply from Ian Pennington on 25th August 2009 acknowledging the receipt of my questions. He told me that he had received many comments and questions from councillors and council officers, and in response to my questions to him he wrote that he was already reviewing copies of S&SSC minutes and reports presumably to get a full picture of the problem areas.

In my reply on 27th August I suggested that if he was widening his scope of investigation, it should include interviewing Mrs Laird, her solicitor, or her barrister, so that he had a full picture regarding the discussions that went on in the run-up to the High Court case. I suggested that this should include the poor external legal advice the council received prior to the court case. I reminded him that I would be asking further questions about this and other matters in a few days time.

I believed there was a strong case for all important matters to be put on the table, and with this in mind I quoted the extract of a report from the Chartered Institute of Housing regarding their achievements under the leadership of Mrs Laird. [Reference – Chapter 23 page 451]

I sent another letter to Ian Pennington on 31st August 2009 with three more questions that I required him to consider.

I asked him to note that Mr Ford the Monitoring Officer was the legal adviser to the S&SSC and the Standards Committee, while at the same time he had registered a grievance against the managing director. I also asked him to consider the role of Cabinet members in the dispute, and in particular those who were also members of the S&SSC dealing with the dispute, which in my opinion was unfair.

I also asked him to consider whether it was right for the S&SSC to make the decision to sue Mrs Laird in the High Court, or whether KPMG thought the matter should have been decided by full council.

Again, I asked whether the names of those who had played the most decisive part in the waste of council taxpayers' money would be published.

One other question that I put to Ian Pennington was whether he would question why the officers' hotel costs and expenses were higher than the total cost of the court case.

Of course, I knew that I was not going to get answers to my questions – all I could hope for was that the investigation by KPMG would cover these points along with all the others and would criticise where necessary and recommend improvements.

In an earlier chapter readers will recall that I wrote about the resolution approved by the S&SCC on 15th January 2009, authorising the chief executive to agree a settlement of the dispute with Mrs Laird. I informed KPMG by email on 12th September 2009 that the resolution was unanimously agreed by the committee. I also suggested that as they had the power to find out the answers to any questions posed, *"Would KPMG take the necessary steps to seek out the terms of the alleged settlement so that we can all see whether it was reasonable in all the circumstances?"*

On the 14th September I received a reply from Ian Pennington confirming that they would be looking into the matter as part of the review process.

At least it sounded as though we were going to make progress.

Another important area of concern to residents was the health of Mrs Laird. Everyone knew by the end of the trial that she was in a very poor mental state of health, but what about the period 2002 to 2004 when she was subjected to a disgraceful ordeal, meted out to her by the Leader of the Council and his Cabinet colleagues?

Mary Nelson emailed me on 16th September explaining that the risk to Mrs Laird's health during the dispute was very important. She wrote: "Instead of using her health risk as a significant factor to be taken into account in weighing up the risks involved by continuing with the court case (especially at the S&SSC meeting on 15th January 2009), CBC only appeared to consider her, by then, very poor state of health as a bargaining, or blackmailing tool, in an attempt to try to get Mrs Laird to settle on their terms and at a high cost."

Mary Nelson thought this was a "disgraceful tactic" and she was right.

David Hall, who was a councillor at the time and a member of the S&SSC, confirmed to me that Mrs Laird's health was not considered by the committee.

The only time it was used, he claimed, was "A justification for hounding her through the courts."

In his email to Mary Nelson on 17th September he wrote: "She was subjected to a stream of vicious and derogatory abuse by Cllrs McKinlay and Hay; and to a lesser extent by Cllr Barnes at meetings in November 2008 and January 2009."

He also remembered that "Mrs Laird was called a liar by Cllr McKinlay at the November 2008 meeting, amongst a number of other things. Cllr Hay, on the other hand called Mrs Laird a serial offender and manipulative at the January 2009 meeting." Cllr Hay claimed, "She was also trying to bring down the Liberal Democrat administration."

Cllr Hall concluded his comments by asking "Can anyone imagine committee members talking about the state of health of Mrs Laird in such a climate of hate?"

I am sure Mary Nelson was pleased with the reply she received from Cllr Hall, but the matter of the Management Risk Register and the state of Mrs Laird's health was going to come up again and again in the forthcoming weeks.

There was a period of silence following the media release and the council meeting, but it did not last long. It was the lull before the storm, which gave way to a wave of questions from the public to their ward councillors. One of the most persistent questions from my constituents was to ask me to explain what was going on behind the council doors. They were even more concerned when I told them that I didn't know anything more than they did, which was true. They asked me questions about the involvement of KPMG; they wanted to know whether the working group had started their review, and whether the costs were as bad as the rumours had indicated.

They had high expectations of what should come out of both reviews. I was repeatedly asked if the working group had come out with decisions; whether they had already been published, and were they being kept from public view.

There was one thing that was made clear to me, local residents were concerned about the revelations concerning the dispute, and they were going to ask plenty of questions about the working group and what decisions they were likely to make. But the answers given by me and other councillors in the early stages were often negative, not least because very few councillors knew what was actually going on.

Even though the PAB Group had a representative on the working group, there was a period of silence, which was understandable and accepted at the time.

On 7th September 2009, my colleague Cllr Diane Hibbert sent an email to me and to Cllr Malcolm Stennett informing us that the working group had met with auditors from KPMG that very day, and an outline of their work plan had been agreed.

She thought it was useful to know what the scope of their work would be and suggested that we meet to go through it with her. Other information in the email informed us that the working group would meet again on 16th September.

Now that the review was underway, the borough councillors would soon have information that could be passed on to the public.

Whether this little piece of information was the reason for a 'surge' in the public's reactions I do not know, but a letter written to Mr Ian Pennington from Mary Nelson on 6th September 2009 "Officially recorded a complaint against Cheltenham Borough Council's accounts for the period 2008–2009."

To support her complaint she told the auditor "...the current overall cost is in excess of £1.6 million, and was an unbudgeted and unplanned expense."

She wanted to know why the council had pursued the prosecution to the High Court when the legal advice gave only a 60 per cent chance of success. "As an elector" she said, "she was concerned that the council had not paid sufficient attention to their own Risk Management Policy, and questioned whether it was adequate".

Having attended the Extraordinary Council Meeting and left unconvinced by the answers she had been given to her questions, she requested the auditor to "investigate and produce a full Public Interest Report (PIR) to fully address her concerns."

This letter to Ian Pennington had 'lit the blue touch paper'; it was a formal request that they could not ignore and it was soon followed by other residents writing in to KPMG with similar requests.

Letters started to appear in the local paper with headlines:

'We have a right to know the facts' and 'Are councillors to be trusted?'

One letter to the local newspaper on 5th August 2009 was from Sally Stringer (see previous chapters), which is worth quoting. She wrote:

"As a former borough councillor, I am appalled, but not surprised at the extraordinary waste of taxpayers' money in pursuing former council MD Christine Laird with claims of fraud and negligence.

Having also been on the receiving end of the Liberal group dishing out its venom a few years ago, I sincerely hope that Mrs Laird finds an inner strength to get better.

Cheltenham has seen its fair share of wastefulness by the Liberal administration over the years and this fiasco along with the free piece of land given to the John Lewis/Waitrose development, has cost the tax payers' millions of pounds that should have been invested in the infrastructure to benefit all, not just the egos of a few.

Following the meeting on Monday (August 3rd), when the council began a review into the fiasco, I sincerely hope that those implicated in this vindictive campaign should do the honourable thing and resign."

Unfortunately, in spite of pleas by Sally Stringer and others, no-one from the council or the Liberal Democrat group resigned after the court case, or in fact after the Public Interest Report by the auditors KPMG.

On Friday 7th August 2009, the *Gloucestershire Echo* published a full page article headed: 'How the council spent £500,000 of YOUR money'

The *Echo* reported that Cheltenham Borough Council had released information about the Laird case expenses in the form as hundreds of entries under numerous columns. The breakdown was as follows: accommodation and expenses when staying in London amounted to £15,398.92. According to the article, the hotels used were Swissotel and Strand.

Hotel accommodation for Andrew North amounted to £277.04 for two nights, and Cllr Andrew McKinlay who spent five nights cost the council £856.49.

The council's legal team had to spend 42 nights between them at a cost of £8,134.90.

Miscellaneous costs amounted to a total of £27,195.43 which included payments to a PR agency (Media Friendly) and to couriers who delivered papers to London and to Bristol. Transport costs, getting witnesses and legal staff to London, amounted to £7,052.24. Legal fees and the cost of expert witnesses amounted to £409,109.25.

The figures will be of interest to readers because they are associated with the names of the principal characters in previous chapters.

Timothy Kerr QC, the local authority's leading Counsel, was paid £311,049.69 from 2006/07. His junior barrister, James Cornwell, was paid £83,642.01. Dr Aylard was paid £4,500 and £3,000 was paid to consultant physician Dr McNamara, and £1,190 was paid to Bryony Houlden, who now works for Somerset County Council.

Apart from the external legal fees, the dispute took up sufficient time of the council's own legal officers that it cost £51,000. This is not an additional cost because they are salaried officers of the council; in other words, if they had not been working on the CBC v Laird case, they would have been able to work on other council matters.

In order to bring the case to court, the council had to pay £3,955 in court fees.

The final item was stationery, which the *Echo* reported amounted to £319.41.

Of course, this was only a fraction of the total cost that the council had incurred during the dispute period, so it had come as a shock to the people who telephoned me after the *Echo* publication, to learn that the final cost was going to be in excess of £2 million.

Several people wanted to know who was responsible for bringing the court case – so I told them the truth. Whilst it was little comfort to them to hear from me that it could have all been avoided if certain councillors had not pursued a vicious campaign of hatred against Christine Laird, they were grateful for my explanation.

They also wanted to know if the councillors responsible would be surcharged, and some thought the situation was so bad that they wondered whether they would be entitled to withdraw paying their community charge.

There was no doubt that the publication of the costs had stirred the minds of the population, and even though there had been regular reports in the *Gloucestershire Echo* throughout the dispute period, it was clear they had not given enough thought or attention to what had been happening in the past, and now they regretted it.

Apart from the telephone calls, the publication of the costs also caused people to write letters to the local newspaper. One letter, which is too long to quote, came from John Webster. Readers will remember from an earlier chapter that John Webster was once an officer of the council. His boss was Christine Laird, although his line manager was Christopher Huckle. A disciplinary report about the conduct of Mr Webster had been discussed, which should have been acted upon, but instead he was allowed to take early retirement, leaving the council with a substantial sum of money. Along with one or two others, I opposed the proposal, saying that the disciplinary matter should have been dealt with first and then consideration given to the question of his early retirement. Mrs Laird spoke in favour of Mr Webster being allowed to go, and she persuaded others to support and to vote for her proposal.

He left the council with his 'financial settlement' only to return to the council as a Liberal Democrat councillor, and later became the Cabinet deputy for finance and community development.

But, in spite of Christine Laird's earlier efforts on his behalf, he wrote what I would describe as a vindictive letter to the *Echo* on 29th August 2009, parts of which were incorrect.

His exaggerated claim that his former boss had taken more than eighteen months off sick was not referred to in the judgment. In fact, the first fifteen months of Mrs Laird's employment was without sickness absence.

John Webster's comment in his letter that Mrs Laird had been backed by a small number of councillors, who had supported her through 'thick and thin', was snide.

It was probably aimed at me and my PAB colleagues, but I am pleased to say that throughout the dispute we tried hard to steer the council away from the direction they were going. If they had listened to PAB councillors and other strong characters in the Conservative group, the council would not have landed itself and the local taxpayers in the mess they did.

It was interesting to read in the letter that John Webster believed if the court had concentrated on the medical questionnaire and its wording, rather than the other things, then the trial would have been over in a few days. Correct in one sense, but it was his Liberal Democrat colleagues, supported by officers, who were responsible for prolonging the whole process. They had tried every way they could to do so, both legally and effectively illegally, including making aberrant accusations to another local authority.

John Webster's letter brought responses from other readers. One letter accused him of continuing his assault on Mrs Laird, even though the case had been lost. With reference to his comments about Mrs Laird's financial settlement, the writer suggested that "Cllr Webster would not like details to be made public of the lump sum and pension he received when he was 'retired' (by Mrs Laird) as an officer of the council." The letter writer's final comment read as follows:

"For Cllr Webster to call for a line to be drawn under this affair is rich indeed. Had he and his colleagues drawn a line under this issue before embarking on High Court action, Cheltenham would still be paying Mrs Laird her ill-health pension entitlement and not now be landed with the huge costs of this case, in both money and reputation."

Another letter dated 7th September 2009 in response to Cllr Webster's letter is worth quoting in full. It reads as follows:

> "With reference to the letter by Cllr Webster about the cost of the Christine Laird case and the latest expose saying that the council spent a further £10,000 on public relations. There is much we still have to learn about this affair, but it seems Cheltenham Borough Council would have been much better to have spent money on advice in human, instead of public, relations.
>
> He has had his chance to put history to the courts and the judgment went against the council, therefore why does he expect any praise for failure? He may think Cheltenham to be a high-performing council and I wish I could take comfort in him being in charge of council finances, but I'm not able to.

The council should face up to the fact that it got it wrong and be ready to carry out action against those responsible, instead of asking us to just sweep it under the carpet. Gambling with our money seems to be the norm for this council".
Signed MWD (Cheltenham)

The most unexpected letter in the *Gloucestershire Echo* at the time came from Cllr John Rawson (Liberal Democrat). In his letter dated 9th September 2009, he referred to the council's expenditure of £9,500 for public relations, which had been quoted by a previous letter writer. Cllr Rawson quoted the article that claimed the amount was agreed by the council in January. He wrote "This might be taken to imply that it was part of the budget, which I presented to the council, as finance member of the Cabinet, at around that time. I can assure you it was not."

Cllr Rawson went on to say, "Neither the full council nor the Cabinet had any say in the decision to spend this money. It was taken under delegated powers by officials with the agreement of the cross-party Staff & Support Services Committee, the same body that launched the lawsuit against Mrs Laird."

Whilst it seems that Cllr Rawson was given an assurance that the decision had nothing to do with him, he admitted in his letter that in retrospect, he wished he had resigned over the issue. The reason he gave for not doing so he wrote "... we were halfway through the budget process at the time and it would have been difficult and maybe irresponsible to do so."

He added "I do not know what advice the PR agency Media Friendly gave, and it may well have been good advice. However, the council's public relations during the Laird case were hardly a triumph. The auditor who is investigating the whole saga of the lawsuit will no doubt want to investigate whether the decision to spend the extra money on public relations was properly taken. This is especially important in view of the fact the council had not approved a budget for it, so it had to be taken from the council's general reserves."

The letter was of great importance at the time and it was hardly a ringing endorsement that the council knew what they were doing with the public finances.

When the Review Working Group met on 16th September 2009 it considered the scope and timetable for carrying out the review, in accordance with the council resolution.

It also considered whether to appoint two independent members who were not councillors or officers of Cheltenham Borough Council.

Cllr Diane Hibbert briefed me and Cllr Stennett on 23rd September with the news that KPMG had revealed that they would not have their report ready until December at the earliest. They had produced a chart setting out the programme of work including a list of the relevant issues and points they intended to pursue. Listening to the explanation given by our colleague Cllr Hibbert, it seemed all the issues that had been at the heart of the dispute would be investigated. We were also comforted by the fact that KPMG were open for any additional points to be made, or for additional material to be sent to them.

The item on the working group agenda on whether to appoint two independent members to the group was hotly debated. The PAB Group had put forward the name of Stan Jones as a suitable independent person, not least because of his intimate knowledge of councils within the southwest region of England.

We were aware that he was the managing director of Gloucestershire First, an organisation that promotes the county as a location for business, for visitors and for investors. He previously worked for Gulf Oil as their Director of Human Resources, so we knew his credentials were impeccable.

In spite of this, Cllr Hibbert revealed that the Conservative member on the working group, Cllr Tim Cooper, objected to Stan Jones being appointed to the group because he was known to have supported PAB candidates in previous elections.

How he came to know this is worrying considering the election of any candidate is a secret ballot. Stan Jones is not the sort of person to go around telling everyone who he voted for in a local election, of that I am sure.

The fact he may have agreed with PAB that 'politics should be kept out of local government' should have been seen to be to his credit as a possible independent member of the working group. Because Stan Jones lived in Prestbury and probably voted for Cllr Stennett and me, only showed that like the other thousand plus residents who voted for us, he thought we had done good work for the community.

If the blinkered mind of Cllr Cooper could only come up with a jaundiced view like that, then it didn't augur well for the working group coming up with sensible recommendations. One can only presume from Cllr Cooper's objection, that if he had believed Stan Jones to be a Conservative voter, then presumably he would have been acceptable to him.

Even more disappointing was the news from Cllr Hibbert that Grahame Lewis, the Strategic Director of Operations and a member of the working group, had spoken against the appointment of Stan Jones.

This information was a great disappointment to me. Grahame Lewis had had more contact with Stan Jones than anyone else in the council. By the very nature of their respective jobs they were in close contact with each other. As MD for Gloucestershire First, Stan Jones had given talks to CBC councillors and officers whenever he was asked to do so, probably by Grahame Lewis. He also worked closely with the county council and the Southwest Regional Assembly, not because he was politically driven, but because he had an independent and incisive outlook on the things that needed to be done in Cheltenham and the wider county areas.

Grahame Lewis knew this and had always spoken highly of him, so it would seem that his comments about Stan Jones had been false, or other forces had been at work which had made him change his opinion.

I have to admit that following the briefing from Cllr Hibbert, my opinion of Grahame Lewis changed completely. He simply was not the man I thought he was.

Stan Jones is as honest as the day is long – his task in life has always been to help others whenever he could. A paradigm no less, and he would have been an asset on the Review Working Group.

I learned that the council's audit committee would be meeting on 13th January 2010 and not in December as previously reported, which was disappointing. But it was good news to hear that one of the items to be discussed was a report by the council's chief finance officer and a representative from KPMG.

During the months of October and November 2009 I felt a groundswell of opinion from my constituents and from residents across the town that nothing short of a Public Interest Report (PIR) from the auditors would be acceptable.

Mary Nelson had already started the ball rolling by asking for a PIR on 6th September 2009, but there was a view that KPMG would not act on the request of just one person, so the 'request procedure' needed to be broadcast in order to persuade other residents to make the same request.

I did not expect the Liberal Democrat councillors to go out and encourage their supporters to ask KPMG for a public interest report, and they did not do so. It would have been an interesting turn of events if they had, and it might have shown to the general public that in spite of their former behaviour, by supporting a PIR they had nothing to hide.

The records show, however, that not once did the Liberal Democrat councillors support a request by the opposition councillors to have an investigation (including the request for the Extraordinary Council Meeting).

In fact, they often went to the other extreme and tried to denigrate the work of those who had been doing their best to find a solution. Take for example the email from Cllr Webster on 12th October 2009 to Cllr Diane Hibbert.

> "Dear Diane,
> In the Autumn issue of the PAB Newsletter there is an article entitled 'The Laird Dispute with Cheltenham Borough Council'.
> Can you tell me:
> 1. if you were the author of this article, and
> 2. if you agree with it as a member of the PAB Group?
> Cllr John Webster."

There was a swift reply from Cllr Hibbert in which she confirmed, "she was not the author of the article, neither did she have any input into its compilation, or its publication." She reminded Cllr Webster "PAB councillors are independent, and do not have to respond to a party whip."

The email was an attempt by the Liberal Democrats to stop Diane Hibbert from being a member of the working group, and it backfired. The fact that the name of the promoter and the publisher was printed on the back page of the *Newsletter* seems to have escaped Cllr Webster's notice.

It was a sly attempt by the Liberal Democrats and it didn't work.

On 18th November 2009 I received a letter from Ian Pennington informing me that KPMG would be undertaking a review of the decision making process for the Laird High Court case. In order to do this they would be conducting a survey of councillor members of the Staff & Support Services Committee.

Enclosed with the letter was a questionnaire, which I was required to complete and return by 25th November 2009. Although the questions were basic, they needed to be put to all the committee members in order for KPMG to get their opinions on what had happened at the S&SSC meetings. I had no doubt that my answers would be different to those given by those responsible for the dispute, and I was sure that some of their answers would be of the 'not-me–guv' variety.

As a member of the S&SSC, I was asked to state who I thought was responsible for taking decisions for the High Court action against Mrs Laird and Rhondda Cynon Taf Borough Council (RCT). KPMG wanted to know whether it was the Monitoring Officer or another officer, the S&SSC or another committee.

Another question asked whether members were clear what the council's objectives were in taking legal action against RCT and Mrs Laird.

The questionnaire also asked whether I had been sufficiently informed about the options open to the council, including the risks and possible costs associated with the two actions when key decisions were taken.

There were questions related to the decision to discontinue the action against RCT in November 2008 and the now infamous 15th January 2009 meeting when the S&SSC decided to continue with the action against Mrs Laird.

Both questions were extremely important, but the 15th January meeting was also about the matter of the resolution approved by the committee, which had instructed the chief executive 'to attempt to settle the dispute out of court'.

The questions would present an opportunity for further and more detailed explanations to be made about the events leading up to and during both meetings. And, not least, a definitive answer still needed to be given to the question of whether or not any negotiation took place with Mrs Laird or was it just a question of 'this is what we think you should agree – take it or leave it'.

From the information supplied by Cllr Hall in previous chapters, the S&SSC meetings were not well conducted and the language used by members was often crude and defamatory. So the review would give anyone the opportunity to open up and 'come clean' about the events surrounding these important meetings, even though the answers would only be made to the appointed auditors.

In my view, the answers to all the questions in the questionnaires should have been made public.

Cllr David Hall, who was a member of the S&SSC during a critical period of the dispute, responded to the letter and questionnaire from KPMG on 19th November 2009. He gave me a copy of his answers together with a copy of the covering letter to the auditor. He went into a lot of detail with his answers, which were clear and precise.

I have included his letter and answers to the questionnaire. (See Appendix 3).

January 2010 was the coldest January in twenty three years with an average temperature of only 0.6C. Snow or sleet fell on twelve days in the first two weeks totalling 17 centimetres of snow, which reached a maximum depth of 11 centimetres on the sixth and seventh days of the month.

Night temperatures fell as low as minus 10.

The wintry conditions we had experienced from the middle of December caused widespread delays nationally to road, rail and air travel. Schools were closed and the wintry conditions caused several accidents on the roads.

It was a relief when rain began to fall in the second half of January, but all in all, it was very depressing with little by way of comfort in the local news.

Depressing though the weather was in January 2010, it didn't stop Mary Nelson from writing to Ian Pennington on Monday 4th January reminding him that he had promised that a report on the Laird prosecution case would be presented to the Audit Committee in January. She wanted to be assured that this was still the case and she also wanted confirmation that the report by KPMG would be a Public Interest Report (PIR).

The answer from the auditor dated 6th January was as follows:

> "We will not now be taking the report to the council's audit committee on 13th January. The strong likelihood is that we will take it to full council at a date to be decided. I will let you know when that has been arranged.
>
> We have not yet finally concluded on whether the report will be a PIR or not, again, I will let you know."

I do not know whether the reply from Ian Pennington compensated for the cold weather we were experiencing, but I took the view that at least the auditors were thinking about a Public Interest Report, and, perhaps, a bit more pressure from other people might just tip the balance in favour of it.

I received copies of two letters sent to KPMG from two local residents dated 11th January 2010. The first accused Cheltenham Borough Council of making "...a horrendous, serious and costly error in pursuing the case against Christine Laird" and then suggested that "Councillors, keen enough to make promises and seek our votes at election times and who would have crowed about their success had CBC won this appalling case, must by the same token, have sufficient integrity to acknowledge their part in pursuing it. KPMG has a duty to the people of Cheltenham to ensure there is a Public Interest Report and we request that you waste no more time in agreeing so to do."

The other letter was from Dr Frank Clayton dated 13th January to Ian Pennington, which simply stated:

> "He hoped KPMG intended to issue a Public Interest Report under Section 8 of the Audit Commission Act (1998) about the Christine Laird case, which you are investigating. It is my belief that the council tax payers of Cheltenham, who are the unhappy people bearing the costs of the unfortunate court action, have the right to see a full report with all the facts and judgments. Without full information, how can the democratic process be considered complete?

I notice that PIR's have been issued after other audits involving much smaller amounts and for minor transgressions of procedures."

Letters to the editor of the local newspaper are always helpful in putting a particular point across. I am sure that the KPMG staff made sure that any articles or letters in the *Gloucestershire Echo* concerning the Laird dispute, the prosecution case, or the ongoing review by the auditors and the council's working group, were read and passed on for consideration.

One letter to the editor suggested that the "Laird case must be investigated further." The writer made the point that as a local taxpayer who will have to pay his share of the wasted £2 million, he was entitled to know what went wrong and that the answers should be made public. He could not believe that legal advice supported a High Court case when the risks of huge losses were likely to occur.

There were other letters submitted on a similar theme and one that added "...to suggest that Mrs Laird's mental health was the reason for the shambles is reprehensible."

Once again, Cllr John Webster couldn't resist the temptation to have another go at his former boss by writing another cryptic and largely erroneous letter in response to the letters published in the local press.

It had been clear for a long time that he would never accept his actions and those of his Lib/Dem colleagues brought Mrs Laird to the edge of mental depression in 2004. Not then, nor during the trial, or even at a later time, has there been an apology from John Webster, or any other member of his Liberal Democrat group, suggesting that maybe, just maybe, the method they used to discredit Christine Laird was totally anathema to human decency.

It is clear from the records that Cllr Webster and his colleagues, indeed the council officers too, knew that the stress Mrs Laird had been put under brought on the depression. She needed help and support, but none was forthcoming.

Statistics published in 2012 show that more than 70 per cent of people who suffer from depression are discriminated against; the World Health Organisation (WHO) thinks that by 2030 depression will be the leading cause of disease on this planet.

Notwithstanding this and in spite of his earlier letter to the local press, to which I have already referred, he restated his assumption about the amount of money the former managing director would receive without mentioning how much she would have to pay in order to defend herself. Again, he claimed that Mrs Laird had a long history of health problems that she had not declared on her application form.

Readers know that the claim by Cllr Webster was not supported in the High Court judgment.

It was following the letter from Cllr Webster that prompted Hugh Laird to write to the local paper on 18th February 2010. This is what he wrote to the editor:

"Cheltenham councillor John Webster seeks to justify spending nearly £2 million pursuing Christine Laird through the high court by repeating aspects of the borough council's failed legal case. It's been a long time since my wife Christine worked for Cheltenham Borough

Council; time has clearly clouded Cllr Webster's memory, or perhaps it is distorted by thoughts of revenge.

Let's face it, your readers can either believe Cllr Webster, who appears to be biased, and as deputy leader of the council, would have had a say in deciding to bring the failed court action and the wasting of so much public money; or believe my wife and Rhondda Cynon Taff Borough Council, individual councillors and residents who have supported her over the last six years; the NHS, the Department for Work and Pensions, the Local Government Pension Fund, her Member of Parliament, and last but by no means least, a High Court judge!

The council's auditor has used his legal powers to investigate precisely why my wife was falsely accused of fraud and wrongdoing by the council. That investigation has now ended and KPMG are due to report shortly.

If the council has done nothing wrong and their actions were justified then the Auditors will say so. Alternatively, if the council was wrong, the report will say that. If the council is guilty of misconduct and misusing public funds, a public interest report will be issued and the council will be publicly named and shamed.

So, before people start jumping to conclusions, or flinging wild accusations around, I suggest everyone just waits for KPMG to publish its findings. If Cllr Webster is right, he will be vindicated, and if not, then he will have some explaining to do."

It was nine months since the High Court judgment was published and members of the general public were making their views known about what they believed to be a deliberate attempt to delay the publication of any report by the council or KPMG.

A report was a long time coming and I believe KPMG made matters worse by continually stating that 'they hadn't made up their minds whether to publish a public interest report or not'. It certainly didn't help, and the number of telephone calls I received during January and February was testimony to this fact.

KPMG intended to keep their cards close to their chest, so it came as a complete surprise to learn in February that they would be publishing their report on 2nd March 2010 and that it would be a Public Interest Report. This information came as a great relief to the public and to the councillors who had been asking for a PIR for a long time.

We knew from the published document that the council must have been kept informed of KPMG's intentions and probably received a draft copy of the report for the chief executive to study and to produce a response.

The chief executive did write a response and it was included as an appendix at the end of the PIR report.

So the gestation period was nearly over and the auditors' recommendations were awaited with bated breath. It would be interesting to see whether the processes leading up to the High Court case had been thoroughly examined as promised. Councillors would have also been interested in reading if any of the answers they had given in the questionnaire had been included in the report, and particularly whether any of their submissions had formed the basis to any of the KPMG's 26 recommendations.

PAB councillors received their copies of the Public Interest Report in February.
2010. Having read my copy, I wrote to Ian Pennington on 11th February 2010
informing him that there were a number of paragraphs in the report where he had
only briefly touched upon the causes of the enormous cost to the taxpayer.

I also expressed my concerns about the paragraphs where he mentioned the
costs, but had failed to enlarge upon the faults that were associated with them.

My letter consisted of five pages and I referred to those paragraphs that clearly
needed to expose the names of the councillors and/or the officers who were responsible for the escalating costs, as well as continually preventing the ending of the
dispute. "My constituents", I wrote, "would want to know the answers to these
questions because the report was silent on these particular points."

There was an introduction to the report and in it the following sentence caught
my eye: "We are making this report in the public interest because of the scale of the
financial costs involved, the number of recommendations being made and the level
of interest being expressed by the public."

This was a good start and I was confident that KPMG had done a reasonable job.
The few councillors and members of the public who had tried so hard to expose
what had been going on at Cheltenham Borough Council from 2002 onwards were
about to be vindicated.

Of course, the report would have been better had it named those responsible for
the dispute and all that went with it, but at least the report was a start.

The *Gloucestershire Echo* wasted no time in publishing a front page article on 12th
February 2010 headed:

'Council faces 26 issues in Laird inquiry'.

"Auditors have criticised Cheltenham Borough Council over its failed bid to sue
Christine Laird, which left taxpayers footing a £2 million bill.

KPMG's critical report on the attempt to claw back £1 million pension and sick pay
from its former managing director highlights a string of complaints and lists 26
recommendations for change. It scolds the council for launching into a blinkered
drive to the High Court without taking into account the full implications of the case.

The 36 page document also criticised the lack of leadership leading up to the end
of the dispute last year, which it calculates to have cost £2,132,000 of public money."

Ian Pennington was reported as saying: "The council was right in trying to
consider how it could have recovered some of its costs and the authority made
mistakes that ultimately increased the sum it was forced to shell out when Mr Justice
Hamblen dismissed its claims in June 2009. Part of the legacy of this dispute is that
it continues to absorb time, energy, attention and money. The council needs to
move on and we encourage members of all political groups and officers to put the
turmoil behind them and build positive working relationships that will benefit the
people of Cheltenham."

Few people disagreed with the sentiments expressed by Ian Pennington, but they
wanted to know why the council's auditors did not intervene long before the High
Court case began, because all the signs were there for the auditors to see.

If they had carried out a preliminary investigation using the same principles of using the questionnaire and talking to the councillors who were in the 'front line' of the dispute, a lot of the pain could have been spared and the costs could have been reduced or avoided.

The chief executive Andrew North said when interviewed "We have supported the investigation each step of the way as we are aware that it covers an issue of considerable importance to the people of Cheltenham. Of course there are lessons we have learned from this case, and in recent years as KPMG have recognised, we have made considerable improvements to the way we do things."

It was reported that the council would consider the KPMG report at the next council meeting on 22nd March and the public had been invited to submit questions to both the council and to KPMG.

'Moving on' is always a fine gesture; recommended by the judge, the chief executive and now Ian Pennington, but the fact will always remain that the dispute should and could have been terminated on more than one occasion, as previous chapters have pointed out.

Cllr John Rawson who was the Cabinet member for finance during the High Court case told the *Echo* that he agreed with the criticism of the council for delegating decision-making – largely to its Staff and Support Services Committee. He commented:

> "The auditor's report confirms many councillors, me included, were shut out of the decision-making process that led to this lawsuit. It was a grave mistake to allow such an important decision to be taken by a small committee of councillors. It gave disproportionate power to a small number of members in both parties who were obsessive about the Laird dispute and who wanted to keep it going long after it should have been laid to rest. If the full council had been allowed to make the decision, there might have been a different outcome and we might have been spared this disaster."

I welcomed Cllr Rawson's comments; they were honest and meaningful. Members of the public contacted me to say how pleased they were to see his comments in the local newspaper.

Cllr David Hall said: "The decision to go to court was motivated by Liberal Democrat councillors on the council who felt that Mrs Laird had tried to force them out of power. I did not think the council's case was strong enough. I am not a gambler, and betting on a 60–40 chance with other people's money to satisfy a politically-motivated claim is not the way forward."

The chief executive said he may have handled the dispute differently if he had taken the top job earlier than 2006. He added, "My hope is that we will soon heed the auditor's advice to put this dispute behind us and move on."

I shall not spend time writing about every one of the twenty six recommendations in the report, but it is important that I comment on those issues that are clearly related to the events I have included in earlier chapters. The KPMG report is a public document and can be obtained from various sources and I would urge those who have been interested in the CBC v Laird case to obtain a copy.

One issue that was important at the time was consideration of the events that resulted in the resolution being passed by the S&SSC at the 15th January 2009 meeting, authorising the chief executive to 'negotiate a settlement' of the dispute before it reached the High Court.

Paragraph 32 of the KPMG report states that the chief executive was authorised to 'explore the potential for settlement', which is quite different to what was approved.

The paragraph goes on to claim, 'the chief executive was unable to speak to the representative of the third political group (PAB), but already had clear indications in writing of that individual's views on the matter'. That was news to me and I hope I am given the chance to see what my alleged views happened to be.

Readers will recall that I was in Australia at the time, and my deputy Cllr Malcolm Stennett assured me on my return that he was not contacted about the terms of the settlement that were going to be offered to Mrs Laird.

The final part of paragraph 32 stated that Mrs Laird rejected the council's settlement proposals, and the council did informally explore whether there was 'the possibility of *further* negotiation on this matter.' (My italics)

I can only repeat what I have already written on this; negotiation in my view is where two sides sit down and discuss what is possible, or not possible. Sometimes a compromise is reached, other times the talks fail. I am assured that this is not what happened in the so-called 'exploration of a potential settlement'.

Having sought confirmation from Mrs Laird of what happened at the time, I restate that only a letter was received from the council by Mrs Laird's solicitor suggesting that the two sides pay their own costs and 'walk away' from the dispute and the impending trial.

That is not a negotiation.

Considering the Lairds had already spent a lot of money in legal representation, the prospect of walking away and paying their own costs, which could amount to a figure in excess of £200,000, was not attractive. They thought at the time that they had more than a good chance of defending themselves in the High Court, and their legal advice was to 'reject the offer'. (Remember it was the council suing Mrs Laird, not the other way round).

In my letter dated 10th March 2010 to KPMG, I suggested that it was inconceivable a large organisation such as CBC, who was suing an individual for damages amounting to nearly £1 million, should ask the accused to make an offer to stop the litigation going ahead.

I asked KPMG whether they agreed that Mrs Laird had no good reason to put forward a 'counter-offer' and that it was up to the council to make the running.

Although I asked several questions related to the above matter, I didn't expect direct answers, and to be fair to KPMG, they did embody some of my concerns in the PIR.

Writing about it now and in retrospect, the legal advice given to Mrs Laird was far better than that given to the council from their external legal advisors.

Paragraph 46 in the KPMG report referred to Mrs Laird's contract of employment in 2003. It stated that the contract came under the auspices of the S&SSC when she was an employee and throughout the period of the dispute. But as the paragraph stated, 'the arrangement rolled on when the dispute changed to become a High Court claim and the council did not recognise that the issue it was managing had changed from an employment dispute to litigation for the recovery of damages'. Indeed, even up to the January 2009 S&SSC meeting (the last meeting before the High Court case commenced) the committee agenda was still referring to "an employment matter" when in reality it had become a legal matter. No-one had questioned whether it remained appropriate for the S&SSC, with its terms of reference centred on internal staffing matters, to continue with this role rather than to refer the matter to the Cabinet or establishing an alternative arrangement.

This was, of course, the nub of the matter, because the S&SSC had usurped the responsibilities of the Cabinet, the scrutiny committee and the council.

As paragraph 47 stated, "The S&SSC's initial consultative role was partly intended to remove potential party political or individual member bias from decision making. However, in reality, the S&SSC remained a political forum."

Probably the most telling paragraph in the report was paragraph 64 and I quote it in full.

> "The Council acted throughout as if it expected to win and this influenced its decisions. Throughout the development of the case, the Council received consistent advice that its prospects of winning were 60:40 in its favour. It was consistently told it had 'a strong case'. This clear message, combined with other factors, furthered the Council's resolve to pursue the case. It did not, however, give sufficient attention to the flip-side of the legal advice, that there was a 40 per cent chance it would lose."

On Risk Management, KPMG wrote that the council had 'tracked the Laird dispute as a corporate risk, but throughout much of the process, it was monitoring the wrong risk. It then removed it from the register when its risk exposure was actually increasing'. (Paragraph 82)

The document was worth waiting for. It was an easy to read statement of the reasons why the council did not win the court case. It set out 26 recommendations to the council, which, if they are carried out in full, will make a vast difference to the way the council is run in the future.

Long before the 'special' meeting on 22nd March 2010 to discuss the KPMG and working group report, Cllr David Hall had written to Sara Freckleton (MO) on 30th October 2009, setting out fourteen lengthy questions, which he wanted to be considered by the Review Working Group.

The introduction to the questions was the well-known and well-rehearsed history of what had happened during his time on the S&SSC and the council's Standards Committee.

Most of the information is contained in previous chapters.

Cllr Hall was never happy with the working group being established, because, like other councillors, he felt that there were a lot of guilty parties who had formed a chorus of pleas for the working group not to blame and shame anyone for what had taken place in the past.

He had made it clear on more than one occasion that the whole case should have been reviewed by an independent examiner. His opinion, which I believed was a valid one, was that the period 2006 to 2009 concerned the heavy debt that had been incurred and who had been responsible for it. The other period 2002 to 2004, in his view, was the critical period when all the damage was done. This period was going to be examined internally, which, in Cllr Hall's opinion, was unacceptable.

The MO replied to Cllr Hall on 21st January 2010 telling him that 'the working group could not review the decisions made by either the Standards Board for England or the High Court'.

Cllr Hall took the view that the review would be a 'whitewash' if the details of the decisions were not examined and lessons learned. He thought that if the working group were only going to discuss 'recruitment matters' and 'conflict resolution' then very little would be helpful to the council in the future.

The council meeting was chaired by Cllr Lloyd Surgenor, who readers will recall from the previous chapters, was a member of the Cabinet that played a part in trying to terminate the employment of Mrs Laird throughout the period of the dispute.

There were only two items on the agenda and councillors were made aware that Ian Pennington from KPMG, assisted by his colleague Darren Gilbert, would present the PIR to council followed by questions.

He began by thanking the council for giving KPMG the opportunity to present their report and explained that a PIR was a rare occurrence, which allowed a relatively serious matter to be brought to the public attention. He gave a glimpse of the background and then urged councillors to be constructive in their debate and to focus on the future.

Several councillors asked questions covering the legal aspects of the process, but Mr Pennington thought it was not the job of auditors to advise the council on such matters, but they would be keen to see that decisions were made following a clear assessment of the options and the risks involved.

In response to a question from Cllr Roger Whyborn who asked if KPMG had found evidence that one particular group had been responsible for the £2 million financial loss resulting from the dispute, or that it was a personal vendetta between the then Leader of the Council and Mrs Laird, Ian Pennington replied that he had not found any evidence of a personal vendetta.

There are no prizes for guessing to which political party the questioner belonged, but it is interesting to note that the answer given by Mr Pennington concerned only the question about a 'vendetta' and not about the 'financial loss' involving one particular group. This shows the importance of asking one question at a time. The first question about responsibility for the £2 million loss was not answered.

Given that Mr Pennington was silent about where that responsibility lay, I often wonder whether Ian Pennington, and others for that matter, providing they had read this book, and read the official 'Statement of Reasons for Decision' of the First Tier Tribunal case on 10th November 2010, would still have the same opinions regarding the dispute and responsibilities as they did in March 2010.

The minutes of the 22nd March 2010 council meeting do not show every question asked, but more importantly, they do not reveal the names of the councillors who asked the questions. Considering KPMG had commented on the poor state of the minutes of past meetings, and the failure to identify the names of councillors, I wondered what they would have thought about the quality of the minutes of the March council meeting had they been shown to them.

All my questions to the auditors started with a long preamble, none of which was recorded in the minutes, but I felt the words were needed to be said in order to give future readers of the minutes a flavour of what I thought about the way the council had behaved towards an individual. I was certainly not happy about the events at the 15th January 2009 S&SSC meeting and the view taken by KPMG in its report, not least because of its significance about the way the council was being run at the time. I was disappointed that KPMG did not recognise it as such.

Another question I asked with a long preamble and not recorded was as follows:

> "The people I represent will be disappointed to learn that neither the council, nor any individual, will be held accountable for the decision to pursue a legal case, when all the portents pointed to possible failure rather than an overwhelming success for the council. If the council believes that the legal advice was poor, should it not be trying to reclaim back some money from the external legal advisors for giving the council poor advice, not just in the Laird case but on the Rhondda Cynon Taf claim as well?"

I have no recall of the answer given to my question. Without a recorded account of who said what and to whom, I can only think that the answer was 'no'.

The public gallery was packed with members of the public who wanted to hear the council give it's debrief on the auditor's critical report and the working group's review. They had come to the council chamber to ask questions of those who had held senior council positions such as why had they behaved in the way they did, which had resulted in a high cost for the council taxpayers.

Numerous questions were put by members of the public concerning the KPMG and working group reports, and some I have recorded here.

Mr George Readman asked whether 'Mrs Laird's legal team had advised the council that their client had no money, and if so had this information been provided to the District Auditor'.

Cllr Jordan confirmed that the former was correct and the council were trying to verify the latter.

Anne Brookes asked the following question:

"The chief executive's response included in the PIR (Appendix 3) is an insult to the taxpayers of Cheltenham. To extract a couple of irrelevant paragraphs from the KPMG summary and ignore the specific points of criticism and failure is smug and complacent and unworthy of someone holding his position. The people of Cheltenham deserve and expect their officers and councillors to do the job they are employed or elected to do, and it is clear from this report that at some point somebody did not do their job, but allowed this most personal and often vindictive case to proceed beyond what was rational, sensible, or in the interest of the people of Cheltenham.

We need someone in charge who can offer leadership to officers and advice to members, make decisions and exercise clear judgment. He showed none of these qualities as this case progressed and has shown no regret since.

When is the chief executive going to acknowledge that pursuing this case was not in the best interests of Cheltenham, accept his responsibility and apologise to the people of Cheltenham?"

There was a period of silence before the chief executive gathered his thoughts and answered the question.

This is what he said:

> "Presumably, the alleged 'irrelevant paragraphs' referred to in the question are the ones that point out that this was a proper case for court and that the decision might have been to proceed even if there had not been governance weaknesses.
>
> The importance of my trying to get these points over is demonstrated by the questioner herself, as despite my comments in Appendix 3 (PIR report) she wrongly assumes in both her written questions that KPMG's conclusions on governance issues automatically lead to the conclusion that the court case should not have been pursued.
>
> As to my personal responsibility, I believe that I have throughout supported effectively the constitutionally correct decisions of the council regardless of my own personal position on the issues; this I believe to be the proper role of a chief executive."

Another question, this time by Mr David Hyett, referred to paragraph 79 of the PIR and its concerns about a 'strong corporate focus' and 'the oversight of the corporate register'. He asked: "Why did the Board of Directors consider this issue to be of insufficient weight for their involvement when it included legal action, a large financial risk, concerned a former managing director and was regularly featured in the press at local and national level?"

Cllr Jordan replied that the Board took the view that the focus and attention should be on moving the council forward. Their responsibility was on ensuring that the organisation had the capacity and resources to deliver the strategic outcomes identified by members, enabling good quality services valued by the customer.

Questions about the financial cost of the dispute, and the poor legal advice given by the council's external legal advisors were put. Other significant questions concerned the involvement of the Liberal Democrats in their pursuit of Mrs Laird, but the answers to all the questions by Cllr Jordan were either dismissive or claimed that it was nothing to do with the Liberal Democrats.

Mr David Woore asked whether the Leader of the Council would accept that some members of the Liberal Democrat administration acted with 'vicious intent throughout the dispute with Mrs Laird and showed lack of leadership in taking appropriate steps to prevent the escalating costs of a high court action'.

'No' was the answer from Cllr Jordan. But, if it wasn't them, then who on earth could it have been?

A question along similar lines from Cllr David Hall who asked: "Are you satisfied that Mrs Laird was treated with respect at all times during the time she spent as the Borough Council's Head of Paid Service"?

The answer from Cllr Jordan: "From my point of view, yes."

I asked the Leader of the Council to tell me why the HR Department did not take up the matter of the medical questionnaire directly with the managing director during the first 15 months of her employment, if the matter was of such great importance that it ultimately became a major point in the High Court action?

The non-answer from Cllr Jordan was that neither the questionnaire, nor its content, was disclosed to the council during this time by the Gloucestershire Occupational Health Unit (GOHU).

Therefore, it would seem that any applicant offered a job by the council would be asked to complete a medical questionnaire and upon completion would be asked to send it directly to the GOHU. Presumably, in a prepaid envelope?

Apparently, there was no importance attached to the content of the questionnaire by the council, at least not at the time and why should there be? It was only two years later that an officer or a councillor thought that as Mrs Laird was absent from work through a stress-related illness, it might be worthwhile asking GOHU to send the questionnaire to the council, so that the council could look at it and see if there was a similar pattern of illness recorded by Mrs Laird.

Why the council did not see the completed medical questionnaire in the first place, and then send it to the GOHU for their comments, is simply unbelievable.

However, as we learned during the course of the trial, this escapade, because that is what it was, turned out to be the council's undoing.

In a supplementary question on the same subject, I asked Cllr Jordan to confirm that Mrs Laird's first fifteen months record of employment showed no absence through illness.

Sara Freckleton the MO, informed members that she had already rejected my question in accordance with the council's rules on public and member questions. My immediate response was to remind the solicitor that I had already asked Mrs Laird for permission to allow disclosure, and that she had agreed to my request.

Mrs Laird had nothing to hide because she had a good record of employment, but it obviously didn't suit the council for this very good work record to become general knowledge.

The *Gloucestershire Echo* published an article on 23rd March claiming:
  "Council chiefs admit £2 million 'error' of suing former MD".

"Senior council officers have admitted a failed bid to sue its former managing director, which left Cheltenham taxpayers footing a bill of more than £2 million was a 'mistake'. In the face of severe public criticism, chief executive Andrew North told an extraordinary meeting of the full council, he would have done things differently in hindsight."

The *Echo* article went on to say that neither Mr North, nor the Liberal Democrat leader Cllr Steve Jordan, would accept that 'they acted inappropriately when deciding to take Christine Laird to the High Court'.

"KPMG scolded the council" the article went on "for launching into a blinkered drive to the High Court and not appreciating all the risks entailed in the lawsuit."

Questions were taken from members of the public, which gave Ken Pollock the opportunity to "accuse the Liberal Democrat administration of pursuing the case because of personal prejudices against the former managing director."

Cllr Jordan disagreed with the questioner.

The article also revealed that when the council attempted to prove in court that Mrs Laird had disguised a history of mental illness when she took on the job of MD, which was subsequently thrown out by the court, it incurred an estimated £550,000 share of Mrs Laird's legal fees on top of its own outlays of more than £1 million. Is it any wonder that Mrs Laird rejected the so-called 'settlement offer' following the 15th January 2009 Staff & Support Services Committee meeting?

One of the more interesting moments in the council chamber came after the working group report had been presented to council. Cllr Hall, who was critical of the report for the reasons mentioned above, was hardly into his speech before Liberal Democrat councillors started to show their disapproval of the points he was trying to get across. Clearly, they did not like what he was saying, and the mayor joined in and tried to stop Cllr Hall from speaking. Cllr Hall was told to sit down, which he refused to do, and the mayor as a last resort, switched off Cllr Hall's microphone.

It was all good fun and livened up the proceedings.

Cllr Whyborn, who was new to the council, moved next business, but thankfully this proposal was not supported by other council members and the discussion continued.

The important point here is to question the purpose behind Cllr Whyborn wanting to move 'next business'? Was it an attempt to silence Cllr Hall, or did he not realise that by 'moving next business' and if it had been agreed, then it would have ended any further debate on the review report of the working group?

In what should have been the last word on the disastrous period in the council's history, was the article in the *Gloucestershire Echo* the following night, which claimed: **"We'll say sorry over Laird case 'errors', vows council".**

"Taxpayers in Cheltenham will receive an official apology from councillors over the failed attempt to sue Christine Laird, which cost more than £1 million of public money", said the article.

The motion to do this was the result of a spontaneous proposal by Cllr Duncan Smith at the end of the March 2010 council meeting. Cllr Smith thought it would be appropriate to "make some sort of gesture to show we are willing to say we are sorry."

The task of drawing up a suitable statement would be the responsibility of the three Group Leaders, but I was not at ease with what had been proposed. The PAB councillors had nothing to apologise for, on the contrary, we had done everything possible over four painful years to get the other political parties to see the folly of their ways and to draw a line under the whole matter. Our suggestions had been constantly ignored, so I was not surprised that the two main political parties thought it was a good idea. Not surprisingly, Cllr Jordan, Leader of the Council and Leader of the Liberal Democrats, thought it was a great idea.

According to the *Echo* article, this is what he said:

"I think a general apology for the errors made by the council is right. It will also make it clear this is a cross-party issue and not the sole responsibility of one party. I'm not sure how it will be worded yet, but that will be dealt with in the next few days."

Inwardly, I was seething. How dare the Leader of the Council implicate the PAB group in the sordid behaviour of members of his group during the dispute by suggesting that a belated apology to the people of Cheltenham should be signed by all groups? Whilst he was right to say that it was not just his political party that had brought on the agony, because readers will know from the previous chapters that some members of the Conservative party were more than content to make life difficult for Christine Laird in 2002 and beyond.

PAB had persistently taken the opposite view, which had even caused Mr Ford, the Monitoring Officer at the time, to report me to the Standards Board for England 'accusing me and my group of acting on behalf of the former MD'.

This is what the *Echo* reported: *"Les Godwin, leader of the PAB group, said he had doubts over whether to support a common apology. If we do that then it would be an admission of culpability, when in fact, we had nothing to do with it. I will talk to my members before I make a decision to sign an apology."*

Apart from the outstanding matter of the letter of apology, I came away from the council meeting believing that we had finally come to the end of the road as far as the CBC v Laird dispute was concerned. Surely, nothing else could emerge that could upset the apple-cart? Yes, it could.

The following day I received a telephone call from the chief executive, Andrew North. He was clearly irate and he made what I thought were ill-founded accusations about my questions to KPMG. As readers will know, I did ask a number of questions, some of which are recorded in this chapter, but he said my questions to KPMG appeared to be related in some way to the questions posed by the public.

What a strange thing to say: of course they were related because the subject matter, on which the questions were based, was the same for councillors as it was for members of the public. It was inevitable that the questions posed would be about the huge financial loss, the behaviour of councillors and officers during the dispute, and the poor legal advice that had been given to the council.

I told Mr North that with such a small canvass the questions were going to be broadly the same, and some duplication was bound to happen.

He was not satisfied with my response and suggested that I had something to do with the formulation of the public questions. I thought his accusation was outrageous, not least because he was suggesting that the members of the public had been incapable of formulating their own questions.

He told me that he thought I had been undermining him in the council meeting, as well as on other occasions and sought an assurance from me that this was not the case.

Of course it was not the case and I gave him the assurance he was seeking.

But, why did Andrew North feel so threatened?

Unfortunately, the matter did not end there. On 26th March 2010, I received an email from Mr North, which was copied to my colleagues Cllr Diane Hibbert and Cllr Malcolm Stennett. This is what it said:

> "You will gather from our conversation earlier in the week that I am concerned that you may be involved in encouraging members of the public to voice personal criticism of me in council meetings and elsewhere arising out of the KPMG report.
>
> Although you disputed this I felt your response was half-hearted and insufficiently specific to amount to a full denial of my concerns.
>
> This is the only reason I am unwilling to sign a public letter – my fear is that you or members of the public close to you will use my signature on the letter against me at some point in the future.
>
> Clearly, I may be wrong in my concerns and I am entirely willing to accept your unequivocal written assurance that you have not (and will not in the future) behave in this way. After all, such behaviour is exactly the sort of bullying conduct which you complain Mrs Laird was subjected to by Cllr McKinlay.
>
> As you know, I and pretty much everybody else wants now to move on. If I am sure that you will not try to present my signature on the letter as reason for personal criticism, or as any admission by me (any more than you yourself) of culpability in this affair then I will sign the letter so as to enable you to do so.
>
> I suggest I prepare an appropriate undertaking dealing with these matters and invite you to sign it on Monday morning so that we can proceed.
>
> As you will be signing (or refusing to sign) as a representative of your group, I feel that Diane and Malcolm should know my position."

It took me a little while to recover after reading the email. What planet did Andrew North think he was on? I could not relate his concerns to what had happened at the extraordinary council meeting in any way at all. Having been a councillor for thirty years, I knew an inordinate amount of Cheltenham people, my time as mayor had certainly brought me into contact with hundreds of people. Often the same people came to council meetings and to planning meetings and we often acknowledged each other in the normal respectful and courteous way. To accuse me of writing their questions and presumably their speeches when they addressed the meeting was, and still is, an outrageous accusation to make.

Having received a copy of the email, Cllr Diane Hibbert responded immediately to Andrew North's email and this is what she wrote:

"Thank you for copying in this email to me. I am shocked and dismayed to read your suggestion that members of the PAB group are involved in some kind of personal action against you.

Members of the public who asked questions at full council were more than capable of reading the KPMG report for themselves and have no doubt drawn their own conclusions and have asked questions on the strength of what they had read. Your suggestion that they have been encouraged by Les to voice personal criticism of you is both an insult to Les and even more of an insult to the members of the public. You should give the public more credit. The whole point of the council meeting was to provide the opportunity for the general public to express their views and to put the matter to rest.

Whilst I can understand that you may have found some of the questions uncomfortable, my own perception of the proceedings was that some awkward questions were asked, but you, along with others, answered sufficiently and that the public should have been content.

There is no escaping the fact that the KPMG report was, in part, very damning of the leadership, whether that be from the political leadership or the corporate leadership. This is what KPMG say, PAB cannot be blamed for the content of the KPMG report. In light of the content of the report, you should not be surprised that there has been some criticism. We all have to be big enough to accept it with good grace.

Furthermore, the review working group did some very good work in finding a way forward rather than dwell on who or what went wrong in the past. The chairman of the group was very clear that trust and communication between officers and members needed to improve.

You are making some very serious accusations of devious action and pursuing this line will quickly undo all the good that has been achieved in the past few weeks. It is certainly not the right way of encouraging or displaying trust.

I trust that Sara Freckleton will suggest suitable wording in the letter (of apology) that will be acceptable to all to sign."

The email to Andrew North from my colleague Diane Hibbert was most welcome. It inspired me to reply to the chief executive by letter on 28th March 2010. It was a long letter, but there were issues that needed to be said, and this is a copy of my letter.

"Dear Andrew,

The Extraordinary Council Meeting held on Monday, 22nd March 2010 ended with the Councillors unanimously accepting the KPMG Public Interest Report, and, with one exception, accepting the Review Working Group Report.

I came away from that meeting believing that the matter was now closed, and, in the words of several people "we should now move on". It was clear to me that questions that needed to be put had been put and answers given by you, KPMG and the members of the Working Group. Inevitably, it would remain a personal thing by all involved whether satisfaction with the answers had been achieved.

My assumption that the 'matter was now closed' was shattered by your inappropriate phone call the next day, in which you made accusations against me, saying that "my questions to KPMG appeared to be related in some way to the questions posed by the public."

As you know, I found your accusations offensive, not least because you appeared to be saying that members of the public did not have the right to put whatever questions they thought appropriate, and, secondly, I had something to do with their formulation.

I told you that I did not see the list of questions until I sat in my place in the Council chamber. It is on record that some members of the public decided to send their questions to councillors ahead of the meeting, but that was their prerogative.

You asked for assurances from me that I was not 'undermining you' which I found extraordinary, but I willingly gave it in the hope that we could all 'move on'.

I come now to the question of the letter of apology, which was proposed by Councillor Smith and debated by Council members. The Motion proposed that the Chief Executive and the Leader of the Council should sign a 'letter of apology, which was generally accepted, but the Leader of the Council wanted all Group Leaders to sign it.

The Mayor intervened and suggested that his signature should be added, although this is not noted in the Minutes of the meeting.

On 24th March, Miss Freckleton sent a first 'draft' copy of a letter of apology to which I responded on Thursday 25th March. I suggested that the letter was too long and contained matters that appeared to be irrelevant in a letter of apology.

I asked one other point for clarification, which was whether the letter was going to be signed by the Group Leaders and the Chief Executive.

You replied immediately to point out that "the letter is to be signed by the Group Leaders only." You continued by saying that "This is what Council decided."

You finished the sentence by claiming "that there appears to be an orchestrated campaign against you and you were not inclined to put your head above the parapet on this one."

Again, I thought your comment was misguided in the light of the Council decision at the Extraordinary Meeting on Monday, 22nd March and didn't indicate to me that we were going to 'move on' as we all thought.

However, on the basis of your reply, I contacted my Group and sought their advice, which is my normal practice. My Council colleagues thought that even though we had the least involvement in the Council's claims against RCT and the former managing director, for the sake of 'moving forward' I should sign the letter, but only if the Chief Executive signed it too.

That response only brought more outrageous comments from you in your email dated

26th March accusing me of "encouraging members of the public to voice personal criticism of you in council meetings and elsewhere arising out of the KPMG report."

You also made it clear that you did not accept the assurance I gave you over the telephone on Tuesday, 23rd March on the spurious claim that it was only 'half-hearted'. You didn't say at the time that you didn't accept my assurance, which again, is regrettable.

The claims in your email are particularly hurtful when I consider that throughout the events leading up to and including the High Court hearing, I was particularly careful, in spite of numerous requests from the Press and media, not to fall into the trap of going public with all the consequences that usually flow from that.

Others did, in fact, go public on more than one occasion, which only brought the name of Cheltenham Borough Council into disrepute.

You must realise that there are a lot of angry Cheltenham people who feel strongly about the financial consequences of the failed claim by the Council against the former Managing Director.

I am sure they realised after reading the Public Interest Report that they were entitled to air their views and feelings through the process of letters to either the District Auditor, or, to the Borough Council; and I am equally sure they would be further annoyed if it became known to them that you thought their questions to KPMG, or the Council, was either inspired or suggested by me. PAB councillors are independent 'free thinking' councillors who are quite capable of working out things for themselves and acting accordingly. They certainly would not expect me to try to influence them on any issues and I wouldn't anyway. The same applies to anyone who makes up our management team or even individual members.

I will be attending the meeting tomorrow morning (Monday 29th March) at 9.30 a.m. but I will not be signing or discussing the pros and cons of some 'written assurance' along the lines you are suggesting. I will be there to discuss the content of the letter and when a final 'draft' is given to me for signature I will sign it in accordance with the resolution that was passed by Council on the 22nd March 2010.

Perhaps, after the meeting tomorrow morning we can actually 'move on' and leave all the rancour behind us.

Councillor Les Godwin."

Needless to say, I did not sign any 'agreement', but I did sign the letter of apology that was printed in the *Gloucestershire Echo*, albeit reluctantly.

The date of the publication was April 1st 2010 – April Fools' Day.

As I anticipated, a number of members belonging to the PAB group contacted me to express their disappointment in me for signing the letter of apology. They had followed the CBC v Laird dispute from the start and they quoted back to me the statements that had been previously reported and the negative minutes of the S&SSC.

They also felt that the summary of confidential proceedings, which the public were entitled to see, had been either non-existent, or sketchy if any were ever produced.

Thankfully, we did not lose any members because of my 'reluctant' signature, and

PAB county councillors Diane Hibbert and Dave Prince with Barbara Cromwell following 2005 election.

it was clear to me that what had saved the day for me and the PAB group was the Public Interest Report. It had vindicated those who had constantly claimed that the council were wrong, and secondly, the local newspaper reports of the incisive questioning of KPMG and the officers of the council at the extraordinary council meeting, outweighed their disappointment with the apology letter.

For the council, the end of the road had been reached as far as the High Court case and the PIR were concerned. But I am sure they knew that once the dust had settled, there would be the matter of payment of costs, further expenditure and the prospects that the former managing director might claim damages from them.

The next chapter will describe the process of Christine Laird's industrial injury claim and the consequences that flowed from it.

CHAPTER 26

The Aftermath

Industrial Injury And The First-Tier Tribunal

A long line of cases shows that it is not merely of some importance, but is of fundamental importance that justice should not only be done, but should manifestly and undoubtedly be seen to be done.

Gordon Hewart (1870–1943)
British lawyer and politician

I have written about the CBC v Laird dispute in the previous chapters because it was a period when the People Against Bureaucracy Group (PAB), like the other groups, had no choice but to play a part in what became known as the 'most bizarre and messiest local government squabble to end up in the High Court'.

It is true that because our group was small, we were often excluded from the discussions that were going on behind the doors at the council offices.

The PAB group was only ever involved in discussions through me as the group leader, and this was evident in the early period of the dispute before it reached the 'litigation' stages. Added to this were my 'declarations of interest' whenever 'the employment matter' was to be discussed, which resulted in my self-imposed exit from the meetings, which resulted in the group being unaware of the decisions that had been taken.

I have also chronicled some of the events as I saw them, but most of the historical facts used have been obtained from the documented evidence and the voluntary provision of useful information from various sources.

This chapter, therefore, centres round the period following the court case, which for the record had ordered the local authority to pay its own costs and to pay 65 per cent of the costs of its former managing director, Christine Laird.

A decision later upheld by the Court of Appeal in February 2010.

It was never going to be easy for Christine Laird following the high profile court case, to get sympathy or concessions from Cheltenham Borough Council. Any claims for damages or allowances were going to be resisted at every attempt and at every level by the council, and from the facts that have been obtained, some of the sums involved were so small and the alleged periods of time were so short, it was difficult to understand why the council continued to make such hard work of it all.

Due to the PAB group's exclusion from meetings when financial matters associated with the Laird case were being discussed, it was some time before we became aware that Christine Laird had been trying to obtain money that was due to her from the council and benefits following appeals to the Secretary of State.

She made a request to the council in 2010 for an annual injury allowance under the Local Government (Discretionary Payments) Regulations 1996. This was considered by the Staff & Support Services Committee (S&SSC) in February 2011 and they made a recommendation to the council on the 25th February 2011, which included an acceptance that Mrs Laird's request satisfied the criteria laid down by the Regulations, but did not accept that the council had been liable for the 'injury' claimed by Mrs Laird. The committee recommended an annual allowance of £1,000 payable from July 2009 and subject to review. When I checked the facts with Christine Laird, she admitted that she was surprised by the council's response and felt the sum was derisory and insulting.

She was aware that there were several options open to her such as a judicial review, an appeal to the Secretary of State, or a formal complaint to the Pensions Ombudsman on the grounds of maladministration.

From these options she decided to appeal to the Secretary of State in September 2011. His subsequent investigation determined that

a. he had jurisdiction to determine the appeal following the council's decision not to backdate the award to August 2005,
b. the council had the right to determine the amount of the allowance, but
c. it should be backdated to 9th August 2005.

The Secretary of State's decision was not accepted by the council and it could have been challenged by way of a judicial review on legal technicalities, but the council decided not to do so.

What would have concerned the council taxpayer at the time was the pointless position of the council quibbling about the backdating issue when the amount of money involved was so small. When set against the costly external legal advice the amount of money was 'peanuts'.

If the council was trying to establish a point of principle then most sensible people would have urged the council to 'settle the matter' rather than continue a fruitless path of trying to prove it.

It is alleged that once again the council sought external legal advice, which, unless the council went to other legal chambers, would have involved using the same barrister that had advised the council leading up to the High Court case. Bizarre, maybe, but the cost for further advice would not be cheap, and the Advice, it seems, produced yet another stalemate.

It is also alleged that at least one member of the council suggested a larger sum in settlement of the claim and advised it would be worth it in the long run. As in the past, this sound advice was ignored and the matter continued to rumble on.

On this and other matters Mrs Laird decided to make a complaint to the

Pensions Ombudsman in an effort to prove her point that the council were continuing to be at fault as far as her situation was concerned.

An application by Mrs Laird to the Department for Work and Pensions (DWP) for a Disability Living Allowance was successful following a medical examination, but it was subject to a biennial medical review. However, in September 2011, the DWP informed Mrs Laird that following a review of her case history, they had determined her benefits would no longer be subject to biennial medical reviews, which meant she had been considered as a long term disabled person.

It was not a surprise to learn that in the period following the termination of Mrs Laird's employment, she made several applications for benefits to which she was entitled. Apart from those already mentioned, she made an application for industrial accident benefit on 27th August 2009, but the DWP determined that only one 'industrial accident' had occurred in March 2003.

I make no claim to knowing what went on regarding the numerous discussions in committee and council, because of my acceptance that anyone being in attendance at either, having participated in any of the previous debates, would not have an open mind regarding the claims that the former managing director had made.

It was also clear from past evidence that no matter what arguments would be put forward on Mrs Laird's behalf; the council and the administration had made up their minds a long time before any discussions took place about an annual award, that the dispute was entirely the fault of the former managing director. There was not going to be any award as far as they were concerned; and should the council be forced into accepting the inevitable, then one could rest assured that any award made would be the smallest amount possible.

On 13th August 2009, Mrs Laird had made an Industrial Accident Declaration and for appropriate benefit; the delay in accepting the decision for an injury allowance, or filibustering by the council had caused Mrs Laird to seek redress from an Industrial Injuries Tribunal on 10th November 2010.

A First Tier Tribunal Hearing was held in Bristol before Judge Martha Street.

The hearing was held to establish whether the mental illness suffered by Christine Laird towards the end of her employment and then subsequently, were the result of various incidents that occurred during her employment. (In Tribunal jargon an 'incident', if proved, becomes an 'industrial accident' for pension purposes).

Surprisingly, the Department for Work and Pensions did not attend the hearing, nor, I am reliably informed, did Cheltenham Borough Council (CBC).

On the evidence before her, Judge Martha Street came to the opinion that from the moment CBC changed political control in 2002, the new Leader of the Council "considered ways of terminating her contract of employment."

She accepted that on 5th March 2003, the Deputy Leader of CBC bullied Mrs Laird and asked her "What would it take for you to go."

Judge Street remarked that the incident has been accepted as an industrial accident by the Secretary of State. She also confirmed that "it was earlier accepted as a repudiatory breach of contract by the High Court."

Judge Street said: "The financial inducement of £63,000 by the deputy was unlawful, but from then on it was common knowledge that the Council Leader was trying to terminate Mrs Laird's employment."

With Mrs Laird's permission I read the Tribunal Statement of Reasons for Decision and whilst it brought a smile to my face, it was not because the detail I was reading was identical to the points I had made in all the previous chapters, but a smile that must have crossed the face of David as Goliath lay mortally wounded before him.

It is a great pity that the council taxpayers were denied the opportunity to read the words of Judge Martha Street: I am sure it would have changed the views of most of the 'doubting Thomas's'.

The quotations I have made from Judge Street's decision coincide with the Laird Radio 5 interview on 7th December 2011, which will be mentioned later.

The incident about the anonymous letters and emails in July 2003 "... triggered her illness and absences from work." Judge Martha Street said:

> "They were malicious and unpleasant, calculated to cause personal distress and to damage her reputation.
>
> It was because she learned that steps to suspend her without grounds during the course of a council meeting caused Mrs Laird to collapse after the meeting.
>
> She was signed off from work with immediate effect for acute anxiety, work related stress and associated reactive depression. The illness lasted for several months.
>
> But before Mrs Laird was well enough to return to work, she read in the local newspaper, on or around 10th October 2003, that a special meeting had been convened to discuss disciplinary charges against her for unspecified misde-meanours. The intention was to lead to the termination of her employment."

According to Judge Street "She suffered a major panic attack, thought at the time to be a heart attack, as a result of the news, and she was temporarily admitted to hospital."

Mrs Laird's absence from work continued until 10th December. On her return she requested an adjustment to her working hours while she adjusted to the return to work. Whilst most of the drama and the abuse mentioned in Judge Street's Statement of Reasons were not new to me, I was unaware that the former managing director had made a request for an adjustment to her working hours, and I was not made aware that the request had been granted. The normal practice in any well-run personnel function is to grant such a request to any employee following a long absence from work.

It was obvious that the pressure on the former managing director was going to continue unabated until she left the council's employment. Judge Street referred to the "threats of suspension" and the informality of proper procedures "including on the grounds of medical incapacity for 'becoming slightly crazy' presented in a manner that was inappropriate and untoward and implying manipulation to secure that outcome."

Being told by telephone that she had been suspended following the emergency council meeting, which caused her to suffer a severe panic attack, lose consciousness and requiring sedation by her GP was bad enough, but to be copied into a letter sent by the council, which accused her of faking her illness before they had received any independent medical advice, were some of the instances referred to by Judge Martha Street. And, as the judge reported in her statement – 'the allegations continued'.

In addressing the issues covered by law, the Judge made the point that the Laird Appeal was not a case in which there was a physical accident or assault.

But, in explaining the relevant section of the Social Security Contributions and Benefits Act 1992, she made the following observations:

> "It was well established that psychological injury can be caused by untoward words spoken in interview or conversation or otherwise communicated. What is the essence of a non-physical accident is the nature of the event, the manner of the communication, not the content. There clearly were issues of some weight between Mrs Laird and her employer. Her conduct was not beyond question nor was her account wholly accepted by the High Court. However, what is at issue here is not what arose in the normal course of an employment dispute. What is at issue is the effect of the manner of carrying on the dispute."

It was not as though CBC were unaware of the way certain individuals were treating Mrs Laird throughout her time as managing director: they were aware and were repeatedly warned by opposition councillors, but they always thought they knew better than anyone else.

Seeking advice from lawyers who specialised in the requirements of the Social Security Contributions and Benefits Act 1992 would have been a better option for CBC rather than the expensive litigation route to the High Court that they had chosen.

In allowing the appeal Judge Martha Street recognised that the incidents referred to above and others not mentioned, triggered Mrs Laird's illness and absence from work. She was significantly affected by her stress related illness and unable to attend work. She referred to a section of law that "A person must be considered with whatever extra sensitivities, physical or mental, she has. If she was well before the first accident (incident), she does not lose entitlement to benefit by reason of a previous history of depression which was over."

The final paragraph of the Decision Notice is as follows:

"While she suffered prolonged exposure to stress or trauma in the course of or linked to her former employment, the Tribunal finds that the trigger for the serious mental illness has been the incidents now identified as accidents."

Judge Street was assisted by Mr MH Young at the First Tier Tribunal Hearing in Bristol on 10th November 2010.

News that the BBC would be conducting an exclusive interview with Mrs Laird on the Victoria Derbyshire Radio 5 show on Wednesday 7th December 2011 was good news. Christine Laird had resisted previous attempts for a radio interview, but some people, myself included, thought it would be a good opportunity for the facts of the dispute to be revealed by the one person who had suffered so much following the appalling behaviour of officers and elected members of the local authority between the years 2002 and 2005.

Having written several chapters of this book, which included the period of the dispute, I was sufficiently confident that any interview with Mrs Laird would confirm my assessment of the situation, just as the First Tier Tribunal Judge Martha Street had done twelve months earlier.

It would certainly help to vindicate people such as Cllr David Hall, who had produced damning evidence of what went on behind the 'closed door' meetings, and he had suffered similar abuse by the same people for his efforts in trying to get accurate records of the meetings. The various documents he supplied setting out the details of those times were often derided by Liberal Democrat councillors, but they were about to be confirmed as accurate accounts of the situation.

It would also vindicate those who had played an important part in achieving a Public Interest Report and the examination of the council's accounts during the dispute, by KPMG.

So, the thought of being able to listen to the one person who had suffered most during the dispute without interference from others was something to look forward to. I recorded the interview, which will remind me, if I will ever need reminding, of how one group of people can be so spiteful and vindictive towards another human being over such a long period of time.

The radio interview was thorough and it highlighted the mental health issues suffered by Mrs Laird and, as she stated, they continue to do so. The interview lasted forty minutes.

The BBC website advertising the broadcast, reported that "A former council chief executive whose employers tried to sue her for a million pounds after she failed to reveal her history of depression speaks exclusively to Victoria Derbyshire. A High Court judge dismissed the case brought by Cheltenham Borough Council against Christine Laird – who has now been awarded maximum disability benefits for life."

The interview attracted good listening figures, which included mental health organisations; support and sympathy came from individuals during the broadcast although some listeners were unsympathetic towards Mrs Laird.

By the end of the interview, however, there was a stream of supportive emails, texts and telephone calls from all parts of the country; the majority criticising CBC for their 'outrageous behaviour'.

In describing the state of her health as it deteriorated due to the constant stress at work, she told the interviewer "I was very frightened, I had lost a lot of weight, I couldn't sleep and when I did I had nightmares. I constantly vomited and my head hurt a lot."

When asked to explain what caused her condition, she said the bullying conduct of a group of people, the insults, abuse and anonymous letters, was simply too much.

She said "Officers who originally supported me suddenly stopped doing so, which I believe was through pressure and the thought of losing their jobs."

Victoria Derbyshire said the local authority had accused Mrs Laird of having withheld a depressive illness when she applied for the job, and she asked if this was true.

Christine Laird replied that if she had been asked the question in the medical questionnaire she would have answered the question truthfully. She said the matter of a previous stress-related illness with her previous employment had been aired in the High Court and it had been dismissed by the Judge.

The fact that she had taken only ten days of sickness absence over a two year period was testament to her reasonably good health. She added that most people have more absences from work due to the common cold.

When asked to explain her treatment by the council, Mrs Laird said the unpleasant comments made her feel unwanted, she was filled with self-doubt and 'wondered what it was that these people did not like about me'.

She constantly asked herself what she could do differently in order to make a difference and to please those who were spiteful to her. Nothing she did, it seemed, made any difference. She said "It was a horrible situation to be in."

Victoria Derbyshire made several references to the comments made by Judge Martha Street during the Industrial Injury Hearing, some of which I have referred to above.

The Judge ruled that the treatment she received from the council was "calculated to cause personal distress" which said it all.

Mental illness is described in most pieces of literature on the subject as 'an illness that feels just as bad as or worse than any other illness, it is just that you cannot see it'. The illness covers a whole range of different types, but words used in everyday conversations are usually 'depression' or 'anxiety'. Whilst these words are easily understood, they often underestimate how serious the illness can be.

Depression lowers one's mood, can make the person feel hopeless, worthless, unmotivated, and in an effort to overcome the symptoms, makes the person feel exhausted. The worse the person feels the more depressed they get.

Anxiety often means an unrealistic worry about the aspects of daily life. It can cause all sorts of problems such as sleeplessness, stomach upset and muscle tension.

Severe anxiety can cause panic attacks and an increase in one's heartbeat.

None of these illnesses should be brought on by the activities of others; they are bad enough in their own right. The fact that one in four people in the United Kingdom are affected by mental health problems shows how common the illness is.* (see footnote)

Unfortunately, the stigma and discrimination towards people with mental health problems is still common and often accompanied by myths about what the different diagnoses mean.

*Mental Health Statistics – Mental Health Foundation.

As I mentioned in an earlier chapter, good employers are aware of the Disability Discrimination Act 1995 and abide by its regulations.

It may be of some comfort to Christine Laird to learn that she is not alone in the often dark world of depression; celebrities in television, sport and the film industry have suffered from depressive bouts of mental illness. Such names as Ruby Wax, Catherine Zeta Jones and Mel Gibson have been sufferers and have preferred to keep silent about it in the early part of their careers.

Ian Thorpe and Michael Phelps, both world swimming and Olympic champions have suffered from depression too. Thankfully, like so many other sufferers, they have spoken out about their own mental health problem, which in some ways act as a comfort to those who still suffer from it.

CHAPTER 27

'Garden Grabbing' – Unwanted Development

Flooding And Protecting The Green Belt

"You can never plan the future by the past".

Edmund Burke 1729–97

Whilst the arguments and recriminations over the CBC v Laird dispute continued long after the Bristol Industrial Tribunal had ended, other matters of equal importance to the Cheltenham council taxpayer were also being considered.

One of these was whether it was right for homeowners to be able to sell off their back gardens to a developer. It was very controversial at the time with neighbours falling out with each other and the political parties spending long hours debating whether it was socially and environmentally correct for the council to allow it.

PAB councillors had long taken the view that if we were to continue with our policy of protecting green open spaces from development, then back gardens needed to be included in our policy.

We believed that back gardens played an important part in the character of a neighbourhood and their continual loss would not only intensify the urban capacity, but also rob the area of important green lungs and wildlife as well as increase the risk of flooding.

In 2007, back gardens were classified as brownfield areas, which put them in the same classification as derelict factories and former military establishments. This meant they were unprotected from development.

How central government could place a carefully manicured green lawn with flower beds in the same category as a derelict factory site was a mystery to PAB councillors. It was something we aimed to challenge at every opportunity.

We believed that the only way to curb the growing number of back garden planning applications was for the council to introduce a Supplementary Planning Document (SPD) that would define the way a back garden site should or should not be developed even with the unhelpful classification.

Some councillors, supported by planning officers, were not in favour of a SPD mainly because it would curtail the number of houses that could be constructed in the town. This was a puerile argument at the time because the council was meeting its housing targets without the need for this type of 'windfall' site.

The fact that uncontrolled development in back gardens could change the character of a neighbourhood and result in the loss of an open space, did not concern those who were opposed to an SPD.

Central government didn't help the situation by refusing to change the status of back gardens; they reinforced their view by stating that all garden spaces within the curtilage of the dwelling were to remain as "previously developed sites".

In spite of this, PAB councillors made several requests to the council for it to set up a working group to see whether a SPD was possible in order to control back garden applications, which would in turn give the planning department better control of the back garden planning applications.

The reaction from some councillors was amazing. Listening to some of the comments one would have thought that we had asked for something that was outrageous, detrimental to the town and its open spaces, rather than the opposite.

Indeed some thought that an SPD would be a tool to ban all developments on back gardens including properties with very large rear gardens.

However, in spite of the opposition, PAB councillors managed to persuade enough members of the council to agree that a Garden Land Working Group (GLWG) should be established to see whether an SPD was needed. The working group would explore the possibility of producing a document that would set down guidelines that would eliminate inappropriate development on back gardens.

The document, in our view, would enable planning officers to make the right recommendation, but only for a development that was in keeping with the character of the neighbourhood and not harm the amenities of the adjoining neighbours. These were simple requirements, in our view, yet the document's passage through the various stages was far from easy.

Because so many back gardens were being lost through unwanted development, PAB councillors urged other councillors to support an early timescale for the SPD. However, at the 28th July 2008 Cheltenham Borough Council (CBC) meeting, Andrew North, Chief Executive (CE) in his report on the subject recommended a timescale of July 2010.

This was unacceptable to PAB councillors who immediately submitted an amended resolution calling on the council to agree a timescale of July 2009.

After more heated words from several Lib/Dem councillors, who supported the timescale proposed by the CE, council approved the PAB amendment.

Cllrs John Morris and Roger Whyborn (Lib/Dems) and Cllr Robin MacDonald (Conservative) abstained from voting on the amendment.

Members of the GLWG were Cllrs Malcolm Stennett and Les Godwin (PAB), Cllr Jacky Fletcher (Conservative), Cllrs John Morris and John Webster (Liberal Democrats)

As I recall, the working group meetings were far from being happy occasions. There were bitter exchanges about the content of an SPD, and sometimes it spilled over between members. On one occasion when Cllr Stennett and I tried to insert a condition that a rear garden development must have its own separate entrance if the application was to succeed, this caused Cllr Morris to walk out of the meeting.

Support for this addition received little support from the planning officers either, but a suggestion by them of inserting the words "would not normally be granted" was agreed, but without the support of the PAB councillors.

The wording was woolly and we knew that its inclusion would be used by applicants and planning officers to allow back garden developments to continue to take place.

We were right with our presumption; more than 90 per cent of back garden applications have received a recommendation to permit since the SPD was published. On rare occasions the planning committee disagreed with the officer's recommendations, and sometimes when the applicants went to appeal, the planning inspector would agree with the committee members' decision and dismiss the appeal, (but not often enough, in my opinion).

The SPD cost CBC council taxpayers £70,000 to produce. Some people would say that it was a waste of money and they would be correct. PAB councillors have tried repeatedly to get the Liberal Democrats to allow a review of the SPD, so that the woolly wording could be deleted. They have refused the PAB request on every occasion, and until they agree to amend it, those who have suggested it was a waste of money will have been proved to be right – it will have been a complete waste of money.

On July 28th 2008 council members were reminded by the CE that in March that year council members had agreed 'in principle' to prepare a Joint Core Strategy (JCS). He added: "A significant resource had been invested by the three councils CBC, Gloucester and Tewkesbury together with the Gloucestershire County Council to develop a framework within which to operate joint working within agreed timetables.

The aim of the JCS would be to put in place a robust plan-led approach to manage major growth focused upon the main urban areas of the three areas over the next 20 years."

Although there was a link between the SPD and the JCS in the council report, I didn't think the significance of the report registered in the minds of those who were sitting in the council chamber.

The CE report stated: "The JCS would provide an opportunity to develop policies setting out the context of housing delivery, including the role and contribution of garden land." So, even before the GLWG got to work on the SPD to prevent "garden grabbing", as local residents called it, it seemed as though the document was doomed.

In August 2008, out of sheer frustration, I wrote a seven-page document entitled "How To Achieve A Supplementary Planning Document When The Odds Are Against You".

It stated the facts and it ended with a personal apology to my constituents.

The SPD was finally approved and published in June 2009. In spite of the assuring words by Cllr Morris that I was seeing obstacles where none existed, I knew deep down that the battle to prevent 'garden grabbing' would be a long and arduous one, with few successful stories to tell; a long battle which is still being fought today.

In less than one year after its publication, the number of back garden permissions that have been allowed exceeded those that were refused by as many as 3 to 1.

On 21st January 2010, Housing Minister John Healy issued a statement promising new guidelines to help prevent development in back gardens. He also reminded local authorities that they 'did have sufficient powers to act, should they care to use them'.

Cllr John Morris, according to a *Gloucestershire Echo* report by Stephen Hackwell, said he was infuriated by the criticism adding "... the Minister should not blame local authorities. In Cheltenham we have done all we can to address the problem but our hands have been tied to a large extent by central government."

Walking out on a Garden Land Working Group meeting because PAB councillors were trying to strengthen the 'draft' document, hardly gave Cllr Morris the right to criticise the statement by the central government minister.

The *Echo* report also reminded readers that the council had introduced an SPD in 2009 after several controversial cases of 'garden grabbing'. The document it said "...aims to tighten up the development of garden land and in-fill sites."

Even when central government reclassified back gardens from brownfield to green open spaces, it made little difference to the number of applications submitted, nor the recommendations to permit by the planning officers.

Judging by the number of letters to the *Gloucestershire Echo* from disgruntled Cheltenham residents, it was clear whose side they were on. Both the PAB and Conservative groups on CBC constantly raised the matter of doubtful recommendations by the planning officers, but it had little effect.

Once again, an *Echo* report by Stephen Hackwell on 27th February 2010 said, "New homes for gardens sparks heated debate".

The report stated: "Plans for stricter monitoring of 'garden grabbing' applications sparked bitter debate at a Cheltenham Borough Council meeting. Calls from Conservative and People Against Bureaucracy councillors for planning officers to adhere to guidance brought in as a deterrent to development bids in the town's back gardens prompted an hour of fierce debate. Liberal Democrat councillors rejected the stance that Conservative and PAB councillors had taken."

The article concluded by reminding readers that "... the council had spent £50,000 producing an SPD last year which placed more stringent controls on which back garden developments should be given the thumbs up."

A motion by the Conservative Group, which the PAB Group seconded, asked the planning officers to stick to the guidance and to issue a report of 'garden grabbing' applications to the council planning committee.

The majority of the Liberal Democrat councillors voted against the motion.

The debates and arguments about unwanted development on back gardens continued throughout 2010, 2011 and 2012. PAB councillors with the support of Conservative councillors tried desperately to strengthen the SPD by seeking reviews of the document at every opportunity.

At a council meeting in February 2012, Cllr John Rawson rejected a PAB suggestion that the SPD was 'full of holes' and that a 'horse and cart' could be driven through the borough's planning laws. He added: "It was nonsense to say that the document was ineffective."

Very few residents, whose lives have been changed by a neighbour's thoughtless construction of a dwelling in the back garden, would agree with Cllr Rawson. Perhaps as the cabinet councillor with responsibility for financial matters, the prospect of more money from the New Homes Bonus scheme (a central government initiative) for each new dwelling, was more important than preserving the character of an area.

The report of the debate in the *Gloucestershire Echo* on 21st February 2012 by Max Wilkinson the newspaper's political reporter, carried the following headline: "Gardens not at risk from changes to planning rules".

The article was an account of what Cllr Rawson had said at the meeting with no reference to any comments made from members of the opposition.

Max Wilkinson became a Liberal Democrat candidate in the Cheltenham Borough Council elections in 2014.

The period 2009 to 2014 was an exceptionally busy period for local authorities. Central government had long urged them to share services with adjoining councils. There was plenty of scope for this and one service that readily came to mind as a joint sharing exercise was refuse collecting.

Following extensive consultations, CBC now shares a range of services with Cotswold, Forest of Dean and West Oxfordshire District Council. It works well and plays a major part in reducing council costs.

It was agreed in June 2009 that CBC and Tewkesbury Borough Council (TBC) should look at the potential for a shared legal service. The Local Government and Housing Act 1989 requires every council to designate one of its officers as the Monitoring Officer with certain statutory powers and responsibilities, which they must exercise in relation to the council.

A temporary arrangement of sharing a Borough Solicitor and Monitoring Officer with TBC had been in place since February so it made sense to formalise the secondment arrangement with effect from 1st July 2009.

As a result of the council's recommendation, Sara Freckleton the TBC Borough Solicitor became the Monitoring Officer for CBC for the purposes of Section 5 (1) of the Local Government and Housing Act 1989.

It was a unanimous decision of the council and I was pleased for Sara as I had always found her to be very efficient throughout my time as a TBC councillor.

She joined the council as a trainee legal executive in July 1977. The council sponsored Sara's training and once she had qualified as a legal executive the council supported further training to enable Sara to qualify as a solicitor.

She qualified in 1986.

In 1987, Andrew Chapman the TBC solicitor left the council to go into private practice and the post was advertised. Sara applied for the vacant job and she was appointed as the Solicitor to the Council in May 1987.

In 1989 when the requirement to appoint a Monitoring Officer was introduced, Sara applied for the job and was later appointed Monitoring Officer.

So, with the appointment of Monitoring Officer for CBC in 2009, Sara had come a long way in her legal career.

The fact that Sara Freckleton had not been involved in the CBC v Laird case meant that when the matter of the KPMG Public Interest Report was in the public domain [referred to in previous chapters], she could look at its contents in an unbiased way.

Sara has been a loyal servant of both TBC and CBC; she offers knowledgeable and reliable advice through which she has gained respect from all sides of the council chamber.

Nick Tucker-Brown, a well-known local developer, spent a number of years trying to convince local residents and the CBC planning officers that there was a case for developing the Green Belt along the north side of Swindon Lane. Finally he submitted an outline planning application to construct 190 dwellings on land known as the Hunting Butts.

The application was submitted on behalf of Galliard Homes Limited. It came before the planning committee on Thursday 18th February 2010 with a planning officer's recommendation to refuse.

The recommendation came as no surprise to PAB councillors. The Hunting Butts is adjacent to the land at The Paddocks, which is referred to in a previous chapter, where the owner of the site tried repeatedly to breach Green Belt policy, but was finally denied by an independent planning inspector.

The planning officer's report to the committee on 18th February rightly referred to the site being "... wholly within nationally designated Green Belt and located outside the principal urban area of Cheltenham."

It also emphasised that "National planning policy as set out in Planning Policy Guidance (PPG2) contains an explicit presumption against development in the Green Belt, in order to maintain the openness of the land."

Philippa Dalton on behalf of Galliard Homes when addressing the planning committee stated: "... the application reconciled a number of challenges, but would help to maintain a strong and effective Green Belt between Cheltenham and Bishop's Cleeve, while making good use of the existing landscape."

She added: "The proposal would provide much-needed family homes in easy distance of Cheltenham, including a large proportion of affordable homes."

Cllr Malcolm Stennett (PAB) responded by reminding members "... the council had spent a lot of money on the Cheltenham and District Green Belt Review, and the Hunting Butts had come out as being of particular high value."

He added: "It would be a travesty if any development was allowed on this land."

The planning committee voted unanimously to support the officer's recommendation to refuse.

Following the planning meeting the *Gloucestershire Echo* contacted me to ask for my views and whether I would be willing to write an article for their column "Speaking Out" published every Saturday. This is a précis of my article:

"Prestbury residents will no doubt be pleased that plans to build 190 homes on Green Belt land near the Racecourse were unanimously rejected by the CBC planning committee. The land is not included in the much-maligned Regional Spatial Strategy and on this fact alone should not be included in the emerging Joint Core Strategy proposals.

Whichever of these two documents is adopted for the future, we should be assured that the land will not be developed for the next twenty years in a future development framework.

The concept of a Green Belt is to stop the coalescence of two settlements and it is also a means of checking unrestricted urban sprawl into the countryside. The swathe of land on the north side of Swindon Lane is the most important buffer to keep Prestbury and Bishop's Cleeve apart.

Since the PAB group was formed in 1976 it has been successful in defending it; forever keeping vigil against those who would wish to spoil it.

In 2006 CBC engaged independent consultants Applied Environmental Research Centre Ltd (AERC) to conduct an extensive review of the Green Belt in readiness for a future Local Development Framework, which will supersede the present Local Plan in June 2011.

The PAB group were delighted to learn when the findings of the review were published that the land on the north side of Swindon Lane and on the south side of the Racecourse was classified as 'high value Green Belt land'.

I have no doubt that there will be further attempts by developers to build there in the future, and I know that the PAB group, along with the local residents, will stand firm against all-comers.

The lesson to be learned here is that there are substantive planning policies that spell out clearly what should happen in any set of given circumstances and, providing those who have the power to interpret them do so correctly, then we have nothing to fear."

In May 2011, I was informed that Galliard Homes had submitted another planning application for 135 dwellings. On the basis that only the number of dwellings had been reduced with nothing else changing, I agreed with the planning case officer, after consultation with my colleague Cllr Malcolm Stennett, that the application should be refused for the same reasons as before. Accordingly, the case officer refused the application using his delegated powers to do so.

Within the appropriate time scale Galliard Homes requested an appeal hearing. The four day hearing was held in the Municipal Offices starting on 22nd March 2012. It was a costly affair mainly because the applicant was represented by a barrister who called several 'expert' witnesses to support his client's case. CBC also appointed a barrister with additional external planning support.

It was estimated that the cost of defending the appeal would be around £70,000 plus the cost of officer time. Time will tell whether it was money well spent in order to defend the Green Belt along the north side of Swindon Lane.

UNDER THREAT.

The Hunting Butts farm – Swindon Lane

Prestbury residents doing their best to save their palying field from development

The issue was straightforward – the applicant was seeking planning permission for the erection of up to 135 dwellings on agricultural land that was in a designated Green Belt area.

The council's response to the planning inspector was that development around the periphery of Cheltenham was constrained by both the Green Belt and the Cotswold Area of Outstanding Natural Beauty (AONB).

The inspector was aware that part of the reason for the three councils of Cheltenham, Gloucester and Tewkesbury promoting a Joint Core Strategy (JCS) was to take a coherent approach to development. He also accepted the view of CBC that should the land at the Hunting Butts be released for development it would undermine that coherent approach.

This was a very important point to remember when the JCS was being prepared for public examination in 2013.

More on this in the next chapter.

Several local residents attended the hearing and some were allowed to address the inspector with their concerns about the consequences for them and their neighbours should the appeal be allowed.

As the local councillor for the area and a member of the CBC planning committee, I was given the opportunity to speak on behalf of my constituents.

I had prepared copies of my statement which I gave to the inspector and the two barristers before I gave some background information to the inspector on the numerous attempts to develop land on the north side of Swindon Lane during the past thirty years.

In my statement and to the inspector directly, I asked him what I should do as the people's representative should the appeal be allowed and the owner of the adjoining land submits a planning application? "A precedent would have been set", I said, "So how do I defend the situation before the planning committee?"

I may be wrong but I believe I did see a very slight 'nodding of the head' as I continued along this line.

Readers can make their own judgment by reading the following paragraph in the inspector's letter of dismissal of the appeal. This is what he wrote:

> "The council argues that if the appeal proposal were to be approved then it would constitute a salient of development into the Green Belt that would mean that the boundary provided by Swindon Lane would cease to be regarded as permanent. In turn this is likely to lead to further applications on nearby land using similar arguments to those advanced here. In support of this, the council points out that nearby land has previously been the subject of both planning applications for residential development and promotion through successive development plan processes, again for residential development.
>
> I have sympathy with the council's view that approving this proposal would make it more difficult to resist future applications nearby."

In his final conclusion he made the following comment: "In this case I have found that despite the clear benefits of the scheme in meeting some of the housing needs, the particular characteristics of the site means that the totality of the harm would not be clearly outweighed by other considerations and the very special circumstances necessary to justify the development do not exist."

Whilst PAB councillors are devoted to the task of retaining open spaces within the town, we are equally concerned that the local authority has a duty to provide housing for its growing population.

We also recognise that building land is a diminishing resource and unless the council looks at all suitable options for development then we are not going to meet the demand and more pressure will be applied to redraw the Green Belt lines around Cheltenham.

Apart from housing there is also a growing problem with car parking to meet the needs of local people and the thousands of tourists on whom we rely to boost the town's income.

PAB councillors have studied both problems for a long time; we came to the conclusion that as the local authority owns a number of reasonably sized car parks it should offer them to developers for residential development. The quid pro quo would be for the developer to construct underground parking for at least a similar number of car parking spaces and provide houses for those who need them on the land above. A simple equation!

Similarly, we believe that there have been too many lost opportunities to construct underground parking when large scale developments have been approved. My colleague Cllr Malcolm Stennett has repeatedly asked the planning department to amend its planning policies in order to force developers to provide underground parking instead of the easy option of providing wasteful and unattractive surface car parks across the town.

The excuse given by officers, supported by the Liberal Democrat administration, is that underground parking is too much to ask the developer to provide. 'It would cost them too much and the River Chelt, plus the sandy soil, would make it difficult for the contractor to go too deep'.

If one talked to any Civil Engineer they would say that using those kinds of excuses is nonsense; anything is achievable in civil engineering terms.

As for the cost – the town's needs are more important than a developer's profit, in our view.

In recent years the planning department allowed a small development of flats with underground parking to be built in a residential street.

It seems that even the smallest underground parking facility is worth the cost of construction.

In the heart of town there has been a large underground parking facility once used by staff at the Cheltenham & Gloucester Building Society before they moved to Barnwood, Gloucester in 1989.

Another that easily comes to mind is the underground car park in Hyde Park,

London, next to the River Serpentine; our twin town in Annecy, France, has a large underground car park next to the Annecy Lake, so what is the real excuse for not constructing underground parking in Cheltenham?

The Cheltenham General Hospital (CGH) site has large surface car parking areas at the front and at the rear of the site. Apart from the poor utilisation of the available land, it still fails to provide adequate parking facilities for members of its staff and hospital visitors.

A few years ago CGH applied for planning permission to extend the hospital site. PAB thought this would be a good opportunity to tidy up the external appearance of the site and suggested that a major underground parking project should be included in the planning permission.

PAB suggested that if we agreed as a planning authority that there was a need for underground parking then it should not only be constructed under the hospital site but under Thirlstaine Road and the land on the opposite side of the road as well.

Of course, our proposal was immediately met with derision from the Lib/Dem administration; they offered no reasons why it should not be allowed.

PAB councillors were not surprised at the Lib/Dem's answer to our request; it was similar to other suggestions we had made to solve the town's parking problems when we asked for underground parking to be installed under Montpellier Gardens. This was scoffed at too.

We are convinced that in a few years time CBC will see the folly of their ways, show a bit of vision and start looking seriously at the enormous benefits to the town that underground parking can bring.

We are not alone in our thinking about underground parking. An article in the *Gloucestershire Echo* on 15th October 2011 had a headline:

"Major scheme 'could have had underground parking'" It read as follows: "Underground spaces could have been a feature of a £65 million redevelopment of two Cheltenham car parks, according to an architect.

Richard Stanley, of the town-based Stanley Partnership, said there was no reason for developers not to include them in the North Place and Portland Street scheme.

But the firm behind the scheme, Augur Buchler, said it did not want to risk damaging nearby buildings by disrupting water channels. Mr Stanley replied that it was nonsense to say that they could not have included underground parking because they couldn't afford it. It is more about whether it is appropriate for the area, not whether it is affordable.

It is certainly dearer than overground parking, but if you are talking about a supermarket as part of the development, then they could certainly pay for it."

Mr Stanley's view, according to the Echo report, "... came after members of the People Against Bureaucracy Group called for spaces below ground in the scheme."

"The PAB leader Les Godwin said he was delighted that the Stanley Partnership supported this sort of development and we now want more people to support the development in principle. Of course it will be more expensive, but it is about having a vision for the town. If we want the town to stay as it is for the next 50 years then we should carry on with the same sort of development that is being planned for North Place."

Is it simply that the council's 'cash-cow' as Cllr Stennett often puts it, rakes in so much easy money each year from the motorists that they are blind to the fact that investment in underground parking is not only wise, but also it frees up land above it for much needed residential development.

In a letter to the *Gloucestershire Echo* from the person responsible for the council's finances, Cllr John Rawson wrote: "Whether the parking is underground or on the surface is academic, except to the most determined underground parking enthusiast."

A strange comment, but perhaps on this occasion Cllr Rawson let the cat out of the bag. It is precisely because Cheltenham councillors view every suggestion put to them as 'academic' that so little gets done. The list of lost chances grows every year, which is why CBC is always playing 'catch-up' to Gloucester and Bristol because we lack vision for the longer term prospects for the town.

The dictionary meaning of the word 'vision' is foresight, imagination, insight, inspiration, innovation, creativity, farsightedness and many other similar words. But, if CBC fails to get the message, not the academic one, the town will fall further behind our neighbours.

There is no doubt in my mind that one of the most important achievements of the PAB Group during its thirty six years' existence was the installation of several flood alleviation schemes in the parish of Prestbury. The fact that it took most of the thirty six years to achieve a successful resolution of the flooding problems in the village is an indication of how dedicated and persistent PAB councillors have had to be to achieve benefits for their local communities.

To witness the terrible flooding of people's homes every time there was a heavy downpour urged me to do something to alleviate their misery. I had no idea what was necessary in order to prevent the flooding of homes, but I was determined in 1985 to make the lives of TBC officers just as miserable until they agreed to introduce a scheme that would prevent the flooding of homes in Prestbury.

It wasn't easy by any means, and there were those who argued against my proposals on the grounds that they would be a waste of money; others argued that the parish might be transferred to CBC as a result of boundary changes and used this as a means of delaying the decision.

TBC, however, to their credit, did come up with a scheme costing around £265,000 which involved the laying of a pipe from the front entrance of Idsall House in The Bank to a point in Mill Street. It didn't appear to be a very big job and we couldn't forget the fact that it was not connected to anything at either end.

In 1991, as forecast, Prestbury was transferred, along with other peripheral parishes, to Cheltenham.

The first task for PAB councillors was to make sure that CBC kept their side of the bargain by investing money towards the completion of the flood alleviation scheme. The commitment appeared to be on the record and we asked for the pipe placed in the ground by TBC to be connected to the Noverton Brook, which would take excess water directly to the Mill Stream.

Later, with the support of Cllr Stennett, we persuaded CBC to install a flood relief overflow drain from the Racecourse (underground) to Bowbridge Lane.

It was our view that once CBC had completed their work it would automatically be decided that the TBC and the CBC pipes would be connected as quickly as possible.

It was wishful thinking on our part; no matter how often we raised the subject, the two sets of pipes costing £1 million, lay in the ground doing absolutely nothing for several years.

We knew that the amount of ready cash needed to carry out the connecting of the two sets of pipes, was never going to be readily available. But with the support of Michael Smith, (CBC Borough Engineer), a sum of money was added to the 'flood relief' budget each year which was 'ring-fenced' until the sum required to complete the work was reached.

In January 2001 I was informed that tenders had been received for the connection of the two schemes. The estimated cost of the project was put at £490,000. Although this sounded like a lot of money, which it was at the time, it included civil engineering work, culvert manufacture, landscaping, compensation to land owners and overall supervision of the work.

After all the previous disappointments we felt that we were at least going to make some progress and see the pipes connected within the projected three year project.

However, for three years nothing happened in spite of questions being put to officers and members of the CBC cabinet by PAB councillors.

At a council meeting in July 2004 we asked why the connection of the two sets of pipes had not been made with the 'ring-fenced' money. The Leader of the Council informed members that the money had been used for other purposes.

In other words, the money had been 'hi-jacked' by the Lib/Dem administration.

PAB councillors were stunned to hear the answer to our question, and so were other members in the council chamber.

Apart from the sheer arrogance of the statement, I had not even been given the courtesy of a call from the Leader of the Council to tell me what had happened to the 'ring-fenced' money.

The report of the meeting by *Gloucestershire Echo* reporter Jenny Hardcastle on July 29th 2004 had the following headline: "Plug is pulled on anti-flood project – £1 million pipes are laying useless underground".

She reported: "A desperate attempt by Prestbury councillors to salvage a £1 million project to ease flooding in their ward has been rejected. The councillors wanted £50,000 of the CBC underspend to be put towards the drainage scheme.

About £1 million worth of drainage pipes are laying useless underground because the council cannot find the money to connect them.

Cllr Les Godwin told the meeting it was a scandal that £1 million worth of council taxpayers' money is laying in the ground when this project could have been done 10 years ago. He reminded them that cash put aside for the project had vanished into other schemes. We did all the design work and put aside £200,000 to complete the scheme and the money was 'pinched.'"

Cllr Stennett proposed that £50,000 of the underspend money should be earmarked and put into a separate account so that the work could eventually be undertaken.

The amendment was lost by 14 votes to 15 with two abstentions.

Like many parts of the country, Cheltenham suffered from the unprecedented rainfall during July 2007. Prestbury village, because it lies at the foot of the Cotswold Hills, is always vulnerable to flooding. Most of the problems have been caused by poor and inadequate drainage facilities, which successive PAB councillors have been highlighting for a number of years.

It took the flooding in 2007 to make the Highways Department and the Environment Agency realise what we had been saying for years – that the drainage system in the village was poor.

The situation at the time seemed an admirable opportunity for me to write to the Secretary of State for the Environment on 22nd July 2007 explaining the history of the two sets of pipes worth £1 million doing nothing because the local authority and the Environment Agency have refused to fund a scheme that would enable the connection to be made.

I suggested to him that he should write to the Environment Agency urging them to complete the Prestbury Land Drainage Scheme.

A few days later I received a letter from Julius Hinks (Defra Customer Contact Unit) thanking me for my letter and informing me that the Rt. Hon. Hilary Benn MP would be visiting Cheltenham in a whirlwind visit to Gloucestershire to see for himself the flood damage.

Mr Hinks informed me that I could speak to Mr Benn at the Municipal Offices and confirm to him the problems facing my constituents in Prestbury.

This I did, but the 'whirlwind visit' lived up to its name. It was manic in the building with everyone flapping around as if it was a royal visit. All I could do was to confirm to him that a million pounds worth of pipes were lying in the ground and he was gone. I was not impressed.

I wrote a second letter to Mr Benn on 9th August expressing my disappointment with his visit because it appeared that nothing was going to happen regarding the connection of the two sets of pipes.

In conclusion I wrote:

"Mr Julius Hinks (Defra) wrote to remind me that the 'clearing of the existing culvert on the Noverton Brook was carried out last year'. That did not stop the water flowing into people's homes in July, just as it has not stopped the water damaging people's properties for the last twenty years. What is needed, as I explained above, is a connection into the Tewkesbury culvert.

> *Please take another look at the Prestbury Land Drainage Scheme and agree that the two sets of pipes should be connected. When you do this, please take into consideration the awful situation that local residents have to endure each winter, or whenever there is an excess amount of rain*
> *Yours sincerely."*

I didn't receive any other communication from the Secretary of State, so I have no idea whether my letter had any effect at all. However, I did receive a telephone call from the Environment Agency (EA) a week or so later inviting me and Cllr Stennett to a meeting at their Tewkesbury Offices.

Again, the news that central government were proposing to change the status of brooks and streams into rivers meant that from here on in, the EA had responsibility for Noverton Brook and the Mill Stream, which helped our case.

This made our task much easier; we were now able to ask the EA to check out the old schemes and to make a case for investment to improve them.

The situation had changed dramatically in a short space of time; Cllr Stennett and I were invited to attend several meetings with the EA and Gloucestershire County Council (GCC) officials in the Tewkesbury offices of the EA.

We discussed various flood relief options, but in order to reach a successful conclusion we knew that we had to 'broker a deal' between the EA, GCC and CBC to reach a funding arrangement for any flood relief schemes.

Once that had been approved the EA set about devising a number of schemes, some of which interlocked and others that acted independently – all with the purpose of ending the misery of flooding in Prestbury.

It was over a quarter of a century ago when TBC were persuaded to install the first flood relief overflow drain to capture excess water from Noverton Brook.

Since then new improved schemes designed by the EA have been installed. New road drains have been installed in Shaw Green Lane to replace the soak- aways, St. Mary's School has been protected from flooding with flood defence walls. Water is now drained away from New Barn Lane into an underground overflow culvert installed across the Parish Council owned playing field, and there are other schemes too that are equally important.

By 2011, Cllr Stennett and I came to the conclusion that the total amount spent on the Prestbury Flood Alleviation Schemes had passed £2 million, which is quite an achievement for a small independent group such as PAB.

I would not be forgiven if I didn't add a comment that the ditch at Piccadilly Way was dredged and foliage removed, which is now an annual exercise.

Of course with all import schemes such as this one there has to be an official ceremony of cutting the ribbon to announce that the scheme was now officially open.

Laurence Robertson, the Member of Parliament for Tewkesbury and Dafydd Evans from the Midlands Environment Agency did the usual photo shoot of digging a make-believe hole in the ground to allegedly commence the scheme.

Flood water in New Barn Lane, Prestbury, April 2009

After 28 years of discussion, Malcolm Stennett and me welcomed the final phase of the Prestbury Flood Alleviation Scheme in 2013

In the group photograph, I couldn't resist the temptation to produce a hand-written notice which I held in front of me which simply said AT LAST.

On 19th October 2011 the *Gloucestershire Echo* carried a front page headline that read 'Cheltenham-Gloucester greenbelt up for grabs?' It revealed that 'Up to 36,800 homes planned for Gloucestershire in 20 years'.

It was a stunning headline that brought a flood of letters as well as creating groups of objectors across the whole of the county.

The Joint Core Strategy proposals had been released: were they better or worse than the proposals contained in the much derided Regional Spatial Strategy?

The next chapter will set out to answer this question.

CHAPTER 28

Cheltenham, Gloucester And Tewkesbury
Joint Core Strategy

A party of order or stability, and a party of progress or reform, are both necessary elements of a healthy state of political life.

John Stuart Mill (1806–73)

The main theme of this chapter is to explain the beginning and subsequent development of the Joint Core Strategy and the important role the Member Steering Group played in progressing and supervising it.

There are references throughout this chapter to documents that have long ceased to exist, or their title changed to accommodate public and council decisions. The Regional Spatial Strategy (2004 – 2006) for instance, which was the forerunner of the Joint Core Strategy, no longer exists.

The term Local Development Framework is a title used across the country by other local authorities engaged in producing a 20 year development plan, but in Cheltenham recently the term Cheltenham Local Plan appears to be the choice for the future.

At the end of the day it makes little difference what a local authority calls its plan or framework, it will be a document that not only indicates where housing development will take place, but include policies that will protect the parks, open spaces, Conservation Areas and the historical buildings in Regency Cheltenham. The Joint Core Strategy, should it be approved by the Secretary of State, will be a part of the new Cheltenham Local Plan.

Before this stage is reached, it is important to put on record my version of events and the small part I played at the member steering group meetings.

It was at the Cheltenham Borough Council meeting on 17th March 2008 that chief executive, Andrew North, presented a report to members of the council on the 'Local Development Framework – Joint Core Strategy'.

He explained that the Government for the South West had requested an 'in principle' view from Cheltenham, Gloucester and Tewkesbury councils on whether there was any scope/support for the concept of a Joint Core Strategy (JCS) for the three areas.

Although the report had the unanimous support of council members a number of concerns were expressed about the proposed urban extensions and the housing allocation referred to in the Regional Spatial Strategy (RSS) panel report.

The chief executive confirmed that Gloucester City Council (GCC) had agreed in principle to the approach and that Tewkesbury Borough Council (TBC) was 'thinking about it'.

It is worth remembering some of the detail of the RSS report that was published in March 2006 because it caused a storm throughout the county.

A *Gloucestershire Echo* article had a headline: "Say goodbye to county greenbelt – 6,000 homes will be built over 20 years".

The article by Marc Rath suggested that the RSS proposals "…paved the way for hundreds of homes between Bishop's Cleeve and Swindon Village." He added: "Land north of Swindon Village and around Innsworth and Longford looks set to be developed over the next 20 years."

This was only part of the proposals, but the proposal in the RSS report that CBC should provide 8,500 homes over the same period seemed reasonable to me – only because the allocated number of homes in the then current CBC Local Plan (1991 – 2011) was 7,350.

The figure of 8,500 was reduced by the Secretary of State to 8,100 which was even better than the original figure.

It was a point I emphasised at several meetings between 2008 and 2013, and what is more, I still believe that the proposals in the RSS were a better option for Cheltenham than the proposals put forward by the JCS team in July 2013.

There were other interesting points in the RSS such as a reference to the land at Leckhampton, which had been threatened with development in the past; declared safe from development.

According to Marc Rath's report, the chairman of Swindon Village parish council was against the move to remove the Green Belt status from around the village. And Cllr Jordan, according to the report, alleged that he had asked for the Green Belt around Swindon Village to be saved.

The reader will be interested to know whether the alleged comments made in 2008 stood the test of time and whether they will be repeated again later in this chapter.

The existing Local Plan expired in June 2011 and preparations for its replacement began when the JCS was launched in 2008. It was Tracey Crews, the Strategic Land Use Manager, who was in charge of putting together the set of new planning documents which would form the LDF.

A daunting task! But I among several other people believed that Tracey had the skill and determination to achieve the LDF if everything fell into place. There were however many difficulties because the process of achieving a JCS, which ultimately would need to satisfy all three local councils, dominated the process.

Having given approval for an LDF at the 17th March council meeting, councillors then 'tasked the officers across the three local authorities to draft the procedures which would demonstrate how a JCS can be delivered'.

Throughout 2008 there were numerous discussions about the LDF, often centred around other matters such as the development of garden land and infill sites and the possible effect the Supplementary Planning Document (SPD) would have on a

Tracey Crews, Head of Planning, explaining the Leckhampton planning proposal to Alice Ross, a Save the Countryside campaigner

future LDF. [The SPD and its ramifications were described in the previous chapter].

In October 2008 the Secretary of State formally modified the RSS proposals. The result, like the curate's egg, was good in parts – some areas saw an increase in the number of dwellings, and other areas enjoyed a reduction.

At the 17th December council meeting the Leader of the Council, Steve Jordan, updated members regarding the RSS, but the mood of the meeting soon changed when he referred to the council's "frozen funds in the Icelandic banks". His only words of comfort were that the Regional Assembly had urged the Government to support businesses, charities and local authorities with funds deposited and frozen in Iceland – whatever that meant.

There had been plenty of reports in the media about the plight of the banks in Iceland and the possible loss of large sums of money for the investors.

The Chief Finance Officer issued a briefing note explaining that CBC had deposits in three Icelandic banks amounting to £11 million, so there wasn't much comfort in knowing that other local authorities were in the same predicament or that central government were being asked for support.

What PAB councillors wanted to know was how the council had come to invest in foreign banks promising unusually attractive interest rates, when they usually turn out to be a 'dodgy' investment?

The answer given was that the council relied on the advice of external financial advisers; a similar answer given to the questions put by the public when the investment of £22.5 million on the money markets took place in January 1999. [Chapter 15 refers]

Whichever way one looked at it – it seemed that the lessons of 1999 had not been learned.

In February 2008 CBC set up a JCS Member Steering Group (JCS/MSG).

According to the minutes of that meeting which took place in Tewkesbury Borough Council, it was by invitation only and consisted of officers from the three councils, the county council and the leaders of each council.

Grahame Lewis the Assistant Director, Built Environment, was chairman, and Andrew North presented the JCS context and a programme framework for the JCS management team.

A report from the JCS team stated that the JCS was the most important part of the LDF. It added that it would set out the strategic vision for the JCS area and that it would show how the RSS for the south west would be delivered locally.

The meeting agreed to hold bi-monthly meetings of the JCS/MSG and its membership would consist of officers and cross-party councillors from each of the three areas.

An ambitious timetable was proposed with an adoption date of May 2011, but it didn't take long for the timetable to be regarded as nothing more than wishful thinking.

In July 2010 central government announced major changes to the planning system. They also announced their intention to scrap Regional Spatial Strategies, which had set targets for housing and jobs and had subsequently acted as a guideline for joint core strategies across the regions.

Local authorities, according to central government, should establish their own local needs through the local planning system. A Bill to formally scrap Regional Spatial Strategies has still to be presented before Parliament.

Nevertheless, Cheltenham, Gloucester and Tewkesbury councils continued to fill the apparent 'policy vacuum' left by the old RSS, and the JCS team continued the work of completing the strategy based on locally-determined development needs.

With the assistance of external sources, work got underway in 2009/10 to forecast economic and population growth in the JCS area.

The JCS/MSG held regular meetings to determine levels of development; identify possible locations for housing and job creation; and to find ways to foster growth in the local economy which would take the strategy to the year 2031.

However, whilst the process looked easy on paper, in reality, the JCS was constantly changing. One significant change was the removal from the strategy of detailed local development management policies, although they were reinstated later as supporting documents to the JCS document.

In October 2010 the anticipated public consultation period planned for the summer of 2011, was changed to the summer of 2012.

Accompanying the announcement was a caveat reminding everyone that until the adoption of the JCS in 2012, councils would be required to continue using the Gloucestershire Structure Plan and the Local Plan 'saved policies' to guide development in the JCS area.

Unfortunately, planning officers seldom made their recommendations based on the so-called 'saved' Local Plan policies, which often meant that any planning application for development could be recommended for approval.

PAB councillors repeatedly asked the council to update the existing Local Plan in order for the committee, and more importantly the communities, to have control over development in their areas.

There was much talk during 2010 about the intention of central government to introduce a Localism Bill that would devolve greater powers to councils and neighbourhoods. It would, we were told, give communities more control over local housing and planning decisions; empower local people; give communities a real share in local growth, and create a more efficient local planning system.

It sounded as though central government had listened to the voices of the people. The Localism Act was published in November 2011.

Most people have waited patiently for the benefits outlined in the Localism Act to become a reality. Nothing so far has been worthy of any mention, and it looks very much as though the copies will gather dust on the shelves.

The year 2010 was also notable for the number of presentations made to members of the MSG by council officers and external consultants. They were interesting and informative but the content of them was so technical and graphical it was difficult to remember much of it.

Entec UK Limited carried out an 'Urban Extensions Boundary Definition Study' for Cheltenham, Gloucester and Tewkesbury councils and produced a 148 page report on their findings in July 2010.

It was a very comprehensive report providing an up to date assessment of land within the five areas of search that had been identified in the draft revised RSS. It also aimed to define the most appropriate boundary for the urban extensions and the Green Belt.

The five areas of search were north of Gloucester, south of Cheltenham, east of Gloucester, north of Bishop's Cleeve and northwest Cheltenham.

As a Cheltenham councillor I was particularly interested in the chapters relating to the areas south of Cheltenham and northwest of Cheltenham.

Although it was a study document for the members of the MSG, there was a strong emphasis from the officer side that the five areas were the best areas to accommodate future housing and employment requirements.

The five areas of search had potential, but my view at the MSG meeting was that the areas of search should be much wider before any hard and fast decisions were made by the JCS team.

My view was not supported.

Chapter 5 (South of Cheltenham) concerned Leckhampton and Shurdington.

The largest part of the area is located in TBC, but a part of the Leckhampton site is in CBC. The study referred to the fact that there was no relevant planning history, although the land had been considered at the Cheltenham Borough Council *Local Plan Second Review Inquiry* in November 2004.

I had attended the Inquiry and I was interested in what the study had to say about "…the revision of the Green Belt boundary to include the land put forward for the development of 550 dwellings."

The study also referred to the Planning Inspector's comments where he concluded that "… such development would materially harm the rural character and appearance of the area and in particular the contribution it makes to the landscape within the site and when seen from the AONB."

These comments were welcome because I had been one of the objectors at the Inquiry who were concerned about the future of the land.

Entec's assessment of the Green Belt in the Leckhampton area was unclear and inconsistent. In one part it talked about the land not making a significant contribution, and in another it quoted the *Urban Extension Evidence Base Review* which concluded "… the land played a significant role in safeguarding the countryside and preventing the coalescence of Cheltenham and Shurdington."

Although the land at Leckhampton did not rate highly in the *Cheltenham Green Belt Review* in March 2007, it is worth quoting the Inspector's words at the public inquiry when he looked at the longer term prospects for the area. This is what he said:

> "This may not, of course, lead to a change in policy, since the concerns which I have expressed for the landscape of the area may prevail even in this wider geographical context and longer timescale. This work is for other people at another time, however, and here I have tried to consider the approach to be taken within the lifetime of this Plan that best serves the Council's aim – which I support – of protecting this land."

Protecting the countryside and the attempts by PAB councillors in June 1995 to change the status of the land at Leckhampton, which would have given it permanent protection, has been explained in previous chapters.

North West Cheltenham was another area of search carried out by Entec.

The land is located on the north western edge of Cheltenham and is mainly within the administrative boundary of TBC whilst a small north eastern section is located within Cheltenham Borough.

There are a number of settlements within this area of search including the village of Elmstone Hardwicke and a part of Uckington, which is situated beside the A4019 Tewkesbury Road.

The land use is predominantly arable agriculture similar to the farming areas around Swindon Village.

The Green Belt assessment by Entec confirmed that the urban area to the north west of Cheltenham was under severe development pressure. Entec supported the *Strategic Green Belt Review* which had found that the land only fulfilled the Green Belt purposes by encouraging the 'recycling' of brownfield land, which would cause the least potential harm to the Green Belt.

The *Cheltenham Green Belt Review*, which only considered land within Cheltenham, concluded that the area offered a sustainable development option and it

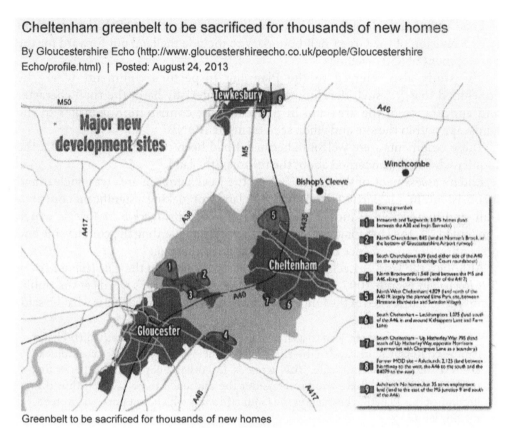

Cheltenham greenbelt to be sacrificed for thousands of new homes

By Gloucestershire Echo (http://www.gloucestershireecho.co.uk/people/Gloucestershire
Echo/profile.html) | Posted: August 24, 2013

Greenbelt to be sacrificed for thousands of new homes

Cheltenham greenbelt to be sacrificed for thousands of new homes

contributed least to Green Belt purposes. The study also concluded that the existing
Green Belt boundaries at North West Cheltenham were relatively weak.

It was disappointing to read the conclusions in each review, which would make it
extremely difficult for local residents to offer a counter-argument.

Subsequent reviews and assessment of the land in NW Cheltenham by the
consultants Environment & Infrastructure UK Limited (AMEC) in September
2011, only confirmed the views expressed by other organisations.

So the five areas of search by Entec in their final report in July 2010 became the
principal discussion points whenever the MSG met.

The CBC Local Plan (1991 – 2011) officially came to the end of its 20 year cycle
on 30th June 2011. Whilst central government had agreed that policies in the Plan
should be saved, PAB councillors took the view that an updated Local Plan would
be more effective as a planning tool when dealing with planning applications.

We tried repeatedly in 2011 and 2012 to persuade the Liberal Democrat administration to agree to set up a working group in order to bring the Local Plan up to
date. On every occasion our proposals were turned down.

It was difficult to understand why the Liberal Democrats were so adamant in refusing to have the Local Plan updated when it could have established new tables setting out the locations that would have been suitable for housing development within the Borough.

If the working group, for example, had decided not to include the land at Leckhampton and New Barn Lane as sites for development, then they would have remained open spaces for the local communities to enjoy.

The open countryside at both locations would have been safe from predator developers.

Additionally, the working group would have had the opportunity to include the land at Gloucester Road, the Oakley (GCHQ) site, Bouncers Lane and many others in an updated Local Plan.

Furthermore, the council could have heeded the advice from Eric Pickles, Secretary of State for the Environment & Local Government, who urged local authorities to update their Local Plans. Again, the council ignored this advice, just as they have repeatedly ignored the same advice in the National Planning Policy Framework (NPPF) document published in March 2012.

The NPPF states clearly in several paragraphs that Local Plans should be brought up-to-date. Paragraph 12 states: *"The NPPF does not change the statutory status of the development plan as the starting point for decision making. Proposed development that accords with an up-to-date Local Plan should be approved and proposed development that conflicts should be refused unless other material considerations indicate otherwise.*

It is highly desirable that local planning authorities should have an up-to-date plan in place."

Nothing could have been clearer, but the Liberal Democrat administration preferred not to have an up-to-date Local Plan, which meant that any planning application submitted was invariably recommended for approval.

Paragraph 14 stated amongst other things that *"...where the development plan is absent, silent or relevant policies are out-of-date, means granting planning permission..."*

In nearly every planning application case, the reason given for allowing development was on the grounds that it was "sustainable development". Of course they were "sustainable" because there was no up-to-date Local Plan to indicate that the sites that were suitable; or whether the local circumstances had been taken into account.

On 12th July 2012, CBC arranged a presentation for council members by a leading member of the Cambridge Centre for Housing and Planning Research (CCHPR).

His brief was to explain the possible changes in population projections, which could affect the final JCS proposals.

To give support to the presentation, CBC invited Celina Colquhoun, a London barrister, who is regarded as a leading planning junior in her Chambers. She specialised in all aspects of planning, environmental and compulsory purchase law, as well as Local Government & Public and Administrative Law.

The lady had an impeccable background and I am sure that her presence brought in extra officers and councillors wanting to hear what she had to say.

My colleague, Cllr Malcolm Stennett, who was sitting next to me, asked Celina Colquhoun whether local councils should update their Local Plans. "Yes councillor" she answered, "Tout de suite."

We could not have wished for a better reply from an independent leading planning lawyer in our efforts to achieve an updated Local Plan that was worthy of the name.

Following the seminar I wrote to Celina Colquhoun to tell her that in spite of her encouraging words, CBC did not intend to update its Local Plan.

Whether it was coincidence, or whether it was due to the constant pressure from PAB councillors, CBC announced that a JCS Planning and Liaison Overview and Scrutiny Working Group (PLWG) would be established.

Its purpose would be to act as a sounding board for the JCS/MSG meetings and to develop a future LDF.

[The LDF would incorporate policies from the final JCS document as well as existing Local Plan policies].

The working group had a wide brief which included the task of evaluating alternative methods of assessing household formation rates over the JCS plan period and then feeding their conclusions and recommendations into the JCS "Preferred Option" process for consideration by the MSG.

Cllr Ian Bickerton was elected chairman of the PLWG and he was good at the job. He understood national population movements including net migration figures, birth rates and deaths over various periods of time.

He was able to transform them into easily understood statistics, but his knowledge on this and household sizes, plus his repeated claims that the figures used by the JCS team were flawed, often got under the skin of the officers.

Nevertheless, his study and eventual calculations usually turned out to be more accurate than those supported by the officers, and surprisingly his stance against accepting whatever figures were put in front of him was looked upon with disdain by his Liberal Democrat colleagues rather than supporting him.

He also held the view that unless the Local Plan was updated it would be an 'open door for the developers'.

With Cllr Bickerton on my side I tried to persuade the PLWG to support the idea of an updated Local Plan, even quoting the words of Mr Pickles who said: "The NPPF states that every local planning authority in England should have a clear, up-to-date Local Plan, which conforms to the framework, meets local development needs and reflects local people's views of how they wish their community to develop."

Whilst some of the working group members added comments in support of an updated Local Plan, when it came to supporting it at the council meeting, they simply followed the 'party political line'.

In an email response to me on the same subject, Tracey Crews wrote: "...the intention behind the adoption of these policies [Local Plan] was to accommodate the *housing requirement for Cheltenham up to 2011. The Plan does not cover housing and employment need which will continue to arise after that date. Therefore, the location sites mentioned in policies PR1 and PR2 cannot now be seen as the only locations which should be developed."*

Tracey Crews was right. The Local Plan should have been updated in 2011 so that it would have specified the sites that were suitable for housing and employment development.

The problem as far as I could see was that the officers did not accept this logic, which explains why some sites have been developed and other green field sites are continually under threat.

An updated Local Plan could have contained the various brownfield sites that have remained vacant and derelict for years: with a caveat that sites with or without planning permission would be compulsory purchased within three years unless they were developed.

That would have solved Cheltenham's housing problem. But a local authority without the vision of encouraging underground parking is less likely to take even bolder steps to solve its housing problems.

In a letter to the *Gloucestershire Echo* on 29th February 2012 I covered the same points. This is a précis:

"One of the largest brownfield sites in Cheltenham, North Place with its public surface car parks, was a golden opportunity to take the pressure off possible countryside development. A new well-designed urban structure creating improvements to the public realm, including attractive housing and a town centre gateway with links to the principal points in the town was the way forward.

Instead, the Lib/Dem administration opted for fewer homes, more surface car-parking, a hotel and a food store – just what we didn't need."

A later proposal included a multi-storey car park, which only added to my despair. In my view, the North Place site was ideal for the start of an urban renaissance of the town centre, which would have created much needed vitality.

However, a further set-back came with the house-builder pulling out of the project, which meant that the start has been further delayed while we await a new bidder in September 2014.

Three years after the *Gloucestershire Echo* published its startling headline: "Say goodbye to county Green Belt", it published another edition on Wednesday 19th October 2011 with another headline claiming 'Cheltenham-Gloucester Green Belt up for grabs'.

It claimed that 36,800 houses could be built over the next 20 years.

The article by Robin Jenkins said:

"Greenbelt land between Cheltenham and Gloucester could be up for grabs if a long-term plan to build tens of thousands of new houses gets the go-ahead.

Under a draft version of the Joint Core Strategy being put together by the district councils of Cheltenham, Tewkesbury and Gloucester, the possible development of some land between the two main urban areas is suggested. It includes the site occupied by Gloucestershire Airport.

It forms part of a document which, if approved, could see 36,800 houses being built over the next 20 years – that is the equivalent of a town nearly half the size of Cheltenham."

The article then went on to state that "Green Belt sites at Swindon Village, Uckington and Leckhampton have been included as areas which could be built on, despite campaigners having battled against such a move for years."

The article about the JCS proposals covered two pages, and it surprised me to read about the detail that had been discussed at the MSG simply because the MSG is a non-voting member steering group, so I wondered how and why the article came into the hands of the local newspaper.

Not that the article was incorrect in any way, and not that the general public should not be made aware of such important proposals, but it would have been nice if the members of the MSG had had sight of the document before it appeared in the local newspaper.

Needless to say, the matter of disclosure was debated at subsequent meetings and it was agreed that a 'Joint Core Strategy – Developing a Preferred Option (Summary Guide)' would be published in January 2012.

This guide explained the purpose of the JCS; the period it covered and four scenarios which it invited the general public to comment on.

They were Scenario A 16,200 houses: Scenario B 33,200 houses: Scenario C 36,850 and Scenario D 40,500.

The consultation period was three months and a number of venues staffed by officers from the three councils answered numerous questions from members of the public.

Not surprisingly, the majority of those who attended the exhibitions voted for Scenario A, a lesser number for Scenario B and only a few opted for Scenarios C and D. But having asked the public for their views and opinions, the JCS team ignored the findings. It still rankles with the campaigners and it did raise the question that if the JCS team were hoping that everyone would opt for Scenario B, or even C or D, then why did the 'team' bother to put Scenario A in the consultation document.

By this time the JCS/MSG, which incidentally was chaired by Cllr Steve Jordan (CBC), studied several reports about housing needs for the JCS area, much of which I have to confess went over the top of my head.

I was not alone about this, and in all honesty and with the greatest will in the world, it was very difficult to take in all that was written in the pages of the numerous reports that came before the elected members of the MSG.

One fifty-page report, plus tables and appendices, on "Assessment of Housing Needs" was presented to the MSG by the authors Nathaniel Lichfield & Partners (NLP) on 12th September 2012.

The presentation by NLP was very professional. It supported the higher number of houses for the JCS area. The presentation was, without doubt, aimed at the councillors on the committee – we were the ones, after all, who had to 'sell' the report to our group members.

But it was on the content of the NLP report that the officers, particularly those who sat on the Cross Boundary Programme Board (CBPB), had come to the conclusion that the methodology used in the future would be based upon data from the Office of National Statistics (ONS) and data from the Department for Communities & Local Government. The officers claimed "…it was because the information will be consistently available and subject to on-going updating".

All the information that the MSG members were given over the following months was part of what was repeatedly called "developing the preferred option".

Apart from the constant projection of different sets of figures, the MSG, at the September meeting, agreed:"The JCS needs to balance environmental, social and economic issues and that the social and environmental impact of the 'objectively assessed housing need' will be considered in preparing the preferred option."

2012 was a busy year for the CBPB, the MSG and the members of council staff who produced the discussion papers. Most of the early months of 2012 were taken up with: –

> Agreeing a JCS programme,
> A study of the impending NPPF,
> A presentation by the Planning Advisory
> Service (PAS) on 'taking the JCS forward',
> A review of public consultation, and
> A review of a consultant's report on 'housing assessment'.

In September we received reports from NLP and the CCHPR on new household projections and their implications for the JCS area.

Further discussions on objectively assessed needs, an infrastructure delivery plan, flood risks, habitat regulations and gypsy traveller sites, were only a few of the topics discussed at the regular meetings.

Cllr Steve Jordan the Leader of CBC and chairman of the JCS/MSG was finding it increasingly difficult, in my view, to act as an independent chairman.

From my perspective, I thought he was finding it difficult to be loyal to the MSG and to the CBC Liberal Democrats with news about the 'preferred option'; and the possible loss of Green Belt land in the Cheltenham area.

I was not surprised therefore, to learn that steps were being taken to find someone who was independent of the MSG and who preferably lived outside the JCS area.

In December the MSG discussed the possibility of establishing programme 'gates'. These were break-points where the proposals were of such high merit, the MSG had to agree that they should 'pass through the gate' to allow the next stage of the strategy to commence.

It was an unusual alternative to the long-established voting system, but upon reflection, if voting had been part of the terms of reference of the MSG, rather than the 'passing through the gate' system, I wonder if the conclusions in 2013 and 2014 would have been any different.

At the 19th December meeting, members of the MSG were introduced to Jim Claydon who had agreed to become the new independent chairman.

Jim is a town planning consultant with 40 years experience in local government. He offers advice and his expertise to organisations in both the public and private sectors.

Among Jim's skills is the ability to lead projects and to manage teams involved in spatial planning, master planning, marine planning and regeneration.

Jim Claydon outlined his background and he confirmed his understanding of the terms of reference for the independent chairman.

I soon became impressed with Jim's style; he seemed to be the ideal person to lead the JCS/MSG through what I believed was going to be a difficult period.

He soon got into his stride at the meeting – I suspected that he had been very well briefed before he took on the job.

The matter of household formation rates and a discussion on the economic assessment project by the Local Economic Partnership (LEP) soon showed that Jim was on top of his brief.

In January 2013 the MSG had a presentation by Capita Symonds on "Flood Risk Assessment", and another presentation by CCHPR on the work of the new CBC Overview and Scrutiny Working Group on the recommendations contained in a household formation report.

Not to be outdone, Gloucestershire First representatives gave a presentation on their emerging economic plan, and once more MSG members debated the Objectively Assessed Need (OAN) for the JCS area.

All of it interesting information, but I am sure, like me, a great deal of it went over the heads of my councillor colleagues. It was comforting to know that the councillors did not have to vote on any of it, and none of it was so crucial that it needed to "pass through the gate".

At the conclusion there was agreement that the issue of household formation rates had now been completed and the issue was now closed.

On 17th May 2013 a presentation was given by NLP on housing figures; another presentation on household formations in the JCS area was given by CCHPR.

Tracey Crews gave a presentation on objectively assessed need and the urban capacity with a strong reference to the 2011 census figures. She also spoke about the work of LEP and their statement on projected growth covering the period up to 2025.

Some councillors questioned the reliability of the 2011 ONS figures particularly as household formations in the JCS area had changed dramatically in recent years. It was agreed that there were a number of factors bringing about the change; young people spending longer times with their parents; more people going into shared households rather than forming 'couple households'. These two factors alone gave concerns among the members that the final house numbers may not be as many as was originally projected.

Neil McDonald (CCHPR) accepted the possibilities of change, but added a note of caution that as the economy grows so would the projections.

Earlier work of the council officers had included the evidence-based information and a forecasting model.

The forecast revealed a need for up to 46,000 dwellings.

MSG members noted that the work done by CCHPR reflected the latest census data leading to a recommended ONS figure in the range of 33,200 to 37,400.

I noted that the figure had come down but not nearly enough in my opinion.

The figures apparently had been endorsed by NLP.

An unexpected but interesting question by Cllr Steve Jordan at the start of the meeting asked "Whether consultation on the Cheltenham Borough Local Plan and the Joint Core Strategy should take place at the same time or separately." The response from an officer was that "the matter is under consideration".

I tried to get a discussion underway on the out-of-date Cheltenham Local Plan, on the strength of the question, but was told that a new Local Plan was being considered, and at the appropriate time it would run in parallel with the JCS.

Of course, it was idle rhetoric; the Local Plan has continued to remain out-of-date and will remain so until the JCS is approved sometime in 2015.

The PAB group considered the answer inadequate.

We have remained concerned that during this void period, planning applications will continue to arrive in the planning department, and with no 'site locations' policy, local councillors will continue to find it difficult to argue against unwarranted development on behalf of local residents.

The format for the MSG meeting on Friday 7th June 2013 was different. Members received supporting documents to the agenda items, which centred on a possible future joint core strategy.

A quick look at the supporting documents and I soon came to the conclusion that after five years of listening to presentations and officer reports, we were approaching the end of a long road leading to a structure that would prove to be difficult for people to accept across the JCS area.

The chairman introduced three additions to the JCS team: County Councillor Will Windsor-Clive; Barbara Maksymiw, an officer from Gloucester City Council; and Julie Wood, an officer from Tewkesbury Borough Council.

Were these additions to the JCS team to give added weight to the CBPB, or did they have a specialist input to the strategy? Only time would tell.

This was followed by the distribution of a draft copy of a Vision Statement by the JCS/CBPB on behalf of the three local authorities. It was debated and approved. [A copy of the Vision statement is included at Appendix 4].

Then Tracey Crews introduced and explained the approach to a distribution strategy centred around three headings – rural dispersal, new settlements and urban extensions.

She then defined a draft policy, which she hoped "would provide a clear steer and support for the overall approach".

The draft distribution strategy over the plan period, we were told, would provide between 21,800 and 28,200 new jobs and 33,200 to 37,400 new homes together with supporting services, facilities and infrastructure.

She emphasised that the figures were based on latest housing and population forecast work and would be disaggregated down to the district and JCS areas.

There was a lot of detailed information in the presentation, but I was particularly interested in the part of the distribution strategy that centred on the Green Belt.

It stated that the Green Belt boundary would be redrawn to accommodate growth and to provide an enduring boundary which would protect Cheltenham and Gloucester and Cheltenham and Bishop's Cleeve from coalescing.

The Green Belt seemed less secure however when Tracey Crews said that the strategy would contain a presumption in favour of development based on standard policies for all plans and based on advice from the planning inspectors.

The chairman concluded the meeting by saying that the next meeting of the MSG would take place on 28th June when information concerning spatial policies and a summary of the strategic sites would be presented to the committee.

I had already come to the conclusion that development on brownfield sites and 'white' land should not be included as possible location sites where there were poor transport links, poor community facilities, and no provision for public green spaces.

As for Green Belt land, it would be a 'no-go' area for development if the land satisfied any of the five recognised purposes set out in Chapter 9 in the NPPF.

The five purposes of the Green Belt have been the bedrock on which planning applications have been determined in the past, and clearly stated in the former Planning Policy Guidance PPG2 as well as the current NPPF.

[The five purposes can be seen at Appendix 5].

The next meeting of the JCS/MSG took place at CBC on 28th June 2013.

I felt a tenseness as I entered the room; I had no idea what was in the Strategic Sites Presentation but I feared the worst.

The chairman introduced the agenda item and explained that the objective of the meeting was to consider the recommendations put forward by the CBPB and to look at their choices. There would be time to reflect and consult with those who needed to know, and at the next meeting on 11th July members would be in a position to decide whether the document was a sound basis on which to proceed with the JCS.

The chairman added: "The CBPB have recommended 21 areas/broad locations around the edge of Tewkesbury, Cheltenham and Gloucester as well as other locations that were capable of providing deliverable development.

The Cotswold Area of Outstanding Natural Beauty has not been considered."

My first reaction was one of surprise – 21 broad locations. When had we been given the slightest hint during the numerous presentations by consultants or officers that there were going to be 21 sites presented for consideration?

When the Regional Assembly's ill-fated Regional Spatial Strategy had been discussed in earlier meetings, we had been left in no doubt that only the areas of Swindon Village and Leckhampton would be included in the JCS, but not others in the Cheltenham area.

I looked at the first page of the recommended potential locations and my worst fears were realised. Cheltenham C2 Option 1 showed land from the level crossing to the old Honeybourne railway line in Swindon Lane as being a potential development site.

C2 Option 2 was even worse; it showed the same area as in Option 1 plus the addition of the Hunting Butts site, which CBC had successfully defended at a planning appeal in May 2012.

[Readers will recall that defence of the Hunting Butts appeal had cost the council taxpayer more than £70,000].

How could the CBPB make such a recommendation when they were well aware of the history concerning the land on the north side of Swindon Lane; the cost of the appeal; and the important fact that the land had been classified as significant Green Belt land by two independent consultants? (AERC and AMEC).

The three councils knew this so why had they ignored it?

As expected, the land at N W Cheltenham (Swindon Village) had been included, and three options were submitted for the land at Leckhampton. I knew in my heart of hearts that the land was vulnerable, and it didn't help when I remembered the valiant efforts of PAB councillors to amend the CBC Local Plan when it was reviewed in 1995.

There was worse to come. The CBPB had recommended that the Green Belt land on the south side of Up Hatherley Way should accommodate residential or a mixture of residential and employment development.

To support their proposal, which would have meant the breaching of a robust and permanent Green Belt line at Up Hatherley Way, the CBPB suggested that a new strong line could be created along Chargrove Lane.

They clearly had not visited the area, for if they had, they would have seen that Chargrove Lane is half the width of Up Hatherley Way and more importantly, Up Hatherley Way is part of the South West Distributor Road that connects the A46 with the Golden Valley.

There were, of course, other sites in the Tewkesbury and Gloucester areas, and representatives from these areas expressed similar concerns with the proposals.

Perhaps the biggest surprise was to find proposals to allow housing, or a mixture of housing and employment, on land at Gloucestershire Airport.

It was an unbelievable suggestion because the same people, who had recommended the proposals, were telling the MSG in previous meetings that the economic success for the county during the JCS period depended to a large degree on the continuing success of the airport.

The land around the Hayden Works was proposed as being suitable for employment purposes, and we were told that discussions with Severn Trent would be undertaken.

Discussions also took place on the Highnam G8 recommendations for urban extensions and the allocation of some land for employment purposes. Considering that land around Highnam is unallocated land (white land), it seemed to me that it was an ideal location for some housing due to its closeness to Gloucester.

Cllr Derek Davies, the senior representative from Tewkesbury, did not agree with the suggestion and there was some exchange of views between him and representatives from GCC as well as disagreement with him from members of his own council.

But when the discussions became heated, the officers intervened by claiming that the inclusion of the Highnam site depended on its alignment with the core strategy and known infrastructure problems, before it could become accepted as a potential site.

If that was the case, then why had the CBPB included Highnam in the 21 allocations, unless it had been included only to look generous by removing it later?

In my opening comments I referred to the discussions that had taken place regarding the location sites within the JCS area, but what had been presented to the MSG that day were sites that had not been mentioned once in the previous five years.

I added: "Once again, the 'goal posts' had been shifted and it was not good enough".

Cllr Steve Jordan referred to C2 Option 1 (Swindon Lane) claiming that it "contradicted all aspects of the Green Belt, therefore why not include all Green Belt land".

Tracey Crews appeared to agree with him stating that "the officers had similar concerns".

My response was to tell the meeting that the significance of the Green Belt along Swindon Lane was there for all to see, and any attempt to change its status would be met with strong resistance from me and the local residents.

Each proposal was debated at length and some of the alternative options were removed from the document.

It was not a good meeting from my perspective and I sought clarity about the release of the 21 options to members of the public.

Andrew North, chairman of the CBPB said: "There was a need for confidentiality, but he was not unhappy with elected members sharing the information with their groups but it would be premature to share the information with the general public."

It made sense, if only on the basis that the next meeting of the MSG on July 11th would be a further review of the sites to determine which sites should be included in a preferred option document.

Prior to the next MSG meeting CBC councillors were invited to a briefing seminar by Tracey Crews on objectively assessed need and potential JCS strategic sites.

The seminar was well attended and she explained that 21 broad locations had been searched for development opportunities around the JCS area. This included 4 broad locations around Cheltenham.

Tracey then explained which areas of the broad locations had been identified as having initial suitability for further investigation as to their development potential. "The first site" said Tracey Crews," was North West Cheltenham (Swindon Village), providing the necessary infrastructure was put into place."

Members were aware that the site was close to the retail park and other employment areas, making the site a sustainable option.

But the second, third and fourth locations at Swindon Lane, Leckhampton and Up Hatherley were not accepted as suitable by the councillors and they questioned the methodology used by the officers in order to come to their conclusions.

There were other comments about the significance of the Green Belt at Swindon Lane and Up Hatherley; officers were vigorously questioned on why the two areas had been included.

I reminded the meeting that two independent Green Belt Reviews had taken place in 2007 and 2011, confirming their importance as Green Belt.

I recalled the result of the 1995 planning inquiry into the Leckhampton land, and the planning inspector's suggestion that the 'white' land should be treated as though it was Green Belt.

Philip Stephenson, who had been introduced as a member of the CBC strategic planning team, explained that he had been asked to look at the inevitable changes to Green Belt boundaries should the proposed sites be approved.

He then surprised members by declaring that it would also be an ideal time to look at all Green Belt boundaries including the land on the south side of the Racecourse abutting the rear of the properties in New Barn Lane.

My response was immediate. I told him that it was an ill-thought out suggestion and it was unworthy of the council to even think about changing the status of the Green Belt around the Racecourse.

I suggested to him as a new member of the JCS team that he would be wise to look at the past history of the site including a planning inquiry that had taken place in 1984. I told him that the inspector had dismissed the appeal for 46 dwellings because the Green Belt played an important part in preventing the northern part of Cheltenham from merging with Bishop's Cleeve.

The response I received from Mr Stephenson was that it was "only a tidying-up exercise" which would enable more commercial development to take place within the Racecourse.

It was total nonsense of course; development within the built-up area of the Racecourse had taken place for the previous thirty years.

The longer the seminar went on the more I came to the conclusion that it was a softening up exercise prior to the MSG meeting in a few days time.

The 11th July 2013 meeting of the MSG, which took place at Gloucester City Council (GCC), was unusual for a number of reasons; Cllr Steve Jordan was absent, and so was Andrew North (CBC Chief Executive).

Cllr Paul James, Leader of GCC was absent, so was Mike Dawson (TBC Chief Executive).

Cllr Roger Whyborn (Up Hatherley) deputised for Cllr Jordan and Cllr Gerald Dee for Cllr James.

I am always suspicious about the absence of key players at a special or important meeting. Cllr Steve Jordan had not been absent from a previous MSG meeting, as far as I could recall, since the MSG had been established in 2008.

Was it because the discussions on the Up Hatherley Way and Leckhampton sites would place him in a difficult position in view of his position as Leader of the Council as well as being the group leader of the Liberal Democrats?

Being the former chairman of the MSG might also have been a further embarrassment to him should he be called upon him to state his preferences on the two sites. On the other hand, he may have had other reasons.

However, Cllr Whyborn deputised for him.

The chairman opened the meeting by reminding members that the main purpose of the meeting was to get the preferred options 'through the gate'. [This was an expression used to signify MSG approval].

In the 'explanation of the preferred option' document a reference was made to Highnam not aligning with the spatial strategy. It also re-stated that the village had infrastructure issues. The report added a note that there was no known developer interest in Highnam. Not at Up Hatherley either.

It seemed that these points were only applicable to the Highnam site, but my view was that they could be applied to any other site as well.

Cllr Derek Davies, lead member for TBC, "noted the sterling work of the JCS team", adding "TBC is a large contributor of land, and the basic JCS plan should be agreed."

Cllr Davies also stated that TBC was in general agreement that the plan should be the basis for the preferred options, but Cllr Jude Perez (Lib/Dem), a TBC councillor, made it clear she was not of the same opinion.

I restated the importance of the Green Belt along Swindon Lane and Up Hatherley and I made it clear that I would not support the preferred options while they contained these two areas.

Cllr Whyborn spoke for several minutes about the strategy and the preferred options, but I found it hard to follow his logic regarding the housing numbers for Cheltenham and the suitability of Leckhampton and Up Hatherley as strategic sites.

He thought the housing numbers were too high suggesting that "a figure of approximately 33,000 should be put forward with a smaller number of sites".

He also thought that Cheltenham could contribute substantially to the 10,000 dwellings figure for Cheltenham but predicated on completion of Junction 10.

As for the Leckhampton and Up Hatherley sites, Cllr Whyborn stated: "... the sites were predicated on decent infrastructure; a park and ride facility; the alleviation of traffic problems; and provision of green spaces."

With regard to Up Hatherley specifically, Cllr Whyborn said: "... there was a significant problem with over-development and the site would need a substantial green buffer along Up Hatherley Way."

I listened to the comments with interest, but it wasn't what I wanted to hear.

Tracey Crews, on the other hand, thought that the comments made by Cllr Whyborn on the Cheltenham housing figures and the need to "finesse" them , as he had put it, were sensible because the final figure must 'stack up at examination'.

Each of the proposed sites was examined in detail and the councillors representing the JCS areas spoke at length on most of the proposed locations.

Gloucester councillor Jeremy Hilton (Lib/Dem) argued strongly that Highnam should not be discounted in the preferred option, adding that it was closer to Gloucester than the sites at Innsworth and Churchdown, which was true.

In my final comments to the committee I said:

> "There appears to be reluctance on the part of several members of the MSG to accept the package in its present state. Amendments and deletions could be made so that the preferred options could be approved.
>
> I am particularly concerned about the disregard that has been shown concerning the breach of the Green Belt at Swindon Lane and Up Hatherley Way, which is part of the South West Distributor Road. Whilst there are some aspects of the proposals that are defendable, I am not prepared to vote for the proposals as they now stand.
>
> And I would certainly not support any proposal that breached existing Green Belt lines which have been established over a long period of time, and re-established by both AERC and AMEC consultants."

The matter of Highnam being included as one of the location sites came up repeatedly from several councillors, but on each occasion there was a robust refusal by Cllr Davies to have the village included. After one intervention he stated that 'he had already agreed with the proposal put forward by Tracey Crews, and that it was totally wrong to discuss the Highnam site that was not even included in the proposals'.

Cllr Philip Workman (TBC) told the meeting 'he was disappointed with what he had heard, adding that the people of Tewkesbury had been hoping for a different outcome especially as Tewkesbury was taking a lot of the development'.

He stated: "The complaints regarding the Cheltenham area were being raised at a late stage in the process, which was disappointing"

Considering that some of the sites had been included at a late stage in the process, it was not surprising that they were the subject of discussion by so many councillors.

Jim Claydon, the MSG chairman, asked members to consider the package which he claimed would be for public consultation and comment.

Much to my surprise he then stated that in order to get a consensus of views, he would be calling for a vote.

As a result, the official record showed that those in favour of the 'package' were Cllrs Paul James (GCC), Tim Harman (CBC) Derek Davies (TBC) and Cllr Phil Workman (TBC).

Councillors against the 'package' were Cllr Les Godwin (CBC), Cllr Roger Whyborn (CBC), Cllr Jude Perez (TBC) and Cllr Jeremy Hilton (GCC).

With apologies from the chairman for breaching the terms of reference of the MSG, he announced that the voting was even at 4 votes for and 4 against.

It had not been a good meeting. Apart from the 'battle' lines that had been drawn, we knew who stood for what and which locations should be added and those that should be removed from a future consultation document.

From what had been said at the meeting, there was a lot of work to be done by the JCS team before any consultation document was presentable to the general public.

The MSG meetings that took place in August 2013 were mainly about the steering group looking at proposals and changes that had been made by the CBPB to the 'draft' document. The group reviewed a 'draft core strategy for the JCS area', which would be presented as a 'draft' consultation document later in the year, subject to further amendments.

In spite of my comments regarding the inclusion of land at Up Hatherley Way and the supposed 'tidying-up' of the Green Belt around the Racecourse, the document received tacit approval.

At the MSG meeting on 14th August the chief executives reported that discussions had taken place within their councils on the preferred options, and although there had been some adverse comments by some members, they were all fairly confident that the 'draft' document would be approved by their respective councils in September.

The MSG agreed that the next meeting would take place on 20th August to recap and note any changes that may have been made. They would agree a timetable when all three councils would discuss the JCS team's report.

The timetable for the three councils was as follows: 3rd September – Tewkesbury: 5th September: Cheltenham: 12th September: Gloucester.

Jonathan Dibble (Programme Manager), reminded members of the recommendation that would be submitted at the 20th August meeting. It would state:

"1.   The councils would approve for public consultation the Draft Joint Core Strategy.
2.   The Response Report on consultation carried out to date will be published as part of the consultation exercise."

Another added item read:

"That authority is delegated to the lead officer in consultation with the lead member and the JCS MSG, to make any necessary minor amendments to the draft JCS as considered appropriate by the three councils in the partnership."

The statement, in my view, was woolly and did not amount to very much. If only 'minor' amendments were going to be allowed and only if they were deemed necessary, then I felt the councils (all three of them) had a 'fight' on their hands.

There was much speculation about the outcome of the CBC meeting to be held on Thursday 5th September 2013.The news that the council meeting would decide whether to accept the JCS document, allowing it to go out for public consultation, was always going to attract a full public gallery.

The *Gloucestershire Echo* gave the meeting plenty of publicity and not unexpectedly, the gallery was full with standing room only.

The mayor, Cllr Wendy Flynn (Lib/Dem) opened the meeting by welcoming the members of the public to the meeting. She explained how she would conduct the meeting, which was in essence going to be a strict adherence to the council rules. The prospect of a debate across the floor of the chamber was shattered when she reminded members that their time to speak on the JCS Consultation Document would be no different from any other agenda item.

In other words, speeches on the main topic would be limited. Clearly, at the pre-council briefing in the mayor's parlour, this decision had been made in order to restrict debate, particularly for those who would be against the document being approved and going out for public examination.

The mayor has the power to "suspend Standing Orders" which enables councillors to speak longer than five minutes and on more than one occasion.

Considering it was an important matter, probably the most important one the council had had to deal with for a long time, one would have thought that in the interests of democracy, the Standing Orders would have been suspended.

After all, the council had suspended standing orders when dog-fouling in the town was discussed only a few months earlier.

Public and members questions were the first item on the agenda and there were several. They were all dealt with in the usual manner, but no public debate on any of them was allowed.

The draft public consultation document was introduced by Cllr Steve Jordan, Leader of the Council. He told council that the Joint Core Strategy was the strategic plan being prepared in order to provide a framework for development in Gloucester, Cheltenham and Tewkesbury up to 2031.

He said: "The report summarises the draft JCS and seeks council approval to publish the document for public consultation." He added, "Subject to the approval of the JCS for public consultation, the outcome will be reported back to the council together with the draft Pre-Submission version of the plan. There would be further consultation prior to the formal submission to the Secretary of State for an examination in public by the independent planning inspectorate."

The mayor invited councillors to ask questions on the report, which would be answered by the Leader of the Council or the Head of Planning, Tracey Crews.

A number of questions were asked including what 'weight' the document would have in a future planning application. Other questions on household formation rates and their review during the consultation period, plus population projections for the end of the plan period in 2031 were also put.

They were all answered positively by Tracey Crews, but unfortunately the minutes of the council meeting do not indicate which councillor asked which question. I can, however, refer to my questions which were as follows:

1. The penultimate paragraph on page 28 refers to "an increased risk of speculative planning applications" – in Cheltenham's case, isn't this because we do not have an up-to-date Local Plan?
2. With reference to the third paragraph on page 38 "In the absence of a 5–year supply of housing land", what weight should councillors give to this statement when a joint letter dated 22nd November 2012 to the developer of the Kidnappers/Farm Lane proposed development stated that 'CBC does not consider that it has under-delivered in the provision of housing; that it has a shortfall of 315 houses when compared against the draft Regional Spatial Strategy (RSS) requirements; considers it has met its housing requirements under the Gloucestershire Structure Plan'.
3. With the permissions granted since November 2012 to the present day, would it be wrong for councillors and the general public to believe that even the shortfall of 315 houses would have been met by now?
4. The recent Briefing Note from the planning department informs us that 'in the absence of an up-to-date Local Plan, Cheltenham's housing supply continues to be monitored against the draft RSS figure of 8,100 dwellings between 2006 and 2026'. This figure equates to 405 dwellings per year.

The JCS minute records that during the period June 2006 and April 2013, 4,400 dwellings had been constructed or planning permissions granted, which equates to 628 dwellings per year, or 52 per month.

If the same pattern continues to 2031, something like 11,311 dwellings will have been constructed. Can the Head of Planning tell me where the proposal for 10,000 dwellings for the Cheltenham area fits into the equation?

What is the housing requirement figure after the deductions have been made and how do the two periods of time fit together?

Unfortunately, instead of welcoming the detail I had put into my questions, some Liberal Democrat councillors became agitated and rude about the number of questions for which I was seeking answers.

Their responses only showed that when the time came for voting on the document, they were inadvertently 'showing their hand' by their impatience.

Most of the answers to my questions were negative, and with some answers it was either a matter of 'wait and see', or we will monitor the points I had made and report on it later during the JCS process.

The last question by a councillor was directed to Cllr Jordan. It asked: "If the majority of the public rejects the JCS proposals, what would be the next step?"

Cllr Jordan replied: "The public consultation is not a referendum. There was an imperative for the council to have a JCS in place to demonstrate needs and how they intended to meet those needs; a decision would be made on that basis."

After a short break the Leader of the Council introduced the Response Report on the draft JCS consultation document. Cllr Jordan began by thanking the officers for their hard work in bringing together the evidence; members for their contributions at the working group meetings and those who had attended the seminars.

He also informed council members that TBC had approved the consultation document at their meeting on 3rd September.

The Leader highlighted the difficult balances that needed to be addressed; housing shortages, protecting the AONB and the Green Belt and the need for a sound strategy.

Why the Leader of the Council mentioned the AONB was a mystery to me because it had never figured in any of the debates at the MSG meetings.

However, he did emphasise the need for the council to accept that the concept of the JCS had been dictated by the National Planning Policy Framework.

Cllr Jordan made two points that I supported. The JCS must be sound and evidenced based on up-to-date figures; and the importance of joint working with Gloucester and Tewkesbury.

Whilst the second point was based on the fact that Gloucester and Tewkesbury had more land, both brownfield and 'white land', I had long taken the view that being part of the consortium was one thing, but not to accept its decisions at any price was another.

I was also concerned with the Leader's comments regarding the protection of the countryside when he stated: "...it was inevitable that this could not be totally preserved if the housing need was to be met." He then added: "The JCS proposals would still mean that 80 per cent of the Green Belt would be protected."

Earlier he had talked about protecting the AONB and the Green Belt from development and then five minutes later claimed that only 80 per cent of the Green Belt would be protected.

Cllr Jordan concluded his report by encouraging council members to support the consultation document, claiming that by not doing so would open the door to speculative development.

I could not agree with these remarks for two reasons.

1. Any planning application for development in the Green Belt now or in the future would be subject to the "saved" policies of the Local Plan, and the five purposes of the Green Belt which are published in paragraph 80 of the NPPF.
2. The JCS consultation document had not been 'approved' or 'passed through the gate' at the previous MSG meetings because 50 per cent of the councillors had decided that a better set of proposals could have been included rather than the ones that now made up the consultation document.

I know it is easy to criticise any sites being presented in a JCS consultation document, but I found it very hard to reconcile the fact that with so many other sites available, the best the CBPB could come up with were nine locations – seven of which were in the Green Belt.

And then to make matters worse, the JCS team suggested taking away the Green Belt status from the land around the Racecourse, leaving it vulnerable to speculative development – the very thing that the Leader of the Council had warned against earlier.

One councillor, in support of my comments, spoke against Cllr Jordan's recommendation saying that the housing numbers were wrong which could result in an over-supply of houses which would jeopardise the Green Belt. He added: "If getting the figures right and delaying the JCS with the prospect of curtailing speculative development, I believe is a risk worth taking."

The Leader of the Conservative Group, Cllr Duncan Smith, proposed the following amendment: *"That the consultation document should be amended to remove the Leckhampton and Up Hatherley sites as identified sites for development."*

In proposing the amendment, Cllr Smith accused the Leader of the Council of giving too many excuses and in his view the consultation document should not have been brought before the council for approval if it was not fit for purpose.

Cllr Smith concluded: "The Leader had reservations about the proposals, and it was clear that the people of Cheltenham did not want this housing because the proposals would not keep the town special and unique."

A number of councillors spoke in support of the amendment and some spoke against it. One comment suggested that if the council did not have a plan then the town would be at the mercy of the developers, adding that it was imperative that a JCS and a Local Plan were in place to protect neighbourhoods.

The councillor didn't explain whether the Local Plan had to be up-to-date, but if it had to be then surely the Lib/Dem administration should have been taking steps to provide both documents simultaneously?

Cllr Andrew McKinlay (Lib/Dem) the local councillor for the Up Hatherley ward spoke against the amendment. This is what he said:

> "To pass this amendment would effectively be a resignation from the JCS process and would not protect the land at Up Hatherley. The area is within Tewkesbury Borough, they would be likely to continue the JCS process and allocate the housing figures to their needs rather than Cheltenham's. This in turn would result in a shortfall of 2,000 properties for Cheltenham, which would have to be found elsewhere in the town.
>
> The amendment was at best devious and at worst dishonest and would result in development by appeal. Any plan would be declared unsound by the inspector if it ignored expert evidence on population growth and had not considered all application sites."

Although the councillor for Prestbury, I was also an Up Hatherley resident, and here was my councillor speaking on my behalf and criticising an amendment which, if approved, would have removed Up Hatherley Way from the JCS location sites.

Apart from being my councillor, Cllr McKinlay was a member of the CBC planning committee. This was a worrying factor because if he believed in the words he had just spoken then he clearly did not understand the planning basics that normally determine whether a planning application should be allowed or not.

If Tewkesbury Borough went it alone (unlikely because with the current JCS proposals, Tewkesbury benefited most with 90 per cent plus of the revenue from the New Homes Bonus Scheme), they would still have to conform to the existing procedure of consulting with the neighbouring local authority.

As a cabinet member as well as a member of the planning committee, the councillor should have been aware of the attempts by the JCS team to persuade Stroud District Council to

a. join the core strategy, and
b. to release non-Green Belt land on their border with Gloucester.

In each case the JCS team have been unsuccessful.

Although Cllr McKinlay did not mention the Green Belt status of the land at Up Hatherley Way, he should have known, as a member of the planning committee, that the land had been confirmed as 'significant Green Belt' in preventing the coalescence of Cheltenham and Gloucester by two independent consultants in 2007 and 2011.

However, Cllr McKinlay was not alone in his opposition to the amendment. One member remarked that those who supported the amendment "…were trying to derail the JCS process which was irresponsible". Another said: "The amendment could lead to other developments which could impact on communities to a greater degree".

One Lib/Dem councillor accused those who supported the amendment of "being parochial and disingenuous, adding that there were no alternatives".

It would not have made sense if I had not supported the amendment because I had spoken against Up Hatherley being included in the draft consultation document at the MSG meeting. I had also voted against the document going forward for public consultation in the "illegal" vote called by the chairman.

I told the council meeting that I had been disappointed to learn that the CBPB had added the Up Hatherley site at the eleventh hour, even though there was strong evidence available which showed that if any development took place there it would close the gap between Cheltenham and Gloucester.

I urged members to support the amendment.

Cllr Jordan responded to the amendment. He said: "Passing the amendment would destroy the JCS agreement which would result in the risk of development in Leckhampton being increased not decreased." He added, "The Government had made it clear that if the council failed to have plans in place to meet needs, then they would have no credibility."

I listened carefully to the Leader's response, but I could not understand the points he was making – they simply didn't make sense because he and his colleagues had repeatedly refused to have an updated Local Plan in place which would not have increased development in Leckhampton.

When the vote was taken the amendment was lost by 9 votes to 19 with 6 abstentions.

Cllr Ian Bickerton (Lib/Dem) then proposed an amendment that asked for four additional recommendations to the substantive motion.

1. Accept that the JCS sites and housing targets were contingent on updated and verified ONS population projections.
2. Guarantee Strategic Housing Market Assessment and Saturn traffic modelling for all sites.
3. Consider the input from parish councils in the form of Neighbourhood Planning documents, NPPF Green Space applications and existing Town and Village Green Applications.
4. Council to produce a policy of brownfield sites first in the consideration of future planning applications.

In his speech Cllr Bickerton asked members to consider his amendment as being a 'light touch' to the document, which would make the resolutions contingent on having the data available.

He told the meeting that he had been informed by the Office for National Statistics that the population projections were interim and only valid for two years. On this information he had come to the conclusion that the statistics needed to be right to ensure that the evidence base was there before sites were being proposed on the Green Belt.

In seconding the amendment, I reminded members that Cllr Bickerton probably knew the statistics better than many taking part in the JCS process, and members should heed his excellent advice.

Some members recognised the points that Cllr Bickerton had made and that they should be taken on board prior to the final JCS document being submitted at the Examination-in-Public.

In responding to the amendment, Cllr Jordan asked members to reject it. He did state that he had sympathy with the content, but he felt they could lose control of the process if it was made contingent on other factors.

The amendment was rejected by 8 votes to 20 with 5 abstentions.

A third amendment was proposed by Cllr David Prince (PAB). His amendment asked the council "... to keep the existing Green Belt boundary around Cheltenham Racecourse".

In proposing the amendment, Cllr Prince referred to the Hunting Butts planning application, highlighting the words the planning inspector used when he said that the land contributed to the open aspect of the Racecourse and needed to be protected.

Cllr Malcolm Stennett (PAB), when seconding the amendment, stressed that the land to the south of the Racecourse was not a strategic site and that it was an important area to preserve.

In supporting the amendment, I reminded the councillors that the Green Belt Review by AERC in March 2007 had recommended that the Green Belt status on the south side of the Racecourse should be maintained.

Tracey Crews in response said that it was only a 'tidying-up' exercise, and then in the next breath claimed that the NPPF states that amendments could only be made to the Green Belt at a strategic point of planning, i.e. the joint core strategy.

Cllr Prince in his summing up made it clear that the so-called 'tidying-up' of the Racecourse land would only encourage developers to submit planning applications once the Green Belt status had been removed.

Cllr Jordan in his response stated that he had no strong views about it and it was only a minor change. He accepted the professional view that the Green Belt boundary in the area needed to be clearer.

He concluded his comments by stating that once the JCS was out for consultation and there were substantial objections to it, then it might be possible to withdraw the proposal, but it depended on the feedback.

The cause of the irregular line of the Green Belt to the rear of the houses in New Barn Lane has come about by planning officers recommending approval for development in contravention of Green Belt policies.

When an application is submitted in this location it is almost bound to be challenged by those who are going to be affected by the planning decision. There is more on this later.

The amendment was lost by 10 votes to 19 with 3 abstentions.

It was clear from the results of each of the proposed amendments that the Liberal Democrats had decided at a party group meeting that the amendments should not be supported. The voting showed that a three-line whip on their councillors had been applied.

As there were no further amendments, the mayor invited councillors to debate the substantive motion, which was to approve the JCS Consultation Document as presented by the Leader of the Council with no amendments.

Several councillors spoke in the debate, mostly from those who were in favour of the JCS Consultation Document. Those who spoke against the document going out for public consultation claimed that the document was flawed and the figures used by the JCS team were out-of-date.

It was noticeable that the Conservative members appeared to be equally split in their support or rejection of the document, and the Liberal Democrat councillors who represented Leckhampton and Swindon Village sat in silence until the debate was drawing to a close. There was a reason for this which I will explain later in this chapter.

I thought long and hard on what I would include in my speech to council and this is a précis of what I said:

"Madam Mayor, By all means have a Joint Core Strategy, but we should not ride roughshod over established planning policies, which I am sure the Planning Inspectorate may have a view on.

Having been a member of the JCS/MSG since its formation, and listened to various officers and consultants putting forward fresh information at each meeting – it felt as if the goalposts were constantly being moved.

As we moved towards the 'Preferred Option', the changes became more dramatic – thankfully, most were rejected.

After two or more years of listening to different proposals and several presentations by consultants, I came to the conclusion that the MSG was more concerned with their 'end goal' rather than taking into account the historical facts about each area.

One example was the Green Belt Review carried out on behalf of CBC in March 2007 by AERC, which had come to the conclusion that the purposes of the Green Belt had been met. But this was put to one side by the JCS team who promptly commissioned another consultancy (AMEC) to carry out another Green Belt Assessment in the JCS area.

AMEC's findings and recommendations were similar to those of AERC, yet the JCS team have accepted some of the findings but not others.

AMEC came to the conclusion that the land between Cheltenham and Gloucester and Cheltenham and Bishop's Cleeve made a significant contribution to the purposes of the Green Belt and recommended that land between these settlements should not be developed in order to prevent their coalescence.

The PAB group have repeatedly supported this view.

Both Leckhampton and Up Hatherley came out favourably in the reviews – so why commission consultants, no doubt at great expense, if their recommendations are going to be ignored?

I would urge members to look carefully at the discussion papers on the 'Preferred Option' – the latest proposal to remove the Green Belt status south of Cheltenham and to the north of Gloucester (as shown on the Map) would result in the gap between Cheltenham and Gloucester becoming smaller.

Both AMEC and AERC have made this point in their recommendations.

The JCS proposals as they stand ignore another established fact – any designated Green Belt must have a strong and permanent boundary, which we have along Up Hatherley Way.

The South West Distributor Road (Up Hatherley Way is a part) has prevented further encroachment into the Green Belt and it is a classic example of a robust defence of the Green Belt line: the NPPF at paragraph 79 states: 'The Government attaches great importance to Green Belts. The fundamental aim of Green Belt policy is to prevent urban sprawl by keeping land permanently open; the essential characteristics of Green belts are their openness and their permanence'.

AMEC, whilst admitting that extending Green Belts was a limited option, did believe that a case could be made for the land immediately south of Cheltenham (Leckhampton). And in their report they suggested that this land should be included in the Green Belt, and I agree with that just as I agreed with the Inquiry Inspector in 1995.

So, Madam Mayor, unless the content of the consultation document is re-examined, I will not be voting for it."

I sat down fully expecting other councillors to respond to what I had just said – there was not a murmur from any of them.

The mayor then called the Lib/Dem councillors who represented Leckhampton and Swindon Village to speak. The timing and the content of each of the speeches showed clearly that the performances had been organised at a pre-council meeting of their group. The message from each of them urged the members of the council not to support the consultation document.

Cllr Jordan summed up the debate as follows:

> "I acknowledge the general feeling that the assessment needs set out in the JCS may be too high. Nevertheless, the consultation document is not a referendum, but it did provide an opportunity to challenge the evidence base, and the council will continue to do that.
>
> The green buffers referred to in the debate were crucial for the quality of life of residents, and it would be further explored during the consultation.
>
> There are missing elements of infrastructure funding, but it could only be secured through following the JCS process. The community levy would only be payable if the council had a robust plan in place.
>
> Having debated the report in detail, it was now a key moment for members to make their decision. In my view, the best thing for Cheltenham is to maintain the JCS process and the team effort between the three councils.
>
> The worst outcome would be for this joint working arrangement to break up."

The Leader then read out the three resolutions before voting took place.

1. The draft Joint Core Strategy be approved for public consultation.
2. Authority be granted to the Chief Executives in consultation with the Lead Member and the JCS Member Steering Group, to make any necessary minor amendments as considered appropriate by the three JCS Councils prior to publication.
3. The JCS Authorities note that through housing allocations and expected supply across the plan period, the draft Joint Core Strategy meets the needs of the three authorities as a whole.

   However, taken individually the needs of each authority are not exactly matched with the supply of homes the Joint Core Strategy is expected to deliver for each area.

   Following consultation and taking account of additional evidence produced during this period, housing and employment allocations will be reviewed to improve this relationship between need and supply for each area.

A recorded vote was requested and approved. 20 councillors voted for the consultation document and 13 voted against. Cllr Penny Hall (Conservative) abstained, Cllr Garnham had declared a personal and prejudicial interest in the JCS, and there were six absentees.

Immediately the vote was announced Cllr Bickerton rose to his feet to speak but was told to sit down by the mayor and by Lib/Dem councillors sitting behind him. Ian persisted with his speech but it was difficult to hear what he was saying – the one thing that councillors in the chamber did hear was that he was resigning from the Liberal Democrats with immediate effect and he would be sitting as an Independent.

There were cheers from the PAB councillors and one or two slapped him on the back. It was quite a night and one to remember.

Not only was it a memorable night with the resignation of Cllr Bickerton, but the meeting had, with its decision, set the population in each of the location sites firmly against the council and most of its councillors.

I must make it clear: although the majority of the Liberal Democrats voted for the document, so did a handful of Conservative councillors. But was it just a coming together of political minds, or was it something even more bizarre?

It was not until I had spoken to Cllr Bickerton on the telephone the following day that some of the reasons for the unusual voting fell into place.

Cllr Bickerton alleged that the Lib/Dem hierarchy had received representations from Cllrs Whyborn, Fisher, Massey and Sudbury, claiming that unless they were allowed to speak and vote against the JCS consultation document, there was a possibility that they would lose their seats at the next election.

According to Cllr Bickerton there had been a 'private' meeting of Lib/Dem councillors who discussed the options that were open to them: 1. Not to enforce the 3–line whip: 2. Cllr Jordan to speak to Cllr Garnham (Leader of the Conservative group) to ascertain how many Conservative councillors would be likely to vote for the document: 3. The speeches that Cllrs Whyborn, Massey, Fisher and Sudbury would make would be in the closing session of the debate, and would be agreed before the council meeting on September 5th.

Cllr Bickerton alleged that the Lib/Dems wanted to make sure they had enough 'votes in the bag' before they agreed to allow some of their members to speak and vote against the JCS substantive motion that would be put to the council.

"They knew" Cllr Bickerton said, "they did not have the support of the PAB councillors, and they were also aware that for various reasons, some Lib/Dem councillors would be absent from the meeting."

Having received an assurance that enough Conservative councillors would support the document, it was odds-on that the voting at the end of the debate would be 20 votes for with 13 against.

"So no matter what was said in the council chamber" said Cllr Bickerton, "the voting would be 20 votes against 13."

What a surprise? All carefully worked out it seemed and caused me to raise my eyebrows if nothing else.

Cllr Bickerton assured me that this calculation of votes prior to a council meeting was not unusual in the Lib/Dem group, because he claimed "...there were councillors like him and one or two others, who the Leader of the Council could not always rely on."

The telephone conversation continued with Cllr Bickerton alleging: "Agreement had been reached that Cllr Massey would make a forceful speech against the consultation document towards the end of the debate. He would declare that he and some of his colleagues were against the document, and he would then rise from his seat, before any other councillor could beat him to it, and ask the mayor for a 'recorded vote' to be taken.

The Lib/Dems had predicted that PAB councillors would get to their feet, but it would read better if the request came from Cllr Massey."

I suggested to Cllr Bickerton that from what he had said the whole business undertaken by the Liberal Democrats, albeit aided and abetted by a number of Conservatives, was a charade from start to finish.

"It was done" said Cllr Bickerton, "to ensure that the vulnerable Lib/Dem seats in the forthcoming local council elections were held."

I responded to these comments by reminding Cllr Bickerton that Cllr McKinlay was the councillor for Up Hatherley and he had spoken in support of development and opposed the amendment to remove Up Hatherley from the document.

"Perhaps" suggested Cllr Bickerton, "Cllr McKinlay, who was well-known to have unshakeable views in private, did not want to align himself with the others."

It was not a line I felt was worth pursuing, so I asked Cllr Bickerton if he had any other points he wanted to tell me about.

Cllr Bickerton's final comments were to warn me 'not to expect the names of the opposition councillors to appear in the minutes of the council meeting'. He stated that the minutes are always vetted by the Lib/Dem cabinet before they are published. He alleged: "Should the minute-taker include the name of a speaker who is an opposition councillor, then the name is replaced with the words 'a member said.'"

This information did not surprise me because on numerous previous occasions both PAB and Conservative councillors have tried unsuccessfully for the practice to end.

We agreed to meet again in the Municipal Offices on Thursday 12th September 2013, which happened to be the final day of the Prestbury Village Green application in the council chamber.

During the break for lunch, Ian Bickerton and I had another chat about the 'behind the scenes' activities at Liberal Democrat group meetings. Ian said he had been disappointed that his resignation speech had not been reported in the *Gloucestershire Echo*. He was particularly unhappy because he had contacted Jack Maidment the *Echo* political reporter prior to the council meeting who had assured him that "he would do something about it in a few days time."

According to Ian, he had contacted the *Echo* again, only to be told that there was an embargo on the consultation document and the council meeting.

He was not sure that an embargo had been requested (I was not aware of it as the PAB group leader), which made him suspicious that 'forces' had been at work that had prevented the news of his resignation from being published.

Although I was not sure that Ian was right about the embargo, I questioned him on whether he thought the so-called 'embargo' was the result of a discussion between the Liberal Democrats and the *Gloucestershire Echo* in order to keep it unreported.

Ian believed it might be the case, particularly as the *Echo* reporter had not contacted him as he had promised to do.

Pressing him on this point, I asked Ian whether, with his inside knowledge of what went on at the 'closed' Lib/Dem meetings, he could say that there was some sort of 'arrangement' between *Echo* reporters and the Lib/Dems when it came to the reporting of council meetings?

Ian asked me to look again at the *Echo* report of the council meeting, complete with photographs. "These were the councillors" he said, "who had 'duped' the readers of the *Echo* by their pre-council arrangements. And if you don't believe what I have already said, ask yourself where in the *Echo* report is there any reference to your critical comments that you made in your speech?"

I agreed that he had made a good point.

Going back to the matter of accuracy of the council minutes, Ian said that neither I nor members of my group should expect to read an accurate account of the meeting. Then out of the blue, he said: *"The Liberal Democrats fear you most, which is why they will not allow the minutes to contain any of your criticisms of them, or the way they do things. They know that you know more than they do about planning, the environment and things associated with it; you produce historical evidence that they cannot dispute and this irritates them. "*

Ian's allegation came as a shock although I did respond to his comments by admitting that I had been aware of their antipathy towards me for many years.

However, the next comment from Ian Bickerton surprised me even more.

He alleged that Cllr Colin Hay had been given the job of neutralising any comments I made in the council chamber, or at a committee meeting.

I wasn't cross – I was flattered, and it did help to explain why Cllr Hay had been so aggressive in his words and manner towards me over recent years.

Our discussion ended with Ian Bickerton explaining that the Lib/Dems attitude towards me, my group and others was probably due to the perceived superiority complex they had developed by having such a large majority on the council. *"They hate anyone else coming up with alternative proposals, or those who challenge the adopted line that they have previously agreed. That is why they don't like me either,"* he said.

The next meeting of the MSG took place on Thursday 26th September when Barbara Carroll of Enfusion provided a presentation to members on the Sustainability Appraisal Report.

Wayne Dyer and Tim Durant of ARUP provided a presentation on the Infrastructure Delivery Plan and Jonathan Dibble gave members information regarding minor changes to the draft JCS document.

Tracey Crews reported the three councils had agreed that the JCS Draft Consultation Document should be published. She added that a full colour tri-fold A5 leaflet giving details of the consultation would be ready for distribution in a few days time.

Jonathan Dibble confirmed that the Draft JCS Document would be made available at public libraries, but the supporting evidence would only be available on the JCS website.

So the time had come for the general public to state their opinions on the Preferred Options after reading the consultation document.

The document included a summary giving a brief overview of what the JCS team had been doing following consultation and evidence gathering over recent years. It also stated that the work had been used to develop the preferred approach to development across the three JCS areas.

Now that we had reached this stage, my first task would be hold public meetings in Prestbury and Up Hatherley as quickly as possible to appraise the local residents of what the consultation document contained.

I also wanted to know what they thought about the proposals and to urge them to respond to the document as quickly as possible.

My first meeting was held on Tuesday 8th October in the home of Mr and Mrs Banks. It was only a small gathering of local people but they were very concerned about the possibility of the land to the rear of their properties, which overlooked the Racecourse, being downgraded.

Naturally they were concerned about the so-called 'tidying-up' proposal by CBC, and after I had explained the situation I urged them to write to the JCS team and the chief executive (Andrew North) setting down their reasons why the land should remain as Green Belt.

My next meeting was with Ian Renton, the chief executive of Cheltenham Racecourse, on Friday morning, which was an informal chat about the land on the south side of the Racecourse and its future.

I explained to Ian Renton the present position and the likelihood that the status of the Green Belt may be downgraded leading to possible development.

Ian was not pleased with this prospect.

I also explained the background history of the land; the planning applications and the public inquiry in 1984 and the JCS proposal, which he welcomed.

I explained to him that in spite of this, CBC had designs on the land being developed in the future in order, as they put it, to allow the Racecourse to expand its operation. This statement, according to Ian Renton, was not the case. He would be opposed to any development around the perimeter fence because it would be dangerous for the racehorses.

I asked him whether he was aware that CBC insisted that it was the Racecourse who wanted to develop the land. He refuted this. He claimed it was CBC who, allegedly, 'badgered him into looking at the development potential of the land on the south side of the Racecourse'.

He added: "They should realise that the Racecourse only owns a portion of the land; others have a stake in it as well."

Before I left Ian Renton's office he kindly arranged for me to have a copy of a map showing the land on the south side of the Racecourse and the area that belonged to the Racecourse Company.

His parting words to me were that the Racecourse was in the process of re-building the main stands and other accommodation at a cost of £42 million, so it would be some time before they would be looking at further development.

It was a useful meeting, and it gave me food for thought as I pondered what my responses would be when I confronted those who had come up with the crass suggestion of downgrading the Green Belt.

On Friday 1st November, the Leckhampton Green Land Action Group (Leglag) held a public meeting at the Leckhampton Primary School to discuss the JCS and its implications.

Although the leaflet indicated 'all local residents welcome', I attended as a member of the public who was interested enough to hear what the speakers had to say on the consequences for Leckhampton should the JCS Preferred Options be adopted by the three councils. I was not alone; there were other residents from Up Hatherley in the audience who were just as interested in the future of the land and the effect it would have on Up Hatherley and the setting of Cheltenham.

Kit Braunholtz introduced the speakers; Adrian Phillips, a well-known local conservationist, Martin Horwood MP and Cllr Duncan Smith (Conservative Party).

Adrian Phillips gave an excellent talk with slides of his work with CPRE, the Cotswold Area of Outstanding Natural Beauty, and Leglag.

Anyone listening to his presentation could not fail to be impressed with his love of the countryside, and particularly the land in the Leckhampton area, which was, as he said, "under threat should the development proposals go ahead".

I was tempted to ask him if he was aware of my efforts to get the same land designated Green Belt in 1995: and whether he was aware that my efforts were blocked by the CBC Lib/Dem administration.

I didn't think it was the right forum to reveal this important historical fact – the audience were more in the mood to condemn the current JCS/MSG members, than the culprits in 1995 who could have given the land a better chance of protection than it currently had.

Martin Horwood MP told the audience that the council had a current Local Plan which had been ignored by the JCS team. "The Leckhampton land was not included in the CBC Local Plan", he told them.

Again, I felt the urge to tell him and the audience that it was not the JCS team but the Lib/Dem administration that had refused to update the Local Plan.

Although the Local Plan policies had been "saved" by the Secretary of State, they were out-of-date, and therefore the 'saved policies' had little or no weight in the planning point he was pursuing.

He stressed the importance of the town having a Local Plan, which is why PAB councillors had tried so hard to get it updated.

I could have reminded him and the audience that the same people he was criticising had produced a paper called 'Cheltenham Plan – Scoping Document' in June 2013. The authors claimed it would help to guide development in the borough over the next 15 to 20 years, adding that the council were very keen to bring forward the 'Cheltenham Plan' as soon as possible [latest forecast 2015]. One reason for this, the document stated, "Is that the existing Local Plan is now out of date, and although we have policy cover in the form of the NPPF, it has some stringent default provisions and is not sufficiently able to reflect local nuances and issues that are of concern to Cheltenham."

I would have thought that the Member of Parliament would be aware of such a document – it might have persuaded him to talk to his councillor colleagues and urge them to support the updating of the Local Plan until the new Cheltenham Plan came into existence.

Cllr Duncan Smith reiterated the importance of the Leckhampton land and urged the audience to take the opportunity that the consultation period offered them, to write to the JCS team expressing their reasons why the land should not be included in the JCS.

As I listened to the questions, I felt sorry for the local residents. They asked many questions about the detail contained in the JCS proposal; loss of green open space; traffic problems and the lack of schools, but they clearly were not aware of the fact that they had been put in this insidious position by the same people who had failed them in the past.

I came away from the meeting feeling depressed.

Throughout November I spoke at 'house meetings', parish council meetings and public meetings in an attempt to explain the details of the JCS, and to advise those present to write letters to the JCS team objecting to the development proposals.

On 6th November I had a one-to-one meeting with Tracey Crews (Head of Planning), which was worth recording.

It was a friendly atmosphere and we agreed to be honest and open with the points we both wanted to make. I asked Tracey Crews (TC) about the AMEC document; why the council, having commissioned the company to carry out the Green Belt Review, had ignored its recommendations.

She didn't agree that the JCS team were ignoring the advice so I referred to the council's intention of removing the Green Belt status from the land around the Racecourse as being just one example. TC responded by referring to the planning application for a dwelling in New Barn Lane, which had resulted in the neighbour going to the Local Government Ombudsman (LGO) and winning a substantial amount of compensation. She added that the council was not going to be 'caught out' again, which is the reason why the council intend to 'tidy-up' the Green Belt on the south side of the Racecourse.

"Hang on a bit" I said, "are you saying that because a planning officer wrongly recommended permission for a dwelling in the Green Belt, and a resident challenges the decision by writing to the LGO, is the reason why the council want to change the status of the land?"

TC replied: "The council were caught out then and we don't intend to be caught out again, which is the reason for the 'tidying-up' exercise."

This prompted me to say: "Do you not think that instead of doing what you are suggesting, you should strengthen the Green Belt at the Racecourse, not weaken it, and applaud the action of the resident, not criticise him?"

TC did not agree with me. She then used the excuse that the land with its current status prevented any further commercial development in the Racecourse area. I refuted this as past planning permissions would show.

We did agree about some things including the spending of £70,000 to save the breaching of the Green Belt at the Hunting Butts. When I reminded TC that the land at the Hunting Butts was part of the Green Belt buffer between Prestbury and Bishop's Cleeve, and the land at the Racecourse was part of that buffer, she had no answer.

I wrote letters of objection to the proposal to include C6b (Up Hatherley Way) in the Joint Core Strategy, and the proposal to remove the Green Belt status from the land around the Racecourse on 10th December 2013. [Copies of my letters at Appendix 6a and 6b]

The main thrust of my objections was that the JCS team should realise there was overwhelming evidence from two different consultants that both tracts of land were significant in keeping settlements from merging.

I also referred to past planning appeals that confirmed these opinions, adding that I would attend the Examination-in-Public and put the same case to the Planning Inspector.

With the consultation period ending on 13th December, the meeting of the JCS/MSG on the preceding day was bound to be interesting.

The chairman, Jim Claydon, opened the meeting by reminding members that they provided the strategic oversight of the JCS, and that it was important that the MSG maintained that approach.

Listening to the chairman's words I could not help thinking they would have been more purposeful if the 'approach' that he referred to had been a fairer set of options than those the councillors were expected to accept.

It was reported that 900 people had attended the 'consultation events' in the JCS area, and there had been more than 2,000 representations made by local residents, many of them sent online to the JCS website.

These would be analysed and a summary of the responses would be presented to the MSG meeting in January 2014.

In answer to several critical remarks, it was revealed that the representations already made would not be reported verbatim, but grouped by policy area with a summary of the comments made within each of the areas.

Members wanted a summary report, but this was refused. It seemed as though there was not going to be a free and open review of the submissions for all to read.

The reason given was that there were insufficient resources to do it.

One comment that took my attention was made by Holly Jones, Planning Policy Manager (TBC), when she reported on the Strategic Sites. She admitted that 'there may be further work required following the outcomes of the consultation processes'.

Did this mean that some of the submissions made were so strong that the CBPB were seriously thinking about a revision of their former proposals?

Tracey Crews seemed to be endorsing the words of Holly Jones when she reported that work was taking place with internal consultees, and the drafting of the JCS Pre-Submission document would draw upon the outputs of this work together with consideration of responses received.

It wasn't clear what was behind the comment, but at this stage in the process, I was 'clutching at straws' in the hope that changes to the proposals might be forthcoming.

Later, we listened to a presentation from Neil McDonald (CCHPR).

He reported that the housing projections from the Department for Communities & Local Government (DCLG) were lower than those that had been received from Experian, Cambridge and Oxford. "The DCLG figures were trend-based projections" he said, "with a line going forward, but," he warned, "'just projecting forward on that basis is not advisable.

DCLG would review their housing projections now that the new information from the Office of National Statistics (ONS) had been released. Any revised information from DCLG was unlikely to affect the JCS plan as it had already assumed a 'return to trend.'"

Neil McDonald concluded his presentation by saying, "There was no reason to do anything different. The evidence did not unpick the joint core strategy."

As I listened to the presentation, I couldn't help wondering whether Neil McDonald had securely tied his colours to the mast from the moment he had given his first presentation to CBC councillors. It sounded as though any changes in the projections would need to be of seismic proportions for Neil McDonald to revise his views.

The next item on the MSG agenda was called "Crunch Items for Discussion", and I would be the first to admit that it was this item on the agenda that filled me with great expectations.

I had submitted my objections to the JCS proposals, but I had been concerned that if we were going to win the hearts and minds of the residents in the JCS area, then the projections and the development locations had to be more realistic than the ones the CBPB were proposing.

I asked the chairman if I could make a statement at the start of the agenda item. Jim Claydon agreed and this is what I said:

"Chairman, we have been listening to presentation after presentation since the MSG was formed in 2008. Most of the reports and presentations, albeit good, have been over the heads of most people sitting round the table. We are now in a mess.

Look at the minutes of the MSG meetings since July 2013 onwards and one can see that from that time things started to go 'pear-shaped'.

All we have managed to do is to incur the wrath of large sections of the community in all three areas. There is a growing swell of anger among our critics who believe the JCS team have chosen the wrong sites for development in the three areas.

They have argued, rightly in my view, that there are several non-Green Belt sites that could have been considered first – Highnam, Brookthorpe/Whaddon and the MOD site at Ashchurch. I am sure other members could put forward other sites.

From Central government down, the advice has been to use brownfield and 'white land' first – we have constantly refused to take this advice, just as we have ignored the advice from the Green Belt Reviews in 2007 and 2011.

The general public believe that the JCS team prefers to ignore the five purposes of the Green Belt, which have been spelt out in Local Plan policies, the former Planning Policy Guidance (PPG2) and more recently, the NPPF.

But chairman, in spite of what I have said, all is not lost.

We are fortunate in that we have the opportunity to have another 'bite-of-the-cherry' before the final proposals go forward for consultation.

I hope we put the next few months to good use – take note of what has been said by the population – re-examine the current proposals in a more meaningful manner, and you may be surprised at the result.

May I suggest, as a first step, that having councillors from the three areas on a re-examining panel would be a step in the right direction. Thank you."

I didn't expect a round of applause and I didn't receive one. The chairman appeared to be nodding his head with some of the points I had made, and he did make an encouraging comment about my statement to the meeting.

Cllr Derek Davies commented: "The Green Belt is not sacrosanct."

Cllr Steve Jordan, on the other hand, said: *"I agree with most of the things Les has said."*

This was encouraging. I did send him an email the following day thanking him for his support at the MSG meeting. I also asked him to let me know what the other points were that he didn't agree with.

I didn't receive a reply.

CHAPTER 29

A Little Silver Lining

Patience is a virtue.

Proverbs – late fourteenth century.

Following the December MSG meeting I wrote to Andrew North.

I told him I was pleased that the chairman had let me speak for so long and that I believed it was necessary for me to make the various points so that the officers, at least, heard the views of an elected councillor.

I was concerned about the broad location proposals and the method used by the JCS team of choosing Green Belt sites before brownfield and white land.

I also referred to the comment made by Cllr Davies.

It is important to the reader that I write my comments in full, because I still believe that my exchanges of emails with Mr North helped to change the thinking of the JCS team. This is a copy of my email:

"No-one has said that the Green Belt is sacrosanct, which is why the proposed development to the North West of Swindon Village has not been challenged at any MSG meeting that I can recall. Generally, apart from members of the 'Save Our Countryside' group, people believe that because the land does not meet any of the five purposes of the Green Belt it is vulnerable for development.

The stance of Cllr Davies is totally different now to the time when he was chairman of the TBC planning committee in 1995, when his committee were at odds with CBC regarding his council's position on the possible loss of Green belt at Staverton and the south west of Cheltenham.

I have a photograph of me presenting a petition with a thousand signatures to Cllr Davies, in the presence of Ron Wheeler (Borough Secretary) and Chris Shaw (Chief Planning Officer), urging them to stand firm against the loss of Green belt between Cheltenham and Gloucester, which was being advocated by CBC, which would have brought the town and city closer together.

I can only come to the conclusion that Cllr Davies believes that by supporting and urging development in the Green Belt, it will distract everyone's attention away from the 'white land' at Highnam, which AMEC recommended 'being capable of taking a large number of dwellings'.

Cllr Davies' comments that 'the Government and the Planning Inspectorate will automatically allow development in the Green Belt, even that which is classified as significant to the five purposes of the Green Belt', is simply spurious nonsense.

My conversations with DCLG over a long period of time have shown that the Government attaches great importance to the 'five purposes of the Green belt', as set out in the NPPF.

They have also emphasised again and again that non-green belt land should be developed before other land is considered.

The planning inspector's letter regarding the Hunting Butts appeal, plus other evidence will be vital at the Examination–in–Public, should significant Green Belt areas be proposed.

As I said in my speech yesterday, we have a second chance in the weeks ahead, for the Cross Boundary Programme Board to come forward with some sensible changes.

Thank you for your time.

Cllr Les Godwin."

I received an immediate reply from Andrew North. He wrote:

"It was a good speech you made yesterday and I totally agree with you that the key issue when we make choices about which parts of the Green Belt to sacrifice (if we are forced to do so), is how the land performs in terms of the five Green Belt purposes.

The brownfield land issue we have tried to address by trying to put as much of the necessary growth as possible into existing urban areas (55 per cent I think it comes to across the JCS area). However, we cannot always control land owner and developer decisions on the use of such land, and (on the whole), the more viable sites may be on open land on the urban fringes.

I really do hope that amidst all of this turmoil of controversy, conflicting evidence and unwelcome policy, we end up with something that can be broadly supported politically.

Regards.

Andrew North."

Malcolm and me with our wives attending a celebration evening following the Hunting Butts decision

On Tuesday 17th December, I was invited to a one-to-one meeting with Andrew North in his office. It was both interesting and positive, which prompted me to send the following email to him so that my version of our conversation was correct. This is what I wrote:

> "I found our meeting yesterday to be positive and encouraging. Thanks again for your kind comments about my speech to the MSG last Thursday – perhaps I or someone else should have made the comments much earlier. I only hope the message has now got through.
>
> Secondly, thank you for your favourable comments about the possible removal of the Up Hatherley site before any re-submission is made.
>
> I think we both agreed that there are alternative sites available and your reference to table SP-2a (Distribution of Development) showing net additional dwellings of 2,740 for the 'rural service centre and service villages' (TBC), means that Highnam 'will take some of the strain'.
>
> Not that you need to be reminded, but I hope you can bring your influence to bear on the point I made about the next three MSG meetings (Jan/Feb/March) being used to agree the changes; putting the results in the public domain immediately. This would be better than waiting for the final pre-submission document to be presented to the three councils.
>
> Thank you for your opinion regarding the Green Belt land around Cheltenham Racecourse. There is enough positive evidence to show that the removal of the Green Belt status from this land would be a retrograde step. It would fly-in-the-face of all the conclusions by the planning inspectors, as well as the recommendations by the planning consultants AERC and AMEC.
>
> The same point about the robustness and permanence of the road that defines the Green Belt boundary at the Racecourse is no different to the robust South West Distributor Road that defines the boundary at Up Hatherley Way.
>
> In conclusion, I believe the discussion we had yesterday could pave the way for further discussions between us on the same subjects in the weeks ahead.
>
> If you think it is a good idea then please let me know.
>
> Cllr Les Godwin."

In reply, Andrew North said that another meeting would be arranged towards the end of January or early February 2014, which was good news.

Before the end of December 2013 the 'notes' of the MSG meeting held on the 12th December were published. The 'notes' didn't usually shock me but this time they did. There was no record of my speech.

I sent an email to the chairman Jim Claydon, complaining about this omission and reminded him about his comments at the end of my speech and the words of Cllr Jordan in response.

He responded as follows:

> "Councillor Godwin, As you probably know I don't have any control over the notes of the meeting, which I saw for the first time today in the same email that you received. Also I have no notes of my own of the meeting. However, I do remember you pointed out that this was the last opportunity for the MSG to take stock of the strategy and that if any

adjustments are made the implications for the plan as a whole needs to be considered.
I also remember you making the point about the significance of the Green Belt and
others responding that this was the only time at which such adjustments should be
made.
I have a good deal of sympathy for the note-taker and appreciate that it has never been
the intention to produce verbatim 'minutes' of these meetings. If you would like to
propose amendments to the notes that more clearly reflect the content of your contribution I should be happy to support the inclusion of the above points. I suspect there may
be others who feel likewise.
Regards.
Jim."

I was disappointed with the chairman's reply because it read as though he had missed the point of the omission. Was he defending the 'note-taker', or did he not want my words recorded in the 'notes' of the meeting?

To offer the excuse that the 'notes' of MSG meetings are not verbatim would have been more acceptable if at least some part of my speech had been recorded.

To suggest that the onus was on me to propose amendments at the next meeting was unhelpful – how could I propose amendments if there was nothing in the 'notes' to amend? In any event, a summary of what I had said had been accepted as a worthwhile contribution to the debate and should have been recorded.

In my reply to the chairman on 31st December, I assured him that I was not asking him to amend the 'notes', but to have words with the person responsible for taking the notes. I added that it was disappointing to find no reference to my speech because I thought the main content of it, if accepted, could have acted as the catalyst for making the much-needed changes leading to a more acceptable JCS document.

Unhappy with the response from the chairman I spoke to Andrew North who was sympathetic to my cause and suggested that I let him have a précis of what I had said and he would deal with the matter.

I was more than happy with the suggestion, and when the 'notes' were published a second time a précis of what I had said had been included.

[The notes containing my speech were accepted by the MSG meeting on 30th January 2014].

On Saturday 18th January the Up Hatherley community were shocked to learn of the sudden death of David Hall. He was, as readers will have read in earlier chapters, a stalwart in the community who played no small part with me in opposing the TBC's 'front-gate refuse collection system' in 1976.

He had been chairman of Up Hatherley parish council for 25 years as well as a borough councillor on both TBC and CBC. The parish had lost a truly great guide and mentor to those inside the parish and across the wider area.

Before the next MSG meeting on 30th January, Andrew North invited Group Leaders to a 'special' meeting in his office to discuss issues that were proving to be contentious.

The timing was perfect, but would it be the forerunner of possible changes to the JCS document?

I attended the meeting with Cllr Steve Jordan and Cllr Andrew Chard, who was deputising for Cllr Robert Garnham (Conservative Group). Also in attendance were Mike Redman and Tracey Crews.

Andrew North informed us that the purpose of the meeting was "to review where we are in the programme and the next steps we need to take."

The first item discussed was the Objectively Assessed Need (OAN) and the latest available information. The Group Leaders believed that with the inward migration figure being lower than at first thought, there would be a good case for reducing the JCS figure of 33,200 dwellings down to 31,000.

It was generally agreed that the evidence was strong and we could safely propose that Up Hatherley could be removed from the JCS proposals.

To give weight to our proposal, we all agreed that should the reduction in the overall figures to 31,000 not be accepted by TBC and GCC then we (CBC) would advocate that sites such as Highnam and other areas should be considered.

We discussed the merits of the MOD Ashchurch site, which is brownfield, and the meeting agreed with my suggestion that the site should be used for residential development and not divided between residential and employment.

The content of the NPPF was debated at length including the chapter on protecting Green Belt land. We also discussed the chapter that dealt with the "Duty to Co-operate" between local authorities. We agreed that if the principle is upheld then Stroud District Council should not oppose development of the non-Green Belt land at Brookthorpe/Whaddon.

We felt that the Examination-in-Public of the Stroud Local Plan could result in the land being released, which we agreed would alleviate the pressure on Green Belt land at Up Hatherley and elsewhere.

The matter of the land at Leckhampton was discussed and it was agreed by Cllr Jordan and Cllr Chard that combining Leckhampton with Up Hatherley would make it harder to remove Up Hatherley from the JCS.

The land at the Racecourse and the so-called 'tidying-up' exercise was discussed, and from the comments around the table, with the probable exception of Tracey Crews, we were not in favour of interfering with the long-standing position of its Green Belt status.

Andrew North called for a 'straw-poll' around the table and individually we agreed that the land at the Racecourse should remain Green Belt.

"What about you Tracey?" said Andrew North, "Do you agree?"

She looked at me and said: "I had better agree otherwise Cllr Godwin will kick me into the ditch."

Everyone laughed and we all agreed that the meeting had been useful.

As I left the building I could not help reflecting on what had been said and what was behind the meeting – why had there been a change of heart?

But whatever my thoughts, there seemed to be a possibility that both Up

Hatherley and the Racecourse might soon be removed from the JCS proposals.

The following day was the next scheduled meeting of the JCS/MSG, which was held in the Municipal Offices. The agenda contained reports on 'crunch issues' affecting housing, location sites and an update on the Stroud Local Plan.

There were 19 attendees at the meeting, which was probably a record. I noted that all three chief executives were in attendance, plus another seven senior officers, and with only Cllr Phil Workman (TBC) absent I couldn't help thinking that the meeting was going to be something special.

The chairman confirmed that the summary of my statement to the MSG on 12th December 2013 was accepted as an accurate reflection of what I had said.

Barbara Maksymiw (GCC) gave an update on the consultation work stream – over 800 people had attended 13 public events.

She reported that around 4,000 responses to the consultation document had been received, adding that the quality of the responses were very high.

Regarding the housing 'crunch issues', Holly Jones reported that Cheltenham and Gloucester could not meet their housing needs and were looking to urban extensions to help facilitate this through the 'duty to co-operate'.

She added that neither Bishops' Cleeve nor Highnam had been identified as urban centres within the draft JCS. "Highnam is very close to Gloucester" she said, "but it is not and cannot be seen as an urban extension, but could include a level of development. However, if Highnam is included as a strategic site, there would have to be a re-appraisal and further consultation and it would impact on the timescales."

Cllr Derek Davies quickly responded by saying that he didn't agree with what had been said and urged the committee to "get on with producing the final document".

Once again, at the mention of Highnam, Cllr Davies attempts to divert the MSG away from the subject and urges everyone "to get on with it".

Presumably, the sooner a Pre-Submission document is approved the safer it will be for Highnam not to have any development.

I contributed to the discussion by stating that the driving force behind the strategy appeared to be 'hung-up' on the matter of urban extensions. "What is paramount" I said, "is whether development is beneficial to the community. To ensure this, the JCS needs to be more informative and incisive as to where the developments in the three areas should be."

Cllr Jordan added: "The JCS team needs to sort out 'crunch issues' and not carry on regardless. I do not disagree with the strategy but with the interpretation of it. Up Hatherley is the single issue of most concern as indicated by those who have corresponded; the land is high value Green Belt and it would be sensible to delete it entirely."

It was the first time I had heard Cllr Jordan refer to Up Hatherley in a MSG meeting, and of course, I agreed with his comments.

Cllr Jude Perez (TBC) did not agree with Cllr Jordan and claimed that 'if Up Hatherley is removed then other Green Belt sites should be looked at'.

In spite of the comment from Cllr Perez, I felt confident following the recent meetings in Andrew North's office and the general tone of the MSG meeting – plus perhaps the presence of all three chief executives – the JCS team and the MSG were moving in the right direction.

We were informed that the Stroud Local Plan had been submitted and the Examination-in-Public was due to take place on 1st April 2014; representatives from the JCS councils would be attending and they would be putting the matter of 'duty-to-co-operate' to the planning inspector.

Andrew North confirmed that the dates when the three councils would discuss the Pre-Submission document were 7th April (TBC), 8th April (GCC) and 9th April (CBC).

He then summarised some of the main points so that everyone was clear where the JCS stood at the end of 2013.

1. The OAN issue had been questioned. The projections by CCHPR have not been superseded by further data and their advice is that we should stick with the figures as previously indicated.
2. Issue re Highnam – it is acknowledged that some development will take place and that problems will be caused with the plan if it becomes a strategic site due to the scale of development.
3. Up Hatherley site – this provision is matching an identified need in different places.

Cllr Davies had the last word. He praised the officers for their tremendous work and he noted that the JCS was making progress. He said that Highnam is not an issue and should not become one.

Bridget Farrer, who lived locally, formed the Hatherley and Shurdington Triangle Action Group (HaShTAG). Its purpose was similar to other action groups – it was opposed to the JCS proposal to develop the land along Up Hatherley Way.

Bridget, together with Stuart Fowler, chairman of Up Hatherley parish council, held a Forum in the village hall on Tuesday 4th February to discuss the JCS and to hear comments from the local councillors (Cllr Roger Whyborn and Cllr Andrew McKinlay).

Stuart Fowler opened the Forum by informing the 50 plus members of the community that the local councillors had been invited to the meeting, but they had declined to attend using the excuse that they had nothing to add to the current situation. "However" said the chairman, "much had happened regarding the JCS and we are fortunate to have Cllr Les Godwin here tonight, who lives in the parish, and who will provide an update for us."

I reminded the audience of the 'lost opportunity' on 5th September 2013 when CBC councillors could have removed Up Hatherley from the JCS consultation document, but they had refused to do so.

"Since that time", I told the meeting, "I had met Andrew North several times in recent weeks in order to keep the matter of Up Hatherley Way and its removal from the JCS document in his mind and in the minds of those who formed the Cross Boundary Programme Board (CBPB)."

I had met Andrew North in the afternoon, mainly to inform him that I would be speaking at the Forum in the evening. I wanted Andrew to know that I would be updating the local residents on the JCS and that I would welcome any good news he had and thought I should pass on to the local residents.

He reminded me that Neil McDonald (CCHPR) believed that unless substantive evidence can be produced to reduce the numbers from 33,200 to 31,000 then the JCS team should hold fast on the numbers. Adding

> "Unless we can do that, then it will mean that alternative locations will have to be found to allow Up Hatherley to be removed. It is fashionable to talk about using the land at Highnam, but I can tell you that the Conservative group on TBC are saying 'hands off Highnam' and threatening to pull out of the JCS arrangement if Highnam is included in any modified proposals."

It was not encouraging news, but I half-expected it.

When I explained to Andrew North my reasons why I thought the selection of the land at Up Hatherley Way was a serious mistake by the JCS team, he agreed that the South West Distributor Road was a strong argument to stop further encroachment into the Green Belt.

He went on to admit that 'the other chief executives were not against withdrawing Up Hatherley from the JCS, although the senior officers on the CBPB were not of the same view'.

I relayed to the Forum meeting in the evening the gist of my conversation with Andrew North. However, the Forum attendees were not impressed with the last point, and someone suggested that I should tell these officers that they are the 'servants of the people and not the other way round'.

Generally, the residents attending the Forum were encouraged by the optimistic comments I had made, and I promised to give them a further update at the next meeting on 11th March.

On Monday 11th February I reported to Prestbury parish council my one-to-one meeting with Andrew North the previous Tuesday afternoon when we discussed the land around the Racecourse. I told the parish council that I had sought confirmation from Andrew North that the proposal to remove the Green Belt status of the land would not be included in the Pre-Submission document that would go before the borough council on 9th April 2014.

I reported that Andrew North had told me that 'no-one was in favour of the Racecourse land being included, but the matter of the land had not been put to the other two councils'. (Gloucester and Tewkesbury).

If that was the case, I told the parish council, its inclusion must have been of such little importance that CBC had not even bothered to share the situation with their colleagues in the JCS team.

The fact that the land was not subject to housing figures indicates that it should not have become an issue for the JCS in the first place.

I told the parish council that Andrew North agreed with my comments.

The next meeting of the MSG was on 6th March. The day before, group leaders were invited to a meeting with Andrew North.

I assumed that the Group Leaders would be told that the previously agreed positions on the Up Hatherley and Racecourse land would be the subject of the discussion. It wasn't, but worse still it seemed to me that Andrew North was back-tracking on the assumptions he had made at the previous group leaders' meeting. It was confusing. I could only think that his previous strong words of encouragement had not been received favourably by the other chief executives. It also hit me hard when I thought about the position I would be in when I explained to the two parish councils that all the previous promises I had given them might prove to be worthless. The meeting was nothing more than a declaration by Andrew North and an apology of being sorry for having to tell me the 'bad news'.

In spite of my protestations there was no support from anyone else in the meeting.

My first task as soon as I returned home was to write a long email to Cllr Steve Jordan, Leader of the Council, expressing my disappointment in the outcome of the meeting. It hadn't escaped my notice that throughout the meeting Cllr Jordan had said nothing in support of my position, or the position of the residents in both Up Hatherley and the Racecourse areas.

Hashtag supporters marching to save the Green Belt at Up Hatherley Way

The following is a précis of my email to Cllr Jordan:

"Having now got over the shock of this morning's briefing by Andrew North, I find the whole JCS process disappointing. It seems that decisions are continually made 'on-the-hoof' making it difficult to understand the logic behind them.

The Up Hatherley and Racecourse Green Belt land was thrust into the 'arena' at the 11th hour (August 2013), and the Racecourse land was described at a seminar by Tracey Crews and Philip Stephenson as being only a "tidying-up" exercise.

When I saw Andrew North soon after the seminar, he too repeated that it was only a 'tidying-up' operation, as though it was insignificant.

Taking away the status of any green belt means it becomes 'white land' like Leckhampton, and it immediately becomes vulnerable to predator developers.

At the 5th September 2013 council meeting when the JCS consultation document was debated, you will recall that PAB put forward a motion asking for the Racecourse Green Belt land to be removed from the document.

After I had spoken in favour of the motion, you told the council "it was only a tidying-up exercise" and you couldn't support it.

The council or a majority of the members voted against the motion.

Ever since that vote, my colleagues and I have been arguing the case for the Green Belt status to stay as it is on the south side of the Racecourse, because, as the Planning Inspector said in 1984, and I quote:

"In my opinion, the possible impact of the proposed development on the character and environmental setting of the Racecourse is a prime consideration, irrespective of any arguments regarding the Green Belt boundary. It is distinguishable from the adjoining Pye site, largely on account of its contours and its visual domination of the Racecourse. The site in conjunction with the other open land to the west, provide an attractive, grassland buffer between the New Barn Lane housing and the Racecourse. From the southern part of the appeal site, fine views are obtained across the Racecourse to Bishop's Cleeve and Southam.

In my opinion, the existing natural grassland setting of some 150 to 200 metres in depth would not be adequately replaced by a landscaped strip of some 35 metres. Not only would the visual character of the area be entirely altered, but the location of residential uses and their associated activities in such close proximity to the Racecourse, would contribute to the urbanisation of the surroundings."

But even if that is not conclusive, the words of the consultants (AERC and AMEC), commissioned by the Borough Council, substantiate the importance of this critical Green Belt on the south side of the Racecourse.

AMEC reported: "Maintenance of the separation between Cheltenham and Bishop's Cleeve is critical to fulfilling the purpose of the Green Belt designation. These segments play an important role in this.

Therefore, this area does not merit further consideration for release from the Green Belt at this stage unless other elements of the evidence base strongly suggest otherwise."

I come back now to the nonsense about 'tidying-up' the Green Belt at the Racecourse: It must still be fresh in your mind when at the meeting in Andrew North's office on Wednesday 29th January 2014, he, Tracey Crews and Mike Redman told you, me and Cllr Chard their views on the JCS.

Primarily, the discussion centred on the Up Hatherley site and the Racecourse Green Belt.

The meeting ended with Andrew North giving his assurance that he would continue to fight for Up Hatherley to be removed from the JCS proposals, and announced that no-one appeared to be in favour of supporting the removal of the Green Belt status from the land around the Racecourse. It was because of what had been said at that meeting that I gave positive updates at the Prestbury and Up Hatherley public meetings.

We left the office that day in an upbeat mood, and I would remind you that I supported your comments about reducing the numbers which I thought had tacit support from the officers. Now I am not so sure.

We should not let Tewkesbury dictate the agenda especially when the brownfield site at the MOD Ashchurch and the white land at Highnam are begging to be developed first.

Regards.

Les."

The outcomes of the MSG meeting on 6th March were predictable. More presentations on employment land and transport modelling, and a further update on the 'duty to co-operate' between the three JCS authorities and Stroud. The Stroud Inquiry had ended and it was a question now of waiting for the Inspector to make known his findings.

On Monday 10th March I faced the members of Prestbury parish council again and gave them the details of the meeting with Andrew North. I told them that in spite of what appeared to be an 'about-turn' the land at the Racecourse was still under scrutiny and could still be removed.

The following night I attended the second Up Hatherley Forum meeting. The meeting was well-attended – 70 residents were recorded as having attended and the chairman Stuart Fowler welcomed them all.

Stuart in his opening comments referred to the recent publication of a letter from Nick Boles MP, Parliamentary Under Secretary of State (Planning), who had emphasised to local authorities that they must take into account the views of local communities when planning for the future.

He had also made it clear in the letter that central government would maintain key protections for the countryside and, in particular, for the Green Belt. He reiterated that a Green Belt boundary could only be altered in exceptional circumstance; its permanence was important in future planning. [Paragraph 83 NPPF]

Stuart Fowler emphasised that the Forum meeting was important because the publication of the JCS Pre-Submission document was only a few weeks away. It would be up to the three councils to vote for or against it.

"It is unfortunate" said the chairman, "that the two local councillors for Up Hatherley had not responded to the invitation to attend the Forum meeting."

In my opening comments I referred to the Nick Boles MP's letter, which I told the meeting also carried a comment that 'unmet housing need cannot expand into the Green Belt'.

"This was good news", I told the meeting, "because since my last update to the parish, there had been a lot of 'shifting of feet' by the officers on the matter of removing the land at Up Hatherley from the forthcoming Pre-Submission document. In spite of promises made at previous meetings, I believe the officers were now trying to renege on those promises. I also believe that they have been under pressure from TBC officers, who must realise that removal of Up Hatherely from the document would probably put pressure back on the land at Highnam and elsewhere in the Tewkesbury area."

I answered several questions regarding the reliability of the officers and the final document. My response to other questions along similar lines was that we do not have anywhere else to go – we needed the officers and particularly those on the CBPB to support our position.

I told the meeting that I would continue to press them between now and the council meeting on April 9th.

I was asked about the dependability of the two local councillors when the next vote is taken. "That was a difficult question to answer" I told the questioner, "they let us all down on 5th September, and despite their recent letters claiming that they are now against development at Up Hatherley, I could not say to you that they would not change their minds again in the future."

In answer to another question about Highnam, I told the questioner that I could only keep pressing the point that the land at Highnam is 'white land' and should be considered in the same way that the 'white land' at Leckhampton had been considered.

There had been a lot of criticism levelled at the JCS team and the CBPB during the course of the evening, and it was clear the changing scene that I had explained had frustrated the local residents as much as it had me.

The reports in the local press alleging that CBC officers had not come to the same conclusions about the Nick Boles MP's letter as the rest of us put further doubt into the minds of local residents.

I had no difficulty in understanding the content of the letter, and my opinions were reinforced when I received a copy of a three-page document issued by the Department for Communities and Local Government (DCLG) headed 'Written Ministerial Statement'.

It referred to the commitment of the Coalition Government in the first paragraph, and then used the rest of the Statement to explain where the DCLG stood with reference to the 'Review of Planning Practices' carried out by Lord Taylor of Goss Moor in October 2012.

The Review had confirmed the Government's position on protecting the Green Belt, adding that "unmet housing need is unlikely to outweigh harm to the Green Belt and other harm to constitute very special circumstances justifying inappropriate development."

It also stated that the Government wanted to make it clear that "windfalls can be counted over the whole Local Plan period, and it was important that councils brought brownfield land into use . . ."

The three-page document was useful and it was clear to me that the JCS team had an important responsibility to take the Ministerial Statement into account before they made known their final proposals for the Pre-Submission Document 2014.

Each public meeting brought a spate of letters to the *Gloucestershire Echo* from angry residents. And when *Echo* readers read that CBC had put a different slant on the words of Nick Boles the Planning Minister, Peter Shield, a Cheltenham resident wrote the following:

> "Shame on you Andrew North in your role as chairman of the JCS programme board (Echo March 12). You are a public servant and we expect better of you than to behave like a barrack-room lawyer looking for a legal loophole to frustrate the clear intentions of Parliament as expressed both in the NPPF and written Ministerial statements.
>
> If you are correct, then Green Belt protection is effectively worthless as, every five years or so, when a Local Plan is prepared or reviewed, the Green Belt boundary is simply changed to accommodate the developers' thirst for prime greenfield sites.
>
> It does no good to excuse yourself with the plea that you have to plan to meet housing needs. One new house for every four that now exist over the next 17 years is clearly excessive and not justified by either population growth or economic prospects for the region.
>
> Let us hope our elected representatives will be able to rein you in."

On 20th March I met Laurence Robertson MP at a resident's house in Linden Avenue, Prestbury, where he had been invited to look at the Green Belt land over-looking the Cheltenham Racecourse.

It was a short visit and the local Member of Parliament left with a promise that he would speak to the Minister in the course of the next few days.

I knew Laurence Robertson MP from other occasions when we had to put our heads together to either stop or achieve something for the local community. I knew he would be committed to do all he could to protect the Green Belt. He had been against accepting the JCS Consultation Document, when it was presented to the council for approval on 5th September 2013.

The following day was also a significant day for the JCS area.

The controversy over the interpretation of the Nick Boles MP's letter had resulted in a special meeting taking place with two senior Civil Servants from DCLG and invited members. The meeting took place in TBC.

Jane Everton, Deputy Director (DCLG) and Lucy Hargeaves (DCLG), plus Keith Holland (Planning Inspectorate) attended: the three councils were repre-sented by the three chief executives, plus the senior councillors from each council.

According to the notes of the meeting there were also invited guests.

Once the news reached the ears of the general public, there was a spate of emails asking why the meeting had to be behind closed doors, and the Cheltenham Alliance formally asked Andrew North for permission to attend.

The request was not granted, which prompted Martin Horwood MP to take up the issue on behalf of the Cheltenham Alliance.

Whilst I did not have any say in the matter, I did express the view that a limited number of people from the Alliance should have been allowed to attend. When the meeting started I noticed that there were a number of people sitting in the public gallery (probably invited guests), so the meeting was not as 'closed' as some people wanted it to be.

The notes of the meeting stated that the meeting had been convened following the recent interventions by Nick Boles MP, on the subject of Green Belts.

"These interventions" according to the notes, "took the form of letters between him and Sir Michael Pitt (Planning Inspectorate) and a written parliamentary statement. The purpose of the meeting was to clarify policy in relation to Green Belts and to consider the implications for the Joint Core Strategy being prepared for the three planning authorities."

As the meeting progressed it became clear that most of the comments and questions were centred on the Green Belt. The DCLG representatives were asked for their interpretation of the Nick Boles MP letter, and the Government's position regarding protection of the Green Belt.

Predictably, they defended what the Minister had written in his Statement and Jane Everton confirmed several times that the Government's policies regarding the Green Belt were clear and substantiated in the NPPF.

Keith Holland told the council representatives that planning matters concerning the Green Belt were entirely the choice of the politicians. Whilst the answer was correct, it was my view that officer recommendations should be in accordance with planning policies too. There is no point in having strong Green belt policies if recommendations made by planning officers are not in accord with those policies.

It seemed that this view was shared by others.

The meeting covered the 'duty to co-operate' and the housing need as established by the 'objectively assessed need' (OAN). DCLG representatives emphasised 'the importance of a five-year supply of residential land across the JCS area, and warned that failure to provide sufficient housing allocations to meet OAN or failure to agree a Local Plan may make the sites vulnerable to planning applications and appeals including sites in the Green Belt'.

It was also made clear in the concluding remarks that when the JCS proposals are examined by the inspector at the Examination-in-Public, he will test the strategy to see if it can deliver the need, but he will not propose alternative strategies. This was an important point because there was a general perception that this may be the case at the examination.

There was a break for a buffet lunch followed by a meeting that had been scheduled as a 'dispute resolution' meeting between the representatives from CBC and representatives from TBC.

The purpose of the meeting, which was chaired by Jim Claydon, was to have an open and frank discussion about the key issues of the JCS programme especially having heard direct from the representatives of DCLG and the Planning Inspectorate.

Andrew North, chairman of the CBPB, opened the meeting by giving a summary of the JCS programme.

The chairman then invited each elected member to make any comments on the present situation which would ensure the most suitable and correct development for the JCS area.

He then followed this up by referring to the potential reduction of the bottom range figure for the OAN in the context of the CCHPR paper, and asked whether this was the process or rationale for removing any site from the document.

He added: "To do so must not make the plan unsound, and that the removal has a political buy-in to the plan."

The discussion that followed seemed to be whether the Up Hatherley site should be removed from the plan, although there was no mention of this in the opening comments by the chairman.

Cllr Jude Perez (Lib/Dem) made her usual plea for the Brockworth site to be considered in the same context as Up Hatherley.

Whilst I found it difficult to hide my delight in debating the possibility of removing the Up Hatherley site from the JCS document, I knew that it was not going to be an easy.

Listening to the opinions expressed by both sides, I came to the view that Andrew North had been doing some 'behind-the-scenes' discussions with TBC. We were simply going through the motions of getting the 'political agreement' that the chairman had mentioned earlier.

After 40 minutes the two sides came to an impasse. The TBC representatives called for a 15–minute break in order for them to discuss privately the issue of Up Hatherley and its importance to the JCS.

After fifteen minutes a request came from the TBC members for an extension.

This was agreed and on the Cheltenham side we couldn't make up our minds whether it was good news or bad. It was a frustrating period with lots of pacing up and down as we tried to pass away the time.

Eventually, we were told that TBC wanted to re-convene the meeting and we all sat with bated breath to hear their decision. Robert Vine, TBC Leader of the Council, announced that they had agreed that the Up Hatherley site should be removed as a result of the lower housing figures. He emphasised that it had not been an easy adjournment for them, but they were keen for the JCS to go forward.

There was an intake of breath when I heard Cllr Steve Jordan ask whether there was any possibility of talking about Leckhampton. There was an immediate response from a TBC councillor who said: "If you want to talk about Leckhampton, we will walk away from the meeting."

Nothing else was said. It was obvious that the TBC group in their adjournment had agreed, perhaps as a compromise that any removal from the JCS was solely Up Hatherley and nowhere else.

The meeting ended with a summary from the chairman, and we all made for the exit door – there were none of the usual pleasant homilies from either side as we walked towards the car park.

I was relieved that the discussion concerning the land at Up Hatherley was now over, and I was anxious to relay the good news to Stuart Fowler, chairman of the parish council, which I did on the way home from Tewkesbury.

On Monday 24th March I received a copy of an email from Cllr Steve Jordan to Robert Vine (TBC). It was copied to Paul James (GCC). It read:

> "Hello Rob, Thank you for your input on Friday, I think it was a very useful discussion and made progress towards agreeing a JCS.
>
> Agreement on reducing the OAN and removing Chargrove from the allocated sites was very helpful. I assume Tewkesbury and Gloucester will be further discussing a specific proposal at Twigworth as I'm not sure exactly what we ended up with. I also confirm the Cheltenham commitment to meeting our urban target without needing to extend the Green Belt at the Racecourse.
>
> One of the other loose ends was the request for me to consider 'reserving' the Chargrove site. Thinking about that option, I don't think it helps as it would still mean Chargrove being available for immediate development if there are any problems elsewhere. Since the 'threat' to develop Chargrove came from left field, I don't think anyone will be convinced unless it is clearly removed.
>
> Taking it out of Green Belt and leaving it as 'reserved' will just seem like weasel words. Given the debate about Nick Boles' statement, it will be useful for us to show that even if some Green Belt is to be developed, we are prepared to defend Green Belt such as this which is flagged red in our own review.
>
> Given that we are already to reserve or safeguard areas west of Cheltenham and northwest Cheltenham (at Junction 10), we don't need to include Chargrove Lane. That is one of the advantages of reducing the OAN. It would also mean that all safeguarded/reserved sites in the JCS are on the edge of Cheltenham, which is politically difficult to justify. For all the above reasons I don't support 'reserving' Chargrove and support removing it as an allocation.
>
> I hope this helps to avoid any confusion in on-going discussions this week.
> Steve."

The email was also sent "for information" by Cllr Jordan to Andrew North and to Cllr Tim Harman.

The email was difficult to understand in some respects, such as the reference "to extend the Green Belt at the Racecourse"; did he mean "remove" rather than "extend", and what did Cllr Jordan mean when he wrote: "... Chargrove came from left field"?

The thrust of the email from Cllr Jordan to Cllr Vines seemed more like confirmation of a behind-the-scenes 'discussion' on two important parts of the JCS. Why would only Andrew North, Cllr Harman and I be told by email of a discussion between the group leaders of Cheltenham and Tewkesbury that could still have serious consequences for the JCS?

There was a special meeting on Monday 24th March in Andrew North's office to discuss the outcome of the DCLG and the CBC/TBC 'special meeting'.

The general consensus was that any future Green Belt planning applications should be dealt with in accordance with the five purposes set out in the NPPF.

We were pleased that agreement (although tenuous), had been reached with TBC and we agreed that we should present a united front at the next MSG meeting on Wednesday 26th March.

I also had a telephone call from Chris Joyner, a resident of Brockworth, who had attended one of the public meetings in Up Hatherley.

Chris wanted to meet me with a colleague at my house on Tuesday 25th March to discuss the recent meeting with DCLG and the JCS. I agreed to the meeting.

At 7.30 pm. I welcomed Chris Joyner, Cllr Jude Perez (Lib/Dem) and Cllr Vince Perez (Lib/Dem) to my home and we talked generally about the JCS; its progress through the years and its proposals.

In spite of the fact that the two councils had met on the previous Friday to discuss and finally approve the removal of Up Hatherley from the JCS, the Brockworth people seemed to want to go back over the detail behind the proposal, in which they seemed to think I had had a big input.

Cllr Jude Perez particularly, kept asking me why I thought Up Hatherley was so special that it should be withdrawn, given that Brockworth was of equal value to the people who lived there.

I reminded Cllr Perez that the choices had been made on the basis of the two Green Belt Reviews, and it was my understanding the land at Up Hatherley was more significant to prevent the merging of Cheltenham and Gloucester, than Brockworth.

After the visitors had departed, I wondered why they had taken the trouble to travel to Up Hatherley when the deal had already been done, and there was nothing that anyone could do about it.

I did wonder whether they were giving me notice that as far as they were concerned the removal of Up Hatherley from the JCS was not over yet. The three councils still had to endorse the Pre-Submission document in April and they would have something more to say about it when the TBC meeting took place on 7th April.

The MSG meeting on 26th March began with an overview by the chairman of the meeting with DCLG. He believed there was no change in Green Belt policy and that the representatives from DCLG and the Planning Inspectorate had made it clear decisions had to be both planning and political.

The duty to co-operate was also made clear, and I noted that the "notes" of the meeting would be posted on the JCS website.

The chairman concluded his summing up by referring to one of the comments made by the officials: "It was the choice of the councils and no-one else to make the decision".

The above are my notes of the DCLG meeting, and I have no other notes of the summary update of the draft JCS, or the 'Final Suite of Policies' that were discussed at the meeting.

It was my last attendance at a JCS/MSG meeting as I had made up my mind some time earlier that after nearly 36 years as a councillor on both Tewkesbury and Cheltenham Borough Councils, it was time for me to retire and let others carry on with the good work that had been achieved.

Having played such an important part in getting the land at Up Hatherley Way removed from the JCS, I was delighted to read the front page article by Jack Maidment in the *Gloucestershire Echo* on Saturday March 29th. It reported:

'Housing plans: 800 greenbelt homes removed. Two sites taken off disputed strategy'.

Alongside a photograph of the land at Up Hatherley, Jack Maidment wrote: "Green Belt land earmarked for almost 800 homes in Up Hatherley has been removed from a controversial housing plan. The site at Chargrove Lane has been saved from development after Cheltenham, Tewkesbury and Gloucester councils reduced the number of homes to be built across the region between 2011 and 2031 from 33,200 to 30,500.

Andrew North, chairman of the Joint Core Strategy Programme Board, said: 'We have been working extremely hard to ensure the feedback from the last consultation and the latest evidence available is incorporated, where appropriate, into this version of the Joint Core Strategy. This is now the version that we, as officers, feel is ready to be presented to the planning inspectorate.'

Meanwhile, the proposal in the blueprint to build more than 3,000 homes on greenbelt land at Twigworth and Innsworth has been amended to remove the Twigworth half of the site."

It was a good article giving a lot of detail on all the JCS proposals.

The article would not have pleased everyone, but two sites had been removed from the JCS following determined work from councillors in each of the three councils, and that was important.

Not unexpectedly, there was apprehension among the local residents in the areas most likely to be affected by the JCS proposals, as they waited to hear the results from the three council meetings on the 7th, 8th and 9th April 2014.

I attended the TBC council meeting on Monday 7th April with my friend and colleague Patrick Durkan.

From the rear of his property, Patrick overlooks the swathe of Green Belt on the south side of the Racecourse, which is why he became a stalwart in the fight against the so-called 'tidying-up' exercise that was supported by Tracey Crews, Andrew North and Cllr Jordan.

The public gallery was packed. A committee room was made available for the overflow of residents and councillors who wanted to listen to the debate.

I was not impressed with the presentation, or the comments that were being made by TBC councillors. Those who were promoting the Pre-Submission document were dismissive of anything their opponents raised, using the theme that "this was the best that could be achieved, and we are where we are and there is no alternative but to accept what is before us".

The opponents to this kind of rhetoric used stronger language than was usually expected in a council debate, and they repeatedly missed the point when putting an alternative point of view.

From my perspective, they made 'heavy weather' of whatever case they had by continually making unfair comments, directed mainly at the councillors in CBC, whom they accused of persistently pushing the case for the removal of Up Hatherley and Leckhampton. This was not true. A case had been made several times to remove land at Twigworth and Innsworth from the JCS strategic allocations.

It was an unnecessary accusation in my view; the MSG was the first place for objections to the strategy to be made. Apart from Cllr Perez, I do not recall other representatives from TBC stating they were opposed to the JCS proposals.

After nearly four hours of listening to the same diatribe I left the meeting, leaving Patrick Durkan to endure more of the same, but I knew he was a reliable source to listen to the final stages of the debate and to report back to me in due course.

There was a lot to think about as I drove home, in particular my speech and what I should include when I addressed the council on Wednesday afternoon.

On Tuesday evening GCC approved the JCS with a comfortable majority.

The CBC public gallery on Wednesday was full with standing room only. Public seats in the council chamber too were full with residents ready to put their questions to the Leader of the Council and the planning officers.

Cheltenham councillors approving the JCS document at a council meeting in April 2014

The twenty-page report to council was presented by Cllr Steve Jordan. He confirmed that 'the report summarises the Pre-Submission version of the Joint Core Strategy and that it seeks council's approval to publish it'.

Members of the public put their questions to the Leader of the Council and, where appropriate, supplementary questions to the Leader were allowed.

Cllr Anne Regan proposed an amendment to the report asking council members to defer the publication of the document to allow more time to study the JCS documents and the evidence base.

Cllr Tim Harman seconded the amendment.

Following a recorded vote the amendment was lost by 7 votes to 21.

Another amendment proposed by Cllr Ian Bickerton and seconded by Cllr Duncan Smith asked the council to await the latest ONS figures which were due out at the end of April. However, I had already arranged with Andrew North and Cllr Jordan for the latest ONS figures (should they show a downward trend) to be a reason for the MSG to be reconvened to discuss them.

The amendment also called for a 'brownfield first' policy to be adopted and the establishment of green spaces in any new developments.

The amendment was lost by 10 votes to 20 with 2 abstentions.

I took up the thrust behind the amendment and the purpose of the ONS question by asking the Leader of the Council whether the notes at the bottom of his report could reflect three important points:

1. Possible changes to the ONS figures.
2. The results of the traffic modelling.
3. The outcome of the Stroud District Council planning inquiry, with particular reference to the land at Brookthorpe/Whaddon?

"All three" I said, "could have consequences for the Pre-Submission document before it goes to the Examination-in-Public at the end of the year."

I was given the assurances I was seeking.

There were several speeches made both for and against the Pre-Submission document being published. The following is my speech to council:

> "Madam Mayor,
>   There is no doubt that we have reached a critical stage in the JCS process.
>   Whilst I would have been happier not to have been given the opportunity to consult a document and then submit my objections to the JCS team following the 5th September meeting last year – and a lot happier if the council had supported the amendment put forward by Cllr Duncan Smith, calling on the council to remove Leckhampton and Up Hatherley from the joint core strategy. However, that is now 'water under the bridge' and as is often said by others, we are where we are and we should now get on with it.
>   Madam Mayor, as this will be the last speech I shall make in this council chamber, I will try to do what my long-suffering wife told me to do before I left home today – "make sure you make it a good one".

I will try, with your indulgence of course.

I cannot say that I am pleased to be where we are with the Joint Core Strategy, and I repeat what I said earlier when we debated the amendments, that it was my intention to suggest in the main debate that the joint core strategy should be deferred to enable the three councils to 'go back to the drawing board' and come forward with better proposals.

I put it to you Madam Mayor, a strategy where 70 per cent of the location sites are in the Green Belt cannot be a sensible document, especially when other non-Green Belt sites exist.

I made a similar plea to the JCS Member Steering Group on 12th December 2013 – I also suggested at that meeting that if a new strategy was forthcoming, the Cross Boundary Programme Board should also include elected members from the three councils.

My suggestion was listened to but not acted upon, and now four months later, we find ourselves at a critical stage of the process.

On Monday, I sat with other members of the public and listened to the debate on the JCS proposals in the Tewkesbury Borough Council chamber.

It was not a good debate by any stretch of the imagination, and like many other people I was appalled at the accusations constantly being levelled at Cheltenham Borough Council, Up Hatherley and Prestbury councillors.

And for good measure, the people in Prestbury who had staged a protest against the eleventh-hour inclusion of the Green Belt land at the Racecourse also came in for criticism.

Madam Mayor, by 9.30 pm I had had enough of listening to this bile and I left the council building.

As I drove back to Cheltenham I pondered on what I had heard – it seemed to me on the face of what I had just heard – that to postpone the decision on the JCS, or even scrap it altogether, would only result in another document being prepared and all the old arguments over whether Up Hatherley and the Racecourse should be included debated again and again.

We would argue around the old hoary chestnut of whether Cheltenham should take more housing and Tewkesbury less, and we would probably finish up with a document similar to the present one.

The proposals before us today are not perfect, but if, as we have been told by many people, that the population projection figures are wrong and the later ONS figures may prove this to be the case, then the assurances we have been given in the recommendations at the bottom of page one, will give the three councils the opportunity to take a fresh look at the allocations should new figures come out, and adjust accordingly.

Not only that, but the assurances also allow further time for the traffic modelling to be accurate, which should meet the requirements which are essential for the areas that will be directly affected by any future development.

Remember too that other areas will feel the impact of the additional traffic that will be created.

And thirdly, and this one is equally important, is the outcome of the Stroud Planning Inquiry and the 'duty-to-co-operate'. If the planning inspector thinks that the Stroud document is unsound; it may result in the land at Brookethorpe/Whaddon being included in the list of sites suitable for development.

Madam Mayor, there is still a long way to go and I am sure there will be representations made to the inspector at the Examination-in-Public.

I wish you all well in your earnest endeavours."

For a moment there was silence, but it was broken by Cllr Barbara Driver, who called out: "We shall miss you on planning, Les."

It was a typical off-the-cuff remark from Cllr Driver, who had been one of the few councillors on planning who fought for what she believed was right, and she was often more right than wrong.

I looked across the chamber to where Cllr Derek Davies and Cllr Robert Vine were sitting – they had long faces, which was to be expected after my criticism of the Tewkesbury Borough Council meeting.

My announcement that I was making my last speech to the council came as a surprise to many councillors – some were gracious enough to pass comment on my years of service in their speeches.

After a long debate, the council members agreed in a recorded vote that the Joint Core Strategy Pre-Submission document should be published under Regulation 19 of the Town and Country Planning (Local Planning) (England) Regulations 2012. The council also agreed that the Pre-Submission document should be submitted to the Secretary of State for independent examination.

18 councillors voted to approve the report with 14 against.

An analysis of the voting pattern is interesting. Cllr Malcolm Stennett and I voted for the Pre-Submission document for the reasons I have referred to above. The Lib/Dem councillors voted precisely the same way as they did at the 5th September 2013 council meeting, but several Conservative councillors having previously voted for the consultation document, voted against the Pre-Submission document.

It was inevitable that as soon as it became known that the Pre-Submission document had been approved by all three councils, planning applications for development of land in the JCS area would be submitted.

The document would be examined for soundness by a government inspector towards the end of the year or in the early part of 2015. This would mean that the inspector would put as much weight on the document that he thought was appropriate.

If nothing else, the next few months for councillors and members of the public, were going to be exciting times.

It would also be a time for me to reflect on my 35 years and nine months as a borough councillor and a representative of the people in Prestbury. It had certainly been a long journey from February 1976 to June 2014 with many pitfalls along the way, but it also had so many delightful occasions that they will remain with Pam and me for the rest of our lives.

The time had come to hand over the baton to someone else whom I could trust to carry on the true PAB traditions of putting people before politics and protecting the beautiful countryside.

That person I am pleased to say is John Payne, a loyal man in every respect; a voluntary worker for the parish and the wider community.

He along with Malcolm Stennett, Dave Prince and Adam Lillywhite will be true ambassadors for the PAB Group and I know each one of them will work assiduously for their communities and for Cheltenham.

CHAPTER 30

Epilogue

I am glad that I succumbed to the pressure from my friends and colleagues to put down on paper the principal historical moments in the creation and long existence of the People Against Bureaucracy Group (PAB).

I am also pleased that I had either foresight, or was it untidiness in my psyche, not to throw anything away during my 35 years and nine months service as a borough councillor.

My archive of documents, reports and emails covering the period 1976 to 2014 was not complete by any means. Missing information was often supplied by others who believed that by filling in the gaps it would contribute to a worthwhile record of the ups and downs of a non-political group of people who passionately believed that people should come before party politics.

When I stood in the by-election in Prestbury in 1978, I did feel strongly that those who lived furthest away from the centre of activity at Tewkesbury, were not only left out, but in their view, were 'shackled' by local bureaucracy. It seemed to me that it would be a good opportunity to try to free the people from it and at the same time, liberate them from the strictures of 'party politics'. It was the message that came across at the inaugural meeting in Lakeside School in February 1976.

It was a big idea at the time and I was far from sure that I was going to win the by-election anyway.

But once I had started out on the journey of trying to win the election for PAB I was determined to make a difference to the lives of the people should I be success-ful. It will be up to the reader to decide whether I have been successful or not.

In recent times, the redevelopment of North Place has been a shambles. The Lib/Dem governing body missed a golden opportunity to tell the council that nothing but the best was acceptable for the site. All the community got for their money were proposals for a food store, a multi-storey car park and inevitable traffic problems that go with it.

It was not beyond the wit of architects to come forward with a scheme of residen-tial development around a central plaza containing water features and attractive landscaping. And of course, the provision of underground parking to ensure the surface area was free from parked cars.

The local community pleaded for houses and a complex of small shops but their pleas as so often happened in other communities, fell on deaf ears.

There is still time to make this part of the town centre an attraction for visitors, providing the council administration have the wherewithal to insist on something better.

While I am proud of what the PAB group have achieved during the past thirty eight years, there have been disappointments too – for example the regular rejection of the opportunity to update the Cheltenham Borough Local Plan. Sites and important green lungs would have had a better chance of preservation if the Plan had been updated.

The new Local Plan, whenever it arrives, should protect the existing green spaces and create new ones in areas that are without them. Steps to strengthen the gap between Cheltenham and Gloucester and Prestbury and Bishop's Cleeve must be included.

The settlement of a dispute in a court of law should always be avoided if at all possible. Sometimes there are winners and sometimes there are losers, but the council's dispute with Christine Laird ended with both sides losing.

The council lost a substantial amount of money and so did the Laird family. But added to the financial loss in Christine Laird's case, was the breakdown in her health, which still requires careful nursing to this day.

The provision of underground parking is still as far away as ever but it remains an ambition for the PAB Group.

Ian Bickerton lost his Leckhampton seat in the 2014 local elections.

He was elected chairman of the Leckhampton Green Land Action Group (LEGLAG) and continues to campaign against development in the Leckhampton area.

Whilst Prestbury is comparatively free from flooding because of the steps that were taken by PAB councillors, there remains a continuing problem of flooding across the town,

Pressure must be exerted on the Highways Department to cure the drainage problems that exist in known problem areas.

The acceptance of a joint core strategy for Cheltenham, Gloucester and Tewkesbury was always going to be a difficult process. It took five years to come to a set of proposals, albeit, far from perfect, but accepted by the majority of elected councillors representing the three areas.

There will be time for a re-assessment of the content of the strategy should the central government inspector decide that the strategy is unsound. But further delay will only result in the loss of more important sites in Cheltenham, Gloucester and Tewkesbury whilst more valuable time is used going through the same processes again that brought so much heartache in the past.

Although the journey has ended for me, the business of putting people before party politics is never finished. There is still much to be done by others and the rewards are there for those who want to do good for people who feel they have been left behind in this fast-moving world.

There will be many pitfalls along the way, and unfortunately there will be a continuous flow of political 'stooges' who will say one thing and do another.

Independent-minded thinkers will be criticised, not for their thinking, but because they have not followed the 'herd' and become prisoners of the political system.

Sometimes, party political councillors will see the folly of their ways and resign as a member of the 'herd' and become independent of the party political system. They will have the freedom of being free-thinkers, which is the best option for them and for the people they represent.

I end on a note of optimism. I believe that with the change in political thinking, more people will come to realise that 'people power' is worth pursuing. People will realise that without the shackles of party politics in local government, better things can be achieved for local people.

I would like to thank:

My friends and colleagues who encouraged me to write the book in 2011. Council officers, past and present at Tewkesbury and Cheltenham councils, who kept me supplied with dates and records.

All my friends and well-wishers who supplied me with letters and emails – too many to mention by name, but they know who they are and I shall always be indebted to them.

David Hall for his inspiration and insatiable appetite to find the truth behind the headlines.

Sara Freckleton for reading the early chapters of the book.

Don Gillanders, an excellent member of the legal fraternity and a long-time friend, for coming to my 'rescue' and reading the book from start to finish.

Hugh Laird for giving me daily updates of the High Court proceedings.

Neil Parrack, who, without his guidance and wisdom, the book would not have been completed. His proof-reading of every page was invaluable: a constant guide and mentor throughout the journey.

Robin Brooks, Commercial Features, Gloucestershire Media, for providing the photographs of Christine Laird in the 2002–2010 period.

Patrick Durkan for his telephone calls and words of encouragement.

Gerald Seal for his forensic examination of the typescript and helpful suggestions.

David Hyett for his photographic skills with the design of the front cover.

Tim Bacon, who never tired of distributing hundreds of leaflets about the book.

The residents of Up Hatherley and Prestbury who have been loyal and supportive along the way.

And finally Pam, whose patience and understanding of the demands on me during the period of writing the book and being a councillor, was always appreciated.

The book is dedicated to my family.

APPENDIX 1

HIGH COURT
CBC V LAIRD
WRITTEN STATEMENT

I, David John Hall of 12 Barton Way, Up Hatherley, Cheltenham, do hereby state that I am not speaking on behalf of either the prosecution or the defence. This statement is simply an expression of the concern I have about the conduct of the case, that I think should be brought to the attention of the court. I also think that I have a duty, to those whom I represent, and to the public at large, to make these concerns known to those who are sitting in judgement.

I seek protection under the terms of the Public Interest of Disclosure Act 2000 Section 97, in making this statement. I have made known my concerns to both the solicitor and Chief Executive of Cheltenham Borough Council.

I have been involved in local government for a number of years. I was first elected to my local parish council in 1973, and became its chairman in 1981. I was to remain chairman until 2006. I have represented the parish at Borough Council level for fifteen years. From 1980–1991 on Tewkesbury Borough Council, and at transfer of the parish to Cheltenham Borough Council until 1992. Then, from 2006 until the present time as a member of Cheltenham Borough Council.

I have served on numerous committees and boards of governance over the years representing both Parish and Borough Councils. I was elected to represent the five parish councils, on the Borough Council Standards Committee in 2001, as its first Parish Member.

I had a brief acquaintance with Mrs Laird at a professional level, whilst representing Up Hatherley Parish Council on a couple of issues. Firstly, in connection with Borough Council's Parish Boundary Review held in 2001/2002, and secondly, in arguing against the continued use of Area Committees. The 1-2-1 discussions I had with her, and the way she facilitated the committees that decided the way forward on these subjects, was impressive, she was always well informed, and her marshalling of evidence was impeccable.

As stated above I believe that a miscarriage of justice may occur if the concerns I have about the conduct of this case are not disclosed. The concerns fall into two areas. Firstly, the part played by the local standards committee during the time of the breakdown of governance. Secondly, that the action is being driven by malice and not in a temperate manner.

I am also deeply concerned about the health and well-being of the person who is being prosecuted. I have some knowledge of disability, having been a Director of Carers Gloucestershire for five years, and for two years the Vice Chairman of the

Board of Directors. Some of the comments that have been made about employing people with mental health problems have, in my view, been discriminatory.

As stated above I was a member of the Borough Council's Standards Committee, from 2001 to 2006. Being for a time its Vice-Chairman. During the early period of the break down in relationships between the Managing Director and the Leader of the Council, the Standards Committee was not involved, other than being briefed by the Monitoring Officer that things were taking their course in accordance with the rules and procedures of governance. The committee was not asked to do anything. We were told that the complaints made by Mrs Laird the leader, Cllr McKinlay, were being investigated by the Standards Board of England, and at the conclusion of the investigation they were all dismissed, with just one exception.

I remember, also, being told by Mrs Hudson-Bendersky, the Standards Committee Chairman, at this time, that she had occasion to meet with Cllr McKinlay, and that he had told her that the Standards Committee was a waste of time and money, and that if it were up to him he would disband it. I also recall expressing my concern, in a letter to the chairman dated 19 May 2004, about a letter the committee had received from Cllr Godwin, dated 18 May 2004, which drew attention to alleged irregularities in the conduct of the case. He went on to tell us that Mr Ford had himself lodged a complaint against Mrs Laird, and I asked her whether or not Mr Ford should continue advising us, with this being the case. I seem to remember that the reply was from Mr Ford, who assured me that the matters were all being dealt with in strict accordance with the code of governance, and there was nothing to worry about.

I subsequently learnt that Mrs Laird had requested that the Borough Council's Standards Committee look into the issues and provide an independent assessment of the points that both she and the Leader of the Council had raised, with a view of coming to some sort of conciliation, between the two parties. This course of action did not happen and the grievances were heard and pronounced upon by panels of elected members. Because of this, I consider the judgements made by these panels to be unsafe.

I have also subsequently learnt that the abuse to which Mrs Laird had been subject started in 2002, and went on way into 2003. What is more I have formed the view that her complaints about this abuse, along with her concerns about people conspiring against her were justified, and that her breakdown was understandable. I am further concerned that the arms length investigation carried out by the Standards Board of England was totally inadequate, not least because it was carried out by telephone, and that the Standards Board of England's representative on the spot, Mr Ford, the Council's Monitoring Officer, was a person who had himself been harbouring grievances against Mrs Laird.

It has also come to my attention that Group Leaders had submitted a complaint about the competence of the Monitoring Officer, in his handling of Mrs Laird's Contract of Employment.

This then is the first of my two key concerns. Mr Ford should not have been advising the local Standards Committee and liaising with the Standards Board of England at the same time as being subject to complaints by members, and harbouring a grievance against Mrs Laird. The SBE judgement of Mrs Laird's complaints about Cllr McKinlay's conduct is, because of this, unsafe.

Turning now to my second point of concern. My understanding was that the Borough Council took its action against Mrs Laird to recover money that the Court may decide was not spent in the public interest.

As a recent member of the Staff. And Support Services Committee (I became a member in May 2008), I as present at a scheduled meeting of the committee dated Monday 24th November 2008. The Borough Solicitor and Ms Farooqi provided a situation report on the High Court case. Cllr McKinlay, led the attack against Mrs Laird, aided by Cllrs Barnes and Hay. He raked over her past misdemeanours, and called her a liar. He contradicted me when I suggested that the Counsel's recommended odds of victory being 6–4 on, were not especially attractive, by saying that the odds were good, and argued that the case be pursued. When the question was put to the vote I abstained. I subsequently remarked to the Chief Executive that I was surprised that Cllr McKinlay, who had played such a pivotal role in arguing for the case to proceed, had not declared an interest in proceedings.

I thought that was it.

Another Meeting was convened for 15 January 2009. On this occasion Cllr McKinlay was not present. I was horrified by the stream of abuse against Mrs Laird declared by Cllr Hay, and as a member of the Standards Committee I thought I had a duty to take the matter further. I subsequently took the matter up with the officer presiding, and she passed my e-mail letter to the Monitoring Officer, Mr Lewis. My questions about Cllr Hay's conduct have been acknowledged, but I am awaiting a detailed reply.

This abuse supported by Cllr Barnes, a continuation of the abuse meted out by Cllr McKinlay at the November Meeting, has led me to believe that the motive behind the case has been driven by malice, and not as I had thought in the first instance by temperate action. Because of this I do not consider the case to have been expedited in the public interest.

Finally, I would like the court to know that at a Staff and Support Services Meeting held on 16 March 2009, the exempt minutes of these two meetings were tabled for accuracy. When the minutes of the November Meeting were addressed. I stated that they did not include reference to the remarks made by Cllr McKinlay, and did not record that he had argued for continuance of the action against Mrs Laird. Cllr McKinlay, who was, surprisingly, present, denied that he had played a pivotal roll in the proceedings and that he had not argued that the proceedings against Mrs Laird should continue. When the vote on accuracy was put, I voted against.

Before the minutes of the meeting of 15 January 2009 were presented Cllr McKinlay was asked by the chair if the intended to declare an interest. Cllr McKinlay answered, "no". The chairman then stated that he had been given advice by the monitoring officer that Cllr McKinlay should declare a prejudicial interest and retire from the meeting. He then left the meeting. The exempt minutes were then considered for accuracy. I asserted that they did not include the remarks made by Cllr Hay, and that his demand that the Chief Executive, who had been tasked to reach an out of court settlement, should drive a hard bargain, was not included. It was agreed that Cllr Hay had made this comment, but it was not thought necessary to include it in the minutes, because it was not a resolution. I countered this by making the point that such a comment would surely have influenced, albeit unwittingly, the chief Executive in his subsequent handling of the negotiations, and should, because of this additional pressure being applied, but included in the minutes. This point too was dismissed as being irrelevant, and when the question was put, I voted against on the grounds of inaccurate reporting.

After the meeting, I was making my way to the members room, when I noticed Cllr McKinlay in conversation with Cllr Barnes. As I approached Cllr Barnes walked away. When I neared the door to the room, Cllr McKinlay sidled up to me, and thrust his face close to mine and whispered in menacing tones, "You've got a short memory, haven't you Councillor". With that he pulled back, as another member approached us. I asked him, as he was walking away, if I may quote him, and ask him to explain his behaviour, and he responded in the affirmative. I wrote to him immediately I returned home asking him to explain his actions, and I copied the note to the Chief Executive. I await his reply.

To conclude. I wish my concerns about the part played by the local standards committee, and the Standards Board of England in the conduct of the dispute, between the Leader of the Council and the Managing Director, to be noted by the Court. Also, to note my concerns that the case has been driven by malice, which I consider to be inimical to the public interest.

David Hall
Elected Member
Cheltenham Borough Council
19 March 2009

APPENDIX 2

Mr Ian Pennington,   August 19th 2009
Director,
KPMG LLP,
Marlborough House,
Fitzalan Court,
Cardiff.
CF24 0TE

Dear Mr Pennington,

REVIEW OF LEGAL ACTION AGAINST MRS CHRISTINE LAIRD

As you are probably aware, I have been a Borough councillor for more than thirty years, serving on both Tewkesbury Borough Council and Cheltenham Borough Council.
As an opposition group leader I was heavily involved on the dispute between Cheltenham Borough Council and its former managing director, Mrs Christine Laird. Since the formation of the Staff & Support Services Committee (S&SS), which I believe was introduced by Mrs Laird, I have been a member of that committee. Therefore, I have been involved with the various processes and decisions of that committee.
I stress 'involved' because I was not always 'at-one' with the decisions of the committee.
I have a reasonably good memory and, of course, I have my own record and notes of events, including meetings and the Minutes.

As you asked me to contribute to the review in your letter dated 7th August 2009 I have set out below a number of questions in an attempt to be the first tranche of questions that I believe should be asked.
I hope you agree?

Question 1. In a number of Minutes of the Staff & Support Services (S&SS) the record shows the details of the spiralling costs of the disputes, including external legal costs, staff costs, and other external costs and so on.
It also records in several Minutes that "the District Auditor has been kept informed of the financial situation."
Is this correct?

Question 2. If the answer above is 'yes' and the District Auditor was informed can you indicate to me at what point the District Auditor would have intervened, if, as we are now told, it was only because the request came from one of the local Members of Parliament that KPMG became involved?

Question 3. Were you or the District Audit office aware that on 13th May 2004 a proposal was put to the S & S S committee that a ceiling should be set on the amount of money spent on the dispute following revelations that the figure could exceed £250,000?

Question 4. Were you aware that the S & S S committee were informed at a later meeting that year that the projected increase in expenditure on the dispute could be a further substantial sum?

Question 5. Did you know that I proposed at a S & S S meeting that all options should be considered to end the dispute including 'retirement on the grounds of ill-health'?

Question 6. In January 2009 the local Press printed an article, which claimed that Mrs Laird had no money and that it would be pointless of the Council going to the expense of the High Court to claim damages.
Was KPMG made aware that Mrs Laird was not in a position to pay damages or excessive costs, whichever way the court case ended?

Question 7. If KPMG were aware of the above facts, did they (KPMG) convey this information to the Council?

Question 8. The chief executive's report to the Extraordinary Council meeting on August 3rd 2009 revealed that the time spent on court proceedings by Legal Services for the period 1st December 2006 to 1st July 2009 had been costed at £50,000. (back-filling posts, which was reasonable).
Can you explain why the claim submitted by the Council in the High Court and undere oath that the cost of pursuing litigation was £190 for every hour expended by Mr P. Lewis and Miss S. Farooqi reaching a figure between £200,000 and £250,000.
Can you explain why the stated figure in the report is so disproportionate to the actual claim in court?

Question 9. If KPMG were aware of the financial position of Mrs Laird in January 2009 (as claimed in my question 6) and the latest projected figure of the total costs the Council will have to pay may be in excess of £1.7 million, do you think that the amount of money expended so far is totally disproportionate to the amount of money claimed by the Borough Council in the High Court action?

I may have further questions, which I will send by email.
Thank you for your help.

Councillor L.G. Godwin

APPENDIX 3

Councillor David Hall

Cheltenham Borough Council

19th November 2009

PRIVATE & CONFIDENTIAL

KPMG
Marlborough House
Fitzalan Road
CARDIFF
CF24 0TE

Dear Sir

Herewith completed questionnaire, as requested.

David Hall

Questions in relation to the legal proceedings leading up to the High Court case

Completed by	**Councillor David Hall**

Date: 19 November 2009

I wish to draw attention to the fact that the answers to this questionnaire have had to rely totally on memory of events that happened nearly twelve months ago.

The reason for this is that I do not have copies of the exempt minutes of the SSS Meetings I attended. I assume the exempt minutes of the 12 June 2008 Meeting were tabled at the 11 September 2008 Meeting, a meeting that I did not attend. The exempt minutes for the Meetings 24 November 2008, and 15 January 2009 were handed out prior to entering exempt business at the 16 March 2009 Meeting. Members were given a few minutes to read these minutes before being asked to approve them. I remember that they contained inaccuracies and omissions as far as I was concerned, (a point that was not agreed by others incidentally), and I voted against acceptance.

The minutes were handed back to the committee clerk at the end of the meeting, and I have not seen them since.

ABCD   *KPMG LLP*
Questions in relation to the legal proceedings leading up to the High Court case
Error! No texts of specified style in document.

Question	Reponse
1. Who do you consider to have been responsible for taking decisions regarding the High Court legal action against Mrs Laird (and RCT Council), e.g. Monitoring Officer, the Staff & Support Services Committee or any other person or committee?	**Elected members of the Staff & Support Services Committee acting on advice from Officer and legal opinion.**
2. Was this allocation of responsibility clearly articulated and understood by the Staff & Support Services Committee?	**I became a member of this committee in May 2008.** **It was always clear to me that this committee was making decisions on behalf of the whole council.** **At the 12 June 2008 Meeting of SSS a verbal update was given on the Court Action. It was reported that the Council had been advised by counsel that it had a strong case for damages against Mrs Laird, and that the case against Cynon Taf should also be pursued.** **I seem to remember that the Chairman reminded members that the Committee had previously delegated authority for the management of the case to the Borough Solicitor, consulting with Group Leaders as necessary. Key decisions were to be decided by the committee.**
3. Did the Staff & Support Services Committee consider whether key decisions regarding the legal proceedings should be referred to, or taken by, an alternative Member forum (e.g. Cabinet, Council etc)?	**No.** **This point was not addressed nor debated.** **The Chairman, at the 12 June 2008 had made clear that the conduct of the case was in the Group Leaders as necessary, and that key decisions were to be made by the Committee.**

ABCD   *KPMG LLP*
Questions in relation to the legal proceedings leading up to the High Court case
Error! No texts of specified style in document.

4. Was it clear to you what the Council's objectives were in taking legal action against Mrs Laird (and RCT Council)? Please can you summarise your understanding. Did the process followed ensure that this objective was clearly articulated and regularly revisted to ensure it remained appropriate and achievable?	**My understanding of the CBC case, was that the action was being taken to recover some, if not all, of the costs, incurred by the Council in dealing with Mrs Laird's protracted suspension and dismissal.** **My understanding of the case against Mrs Laird was that it hinged on the fact that she had failed to disclose on her application form that she had suffered from some form of mental illness at some time. I think I learnt this at the November 2008 Meeting.** **I seem to remember also that this charge was changed some time later to one of fraudulent intent. I have asked for confirmation of this point from the M.O. but have not received a reply.**
5. Were updates from officers (written reports or verbal explanations) timely and sufficient for the Staff & Support Services Committee to reach informed decisions?	**I cannot speak for meetings before May 2008, and I was not present at the September Meeting.** **At the June 2008 Meeting the committee was given a verbal update, but not called upon to make a decision.** **At the 24 November 2008 Meeting a verbal update was given which included a sparse risk analysis. The chances of success against Laird and Cynon Taff were given, and the committee resolved to continue the action against Laird, but discontinue the action against Cynon Taff.** **I was uncomfortable about the risk and the way the case was being managed and I abstained when the question was put to continue the action against Mrs Laird. I took up my reservations with the CE following the meeting.** **At the 15 January 2009 Meeting members were invited to sight briefing papers, under close supervision, the day before the meeting took place. This Meeting authorised the CE, in consultation with the leaders of the each of the Council's political groups, to seek an out of court settlement.**

ABCD   *KPMG LLP*

Questions in relation to the legal proceedings leading up to the High Court case
Error! No texts of specified style in document.

| 6. For those meetings that you attended as a member of the Staff & Support Services Committee did you feel sufficiently informed about the options open to the Council, including the risks and possible costs associated with each one, when making key decisions?

 (This is particularly for the key decisions at the 24 November 2008 meeting, where the claim against RCT Council was discontinued, and the 15 January 2009 meeting where the Staff & Support Services Committee resolved to continue with the claim but to attempt to settle out of court). | **Regarding the 24 November 2008 Meeting, as mentioned above, I was uncomfortable about what was happening, and was of the opinion that the Council was taking on unreasonble risks.**
 As well as making my feelings known to the CE, I informed the Leader of the Conservative Group, Cllr Duncan Smith.
 I repeat that I abstained when the committee resolved to continue the action.
 It should be made clear that it was at the November Meeting that the decisions to continue the case against Mrs Laird was made.
 The ad hoc meeting in January was convened primarily to authorise the CE to seek an out of court settlement, not to discontinue the action. That decision had already been made.

 The reasons for continuance being part of the motion debated in January was that an out of court settlement could not be sought if it had already been decided to discontinue the action. |
| 7. As a member of the Staff & Support Services Committee did you feel able to express your views about the way the Council should proceed with the legal proceedings?
 If no please explain why. | **Yes** |

ABCD   *KPMG LLP*

Questions in relation to the legal proceedings leading up to the High Court case
Error! No texts of specified style in document.

8. Do you have any other comments you wish to make about the Staff & Support Services Committee's role in relation to these legal proceedings?	**1. I was surprised that the Chief Executive,** and other directors, did not play a more active role in advising members about the risks to which the Council was being exposed. Also, I do not think that the sole responsibility for advising on risk should have been left to the Borough Solicitor. **2. I was concerned that key members of the** administration, who had played roles in marshalling and promoting the case against Mrs Laird from its beginning, were taking part in meetings where decisions to commence and continue the action against her were being made. I think these members should have declared both personal and prejudicial interests and have withdrawn from such meetings. Once again, I made by misgivings about this aspect of the case known to both the CE and to the MO, in various 1-2-1s I had with them following the meetings where this alleged code abuse had happened. **3. I was profoundly disturbed by the** behaviour of certain elected members at both the November 2008, and January 2009 Meetings. I made my concerns known to both the MO and CE. Immediately following these meetings. Because of the derogatory remarks and comments levelled at Mrs Laird at both meetings I gained the distinct impression that the case against her was being driven by malice. My concern was that the judgements made by these people being clouded by spite, could well lead to unreliable decisions, which were inimical to the public interest. **4. The exempt minutes of these critical** meetings were poor. Both the November and January Exempt Minutes were tabled for accuracy at the March Meeting. I challenged and voted against acceptance of both sets of minutes, on grounds of inaccuracy and omissions. **5. Exempt minutes of SSS meetings do not** record the presence of officers.

APPENDIX 4

Vision Statement

By 2031 Tewkesbury Borough, Cheltenham Borough and Gloucester City will have continued to develop as highly attractive and accessible places in which to live, work and socialise.

The Joint Core Strategy area will be recognised nationally as enjoying a vibrant, competitive economy with increased job opportunities and a strong reputation for being an attractive place in which to invest.

The character and identity of individual communities will have been retained while improved access to housing will have addressed the needs of young families, single people and the elderly.

New developments will have been built to the highest possible standards of design and focused on protecting the quality and distinctiveness of each community. Established in sustainable locations, without increasing the risk of flooding, they will have been designed with sensitivity towards existing villages, towns and cities and with respect for the natural environment.

As a result of a strong commitment to the housing and employment needs of the existing and growing population, all residents and businesses will benefit from the improved infrastructure, which will include roads, public transport and services, and community facilities.

Five Purposes of Green Belt (NPPF) National Planning Policy Framework

9. Protecting Green Belt Land

79. The Government attaches great importance to Green Belts. The fundamental aim of Green Belt policy is to prevent urban sprawl by keeping land permanently open; the essential characteristics of Green Belts are their oppenness and their permanence.

80. Green Belt serves five purposes:

- to check the unrestricted sprawl of large built-up areas;
- to prevent neighbouring towns merging into one another;
- to assist in safeguarding the countryside from encroachment;
- to preserve the setting and special character of historic towns; and
- to assist in urban regeneration, by encouraging the recycling of derelict and other urban land.

81. Once Green Belts have been defined, local planning authorities should plan positively to enhance the beneficial use of the Green Belt, such as looking for opportunity to provide access; to provide opportunities for outdoor sport and recreation; to retain and enhance landscapes, visual emenity and biodiversity; or to improve damaged and derelict land.

82. The general extent of Green Belts across the country is already established. New Green Belts should only be established in exceptional circumstances, for example when planning for larger scale development such as new settlements or major urban extensions. If proposing a new Green Belt, local planning authorities should;

- demonstrate why normal planning and development management policies would not be adequate.
- set out whether any major changes in circumstances have made the adoption of this exceptional measure necessary;
- show what the consequences of the proposal would be for sustainable development;
- demonstrate the necessity for the Green Belt and its consistency with local Plans for adjoining areas; and
- show how the Green Belt would meet the other objectives of the Framework.

APPENDIX 6A

Councillor L. G. Godwin, J.P.

10th December 2013

Tracey Crews,
Head of Planning,
Cheltenham Borough Council,
Municipal Offices,
Cheltenham.

Dear Tracey,

**Re: OBJECTION TO THE PROPOSAL TO INCLUDE C6b (UP HATHERLEY WAY)
IN THE JOINT CORE STRATEGY**

While most people recognise that there should be a strategy for growth and more houses to cope with a possible increase in employment opportunities in the three local authority areas, it is becoming clearer each day that the selection of possible sites, and the calculation of the figures, is flawed.

To support a strategy for growth, the population in the three areas must be supportive of the proposals. Of course, there will be some people in the three areas who are not directly affected by the JCS proposals. They will not be concerned until they realise that the countryside pursuits they used to enjoy are no longer there, or the alarming increase in traffic volumes start to affect them. But that should not mean that the Cheltenham Local Plan Green Belt Policies that have stood the test of time, and now supported and reinforced by the words contained in Chapter 9 of the National Planning Policy Framework (NPPF), should be cast aside.

The JCS briefing note dated 7th July 2013, headed "Green Belt Review" informs members and those who visit the JCS website, "The purpose of the Green Belt Review is to provide an independent assessment of the Green Belt which falls within the Gloucester, Cheltenham and Tewkesbury Joint Core Strategy (JCS) areas."

The review followed a 'principles based approach' which meant that is assessed the entire Green Belt against the five key purposes of Green Belt Policy, which are contained within PPG2.

**Leader of the Independent Group (PAB) Cheltenham Borough Council Mayor
of Cheltenham 1997/98
Website: www.pad.org.uk**

The five purposes are well-known and have been used many times in previous years to defend the Green Belt from development.

The briefing note went on to say: *"The review will help ascertain whether the Green Belt, as a whole, continues to contribute to these purposes, or whether there are parts which no longer contribute; and to what extent.*

It will also identify whether there is any justification to remove or add areas to the Green Belt."

At the bottom of the briefing note was an invitation to readers to download the JCS Green Belt Review Report dated September 2011. What the briefing note did not explain was that the independent assessment had been carried out by a company called Environment and Infrastructure UK Limited (AMEC).

The review had been commissioned by Cheltenham Borough Council on behalf of the three councils in the JCS area.

The Assessment Methodology that AMEC used was a simple one. The key objective of the study brief was to review the existing Green Belt in the JCS area in the context of PPG2 (subsequently replaced by the NPPF in March 2012) and the five purposes of including land in the Green Belt.

The study brief also stated: *"There are certain areas which do not need to be considered in great detail as their role in meeting the purposes of the Green Belt and the key purpose of designation, separation, is very clear."*

AMEC's 'broad assessment criteria' re-stated the five purposes historically laid out in PPG2 and later in the NPPF.

The results of the assessment were recording in a matrix using a simple 'traffic light' system where the red light indicated an area that made a significant contribution to Green Belt purposes.

The amber light indicated an area that made a contribution to Green Belt purposes: and the green light indicated an area that made a limited contribution to Green Belt purposes.

Using the traffic light system, AMEC placed the land between Cheltenham and Gloucester in the red area because it made a significant contribution to the Green Belt purposes. The land included the segment SE4 (Up Hatherley).

To justify its conclusion that SE4 made a significant contribution to Green Belt purposes, AMEC evaluated the significance of SE4 against the Green Belt purposes. It found that it "checked unrestricted sprawl; made a significant contribution to preventing the merger of Cheltenham with Gloucester; safeguarded the countryside from encroachment, and preserved the setting of the town."

In its recommendation, AMEC endorsed that the area was critical to the separation of Cheltenham and Gloucester, which was the original purpose of the Green Belt designation. It also confirmed: *The land was critical to preventing the closing of the gap between Cheltenham and Churchdown, which has already been intruded in developments associated with Gloucestershire Airport."*

The proposal to construct the South West Distributor Road (SWRD) in the early 1980's was fiercely opposed by local residents in Up Hatherley and The Reddings. The County Council could not persuade the parish councils or the local people that the road would be beneficial to them; neither could they justify the loss of many hectares of Green Belt land for a road they may or may not use.

In spite of PPG2, and local opposition, the road was constructed. The parish councils and Tewkesbury Borough councillors were assured that in spite of the loss of Green Belt land, which they regretted, the provision of the distributor road would be wide and robust and provide a permanent barrier against further encroachment into the Green Belt.

The late inclusion of the C6B proposal (Up Hatherley Way) would extend the built form of the town into the well-defined Green Belt, and would compromise the fundamental aims of Local Plan Green Belt policies and the NPPF.

To replace a robust and permanent road (SWRD) with a weak boundary line at Chargrove Lane is not in keeping with good Green Belt practice.

The 'gap' between Cheltenham and Gloucester is becoming smaller; the C6B proposal will reduce the gap still further, which is contrary to the second purpose of Green Belts – the merging of neighbouring towns and settlements.

To fracture the significant Green Belt area at south Cheltenham, would inevitably lead to more planning applications being submitted.

For some reason, with all the advice and recommendations from the experts, the JCS team (Programme Board) appear to have been extremely selective with their choice of sites for development in the JCS area.

The Highnam location (G8a) is non-Green Belt land and could take a large number of dwellings as part of the overall contribution to the joint core strategy. The AMEC (September 2011) review states: ***"Access is good via the A40 and the B4215."***

Although AMEC admitted that access from the south would require road infrastructure work to be undertaken, that should not be taken to mean that no development should take place.

AMEC also proposed large scale development being possible on all sides of Highnam, with the exception of the eastern side, which has significant flood risks considerations. Their recommendations included the phasing of development at Highnam over a twenty year period.

As the land is not protected by the five purposes of the Green Belt (NPPF), it should have been looked at first before Green Belt land in other areas was even considered.

Similarly, why is the land at Court Farm, Whaddon, south of Gloucester, which is not in the Green Belt, not included as a sustainable growth option in the joint core strategy? The fact that part of the land falls in the Stroud District should not be a reason not to include it in the Cheltenham, Gloucester and Tewkesbury JCS.

By not discussing with Stroud District Council the land at Whaddon may not be in accord with the cross-boundary co-operation principle laid down in the NPPF.

The land at Court Farm, Whaddon, represents a genuine opportunity to provide a sustainable urban extension at Gloucester, without the need for incursion into the Green Belt at Up Hatherley Way (C6b).

Furthermore, until the Regional Spatial Strategy (RSS) is removed from the Statute Book, its housing growth requirements remain part of its evidence base alongside local and national household projections.

The evidence base that informed it still remains a relevant indicator of the sustainability of broad locations for growth within the JCS area.

Finally, would the JCS Programme Board re-assess the brownfield MOD site at Ashchurch for housing rather than a mix of housing and employment?
If the Joint Core Strategy is to progress smoothly to the next stage, then non-Green Belt land should be developed before significant Green Belt such as the land along Up Hatherley Way (C6b) is even considered.

I strongly oppose the inclusion of C6b (Up Hatherley Way) in the JCS proposals.

Councillor Les Godwin.
Joint Core Strategy/Member Steering Group.

APPENDIX 6B

Councillor L. G. Godwin, J.P.

10th December 2013

Tracey Crews,
Head of Planning,
Cheltenham Borough Council,
Municipal Offices,
Cheltenham.

Dear Tracey,

Re: OBJECTION TO THE PROPOSAL TO REMOVE THE GREEN BELT STATUS FROM LAND AT THE CHELTENHAM RACECOURSE

The proposal to remove the Green Belt status from the land on the south side of Cheltenham Racecourse was an after-thought. It was never mentioned during any of the three years of discussion at the Joint Core Strategy/Member Steering Group meetings, which means it never formed part of the core strategy for Cheltenham, Gloucester and Tewkesbury.

Why should it? The land has always played a prominent part in securing the opennesss of the Racecourse, a point recognised by the consultants AERC and AMEC, who were engaged to study the significance of the Green Belt around Cheltenham in March 2007 and again in September 2011.

The Leader of Cheltenham Borough Council claimed at the 5th September 2013 council meeting that the proposal was "only a tidying-up exercise" of the Green Belt, and the Chief Executive claimed at a subsequent meeting with the PAB group councillors, that "he didn't even know it was being proposed".

The Leader of the Council went further, and added to his earlier comment: "By putting the JCS out to public consultation, it would be possible to take out that area depending on the feedback."

On that advice, I strongly object to the proposal to remove the Green Belt status from the land on the south side of the Racecourse and the north side of New Barn Lane for the following reasons.

**Leader of the Independent Group (PAB) Cheltenham Borough Council Mayor of Cheltenham 1997/98
Website: www.pad.org.uk**

In June 1984, an appeal to develop the land was dismissed by the Planning Inspector. This is what he said: *"In my opinion, the possible impact of the proposed development on the character and environmental setting of the Racecourse is a prime consideration, irrespective of any arguments regarding the Green Belt boundary. It is distinguishable from the adjoining Pye site, largely on account of its contours and its visual domination of the Racecourse. The site in conjunction with the other open land to the west, provide an attractive, grassland buffer between the New Barn Lane housing and the Racecourse. From the southern part of the appeal site, fine views are obtained across the Racecourse to Bishop's Cleeve and Southam.*
In my opinion, the existing natural grassland setting of some 150 to 200 metres in depth would not be adequately replaced by a landscaped strip of some 35 metres. Not only would the visual character of the area be entirely altered, but the location of residential uses and their associated activities in such close proximity to the Racecourse, would contribute to the urbanisation of the surroundings."

In March 2007, Cheltenham Borough Council commissioned Applied Environmental Research Centre Limited (AERC) to provide independent advice on the Green Belt for input into the Core Strategy.
The AERC Green Belt Review included "Extensive consultation with Tewkesbury Borough Council, Gloucester City Council, Gloucestershire County Council, and officers of the South West Regional Assembly."
AERC found that three of the four Cheltenham Borough Council Green Belt policies contributed positively to the purposes of the Green Belt, and should be included in a future Local Development Framework without change.
The fourth Green Belt policy allowing "limited infilling at Bowbridge Lane and Shaw Green Lane", would not, in the opinion of AERC, "contribute positively, and would conflict with Green Belt purposes and could be considered unsound."
It did not suggest that the Green Belt status of land at Bowbridge Lane and Shaw Green Lane should be removed, it recommended that "infilling should not be included in a Green Belt policy".

On 5th March 2007, AERC held a seminar at the Municipal Offices for councillors from Cheltenham and Bishop's Cleeve. Officers were also in attendance.
Seminar attendees were given maps of Cheltenham and surrounding district, and they were asked to score against those areas of Green Belt that they considered made significant contributions to the purposes of the Green Belt (prevent merging of settlements). The area that received the highest score was the land between Prestbury and Bishop's Cleeve, including the Racecourse.
The AERC Review when commenting on the 'ranking exercise' said: *"The assessment reflects the view (shared by the stakeholders) that the most important Green Belt purposes in Cheltenham are preventing towns merging, particularly Cheltenham and Gloucester, and Cheltenham with Bishop's Cleeve, and checking urban sprawl."*

Figure F (Map of Cheltenham and surrounding area) of the AERC Review, confirmed the strong, I repeat strong Green Belt boundary that existed along New Barn Lane.

Cheltenham Borough Council, Gloucester City Council and Tewkesbury Borough Council commissioned AMEC Environment and Infrastructure UK Limited to carry out an assessment of the Green Belt in readiness for the Joint Core Strategy.
AMEC published their final report in September 2011.
Their findings on the Green Belt in the Cheltenham and Bishop's Cleeve segment, was similar to the findings of AERC.
AMEC reported: ***The separation between Cheltenham and Bishop's Cleeve is critical to fulfilling the purpose of Green Belt designation (as extended in 1981)."***
Segments NE18 and NE22, which abuts Prestbury, is included in the total segments that make up the land between Cheltenham and Bishops Cleeve. The Green Belt area also abuts New Barn Lane, similar to that shown in the 2006 Cheltenham Borough Council Proposals Map.
AMEC, in its evaluation and recommendations concerning the land between Cheltenham and Bishop's Cleeve, made the following observations:

1. The segments NE18 and NE22, along with others, make a significant contribution towards preventing sprawl in various locations where there is already some evidence of ribbon development.
2. The segments make a significant contribution towards the separation of Cheltenham and Bishop's Cleeve.
3. Safeguards the countryside from encroachment: although there are significant urbanised areas associated with Cheltenham Racecourse and associated development, much of the land is open. There are not strong boundaries to contain development. In its recommendation, AMEC reported: ***"Maintenance of the separation between Cheltenham and Bishop's Cleeve is critical to fulfilling the purpose of the Green Belt designation. These segments play an important role in this. Therefore, this area does not merit further consideration for release from the Green Belt at this stage unless other elements of the evidence base strongly suggest otherwise."***

Your comment at our one-to-one meeting in your office on Wednesday, 6th November 2013, that the reason for the 'tidying up' exercise is due to the recent problem of a planning application in the area, and the Local Government Ombudsman (LGO) case that followed. I suggest is not consistent with the AMEC recommendation above.
The fact that a resident objected to a planning permission given for a development in the Green Belt and was successful with his application to the LGO, should not be condemned, or used as an excuse, but hailed as a success in the defence of the Green Belt around the Racecourse.

For the reasons I have set out above, the proposals to remove the Green Belt status from the land on the south side of the Racecourse, would be a retrograde step, and contrary to the purpose of the Green Belt.

I strongly object to the removal of the Green Belt status of the land on the south side of the Racecourse.

Councillor Les Godwin.
Member of the JCS Member Steering Group.

Index

Lightning Source UK Ltd.
Milton Keynes UK
UKOW07n0412090415

249314UK00001B/6/P